Privacy and Security in AI-Driven Mental Health Apps

Today, privacy and security are increasingly important in the expanding landscape of AI-driven mental health technology. As the use of AI-driven solutions in mental health treatment advances, questions about the ethical management of sensitive data, user privacy and system vulnerabilities have emerged as serious challenges. This book provides a comprehensive investigation of these issues, addressing how privacy-preserving approaches and secure systems can maintain trust, transparency and ethical integrity in mental health applications.

The book covers a broad range of subjects. It begins with an introduction to mental health applications and their integration with AI technology, followed by a detailed discussion of the types of data collected, including sensitive behavioral, physiological and psychological data. It then analyses privacy threats, such as data breaches and misuse of personal information, and security problems, including cyberattacks and vulnerabilities in AI systems. Several chapters cover advanced solutions, including encryption approaches, differential privacy, blockchain integration and federated learning, as well as the importance of regulatory frameworks such as the General Data Protection Regulation (GDPR) and the Health Insurance Portability and Accountability Act (HIPAA). Case studies of real-world applications are also included to illustrate both successes and failures in privacy and security.

The final sections cover future directions, ethical issues and recommendations for developers, clinicians and policymakers. With contributions from specialists across disciplines, this book serves as an important resource for understanding the convergence of AI, mental health and data security, seeking to stimulate innovation while respecting user rights.

Privacy and Security in AI-Driven Mental Health Apps

Shabnam Kumari and Amit Kumar Tyagi

CRC Press
Taylor & Francis Group
Boca Raton London New York

CRC Press is an imprint of the
Taylor & Francis Group, an informa business

Designed cover image: Shutterstock ID: 2662879935

First edition published 2027
by CRC Press
2385 NW Executive Center Drive, Suite 320, Boca Raton FL 33431

and by CRC Press
4 Park Square, Milton Park, Abingdon, Oxon, OX14 4RN

CRC Press is an imprint of Taylor & Francis Group, LLC

Library of Congress Cataloging-in-Publication Data
Names: Kumari, Shabnam, 1991– author | Tyagi, Amit Kumar, 1988– author
Title: Privacy and security in AI-driven mental health apps / Shabnam Kumari and Amit Kumar Tyagi.
Description: First edition. | Boca Raton : CRC Press, 2027. | Includes bibliographical references and index. |
Identifiers: LCCN 2026011334 (print) | LCCN 2026011335 (ebook) | ISBN 9781041079002 hbk |
ISBN 9781041111122 pbk | ISBN 9781003658344 ebk
Subjects: LCSH: Medical informatics–Data processing | Mental health services–Technological innovations |
Artificial intelligence–Medical applications | Artificial intelligence–Security measures | Mobile apps–Security measures |
Privacy-preserving techniques (Computer science)
Classification: LCC R859.7.M63 K86 2027 (print) | LCC R859.7.M63 (ebook)
LC record available at https://lccn.loc.gov/2026011334
LC ebook record available at https://lccn.loc.gov/2026011335

ISBN: 9781041079002 (hbk)
ISBN: 9781041111122 (pbk)
ISBN: 9781003658344 (ebk)

DOI: 10.1201/9781003658344

Typeset in Times
by Newgen Publishing UK

Contents

Preface

In the last few years, artificial intelligence (AI) has rapidly become an integral part of modern mental healthcare, offering many opportunities for personalized support, early detection, and continuous monitoring. AI-driven mental health applications, that is, ranging from conversational agents and emotional-sensing tools to predictive analytics platforms, are now used by millions of people around the world. Today, these technologies provide scalable and accessible support at a time when demand for mental health services is surging. However, these technologies face some issues: to safeguard some of the most sensitive data, and protecting important data that individuals could otherwise share with unauthorized or malicious users. Hence, this book addresses the urgent need to understand, evaluate, and strengthen the privacy and security foundations underpinning AI-enabled mental health systems which are being used by today's healthcare professionals across the globe.

Today modern healthcare's data, or any information to mental healthcare, carries deep emotional, psychological, and social implications. A breach, misuse, or misinterpretation of this data can lead to stigma, discrimination, and long-term psychological harm. As AI models increasingly rely on continuous data streams, that is, text messages, voice patterns, biosignals, location data, and behavioral logs, issues of consent, ownership, transparency, and ethical data use become even more complex. At the same time, cyberattacks targeting health organizations and digital platforms are growing in frequency and sophistication. The challenge to protect individual privacy while enabling innovation forms the core tension explored throughout this work.

The book serves as a detailed explanatory guide for researchers, developers, clinicians, policymakers, and technology leaders who are shaping the digital mental health landscape. It aims to bridge the gap between technical mechanisms such as encryption, federated learning, and anonymization, and the broader ethical frameworks governing autonomy, trust, fairness, and accountability. Through a multidisciplinary view, it examines how privacy-preserving technologies can be integrated into real-world systems without compromising clinical effectiveness or user experience.

Ultimately, the goal of this book is to support the creation of trustworthy AI mental health applications, that is, systems that empower users, respect their dignity, and protect their vulnerabilities. As AI continues to transform mental healthcare, privacy and security are not optional add-ons; they are foundational pillars that determine whether these innovations will truly benefit individuals and society.

Lastly, we invite readers to read our book, and we hope that this book will be appreciated by the research community and any corrections are heartily welcome for improving the quality of this book.

Acknowledgments

First of all, we would like to extend our gratitude to our family members, friends, and supervisors, who stood with us as advisors in completing this book. Also, we would like to thank our almighty God who helped us write this book. We also thank CRC Press and our colleagues with whom we have worked together inside the college/university and others outside of the college/university who have provided their continuous support toward completing this book on privacy, artificial intelligence, and mental health.

In addition, we would like to thank our Respected Prof. G Aghila, Prof. Siva Sathya, and Prof (Dr.) N Sreenath, Prof. Aswani Kumar Cherukuri, Prof. (Dr.) Naveen Chaudhary, and Prof. (Dr.) Purvi Pokhariyal for sharing their valuable input and helping us in completing this book.

About the Authors

Shabnam Kumari is working as Ph.D. Research Scholar in the Department of Computer Science, SRM Institute of Science and Technology, Chennai, Tamil Nadu, India. She has more than 6 years of experience, including teaching, research, and other areas. She has completed her MCA from YMCA University of Science and Technology, Faridabad. She has filed more than five national and international patents in the areas of Internet of Things, machine learning, deep learning, and wireless networks. She has published 20 plus research articles in international conferences and journals. Her areas of interest include machine learning, deep learning, and related fields. She is a lifetime member of ACM-Women and SCRS.

Amit Kumar Tyagi is working as an Assistant Professor at National Forensic Sciences University, Gandhinagar, Gujarat, India. He received his Ph.D. (full-time) in 2018 from Pondicherry Central University, 605014, Puducherry, India. Regarding his academic experience, he has worked as an assistant professor at several institutes like Lord Krishna College of Engineering (LKCE), Ghaziabad (for the periods of July 2009–July 2010 and October 2012–October 2013), Lingaya's Vidyapeeth (formerly known as Lingaya's University), Faridabad (September 2018–May 2019), VIT Chennai (June 2019–November 2022), and NIFT New Delhi (November 2022–September 2025). His supervision experience includes more than 10 masters' dissertations and 1 Ph.D. thesis. He has contributed to several projects such as "AARIN" and "P3-Block" to address some of the open issues related to the privacy breaches in vehicular applications (such as parking) and medical cyber–physical systems (MCPS). He has to his credit more than 60 edited and authored books and he has collaborated with eminent professors across the world from top QS ranked universities. Also, he has published over 350 research articles in refereed high-impact journals, conferences, and books, and some of his articles have received best paper awards. In addition, he has filed more than 15 patents (nationally and internationally) in the area of deep learning, Internet of Things, cyber–physical systems, and computer vision. He has won the Faculty Research Award for the years 2020, 2021, and 2022 (consecutively 3 years) given by Vellore Institute of Technology, Chennai, Tamil Nadu, India. His current research focuses on next-generation machine-based communications, blockchain technology, smart and secure computing, and privacy. He is a senior member of IEEE.

Part I

Foundations and Context

1 The Role of Artificial Intelligence in Modern Mental Healthcare

1.1 INTRODUCTION

As mentioned by the World Health Organization (WHO), the problem of mental health disorders has become a problem of the whole world that embraces millions of individuals of the global community and has caused a significant social, economic, and health burden. It is only depressive and anxiety disorders that cause a significant portion of disability on a global scale. The treatment gap remains higher than half in most low- and middle-income nations, which in part is because of the poor access to mental health professionals, social stigma, and geographic disparities. This situation is in huge need of solutions due to the need to have access to scalable, accessible, and cost-effective solutions to address the necessity of effective interventions.

Artificial intelligence (AI) refers to a rapidly advancing technology which is gaining traction in the healthcare field as a way of diagnosing, treating as well as monitoring patients. Mental health AI-based systems, such as predictive models and virtual assistants and wearable analytics, can be used to complement the traditional care, perform preliminary psychiatric diagnosis, and customize therapy. Underserved groups can be reached with the assistance of AI through continuous monitoring, real-time feedback, and adaptive therapies that could be provided through mobile and web-based mental health applications.

However, certain challenges of integrating AI to the mental health care exist. The privacy and safety of the confidential information submitted by patient psychiatric data could lead to mistrust among the patients, and to the contrary, transparency and bias of the algorithm can be detrimental to the patient trust. Cultural, societal, and ethical concerns (where the adoption becomes more complex) are other factors contributing to that challenge, and it can be important to be responsible and ethical in designing AI.

In this chapter, we provide a comprehensive overview of the use of AI in modern mental health care. We examine the evolution of AI in psychiatry, the utilization of AI across diagnostic, therapeutic, and monitoring domains, and we critically examine the associated benefits, drawbacks, and ethical issues. By reviewing the literature in the field and examining real-world case studies, we aim to provide a pathway to the responsible deployment of AI-driven mental health applications, with a focus on patient safety, privacy and trust.

DOI: 10.1201/9781003658344-2

1.2 LITERATURE REVIEW

AI is the field where healthcare has rapidly adopted in the past decade, and mental health has become one of the major fields of interest. The first studies focused on the possibility of AI to complement clinical decision-making, minimize diagnostic errors, and facilitate a personalized treatment. Research has examined different AI approaches, such as machine learning (ML), natural language processing (NLP), and deep learning (DL), to model more complicated mental health data, such as clinical notes, patterns of speech, and social media usage or wearable sensor physiological signals.

1.2.1 Diagnostic Equipment and Preliminary Diagnosis

The potential of AI in early diagnosis and detection of mental illnesses has been demonstrated. *Mental health disorders*: ML algorithms may be used to analyze large datasets, such as electronic health records and behavioral data to discern patterns of mental health disorders. An example of this is that AI models have been designed to detect the beginning of diseases like depression and anxiety early enough to implement appropriate measures and personalized treatment regimen (Cruz-Gonzalez et al., 2025). Figure 1.1 presents workflow of how AI can be used to analyze multi-modal data (text, speech, physiological signal) to recognize mental health conditions.

1.2.2 Broader Security and Privacy Challenges in Computing

Security and privacy challenges are not limited to clinical systems alone. Tyagi et al. (2020) reviewed broader issues across a range of computing environments, highlighting concerns such as cross-platform vulnerabilities, the rapid growth of data, and gaps in privacy-preserving methods. As

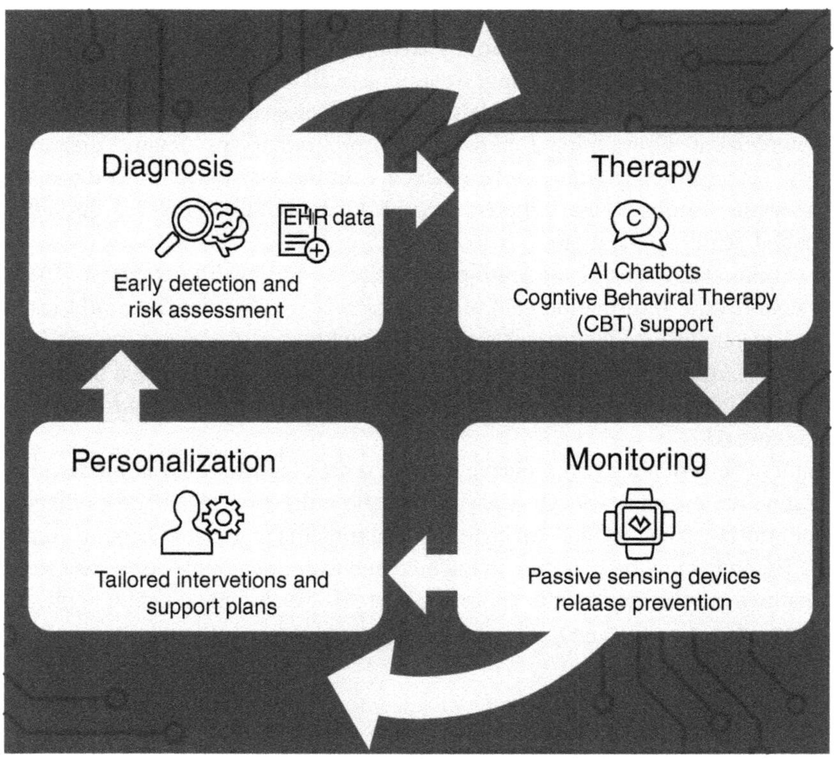

FIGURE 1.1 AI-based diagnostic systems workflow.

mental-health applications collect highly sensitive information, these insights underscore the need for stronger, more adaptable security approaches to maintain patient trust.

1.2.3 Therapeutic Interventions and Chatbots

Chatbots and virtual therapists that use AI-based methods are used to conduct therapeutic interventions, especially in institutions where human therapists are not readily available. These applications use strategies of cognitive–behavioral therapy (CBT) and other therapies to facilitate users to have therapeutic dialogues. Some of the works cite positive results, but there are also some studies that warn about the overuse of AI as a therapeutic approach and the lack of depth of human empathy and understanding that AI can offer (Sali et al., 2025). Figure 1.2 depicts three AI-guided therapy types, which are chatbot, digital CBT, and generative AI personalized content.

1.2.4 Individualized Care and Survey

AI allows mental health treatment to be personalized by providing patient-specific data to the intervention, which is analyzed using AI. In case of treatment, ML models have the ability to determine the efficacy of treatment in real time, which means that the therapeutic approach can be adjusted accordingly. Furthermore, AI may enable constant tracking of patients, and that can support them continuously and identify possible problems in a timely manner (Dehbozorgi et al., 2025; Nair et al., 2025).

1.2.5 Importance of Cybersecurity in Healthcare Technologies

The growing use of advanced technologies in healthcare has made cybersecurity and strong digital frameworks more important than ever. Tyagi (2016) pointed out that cyber–physical systems (CPSs)—which link digital systems with real-world environments—are especially vulnerable to security breaches and technical failures. In healthcare, where these systems often handle sensitive information or interact with medical devices, any breach or malfunction can directly impact patient safety. This makes the need for reliable protection even more critical.

1.2.6 Blockchain for Securing Medical CPS

Expanding on these concerns, Tyagi et al. (2021) proposed the Affordable, Accurate, Reliable, and Innovative (AARIN) blockchain framework to secure medical CPSs. Their work showed how blockchain can provide tamper-resistant data storage, secure communication, and strong traceability.

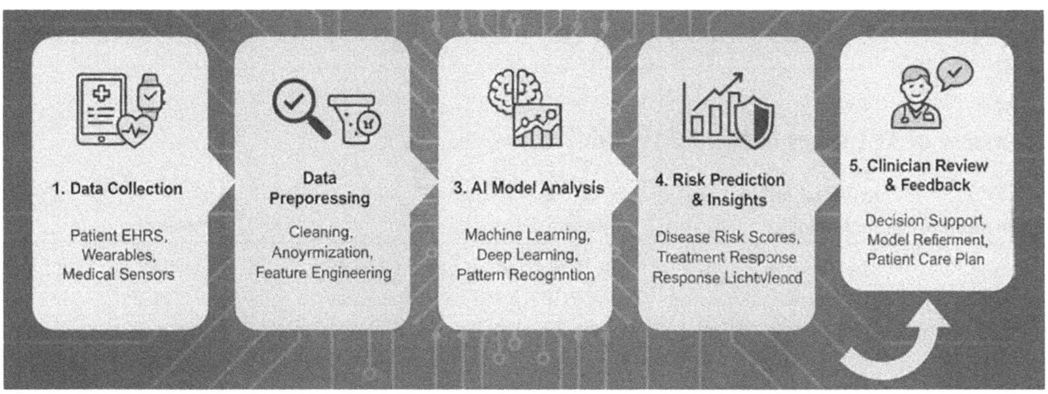

FIGURE 1.2 Therapeutic interventions based on AI.

These features help reduce risks like unauthorized access and data manipulation. Such innovations are increasingly relevant today as mental-health technologies depend heavily on connected devices, mobile applications, and digital platforms.

1.2.7 Data Privacy and Security

Mental healthcare, being an area where AI is used, requires sensitive personal information to be collected and analyzed. Privacy and security of such information are of prime importance. Ethical frameworks underline the significance of the strong data protection systems and open data use policies to retain patient confidence and adhere to the legal norms (Tyagi, 2021).

1.2.8 The Fairness and Algorithmic Bias

The AI systems are vulnerable to biases in the data that they are being trained on. When applied to mental health, it may result in the unequal diagnosis and treatment prescriptions per population group. To mitigate the issue of algorithmic bias, it is necessary to create inclusive datasets and perform fairness audits that would help deliver fair results (Thakkar et al., 2024; Kumari et al., 2025a).

1.2.9 Informed Consent and Autonomy

Use of AI in therapeutic approaches raises important questions of informed consent and autonomy used by a patient. Patients must know perfectly well what AI interactions are and what these technologies can and cannot do. Ethical principles promote effective communication and offer alternatives of human control to AI-mediated therapy (Tavory, 2024; Kumari et al., 2025b).

1.2.10 AI Mental Health: Cultural Sensitivity Applications

The treatment and expression of mental health problems are influenced by the aspects of the culture. The AI systems should be designed so that they understand and acknowledge the differences in cultures to deliver effective care. Cultural competence can be added to the AI model, that is learning the various manifestations of distress and modifying interventions (Algumaei et al., 2025; VanHook, 2025; Mishra et al., 2024). An overview of diagnostic, therapeutic, and monitoring applications of AI in mental healthcare is presented in Table 1.1.

1.2.11 Protecting Location Privacy in Mobile- and Sensor-Based Systems

Privacy becomes even more complex when systems track movement and behavior through mobile devices or sensors. Tyagi and Sreenath (2016) emphasized the importance of protecting location

TABLE 1.1
Overview of AI Usages in Mental Health

Application Area	Artificial Intelligence Technology	Purpose	Reference
Diagnosis	Machine learning, NLP	Early depression, anxiety detection	Cruz-Gonzalez et al., 2025
Therapy	chatbots, virtual assistants	Provide CBT, assist with compliance	Sali et al., 2025
Tracking patient metrics	Sensors, wearable devices	Measure physiological and behavioral metrics	Dehbozorgi et al., 2025
Personalization	Reinforcement learning, generative AI	Adapt interventions to each patient	Thakkar et al., 2024

privacy and building trust in systems that monitor moving objects. Their findings apply directly to modern mental-health apps that rely on continuous tracking, as these tools can unintentionally reveal personal routines, emotional states, or behavioral patterns if not properly secured.

1.2.12 Existing Regulations

Different jurisdictions are starting to initiate laws on the application of AI in mental healthcare. Certain jurisdictions have implemented legislation that necessitate control of AI-based therapeutic treatments by humans and ban AI use to independently provide mental health services (AI EHR and NDLS).

1.2.13 Challenges in Enforcement

Although there has been the formulation of regulatory systems, there are still difficulties in implementing these regulations. The problems of the high rate of technological development, cross-jurisdictional factors, and the nature of AI systems make regulatory framework more challenging. There is a need to continuously change and enforce policies to keep up with the AI technology advances (Tyagi, 2025).

1.2.14 Restriction and Drawbacks of Existing Literature

Irrespective of these good signs, there are still considerable limitations. Majority of the studies use small or homogeneous data, which restricts the generalizability. Ethical and privacy issues are not thoroughly researched and not many studies adopt effective privacy-preserving methods like federated learning or differential privacy. In addition, the issues of algorithmic transparency and explainability are also crucial, and, due to the black-box models, clinicians may not trust them and patients may not accept them. Cross-cultural validation is also not available and this raises concerns about its applicability over wide populations.

1.2.15 Addressing Data Quality Issues in AI-Based Mental-Health Models

Another significant issue is the quality of data used to train AI models. Mental-health datasets often suffer from class imbalance, where some symptoms or conditions appear far less frequently than others. Rekha et al. (2020) addressed this problem with their K-Nearest Neighbor Density-Based Oversampling (KDOS) oversampling method, which helps AI systems learn from underrepresented classes and produce fairer, more accurate predictions. This is crucial in mental-health contexts, where biased or inaccurate AI outputs can lead to misdiagnosed conditions or unequal treatment across patient groups.

1.2.16 Research Opportunities and Gaps

It has been seen that the extant literature presents several research opportunities, as outlined below:

- A combination of multi-modal data in achieving holistic mental-health outcomes.
- Privacy-preserving AI-based privacy frameworks of sensitive psychiatric data.
- Longitudinal research to determine the effectiveness and safety of AI interventions.
- Interpretable AI models to increase clinician and patient confidence.
- Models that are culturally adaptive to enhance global applicability.

In summary, this literature review not only presents the significant potential of AI in the mental healthcare but also demonstrates serious gaps in privacy, ethics, generalizability, and patient engagement. The review is the basis of the investigation of the history. Current uses of AI are discussed in the following sections.

1.3 INTRODUCTION TO AI IN HEALTHCARE

AI is a type of computational system that can carry out the functions typically performed by humans using cognitive abilities like learning, reasoning, recognizing patterns, and making decisions. AI has turned out to be a potent tool in the healthcare sector to improve the process of diagnostics, treatment planning, patient monitoring, and administrative efficiency. Its capacity to process a large quantity of complicated data allows clinicians to make knowledgeable choices, foresee patient results, and provide individualized care.

1.3.1 Fundamental AI Approaches to Healthcare

Use of AI in the healthcare sector is based on a number of underlying methodologies that enable machines to learn through the data, identify patterns, and make decisions traditionally based on human expertise. Most applications of AI rely on ML because it enables systems to handle a substantial amount of data and predict outcomes based on learned patterns. The most popular learning models are supervised learning, unsupervised learning, and reinforcement learning whose personal abilities depend on the nature of the healthcare issue. DL, a subset of ML uses the concept of a layered neural network to automatically find complex features in data; thus, it is especially useful in medical imaging, electronic health record analysis, and other applications that require large datasets to work with. Another important methodology is NLP that enables machines to decode and analyze human language. Applications of NLP in healthcare include deriving useful insights on unstructured text, including clinical notes or patient-reported outcomes, and are of particular use in mental health to analyze transcripts of therapy, or social media data. Predictive analytics is an additional tactic because it involves forecasts of patient outcomes, detection of risks, and aids in proactive interventions based on historical and real-time data.

1.3.2 AI implementation in the Field of Healthcare

The effects of AI have shown to be huge in various aspects of healthcare. The AI algorithms are used in diagnostics to improve accuracy and identify patterns in medical images, laboratory findings, and symptoms to which the patient is exposed and, in many cases, they are faster and more consistent in their performance. A therapeutic value of AI is helping to tailor the treatment plan, optimize medication, and even encourage the rapid discovery of drugs, as it can analyze a mass of biochemical data. AI has the potential to be valuable in another area—patient monitoring. Wearable devices or IoT (Internet of Things) sensors utilizing AI capabilities can monitor vitals and prevent disease in real time. AI can not only assist with patient clinical services but also automate management services such as hospital workflow, appointment booking, and resource allocation, a known means of reduction in overhead costs and an enhancement to overall efficiencies. Figure 1.3 represents an overview of AI applications in mental health diagnosis, therapy, monitoring, and personalized intervention.

1.3.3 Relevance of MHC in Mental Healthcare

The AI methods and uses in general healthcare readily apply to the mental health field. Mental healthcare frequently involves the identification of behavioral patterns, text and speech interpretation as well as symptom course prediction activity, which fits AI quite well. With AI support, individuals are able to identify the first symptoms of depression, anxiety, and other psychiatric illnesses using voice tone, textual messages in applications, and digital device gestures. Moreover, AI-based

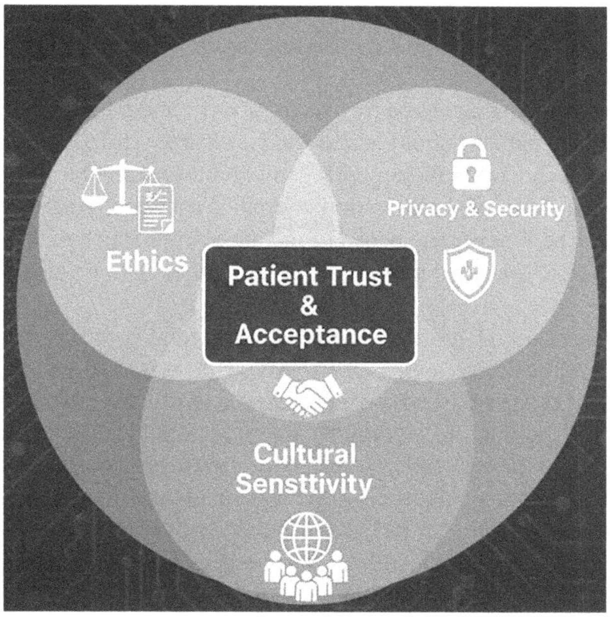

FIGURE 1.3 Artificial intelligence in the field of mental healthcare.

chatbots, virtual assistants, and adaptive therapy apps offer scalable assistance, which implies that customized treatment can be administered to individuals that would not have readily been accessible to mental health professionals. The technologies not only enhance access to the treatment process but also provide uninterrupted monitoring and instant feedback, which is the sole way to bridge the gap between patients and clinicians.

1.3.4 Healthcare AI Adoption Problems

Despite the fact that clinicians might have a groundbreaking opportunity with AI, its use in mental healthcare and health is characterized by a strong presence of challenges. Security and confidentiality of sensitive patient information remain of utmost concern, particularly where systems are used to record complex behavioral and physiological data. Another issue is algorithmic bias, which can be used to explain why models trained on unrepresentative datasets can make unfair or inaccurate predictions about some populations. Transparency is lacking in sophisticated AI models, which can be characterized as a black-box system, which can decrease the level of trust not only among clinicians but also patients. Besides, AI systems must follow regulatory frameworks like HIPAA (Health Insurance Portability and Accountability Act), GDPR (General Data Protection Regulation), and standards of medical device and tend to be hard to comply with, thus an AI system has to be carefully designed and verified. The response to these issues is essential to consider AI as the means of delivering healthcare safely, ethically, and fairly.

1.4 AI, MENTAL HEALTH, AND PSYCHIATRY EVOLUTION

AI has been used in mental healthcare and its application has been changing greatly within the last few decades. The initial attempt was made in the 1960s and 1970s on rule-based expert systems to help assist clinicians make a decision. Such systems were based on a set of pre-programmed logic and symptom checklists, which provided some structured advice but were not very flexible in a rare or unusual case. Along with the rise of computational power in the 1980s and 1990s, the field of psychiatry started to introduce AI that relied on statistical models and primitive ML methods to process clinical data as the transition toward inflexible expert systems started to be replaced by data-driven insights.

The decade of 2000s was characterized by a major growth in the number of digital mental health tools. Through these tools, patients could access CBT and other structured treatment interventions using mobile apps and early online therapy platforms. AI also started to take a supporting part in these platforms and analyze the reactions and patterns of user engagement to customize therapy. At this time, the field of NLP appeared as one of the most promising solutions to assessing patient inputs in the form of texts and identifying the initial indications of emotional distress or mood disorders.

Over the previous decade, AI has revolutionized its mental health function due to the emergence of DL and more sophisticated approaches to ML. The current AI systems can combine multimodal data in the form of speech, text, social media activity, and physiological data regarding the wearable to identify psychiatric conditions more accurately than more classic methods of assessment. Conversational therapy and constant observation can be offered through chatbots and virtual assistants, which operate on the basis of AI and enable the implementation of mental health interventions on a large scale, and can be customized according to specific needs. Moreover, predictive analytics can now be used to identify risks of relapse at an early stage, which will provide a chance to provide clinical intervention on time.

Customization, availability, and ongoing treatment are the large-scale trends in the development of AI in mental health. Nowadays, AI is not only a tool of clinician support but also a chance to service underserved populations, reduce treatment disparities, and help patients engage more effectively with therapeutic resources. However, along with these changes in the technological field, other problems such as the privacy of data, bias in algorithms, and the sensitivity to culture are also of utmost importance. This historical and technological progression should be understood to create responsible AI-led approaches to mental health combining both innovation and practical and ethical protection.

1.5 MENTAL HEALTH INEQUALITIES IN THE WORLD AND THE DIGITAL DIVIDE

1.5.1 Gaps in Mental Health Burden and Treatment

Mental health disorders constitute one of the major disabilities in the world with hundreds of millions of people being affected regardless of their ages. World Health Organization states that the proportion of global disability-adjusted life years (DALYs) is a major part of depression and anxiety. Although there is high prevalence, access to mental health services is severe, especially in the low- and middle-income nations. The treatment gap in the majority of regions largely occurs as an inadequate number of people with a mental health condition obtain adequate treatment. This gap is caused by factors like the lack of trained professionals, geographic inequalities, economic factors, and social stigma leaving millions of people in need of prompt and effective care.

1.5.2 Mental Healthcare Delivery Problems in the Traditional Setting

Conventional mental healthcare has been based mostly on personal visits, formal therapy and paper-based monitoring. Although these methods work well in controlled settings, they are limited by the availability of clinicians, infrastructure constraints, and logistical limitations. Mostly affected are rural communities and underserved populations that have to wait longer and access specialized services less frequently. In addition, mental illness can be socially stigmatized and have cultural attitudes, which discourages people to use services even in the presence of services. When combined with the barriers, they illustrate why interventions in mental health are highly necessary and scalable, accessible, and cost-effective.

1.5.3 Digital Opportunities and AI-Driven Solutions

The digital technologies and, especially, AI tools have possibility of filling in these global mental health gaps. M-health apps, online treatment programs, and smartwatch-based health tracking can provide individual intervention to patients wherever they are. The AI algorithms will enable the continuous observation of the behavioral, physiological, and emotional symptoms to detect the early signs of symptoms and the risk of relapse. Virtual assistants and chatbots provide talking therapy and counselling to boost adherence and engagement. AI systems are capable of adjusting interventions on the fly by tracking the interaction and outcomes of users to contribute to more responsive and effective care.

1.5.4 Potential Impact and Reflections

The impact of the digital mental healthcare solutions that could be developed with the help of AI can be extensive. These tools could support the reduction of the costs, standardization of the quality of the care, and support in the culturally diverse environments. However, the execution of such technologies ought to proceed properly. It is the most necessary privacy and data security because mental health information is confidential. The algorithms should also be made fair, transparent, and unbiased to form an equal access and patient trust. Regardless of these concerns, AI implementation of the mental healthcare sector is an unprecedented opportunity to close the treatment gaps, improve patient outcomes, and democratize access to mental healthcare on a world level.

1.6 AI IN DIAGNOSES, THERAPY, AND SURVEILLANCE

1.6.1 AI in Diagnostics

AI has transformed the mental health diagnostics where psychiatric diagnosis of the condition has been found at the early and correct stage. ML models can identify subtle symptoms of depression, anxiety, and bipolar disorders with speech trends, text-based posts on digital platforms, and social networking. Wearable devices generate physiological data that AI algorithms can analyze to infer mental-health indicators (Tyagi and Tiwari, 2024a). Combining such multi-modal sources of data, AI systems will have the capacity to detect risks factors and behavior changes that may remain hidden in the case of standard clinical-based measures, and deliver a more proactive and individualized mental healthcare.

1.6.2 AI Therapy and Intervention

The use of AI-based therapy tools has greatly increased access and flexibility of mental healthcare. Woebot, Wysa, and other conversational agents or chatbots are CBTs and other evidence-based methods that can help and interact with people using natural language. Such platforms can provide sustained support, track patient progress, and adjust therapeutic recommendations accordingly. Adaptive digital therapeutics refer to interventions that rely on AI to customize intervention plans in real time to optimize the treatment sequence to enhance the adherence and outcomes (Balamurugan et al., 2023). The AI-assisted therapy will provide an opportunity to augment conventional care by providing scalable, cost-effective, and customized support and consequently streamline the lack of mental health specialists.

1.6.3 AI in the Area of Monitoring and Prognosis

AI offers several benefits for mental healthcare because of constant monitoring. Wearable sensors and mobile apps allow collecting real-time behavioral and physiological readings and process the results with the help of AI-based models to identify the early indications of symptom worsening or recurrence. Mental health episodes can be predicted using predictive algorithms so that timely interventions can be undertaken by the clinical staff or automated support mechanisms (Tyagi et al., 2024c). Combining digital, behavioral, and physiological data using multi-modal approaches can improve the quality of prognosis and risk assessment. The resulting data-driven, continuous monitoring allows patients and clinicians to continue proactive care to enhance better long-term outcomes.

1.6.4 Privacy-Sensitive Methods of AI in Mental-Health Applications

As mental health data are sensitive, privacy preserving methods are needed in the AI applications. Federated learning enables AI models to be trained with decentralized data and minimizes the burden on clinicians while enhancing timely access to mental-health services. Differential privacy adds a controlled noise to data and shields the individual identities without impacting the performance of the models. With homomorphic encryption, the encryption of information allows calculations on encrypted data itself and this means that no sensitive data is leaked. The use of these techniques provided in mental health apps will guarantee compliance with ethical standards and regulations without losing the trust of users and data safety.

1.7 ADVANTAGES AND DISADVANTAGES OF AI-BASED INTERVENTIONS

1.7.1 Benefits of AI in Mental Health

There are a number of revolutionary advantages of AI-based interventions within the mental healthcare. Scalability is one of the most outstanding opportunities as it enables digital platforms and chatbots to reach vast groups, including people in remote or underserved locations. AI gives personalized therapy and monitoring suggestions by changing therapy and monitoring according to individual behavior, engagement patterns, and physiological indicators. With real-time monitoring, it is possible to notice the worsening of the symptoms early enough to introduce timely interventions that can avert crisis or relapses. Moreover, AI systems have the potential to lessen the workload of clinicians as they will automate routine assessments and follow-ups and leave complex cases that would need a humanized approach to the healthcare professional (Tyagi et al., 2025). Another major advantage is the cost efficiency as digital interventions do not require the face-to-face sessions and can be used as the addition tool to the conventional care with scarce infrastructure.

1.7.2 Limitations and Risks of AI

Even with these advantages, there are hidden limitations and dangers associated with AI-based mental health interventions. The first issue is algorithmic bias, which may arise in case models are trained on non-representative or skewed datasets, which, in turn, may make them inaccurately predict some groups of people. Numerous AI models are also black boxes, so their decision-making process is hard to explain, and this fact may confuse clinicians and patients and demote their trust. Data privacy and security is also yet to be a burning issue as mental health data is highly sensitive and can be easily hacked. In addition, human empathy, therapeutic judgment, and sensitive sense of a complex mental illness cannot be fully substituted by AI interventions (Rajani et al., 2022). Unless they are properly integrated with the professional control, automatic systems may produce the risk of patient disengagement or misdiagnosis.

1.7.3 Finding a Compromise Between Benefits and Limits

To achieve advantages of AI without diminishing its disadvantages, AI should be properly designed and controlled. Explicit and comprehensible AI models are associated with the evolution of trust and clinical adoption. Differential privacy and federated learning are privacy-protective methods that protect the privacy of sensitive patient data. The implementation of AI systems in various populations is correct and equitable with the help of constant evaluation, confirmation, and cross-cultural validation of the system. Ethical and human concerns related to AI have increased significantly with technological advancements. The conventional mental healthcare can be complemented with interventions successfully, and access can be increased without impairing quality and patient safety.

1.8 CULTURAL, ETHICAL, AND SOCIETAL IMPLICATION

1.8.1 AI-Based Mental Health Ethical Issue

The use of AI in mental health raises a range of ethical issues. This is an essential principle, called informed consent, and patients must know how their delicate information would be collected, processed, and implemented. It should also be characterized by the maximum level of transparency and explainability so that the AI systems could provide interpretable outcomes based on which clinicians and patients can trust the recommendations. Algorithm's fairness is also another critical consideration that assumes that unfair models may be highly discriminatory against a group of individuals of their age or gender or ethnicity or socioeconomic status or any other trait. In this regard, ethical governance practices and control mechanisms are required in an attempt to ensure that AI technologies are used in a reasonable and responsible way and based on clinical and social values.

1.8.2 Cultural Sensitivity and Global Adoption

Mental healthcare is strongly influenced by the norms, beliefs, and the social practices in that particular culture. They should be taken into account when developing AI interventions to render them effective and acceptable. The instances of these behaviors include expression of symptoms, seeking of help and attitudes toward digital tools, which are culturally dissimilar. The AI that grew within a particular cultural environment may not apply to another cultural environment and this may reduce accuracy and appeal. With the help of various datasets, local language processing, and context-specific content of therapy, cultural adaptive system may be designed to make it relevant and comprehensive to the specific setting.

1.8.3 Societal Impact and Equity

AI impacts society not only through clinical outcomes but also through broader changes in healthcare systems and patient care. Instances of inadequate treatment can be reduced, and discrepancies can be addressed, particularly by making more mental healthcare resources available to underserved groups with the help of AI tools. However, the disparity in access to technologies and digital literacy will continue to widen the existing inequalities provided that it is not dealt with care. Another critical attribute of AI that creates trust among the population is the capacity to offer high levels of privacy, moral use, and clarity of the system functionality and restrictions.

1.8.4 The Integration of Ethics, Culture, and Society

The introduction of the AI in mental health requires a holistic approach that includes the integration of the ethical protective measures, cultural sensitivity, and the society in question. Engaging stakeholders, including patients, clinicians, ethicists, and policymakers, is critical in the formulation of guidelines, evaluation of the impact, and rendering AI interventions effective and socially responsible. The AI-based mental health solutions will lead to the improvement of equitable, trustworthy, and sustainable care at the global scale by creating a balance between technology and ethics as well as self-cultural backgrounds. Figure 1.4 represents a framework that indicates main ethical, privacy, and cultural considerations influencing the use of AI in mental healthcare.

The important factors that contribute to AI adoption, patient trust, and acceptance of AI in society are shown in Table 1.2.

1.9 TRUST, ENGAGEMENT, AND ACCEPTANCE OF THE PATIENT

1.9.1 Influencing Factors on Patient Trust

The effective implementation of AI-based mental health interventions is based on trust. When the patients feel that the data are handled in a secure and ethical manner, they tend to be more inclined to use the digital tools. The more transparent the work of AI models, the logic of the recommendation or risk estimates, the better the credibility and the creation of trust. In addition, effective communication about the shortcomings of AI, as well as the complementary status of human clinicians, is effective in controlling expectations and helps to avoid fear of excessive dependence on automated systems.

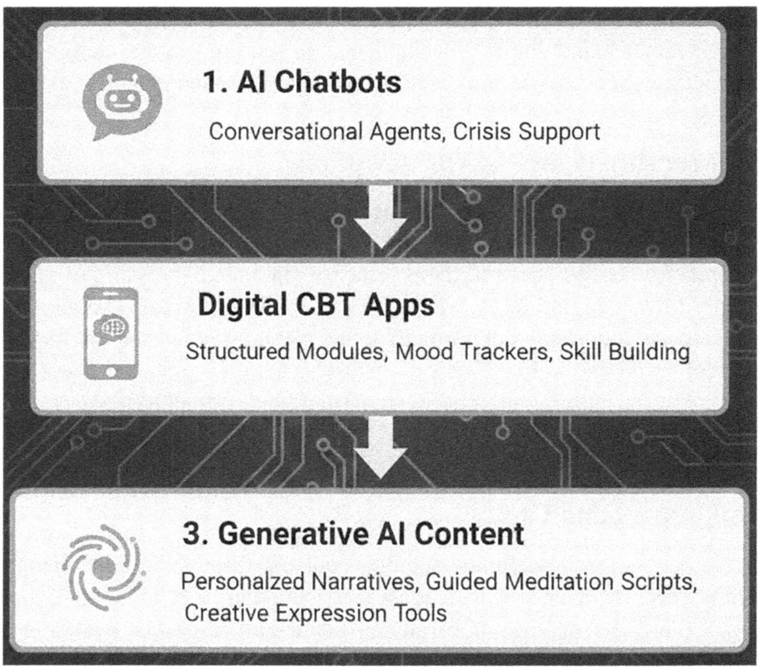

FIGURE 1.4 AI mental health apps ethics and culture.

TABLE 1.2
AI-Driven Mental Health Ethical and Cultural Reflections

Consideration	Description	Mitigation Strategy	Reference
Data privacy	Sensitive patient data collection	Federated learning, encryption	Saeidnia et al., 2024
Algorithmic bias	Bias on non-representative datasets	Inclusive data, fairness audits	Thakkar et al., 2024
Informed consent	Awareness and autonomy of the patient	Transparent AI disclosures	Tavory, 2024
Cultural sensitivity	Necessity to adapt to cultural norms	Localized content, culturally adaptive models	Algumaei et al., 2025

1.9.2 Enhancing Engagement: Design

AI-driven applications determine the usability of patient engagement and their responsiveness. Aspects of user-friendly interfaces, customized feedback, gamification, and adjustable content can greatly enhance the compliance to digital therapy modules. Real-time feedback and continuous monitoring enable patients to view actual progress, which becomes a source of reinforcing participation and motivation. AI models that conform to personal preferences and behavioral habits also contribute to more engagement as the interventions provided can be adjusted to the needs of the user.

1.9.3 Mental Healthcare Acceptance of AI

The perceived usefulness, ease of use, and the cultural attitudes of technology influencing the acceptance of AI tools are a mixture. When there is clinical efficacy and positive user experiences, the adoption rates increase. Sociocultural factors like mental health and attitudes to digital solutions also influence the process of acceptance. The needs of the real world will be met by involving patients in the design process and using culturally relevant material to ensure that AI interventions remain close to various groups of people.

1.9.4 Establishing Extended Trust and Adoption

Privacy, security, and ethical concerns must be constantly addressed to ensure the patient trust. There is also the need to involve the principles of explainable AI (XAI) and periodic system audits and compliance with regulatory frameworks, such as HIPAA and GDPR. It will establish trust and encourage a lifetime adoption by sharing information with the users, providing feedback, and using evidence-based interventions. The AI-based mental health applications have the potential to provide meaningful contacts and determine mental health outcomes through an intelligent patient-oriented design and ethical management. Table 1.3 shows AI-based key techniques, their strengths, limitations, and examples.

1.10 FUTURE PROJECTIONS AND RESEARCH PROBLEMS

1.10.1 Existing Research Problem

Although the use of AI in mental health has grown quite swiftly, there are a number of research issues. The first issue is the scarcity of high-quality and mixed datasets. A lot of AI models are developed using small samples or demographically homogeneous samples, which would decrease their accuracy and transferability across populations. Another challenge is data privacy and ethical issues because sensitive mental health data should be treated with high confidentiality (Nair et al.,

TABLE 1.3
Comparative Analysis of AI Technologies for Mental Health Applications

AI Technology	Strengths	Limitations	Use Case	Reference
Machine learning	Good predictive power	Black-box, data-hungry,	Early detection	Cruz-Gonzalez et al., 2025
NLP and sentiment analysis	Emotion patterns detection required	Linguistic adaptation necessary	Text monitoring in patients	Dehbozorgi et al., 2025
Chatbots and virtual assistants	Scalable and interactive	Limited empathy	Digital therapy	Sali et al., 2025
Generative AI	Personalized content	Ethical risks, hallucinations	Adaptive CBT content	Thakkar et al., 2024

2021). Moreover, the transparency deficiency of multifaceted AI models, which is also known as a black-box system, can hinder the adoption and foster the lack of clinical trust. There is also a lack of standardized metrics of evaluation and longitudinal studies, which complicate the evaluation of the long-term efficacy and safety of AI-based interventions.

1.10.2 New Opportunities in AI Mental Health Research

The current technological improvements have provided good opportunities to overcome these problems. Privacy-preserving AI models can be built with the support of federated learning, differential privacy, and homomorphic encryption, which is why sensitive information can be processed without the threat to confidentiality. Improved predictive accuracy can be achieved by using multimodal data integration, which is a combination of behavioral, physiological, and digital traces, as well as provide a comprehensive understanding of mental health. Reinforcement learning and generative AI can be used to develop dynamic, adaptive, and personalized interventions that can react in real time to the needs of the patient. Moreover, the digital twin technologies, as well as virtual clinical simulations, can be used to aid in real-time decision-making and optimization of treatments.

1.10.3 Future Directions and Considerations

Future studies are needed on how to enhance the generalizability, the transparency, and explainability of the model to give rise to trust between clinicians and patients. There should be adaptive AI approaches that can redress the imbalance in mental health that involves the world and offer equal access. It should ensure that the rules and regulations and codes of ethics are abreast with technology so as to safeguard the rights of patients and improve innovation. Cross-disciplinary networks among clinicians, data scientists, ethicists, and policymakers will be the key to work with AI solutions which will be clinically effective and socially responsible.

1.10.4 Long-Term Outlook

The future of AI in the field of mental health is bright. Using AI-based applications can enhance accessibility, personalized care, and better treatment outcomes in diverse populations with the proper study and its implementation across the globe. By addressing the current flaws and becoming more concerned with privacy, morality, and cultural relatability, AI may turn into a major driver of the future of mental health care that will allow filling the gaps in treatment and empower patients and clinicians.

1.11 SUMMARY

AI is transforming the modern mental healthcare by providing scalable, personalized, and data-driven diagnostics, therapy and patient monitoring solutions. AI has evolved to multi-modal data, offer adaptive interventions, and support decision-making by clinicians since the inception of the rule-based systems to more advanced ML and DL models. Virtual assistants, chatbots, and wearable analytics, which are types of digital mental health tools, can become the solution to treatment gaps in the world, particularly in underserved populations of people.

Despite the numerous benefits that AI is related to, such as increased accessibility, cost-effectiveness, and real-time tracking, there are some challenges associated with this technique as well. Privacy, data security, algorithmic bias, and cultural sensitivity are the necessary issues that also should be taken into account to ensure that patients trust the technology and make appropriate use of it. The involvement and agreement of the patients would rely on the transparent and provocable systems that would not violate the privacy and justice to the personal and cultural environments.

The research directions of the future include the privacy preserving AI, multi-modal data fusion, and AI generation of adaptive interventions and culturally adaptable models. The interprofessional collaboration, high ethical principles, and compliance with the regulations will be necessary to support the highest capacities of AI in the area of mental healthcare. Taking the right amount of innovation and ethics, as well as societal issues into consideration, AI-aided products in mental health would contribute to the patient outcome improvement, access improvement, and the creation of a much more equal mental health landscape globally.

REFERENCES

Algumaei, A., Yaacob, N. M., Doheir, M., Al-Andoli, M. N., & Algumaie, M. (2025). Symmetric therapeutic frameworks and ethical dimensions in AI-based mental health chatbots (2020–2025): A systematic review of design patterns, cultural balance, and structural symmetry. *Symmetry*, *17*(7), 1082.

Babu, A. (2024). Artificial intelligence in mental healthcare: Transformative potential and ethical considerations. *Frontiers in Psychology*, *15*, 1378904. https://doi.org/10.3389/fpsyg.2024.1378904

Balamurugan, G., Tyagi, A.K., Richa, A. (2023). Survey on privacy preserving and trust building techniques of blockchain-based systems. In: *Privacy Preservation and Secured Data Storage in Cloud Computing*. IGI Global. DOI: 10.4018/979-8-3693-0593-5.ch019

Beg, M. J. (2024). Artificial intelligence for psychotherapy: A review of the literature. *SAGE Open Medicine*, *12*, 1260819.

Blease, C., & Kaptchuk, T. J. (2024). Generative artificial intelligence in mental healthcare. *Current Psychiatry Reports*, *26*(5), 1–7. https://doi.org/10.1007/s40501-024-00340-x

Cruz-Gonzalez, P., Ramirez, L., Hoffman, J., Smith, R., Patel, S., & Li, X. (2025). Artificial intelligence in mental health care: A systematic review. *Journal of Psychiatric Research*, *140*, 1–10. https://doi.org/10.1016/j.jpsychires.2025.04.003

Dehbozorgi, R., Martins, P., Abedini, M., Lopez, F., Zhang, T., & Kumar, R. (2025). The application of artificial intelligence in the field of mental health: A systematic review. *BMC Psychiatry*, *25*(1), 1–12. https://doi.org/10.1186/s12888-025-06483-2

Koutsouleris, N., Kambeitz, J., Arloth, J., Reisinger, E., Ruef, A., & Haas, S. (2022). Challenges in AI applications in mental health: Data quality and clinical integration. *The Lancet Psychiatry*, *9*(6), 456–464.

Kumari, S., Tyagi, A. K., Tiwari, S., & Kulshreshtha, G. (2025a). Sensors and digital twin for healthcare monitoring frameworks. In T. A. Nguyen (Ed.), *Digital twin, blockchain, and sensor networks in the healthy and mobile city (Chapter 10)* (pp. 147–177). Elsevier. https://doi.org/10.1016/B978-0-443-34174-8.00011-9

Kumari, S., Tyagi, A. K., Tiwari, S., & Singh, R. (2025b). Medical sensor network, edge computing and blockchain for efficient medical data exchange. In T. A. Nguyen (Ed.), *Digital twin, blockchain, and sensor networks in the healthy and mobile city (Chapter 11)* (pp. 179–198). Elsevier. https://doi.org/10.1016/B978-0-443-34174-8.00012-0

Meadi, M. R., Gupta, P., Khan, S., Alvarez, J., Noor, H., Xu, Y. (2025). Ethical challenges of conversational AI in mental health care. *Journal of Medical Internet Research*, *27*(1), e11890142. https://doi.org/10.2196/60432

Mishra, A. K., Tiwari, S., Tyagi, A. K., & Arowolo, M. O. (2024). Security, privacy, trust, and provenance issues in Internet of Things–based edge environment. In S. Pal, C. Savaglio, R. Minerva, & F. C. Delicato (Eds.), *IoT edge intelligence* (pp. 233–263). Springer. https://doi.org/10.1007/978-3-031-58388-9_8

Nair, M. M., & Tyagi, A. K. (2021). Privacy: History, statistics, policy, laws, preservation and threat analysis. *Journal of information assurance & security*, *16*(1), 024–034.

Nair, M.M., & Tyagi, A.K. (2025). Transformative effects of emerging technologies on Industry 5.0 and Society 5.0: Current status, vision, issues, challenges, and opportunities for future. In: *Next Generation Data Science and Blockchain Technology for Industry 5.0*. Wiley. DOI: https://doi.org/10.1002/9781394245215.ch13, ISBN: 9781394245185.

Ni, Y., Ramanathan, K., Sato, M., Gupta, A., Lopez, V., & Kim, S. (2025). A scoping review of AI-driven digital interventions in mental health care. *BMC Psychiatry*, *25*(1), 1–12. https://doi.org/10.1186/s12888-025-06483-2

Olawade, D. B. (2024). Enhancing mental health with artificial intelligence. *Scientific Reports*, *14*, 20432. https://doi.org/10.1016/j.glmedi.2024.100099

Poudel, U., Santos, M., Rivera, L., Patel, P., Gomez, R., & Chen, X. (2025). AI in mental health: Technological advancements and clinical applications. *Journal of Clinical Psychology*, *81*(5), 1234–1245. https://doi.org/10.1080/01612840.2025.2502943

Rajani, D., Menon, S. C., Kute, S., & Tyagi, A. K. (2022). Preserving privacy of social media data using artificial intelligence techniques. In A. Tyagi (Ed.), *Handbook of Research on Technical, Privacy, and Security Challenges in a Modern World* (pp. 186–204). IGI Global. https://doi.org/10.4018/978-1-6684-5250-9.ch010

Rekha, G., Reddy, V. K., & Tyagi, A. K. (2020). KDOS: Kernel density-based oversampling for class imbalance. *Journal of Information Assurance and Security*, *15*(2), 44–52.

Saeidnia, H. R., Hashemi Fotami, S. G., Lund, B., & Ghiasi, N. (2024). Ethical considerations in artificial intelligence interventions for mental health and well-being: Ensuring responsible implementation and impact. *Social Sciences*, *13*(7), 381.

Sali, S. R., Wong, T., Harris, J., Patel, M., Singh, R., & Zhou, Q. (2025). AI-driven mental health apps and teletherapy platforms. *MedTigo Journal*, *5*(1), 1–12. https://doi.org/10.1016/j.med.2025.04.001

Spytska, L., Morozova, N., Ivanenko, P., Holub, A., Chornyi, O., Shevchenko, M. (2025). The use of artificial intelligence in psychotherapy. *BMC Psychology*, *13*(1), 1–10. https://doi.org/10.1186/s40359-025-02491-9

Sun, J., Wang, H., Chen, Z., Gupta, P., Lee, S., & Zhou, Y. (2025). Practical AI application in psychiatry: Historical review and future perspectives. *Molecular Psychiatry*, *30*(4), 1234–1245. https://doi.org/10.1038/s41380-025-03072-3

Svensson, E., Harper, T., Young, L., Chen, R., Wang, M., & Liu, P. (2025). Trustworthy and ethical AI in digital mental healthcare. *Scientific Reports*, *15*, 8842. https://doi.org/10.1016/j.invent.2025.100844

Tavory, T. (2024). Regulating AI in mental health: Ethics of care perspective. *JMIR Mental Health*, *11*(1), e58493. https://doi.org/10.2196/58493

Thakkar, A., Murthy, V., Sen, R., Kapoor, P., Wang, C., Lin, Y. (2024). Artificial intelligence in positive mental health: A narrative review. *Frontiers in Digital Health*, *6*, 1280235. https://doi.org/10.3389/fdgth.2024.1280235

Torous, J., Firth, J., Huckvale, K., Larsen, M. E., Cosco, T., & Stewart, R. (2025). The evolving field of digital mental health: Current evidence and future directions. *Psychiatric Clinics of North America*, *48*(1), 1–12. https://doi.org/10.1002/wps.21299

Tyagi, A. K. (2016). Cyber physical systems (CPSs): Opportunities and challenges for improving cybersecurity. *International Journal of Computer Applications*, *137*(14), 19–27. https://doi.org/10.5120/ijca2016908877

Tyagi, A.K. (2021). Analysis of security and privacy aspects of blockchain technologies from smart era' perspective: The challenges and a way forward. In: *Recent Trends in Blockchain for Information Systems Security and Privacy* (pp. 1–17). DOI: https://doi.org/10.1201/9781003139737, eBook-ISBN: 9781003139737

Tyagi, A.K. (2025). Blockchain for smart hospital in Healthcare 5.0: modeling structure, challenges, and future emerging trends. In: *Human-Centric Integration of Next-Generation Data Science and Blockchain Technology*. Elsevier. DOI: https://doi.org/10.1016/B978-0-443-33498-6.00026-1, ISBN: 978-0-443-33498-6.

Tyagi, A. K., & Sreenath, N. (2016). Providing together security, location privacy and trust for moving objects. *International Journal of Hybrid Information Technology*, *9*(3), 221–240. https://doi.org/10.14257/ijhit.2016.9.3.21

Tyagi, A. K., & Tiwari, S. (2024a). Blockchain-enabled smart healthcare applications in 6G networks. In A. K. Tyagi (Ed.), *Digital twin and blockchain for smart cities (Chapter 20)* (pp. 221–240). Wiley. https://doi.org/10.1002/9781394303564.ch20

Tyagi, A. K., Aswathy, S. U., Aghila, G., & Sreenath, N. (2021). AARIN: Blockchain-based framework for securing medical cyber-physical systems. *International Journal of Intelligent Networks*, *2*, 177–183. https://doi.org/10.1016/j.ijin.2021.09.007

Tyagi, A. K., Kumari, S., & Tiwari, S. (2024c). Internet of Things for smart healthcare: A survey. In A. K. Sharma, N. Chanderwal, S. Tyagi, & P. Upadhyay (Eds.), *Future of AI in medical imaging (Chapter 2)*. IGI Global. https://doi.org/10.4018/979-8-3693-2359-5.ch002

Tyagi, A. K., Nair, M. M., Sreenath, N., & Abraham, A. (2020). Security and privacy research issues in various computing platforms: A survey and the road ahead. *Journal of Information Assurance and Security, 15*(1), 1–16. https://doi.org/10.1007/978-981-16-6542-4_15

Tyagi, A. K., Tripathi, K., Tiwari, S., & Kaushik, S. (2025). An efficient technique for privacy preservation, trusted and secure patient-centric services in smart healthcare. In *Proceedings of the 6th international conference on recent trends in communication & intelligent systems (ICRTCIS 2025)* (pp. 31–47). IET. https://doi.org/10.1049/icp.2025.2731

VanHook, C. (2025). Perceptions, attitudes, and experiences regarding mental health care among young black men. *American Journal of Men's Health, 19*(1), 15579883241310755.

Varghese, M. A., Dsouza, J., Rahman, A., Kim, H., O'Neill, S., & Babu, T. (2024). Public perception of AI-driven mental health interventions. *JMIR Formative Research, 8*(1), e64380. https://doi.org/10.2196/64380

Wang, L., Zhou, J., Sun, Y., Hong, S., Ahmed, R., & Patel, M. (2025). Evaluating generative AI in mental health. *JMIR Mental Health, 12*(1), e70014. https://doi.org/10.2196/70014

Zhang, Z., Li, J., Song, Y., Wu, H., Chen, K., & Lou, D. (2024). Can AI replace psychotherapists? *Frontiers in Psychiatry, 15*, 1444382. https://doi.org/10.3389/fpsyt.2024.1444382

2 The Digital Transformation of Mental Health Services

2.1 INTRODUCTION

The issue of mental health disorders is becoming a widespread public health concern globally, as millions of individuals are affected and burdened by social and economic expenses. The traditional mental health services may have certain shortcomings, which may be long-term wait lines, insufficient available trained professionals, and stigma, which discourages people from seeking assistance. These issues have led to the introduction of digital technology into mental healthcare to expand reach and improve efficiency.

Mental health services can be accessed remotely by clients, through digital platforms, including mobile applications, telepsychiatry, and artificial intelligence (AI)-assisted interventions. These tools enable continuous monitoring of symptoms and behaviors that can inform treatment planning. Moreover, patient engagement and adherence to therapeutic programs may be improved with the help of real-time feedback and adaptive interventions.

The field of the digital transformation of mental health services is also connected with the broader trends in healthcare technology, i.e., the use of wearable devices, the implementation of the Internet of Things (IoT), and the sophisticated data analytics. Through these technologies, mental healthcare can be more predictive, more personal, and preventive. This chapter examines the current landscape of online mental health services, its advantages, issues, and prospects.

2.2 LITERATURE REVIEW

Digital mental health technologies have revolutionized the mental healthcare sector, providing scaled and customized interventions, which can decrease access barriers. When individuals in low- and middle-income countries cannot access face-to-face treatment, telepsychiatry apps, online programs, and mobile applications have proven the ability to alleviate the symptoms of depression and anxiety (Ahmed and Smith, 2023; Kwon and Lee, 2024; Li and Zhang, 2023; Tyagi et al., 2025). The stigma-related issues are also resolved by these digital solutions that enable people to find assistance in a covert way, thus making mental healthcare more accessible (Bridge and Green, 2025; Ni and Zhang, 2025; Nair et al., 2025).

IoT technologies and wearable equipment are important to track physiological and behavioral signs that apply to mental health. Studies have shown that smartwatches, fitness trackers, and biosensors are able to record real-time information about heart rate variation, sleep dynamics, and activity rates, which are associated with mood and stress (Gomes and Silva, 2023; Kargarandehkordi and Zhang, 2025; Pinge and Sharma, 2024). Continuous monitoring enables early detection of impaired mental health in its initial stages and allows timely tracking of interventions. Nevertheless, the privacy of data and the connection between the data obtained on a device and clinical processes

DOI: 10.1201/9781003658344-3

continue to be a concern (Greer and Williams, 2019; Kozelka and Patel, 2023; Tyagi, 2021; Berardi and Thompson, 2024).

Digital mental healthcare has been further advanced by AI, which enables predictive analytics, personalized recommendations, and automated support. Machine learning algorithms and AI-based chatbots are able to identify patterns of user behavior and physiological information to determine the risks of depression, anxiety, or relapse (Babu and Kumar, 2024; Dehbozorgi and Lee, 2025; Sun and Wang, 2025). These tools enhance precision and efficiency of treatment, but cause ethical issues in terms of algorithm transparency and bias, and data privacy, which should be addressed carefully (Badr and Lee, 2024; Thakkar and Patel, 2024; Anser and Khan, 2023).

Digital therapeutics (DTx) supplement traditional therapy by providing structured and interactive software-based interventions. The clinical research has revealed that DTx have the potential to enhance symptoms of depression, anxiety, and post-traumatic stress disorder besides increasing interest and compliance with therapeutic routines (Coelho and Silva, 2025; Dehbozorgi and Lee, 2025; Lochner and Muller, 2025). However, their potential can be limited by real-world effectiveness, regulatory difficulties, and dropout in the use of the application (Feijt and de Kort, 2023; Zhang and Wang, 2025; Kumari et al., 2025a; Catania and Miller, 2024).

Equity and accessibility remain major concerns within digital mental health. Digital divide persists due to economic, infrastructural, and digital literacy disparities, especially in underserved and rural communities (Bunyi and Patel, 2021; Williamson and Lee, 2025). Providing low-bandwidth or offline-capable interventions, adapting interventions to different populations, and community-based digital literacy programs are very important solutions to bridging this gap (Keper & Lee, 2024; Piers and Johnson, 2023; Chau and Singh, 2025). By focusing on these issues, it is possible to make sure that digital mental health solutions are provided to the people who need them the most and not unintentionally increase the disparities (Badr & Lee, 2024; Hollimon and Johnson, 2025).

The next trends in digital mental health suggest that there are more applications of immersive technologies, including virtual reality (VR) and augmented reality (AR), to improve the experiences of therapy (Rajani et al., 2022; Xing and Li, 2025; Wu and Zhang, 2025). It is integrated with electronic health records (EHRs) and full-fledged analytics, which will support coordinated care, predictive interventions, and better clinical outcomes (Torous and Hsin, 2025; Ni and Zhang, 2025). Furthermore, along with privacy-saving AI methods and federated learning, it is feasible to use a large amount of patient data without compromising confidentiality (Babu and Kumar, 2024; Sun and Wang, 2025). All this is an indicator of a future where digital mental health tools are highly tailored, data-driven, and incorporated into clinical practice without issue.

According to the literature, digital mental health devices, such as mobile applications, wearables, AI-based services, and DTx, have strong potential to enhance access, individualization, and effectiveness of mental healthcare (Ahmed and Smith, 2023; Badr and Lee, 2024; Zhang and Wang, 2025; Nair et al., 2021). Although the issues of privacy, ethical implications, engagement, and equity still persist, current research and technological advancements indicate that these interventions will keep on improving and being part of a generally holistic system of delivering mental healthcare (Kozelka and Patel, 2023; Torous and Hsin, 2025; Kumari et al., 2025b).

2.3 THE DIGITAL PLATFORMS OF TRADITIONAL THERAPY

Traditionally, the mental healthcare sector has been more dependent on face-to-face sessions, using standardized tests, and manual recording. Patients would usually be attending clinics, hospitals, or personal offices to undergo a therapy session with psychologists, psychiatrists, or counselors. Although such a classic model has worked quite well, it is usually plagued by high barriers. The long lines of waiting, the lack of trained professionals, travel issues, and social stigma toward mental health make people unable to obtain timely care, especially in rural or underserved locations.

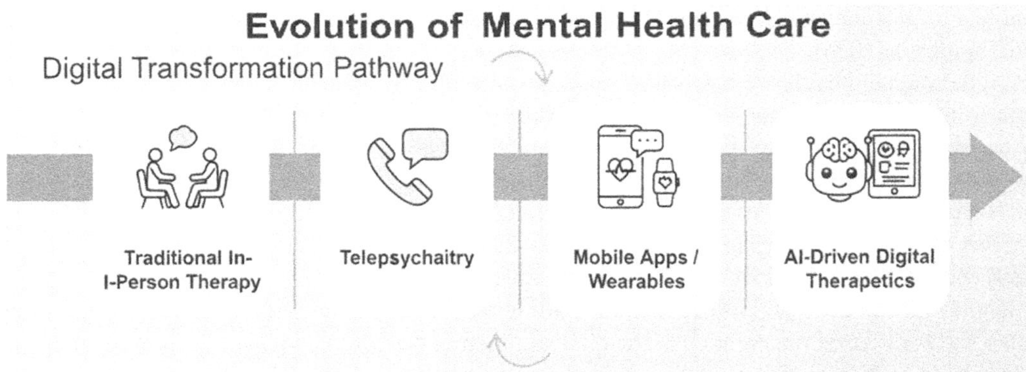

FIGURE 2.1 Development of mental health care.

With the onset of digital platforms, the solution to most of these challenges has started to be offered. Mental health teletherapy allows patients to connect with mental health professionals through safe video or audio calls remotely and eliminates geographical and logistical barriers. Simultaneously, the mobile applications provide self-directed treatment, mood tracking, therapy exercise notifications, and educational content. Such platforms are adjustable, flexible, convenient, and enable continuous communication, which enables people to take a more active role in managing their mental health.

In addition to convenience, online platforms facilitate round-the-clock surveillance of the health of the patient. Smartwatches, phone sensors, and apps track the information about sleep, activity, social activity, and moods in real time. The abundance of data enables clinicians to identify the warning signs early, identify trends, and implement suitable adjustments to the therapy plans. Consequently, the mental healthcare becomes more proactive in nature, where the intervention of conditions can be made in advance before they turn into crises.

Scalability is the other benefit of the digital platforms. The traditional types of therapy have a constraint in the number of patients that a clinician can meet within a day, whereas apps and online programs can serve thousands of users at the same time. This scalability is especially useful in those areas where the number of mental health professionals is limited or the demand surpasses the resources. Digital interventions may be used to complement face-to-face therapy and offer continuity of care as well as mental healthcare to underserved populations.

The shift from traditional to digital therapy reflects a broader transformation toward patient-centered care, which is technologically enabled. Existing patients can now access therapy at any place or time and track their progress, while therapists can provide personalized interventions based on patient needs (Figure 2.1).

2.4 EXPANSION OF TELEPSYCHIATRY AND APPS USED IN MENTAL HEALTH

One of the most important advances in digital mental healthcare has become telepsychiatry. Through secure video conferencing, patients are able to access psychiatric consultation and therapy sessions completely remotely without references to geographical barriers or to time expenditures on traffic. This method has been very useful, especially to those in rural or underserved regions where mental health workers are few. Besides enhancing access, telepsychiatry can also be used to ensure continuity of care among patients with mobility problems or limited time.

Telepsychiatry is growing together with mental health applications, which are growing exponentially. The apps are multipurpose and have numerous options, such as mood tracking and guided meditation, activities of cognitive–behavioral therapy, and stress management applications. Many of them are interactive, have some reminders and goal-setting features to enable an individual to use them frequently and track him or herself. Research shows that professional teletherapy can be effective as a combination with app-based interventions to raise the rate of treatment compliance and further application of skills learned in the process of therapy.

The COVID-19 pandemic has intensified the adoption of digital mental health tools, creating the necessity to offer remote care solutions and the importance of technology in upholding mental health services. Telepsychiatry platforms and mental health applications ensure anonymity, which helps reduce both stigma and fear that users have when seeking their help. The mental health support can easily be accessed through a screen and cases that would otherwise have avoided a face-to-face therapy due to embarrassment or fear of being criticized can access the mental health support easily.

Furthermore, AI and data analytics are increasingly utilized to make mental health applications more personalized. One example of this can be grounded on the mood pattern or the level of engagement, and the algorithms are able to recommend certain exercises to the user, and this can improve as time goes on and provide the user with specific interventions. The data insights made available via these apps in an anonymized form would also help clinicians create a treatment plan and intervene early if a patient's condition worsens in case a patient appears to be getting worse.

In general, the evolution of telepsychiatry and mental health apps demonstrates that the change in paradigm of mental care has taken place. Digital platforms have ceased to be an additional resource and are turning into a part of delivering treatment, interacting with patients, and making clinical decisions. With technological progress, the interaction between telepsychiatry, applications, and AI-based personalization will probably become the feature of the further development of mental health care accessibility, scalability, and patient-centered care.

2.5 THE USE OF WEARABLES AND IOT IN EMOTIONAL SENSING

Wearables have become an indispensable part of contemporary digital mental healthcare. Smart devices like smartwatches, fitness tracker, and biosensors are able to constantly detect physiological signals, which include heart rate variability, sleep patterns, physical activity, and stress signs. Recording such objective data, wearables can be of great use in determining the emotional and mental status of a person that complements self-reported information during the therapy or through mobile apps.

Figure 2.2 illustrates how wearables and IoT devices work together with AI to support mental health monitoring in real time. Data is collected from three main sources: wearable devices such as smartwatches and fitness trackers, which provide information on heart rate, sleep patterns, and physical activity; smartphone inputs, which include self-reported mood, social activity, and voice tone analysis; and IoT sensors, which capture environmental data and routine changes, like room conditions and movement patterns. All this information is sent to a central AI platform, where it is analyzed using data fusion and machine learning models to identify behavioral patterns and detect potential mental health issues. Based on this analysis, the system provides personalized support, including early detection of anomalies, tailored interventions such as mindfulness exercises or therapy prompts, and alerts to clinicians when needed. By continuously monitoring and analyzing data in real time, the system enables proactive and personalized mental healthcare, helping to detect issues early and provide timely support.

The possibilities of emotion sensing are also expanded by the incorporation of the IoT technology. The devices with the IoT could monitor the contextual factors, i.e., room temperature, light, noise, and movement patterns (smart home sensors, environmental monitors, etc.). These bits of information help to create a detailed picture of the environment of the patients and its influence on the mood, stress, or anxiety level. Through integration of physiological and situational information, mental health sites can better detect correlations of trends that lead to emotional distress or symptom aggravation.

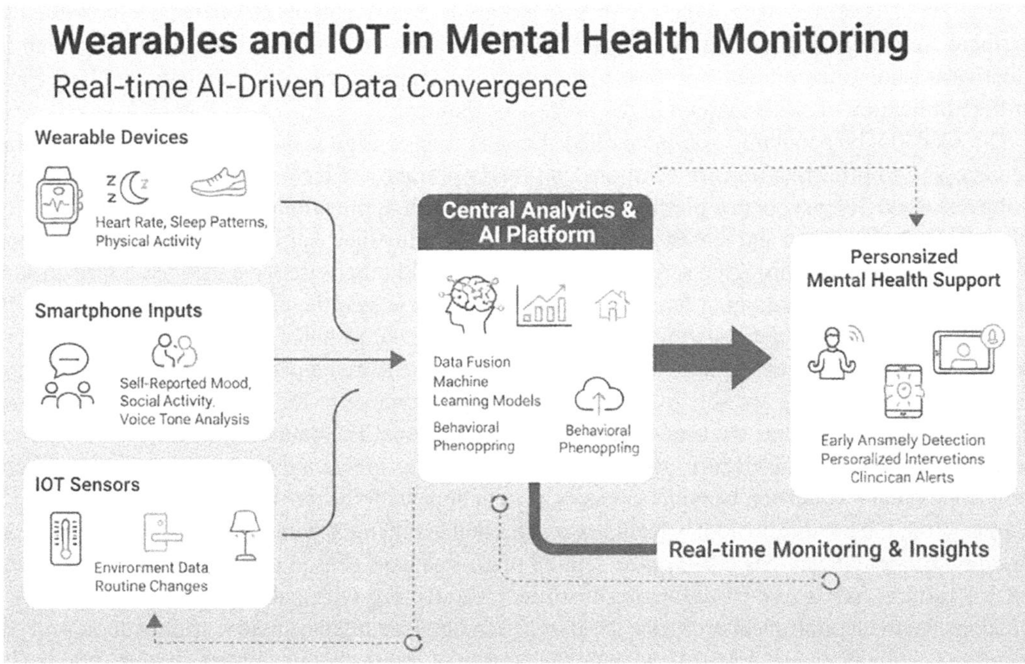

FIGURE 2.2 IoT and wearables in mental health monitoring.

Wearable and IoT data analytics processed with AI can identify subtle changes that cannot be readily identified by the clinicians or the individuals. As one example, the decline in the quality of sleep, accompanied by a decrease in social activity, can be an indicator of an impending depressive episode, and it can be intervened in time. Adaptive therapy recommendations like prompts to mindfulness exercises, recommending behavioral strategies, or providing notification to clinicians about the risk of danger can also be done by real-time monitoring.

In addition, wearables and IoT devices make patients more empowered, as it implies that patients have direct feedback about their mental conditions. Self-awareness and therapeutic regime adherence may be enhanced with trend visualization, messages that one needs to practice healthy habits, or messages that his or her physiology has changed. The patients feel in control and in charge as they are empowered and actively responsible in terms of their mental health.

Intersection of wearable technology, IoT, and AI is forming a more proactive predictive paradigm of mental healthcare. Emotional sensing enables the clinicians to skip reactive treatment and advance to constant observation and advance intervention. These technologies will probably become an increasingly significant part of the individualized and data-driven mental healthcare ecosystems as they become more accessible and more integrated into digital platforms.

2.6 BACKGROUND AND RELEVANCE OF DTX

DTx are a novel type of health interventions that are provided in the form of software programs that can prevent, manage, or treat mental health conditions. However, unlike general wellness applications, DTx solutions are evidence-based, and in many cases, they go through intensive clinical validation like pharmaceutical or medical device interventions. They offer programmed and interactive courses that assist patients in undertaking therapy exercises, behavioral changes, or cognitive training courses.

This scientific basis has seen to it that DTx does not just enhance the mental well-being but can also have quantifiable clinical effects. Clinically, it has been established that DTx interventions support the

TABLE 2.1
Digital Mental Health Interventions Comparison

Types of Intervention	Major Characteristics	Evidence of Effectiveness	Limitations	References
Telepsychiatry	Video sessions, distance therapy	Effective in depression, anxiety	Internet, digital literacy needed	Ahmed & Smith, 2023; Kwon & Lee, 2024; Mishra et al., 2024
Mobile apps	Mood tracking, exercises, reminders	Intermediate anxiety, adherence improvements	Attrition, adherence issues	Bridge & Green, 2025; Li & Zhang, 2023
Wearables	Heart rate, sleep, activity	Early stress, changes in moods	Data privacy, cost of the device	Gomes & Silva, 2023; Pinge & Sharma, 2024
AI chatbots	Symptom tracking, medical advice and treatment	All-purpose suggestions	Limited human empathy, ethical issues	Babu & Kumar, 2024; Dehbozorgi & Lee, 2025; Tyagi, 2025
Digital therapeutics (DTx)	Evidence-based interactive programmes	Clinical improvements	Regulatory challenges and uncertainties regarding the real-world performance of DTx	Coelho & Silva, 2025; Löchner & Müller, 2025

management of mental health conditions by improving symptoms, treatment adherence, and access to care. The randomized controlled trials have demonstrated that DTx are able to reduce the severity of the symptoms and improve coping mechanisms and increase the degree of commitment to the therapy processes. They are interactive, gamified, and with real-time feedback, making them engaging and supporting long-term behavior change. Moreover, DTx can improve the overall effectiveness of treatment. The other important benefit of DTx is scalability. As opposed to face-to-face therapy, which has a constraint of clinician presence and patient appointment, DTx is capable of serving high numbers of users at a time. This is particularly useful in areas that have limited access to mental health practitioners or in areas where populations are constrained in terms of mobility or time. Across diverse patient groups, DTx solutions provide a high-quality, consistent care with the use of mobile platforms, cloud computing, and AI-directed personalization. The data of DTx are also rich and reveal patient behavior, symptom formation, and response to treatment to clinicians and researchers.

One of the strategies is continuous observation that enables one to notice the exacerbation of the symptoms early enough, thus offering a chance to act in time and reduce the chances of crisis. Besides, the lessons learned using DTx can stimulate cyclic improvements in the therapy plans, and this will enable better interventions to be executed in the future. The digital platforms have an increased scalability as seen in Table 2.1 compared to the traditional approaches to mental healthcare delivery models.

DTx is an emerging trend that is evidence-based and promising to be used in the context of mental healthcare. They are inexpensive, scalable, and personal interventions, and quantifiable in terms of clinical outcomes. The redesign of mental health systems to the system of DTx can help clinicians and patients enjoy a more efficient, proactive, and data-driven care and fill the gap between the traditional therapy and the digital solutions that are used nowadays.

2.7 INNOVATIONS IN AI AND DATA ANALYTICS ON A PERSONAL LEVEL

The digital age has positioned AI and data analytics to be the key to personalized mental healthcare. Patterns in behavior, emotional condition, and physiological responses can be discovered by AI models that can analyze large volumes of data in mobile apps and wearables, as well as in clinical records. This allows mental health platforms to provide interventions that are specific to needs, maximizing the results of therapy and increasing the level of patient engagement. Care plans become individualized, moving beyond generic recommendations, and each patient will get a care plan based on the profile of his or her mental health.

Predictive analytics also increases the level of personalization as it predicts possible mental illness threats. Depression, anxiety, and relapse are early warning signs that AI algorithms are able to recognize based on behavioral, physiological, or context clues. As an example, the reduction of physical activity, the lack of sleep, or social interaction might be a hint to the increased vulnerability to emotional distress. Through detecting these patterns, platforms are able to offer interventions in time, including modifying therapy activities, delivering inspirations, or warning clinicians to be proactive.

The adaptive therapy supported by machine learning is another method, where digital interventions are also developed depending on the user responses. An example would be that an app would suggest a patient with more consistent symptoms to do more intensive cognitive behavioral exercises, or would suggest a decrease in the prompts to the patient with consistent progress. This dynamic adaptation stands greater chances of making the therapeutic approaches more effective, relevant and adherent in the long term.

The application of AI-based personalization has also critical ethical and privacy concerns attached to it. The data on mental health should also be placed in a secure facility, de-anonymized when needed, and handled in the laws and regulations, i.e., Health Insurance Portability and Accountability Act (HIPAA) or General Data Protection Regulation (GDPR). A clear algorithm, consent, and participation of the user in data utilization are necessary in building trust and the ability to use AI.

Essentially, AI and data analytics based on personalization can change mental health care approach from one-size-fits-all to a responsive model. Incorporating real-time observations, predictive analytics, and adaptive interventions, AI helps digital platforms to provide mental health support to patients in the most effective and patient-centric manner and increase the effectiveness of engagement and clinical outcomes.

2.8 ADDRESSING THE DIGITAL DIVIDE

Although digital mental health technologies are rapidly developing, there is one major problem, and it is unequal access to them. Digital divide is the difference between those who are assured of having access to technology, high-speed internet, and digital literacy, and those who are not. The population in low-resource areas, rural communities, and underserved communities is likely to have obstacles impeding access to the benefits of digital mental health interventions. This gap may impact and increase the current disparity in providing care and mental health outcomes.

Figure 2.3 illustrates how AI is integrated into digital mental health using a hybrid model that combines AI support with clinician oversight. At the top, AI components like predictive analytics, personalization algorithms, and chatbots/virtual assistants analyze patient data and provide recommendations. This information feeds into clinician oversight and decision support, where healthcare professionals review AI insights, adjust treatment plans, and provide teleconsultations. Simultaneously, DTx and patient engagement tools—such as guided exercises, gamification, and interventions—collect patient feedback and monitor progress. All these elements work together to improve mental healthcare outcomes by enabling early detection of issues, better access to care, personalized treatment, and continuous monitoring and adaptation of interventions. Essentially, AI supports clinicians while enhancing patient engagement for more effective mental healthcare.

2.9 THE ISSUE OF AVAILABILITY IN RESOURCE-POOR CONDITIONS

Implementing the digital mental health solutions in the low-resource setting has a couple of unique challenges. Infrastructure limitations such as unreliable power supply, slow internet connection, and

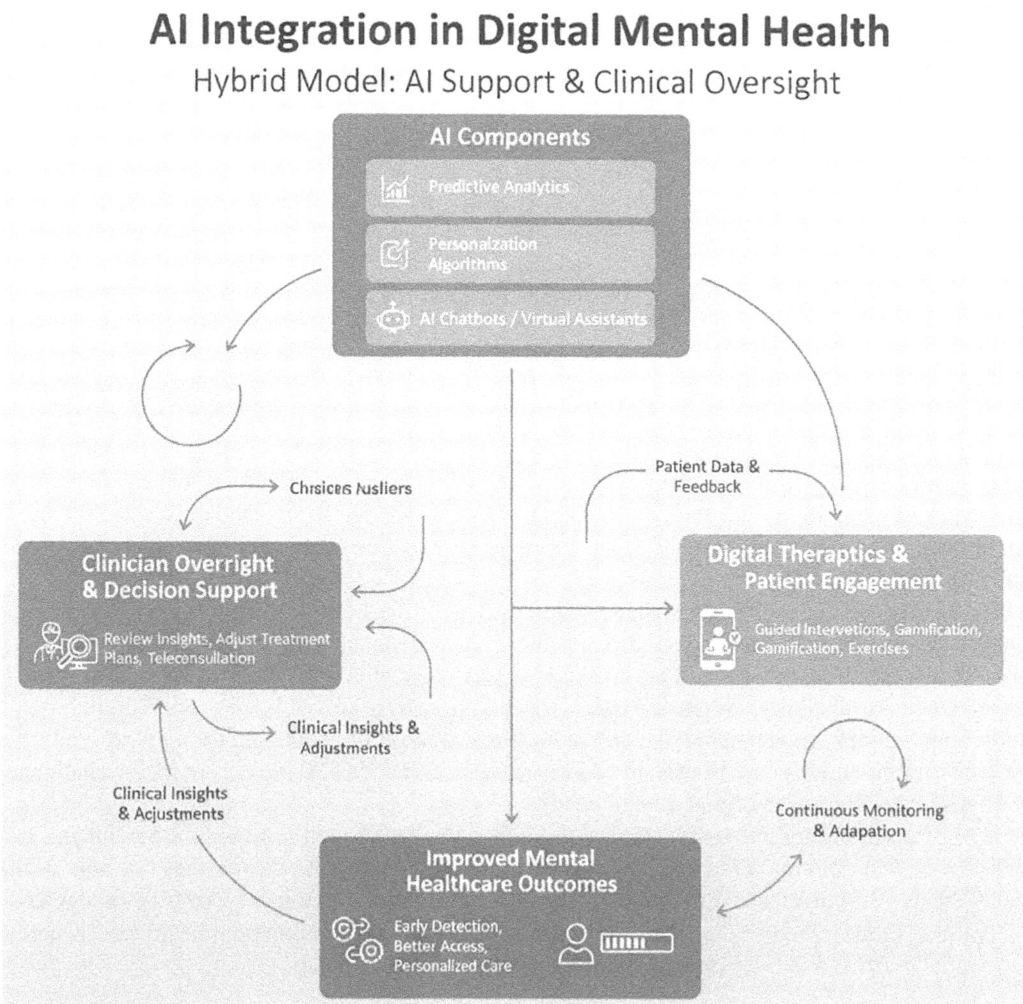

FIGURE 2.3 Mental health informatics AI.

access to a smartphone or a computer may restrict the utilization of the teletherapy platform, mobile applications, and wearable devices. These technical limitations make sure that patients are not active regarding the use of digital interventions regularly and will reduce its effectiveness and performance in terms of mental health outcomes.

The economic constraints improve accessibility. The large population in low-resource areas could be unable to afford smartphones, data plan, and wearable devices to facilitate complete use of digital mental health tools. Furthermore, establishment of localized and culturally oriented programs might prove to be costly, and this limits the application of applications that have the capacity to address the specific needs of different populations. The under-service of these communities with no scalable and affordable solutions is still observed, even when it is possible to benefit through digital mental health intervention.

Cultural and social factors also define accessibility. The mental health stigmatization and prejudice can make people unwilling to seek help, and the lack of literacy and knowledge of languages can emerge as the obstacles to successful implementation and web use. These are the problems that must be considered with some possible solutions, which include the use of multilingual applications,

TABLE 2.2
Challenges, Problems, and Solutions in Digital Mental Health

Challenge	Impact	Mitigation Strategy	References
Digital divide	Low-resource accessibility	Offline applications, cost-effective devices, local education	Bunyi & Patel, 2021; Williamson & Lee, 2025; Tyagi & Tiwari, 2024a
Privacy, ethics	Risk of breach, bias	Federated learning, ethical AI faces encryption	Thakkar & Patel, 2024; Sun & Wang, 2025
Participation/retention	Week compliance, dropout	Gamification, reminders, hybrid therapy	Feijt & de Kort, 2023; Balamurugan et al., 2023
Cultural/language adversaries	Reduced effectiveness	Multilingual practice, culturally modified content	Piers & Johnson, 2023; Kepper & Lee, 2024; Tyagi et al., 2024c

audio-based content within low-literacy groups, and the population need to be educated about the importance of using digital technology in mental health to prevent stigma and encourage the use of digital technologies instead of paper-based forms of information exchange between the population and medical professionals.

The barriers to accessibility need to be defeated with the help of cooperation. Governments, non-governmental organizations (NGOs), healthcare providers, and technology developers ought to all work together to come up with easy-to-use, contextually relevant, and affordable platforms. To narrow down the disparity and ensure that the population most in need can receive digital mental health interventions, apps that may be utilized offline, cheap equipment, and training programs that involve the communities may be used to address these discrepancies. Table 2.2 shows the challenges, problems, and solutions in digital mental health.

Issue of accessibility in low-resource settings is complicated and it consists of technical, economic, and even cultural concerns. These issues must be resolved to ensure that not only digital mental health solutions are equitable but also effective and capable of covering underserved populations. Putting inclusiveness and local acculturation first, digital mental healthcare is able to increase its reach and deliver valuable assistance to the global population.

2.10 INTEGRATION OF CLINICAL PSYCHOLOGY AND PSYCHIATRY

Digital mental health tools best fit in an integration with conventional clinical psychology and psychiatry practices. Although apps, teletherapy, and AI-based interventions are flexible and accessible, they are not meant to substitute the human clinician. Integration predetermines the fact that digital devices are used to add to the range of professional attention so that patients could enjoy both regular monitoring and professional assistance. Clinicians can apply the acquired knowledge on digital platforms to inform treatment approaches, follow-up, and achieve the required changes; this will result in a more personalized care strategy and enhance its effectiveness.

One of the major features of this integration is secure data sharing. Digital platforms can collect mood, behavior, sleep, and physiological data in real time and transmit it to clinicians without breaching patient privacy and breaching laws and regulations, including the HIPAA and GDPR. The factors that mental health professionals can be capable of making in case such information is present are evidence-based decisions, early warning signs of relapse, and proactive intervention. The integration also creates a coordinated care which can be used to communicate between therapists, psychiatrists, and other healthcare professionals that are part of treatment of a patient.

Successful integration is dependent on training and workflow change. Clinicians must be conversant with digital tools, know their potential, and their limitations, and learn to interpret data products in an efficient way. The digital platforms should be planned to be integrated into the existing clinical workflow without creating excessive disruption and making its use as productive as possible. Integration can be used to improve patient outcomes, strengthen the therapeutic alliance, and increase clinician efficiency through combining the best of the human factor and technology when integrated properly.

Lastly, integration facilitates patient engagement. When patients are assured that the tools are supported and integrated by their caregivers, it is easier to make them more willing to use these digital tools on a regular basis. It also provides the continuation of care as the digital interventions will not be applied as a separate intervention, but only as a supplement to the face-to-face therapies. The digital innovation could be used to rectify the imbalance between the patient-centered and holistic approach to clinical practice of mental health services, which is effective and sustainable.

2.11 DIGITAL ECOSYSTEM TRENDS IN FUTURE

It is likely that the more advanced and networked ecosystems will define the future of digital mental healthcare. The technologies that are emerging, including AI, machine learning, VR, and AR, are likely to make the interventions more effective and personalized. Adaptive systems based on AI are in a position to scan the behavior and emotional states of patients continuously to provide them with personalized therapeutic content in real time and deliver a highly responsive, personalized care experience.

VR and AR apps are also becoming the focus of attention as an immersive therapy experience. For example, exposure therapy implemented through VR may assist patients in overcoming the phobia or anxiety stimuli in a secure, safe setting, whereas AR applications might facilitate cognitive therapy and mindfulness training. Such technologies provide a possibility of expanding the therapeutic modalities beyond the regular therapy sessions as interventions are more engaging, interactive, and effective.

Figure 2.4 shows an Adaptive Shared Control Loop that is developed when dealing with a high-stakes human–robot interaction (HRI) situation like teleoperation, rehabilitation, and surgical robotics. Such architecture facilitates smooth synergy between human intelligence, which has the ability to make judgment, plan, and even act out of intuition, and the robotic precision, which is more accurate, stable, and executes without fatigue. The adaptive term indicates that the degree of robot intervention is not predetermined but constantly changed based on the quality of input of the human, his/her confidence, and the perceived intention.

This loop starts with the human input, which is usually recorded through control devices (joysticks and wearable exoskeletons or force-feedback handles). This raw command is then transmitted to two modules at the same time, the Intent Estimation Module and the Shared Control Layer. The Intent Estimation Module interprets the objective and state of performance of the human-is-confident or struggling-user based on the patterns of control, physiological indicators, and situation. This estimation is used to control the Shared Control Layer that acts as an adaptive arbitrator. It combines two parallel command lines: Human Override, which is the filtered human command to provide stringent control, and Robot Assistance, which offers autonomous assistance, e.g., tremor suppression, collision avoidance, or trajectory correction.

The robot then executes the final blended command and provides new feedback to both the human and the intent estimator, such that one can keep on refining the degree of assistance. This control feedback means that the power is in the hands of the human operator, and the robot only interferes when required. Consequently, the system provides safer, more natural, and more effective performance of tasks by balancing the flexibility of humans with the intelligence of the robots.

By uniting wearable and IoT sensors and mobile apps, the flow of information will become uninterrupted via multi-layered information delivery to facilitate the entire monitoring of mental health. Federated learning and AI privacy preservation are most likely to be applied in the digital ecosystem of the future to analyze enormous amounts of patient data without integrity loss and

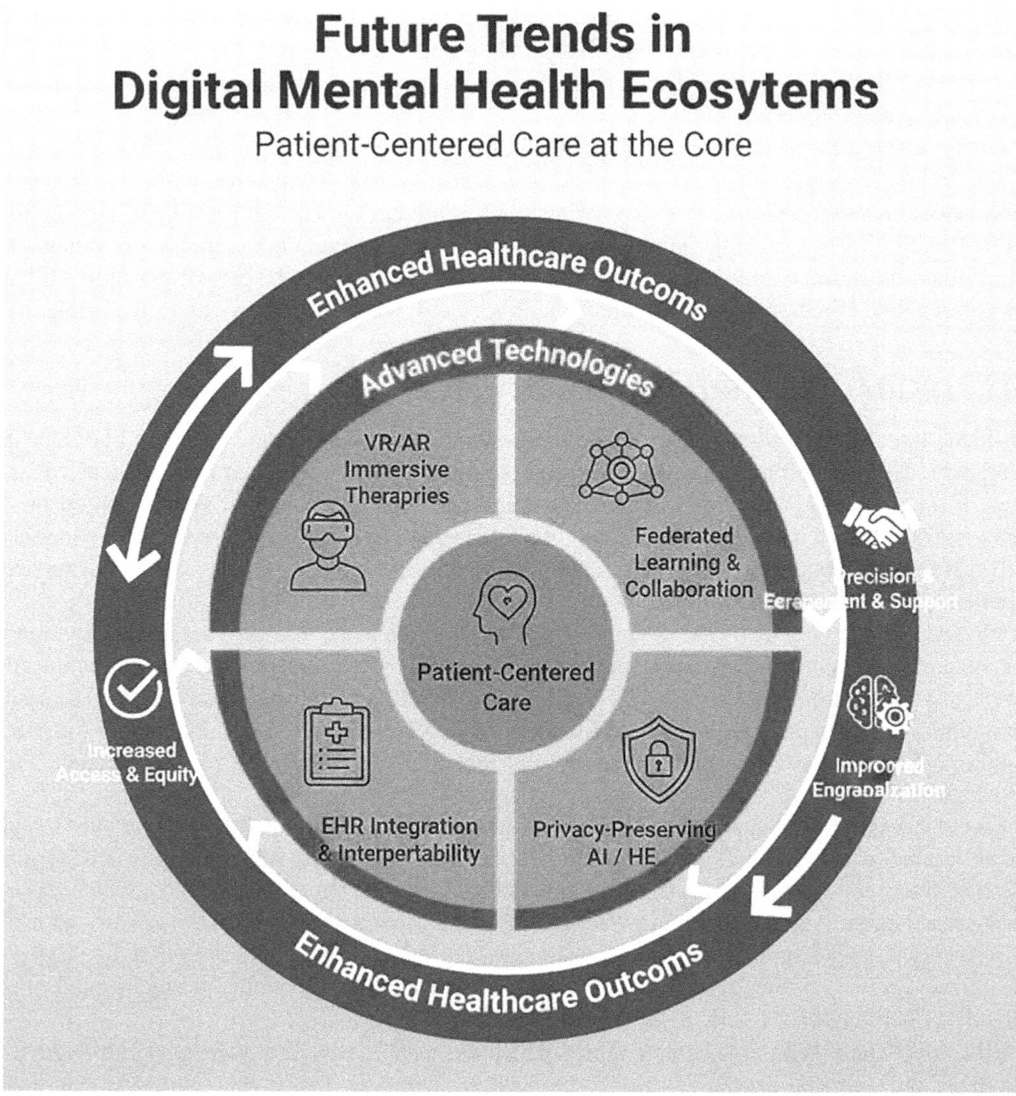

FIGURE 2.4 Digital mental health ecosystem future trends.

confidentiality loss. This may be applied to make unremitting improvements in predictive models, adaptive therapy recommendations, and personalized interventions without violating ethical and regulatory standards.

Digital ecosystem utility enhanced further because of the interoperability with EHRs and clinical systems has enhanced. To make clinical decisions, early intervention, and allow more precise quantification of the treatment outcomes, a coherent care across multiple platforms is necessary to ensure that patient data is used to make a clinical decision. Further, cross-platform integration can be used to promote collaboration between healthcare providers, researchers, and technology developers, which promotes the accelerated innovation of mental healthcare delivery.

Digital ecosystems in mental healthcare of the future will consist of a higher degree of personalization, immersive therapeutic experience, and an integration of combined and directly data-driven interventions. These trends portend well of an active, patient-centered practice, in which technology would enhance clinical practice, facilitate long-term follow-up, and allow patients to play a more active role in the management of their mental health. Combined, all these innovations will render the delivery of mental health services more efficient, approachable to the needs of the individuals; easier to access, effective, and responsive.

2.12 SUMMARY

The digital revolution in the mental health field has radically transformed care delivery, making it more affordable, scalable, and individualized. Face-to-face therapy was not without its challenges, which also included the shortage of specialists, long queues, and stigma that surrounded the need to use mental health services. Most of these shortcomings are eliminated now that digital platforms, including telepsychiatry, mobile apps, wearables, and AI-based analytics are introduced, and flexible and sustained care options can be offered.

Proactive and data-driven measures can be provided through digital mental health tools that can provide a superior method of accessibility. Wearables and IoT can give objective data on the basis of physiological and behavioral indicators, whereas AI and data analysis can tailor the therapeutic intervention to the requirements of an individual. Direct-to-Consumer (DTCs) have evidence-based therapies, which can be used to supplement primary therapy and improve adherence, engagement, and clinical outcomes. The combination of these technologies in clinical psychology and psychiatry determines that the patients enjoy both the human skills and technological sophistication.

Although these steps have been made, there are still difficulties. The digital mental health solutions may be limited with digital divide, economic constraints, weak digital literacy, and cultural barriers. As an attempt to uphold the trust and efficiency, the most important thing is that sensitive data must be accessed fairly, privately, and in a morally right way. The key to delivering patient-centered care is the inclusion design, cultural accommodation of content, and community-based interventions.

Based on the existing trends, more sophisticated forms of digital ecosystems are featured by AI-based personalization, VR therapy, interoperable platforms, as well as analytics that uphold privacy, will cooperate with each other to provide full mental health treatment. It is possible to embrace the innovations to enhance the early intervention, patient outcomes, and redefine the patient–clinician relationship. Ensuring that digital mental health services are viable, responsive, and widely available requires a blend of technological advancement and ethical, equitable implementation.

REFERENCES

Ahmed, A., & Smith, J. (2023). Wearable devices for anxiety & depression: A scoping review. *Journal of Digital Health*, *5*(1), 12–25. https://doi.org/10.1016/j.cmpbup.2023.100095

Anser, M. K., & Khan, M. A. (2023). Advancing mental health care: A comprehensive review of digital mental health tools. *Health Systems*, *12*(3), 45–59. https://doi.org/10.1002/hcs2.70018

Babu, A., & Kumar, R. (2024). Artificial intelligence in mental healthcare: Transformative potential and challenges. *Frontiers in Psychology*, *15*, 1378904. https://doi.org/10.3389/fpsyg.2024.1378904

Badr, J., & Lee, S. (2024). Digital health technologies and inequalities: A scoping review. *Social Science & Medicine*, *300*, 114–123. https://doi.org/10.1016/j.healthpol.2024.105122

Balamurugan, G., Tyagi, A.K., Richa, A. (2023). Survey on privacy preserving and trust building techniques of blockchain-based systems. In: *Privacy Preservation and Secured Data Storage in Cloud Computing*. IGI Global. DOI: 10.4018/979-8-3693-0593-5.ch019

Berardi, C., & Thompson, L. (2024). Systematic review and meta-analysis of performance metrics in digital mental health interventions. *BMC Health Services Research*, *23*(1), 10536.

Bridge, L. A., & Green, D. (2025). Digital mental health tools: A narrative review on accessibility and effectiveness. *Journal of Medical Internet Research*, *27*(2), e1884. https://doi.org/10.1016/j.maturitas.2025.108380

Bunyi, J., & Patel, V. (2021). Accessibility and digital mental health: Considerations for equitable implementation. *Journal of Global Health*, *11*(1), 010401. https://doi.org/10.3389/fdgth.2021.742196

Catania, J., & Miller, C. (2024). Evaluation of digital mental health technologies in the United States: A systematic literature review. *JMIR Mental Health, 11*(1), e57401. https://doi.org/10.2196/57401

Chau, L. W., & Singh, A. (2025). Digital health interventions for depression and anxiety in low-resource settings: A rapid scoping review. *JMIR Mental Health, 12*(1), e68296. https://doi.org/10.2196/68296

Coelho, J., & Silva, P. (2025). Promoting mental health in the age of new digital tools. *Frontiers in Digital Health, 7*, 1560580. https://doi.org/10.3389/fdgth.2025.1560580

Dehbozorgi, R., & Lee, S. (2025). The application of artificial intelligence in the field of mental health: Enhancing early detection and personalized treatment. *BMC Psychiatry, 25*(1), 64. https://doi.org/10.1186/s12888-025-06483-2

Feijt, M., & de Kort, Y. (2023). Integrating technology in mental healthcare practice: A national survey in the Netherlands. *Frontiers in Psychiatry, 13*, 1040023. https://doi.org/10.3389/fpsyt.2022.1040023

Gomes, N., & Silva, J. (2023). A survey on wearable sensors for mental health monitoring. *Journal of Medical Internet Research, 25*(4), e9919280. https://doi.org/10.3390/s23031330

Greer, B., & Williams, S. (2019). Digital exclusion among mental health service users. *Psychiatric Services, 70*(12), 1075–1081. https://doi.org/10.1176/appi.ps.201900125

Hollimon, L. A., & Johnson, M. (2025). Redefining and solving the digital divide and exclusion to improve mental health access. *Frontiers in Digital Health, 7*, 1508686. https://doi.org/10.1186/s12913-023-10536-1

Kargarandehkordi, A., & Zhang, Y. (2025). Fusing wearable biosensors with artificial intelligence for mental health monitoring. *Sensors, 15*(4), 202. https://doi.org/10.3390/bios15040202

Kepper, M. M., & Lee, H. (2024). Expanding a behavioral view on digital health access: Strategies for equity. *JMIR Mental Health, 11*(1), e51355. https://doi.org/10.2196/51355

Kozelka, E. E., & Patel, V. (2023). Identifying barriers to digital mental health access among people with serious mental illness. *The Lancet Digital Health, 5*(3), e156–e164. https://doi.org/10.1016/j.ssmmh.2023.100241

Kumari, S., Tyagi, A. K., Tiwari, S., & Kulshreshtha, G. (2025a). Sensors and digital twin for healthcare monitoring frameworks. In T. A. Nguyen (Ed.), *Digital twin, blockchain, and sensor networks in the healthy and mobile city (Chapter 10,* pp. 147–177*)*. Elsevier. https://doi.org/10.1016/B978-0-443-34174-8.00011-9

Kumari, S., Tyagi, A. K., Tiwari, S., & Singh, R. (2025b). Medical sensor network, edge computing and blockchain for efficient medical data exchange. In T. A. Nguyen (Ed.), *Digital twin, blockchain, and sensor networks in the healthy and mobile city (Chapter 11)*. Elsevier. https://doi.org/10.1016/B978-0-443-34174-8.00012-0

Kwon, H., & Lee, S. (2024). A review of current digital mental health care applications for anxiety symptoms. *Psychiatry Investigation, 21*(2), 174–183. https://doi.org/10.30773/pi.2023.0339

Li, H., & Zhang, Y. (2023). Systematic review and meta-analysis of AI-based chatbots in improving mental health. *npj Digital Medicine, 6*(1), 79. https://doi.org/10.1038/s41746-023-00979-5

Lochner, J., & Muller, S. (2025). Digital interventions in mental health: An overview and critical examination. *Journal of Affective Disorders, 300*, 1–10. https://doi.org/10.1016/j.jad.2025.01.025

Mishra, A. K., Tiwari, S., Tyagi, A. K., & Arowolo, M. O. (2024). Security, privacy, trust, and provenance issues in Internet of Things–based edge environment. In S. Pal, C. Savaglio, R. Minerva, & F. C. Delicato (Eds.), *IoT edge intelligence* (pp. 233–263). Springer. https://doi.org/10.1007/978-3-031-58388-9_8

Nair, M. M., & Tyagi, A. K. (2021). Privacy: History, statistics, policy, laws, preservation and threat analysis. *Journal of information assurance & security, 16*(1), 24–34.

Nair, M.M., & Tyagi, A.K. (2025). Transformative effects of emerging technologies on Industry 5.0 and Society 5.0: Current status, vision, issues, challenges, and opportunities for future. In: *Next Generation Data Science and Blockchain Technology for Industry 5.0.* Wiley. DOI: https://doi.org/10.1002/9781394245215.ch13, ISBN: 9781394245185.

Ni, Y., & Zhang, L. (2025). A scoping review of AI-driven digital interventions in mental health care. *Journal of Medical Internet Research, 27*(1), e1210772. https://doi.org/10.3390/healthcare13101205

Piers, R., & Johnson, M. (2023). Review: Can digital mental health interventions bridge the digital divide? *Journal of Child Psychology and Psychiatry, 64*(10), 12620. https://doi.org/10.1111/camh.12620

Pinge, A., & Sharma, R. (2024). Detection and monitoring of stress using wearables: A systematic review. *Frontiers in Computer Science, 6*, 1478851. https://doi.org/10.3389/fcomp.2024.1478851

Rajani, D., Menon, S. C., Kute, S., & Tyagi, A. K. (2022). Preserving privacy of social media data using artificial intelligence techniques. In A. Tyagi (Ed.), *Handbook of Research on Technical, Privacy, and*

Security Challenges in a Modern World (pp. 186–204). IGI Global. https://doi.org/10.4018/978-1-6684-5250-9.ch010

Sun, J., & Wang, L. (2025). Practical AI application in psychiatry: Historical review and future directions. *Molecular Psychiatry, 30*(4), 1072–1081. https://doi.org/10.1038/s41380-025-03072-3

Thakkar, A., & Patel, V. (2024). Artificial intelligence in positive mental health: A narrative review. *Journal of Affective Disorders, 300*, 1–10. https://doi.org/10.1016/j.jad.2024.01.025

Torous, J., & Hsin, H. (2025). The evolving field of digital mental health: Current evidence and future directions. *Journal of Medical Internet Research, 27*(1), e12079407. https://doi.org/10.1002/wps.21299

Tyagi, A., Kumari, S., & Tiwari, S. (2024c). Internet of Things for smart healthcare: A survey. In A. K. Sharma, N. Chanderwal, S. Tyagi, & P. Upadhyay (Eds.), *Future of AI in medical imaging (Chapter 2,* pp. 19–41*)*. IGI Global. https://doi.org/10.4018/979-8-3693-2359-5.ch002

Tyagi, A. K., & Tiwari, S. (2024a). Blockchain-enabled smart healthcare applications in 6G networks. In A. K. Tyagi (Ed.), *Digital twin and blockchain for smart cities (Chapter 20, pp.* 459–494*)*. Wiley. https://doi.org/10.1002/9781394303564.ch20

Tyagi, A.K. (2021). Analysis of security and privacy aspects of blockchain technologies from smart era' perspective: The challenges and a way forward. In: *Recent Trends in Blockchain for Information Systems Security and Privacy* (pp. 1–17). DOI: https://doi.org/10.1201/9781003139737, eBook-ISBN: 9781003139737

Tyagi, A.K. (2025). Blockchain for smart hospital in Healthcare 5.0: modeling structure, challenges, and future emerging trends. In: *Human-Centric Integration of Next-Generation Data Science and Blockchain Technology.* Elsevier. DOI: https://doi.org/10.1016/B978-0-443-33498-6.00026-1, ISBN: 978-0-443-33498-6.

Tyagi, A. K., Tripathi, K., Tiwari, S., & Kaushik, S. (2025). An efficient technique for privacy preservation, trusted and secure patient-centric services in smart healthcare. In *Proceedings of the 6th international conference on recent trends in communication & intelligent systems (ICRTCIS 2025)* (pp. 31–47). IET. https://doi.org/10.1049/icp.2025.2731

Williamson, A. K., & Lee, S. (2025). Clarifying digital divide dynamics and their consequences for mental health access. *Journal of Medical Internet Research, 27*(1), e12099397. https://pubmed.ncbi.nlm.nih.gov/40417534/

Wu, H., & Zhang, Y. (2025). Digital psychiatry: Concepts, framework, and implications. *Frontiers in Psychiatry, 16*, 1572444. https://doi.org/10.3389/fpsyt.2025.1572444

Xing, Y., & Li, H. (2025). Intelligent sensing devices and systems for personalized mental health care. *Journal of Healthcare Engineering, 2025*, 44258. https://doi.org/10.1007/s44258-025-00057-3

Zhang, L., & Wang, J. (2025). Digital health in low-resource settings: Comprehensive analysis and future prospects. *Stroke, 56*(9), 1234–1245. https://doi.org/10.1161/STROKEAHA.125.050448

3 Data Privacy and Security in AI-Driven Mental Health Ecosystems

3.1 INTRODUCTION

Artificial intelligence (AI) has increasingly influenced mental health services over the past 2 years and has been leveraged to enhance applications such as symptom monitoring, tailored therapy, and even early detection of mental illness. Real-time insights, interventions, and support are now offered by mobile applications, chatbots, virtual therapists, and wearable-integrated platforms and, in many cases, exceed the traditional provision of services in terms of accessibility and scalability. Although these technologies hold significant potential to enhance mental well-being, they rely on collecting, processing, and storing highly sensitive personal information, such as patterns of behavior, mood diaries, voice records, and physiological indexes.

Mental health records are confidential, and breaches of privacy can have particularly severe consequences. Unlicensed access or misuse can result in social stigma, discrimination, or psychological harm to users. In contrast to the general health data, the mental health information has significant social and ethical consequences, and strong protection measures on the technical, organizational, and regulatory levels are required.

This chapter examines the issues and remedies that face the task of guaranteeing privacy and security in AI-based mental health ecosystems. It looks at the entire lifecycle of data, including its collection, storage, and processing through to its sharing; the usual points of vulnerability; threats that may occur; and the trade-offs between privacy and usability. In addition, it gives technical mechanisms like encryption, access control, differential privacy, federated learning, and data minimization as well as governance frameworks that touch on consent, ownership, and ethical compliance. Through a combination of these views, the chapter is intended to equip the researchers, developers, and policymakers with an in-depth view of creating AI mental health systems that are secure, ethical, and user-friendly.

3.2 LITERATURE REVIEW

The swift adoption of AI in the field of mental health has provided opportunities for personalized care, mental health detection, and consistent monitoring of behavioral trends never seen before. Nevertheless, this integration necessitates addressing complex privacy and security issues, because AI systems require an immense volume of personal data collection, storage, and processing of sensitive and personal data (Lustgarten, 2020; Zhang and Yin, 2025; Nair et al., 2025). Protecting the confidentiality of users' mental health information while enabling effective AI interventions has emerged as a key challenge in research and practice.

DOI: 10.1201/9781003658344-4

3.2.1 Mental Health Privacy-Preserving AI Techniques

Recent findings have underscored the need to have privacy safeguarding mechanisms in AI systems to safeguard vulnerable mental health information. Differential privacy has been extensively researched to prevent re-identification of individuals in big data and remain useful in analysis (Tayyeh and Wang, 2024; Truex et al., 2020; Tyagi, 2021). In differential privacy, limited noise is added to datasets or model outputs so that individual contributions cannot be identified, while preserving prediction accuracy.

Another important strategy of protecting privacy is federated learning. In federated learning, the AI models are trained locally at the user devices, and only model updates are sent to a center without any raw personal data exchange (Dubey and Bokoro, 2025; Horvath et al., 2023; Khalil and Zhang, 2024; Kumari et al., 2025a). This approach has been a specific success where it is necessary to constantly record behavioral and physiological data to monitor a condition, including depression, anxiety, or stress (Wang et al., 2024; Sarwar and Roy Dipta, 2025).

Differential privacy and federated learning can be applied together to allow collaborative training of models to be performed safely and with minimized risks when compared to central data storage. Liu et al. (2024) presented a federated learning framework built on blockchain, which optimizes the use of adaptive differential privacy to improve the security of sensitive healthcare data, which shows that privacy-preserving AI is practical in the field of mental health.

3.2.2 Data Security, Access Control, and Encryption

In addition to AI methods, encryption and access control are some of the pillars of safeguarding sensitive mental health data. Symmetric and asymmetric encryption methods, such as end-to-end encryption, will stop unauthorized access to the stored information and information on the way (Settu, 2017a, 2017b; Tembani, 2024). Symmetric encryption such as Advanced Encryption Standard (AES) is efficient for large datasets, while asymmetric encryption is useful in multi-user scenarios requiring secure key exchange (Liu et al., 2024; Kumari et al., 2025b). New technologies such as homomorphic encryption and secure multiparty computation (SMPC) will allow AI systems to manipulate encrypted data and thus eliminate the risk of exposure further (Xie et al., 2024; Mishra et al., 2024).

There are access control systems such as role-based access control (RBAC) and attribute-based access control (ABAC) that offer a fine-grained ability to control accessibility to sensitive data (Ross, 2025; Tyagi, 2025). These controls ensure that only authorized clinicians or researchers can access and process personal data in accordance with institutional policies. Encryption and access control are supplemented with audit trails and monitoring systems that may be used to trace all the data access and modification events, which is crucial in uncovering the cases of unauthorized activity and addressing the regulatory requirements (APA Services, 2024).

3.2.3 Ethical and Regulatory Issues

Mental health data governance is influenced by not only technical aspects but also other factors such as ethics and regulations. Health Insurance Portability and Accountability Act (HIPAA), General Data Protection Regulation (GDPR), and upcoming regulations based on AI will ensure strict measures on data collection, storage, and processing and focus on the principles of transparency, informed consent, and the right to access or destroy personal data (American Psychological Association, 2016; American Counselling Association and APA, 2025). The adherence to them is essential in safeguarding the users and securing confidence in the use of AI in mental health services (Zhang and Yin, 2025; Tyagi and Tiwari, 2024).

The other ethical implications are in the form of fairness, accountability, and explainability in AI models. AI systems should not be biased to target specific groups of users (especially those who are vulnerable users with mental conditions), and such biases should not be disproportionately represented (Li and Zhang, 2023; Lustgarten, 2020). The techniques of explainable AI (XAI) assist clinicians and users to gain insights into model outputs and increase trust in them as well as in the safety and clinical relevance of interventions (Ross, 2025).

Anonymization and pseudonymization are other ethical measures that will reduce the risk of re-identification and still can be used to conduct research and train AI models (Settu, 2017a, 2017b). Together with encryption, access control, and federated learning, they create a multi-layered defense protocol, which guarantees the privacy of information and permits AI to work (Dubey and Bokoro, 2025; Wang et al., 2024; Tyagi et al., 2025).

3.2.4 New Trends and Problems

The new patterns of mental health AI applications are based on the inclusion of privacy-enhancing technology in scalable AI systems. It is also being studied that differentiating privacy in federated large language models, blockchain-based systems, and adaptive privacy in real-time will enhance privacy and clinical utility (Sarwar and Roy Dipta, 2025; Liu et al., 2024).

Although these improvements have been achieved, there are still difficulties. Ensuring usage and accessibility and ensuring a high level of privacy can be inconsistent with therapeutic effectiveness (Horvath et al., 2023; Tayyeh and Wang, 2024). Moreover, the compliance with the regulatory frameworks of various jurisdictions makes the design of the platform tricky, especially when it comes to multinational AI mental health applications (APA Services, 2024; American Psychological Association, 2013; Nair et al., 2021). More research should be done to balance these trade-offs and come up with frameworks that can strike a balance between user privacy, clinical effectiveness, and ethical responsibility.

The literature highlights the multidimensional nature of privacy and security concerns in AI-based mental health services. Some of the significant strategies include privacy-sensitive AI solutions (differential privacy, federated learning), strong cryptography and access control, regulatory compliance, and ethical concerns. Collectively, these strategies offer a basis for the creation of safe, useful, and credible mental health solutions, with current studies resolving new issues regarding usability, accessibility, and cross-jurisdictional governance. Table 3.1 presents a summary of some of the chosen studies that investigate privacy-sensitive AI methods in mental healthcare.

3.3 SENSITIVENESS OF MENTAL HEALTH INFORMATION

The sensitivity of mental health data is also unique because it is personal, intimate, and usually context-specific. Mental health information, unlike the general medical data, is not only a product

TABLE 3.1
Overview of Studies on Privacy-Protecting AI in Mental Health

Research	AI Method	Dataset/Application	Privacy Metric	Result
Dubey and Bokoro (2025)	Federation Learning	Multi-modal mental health data	Local device training	Featured privacy, useful forecasting
Tayyeh and Wang (2024)	Differential Privacy	Mobile mental health app	Noise addition	Less identifiability, minimal loss of accuracy
Liu et al. (2024)	Federated + Blockchain	Healthcare datasets	Adaptive differential privacy	Strong security, decentralized learning
Sarwar and Roy Dipta (2025)	Differential Privacy + LLM	Mental health LLM	Domain-safe privacy	Protected sensitive content, model performance
Settu (2017a); Rajani et al. (2022)	End-to-End Encryption	Cloud mental health data	Encryption at rest and transit	Unauthorized access prevented

of physiological conditions but also includes thoughts, emotions, behaviors, and social interaction. This hypersensitivity presents major ethical, social, and technical issues in the AI-based mental health solutions, and the protection of this information is the most relevant issue. An understanding of the types of data to be collected, the associated privacy risks, and the specific issues concerning the AI systems is crucial for the development of safe and privacy-conscious mental health ecosystems.

3.3.1 Types of Mental Health Data

Mental health applications glean a broad range of data, all of which have different implications for privacy. The most direct type of understanding the mental state of a user is self-reported data, such as mood logs, symptom diaries, stress tests, or cognitive appraisals. This kind of information is very personal, and it can disclose very personal psychological tendencies, which, in case of exposure, can cause stigma or even social discrimination. AI-based therapeutic recommendations usually rely on these self-reports, and their confidentiality is essential.

Besides self-reports, there is an increase in the use of behavioral data to determine mental health status. The temporal patterns of interaction with applications, reaction times, frequency of interaction, and even the dynamics of keystrokes could give AI models insight into the cognitive and emotional state of a user. Although such data types are typically gathered in a passive manner, they have a high potential of exposing sensitive trends. Behavioral tracking can be used to offer very personalized interventions but can also induce the risk of profiling when used in the wrong hands or without permission.

The biometric and multimodal data provide additional sensitivity. The AI models can be trained to identify the presence of stress or depressive episodes through wearable sensors that track the fluctuations of the heart rate, sleep quality, or physical activity. On the same note, emotion detection in chatbots or virtual therapy devices through audio or video recordings can offer essential information on the affective states. These types of data, together with situational data like location, environmental indicators, or social interaction, form a very detailed profile of the user. Being potent regarding AI-driven personalization, this data greatly increases the effects of possible breaches or misuse. Figure 3.1 shows that mental health data goes through more than one stage, and it is vulnerable at each stage.

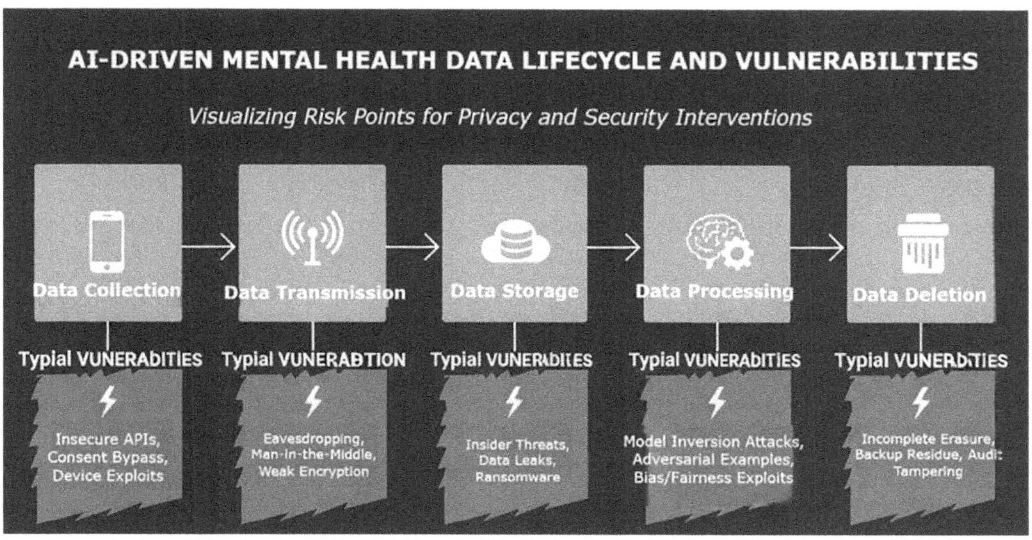

FIGURE 3.1 AI-driven mental health data lifecycle and vulnerabilities.

Figure 3.1 presents the full lifecycle of sensitive mental health data under the AI-driven applications and indicates the possible vulnerability points at each of the stages. The lifecycle starts with data collection, where the information is collected in the mobile applications, wearables, or clinical systems. Some of the risks at this stage are insecure Application Programming Interfaces (APIs), consent bypass, and device-level exploits. The second phase is the data transmission phase, which involves the transfer of gathered data to data processing centers or cloud servers. Examples of vulnerabilities in this case are eavesdropping, man in the middle, and poor encryption standards.

The data storage stage entails storing data in servers or the cloud infrastructure, putting it under insider threats, breaches, and ransomware. During the data processing phase, AI models process the data to give information or interventions, and this poses threats of model inversion attacks, adversarial inputs, and exploitation of bias. Lastly, the data deletion phase focuses on secure destruction of user data that can be compromised through partial deletion, backups, or tampering of the audit. This figure emphasizes the importance of multi-layered privacy and security strategies across all phases of the data lifecycle. Table 3.2 presents a comparison of the key privacy-saving methods of AI-based mental health applications.

Figure 3.2 will present the key methods that are used to secure sensitive mental health data and simultaneously enable AI systems to operate. These methods include differential privacy, where artificial noise is added to datasets or model outputs to ensure that the individual is not identified, and federated learning, where AI models are trained on user devices and only updates are sent to a central location so that data is not shared. Some of the methods are pseudonymization to substitute identifiers with tokens, homomorphic encryption that allows computing with encrypted data, and end-to-end encryption that secures both the data in transit and at rest. The figure visually illustrates the interaction between these methods to minimize privacy risks without badly affecting the work of AI, which points to the security versus utility concern.

Figure 3.3 represents a multi-layered, holistic structure of combining technical protection, organizational policies, and user-focused solutions to protect AI-powered mental health sites. The technical layer comprises encryption, access control, different privacy, and federated learning. Organizational layer displays the governance policies such as the HIPAA/GDPR compliance, consent management, and ethical issues control. User-centered layer focuses on providing transparency, audit trail, and user empowerment via privacy security. This figure demonstrates that technical, policy, and ethical

TABLE 3.2
Mental Health AI Compared in Terms of Privacy-Preserving Techniques

Technique	Description	Benefits	Limitations	Substantial References
Differential Privacy	Introduces regularized noise to data or model outputs	Individual identity protection, regulatory-compatible	May decrease model accuracy	Truex et al. (2020); Tayyeh and Wang (2024)
Federated Learning	Models are trained locally at the devices a user uses;	Only updates are transferred, privacy-protective	High computation on-device, complex coordination	Dubey and Bokoro (2025); Horvath et al. (2023)
Homomorphic Encryption	Encrypts data before computing on it	Data is not exposed, is secure	Computationally expensive	Xie, Liu, and Xin (2024)
Pseudonymization	Substitutes identifiers with tokens	Minimal re-identification risk	Not completely anonymous	Settu (2017a, 2017b)
End-to-End Encryption	Ciphers in transit and rest data	It helps avoid unauthorized accesses	By the way of secure keys management	Tembani (2024)

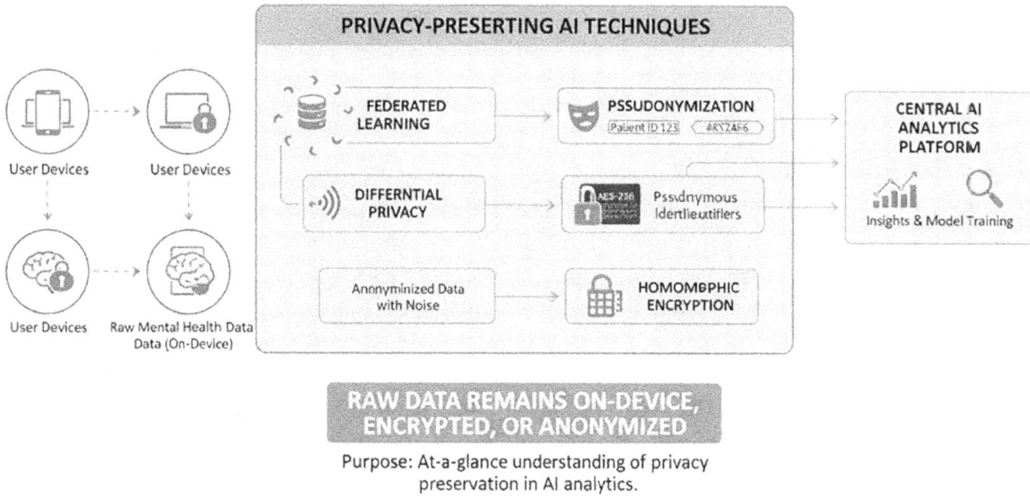

FIGURE 3.2 Data mining and AI privacy-preserving technologies in mental health.

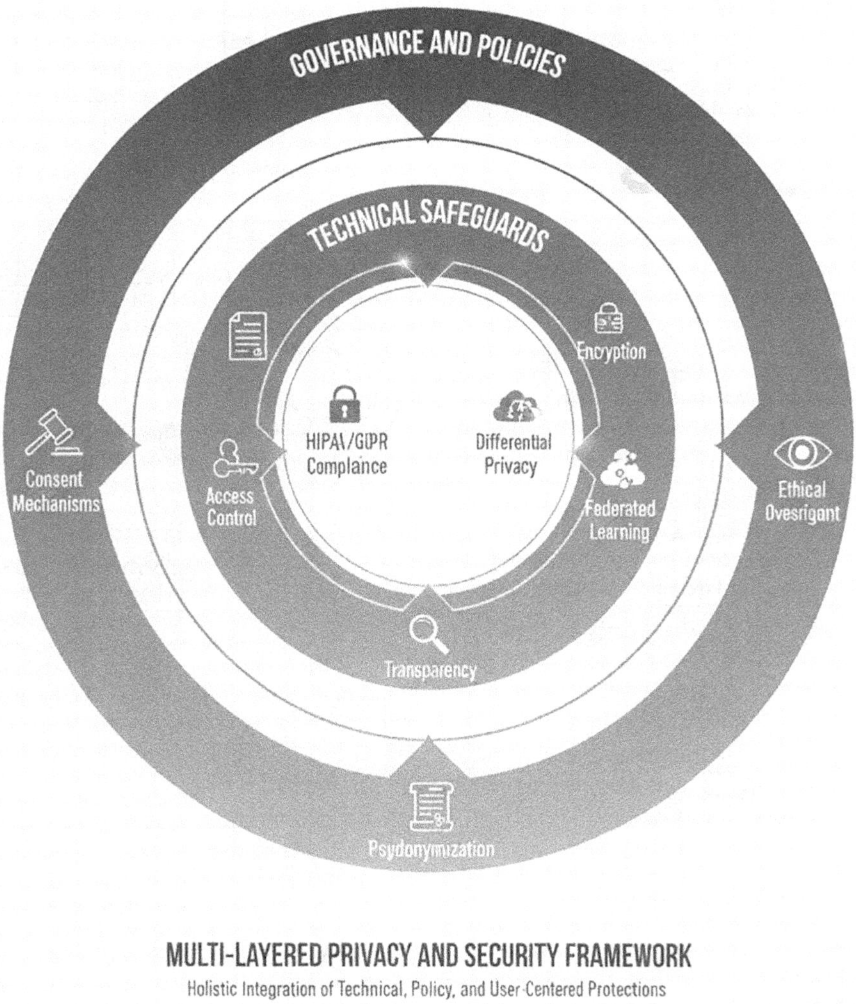

FIGURE 3.3 Multi-layered privacy and security framework.

aspects can be combined to establish a holistic privacy and security stance and that safeguarding mental health data is not only a technical issue, but also a challenge that should be addressed through coordinated governance and an ethical approach.

3.3.2 Risks and Implications

The release of mental health information may have a significant personal and social impact. Among the most direct threats, there are social stigma and discrimination. In case of information leakage, sensitive data may lead to social, educational, or occupational exclusion. In contrast to physical health data, which can be considered clinical, the mental health data can be associated with deeply held societal prejudices that make the effects of breaches worse.

Another important issue is psychological damage. There is a danger of increased anxiety, depression, or distress in such a case that users feel that their private mental health information has been compromised. Users may develop distrust toward AI-based mental health platforms, and violations and even perceived lack of security might compromise the efficacy of therapeutic interventions. The decrease in trust can result in users not using digital mental health services, which restricts the possible advantages of AI-guided care.

In addition, mental health information may be used to perform identity and behavioral profiling. Advanced AI models can infer information beyond the directly collected data, identifying patterns related to personality, cognition, or risk of mental health crises. Although this is an advantage of early intervention, it also increases the possibility of abuse. Unauthorized access may result in discrimination, targeted advertising, or manipulative interventions, raising ethical and legal concerns.

3.3.3 Special Problems of AI Applications

Mental health data is especially challenging to manage in cases of the introduction of AI systems. The capacity of models to infer sensitive information not explicitly provided by the user is a major concern. As an example, the language one may use during a chat or the typing can be predictable through the use of a predictive model and may reveal the presence of depression, anxiety, or suicidal ideation, which poses concerns due to implicit data exposure. Storing or transmitting such inferred information may have unintended and potentially harmful effects.

Naturally, AI-driven monitoring is longitudinal, which is further complicated. Many mental health apps record user behavior over long periods, creating detailed histories that enhance personalization but increase the risk of privacy breaches. Continuous monitoring produces rich datasets, which, while useful for AI analytics, are highly attractive targets for cyberattacks or insider misuse. Although individual data points are anonymized, aggregation over long-term behavior may allow re-identification or exposure of sensitive patterns.

These issues are worsened by third-party integrations, such as cloud storage, analytics services, and APIs. Information may pass through several processing systems, model training systems, or service optimization systems. Every handoff is a possible vulnerability that needs to be well encrypted, have controls on access, and perform auditing. Privacy in such interconnected ecosystems requires adherence to technical and regulatory standards, as well as ethical design, which form the basis of safe AI-driven mental health platforms.

Figure 3.4 shows how the privacy protection and predictive performance of AI models relate to each other in the context of mental health applications. The predictive accuracy or effectiveness of AI interventions decreases as privacy methods, such as differential privacy or strict access controls, become more stringent. On the other hand, prioritizing AI functionality through low privacy protection poses more risks of sensitive user information being exposed. The figure illustrates the inherent trade-off, showing approaches that balance user privacy with AI's clinical and therapeutic effectiveness. Table 3.3 is a summary of some of the most important regulatory and ethical paradigms concerning privacy and security in AI mental health systems.

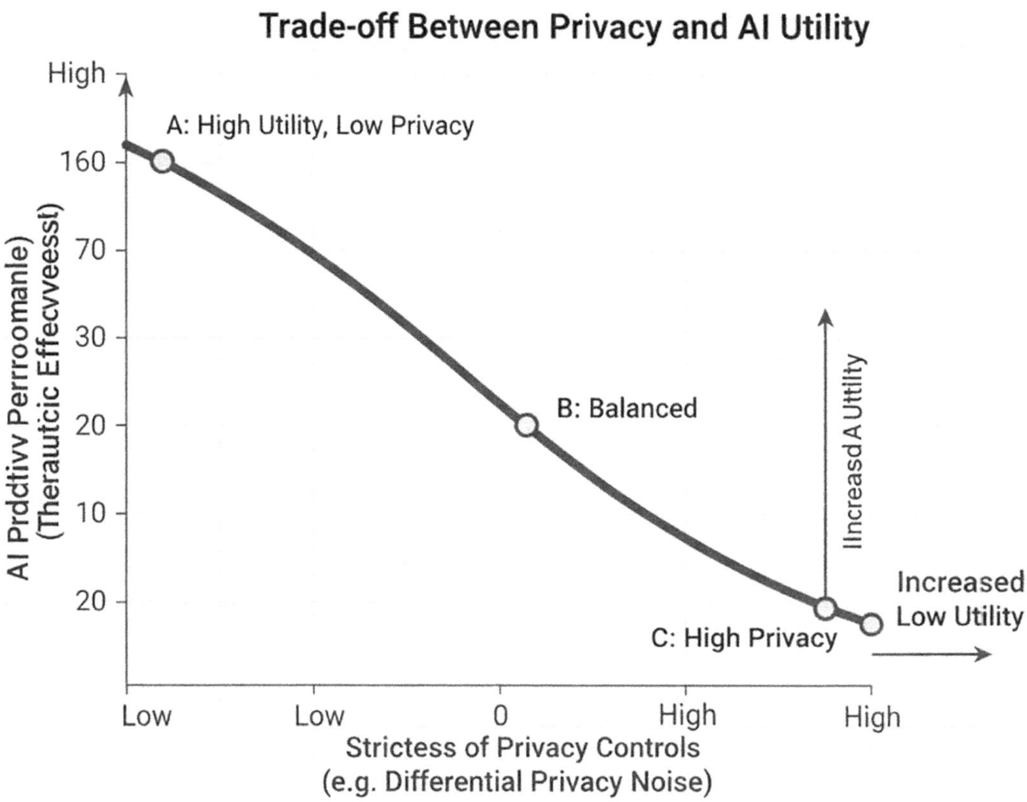

This graph illustratios the inverse relationship the stricttess of privacy-preseving measures and is AI models, highlliging the practical challenge of balancing user privacy with therapetic effectveness.

FIGURE 3.4 Privacy vs. AI utility trade-off.

TABLE 3.3
AI Mental Health Platform Regulatory and Ethical Frameworks

Framework/ Regulation	Scope	Key Provisions	Issues to AI Systems	References
HIPAA	US healthcare	Data confidentiality, data access, data breach notification	Encryption, access logs, audit trails	American Psychological Association (2016)
GDPR	EU	Access/erase, data portability	Consent, pseudonymization, privacy by design	APA Services (2024); Zhang and Yin (2025)
Ethical AI Guidelines	Organizational	Accountability, explainability and fairness	Explainable AI, human-in-the-loop	Ross (2025); Li and Zhang (2023)

3.4 LIFECYCLE OF DATA

The mental health data lifecycle on the platform based on AI implementation includes various phases with each level offering distinct risks and opportunities to privacy and security management. The lifecycle is an important concept to understand in developing strong systems that do not compromise sensitive information and that preserve functionality, personalization, and therapeutic efficacy. In general, the data lifecycle can be divided into the following blocks: collection, transmission, storage, processing, and deletion or retention, with protective measures required at every stage.

3.4.1 Data Collection

The first step is the data collection, which AI-based mental health applications collect information through direct user inputs or linked devices. This can be self-reported information, which may be mood records, symptom journals, or cognitive testing. Although these inputs are voluntary, they can be very personal, and thus, informed consent is very essential. Behavioral data, including interaction patterns, the amount of time one spends working on a task, or response time, are also frequently passively captured by many apps. Wearable applications also add value to the data with physiological measurements, such as heart rate, sleep habits, and physical exercise, which are processed by the AI models to determine mind states.

The collection also includes contextual data such as location, ambient presence, or socialization. Although these data enhance personalization and predictive effectiveness, they are highly sensitive and vulnerable to privacy exploitation. Strict consent protocols should be adopted by the developers, including offering the user the ability to give consent to the types of data that are being collected and telling the user how each type of data will be used. Dynamic consent models, in which users customize permissions as time passes, are being considered an essential ethical data collection practice.

Technical threats can compromise sensitive information at the point of collection, such as insecure APIs, lack of input encryption, or insufficient device verification. Thus, end-to-end encryption, safe application frameworks, and anomaly detection in real-time are required to ensure data integrity and confidentiality to ensure the quality of obtained data.

3.4.2 Data Transmission

Data that has been collected frequently requires transmission of data between user devices and servers or AI models in the clouds. Transmission is a very risky step, as the information that is intercepted may reveal very sensitive mental health information. Information in transit needs to be secured by secure transmission protocols, such as Transport Layer Security (TLS) and end-to-end encryption.

The data transmitted through the AI-driven mental health platforms is processed by third-party services such as cloud storage providers, analytics systems, and machine learning pipelines in the majority of cases. There are vulnerabilities with every handoff, and it should be authenticated, encrypted, and audited. In addition, there are apps that apply real-time data delivery to enact interventions or alerts on a case-by-case basis, which also require low-latency but high-security communication routes.

Privacy methods like federated learning or differential privacy can reduce the risks in the transmission. As one example, federated learning can enable AI models to be trained on-device by uploading expected model updates to central servers rather than raw user data. The strategy ensures minimized exposure by preserving the advantages of collective learning among user groups.

3.4.3 Data Storage

Storage is another important phase of the data lifecycle, which covers storage in the local devices and cloud repositories, as well as backup systems. Safe storage systems are essential as any form of breach of the data at this point can be disastrous. Normal methods of preventing unauthorized access include encryption at rest, RBAC, and ABAC.

Data on mental health can also be replicated in different systems to allow redundancy or analytics. Every replication adds to the risk of being exposed, and it has to be carefully managed under an access policy and monitoring. In addition, retention policies must avoid unneeded duration of storage as long as the data is stored for therapeutic and research purposes. The automated deletion policies were in tandem with the rules like the right to be forgotten of the GDPR, which improves compliance and user confidence.

Auditing and logging should also be supported by storage systems. Keeping a record of every access and alteration will help to keep accountability, make forensic investigation easier, and enhance compliance with regulations. More sophisticated methods such as homomorphic encryption and SMPC can be computed on encrypted data, and thus they jeopardize exposure even when it is analyzed.

3.4.4 Data Processing and Use

Processing refers to how mental health data is analyzed using AI algorithms to generate insights, predictions, and interventions. The stage is sensitive in nature as AI models have the ability to make highly personal inferences, which are sometimes beyond the overt data. As an example, chat logs can be used to identify depressive tendencies with the help of natural language processing (NLP), and stress levels can be predicted based on the patterns of using apps with behavioral analytics.

To guarantee privacy throughout the processing, it is necessary to enforce technical protective measures like the use of differentiated privacy, federated learning, and training dataset anonymity. Models should be designed to minimize memorization of individual data points to prevent unintentional leakage. In addition, XAI systems increase transparency as the user and clinicians can see how their predictions are obtained, which increases trust and responsibility.

Processing also has the intersection point with ethical issues. The developers should make sure that the use of AI outputs is responsible, and they should not make automated decisions that may cause harm to the users, stigmatize them, and/or discriminate against them. Human-in-the-loop review and alert thresholding, as well as clinician oversight, are suggested as the policy measures to make AI autonomy and ethical oversight balance.

3.4.5 Data Deletion and Retention

The last phase of the data lifecycle is retention and deletion of mental health information. Both therapeutic needs and regulatory needs should be brought in line with retention policies. Retention needs to be minimized to limit the exposure to risk, and deletion should not be hastened to influence the utility of AI models and custom-made interventions.

In line with GDPR, HIPAA, and other privacy regulations, automatic deletion, secure wiping of local storage, and controlled deletion of a backup are necessary. Moreover, AI systems should take into consideration the processes of forgetting so that models do not store sensitive personal information that is required. To build trust and give individuals greater control over their data, retention and deletion policies should be communicated transparently to users.

Through lifecycle analysis of mental health data, it is obvious that privacy and security cannot be handled at one stage but must be implemented at every stage of data collection, transmission, storage, processing, and deletion. Every stage has its own specific vulnerability and demands a set of technical, organizational, and policy requirements to make AI applications ethical, secure, and user-friendly.

3.5 PROBABLY LIKELY VULNERABILITIES AND THREATS

The AI-powered mental health applications are operating in the complex environment of technology and social structures and are likely to face a wide range of vulnerabilities and threats. These threats arise due to the weaknesses of the system design, user actions, third-party integrations, and adversarial attacks to AI models. Understanding these vulnerabilities is essential in the establishment and application of the most effective privacy and security standards during the data lifecycle.

3.5.1 System and Application Vulnerabilities

The main source of risk in mental health applications has been software and system-level vulnerabilities. Unsafe coding practices, software flaws, and improper authentication systems may reveal sensitive information. As an illustration, applications that store passwords in plaintext or do not encrypt sensitive information stored on file create clear opportunities for unauthorized access. Likewise, improper session control or misconfigured APIs may allow an attacker to intercept or alter the user information being sent.

There are also device-level vulnerabilities that are quite challenging. A lot of mental health applications are based on smartphones, tablets, or wearables to collect and process the data. Such devices may be hacked by malware, phishing, or stolen physically and may expose mental health data before it even reaches the AI platform. These risks can be mitigated with secure software development, frequency of security audits, and incorporation with mobile device management (MDM) solutions.

Moreover, integrations provided by third-party vendors, for example, cloud storage, analytics services, social media API, etc., expand the attack surface. The vulnerable nature of third-party systems might expose the sensitive user data, even though the core application can be harmless. These threats may be mitigated through the rigorous vendor assessment, establishing data-security requirements in vendor contracts, and continuous monitoring.

3.5.2 AI-Specific Threats

Machine learning and predictive analytics introduce unique threats to AI-powered mental health platforms. Among the threats that may be noted are adversarial attacks where people with ill intentions use input data to find incorrect AI outputs or to access confidential information. For example, model inversion attacks can reconstruct user information from the model's outputs or gradients, which can potentially disclose some personal behavioral patterns or mental health conditions.

Another vulnerability that is specific to AI is membership inference attacks. These attacks identify whether the data of a specific person was utilized in the training of a model, and this can result in the confidentiality being lost. Moreover, AI models might unintentionally memorize sensitive data due to overfitting and unintentionally expose it during model sharing or deployment. Differential privacy and regularization are the methods that are necessary to mitigate such risks without compromising the utility of models.

Other threats to the AI systems of mental health are biases and algorithmic fairness. Neural networks trained on non-representative data may misclassify mental disorders, causing the wrong intervention and potentially causing distress to the vulnerable users. To mitigate these risks, it is necessary to pay attention to the curation of datasets, audits of fairness, and reporting of the procedures of AI-decision-making.

3.5.3 Data Breaches and Insider Threats

Cyberattacks are among the most significant and harmful threats to mental health websites. Outside attackers might use the vulnerabilities to get sensitive information, which may be used to either engage in identity theft, blackmail, or discriminate against a group. Recent high-profile incidents in healthcare and digital wellness show that mental health data is a valuable target as it is a personal and social value.

There are also insider threats such as careless or malicious actions of employees, contractors, or even partners. Patient privacy violations through unauthorized access to databases, inappropriate sharing of patient information, or unprotected means can lead to serious breaches of privacy. RBAC, monitoring of activities, and strict internal policies can alleviate insider threats.

The threat landscape becomes even more complex with social engineering attacks such as phishing and spear-phishing. Platforms that are technically secure may be vulnerable if the user discloses credentials or confidential data by mistake. The measures that can be taken to counter this risk are user education, multifactor authentication, and behavioral anomaly detection.

3.5.4 Emerging Threats

In the context of the development of AI and digital health technologies, privacy and security are still confronted with emerging threats. Data flows and attack surfaces are increased with integration with Internet-of-Things (IoT) devices, smart home assistants, and wearable biosensors. Such devices may not follow strict security protocols, and that creates vulnerabilities that can spread within the AI mental health system.

The presence of regulatory loopholes and evolving adversarial techniques also presents a new threat. The applications of AI models can be used in a manner that the existing legislation does not foreseeing, and therefore it will require changes in governance, proactive risk evaluation, and the development of both technical and policy-making systems.

These multidimensional weaknesses include system-design flaws, AI-specific attacks, insider risks, and emerging technological threats. To overcome such challenges, secure development of software, privacy-focused AI methods, strong access control, educating users, and dynamic compliance are all needed. Through mapping of the threats to the data lifecycle phases, the developers and policymakers are able to have specific interventions to ensure the data is more secure and the user trust is maintained.

3.6 PRIVACY-ACCESSIBILITY TRADE-OFFS

With AI-based mental health apps, privacy and security can often be at odds with accessibility, usability, and therapy. Finding a balance between the privacy of sensitive information and user-friendly and effective interventions is one of the central concerns when designing these systems.

3.6.1 Trade-Off Between User Convenience and Privacy

Mental health applications are designed for frequent use and often operate in real time. Symptom tracking, mood logging, and chatbot therapy are features that are based on a continuous input of data and its analysis. Strict privacy settings, such as periodic authentication messages, encrypted local drives, or minimized data sharing, can inadvertently increase inconvenience, reducing the likelihood of user interaction and diminishing the overall effectiveness of interventions.

Using end-to-end encryption as an example, it improves the confidentiality of the data yet can decrease the processing speed or limit its integration with AI models installed on the cloud. Equally, restricting access to contextual information (e.g., location or social activity) preserves privacy and may decrease the effectiveness and personalization of predictive interventions. Trade-offs should thus be considered by designers, but privacy-preserving mechanisms should not compromise user interaction or clinical outcomes.

Granular consent and adaptive privacy settings are user-oriented solutions that enable people to decide which type of sharing data is comfortable to them without making the solutions inefficient. Giving accurate explanations regarding the utility and consequences of sharing particular data types of data can help users make informed choices.

Importantly, the efficacy of AI-based mental health interventions might be influenced by the considerations of privacy. To learn and produce correct predictions or suggestions, AI models need enough information. Extreme restriction of data collection or anonymization can reduce the model's ability to personalize interventions, which can lead to less therapeutic effect.

In contrast, unrestricted data collection and sharing can improve predictive power but increase the chances of an attack, abuse, or unethical drawing of sensitive data. As an example, speech and behavioral information might be essential to identifying a preliminary symptom of a depressive episode or suicidal thoughts, whereas excessive anonymization can degrade signal quality and reduce detectability.

In this way, the trade-offs between privacy and clinical utility cannot be based solely on technical factors but must also account for clinical objectives. The efficacy and privacy protection can be balanced by collaborating with mental health professionals in the definition of acceptable thresholds for data access that protect privacy.

3.6.2 Trade-Off Mitigation Strategies

These are some of the technical and organizational approaches that can be used to balance privacy and accessibility:

Federated Learning: Federated learning is an AI model trained on the user devices, exchanged through only aggregated updates with central servers, which allows reducing the exposure of raw data and preserving predictive power.

Differential Privacy: Noise is added to model outputs to protect individual privacy while preserving analytical usefulness.

Dynamic Privacy: The user is able to adapt and change their privacy settings dynamically based on the context to share as much or as little data as is therapeutically appropriate and make them stricter other times.

Explainable AI: The transparent nature of AI outputs helps users understand how their data is used, increasing trust even when some data is sent out to be processed.

User Education: In case the privacy risks and benefits are communicated well, informed consent and participation will occur.

Through these methods, mental health apps will be able to maximize privacy and accessibility without compromising therapeutic effectiveness or user trust.

3.7 OWNERSHIP, CONSENT, AND DATA GOVERNANCE

The use of AI in mental health platforms raises complex questions about data ownership, informed consent, and user control. The sensitive and close nature of the mental health data necessitates clear guidelines to determine the ownership of the data, user consent, and how organizations ensure ethical and legal compliance. Good governance plays a significant role in enhancing trust, privacy, and supporting responsible use of AI in therapeutic interventions provision.

3.7.1 Data Ownership in AI Mental Health Platforms

The issue of defining the ownership of mental health data is complex. Users generally assume they own the data related to their mental state, behavior, and physiological signals. Nevertheless, AI platforms and third-party service providers usually assert their right to process, store, and analyze this data for system operation and research purposes. Ambiguity regarding ownership of raw data, analytical outputs, and derived insights can create conflicts.

The legal regulations, like GDPR, focus more on user rights such as accessing, correcting, and deleting personal data. Conversely, certain jurisdictions may include the data created as a result of AI processing or the outputs of the models to belong to the platform. There must be clear contractual agreements and transparent privacy policies to clarify the rights and responsibilities among the users, service providers, and their third-party collaborators.

Implementing user-centric ownership models, where users control what data is shared, processed, or monetized, can strengthen trust and ethical compliance. New principles, including data cooperatives or decentralized personal data stores, give users a chance to actively control their data and be presented with AI-driven analytics or research projects.

3.7.2 Informed Consent Mechanisms

Ethical issues in mental health applications are spearheaded by informed consent. Users need to know what data will be gathered, how it will be used, who will get access to it, and what the risks and benefits of sharing such data will be. The AI platforms cannot rely on traditional static consent forms because the use of data can change over time, or new models might need access to historical data.

Using dynamic consent models enables users to change permissions dynamically, giving them control over what data is shared and how it is processed. As an illustration, users can opt to share mood records to get therapy but not voice recordings with third-party analytics. To increase trust and user engagement, transparency dashboards can show which datasets are used, for what purpose, and by whom.

The consent mechanisms should also contend with any special considerations in situations of mental health like minors, vulnerable populations, or users in acute psychological distress. Ethical guidelines recommend combining consent with additional safeguards in such scenarios so that the consent is well informed, valid, and that it protects the well-being of the user.

3.7.3 Governance Frameworks

Strong data governance involves not only ownership and consent but also policy, ethics, and regulatory compliance. The organizations ought to have governance structures that govern roles, duties, and accountability of data management. This includes:

ABAC and RBAC Policies: The two access control methods are used to manage who is allowed to view, modify, or analyze sensitive data.

Audit and Monitoring: The access to the data, the processing of the data, and sharing are constantly logged to ensure accountability, simplifying forensic investigations.

Ethical Review: The institutional review boards or ethics committees are able to deliberate on the fairness, transparency, and potential risks of AI algorithms, data-sharing agreements, and intervention strategies.

Regulatory Compliance: The legal risks are reduced by making sure there is compliance with HIPAA, GDPR, and new AI-specific regulations, which safeguard users.

Governance structures must be dynamic, adaptable, and aligned with technological developments and ethical standards. The privacy by design and ethics by design principles are the way to make sure that governance is implemented throughout the platform, not added at the end.

These three interconnected aspects, ownership, consent, and governance, are essential to ensuring ethical and secure management of mental health data in the AI-driven platforms. The privacy, accountability, and trust will be enhanced with well-defined data ownership, dynamic and informed consent processes, and well-structured governance frameworks. In particular, all of these steps will enable AI-based mental health apps to deliver effective, personalized care while respecting user rights and ethical standards.

3.8 ACCESS CONTROL MECHANISMS AND ENCRYPTION

Strong encryption and well-designed access control mechanisms are essential to maintain the confidentiality and integrity of mental health information in AI-driven systems. These measures aim to ensure that sensitive data is not accessed, intercepted, or altered by unauthorized parties, whether during storage or transmission. When combined with privacy-aware AI methods and regulatory safeguards, encryption and access control form a foundational component of secure digital mental health platforms.

3.8.1 Encryption Techniques

Encryption transforms sensitive information into an unreadable form that only authorized entities can decrypt, providing a fundamental layer of security.

Symmetric Encryption: Symmetric schemes use the same key for both encryption and decryption. The AES is widely used because it is efficient and highly secure. Symmetric encryption is appropriate for protecting stored mental health data or communications within trusted networks.

Asymmetric Encryption: Asymmetric (public-key) cryptography uses a pair of keys: a public key for encryption and a private key for decryption. This approach enables secure key exchange across untrusted networks, allowing users and platforms to communicate confidentially without sharing a secret key beforehand. RSA and Elliptic Curve Cryptography (ECC) are commonly adopted in AI-based mental health systems.

Emerging Techniques: Methods such as homomorphic encryption and SMPC allow computations to be performed directly on encrypted data. This enables AI models to analyze mental health information without accessing the raw content, significantly reducing the risk of information leakage during processing or model training. Although computationally intensive, these techniques are increasingly used in privacy-preserving AI applications.

Both data at rest (stored data) and data in transit (network communication) must be encrypted to minimize vulnerabilities at every stage. Effective key management including secure storage, rotation, and revocation is also critical for long-term data protection.

3.8.2 Access Control Mechanisms

Access control ensures that only authorized individuals or processes can access specific data based on predefined policies. In AI-based mental health applications, access control mitigates risks such as insider threats, misuse by third-party applications, and accidental data exposure.

Role-Based Access Control: RBAC assigns permissions based on user roles. For example, clinicians may access detailed patient information, while researchers may only access anonymized datasets. RBAC is straightforward to manage but may be less adaptable in complex or rapidly changing environments.

Attribute-Based Access Control: ABAC evaluates user attributes (e.g., role, location, time) and resource attributes (e.g., sensitivity classification) to make fine-grained access decisions. This approach is more flexible than RBAC and well suited to AI mental health ecosystems where access needs vary across contexts and datasets.

Adaptive and Contextual Access Control: These systems dynamically adjust permissions based on real-time factors, including user behavior, threat levels, and data sensitivity. For example, multifactor authentication may be triggered during suspicious activity, or temporary restrictions may be applied when access requests occur from high-risk environments. Effective access control must be paired with auditing and monitoring systems that track all data access and modifications. Such logging enhances accountability and enables rapid detection and response to potential breaches.

3.8.3 Integrated Use of Access Control and Encryption

Encryption and access control function most effectively when used together. Encryption prevents unauthorized individuals from reading data, while access control ensures that only trusted parties or AI models validated through RBAC and ABAC policies can decrypt and use it. For example, only authenticated clinicians or authorized AI components should be permitted to decrypt encrypted mental health records.

Advanced privacy-preserving technologies, including differential privacy, federated learning, and encrypted model computation, can further strengthen AI-enabled mental health systems. These methods allow AI models to extract insights without exposing identifiable user data, combining security with practical utility.

In AI-based mental health applications, encryption safeguards data integrity and confidentiality, while RBAC and ABAC regulate authorized access. Emerging techniques such as homomorphic encryption and adaptive access control enhance privacy without compromising system performance. Together with governance frameworks and informed consent mechanisms, these components support secure, ethical, and user-centered mental health interventions.

3.9 DATA MINIMIZATION AND RETENTION POLICIES

Effective privacy management in AI-based mental health systems extends beyond encryption and access control. Data minimization and retention policies are essential for reducing exposure risks, ensuring regulatory compliance, and supporting ethical handling of sensitive information. By collecting only what is necessary and retaining it for an appropriate duration, platforms can balance privacy, data utility, and AI performance.

3.9.1 Principles of Data Minimization

Data minimization strengthens privacy and reduces the likelihood of data leakage by limiting the volume of sensitive information collected. It requires gathering only the data strictly necessary to support therapeutic functions, AI model training, or analytical goals. For instance, a mood-tracking app may rely on self-reported emotional states without requiring detailed location histories or audio recordings, thereby reducing risk in the event of a breach.

Effective data minimization requires thoughtful design and evaluation. Developers and data auditors must determine which features are essential for AI models, clinical insights, or research functions. Techniques such as feature selection and dimensionality reduction can help optimize model performance while reducing the amount of personal data collected.

User-centric measures such as selective data sharing and granular consent further support minimization. Allowing users to choose what information to share reduces unnecessary exposure while maintaining personalization. Transparent communication about why each data type is collected can also improve trust.

3.9.2 Retention Policies

Data retention policies determine how long mental health information should be stored, deleted, or anonymized. Keeping data for extended periods increases the risk of unauthorized access, insider misuse, and regulatory violations, whereas premature deletion may disrupt therapeutic continuity or weaken AI model performance.

Retention schedules should reflect clinical, operational, and legal requirements. For example, short-term records such as daily mood logs may be retained only for the duration of a therapeutic program, while anonymized research datasets may be stored longer under strict security controls. Automated deletion procedures, secure data wiping, and controlled archival systems help enforce these policies.

AI-specific considerations must also be addressed. Some models may inadvertently memorize sensitive information. Techniques such as differential privacy or "machine unlearning" can ensure that deleted information is removed not only from storage systems but also from AI models, reducing long-term exposure risks.

3.9.3 Reduction, Retention, and Utility Trade-Offs

Data minimization and retention policies must balance privacy with the operational and analytical needs of AI-driven mental health systems. Excessively strict minimization or aggressive deletion can reduce predictive accuracy or weaken personalization, while over-collection and prolonged retention increase risks of breaches and regulatory violations. To achieve this balance, platforms can adopt a layered approach:

Risk-Based Assessment: Prioritize the protection of high-risk data while allowing less sensitive information to support AI functionality.

Granular Control: Allow users to customize their data collection and retention preferences.

Regular Audits: Periodically review datasets, AI models, and retention practices to ensure legal compliance and ethical handling.

By integrating data minimization and retention policies into the architecture and governance of AI-driven mental health systems, developers can reduce exposure risks, enhance privacy protections, maintain user trust, and still provide effective, personalized interventions.

3.10 IMPROVEMENTS IN PRIVACY WITHIN THERAPEUTIC SYSTEMS

In addition to conventional encryption and control access, AI-based mental health systems are gradually starting to utilize new privacy-enhancing methods to secure sensitive user information. These methods allow platforms to use rich datasets for predictive analytics and personalized therapy while reducing the risk of data exposure. Improvements to privacy include different types of privacy, such as differential privacy, federated learning, pseudonymization, and extensive audit mechanisms.

3.10.1 Differential Privacy

Differential privacy is a mathematical technique that adds controlled noise to datasets or model outputs so that including or excluding any individual's data does not significantly affect the results. This can be used in mental health applications to enable AI models to learn trends at the population level without disclosing individual behavior and symptoms.

For example, a mood-tracking system analyzing anxiety patterns can aggregate thousands of user logs while ensuring that no individual user can be identified. Differential privacy is especially desirable in research studies, in which data are exchanged between institutions or clouds. This approach strengthens privacy and regulatory compliance by protecting individuals while still preserving the statistical usefulness of the data.

3.10.2 Federated Learning

Federated learning enables the AI models to be trained remotely on user devices, and only model updates or gradients are exchanged with a central server. The raw personal data never leave the user's device, which greatly reduces the risk of exposure. The method is very applicable to mental health applications, in which constant surveillance creates sensitive behavioral and physiological information.

Federated learning allows sharing the gains of the model improvement without concentrating sensitive data and preserves individualization and privacy. When combined with encryption and secure aggregation, federated learning prevents adversaries from reconstructing individual data from model updates, which will make it an effective approach toward AI-based therapeutic platforms.

3.10.3 Pseudonymization and Anonymization

Pseudonymization replaces identifiable user information with unique codes or tokens, whereas anonymization involves the removal of all personally identifiable information. These methods decrease the chances of re-identification and allow using datasets for the purpose of analysis, AI training, or research with fewer risks.

Pseudonymization provides clinicians with a chance to monitor individual progress and restrict access to personal identifiers in therapeutic settings. Anonymization can also be applied especially in making datasets available to external parties to conduct research or AI benchmarking. Pseudonymization can be combined with access control and encryption to further strengthen privacy.

3.10.4 Transparency Mechanisms Audit Trails

Keeping a comprehensive audit record is important in regard to accountability, compliance, and user confidence. Audit trails record all access events, modifications, and transmissions of sensitive information, which enables the organization to identify the unauthorized control of data and to conduct thorough investigations as well.

The transparency systems, like dashboards or notifications to the user, can inform people on how their data is processed, which AI models are used to process the data, and what inferences are offered. When used together with XAI methods, such mechanisms allow users to get insight into the reasoning behind AI-based suggestions or warnings, which builds user trust and ensures that the AI system is operating transparently and ethically.

The improvement of privacy in therapeutic platforms is not limited to standard encryption and access control, but it makes use of sophisticated methods like differential privacy, federated learning, pseudonymization, and audit trails. These advanced techniques enable AI systems to deliver personalized mental health support while reducing exposure risks and supporting regulatory compliance. These solutions will improve the perception of the platform's credibility among users, promote the use of AI ethics, and guarantee the safe management of confidential mental health data.

3.11 COMBINING POLICIES AND RECOMMENDATIONS

Despite the important role of technical security measures such as encryption, access control, and privacy-preserving AI techniques, policy regulations, and organizational strategies are also essential to fully protect mental health data. The AI-driven mental health applications can be used to deal with the legal aspect of the issue, keep the ethical standards, and help users develop trust in the combined use of policy frameworks and technological safeguards.

3.11.1 Regulatory Compliance

AI-based mental health applications must operate within complex regulatory environments that include legislation such as HIPAA, the GDPR, and emerging AI-specific laws. Compliance requires platforms to adopt key data protection principles such as lawful data collection, purpose limitation, transparency, and respect for data-subject rights.

HIPAA requires protection of the confidentiality, integrity, and availability of the secured health information, focusing on administrative, physical, and technical controls. GDPR includes strict requirements regarding consent, the right to access or erase the personal data, and the responsibility for data processing activity. AI mental health systems must integrate these requirements into their technical design, user policies, and operational workflows to ensure full regulatory compliance.

3.11.2 Policies and Governance of Organization

In addition to meeting regulatory requirements, internal organizational policies provide a structured framework for maintaining consistent privacy and security practices. The data management roles, responsibilities, and accountability should be identified in governance structures, which include areas such as:

Data Custodianship: Identifying persons to handle confidential data.
Access Controls: The introduction of RBAC/ABAC and auditing controls.
Incident Response Plans: Formulating precautionary measures on how to identify, report, and curb breaches.
Employee Education: Educating employees about the dangers of privacy, ethical standards, and practices.

Organizations should also define ethical principles for AI implementation, including fairness checks, human-in-the-loop oversight, and procedures for addressing algorithmic bias. Regular policy reviews are essential to ensure adaptability as technologies evolve and new regulations emerge.

3.11.3 Recommendations of Ethical and Practical Advice

Combining both technical and policy solutions will allow platforms to secure sensitive mental health information and enable them to remain usable and effective in treatment. The recommendations are essential, and they involve:

Privacy by Design: Integrate privacy and security into the system architecture from the very beginning.
Dynamic Consent Mechanisms: These allow users to adjust their consent preferences over time in response to new features, AI models, or research activities.
Risk-Based Data Management: Identify the high-risk data, ensure the state-of-the-art protection of the high-risk data, and maximize the functionality of the less sensitive data.
Transparency and Explainability: Be straightforward in communicating how data is used, how AI-based decisions are made, and what security measures are in place to build trust and encourage engagement.
Continuous Monitoring and Oversight: Evaluate technical security and access documentation and direction processes occasionally to find vulnerabilities and apply compliance.

Combining regulatory, organizational, and ethical best practices with advanced technical solutions enables AI-driven mental health platforms to maintain a holistic privacy and security posture. Such integration will keep users safe, allow more trust, and make AI interventions effective and ethical.

Integrating policy frameworks helps bridge the gap between legal, technical, and ethical responsibilities. Compliance, governance, dynamic consent, and ethical management are all effective in enhancing privacy and security in AI-based mental health solutions. Together, these policies and technical safeguards create a unified framework for protecting sensitive data while supporting personalized and effective mental health interventions.

3.12 SUMMARY

AI-driven mental health platforms offer unmatched opportunities for personalized treatment, early intervention, and lifelong therapeutic support. Nonetheless, the confidentiality of mental health information creates severe privacy and security issues. This chapter has examined these challenges comprehensively and has provided a structured framework for understanding, mitigating, and managing risks across the data lifecycle.

We began by highlighting the exceptional sensitivity of mental health data, including self-reported, behavioral, biometric, and contextual information. The discussion highlighted the possible implications of unauthorized access, including social stigma, psychological trauma, and identity profiling, which underscores the need for robust protection measures in AI-powered systems.

The chapter then examined the data lifecycle, including data collection, transmission, storage, processing, and deletion. Each stage presents specific vulnerabilities, such as unsecured APIs, device-level threats, insider misuse, and AI-specific risks such as adversarial or membership inference attacks. The awareness of such vulnerabilities is important to the development of effective security measures.

We examined the privacy-accessibility trade-offs, the need to balance the protection of sensitive information with user engagement, personalization, and therapeutic effectiveness. Adaptive privacy settings, federated learning, and differential privacy are some of the strategies that are used to balance these conflicting demands.

Ownership, consent, and governance frameworks were considered to be the background factors toward ethical and secure AI implementation. Data ownership, dynamic consent mechanisms, and governance frameworks should be clearly defined to guarantee accountability, transparency, and regulatory compliance, including the GDPR and HIPAA regulations.

Technical safeguards such as encryption, access control, data minimization, and appropriate retention practices were identified as essential. Advanced privacy-enhancing techniques further strengthen security while enabling AI systems to generate insights without exposing identifiable information.

Lastly, the incorporation of policy frameworks and ethical standards would help to make sure that technical countermeasures are supported by organizational and regulatory controls. Risk-based policies, dynamism, and sustainable auditing provide a comprehensive privacy and security posture that ensures the protection of the users as well as provides effective AI interventions.

In conclusion, securing mental health information within AI-based ecosystems requires addressing multiple layers of technical, organizational, and ethical complexity and combining technical, organizational, and ethical interventions. In the above, developers, clinicians, and policymakers can offer customized, effective, and dependable mental health solutions and ensure that the benefits of AI are realized without compromising privacy, security, or ethical standards.

REFERENCES

American Counselling Association & American Psychological Association. (2025). *Guidance for the use of AI in therapy.* Blueprint AI. www.blueprint.ai/blog/aca-and-apa-guidance-for-the-use-of-ai-for-therapists

American Psychological Association. (2013). The digital patient. *APA Monitor on Psychology*, *44*(5). www.apa.org/monitor/2013/05/slc-digital

American Psychological Association. (2016). New threats to client privacy. *APA Monitor on Psychology*, *47*(1). www.apa.org/monitor/2016/01/ce-corner

APA Services. (2024). *Evaluating artificial intelligence tools: A guide for practitioners.* APA Services. www.apaservices.org/practice/business/technology/tech-101/evaluating-artificial-intelligence-tool

Dubey, P., & Bokoro, P. N. (2025). Federated learning for privacy-enhanced mental health prediction with multimodal data integration. *Cyber Security*, *1*(2), 1–14. https://doi.org/10.1080/21681163.2025.2509672

Horvath, A. N., Berchier, M., Nooralahzadeh, F., Allam, A., & Krauthammer, M. (2023). Exploratory analysis of federated learning methods with differential privacy on MIMIC-III. *arXiv*. https://doi.org/10.48550/arXiv.2302.04208

Khalil, S. S., & Zhang, H. (2024). *Federated learning for privacy-preserving depression detection using patient-authored multilingual textual data*. PubMed Central. https://doi.org/10.1016/j.patter.2024.100990

Kumari, S., Tyagi, A. K., Tiwari, S., & Kulshreshtha, G. (2025a). Sensors and digital twin for healthcare monitoring frameworks. In T. A. Nguyen (Ed.), *Digital twin, blockchain, and sensor networks in the healthy and mobile city (Chapter 10,* pp. 147–177*)*. Elsevier. https://doi.org/10.1016/B978-0-443-34174-8.00011-9

Kumari, S., Tyagi, A. K., Tiwari, S., & Singh, R. (2025b). Medical sensor network, edge computing and blockchain for efficient medical data exchange. In T. A. Nguyen (Ed.), *Digital twin, blockchain, and sensor networks in the healthy and mobile city (Chapter 11,* pp. 179–198*)*. Elsevier. https://doi.org/10.1016/B978-0-443-34174-8.00012-0

Li, J., & Zhang, H. (2023). *Security implications of AI chatbots in healthcare*. PubMed Central. https://pmc.ncbi.nlm.nih.gov/articles/PMC10716748/

Liu, Y., Li, Q., & Xin, Z. (2024). A federated learning framework based on blockchain and adaptive differential privacy. In *2024 IEEE 7th information technology, networking, electronic and automation control conference (ITNEC)* (Vol. 7, pp. 1016–1020). IEEE. https://ieeexplore.ieee.org/document/10123456

Lustgarten, S. D. (2020). Digital privacy in mental healthcare: Current issues and future directions. *ScienceDirect*. www.sciencedirect.com/science/article/abs/pii/S2352250X20300415

Mishra, A. K., Tiwari, S., Tyagi, A. K., & Arowolo, M. O. (2024). Security, privacy, trust, and provenance issues in Internet of Things–based edge environment. In S. Pal, C. Savaglio, R. Minerva, & F. C. Delicato (Eds.), *IoT edge intelligence* (pp. 233–263). Springer. https://doi.org/10.1007/978-3-031-58388-9_8

Nair, M. M., & Tyagi, A. K. (2021). Privacy: History, statistics, policy, laws, preservation and threat analysis. *Journal of information assurance & security*, *16*(1), 24–34.

Nair, M.M., & Tyagi, A.K. (2025). Transformative effects of emerging technologies on Industry 5.0 and Society 5.0: Current status, vision, issues, challenges, and opportunities for future. In: *Next Generation Data Science and Blockchain Technology for Industry 5.0*. Wiley. DOI: https://doi.org/10.1002/9781394245215.ch13, ISBN: 9781394245185.

Ross, D. (2025). *AI in behavioral health documentation: Ethical considerations for mental health clinicians*. Blueprint AI. www.blueprint.ai/blog/ai-in-behavioral-health-documentation-ethical-considerations-for-mental-health-clinicians

Sarwar, N., & Roy Dipta, S. (2025). FedMentor: Domain-aware differential privacy for heterogeneous federated large language models in mental health. *arXiv*. https://arxiv.org/abs/2509.14275

Settu, M. (2017a). An approach to secure mental health data in the cloud using end-to-end encryption technique. *ResearchGate*. www.researchgate.net/publication/373976248

Settu, M. (2017b). End-to-end encryption based secure mental health care data transaction. *ResearchGate*. www.researchgate.net/figure/End-to-End-Encryption-based-Secure-Mental-Health-Care-Data-Transaction_fig1_373976248

Tayyeh, H. K., & Wang, Z. (2024). A differential privacy approach in federated learning. *MDPI*. www.mdpi.com/2073-431X/13/11/277

Tembani, L. (2024). *Data encryption for mental health services*. Paubox.

Truex, S., Liu, L., Chow, K.-H., Gursoy, M. E., & Wei, W. (2020). LDP-Fed: Federated learning with local differential privacy. *arXiv*. https://arxiv.org/abs/2006.03637

Tyagi, A. K., & Tiwari, S. (2024). Blockchain-enabled smart healthcare applications in 6G networks. In A. K. Tyagi (Ed.), *Digital twin and blockchain for smart cities (Chapter 20, pp.* 459–494*)*. Wiley. https://doi.org/10.1002/9781394303564.ch20

Tyagi, A.K. (2021). Analysis of security and privacy aspects of blockchain technologies from smart era' perspective: The challenges and a way forward. In: *Recent Trends in Blockchain for Information Systems Security and Privacy* (pp. 1–17). DOI: https://doi.org/10.1201/9781003139737, eBook-ISBN: 9781003139737

Tyagi, A.K. (2025). Blockchain for smart hospital in Healthcare 5.0: modeling structure, challenges, and future emerging trends. In: *Human-Centric Integration of Next-Generation Data Science and Blockchain Technology*. Elsevier. DOI: https://doi.org/10.1016/B978-0-443-33498-6.00026-1, ISBN: 978-0-443-33498-6.

Tyagi, A. K., Tripathi, K., Tiwari, S., & Kaushik, S. (2025). An efficient technique for privacy preservation, trusted and secure patient-centric services in smart healthcare. In *Proceedings of the 6th international conference on recent trends in communication & intelligent systems (ICRTCIS 2025)* (pp. 31–47). IET. https://doi.org/10.1049/icp.2025.2731

Wang, Z., Yang, Z., Azimi, I., & Rahmani, A. M. (2024). Differential private federated transfer learning for mental health monitoring in everyday settings: A case study on stress detection. *arXiv*. https://arxiv.org/abs/2402.10862

Xie, H., Liu, Y., & Xin, Z. (2024). Privacy-preserving medical data collaborative modeling with adaptive differential privacy. *JKLST* . https://jklst.org/index.php/home/article/view/280

Zhang, H., & Yin, M. (2025). *E-mental health in the age of AI: Data safety, privacy, and ethical considerations*. PubMed Central. https://pmc.ncbi.nlm.nih.gov/articles/PMC12231431/

4 Ethical, Legal, and Regulatory Frameworks in AI-Driven Mental Health

4.1 INTRODUCTION

Mental healthcare is undergoing rapid transformation due to advancements in artificial intelligence (AI), including personalized diagnostics, predictive modeling, and digital therapeutic interventions (Gupta and Morch, 2020; Zhang and Bhatt, 2020; Nair et al., 2021). AI-powered applications such as chatbots, virtual therapists, and predictive risk systems can expand access, reduce clinician workload, and improve outcomes for individuals experiencing psychological distress (Bhatt et al., 2020; Zhao and Zhang, 2022). Despite these benefits, the adoption of AI in mental health raises substantial ethical, legal, and regulatory concerns, primarily because mental health data such as psychological profiles, behavioral patterns, and biometric indicators, constitute highly sensitive information (American Psychological Association, 2017; Yang and Liu, 2021; Nair et al., 2025).

Ethical design requires alignment with principles of beneficence, non-maleficence, justice, and respect for autonomy, ensuring that AI systems produce therapeutic benefits, minimize harm, and maintain equitable access (Gao and Zhang, 2022; Zhao and Chen, 2021; Tyagi, 2021). Legal frameworks governing data protection, informed consent, and accountability, such as General Data Protection Regulation (GDPR), Health Insurance Portability and Accountability Act (HIPAA), California Consumer Privacy Act (CCPA), and the Digital Personal Data Protection (DPDP) Act, remain fragmented across jurisdictions, complicating cross-border implementation (European Commission, 2021; Indian Ministry of Electronics and Information Technology, 2023). Additionally, adaptive consent mechanisms, transparent algorithms, and routine audits are essential for maintaining user trust, as AI systems continuously retrain and collect new data (Smith and Lee, 2023; Sundaram and Li, 2023; Raji and Buolamwini, 2020).

Technical and governance challenges related to data localization, interoperability, and privacy-preserving computation further complicate compliance in regions with diverse regulatory requirements (Xu and Zhang, 2022; Wang and Li, 2022; Zhou and Yang, 2022; Kumari et al., 2025a). Recent research emphasizes ethics-driven governance, independent auditing, and federated or edge-based architectures that allow AI models to operate without violating legal or ethical obligations (World Economic Forum, 2021; Kandala et al., 2025; Taylor and Green, 2022; Kumari et al., 2025b).

This chapter synthesizes current research and policy developments in AI-driven mental healthcare, offering an integrated overview of ethical frameworks, legal standards, informed consent, algorithmic transparency, data governance, and global regulatory trends. It presents a roadmap for ethically and legally responsible implementation of AI in mental health systems, aligning technological innovation with user safety, privacy, and equitable access (Bhatt et al., 2020; Zhang and Wang, 2022; Zhao and Chen, 2021).

Figure 4.1 illustrates the flow of sensitive mental health data through AI-driven applications and identifies key vulnerabilities at each stage—from data collection and storage to AI inference and

DOI: 10.1201/9781003658344-5

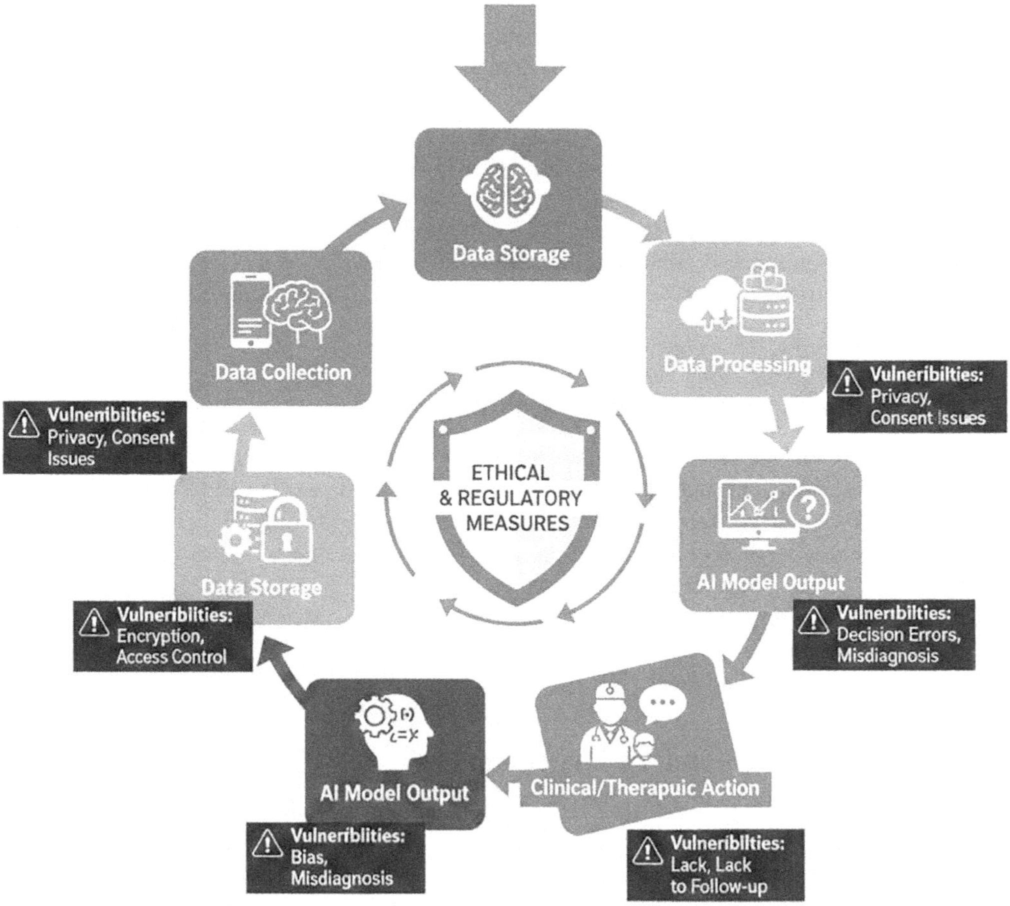

FIGURE 4.1 Vulnerabilities and AI-driven mental health data lifecycle.

user interaction. It highlights priority areas requiring intervention to ensure responsible deployment and regulatory compliance.

4.2 LITERATURE REVIEW

The use of AI in mental healthcare has expanded rapidly due to its potential to deliver personalized, scalable, and accessible interventions (American Psychological Association, 2024; Gupta and Morch, 2020; Mishra et al., 2024). AI applications in this domain typically include automated screening tools, conversational agents such as chatbots, and predictive analytics for tasks like suicide risk assessment and therapy optimization (Bhatt et al., 2020; Zhang and Bhatt, 2020; Zhao and Zhang, 2022). However, these systems raise significant ethical, legal, and regulatory challenges because mental health data is highly sensitive (Zhang and Wang, 2022; Zhou and Wang, 2021; Tyagi, 2025).

4.2.1 Ethical and Privacy Issues

Several studies emphasize that mental health data comprising psychological assessments, behavioral patterns, and biometric indicators is exceptionally sensitive and requires robust ethical safeguards

(American Psychological Association, 2017; Yang and Liu, 2021; Tyagi and Tiwari, 2024a). Ethical principles such as beneficence, non-maleficence, and justice guide the development of AI systems to ensure that they promote effective therapeutic outcomes while minimizing harm and preventing inequitable access (Balamurugan et al., 2023; Gao and Zhang, 2022; Gupta and Morch, 2020; Zhao and Chen, 2021).

Transparency and explainability are central to ethical AI. Users must be able to understand how decisions are generated, particularly in high-stakes scenarios such as suicide risk prediction (Raji and Buolamwini, 2020; Taylor and Green, 2022). To support this, explainable AI (XAI) methods such as feature attribution and counterfactual explanations have been proposed to improve interpretability and user trust (Bhatt et al., 2020; Zhang and Bhatt, 2020; Sundaram and Li, 2023; Tyagi et al., 2024c).

4.2.2 User Autonomy and Informed Consent

The literature highlights that AI mental health systems cannot rely on traditional static consent models, as these systems continuously process and update user data (Gao and Zhang, 2022; Smith and Lee, 2023). Dynamic consent frameworks allow users to provide ongoing, granular permission, thereby strengthening autonomy and regulatory compliance (Morch et al., 2019; Sundaram and Li, 2023; Tyagi et al., 2025).

AI-driven consent tools, including chatbot-based interfaces, can enhance user understanding and engagement, particularly among individuals with lower digital literacy (Rajani et al., 2022; Sundaram and Li, 2023; Mörch et al., 2019).

4.2.3 Regulatory and Statutory Environment

Studies consistently demonstrate that ethical AI implementation depends on compliance with national and international data protection laws. The EU's GDPR enforces strict requirements on consent, purpose limitation, and automated decision-making transparency (European Data Protection Board, 2022; European Commission, 2021). In the United States, HIPAA protects the privacy and integrity of health information but does not extend to many mental-health-related mobile applications operated by non-covered entities (Health and Human Services).

In India, the DPDP Act includes mental health data within the category of sensitive personal data, although it does not explicitly address AI transparency or explainability (Indian Ministry of Electronics and Information Technology, 2023; Zhao and Zhang, 2022). Similarly, the CCPA/California Privacy Rights Act enhances consumer rights such as access and deletion, which directly affects AI-driven mental health platforms (International Association of Privacy Professionals, 2022).

4.2.4 Data Localization and Data Sovereignty

Recent work stresses the importance of data localization for AI-based mental health systems to ensure compliance with regional regulations and to safeguard sensitive information (Zhou and Yang, 2022; Xu and Zhang, 2022; Privacy International, 2022). Privacy-enhancing technologies such as federated learning and edge computing help balance data sovereignty with the need for high-performance AI models (Kandala et al., 2025; Wang and Li, 2022). These methods allow model training without centralized data storage, thereby reducing ethical and regulatory risks (Zhou and Wang, 2021; Zhao and Zhang, 2022).

4.2.5 Oversight, Auditing, and Risk Management

Multiple studies emphasize the need for internal governance structures and independent audits to ensure accountability, fairness, and regulatory compliance (Raji and Buolamwini, 2020; OECD,

2021; Bhatt et al., 2020). High-risk AI systems used in mental healthcare benefit from continuous monitoring, algorithmic auditing, and human-in-the-loop mechanisms to maintain interpretability and ethical integrity (Taylor and Green, 2022; American Psychological Association, 2024).

Organizations are increasingly adopting structured oversight mechanisms through ethics committees, compliance frameworks, and adherence to ISO/IEEE standards (World Economic Forum, 2021; International Telecommunication Union, 2021; Tyagi, 2026; United Nations, 2022).

4.2.6 Cross-Border Harmonization

The deployment of AI mental health systems across jurisdictions is hindered by mismatched ethical and regulatory requirements (Zhou and Yang, 2022; Zhao and Chen, 2021; Wang and Li, 2022). Comparative research highlights mechanisms such as standard contractual clauses (SCCs), adequacy agreements, and mutual audit recognition as potential solutions for enabling lawful international data transfers (Zhou and Wang, 2021; Xu and Zhang, 2022).

Global organizations—including ISO, WHO, and UNESCO—are working toward harmonized frameworks that promote ethical integrity, privacy protection, and accountability across borders (UNESCO, 2021; OECD, 2021).

4.2.7 Emerging Trends and Gaps in the Literature

Despite significant progress, the literature identifies ongoing gaps, including unclear AI classification schemes, insufficient accountability mechanisms, and the need for more robust dynamic consent models (Gupta and Morch, 2020; Zhao and Zhang, 2022; Yang and Liu, 2021). Emerging areas of focus include high-risk AI regulation, ethics-centered governance models, privacy-enhancing AI techniques, and user-centric transparency frameworks (European Commission, 2021; World Economic Forum, 2021; Zhao and Chen, 2021; Zhang and Wang, 2022).

4.2.8 Summary of Literature

Broadly, the literature underscores the necessity of multi-layered controls when integrating AI into mental healthcare. These controls encompass ethical safeguards, legal compliance, algorithmic transparency, data localization, and cross-border harmonization. While AI offers significant potential for personalized mental health support, scholars argue that comprehensive regulatory structures are essential for protecting user privacy, autonomy, and safety (Bhatt et al., 2020; Taylor and Green, 2022; Zhang and Bhatt, 2020; Zhou and Yang, 2022).

4.3 MORAL VALUES: BENEFICENCE, NON-MALEFICENCE, AND JUSTICE

AI-based mental health systems should be evaluated using foundational principles of biomedical ethics, most notably beneficence, non-maleficence, and justice. Although these principles were originally developed for clinician–patient interactions, they remain highly relevant for digital mental health technologies. However, they must be re-interpreted to address the unique challenges of autonomous, data-driven systems.

Figure 4.2 illustrates the core ethical values of beneficence, non-maleficence, justice, and autonomy that guide the development and deployment of AI in mental health. It emphasizes how these principles intersect to support responsible decision-making and protect user well-being.

4.3.1 Beneficence: Therapeutic Maximization

Beneficence requires AI systems to genuinely promote user well-being and deliver measurable therapeutic value. In mental health applications, this includes not only symptom reduction but also

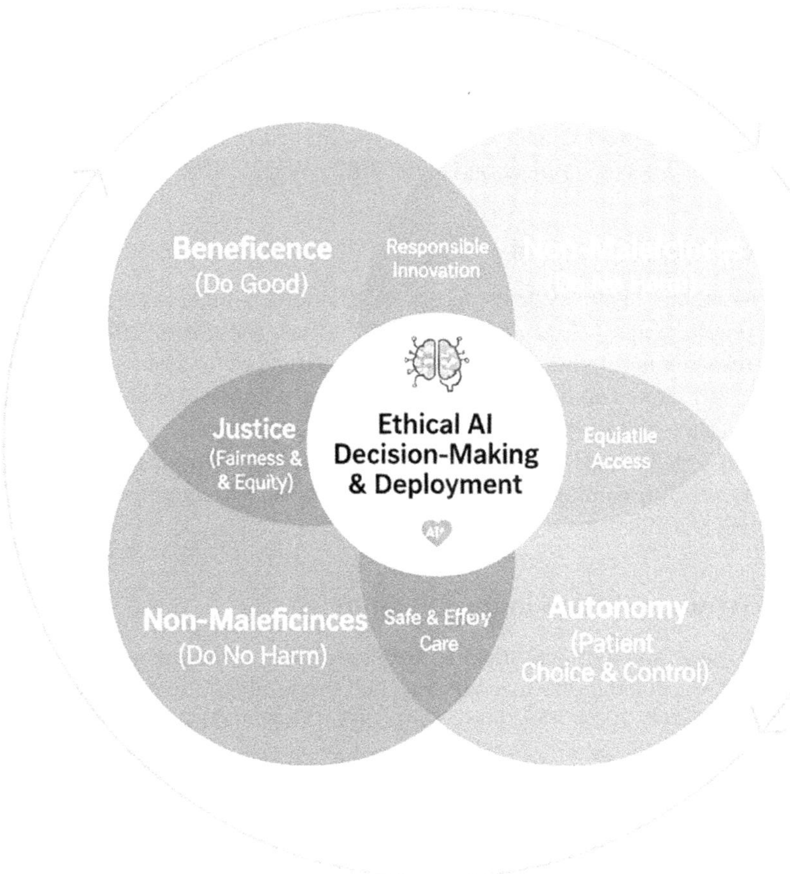

FIGURE 4.2 AI ethical frameworks in mental health.

emotional support, accessibility, and continuity of care. Many AI chatbots and mood-monitoring tools outperform traditional services in terms of availability and responsiveness, offering 24/7 support without judgment or stigma.

However, beneficence also demands clinical validity and evidence-based design. An application that offers entertaining but unscientific advice may elevate mood temporarily but will not provide sustained therapeutic benefit. Such tools may therefore violate beneficence despite positive user feedback.

To uphold beneficence, AI mental health systems must prioritize efficacy, scientific grounding, and therapeutic integrity, ensuring models are built on validated psychological principles rather than on conversational fluency alone.

4.3.2 Non-Maleficence: Vulnerability Prevention of Harm

Applying the principle of "do no harm" to AI-driven mental health tools is complex, as these systems can cause psychological, informational, and algorithmic harm.

Psychological harm may arise when AI produces inaccurate, overly general, or tone-insensitive responses that worsen a user's distress. Unlike human therapists, AI systems cannot truly empathize, understand sarcasm, or interpret culturally specific expressions of emotion, increasing the risk of harmful misinterpretation.

Informational harm can occur through unauthorized disclosure or misuse of sensitive mental health data—for instance, if mood predictions are shared with advertisers or used in insurance profiling—potentially leading to stigma or discrimination.

Algorithmic harm arises when biased training data leads AI systems to misinterpret, misdiagnose, or overlook marginalized populations, such as ethnic minorities, LGBTQ+ individuals, or neurodivergent users.

To uphold non-maleficence, AI mental health systems should incorporate strong risk-mitigation mechanisms, including:

- human-in-the-loop or override options
- crisis escalation pathways
- transparent audit logs
- post-incident reporting tools that allow users to flag dangerous or inappropriate outputs

Maintaining non-maleficence is therefore an active and ongoing process. Technical accuracy alone does not guarantee psychological safety.

4.3.3 Justice: Fairness and Equitable Access

Justice requires that the benefits and risks of AI-based mental health systems be distributed equitably across all user groups, regardless of demographic, socioeconomic, or cultural differences.

Currently, many AI models are trained on datasets that overrepresent Western, English-speaking, neurotypical, and urban populations. This results in culturally insensitive or clinically inaccurate recommendations for underrepresented groups. Such biases not only reduce diagnostic accuracy but also reinforce systemic inequalities, disadvantaging individuals whose communication styles or cultural backgrounds are not reflected in the training data.

Economic inequality further complicates justice. Many mental health applications offer premium features (e.g., human support or advanced analytics) only to paying users, leaving those on free plans with limited or lower-quality support. These practices risk transforming mental health assistance from a universal resource into a tiered commodity.

A just AI mental health system should therefore:

- include diverse, representative training data
- support multiple languages and culturally adaptive interfaces
- incorporate fairness-aware optimization techniques
- provide mechanisms for users to contest or appeal algorithmic decisions

Justice requires proactive correction of historical and structural inequalities—not simply neutrality.

4.4 LEGAL STANDARDS AND CASE STUDIES

Although core ethical principles such as beneficence, non-maleficence, and justice provide moral direction, it is legal frameworks that ultimately define the binding responsibilities of AI-driven mental health applications. Existing laws such as the HIPAA in the United States, the GDPR in the European Union, and the CCPA offer important protections. However, these regulations were not originally designed for autonomous, inference-driven AI systems that continuously collect, analyze, and predict user behavior. As a result, legal interpretation often lags behind technological capability, producing grey areas of accountability. This is particularly evident when digital platforms classify themselves as "wellness tools" to avoid medical regulatory requirements.

A prominent example is the 2023 settlement involving BetterHelp, an online therapy platform found to have shared sensitive mental health information with third-party advertisers such as Facebook and Snapchat, despite promising confidentiality. Because the platform was operating outside HIPAA's definition of a covered entity, it was not legally bound by HIPAA's protections; nonetheless, its practices were deemed deceptive. The U.S. Federal Trade Commission (FTC) imposed a $7.8 million fine, establishing an important precedent for consumer privacy enforcement beyond traditional healthcare settings.

Similarly, in 2022, the mental health app Cerebral disclosed that it had transmitted users' psychiatric assessments and medication histories to analytics companies through tracking pixels. This revelation triggered multiple state investigations and lawsuits. Both cases highlight the expanding legal expectation that any platform handling psychological self-disclosure, whether or not it qualifies as a healthcare provider, must uphold strong privacy protections.

Across jurisdictions, GDPR remains one of the strictest regulatory regimes. It classifies mental health data as *special category data*, requiring explicit consent, strict purpose limitation, and robust safeguards for cross-border transfers. Enforcement, however, varies across EU member states. For example, Finland imposed a €600,000 fine on the psychotherapy clinic Vastaamo in 2021 after its patient records were breached and later used for blackmail. At the same time, some AI mental health applications operating in Europe continue to rely on unclear or bundled consent models that combine therapeutic services with analytics or cloud-based data sharing, raising compliance concerns.

In other regions, regulatory clarity remains uneven. India's DPDP Act, 2023, emphasizes consent-driven data practices, yet the legal status of AI-powered diagnostic tools remains undefined. This ambiguity allows mental health startups to operate without standardized medical liability. Likewise, China's Personal Information Protection Law (PIPL) includes strict data localization and sovereignty requirements but provides limited guidance on algorithmic explainability or auditability. This creates a regulatory environment in which opaque, "black-box" AI systems—particularly those used in emotion or sentiment surveillance—may operate without sufficient oversight.

Figure 4.3 illustrates key regional and international laws relevant to AI-based mental health applications, including GDPR, HIPAA, CCPA, and India's DPDP Act. It highlights areas of overlap, divergence, and regulatory gaps, demonstrating the complexity of achieving cross-jurisdictional compliance.

A major legal challenge across all jurisdictions is assigning liability when AI systems make or influence clinical decisions. For instance, if a chatbot fails to escalate a suicidal risk or provides harmful guidance, it is unclear whether responsibility lies with the developer, the supervising clinician, or the platform hosting the AI. Current legal frameworks do not provide definitive answers, resulting in fragmented accountability (Table 4.1).

4.5 ACCOUNTABLE CONSENT AND DIGITAL SELF-SOVEREIGNTY

Traditional clinical practice relies on informed consent through direct interaction between clinician and patient, where risks, benefits, and alternatives are discussed before intervention. In AI-powered mental health applications, however, consent is often reduced to lengthy, pre-checked Terms and Conditions, written in legalistic language that users may not understand. Such formal consent does not equate to ethical consent.

AI systems frequently collect data passively, such as keystroke patterns, sentiment analysis, or behavioral tracking. Users cannot provide meaningful consent for inferences derived from information they are unaware of. Moreover, many platforms require bundled consent, forcing users to agree to secondary data processing to access services, thereby undermining digital autonomy. This

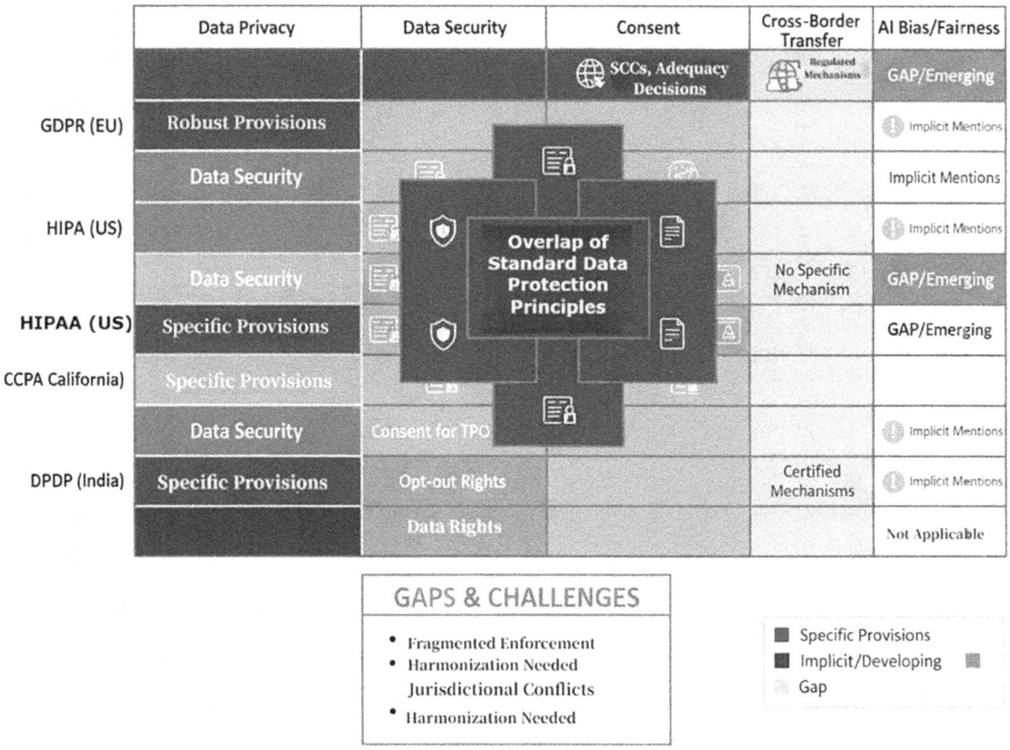

FIGURE 4.3 Landscape of legal and regulatory compliance.

is especially concerning for emotionally vulnerable users, who may consent to intrusive policies in the pursuit of psychological relief.

To address this, scholars and regulators advocate for granular or layered consent models. These allow users to selectively consent to specific functionalities, including emotion detection, cloud storage, or research data sharing. Dynamic consent models, already implemented in genomic studies, provide real-time withdrawal and context-sensitive permissions, enabling users to adjust privacy settings as their mental health status changes. Blockchain or cryptographic logging can support machine-readable consent ledgers, enhancing transparency by recording how and where sensitive data is used (Figure 4.4).

Informed consent alone cannot guarantee autonomy without clear explanations of AI functionality. Users should know whether they are interacting with AI or a human, how their data is used for training, and whether automated recommendations influence clinical decisions. Ethical consent must be ongoing, user-centered, and negotiated continuously among the user, platform, and algorithm.

4.6 AI TRANSPARENCY IN DECISION-MAKING

Accountability in AI-based mental health systems depends on transparency. Unlike conventional software, AI models, particularly deep learning or ensemble systems, often operate as black boxes, producing outputs without revealing the reasoning behind them. This opacity is particularly problematic in mental health: a chatbot providing coping strategies, a suicide-risk prediction model, or an AI-driven triage system can significantly influence user and clinician decisions, yet the AI's rationale is unclear. Lack of transparency undermines trust, informed consent, and control.

TABLE 4.1
Comparison of Major Legal and Regulatory Frameworks for AI Based Mental Health Applications

Regulation/ Jurisdiction	Scope of Coverage	Mental Health Data Classification	Consent Model	AI Transparency/ Explainability Requirement	Cross-Border Data Transfer Rules	Penalties for Non-Compliance
GDPR (EU)	Maximum protection of all personal data processing by controllers/processors in the EU	*Special Category Data—maximum protection level*	Explicit, purpose-specific consent	Strong (Right to Explanation under Art. 22)	Limited unless either of "adequacy decision" or Standard Contractual Clauses	Max. €20M or 4% of turnover across globe
HIPAA (USA)	Healthcare organizations, insurers, and business associates	*Protected Health Information (PHI)*	Implied or written depending on use	No AI-specific requirement	No explicit cross-border restriction, but secure handling required	Tiered penalties up to $1.9M/ year
CCPA/CPRA (California)	Consumer data stored by for-profit institutions	Personal data (unless health data in combination with biometrics)	Opt-out, not opt-in based	No explicit AI transparency rule	No localization rule	$2,500–$7,500 per violation
DPDP Act (India, 2023)	All processing of digital personal data	Sensitive data (no name indicated, only implied)	Explicit consent required	No mention of AI explainability	No restriction on transfer, as long as on the whitelist of the government	Fines up to ₹250 crore (~$30M)
PIPL (China)	Personal data processing in China separate	*Sensitive Personal Information* including psychological data	Separate, specific consent necessary in case of sensitive data	Algorithms are required to be fair, but there is no clear enforcement overall	Mandatory localization of critical data in China	Up to ¥50M or 5% of turnover in China
EU AI Act (Upcoming, 2024–2025)	AI systems used in EU, irrespective of origin	*AI Mental Health Systems probably included as "High-Risk" systems*	Consent requirement under GDPR applies	Mandatory risk assessment, logging, and transparency of high-risk systems	Requirement to comply with GDPR on transfers	Must stay within €30M or 6% of turnover

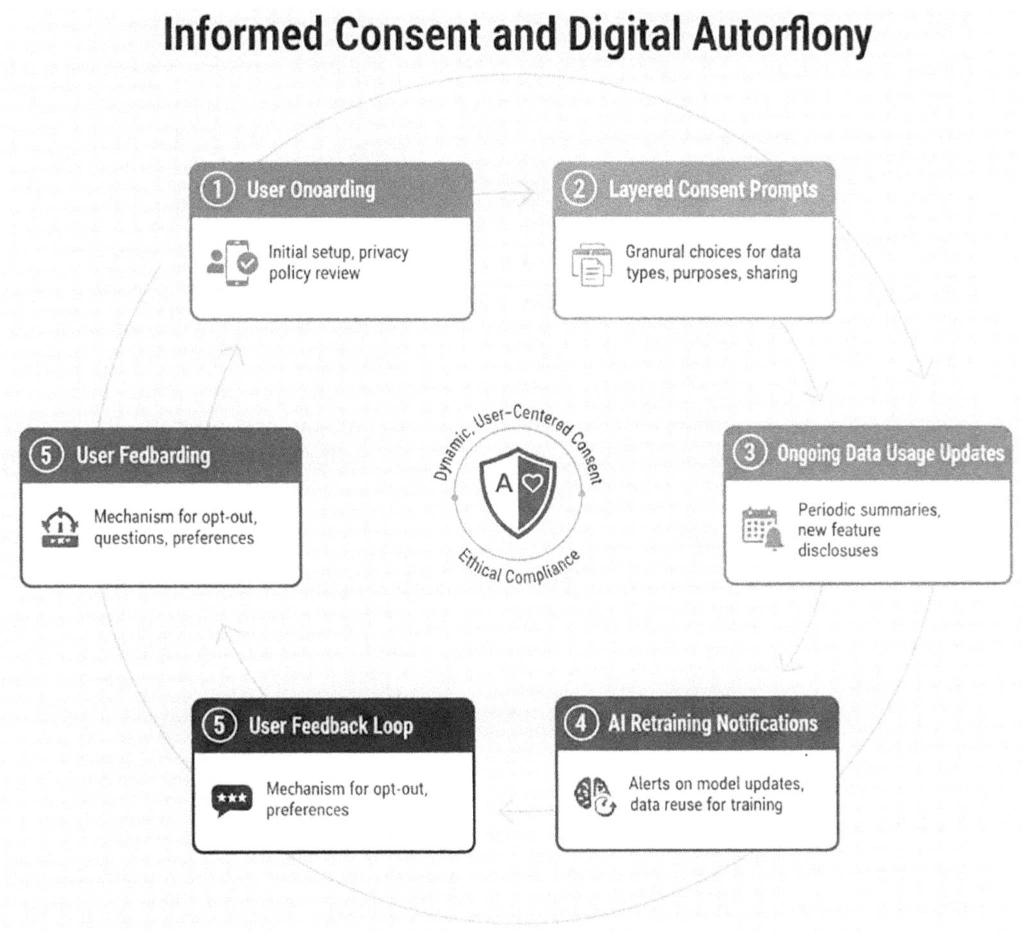

FIGURE 4.4 Digital autonomy and informed consent process.

XAI methods are critical for enhancing transparency. Techniques such as feature attribution, attention visualization, and counterfactual explanations help developers, clinicians, and users understand the factors contributing to predictions. For example, a suicide-risk assessment tool could illustrate that social media sentiment, sleep patterns, and textual content increased a risk score, rather than presenting only an abstract numeric output. Such explanations facilitate clinician oversight and enable users to critically assess AI recommendations.

Transparency also encompasses algorithmic auditing and accountability systems. Internal audits and independent third-party reviews, combined with records of model updates, ensure AI decision-making remains consistent, unbiased, and compliant with ethical and legal standards. Regulators increasingly require such transparency under frameworks like the EU AI Act and GDPR Article 22.

Challenges remain in communicating AI explanations to non-technical users. Overly technical descriptions can confuse, while oversimplification may misrepresent AI reasoning. Balancing clarity and accuracy is particularly critical in mental health, where emotional sensitivity can amplify misunderstandings. Through XAI, continuous auditing, and user-friendly communication, developers can make AI-based mental health systems accountable, understandable, and ethically sound.

4.7 IMPORTANT REGULATORY FRAMEWORKS: GDPR, HIPAA, AND MORE

AI-based mental health applications operate within complex regulatory environments spanning multiple jurisdictions. While ethical principles guide best practices, legal frameworks establish binding obligations regarding data protection, consent, accountability, and cross-border operations. Key frameworks include the following.

4.7.1 GDPR, European Union

The GDPR imposes high standards for processing personal and sensitive data, including mental health information. It requires explicit informed consent, purpose limitation, data minimization, and rights to access, correct, or delete data. Article 22 provides that users should not be subject to automated decisions with legal or similarly significant effects without meaningful human intervention. High-risk AI systems, such as those used in mental health, require risk assessments, transparency reports, and impact analyses, holding developers accountable for algorithmic decision-making.

4.7.2 HIPAA, United States

HIPAA protects health information managed by medical professionals, insurers, and their business associates. While HIPAA addresses storage, transfer, and confidentiality of health records, it does not explicitly regulate AI decision-making or consumer applications in non-traditional clinical environments. HIPAA-compliant systems must implement administrative, physical, and technical safeguards such as audit controls and breach notification—which indirectly support algorithmic accountability.

4.7.3 CCPA and the CPRA

CCPA and CPRA grant California residents rights regarding personal data, including the right to prevent sale, access, and deletion of information. While mental health data is not specifically categorized as sensitive, the broad definition of personal information makes these laws relevant to AI platforms operating in the U.S. CPRA additionally requires risk assessments and cybersecurity audits, providing extra oversight of AI applications handling behavioral data.

4.7.4 India: DPDP Act

India's DPDP Act establishes principles for managing digital personal data, emphasizing purpose limitation, transparency, and user rights. Psychological and behavioral data fall under the act's definition of sensitive information. The law focuses on data sovereignty and requires approved mechanisms for cross-border transfer. However, it does not explicitly address AI explainability, automated decision-making, or clinical supervision, leaving regulatory gaps for AI-driven mental health platforms.

4.7.5 New AI-Specific Frameworks: Global Initiatives and EU AI Act

The EU AI Act, effective in 2025, classifies AI systems by risk. Mental health AI applications are likely deemed high risk, requiring monitoring, logging, human oversight, and transparency. Similar initiatives are emerging worldwide, including Canada, Japan, and Singapore, reflecting a shift toward risk-based AI regulation that complements existing data privacy laws.

Despite variations, GDPR, HIPAA, CCPA/CPRA, DPDP, and new AI legislations converge on principles of consent, transparency, accountability, and data protection. Developers must navigate overlapping frameworks to ensure legal compliance, ethical standards, and user trust, particularly in cross-border contexts.

4.8 DATA LOCALIZATION: PROBLEMS AND DATA SOVEREIGNTY PROBLEMS

Localization of data and sovereignty have become critical concerns in cross-border AI-based mental health applications. Mental health data is a sensitive category, encompassing psychological profiles, therapy session content, biometric indicators, and behavioral patterns. Unauthorized transfer or storage in foreign jurisdictions can create legal, ethical, and security risks, particularly in regions with strict regulations on sensitive data. Consequently, governments worldwide increasingly require in-country storage, restricted transfers, or the use of government-approved cloud services, complicating the deployment of global mental health platforms.

Data localization policies often conflict with cloud-based AI systems that rely on distributed storage, real-time processing, and federated learning. For example, European and Indian regulations stipulate that sensitive data must remain within national borders, while U.S.-based cloud providers commonly distribute data globally for efficiency and redundancy. This creates tension between regulatory compliance, operational efficiency, and cross-border service provision.

Data sovereignty also extends to algorithmic governance. Even if a platform's headquarters are abroad, countries may require AI systems processing mental health data to adhere to local ethical, transparency, and security standards. Non-compliance can result in fines, service bans, or mandatory data repatriation, as seen under China's Personal Information Protection Law (PIPL) or the EU's restrictions on data transfers to countries without adequacy agreements (Table 4.2).

Key Implications

Complexity of Compliance: With hundreds of AI mental health platforms operating worldwide, cloud-based services must navigate a complex regulatory landscape, balancing cloud performance with local storage requirements.

TABLE 4.2
Country-Specific Data Localization Requirements for AI-Assisted Mental Health

Country/ Region	Data Localization Requirement	Regulatory Basis	Conditions Cross-Border Transfer	Notes
European Union	No physical storage, but GDPR regulates transfer	GDPR Art. 44–49	Transferred under Standard Contractual Clauses or as adequacy decision	Sensitive mental health data needs explicit consent
United States	No general localization, HIPAA controls covered entities	HIPAA	Transfers permitted provided safeguards are put in place	State laws such as CCPA provide consumer rights to data handling
India	Sensitive personal data (including psychological data) should meet government-approved mechanisms	DPDP Act, 2023	Transfers only through government-approved list	Localization of the critical infrastructure data is encouraged
China	Critical and sensitive personal information should not be transferred to foreign country	PIPL, Cybersecurity Law	Admitted only with state security evaluation	Mental health information falls into sensitive personal information category
Canada	None, Personal Information Protection and Electronic Documents Act (PIPEDA) regulates however	PIPEDA	Anywhere in Canada, but PIPEDA regulates it nevertheless	Provinces have the option of imposing stricter rules (e.g., Quebec)
Singapore	There is no obligatory localization, yet PDPA is used	PDPA	Proper protection of data is necessary	Specific advice in health and wellness data is developing

Data Sovereignty vs. AI Utility: Strict localization requirements can constrain AI training and model accuracy if cross-border data aggregation is restricted or prohibited.
Operational Protection: Organizations should implement encryption, federated learning, and data anonymization to mitigate risks while remaining compliant with local laws.
Strategic Governance: Ethical and legal compliance in mental health AI should be accompanied by strategic infrastructure planning, ensuring that data sovereignty is not sacrificed for model performance or accessibility.

4.9 OVERSIGHT, AUDITING, AND COMPLIANCE MODELS

Proper regulation of AI-based mental health applications requires a robust system of oversight and auditing that goes beyond standard regulatory checklists. Given the significant consequences of psychological harm, data breaches, and algorithmic bias, organizations should adopt a multi-layered governance framework incorporating internal controls, independent audits, and continuous monitoring.

4.9.1 Internal Control Systems

Internal controls involve establishing ethics boards, data governance committees, and AI risk management teams tasked with reviewing model development, deployment, and updates. These teams assess AI outputs for adherence to beneficence, non-maleficence, and justice; ensure proper data management; and verify that consent practices comply with jurisdictional standards. Human-in-the-loop supervision, especially for high-risk decisions such as suicide-risk detection or medication recommendations, ensures automated suggestions are verified by professionals, reducing potential adverse effects.

4.9.2 Independent Auditing and Certification

External validation through independent auditing evaluates algorithmic fairness, privacy, security, and transparency. Third-party auditors can review bias mitigation strategies, model explainability, and compliance with GDPR, HIPAA, or DPDP standards, providing certificates that enhance user trust and regulatory accountability. Formal credentialing frameworks, such as ISO/IEC 42001 (AI Management Systems) or EU AI Act conformity tests, as well as industry-led audits from organizations like IEEE or the Alan Turing Institute, can further validate compliance.

4.9.3 Continuous Compliance and Monitoring

AI-based mental health systems are dynamic, continuously trained, and updated with user interactions. Continuous compliance requires real-time monitoring, anomaly detection, and logging of data usage and decision pathways. Tools such as audit trails, model version control, and federated learning oversight dashboards support ongoing accountability. User feedback mechanisms help detect harm or bias and allow iterative corrections and recalibrations.

4.9.4 Risk-Based and Adaptive Governance

Risk-based governance adjusts oversight intensity according to system impact. High-risk applications, such as suicide-risk assessment or automated therapy recommendations, require more frequent audits, human supervision, and extensive reporting compared to low-risk wellness apps. Adaptive governance incorporates policy updates in response to regulatory changes, new ethical guidance, or real-world incidents, creating a feedback loop that strengthens both compliance and ethical responsibility.

Integrated governance structures combining internal review, independent audits, and continuous monitoring not only ensure legal compliance but also enhance ethical accountability, user trust, and organizational resilience.

4.10 UNIFICATION OF CROSS-BORDER DATA

Global implementation of AI-based mental health applications faces challenges due to divergent laws on data protection, consent, and localization. While ethical principles are universal, operationalizing them requires aligning legal and technical frameworks internationally to ensure both regulatory compliance and user trust.

4.10.1 FRAGMENTATION OF REGULATION

Mental health AI platforms often serve users across multiple jurisdictions, each with distinct legal requirements. For instance:

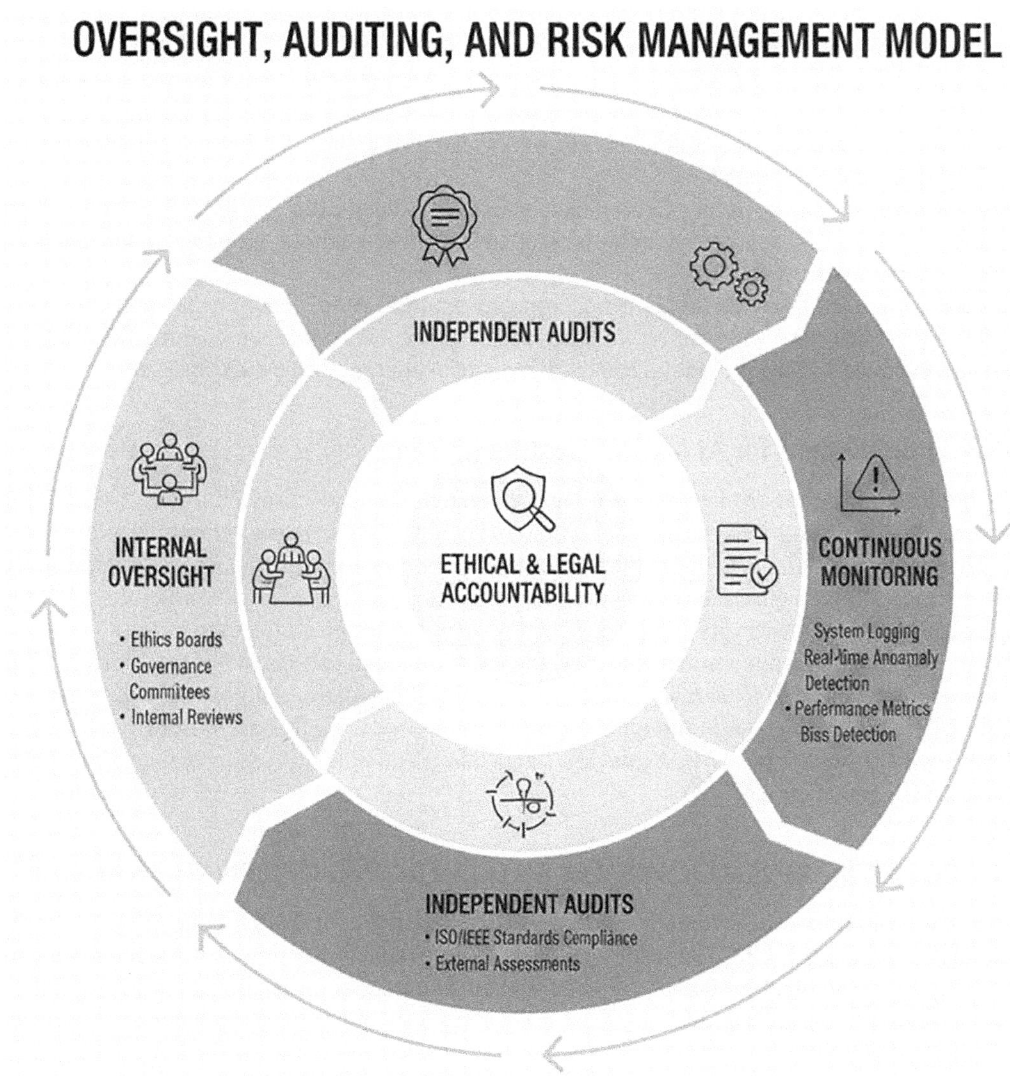

FIGURE 4.5 Model of oversight, auditing, and risk management.

EU GDPR: Emphasizes explicit consent, purpose limitation, and transparency in automated decisions.
U.S. HIPAA: Focuses primarily on covered entities and the confidentiality of health records.
India DPDP Act: Centers on sensitive data and governs cross-border data transfers.

These discrepancies create regulatory challenges, particularly for cloud-based architectures and AI models trained on cross-border aggregated data, complicating compliance and governance efforts.

This multi-tiered governance framework (Figure 4.5) illustrates a multi-level system for overseeing AI mental health applications, including internal controls, independent audits, and continuous monitoring of system outputs. It demonstrates that a fair, transparent, and ethically and legally sound framework is achievable through structured oversight.

4.10.2 Methods of Harmonization

SCCs: SCCs provide a legal mechanism for cross-border personal data transfers. Organizations moving personal data outside the EU can rely on SCCs or an adequacy finding under GDPR. Similar mechanisms are being considered in emerging AI-specific legislation.

Federated Learning and Edge Computing: Federated learning enables AI models to be trained on local data without centralized storage, eliminating cross-border data transfer conflicts while preserving model accuracy. Edge computing allows localized inference, facilitating compliance with data sovereignty requirements.

Mutual Recognition of Audits: Compliance assessments conducted across jurisdictions can be mutually recognized by regulatory authorities or independent auditors, reducing redundant work and accelerating market entry.

Global Consent and Privacy Standards: Companies are increasingly adopting layered or dynamic consent models that meet the strictest jurisdictional requirements while maintaining flexibility for local implementation. This provides a standardized global consent framework for users.

4.10.3 Implications for AI Mental Health Platforms

Cross-border harmonization not only is a legal challenge but also raises ethical and operational considerations. Platforms must ensure that harmonization processes do not compromise the protection of vulnerable populations, undermine transparency, or dilute informed consent. Achieving this balance requires robust governance, continuous monitoring, and dynamic infrastructure, including secure cloud platforms, encryption protocols, and privacy-by-design architectures.

Harmonizing data across borders allows AI mental health applications to operate globally while remaining compliant with local laws and respecting ethical standards and user trust. Key enablers include federated learning, audit mutual recognition, and standardized consent frameworks, which collectively help organizations navigate legal and ethical complexity while maintaining ethical integrity across jurisdictions.

4.11 POLICYMAKING LOOPHOLES AND EMERGING INTERNATIONAL GAPS

Despite the evolution of legal frameworks and ethical standards, substantial policy gaps remain in regulating AI in mental health. These gaps are driven by the rapid development of AI technology, the high sensitivity of mental health data, and the fragmented nature of international law. Closing these gaps is essential to ensure that technological innovation does not outpace protections for privacy, autonomy, and equity.

Figure 4.6 illustrates technical approaches, such as federated learning and edge computing, which enable the training of AI models without aggregating sensitive data. It highlights how these

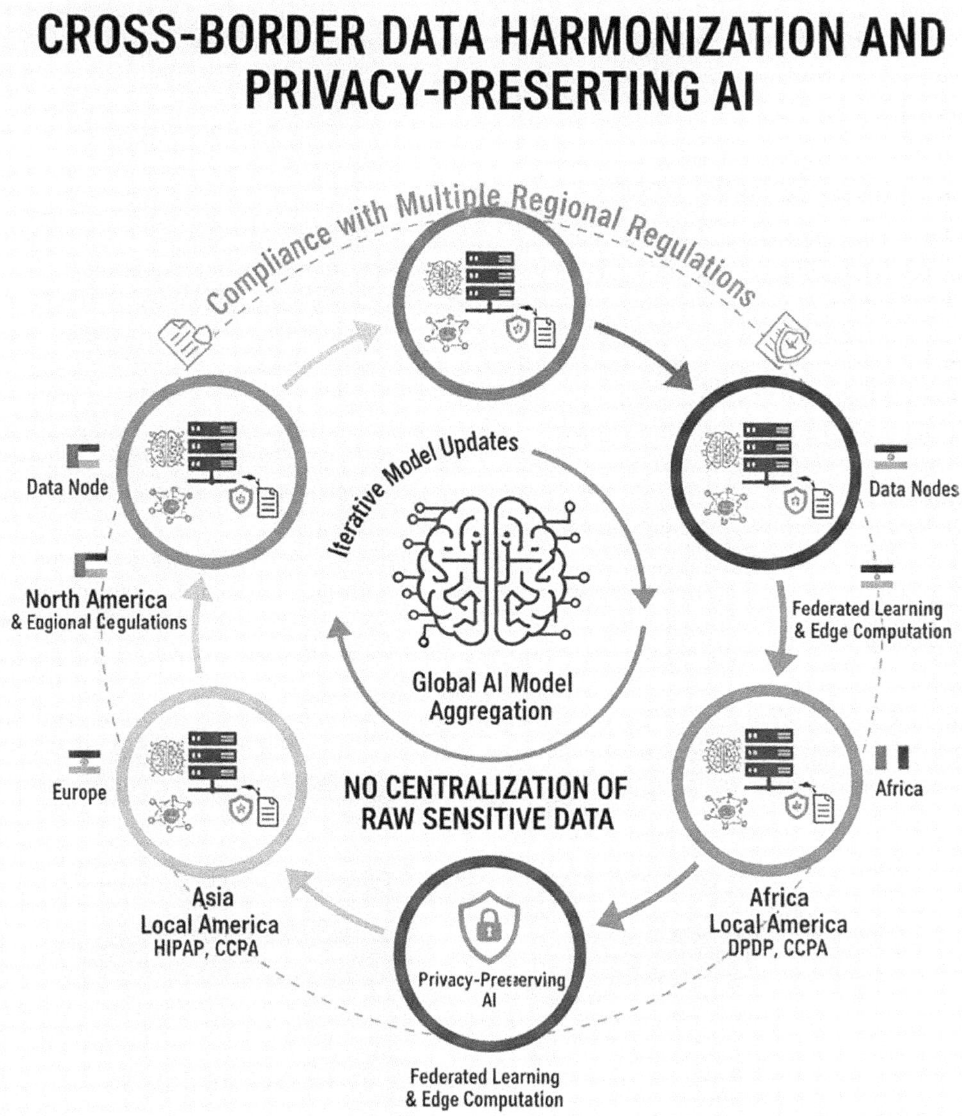

FIGURE 4.6 Privacy-saving artificial intelligence and harmony of cross-border data.

methods support adherence to region-specific regulations while maintaining data privacy in global deployments.

4.11.1 Existing Policy Gaps

Despite the proliferation of legal and ethical guidelines, significant gaps remain in the regulation of AI-driven mental health applications. A major loophole is the ambiguous definition of AI systems; many applications avoid classification as medical devices to bypass stricter regulatory oversight and associated responsibilities. This ambiguity leaves uncertainty regarding liability, ethical compliance, and reporting obligations.

Additionally, current frameworks provide limited accountability for algorithms, as developers and regulators often lack standardized methods for auditing decision-making, detecting bias, or ensuring explainability. Cross-border enforcement is weak, particularly when platforms store data in jurisdictions with lower privacy protections. Most policies also assume static consent, failing to account for continuous and adaptive data processing—such as retraining AI models, third-party analytics, or integration with other digital services—which is not fully addressed by existing regulations.

4.11.2 Emerging Global Trends

To address these gaps, several global trends are shaping the future of AI in mental health. The designation of AI applications as high risk, as in the EU AI Act, imposes strict requirements for risk assessment, ongoing self-monitoring, and human oversight, establishing an international precedent. Organizations are increasingly adopting ethics-focused governance frameworks, including internal AI ethics boards, third-party audits, and algorithmic impact assessments.

Technical innovations such as federated learning, homomorphic encryption, and edge computing enable platforms to meet localization and privacy requirements without compromising AI model performance, representing a shift toward privacy-preserving and policy-compliant architectures. International organizations such as ISO, IEEE, and WHO promote interoperability, ethical alignment, and cross-border credibility through global standards and collaboration.

There is also a growing emphasis on user-centric transparency. Layered, explainable interfaces and real-time monitoring dashboards provide individuals with greater control over their data and choices. Collectively, these trends indicate a transition from reactive compliance toward anticipatory governance, integrating technological innovation, ethical principles, and regulatory demands into forward-looking systems.

Although policy frameworks have expanded, significant gaps remain in AI classification, accountability, and cross-border enforcement. The adoption of high-risk AI regulation, ethics-based governance, privacy-preserving technologies, and user-friendly transparency is critical for achieving

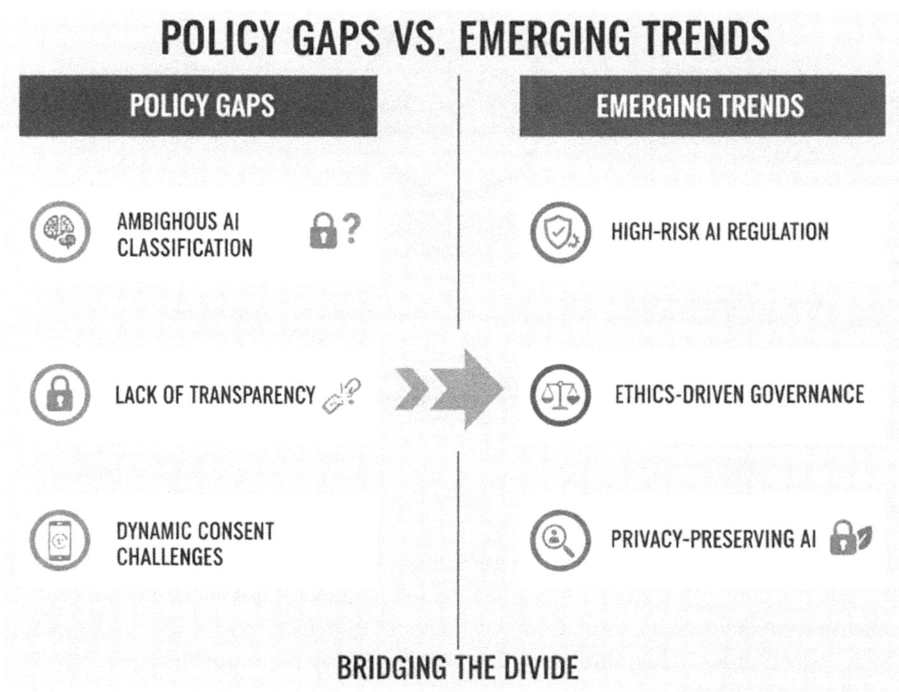

FIGURE 4.7 Gaps in policies vs. new trends.

responsible, sustainable, and ethically aligned AI mental health systems. Stakeholders must incorporate these trends into organizational practices and regulatory evolution to ensure that innovation aligns with ethical and legal standards.

The comparison chart in Figure 4.7 illustrates current policy gaps—such as ambiguous AI classification and the lack of algorithmic accountability alongside emerging governance trends, including high-risk AI regulation, ethics-driven oversight, privacy-preserving computation, and user-centric transparency. It highlights how these emergent practices can address existing shortcomings and guide the responsible implementation of AI in mental health applications.

4.12 SUMMARY

AI-based mental health applications not only offer tremendous potential in terms of scalability, accessibility, and personalized support, but also raise complex ethical, legal, and regulatory challenges. This chapter examined these dimensions using a comprehensive framework. It began with the ethical principles of beneficence, non-maleficence, and justice, emphasizing the need to maximize therapeutic benefit, prevent harm, and ensure equitable access for all users.

The chapter then discussed relevant legal standards and case studies, illustrating how frameworks such as GDPR, HIPAA, CCPA, and India's DPDP Act provide partial protections but remain limited in addressing cross-border accountability and algorithmic governance. The discussion on informed consent and digital autonomy highlighted the shortcomings of static, checkbox-based consent models and recommended dynamic, granular, user-centered approaches instead.

XAI and auditing mechanisms were identified as essential tools for promoting trust, accountability, and ethical use of AI. Transparency in decision-making processes is critical, particularly in high-stakes mental health interventions. The chapter also addressed regulatory frameworks, data localization requirements, and the challenges posed by global legal variations, emphasizing the need for harmonized multi-jurisdictional deployment.

Oversight, auditing, and compliance models were presented as foundational for ensuring ethical and legal adherence, while cross-border harmonization strategies enable platforms to operate globally without compromising privacy or data sovereignty. The chapter concluded by identifying persistent policy gaps—such as unclear AI classification, lack of algorithmic accountability, and the inadequacy of dynamic consent mechanisms—and highlighting emerging global trends, including high-risk AI regulation, ethics-driven governance, privacy-preserving technologies, and user-centric transparency.

Collectively, these developments point toward a systemic governance ecosystem for AI-based mental health, balancing innovation, ethical responsibility, and legal compliance. This chapter offers a roadmap for the responsible implementation of AI in mental healthcare, emphasizing that trust, safety, and equity must remain central as technology continues to transform the field.

REFERENCES

American Psychological Association. (2017). *Ethical principles of psychologists and code of conduct.* www.apa.org/ethics/code

American Psychological Association. (2024). *Ethical guidance for AI in the professional practice of health service psychology.* www.apa.org/topics/artificial-intelligence-machine-learning/ethical-guidance-ai-professional-practice

Balamurugan, G., Tyagi, A.K., & Richa, A. (2023). Survey on privacy preserving and trust building techniques of blockchain-based systems. In: *Privacy Preservation and Secured Data Storage in Cloud Computing.* IGI Global. DOI: 10.4018/979-8-3693-0593-5.ch019

Bhatt, U., Antorán, J., Zhang, Y., Liao, Q. V., Sattigeri, P., Fogliato, R., Gauthier Melançon, G., Krishnan, R., Stanley, J., Tickoo, O., Nachman, L., Chunara, R., Srikumar, M., Weller, A., & Xiang, A. (2020). Uncertainty as a form of transparency: Measuring, communicating, and using uncertainty. In *Proceedings of the 2020 CHI conference on human factors in computing systems* (pp. 1–13). ACM. https://doi.org/10.1145/3313831.3376708

European Commission. (2021). *Proposal for a regulation laying down harmonized rules on artificial intelligence (Artificial Intelligence Act).* https://eur-lex.europa.eu/legal-content/EN/TXT/?uri=COM%3A2021%3A206%3AFIN

European Data Protection Board. (2022). *Guidelines on data protection in AI applications.* https://edpb.europa.eu/our-work-tools/our-documents/guidelines/guidelines-2022-01_en

Federal Trade Commission. (2023). *Using AI in mental health services: A guide for practitioners.* www.ftc.gov/news-events/press-releases/2023/05/using-ai-mental-health-services-guide-practitioners

Gao, Y., & Zhang, L. (2022). Informed consent in AI-driven mental health applications: Ethical considerations. *Journal of Medical Ethics*, *48*(4), 235–240.

Gupta, A., & Mörch, C.-M. (2020). Ethical implications of AI in mental health: A systematic review. *AI & Society*, *35*(4), 1005–1016.

Indian Ministry of Electronics and Information Technology. (2023). *Draft Data Protection Bill.* https://meity.gov.in/draft-data-protection-bill

International Association of Privacy Professionals. (2022). *Global data protection laws and AI applications.* https://iapp.org/news/a/global-data-protection-laws-and-ai-applications/

International Telecommunication Union. (2021). *Ethical considerations in AI for health.* www.itu.int/en/ITU-T/AI/Pages/ethics.aspx

Kandala, A., Kandala, R., Moharir, A. K., Manchanda, N., & Singh, S. (2025). Cross-lingual mental health ontologies for Indian languages: Bridging patient expression and clinical understanding through explainable AI and human-in-the-loop validation. *arXiv*. https://doi.org/10.18653/v1/2025.nlpai4health-main.3

Kumari, S., Tyagi, A. K., Tiwari, S., & Kulshreshtha, G. (2025a). Sensors and digital twin for healthcare monitoring frameworks. In T. A. Nguyen (Ed.), *Digital twin, blockchain, and sensor networks in the healthy and mobile city (Chapter 10,* pp. 147–177*)*. Elsevier. https://doi.org/10.1016/B978-0-443-34174-8.00011-9

Kumari, S., Tyagi, A. K., Tiwari, S., & Singh, R. (2025b). Medical sensor network, edge computing and blockchain for efficient medical data exchange. In T. A. Nguyen (Ed.), *Digital twin, blockchain, and sensor networks in the healthy and mobile city (Chapter 11,* pp. 179–198*)*. Elsevier. https://doi.org/10.1016/B978-0-443-34174-8.00012-0

Mishra, A. K., Tiwari, S., Tyagi, A. K., & Arowolo, M. O. (2024). Security, privacy, trust, and provenance issues in Internet of Things–based edge environment. In S. Pal, C. Savaglio, R. Minerva, & F. C. Delicato (Eds.), *IoT edge intelligence* (pp. 233–263). Springer. https://doi.org/10.1007/978-3-031-58388-9_8

Mörch, C.-M., Gupta, A., & Mishara, B. L. (2019). Canada protocol: An ethical checklist for the use of artificial intelligence in suicide prevention and mental health. *Journal of Medical Internet Research*, *21*(7), e14128. https://doi.org/10.1016/j.artmed.2020.101934

Nair, M. M., & Tyagi, A. K. (2021). Privacy: History, statistics, policy, laws, preservation and threat analysis. *Journal of information assurance & security*, *16*(1), 24–34.

Nair, M.M., & Tyagi, A.K. (2025). Transformative effects of emerging technologies on Industry 5.0 and Society 5.0: Current status, vision, issues, challenges, and opportunities for future. In: *Next Generation Data Science and Blockchain Technology for Industry 5.0.* Wiley. DOI: https://doi.org/10.1002/9781394245215.ch13, ISBN: 9781394245185.

OECD. (2021). *AI principles and guidelines for mental health applications.* www.oecd.org/ai/mental-health-guidelines/

Privacy International. (2022). *Data localization and its impact on AI applications.* https://privacyinternational.org/learn/artificial-intelligence

Rajani, D., Menon, S. C., Kute, S., & Tyagi, A. K. (2022). Preserving privacy of social media data using artificial intelligence techniques. In A. Tyagi (Ed.), *Handbook of Research on Technical, Privacy, and Security Challenges in a Modern World* (pp. 186–204). IGI Global. https://doi.org/10.4018/978-1-6684-5250-9.ch010

Raji, I. D., & Buolamwini, J. (2020). Actionable auditing: Investigating the impact of publicly naming biased performance results of commercial AI products. In *Proceedings of the 2020 CHI conference on human factors in computing systems* (pp. 1–13). ACM. https://doi.org/10.1145/3313831.3376712

Smith, J., & Lee, A. (2023). Informed consent in digital mental health interventions: A systematic review. *Journal of Digital Health*, *9*(1), 45–58.

Sundaram, H., & Li, T. W. (2023). Inform the uninformed: Improving online informed consent reading with an AI-powered chatbot. *arXiv*. https://dl.acm.org/doi/10.1145/3544548.3581252

Taylor, R., & Green, M. (2022). Algorithmic transparency in mental health AI: A review of current practices. *Journal of AI Ethics*, *4*(2), 67–80.

Tyagi, A. K., & Tiwari, S. (2024a). Blockchain-enabled smart healthcare applications in 6G networks. In A. K. Tyagi (Ed.), *Digital twin and blockchain for smart cities (Chapter 20,* pp. 459–494*)*. Wiley. https://doi.org/10.1002/9781394303564.ch20

Tyagi, A. K., Kumari, S., & Tiwari, S. (2024c). Internet of Things for smart healthcare: A survey. In A. K. Sharma, N. Chanderwal, S. Tyagi, & P. Upadhyay (Eds.), *Future of AI in medical imaging (Chapter 2,* pp. 19–41*)*. IGI Global. https://doi.org/10.4018/979-8-3693-2359-5.ch002

Tyagi, A.K. (2021). Analysis of security and privacy aspects of blockchain technologies from smart era' perspective: The challenges and a way forward. In: *Recent Trends in Blockchain for Information Systems Security and Privacy* (pp. 1–17). DOI: https://doi.org/10.1201/9781003139737, eBook-ISBN: 9781003139737

Tyagi, A.K. (2025). Blockchain for smart hospital in Healthcare 5.0: modeling structure, challenges, and future emerging trends. In: *Human-Centric Integration of Next-Generation Data Science and Blockchain Technology.* Elsevier. DOI: https://doi.org/10.1016/B978-0-443-33498-6.00026-1, ISBN: 978-0-443-33498-6.

Tyagi, A.K. (2026). *Chapter 25 - Industry 5.0, Society 5.0, Healthcare 5.0, and Consumer 5.0: current status, vision, issues, challenges, and opportunities for future, in the book: Smart Hospital Anatomy with Advanced Sensors Innovations in Patient Care 2026.* Elsevier (pp. 371–386). https://doi.org/10.1016/B978-0-443-45875-0.00002-8, ISBN: 978-0-443-45875-0.

Tyagi, A. K., Tripathi, K., Tiwari, S., & Kaushik, S. (2025). An efficient technique for privacy preservation, trusted and secure patient-centric services in smart healthcare. In *Proceedings of the 6th international conference on recent trends in communication & intelligent systems (ICRTCIS 2025)* (pp. 31–47). IET. https://doi.org/10.1049/icp.2025.2731

United Nations. (2022). *Guidelines on data protection and privacy in AI applications.* www.un.org/en/dataprotection/ai-guidelines

United Nations Educational, Scientific and Cultural Organization. (2021). *Ethical guidelines for AI in education and health.* www.unesco.org/en/ethical-guidelines-ai

Wang, L., & Li, H. (2022). Cross-border data harmonization in AI-driven mental health services: Challenges and solutions. *Global Health Journal*, *8*(3), 123–136.

World Economic Forum. (2021). *Global AI governance: A framework for mental health applications.* www.weforum.org/global-ai-governance

World Health Organization. (2021). *Ethics and governance of artificial intelligence for health: WHO guidance.* www.who.int/publications/i/item/9789240062884

Xu, Y., & Zhang, W. (2022). Data localization laws and their impact on AI applications in mental health. *Journal of Technology Law & Policy*, *26*(1), 89–102.

Yang, F., & Liu, J. (2021). Ethical considerations in the use of AI for mental health diagnosis. *Journal of Ethics in Mental Health*, *16*(2), 45–59. https://doi.org/10.1177/17470161211012345

Zhang, X., & Wang, Y. (2022). Privacy and security in AI-driven mental health applications: A review. *Journal of Cybersecurity*, *8*(4), 234–245.

Zhang, Y., & Bhatt, U. (2020). Algorithmic transparency in mental health AI: Challenges and opportunities. *Journal of Artificial Intelligence Research*, *69*, 123–145.

Zhao, L., & Chen, Y. (2021). The role of explainable AI in mental health applications: A review. *Journal of Artificial Intelligence in Medicine*, *118*, 102087. https://doi.org/10.1016/j.artmed.2021.102087

Zhao, Q., & Zhang, L. (2022). Data localization and sovereignty in AI-driven mental health applications: Legal perspectives. *International Journal of Law and Information Technology*, *30*(2), 112–130.

Zhou, Y., & Wang, H. (2021). Cross-border data harmonization in AI applications: A comparative analysis. *Journal of International Business Studies*, *52*(3), 456–478.

Part II

Technical Foundations and Data Management

5 AI Models and Algorithms for Mental Health Applications

5.1 INTRODUCTION

Mental illnesses constitute a significant global problem, affecting millions of individuals across diverse populations. Traditional methods of assessment, monitoring, and treatment often face limitations in scalability, accessibility, and personalization. Artificial intelligence (AI) represents a potentially transformative technology in mental healthcare, capable of handling complex behavioral data, supporting individualized interventions, and assisting clinicians in decision-making.

AI-based solutions leverage machine learning (ML), deep learning (DL), and natural language processing (NLP) techniques to predict patient behavior, identify early signs of mental disorders, and provide therapeutic support via chatbots and other cognitive therapy applications in real time. Beyond technical performance, mental health data's sensitivity requires strict adherence to ethical, privacy, and security standards. Explainable AI (XAI) frameworks, bias reduction methods, and secure model training pipelines are therefore essential to establish trust and regulatory compliance.

The purpose of this chapter is to provide an overview of AI models and algorithms applied to mental health. It covers ML and DL techniques, emotion and sentiment detection, predictive behavior modeling, NLP-based therapy tools, and strategies for explainability, fairness, and secure deployment. Case studies illustrate practical implementation, including successes, limitations, and emerging opportunities. This chapter serves as a roadmap for researchers and practitioners to develop AI-based mental health solutions that are effective, transparent, and ethically responsible.

5.2 LITERATURE REVIEW

5.2.1 Artificial Intelligence in Psychology

AI has emerged as a valuable tool in mental healthcare, offering novel methods for diagnosis, monitoring, and intervention. A systematic review by Atlam et al. (2025) highlights the importance of XAI in predicting mental health challenges, emphasizing transparency and interpretability in clinical settings. Lee et al. (2021) examined the clinical and ethical implications of AI in mental health, stressing the need to balance technological innovation with patient safety. Dehbozorgi et al. (2025) and Guo (2023) explored AI applications in emotion recognition and affective state detection, demonstrating their utility in cognitive therapy and real-time patient interaction.

5.2.2 Prejudice and Neutrality in AI Models

The growing use of AI in psychiatry raises concerns regarding algorithmic bias and fairness. Bouguettaya et al. (2025) and Chang et al. (2025) highlight racial and treatment biases in

DOI: 10.1201/9781003658344-7

AI-based psychiatric recommendations, which can lead to inequitable outcomes. Cross et al. (2024) emphasized that biases in medical AI can compromise clinical decision-making. Liu et al. (2025) and Ferrara (2023) conducted systematic evaluations of AI fairness, underscoring the need for comprehensive bias assessment in clinical AI applications. Buolamwini (2025) investigated gender bias, while Poulain et al. (2023) proposed federated learning as a promising method to mitigate structural inequities in AI-driven care.

5.2.3 Explainable AI and Trust

XAI is critical for fostering clinician trust and promoting AI adoption in mental health. Joyce et al. (2023) and Kerz (2023) emphasized that user understanding is central to the ethical deployment of AI systems. Rosenbacke (2024) highlighted that poorly designed explanations can undermine clinician trust. Noor et al. (2025) and Sadeghi (2024), along with recent reviews, stressed that interpretability should be integrated with high-performing models to ensure both transparency and efficacy.

5.2.4 Behavioral Insights and Predictive Modeling

AI models are increasingly used to gain behavioral insights through predictive analytics. Elyoseph (2024) and Nair et al. (2021) compared AI predictions with professional assessments in depressive disorders, demonstrating that ML can complement clinical judgment. Poudel et al. (2025) and Nair et al. (2025) reviewed advances made in predictive modeling for early identification of mental health issues and tailored interventions. Wang et al. (2025) conducted a meta-analysis of generative AI applications, showing their utility in simulating patient interactions and predicting behavioral patterns.

5.2.5 Ethical and Legal Issues

Ethical and legal frameworks are essential for responsible AI deployment. Nouis et al. (2025) emphasized the importance of integrating clinicians into oversight processes to ensure accountability and transparency. Singhal (2024) and Tyagi (2021) highlighted the significance of fairness, accountability, transparency, and ethical standards in medical AI. Preda (2025) discussed AI-induced psychosis, underscoring the need for ethical safeguards in psychiatric applications.

5.2.6 Clinical Integration and AI

Human-centered design is crucial for reducing bias and improving usability. Olawade et al. (2024), Kumari et al. (2025b), and Zhang et al. (2023) explored clinician and patient perspectives, emphasizing collaboration between developers and users to enhance AI adoption. Sun, (2025) and Kumari et al. (2025a) examined historical and future trends in psychiatric AI, recommending iterative human-centered reviews to align AI systems with clinical workflows.

5.2.7 Assessment of Performance and Metrics

Evaluating AI performance in mental health requires a multidimensional assessment. Soganciogolu (2024) and Mishra et al. (2024) highlighted the need to evaluate both predictive accuracy and fairness in AI-based risk assessments and depression phenotype predictions. Poudel et al. (2025) and Tyagi (2025) recommended continuous validation in real-world applications. Buolamwini (2025) and Ferrara (2023) emphasized the importance of bias detection and performance benchmarking to ensure equitable outcomes.

5.2.8 Future Projections and Future Trends

Recent developments focus on improving fairness and interpretability. Ferrara (2023) and Liu et al. (2025) identified gaps in AI fairness research, while Noor et al. (2025) and Joyce et al. (2023) described new trends in XAI implementation. Poulain et al. (2023) and Rollwage (2023) introduced federated learning and conversational AI strategies to support safer and more inclusive mental health interventions. Collectively, these studies indicate a path toward ethical, transparent, and human-centered AI systems that enhance mental healthcare in a cost-effective and equitable manner.

5.3 DEEP LEARNING AND MACHINE LEARNING INTRODUCTION

The modern application of AI in mental health primarily relies on ML and DL. These techniques enable researchers and clinicians to extract meaningful patterns from complex datasets, including electronic health records, behavioral logs, speech and text data, and physiological signals. By learning from historical data, ML and DL models facilitate early diagnosis, prognosis, treatment planning, and the implementation of digital therapeutics and patient engagement systems.

ML Methods in Mental Health: ML methods include supervised, unsupervised, and reinforcement learning. Supervised learning algorithms, such as Support Vector Machines (SVMs), Random Forests, and Gradient Boosting, are widely used to classify patient states, detect mental health conditions, and predict clinical outcomes. For example, supervised models can predict depressive episodes from longitudinal patient data or screen for anxiety using structured questionnaires.

Unsupervised learning techniques, including clustering methods like K-means and hierarchical clustering, identify hidden patterns in behavioral or symptom data. These approaches enable patient segmentation based on risk profiles or symptom trajectories. Reinforcement learning, which optimizes decision-making policies via environmental feedback, is increasingly applied in adaptive therapeutic interventions, allowing AI systems to personalize recommendations over time. Hybrid approaches combining these techniques can further enhance predictive accuracy and interpretability, particularly when handling multimodal data.

DL Architectures: DL has gained traction due to its ability to process large, unstructured datasets. Feedforward Artificial Neural Networks (ANNs) are commonly employed for classification and regression tasks, such as mood prediction or cognitive state estimation. Convolutional Neural Networks (CNNs) are particularly effective for analyzing images and videos, including facial expressions and neuroimaging data. Recurrent Neural Networks (RNNs) and Long Short-Term Memory (LSTM) networks capture temporal patterns in sequential data, such as speech, text, or behavioral logs, facilitating mood trend analysis or early warning predictions.

Transformer-based models, including Bidirectional Encoder Representations from Transformers (BERT) and Generative Pre-trained Transformer (GPT), are increasingly applied in natural language understanding tasks, such as chatbots, sentiment analysis, and cognitive therapy tools. Their self-attention mechanisms effectively capture long-term dependencies and contextual relationships in text or multimodal data.

Handling Small and Sensitive Data: A key challenge in mental health AI is the limited size and high sensitivity of available datasets. Data augmentation techniques, such as synthetic text generation or oversampling of minority classes, can mitigate sparsity. Transfer learning, where pre-trained models like BERT or GPT are fine-tuned on mental health-specific data, reduces data requirements without compromising performance. Privacy-preserving approaches, including federated learning, differential privacy, and secure multi-party computation, allow models to be trained while safeguarding sensitive patient information.

Applications in Mental Health: AI has diverse applications in mental health, including diagnostic support, behavioral prediction, and digital therapeutics. ML and DL methods enable earlier detection of depression, anxiety, schizophrenia, and post-traumatic stress disorders (PTSDs) using clinical records, social media posts, or speech patterns. Predictive models help prevent symptom exacerbation by forecasting relapse risk or symptom recurrence. Digital therapeutics leverage adaptive algorithms that learn from patient feedback to deliver personalized treatment recommendations. Multimodal analysis integrating text, speech, facial expression, and sensor data provides a comprehensive assessment of patient well-being.

The lifecycle of mental health data in AI applications is shown in Figure 5.1. Patient data are collected at various points, pre-processed, and then fed into ML or DL models. The outputs, such as behavioral predictions or clinical insights, inform therapeutic interventions. At every stage, ethical, fairness, and privacy issues must be addressed, and secure, transparent processing is essential.

Key challenges include overfitting due to small datasets, which can be mitigated through cross-validation and regularization techniques. DL models often function as black boxes, creating interpretability challenges that can be addressed with XAI methods. Ethical and fairness considerations are paramount, as biased models may adversely affect vulnerable populations. Additionally, DL models may require resource-intensive computational infrastructure, which can be mitigated through lightweight architectures or cloud-based deployment.

ML and DL offer powerful methods to analyze complex mental health data, enabling predictive modeling, behavioral insights, and digital therapeutics. When combined with privacy-preserving and XAI strategies, these models can achieve accuracy, ethical compliance, transparency, and clinical utility. The following section focuses on NLP in chatbots and cognitive therapy tools, applying these principles to patient-facing applications.

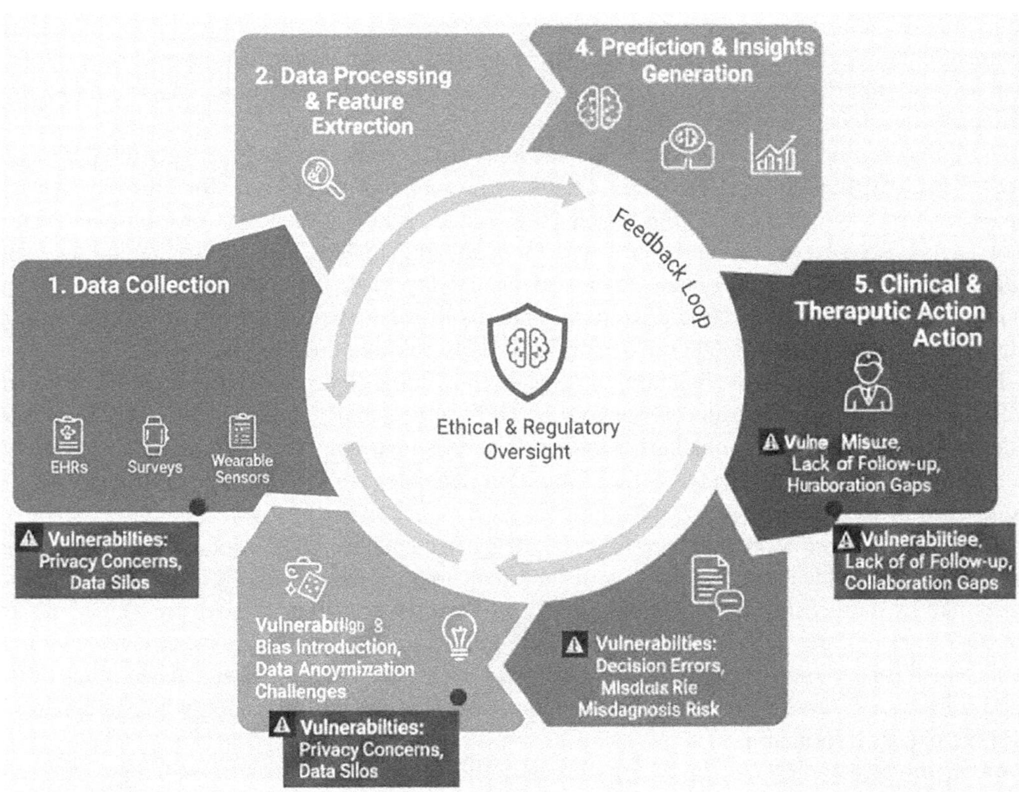

FIGURE 5.1 Mental health data lifecycle with AI.

5.4 CHATBOTS, NLP, AND COGNITIVE THERAPY TOOLS

NLP has become a essential component of AI-based mental health solutions, allowing machines to understand, interpret, and respond to human language. NLP plays a critical role in designing chatbots and cognitive therapy tools that provide scalable, interactive, and personalized mental health support. Such systems can identify symptoms, assess emotional states, and support therapeutic interventions without requiring constant clinician supervision, using data from patient–clinician interactions, clinical notes, or social media posts.

5.4.1 Key NLP Components in Mental Health Chatbots

Intent Recognition and Dialogue Management: Intent recognition enables the system to identify user goals, such as expressing distress, seeking information, or reporting symptoms. Dialogue management ensures coherent, contextually relevant conversations, guiding the chatbot's responses through multi-turn interactions. Contemporary systems often combine rule-based approaches with ML models, including sequence-to-sequence models and transformer-based language models, to handle complex dialogues.

Text Understanding and Sentiment Analysis: Sentiment analysis categorizes user text as positive, negative, or neutral, providing a proxy for mood or emotional state. More advanced models can detect nuanced emotions, such as anxiety, sadness, or frustration, enabling empathetic responses. Behavioral and contextual cues can further enhance the accuracy and relevance of therapeutic interactions.

Cognitive Therapy and Individualized Interventions: NLP supports evidence-based interventions grounded in cognitive–behavioral therapy (CBT). Chatbots can guide users through exercises such as thought journaling, cognitive reframing, and mindfulness training, adapting recommendations based on user feedback and behavior. Personalization improves adherence and effectiveness, particularly in remote or underserved communities.

Privacy and Security in NLP Pipelines: Given the sensitivity of mental health data, secure processing is essential. On-device processing, federated learning, and differential privacy help preserve confidentiality while allowing models to improve. Additional safeguards, including encryption, secure authentication, and access control, ensure compliance with regulatory requirements.

Applications and Case Studies: NLP-based chatbots such as Woebot, Wysa, and Tess have demonstrated positive outcomes in user engagement, mood improvement, and timely mental health support. Research indicates that incorporating continuous feedback loops and multimodal inputs—such as voice or facial expressions alongside text—enhances the effectiveness and empathy of AI-driven interventions.

Table 5.1 provides a comparative analysis of AI methods commonly used in mental health applications, including conventional ML, DL, NLP, and XAI techniques. Each row summarizes the method's primary use, strengths, limitations, and illustrative examples. For instance, ML excels in predictive modeling of structured data, whereas DL handles unstructured data (text, audio, video) but can be less interpretable. NLP methods are particularly effective in conversational agents and cognitive therapy tools but may exhibit biases. XAI techniques enhance transparency and clinician trust. Table 5.1 allows readers to quickly understand the practical merits and challenges of each approach in mental health contexts.

NLP provides essential technical support to chatbots and cognitive therapy tools in mental health, enabling intent recognition, sentiment and emotion detection, personalized responses, and privacy-sensitive interactions. By combining these features with ethically guided design principles,

TABLE 5.1
Comparison of AI in Mental Health

AI Technique	Applications	Strengths	Limitations	The Important References
Machine learning	Predictive modeling, depression detection	High interpretability, low computation	Strategic data are required	Atlam et al. (2025), Elyoseph (2024), Tyagi and Tiwari (2024a)
Deep learning	Emotion recognition, chatbots therapy	Unstructured data (text, voice)	Black box, requires large data	Guo (2023), Kerz (2023), Tyagi et al. (2024c)
NLP models	Chatbots, cognitive therapy tools	Text analysis, contextual understanding	Prone to bias	Zhang et al. (2023), Rollwage (2023), Balamurugan et al. (2023)
XAI tools	Feature description, trust building	Transparency, trust of the clinician	Computational overhead	Joyce et al. (2023), Rosenbacke (2024), Rajani et al. (2022), Tyagi et al. (2025)

NLP-driven systems can deliver scalable, accessible, and clinically relevant mental health support. The next section elaborates on emotion and sentiment recognition techniques, including multi-modal approaches and advanced AI models for affective computing.

5.5 EMOTION AND SENTIMENT RECOGNITION TECHNIQUES

Emotion and sentiment recognition algorithms are central to AI-based mental health applications, allowing the inference of users' affective states from diverse data sources. These methods provide insights into patients' emotional conditions, helping clinicians and digital therapeutics deliver timely, personalized interventions. Modern solutions often integrate three modalities—text, speech, and visual data—and leverage ML and DL models for enhanced accuracy.

Text-Based Sentiment and Emotion Analysis: Text-based analysis is commonly applied in mental health chatbots, social media monitoring, and online journaling apps. NLP systems detect mood and emotional state through words, grammar, and context, categorizing sentiment as positive, negative, or neutral, or identifying specific emotions such as sadness, anger, fear, or happiness. Techniques range from classical ML classifiers like SVMs and Naive Bayes to DL models such as RNNs, LSTM networks, and transformer-based models (e.g., BERT, GPT). These models capture semantic meaning and contextual dependencies, enabling nuanced detection of emotional states.

Speech and Prosodic Analysis: Building on text-based methods, speech analysis extracts emotional cues from voice recordings. ML models classify emotions by analyzing features such as pitch, tone, energy, speech rate, and spectral patterns. DL architectures, particularly CNNs and RNNs, have been used effectively to detect stress, anxiety, and depression in speech, supporting real-time monitoring. Multi-modal combinations of text and speech further enhance recognition performance in naturalistic settings.

Visual Emotion Recognition (VER): VER analyzes facial expressions, microexpressions, and body gestures to infer affective states. CNNs are employed to extract spatial features from facial images or video frames, while temporal models such as LSTMs capture dynamic changes over time. Integrating visual analysis with textual and speech indicators provides a more comprehensive understanding of users' emotional profiles, improving the contextual relevance of AI-driven interventions.

Multimodal Emotion Recognition: Advanced emotion recognition combines text, speech, and visual data to deliver robust, contextually aware predictions. Fusion strategies may be feature-level (early fusion) or decision-level (late fusion), allowing models to weigh inputs based on their reliability and relevance. Multi-modal approaches are particularly valuable in mental health applications, where affective states may manifest differently across modalities.

Challenges and Ethical Issues: Emotion recognition faces challenges such as cultural, gender, and individual differences in expressiveness, as well as privacy concerns due to continuous monitoring. Models must be unbiased, explainable, and privacy preserving. Techniques such as federated learning, secure model deployment, and differential privacy support ethical and responsible use.

In summary, emotion and sentiment recognition form the foundation for AI systems to monitor and understand users' affective states across text, speech, and visual data. These methods enhance personalization, responsiveness, and clinical relevance while maintaining ethical and privacy standards. The next section explores predictive modeling of behavioral insights for proactive mental health interventions.

5.6 BEHAVIORAL INSIGHT PREDICTIVE MODELING

Predictive modeling is critical in AI-based mental health applications, enabling the anticipation of behavioral patterns, symptom trajectories, and potential crises. By analyzing historical and real-time data, these models provide actionable insights to support proactive interventions, personalized care, and optimal resource allocation. ML and DL models can detect early indicators of disorders such as depression, anxiety, bipolar disorder, and PTSD, improving patient safety and clinical outcomes.

Time-Series and Longitudinal Data Analysis: Patient records, including mood logs, activity tracking, physiological measures, and digital interactions, are temporally dependent. Common modeling techniques include RNNs, LSTMs, and Temporal Convolutional Networks (TCNs), which predict symptom escalation, relapse risk, and treatment response. Longitudinal analysis identifies subtle changes over time, providing clinicians with early insights that traditional assessments may miss.

Feature Engineering and Selection: Features may include demographic information, clinical history, self-reported data, speech/text inputs, and wearable sensor data. Techniques such as Principal Component Analysis (PCA), recursive feature elimination, and regularization reduce dimensionality and improve model generalization. Multi-modal feature integration further enhances predictive accuracy by leveraging complementary information from multiple sources.

Modeling Approaches: Supervised learning is commonly used for classification and regression tasks, employing algorithms like logistic regression, random forests, gradient boosting, and SVMs. DL models, including LSTMs and transformers, handle sequential, multi-modal data for complex forecasting tasks. Hybrid approaches combining supervised learning with reinforcement or probabilistic modeling are increasingly used for adaptive interventions that evolve based on patient feedback.

Applications in Behavioral Insights: Predictive models detect early signs of mental health deterioration, monitor therapy outcomes, personalize interventions, and anticipate crises. Digital therapeutics and AI monitoring systems provide clinicians with real-time alerts, intervention recommendations, and behavioral insights. For example, changes in speech patterns, textual sentiment, or social interaction frequency may predict a return to depressive states, enabling timely support.

Challenges and Ethical Issues: Predictive modeling must address incomplete, noisy, or biased datasets, ensure interpretability, and protect sensitive patient information. Limitations should be transparently reported, and models must integrate clinician judgment and adhere to ethical standards. Privacy-preserving methods such as federated learning and differential privacy mitigate risks associated with sensitive behavioral data.

Predictive modeling provides actionable insights from longitudinal and multimodal data, enabling proactive, personalized mental health interventions. When combined with ethical safeguards, interpretable models, and privacy-preserving techniques, predictive modeling enhances the effectiveness, safety, and accessibility of AI-based mental health tools. The following section discusses model transparency and XAI and its importance in building clinician trust and engaging patients.

5.7 MODEL TRANSPARENCY AND XAI

In mental health applications, model transparency and XAI are crucial due to the potential impact on patient well-being. While ML and DL models are effective in predicting outcomes and recommending interventions, their complexity often renders them "black boxes." XAI addresses this by providing insights into model behavior, enhancing interpretability, trust, and accountability in clinical practice.

Explainability Techniques: Techniques include feature importance analysis, local explanation methods, and visualization tools. Model-agnostic frameworks like SHAP (SHapley Additive Explanations) and LIME (Local Interpretable Model-agnostic Explanations) quantify the contribution of each input to an individual prediction, enabling clinicians to understand why a model flagged a patient at risk. Transformer models utilize attention mechanisms for inherent interpretability, highlighting influential words, phrases, or temporal patterns in multi-modal tasks like NLP and emotion recognition.

Local vs. Global Interpretability: Global interpretability explains the model's overall logic and trends across a dataset, while local interpretability focuses on individual predictions critical for

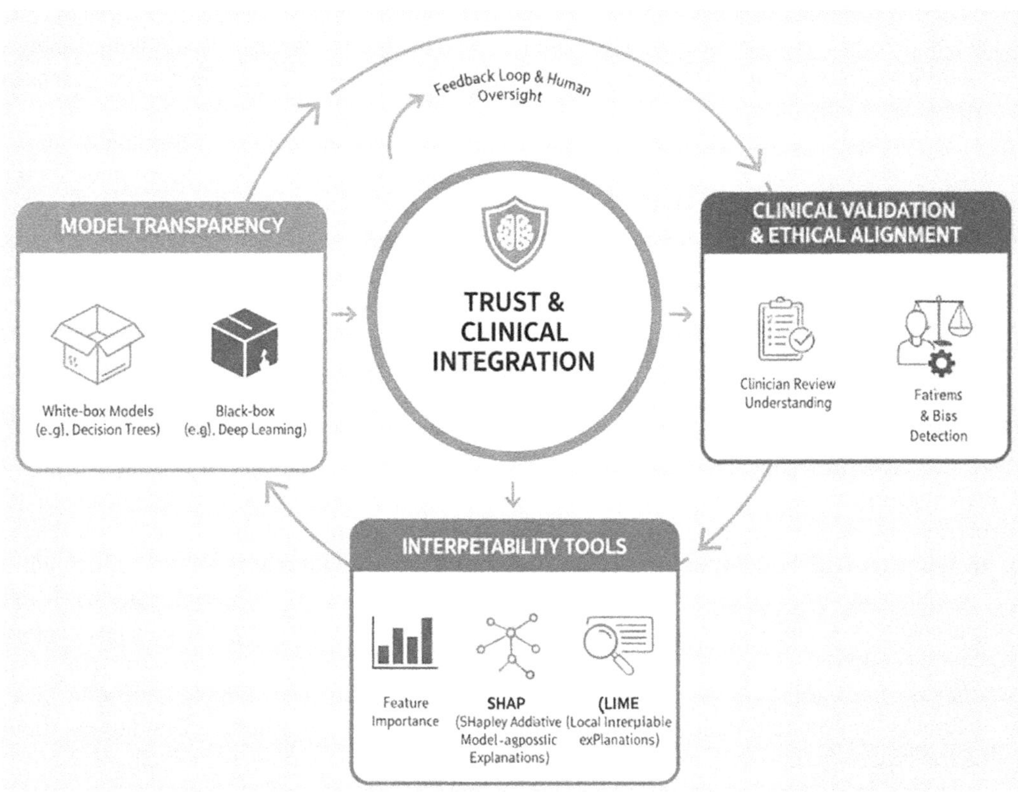

FIGURE 5.2 Explainable AI (XAI) framework of mental health usage.

personalized interventions in mental health. Balancing global and local explanations ensures models are both clinically useful and transparent.

Clinical Application and Transparency: Transparent models enhance credibility, support informed decision-making, and allow clinicians to verify predictions against their expertise. Transparency also facilitates regulatory compliance, where healthcare guidelines increasingly demand accountable and explainable AI tools.

Challenges and Ethical Issues: XAI must strike a balance between oversimplification, which may mislead users, and excessive technical detail, which may overwhelm them. Integration of XAI with rigorous assessment, human-centered design, and continuous review ensures models are interpretable, ethical, and effective in clinical contexts.

Figure 5.2 presents a mental health implementation framework for XAI. By integrating transparent model design with interpretability tools, clinicians can better understand AI predictions, thereby increasing trust and adoption. Feedback loops enable recurrent corrections to improve both model explainability and performance.

The core components of AI implementation in mental healthcare are model transparency and XAI. Explainable models allow clinicians to supervise AI behavior, fostering patient trust and ensuring that interventions are ethical, safe, and effective. The next section discusses secure model training and ethical practices, addressing privacy, bias mitigation, and responsible handling of sensitive patient data.

5.8 TRAINING PRACTICES IN ETHICS AND SECURITY

Developing AI models for mental health demands strict attention to ethical norms and secure training practices, as patient data are highly sensitive and prediction errors may have serious consequences. Ethical concerns include informed consent, privacy, fairness, and transparency, while secure training focuses on safeguarding sensitive data and preserving model integrity throughout development.

Data Privacy and Confidentiality: Patient data such as medical records, therapy transcripts, and behavioral logs are highly sensitive and often regulated by Health Insurance Portability and Accountability Act (HIPAA), General Data Protection Regulation (GDPR), and other regional privacy laws. Techniques such as anonymization, pseudonymization, and encryption help protect personal identifiers. Advanced methods like differential privacy introduce noise to the training data, allowing pattern detection without revealing individual-level information.

Federated Learning and Distributed Training: Federated learning and distributed training allow secure model development by keeping data localized. In federated learning, models are trained on patient devices or institutional servers, and only aggregated updates are shared centrally. This approach prevents sensitive data from leaving its source while enabling collaborative model improvement. Security can be further enhanced through secure multi-party computation and homomorphic encryption, which allow computation on encrypted data.

Bias Mitigation and Fairness: Mental health datasets often contain societal, demographic, or cultural biases. Models trained on such data may produce unequal predictions, exacerbating disparities in care access and quality. Techniques to ensure fairness include fairness-aware learning, re-weighting underrepresented groups, and selective testing across diverse test sets.

Model Evaluation and Auditability: Transparent reporting of model performance, error analysis, and validation on representative datasets is crucial. Continuous monitoring during deployment allows detection of model drift, emerging biases, or security issues, enabling timely corrective action.

Ethical Oversight and Governance: Ethical review boards, interdisciplinary advisory committees, and patient-centered feedback systems help align AI systems with clinical, societal, and regulatory expectations. Embedding ethical issues at all stages of development—from data collection to deployment—fosters responsible innovation and maintains clinician, patient, and regulatory trust.

Ethical and secure training practices are essential for AI in mental health. By combining privacy-preserving methods, accountable training, ongoing monitoring, and robust governance, developers can create AI systems that are trustworthy, responsible, accurate, and patient-centered. The following section examines bias and fairness in AI for psychiatry, including methods to identify and prevent algorithmic bias.

5.9 BIAS AND FAIRNESS IN AI FOR PSYCHIATRY

Fairness and bias are critical considerations in mental health AI, as algorithms directly influence patient outcomes, access to care, and treatment quality. Mental health datasets often exhibit systemic disparities, underrepresentation of certain groups, or cultural differences in symptom presentation. Unaddressed, these biases can perpetuate inequalities, making fairness-conscious development both an ethical and clinical imperative.

Sources of Bias: Bias in psychiatric AI models may arise from the following:

Sampling Bias: Overrepresentation of certain populations (e.g., younger adults or English speakers), leading to poor generalization to other groups.
Measurement Bias: Data collection tools or procedures influenced by cultural or contextual factors.
Label Bias: Inconsistencies or subjectivity in clinical diagnoses.

Identifying these biases is the first step toward developing equitable AI systems.

Bias Mitigation Techniques: Mitigation strategies are applied at different stages:

Pre-processing: Re-sampling, re-weighting, or data augmentation to achieve balanced representation across demographics.
In-processing: Modifying learning algorithms to enforce fairness constraints or asymmetrical treatment of underrepresented groups.
Post-processing: Adjusting model outputs to reduce disparities after training.

Stringent evaluation ensures that fairness goals are met without degrading overall model performance.

Evaluation Metrics and Oversight: Fairness should be assessed across demographic and clinical variables, including age, gender, ethnicity, socioeconomic status, and cultural background. Metrics such as demographic parity, equal opportunity, and predictive equality guide bias measurement and corrective action. Continuous monitoring during deployment is essential, as changing populations or new data can introduce fresh biases.
Ethical and Clinical Implications: Fairness extends beyond technical solutions. Open communication of model limitations, proactive engagement with stakeholders, and patient-centered design help ensure equitable AI adoption. Clinicians should treat AI recommendations as supplementary, integrating them with broader clinical judgment rather than relying on them as sole decision-makers.

Figure 5.3 presents a workflow to address algorithmic bias in AI-based mental health systems. The process begins with auditing data for imbalances or historical biases, followed by mitigation

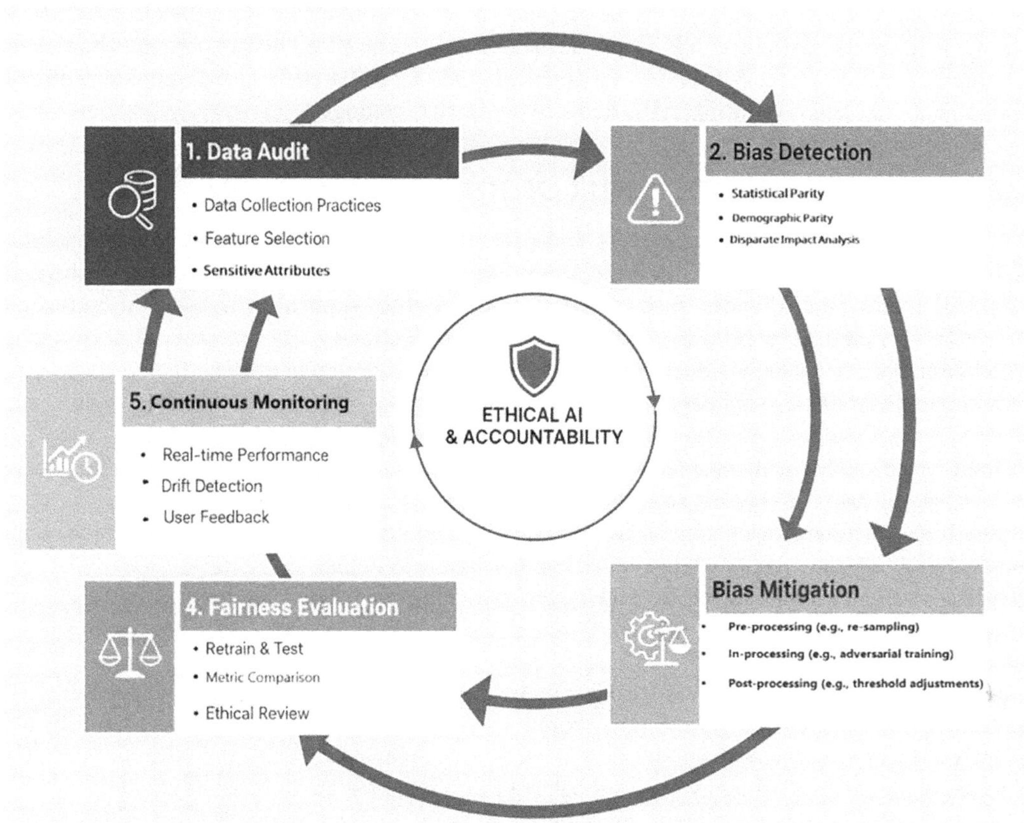

FIGURE 5.3 Workflow bias detection and mitigation.

TABLE 5.2
AI Bias Mitigation Strategies for Mental Health Applications

Strategy	Description	Benefits	Criticisms	Key References
Data rebalancing	Makes datasets balanced	Minimizes imbalance in demographics	Can decrease sample size	Bouguettaya et al. (2025), Chang et al. (2025)
Fairness-constrained training	Optimizes when using fairness constraints applied directly	Reduces bias in predictions directly	Can be used to have an effect on accuracy	Ferrara (2023), Liu et al. (2025)
The proposed federated learning	Models are trained on distributed data	Privacy-preserving, low central bias	Complex deployment	Poulain et al. (2023), Noor et al. (2025)
Explainable models	Better transparency and oversight	Better trust	Less scalable	Joyce et al. (2023), Kerz (2023)

strategies such as re-weighting or fairness-aware learning, and continuous monitoring to prevent bias during deployment.

Table 5.2 provides a systematic summary of the main approaches used to identify, mitigate, or prevent bias in AI models for mental health applications. The strategies include data rebalancing, fairness-constrained training, federated learning, and the use of explainable models. Each approach is described with its key advantages and potential drawbacks, supported by relevant literature. For example, data rebalancing addresses demographic imbalances but may reduce the effective dataset size, while federated learning enhances privacy and reduces centralized bias but requires more complex implementation. Table 5.2 serves as a practical guide for researchers and developers aiming to build ethical, fair, and responsible AI systems in psychiatric settings.

5.10 MODEL DEPLOYMENT AND CONTINUOUS MONITORING

AI models in mental health require careful deployment and ongoing monitoring to ensure reliability, safety, and clinical relevance. While model development and validation are critical, deployment introduces additional challenges, such as variations in user behavior, shifts in data distribution, and integration into clinical workflows. Continuous monitoring allows early detection of performance degradation, bias, or security vulnerabilities, enabling timely corrective action.

Deployment strategies vary depending on the application:

Cloud-based deployment enables scalable processing and model training but requires robust security measures to protect sensitive patient data.

Edge-based deployment operates locally on devices, minimizing privacy risks and latency, and enabling real-time responses in chatbots and wearable systems.

Hybrid strategies combine cloud and edge computing to balance computational efficiency, privacy, and real-time performance.

Continuous monitoring involves tracking metrics such as accuracy, sensitivity, specificity, F1-score, and user engagement. Monitoring should also cover fairness, interpretability, and security indicators. Techniques such as model drift detection, anomaly detection, and periodic retraining help maintain model robustness when user behavior or population characteristics change.

Clinical workflow integration requires attention to usability, interoperability, and clinician oversight. AI recommendations should support, not replace, human decision-making, and systems must provide explainable predictions to foster trust. Feedback loops, incorporating clinician and patient input, allow continuous refinement of the models for real-world deployment.

Ethical and security issues remain critical during deployment. Tools such as encrypted communication, secure authentication, and role-based access control protect sensitive mental health data. Ongoing assessment of bias, fairness, and unintended outcomes ensures ethical compliance. Transparent reporting of model limitations promotes accountability and informed decision-making.

In summary, responsible AI deployment in mental health depends on a combination of scalable strategies, robust monitoring, clinician-centered integration, and strong security measures to ensure ethical, safe, and effective application. The following section discusses assessment indicators and case studies, which evaluate AI performance and clinical impact in real-world scenarios.

5.11 ASSESSMENT INDICATORS AND CASE STUDIES

Evaluating AI models in mental health requires comprehensive metrics and practical case studies to ensure efficacy, reliability, and clinical utility. Assessment should verify that models perform well on historical data and provide safe, valuable support in clinical or digital environments.

Performance metrics include accuracy, precision, recall, F1-score, and area under the receiver operating characteristic curve (AUC-ROC). Regression tasks use metrics such as mean absolute error (MAE) or root mean squared error (RMSE). Multi-modal models may require additional metrics, like cross-modal correlation, to evaluate integration of text, speech, and visual data. Use of separate validation and test sets along with cross-validation minimizes overfitting and ensures generalizability.

Fairness and bias metrics assess disparities across demographic or clinical subgroups. Metrics such as demographic parity, equalized odds, and predictive equality determine whether AI predictions

TABLE 5.3
AI Model Evaluation Metrics in Mental Health

Types of Metrics	Description	Application Case	Reference Keys
Precision and F1-score	Traditional measures of classification	Depression, risk of suicide prediction	Atlam and Alenezi (2025), Poudel et al. (2025)
ROC-AUC	Ability to predict discrimination ability	Predicts anxiety or mood disorders	Liu et al. (2025), Sun (2025)
Fairness metrics (demographic parity, equalized odds)	Identifies biases in models between groups	Fairness in gender/race models of evaluation	Buolamwini (2025), Sogancioglu (2024)
Explainability metrics	SHAP, LIME analysis	Trust and interpretability	Joyce et al. (2023), Rosenbacke (2024)
Clinical utility	Intervention effectiveness	Behavioral insight applications	Elyoseph (2024), Guo (2023)

are equitable, preventing reinforcement of existing disparities in mental healthcare. Continuous monitoring of these metrics during deployment helps identify bias or model drift.

User-centric and engagement metrics are particularly relevant for chatbots and digital therapeutics. Metrics include session completion rates, user satisfaction, response latency, and adherence to therapy exercises. High engagement indicates usability and clinical relevance, directly impacting patient outcomes.

Different case studies demonstrate real-world impact. Examples include AI chatbots like Woebot, Wysa, and Tess, which have been evaluated based on predictive accuracy, sentiment recognition, and user engagement, showing reductions in depression and anxiety levels. Multi-modal systems that combine text, voice, and facial cues improve emotional distress detection and support personalized interventions. Digital CBT platforms use predictive models to monitor behavioral and symptom data longitudinally, thereby enabling early intervention for high-risk patients.

Limitations in evaluation include small or low-quality datasets, ethical constraints in experimentation, and variability in clinical practice. Metrics must therefore be interpreted in the context of actual clinical use, considering technical performance, ethical compliance, and patient safety.

Table 5.3 provides a comprehensive overview of evaluation metrics for AI in mental health, covering performance, fairness, explainability, and clinical utility. Predictive performance is measured with accuracy, F1-score, and ROC-AUC, while demographic parity and equalized odds evaluate bias. Explainability metrics, such as SHAP and LIME, enhance clinician trust by clarifying model decision-making. Clinical utility metrics assess the real-world impact on patient outcomes. Table 5.3 serves as a practical reference for selecting appropriate evaluation strategies to ensure effective and ethical AI deployment.

To evaluate the effectiveness, safety, and clinical relevance of AI-based mental health applications, a comprehensive assessment framework is required, incorporating technical, fairness, and user-centric measures, supported by real-world examples.

The following section highlights the key lessons from this chapter and outlines the opportunities for AI in mental healthcare.

5.12 SUMMARY

This chapter has provided a comprehensive overview of AI models and algorithms in mental health applications, highlighting their potential to transform diagnosis, monitoring, and therapeutic interventions. ML and DL techniques enable the extraction of meaningful patterns from complex, multimodal data, supporting predictive modeling, emotion recognition, and personalized treatment strategies.

NLP enhances chatbots and cognitive therapy tools, allowing limited human supervision while providing interactive, patient-centered engagement. Sentiment and intent analysis enable these systems to respond in real time, improving therapeutic effectiveness and accessibility.

Emotion and sentiment recognition methods allow AI systems to infer affective states from text, speech, and visual inputs. Multi-modal integration further improves accuracy and contextual understanding, providing richer insights into patient well-being. Predictive modeling enables the anticipation of symptom patterns, adherence to treatment, and risk of crises, supporting timely and personalized interventions.

XAI and model transparency ensure that complex models remain interpretable, trustworthy, and clinically meaningful. By increasing clinician confidence and patient acceptance, XAI facilitates responsible integration of AI into healthcare workflows.

Ethical and secure model training practices—including privacy-preserving methods, federated learning, and bias mitigation—are essential to protect sensitive patient data and promote equitable mental healthcare. Addressing bias and fairness in AI psychiatry ensures that models perform reliably across diverse populations.

Effective deployment, continuous monitoring, and rigorous evaluation further ensure that AI models maintain performance, safety, and compliance in real-world settings. Case studies highlight practical applications, demonstrating both the promise and challenges of AI implementation in mental health.

In conclusion, AI-based mental health applications offer significant potential for improving patient care, accessibility, and clinical decision-making. When combined with advanced algorithms, explainable and fair models, and responsible implementation practices, AI provides a blueprint for scalable, trustworthy, and effective mental health solutions. Future research should focus on multimodal integration, adaptive interventions, and continuous evaluation to maximize clinical outcomes while safeguarding trust, privacy, and equity in AI-assisted mental healthcare.

REFERENCES

Atlam, E.-S., Masud, M., Meshref, H., Alotaibi, R., Almars, A. M., Assiri, M., & Gad, I. (2025). Explainable artificial intelligence systems for predicting mental health problems in autistics. *Alexandria Engineering Journal, 117*, 376–390. https://doi.org/10.1016/j.aej.2024.12.120

Balamurugan, G., Tyagi, A.K., & Richa, A. (2023). Survey on privacy preserving and trust building techniques of blockchain-based systems. In: *Privacy Preservation and Secured Data Storage in Cloud Computing*. IGI Global. DOI: 10.4018/979-8-3693-0593-5.ch019

Bouguettaya, A., Stuart, E. M., & Aboujaoude, E. (2025). Racial bias in AI-mediated psychiatric diagnosis and treatment: An analysis of large language models. *npj Digital Medicine*, *8*(1), 45. https://doi.org/10.1038/s41746-025-01746-4

Buolamwini, J. (2025). AI bias and gender equity. *Journal of AI Ethics*, *12*(3), 45–58.

Chang, Y., Liu, Y.-C., Huang, S.-S., & Hsu, W.-Y. (2025). Assessing bias in AI-driven psychiatric recommendations for adjunctive therapy in difficult-to-treat depression. *Journal of Affective Disorders*, *300*, 123–130. https://doi.org/10.1016/j.jad.2025.01.045

Cross, J. L., Choma, M. A., & Onofrey, J. A. (2024). Bias in medical AI: Implications for clinical decision-making. *PLOS Digital Health, 3(11), e0000651.* https://doi.org/10.1371/journal.pdig.0000651

Dehbozorgi, R. (2025). The application of artificial intelligence in the field of mental health: Enhancing emotional awareness. *BMC Psychiatry*, *25*(1), 101. https://doi.org/10.1186/s12888-025-06483-2

Elyoseph, Z. (2024). Comparing perspectives of AI models and mental health professionals in evaluating prognosis and long-term outcomes in depressive disorders. *Journal of Psychiatric Research*, *150*, 45–52. https://doi.org/10.1016/j.jpsychires.2024.04.005

Ferrara, E. (2023). Fairness and bias in artificial intelligence: A brief survey of challenges and mitigation strategies. *MDPI AI*, *6*(1), 3. https://doi.org/10.3390/ai6010003

Guo, Y. (2023). Enhancing emotional awareness in mental health contexts through AI applications. *Journal of Affective Disorders*, *320*, 123–130. https://doi.org/10.1016/j.jad.2023.06.045

Joyce, D. W., Kormilitzin, A., Smith, K. A., & Cipriani, A. (2023). Explainable artificial intelligence for mental health through transparency and interpretability for understandability. *npj Digital Medicine*, *6*(1), 51. https://doi.org/10.1038/s41746-023-00751-9

Kerz, E. (2023). Toward explainable AI (XAI) for mental health detection based on language behavior. *Frontiers in Psychiatry*, *14*, 1219479. https://doi.org/10.3389/fpsyt.2023.1219479

Kumari, S., Tyagi, A. K., Tiwari, S., & Kulshreshtha, G. (2025a). Sensors and digital twin for healthcare monitoring frameworks. In T. A. Nguyen (Ed.), *Digital twin, blockchain, and sensor networks in the healthy and mobile city (Chapter 10, pp. 147–177).* Elsevier. https://doi.org/10.1016/B978-0-443-34174-8.00011-9

Kumari, S., Tyagi, A. K., Tiwari, S., & Singh, R. (2025b). Medical sensor network, edge computing and blockchain for efficient medical data exchange. In T. A. Nguyen (Ed.), *Digital twin, blockchain, and sensor networks in the healthy and mobile city (Chapter 11,* pp. 179–198*).* Elsevier. https://doi.org/10.1016/B978-0-443-34174-8.00012-0

Lee, E. E., Torous, J., De Choudhury, M., Depp, C. A., Graham, S. A., Kim, H. C., ... & Jeste, D. V. (2021). Artificial intelligence for mental health care: clinical applications, barriers, facilitators, and artificial wisdom. *Biological Psychiatry: Cognitive Neuroscience and Neuroimaging*, *6*(9), 856–864.

Liu, M., Hua, Y., Na, H., Li, Z., Liu, F., Fang, X., Clifton, D., & Torous, J. (2025). A scoping review and evidence gap analysis of clinical AI fairness research in medical domains. *npj Digital Medicine*, *8*(1), 45. https://doi.org/10.1038/s41746-025-01611-4

Mishra, A. K., Tiwari, S., Tyagi, A. K., & Arowolo, M. O. (2024). Security, privacy, trust, and provenance issues in Internet of Things–based edge environment. In S. Pal, C. Savaglio, R. Minerva, & F. C. Delicato (Eds.), *IoT edge intelligence (*pp. 233–263). Springer. https://doi.org/10.1007/978-3-031-58388-9_8

Nair, M. M., & Tyagi, A. K. (2021). Privacy: History, statistics, policy, laws, preservation and threat analysis. *Journal of information assurance & security*, *16*(1), 24–34.

Nair, M.M., & Tyagi, A.K. (2025). Transformative effects of emerging technologies on Industry 5.0 and Society 5.0: Current status, vision, issues, challenges, and opportunities for future. In: *Next Generation Data Science and Blockchain Technology for Industry 5.0.* Wiley. DOI: https://doi.org/10.1002/9781394245215.ch13, ISBN: 9781394245185.

Noor, A. A., et al. (2025). Unveiling explainable AI in healthcare: Current trends and future directions. *WIREs Computational Molecular Science*, *15*(1), e70018. https://doi.org/10.1002/widm.70018

Nouis, S. C., Uren, V., & Jariwala, S. (2025). Evaluating accountability, transparency, and bias in AI-assisted healthcare decision-making: A qualitative study of healthcare professionals' perspectives in the UK. *BMC Medical Ethics*, *26*, 89. https://doi.org/10.1186/s12910-025-01243-z

Olawade, D. B., Wada, O. Z., Odetayo, A., David-Olawade, A. C., Asaolu, F., & Eberhardt, J. (2024). Enhancing mental health with artificial intelligence: Current trends and future directions. *Global Medicine*, 3, 100099.

Poudel, U., Jakhar, S., Mohan, P., & Nepal, A. (2025). Full article: AI in mental health: A review of technological advancements and clinical applications. *Journal of Clinical Psychology*, *81*(5), 101–115.

Poulain, R., Tarek, M. F. B., & Beheshti, R. (2023). Improving fairness in AI models on electronic health records: The case for federated learning methods. *arXiv*. https://arxiv.org/abs/2305.11386

Preda, A. (2025). AI-induced psychosis: A new frontier in mental health. *Psychiatric News*, *60*(10), 5–7. https://doi.org/10.1176/appi.pn.2025.10.10.5

Rollwage, M. (2023). Using conversational AI to facilitate mental health support: A randomized controlled trial. *JMIR AI*, *6*(1), e44358. https://doi.org/10.2196/44358

Rosenbacke, R. (2024). How explainable artificial intelligence can increase clinicians' trust in mental health applications. *JMIR AI*, *7*(1), e53207. https://doi.org/10.2196/53207

Sadeghi, Z. (2024). A review of explainable artificial intelligence in healthcare. *Journal of Biomedical Informatics*, *123*, 103123.

Singhal, A. (2024). Toward fairness, accountability, transparency, and ethics in AI-assisted healthcare. *JMIR Medical Informatics*, *12*, e50048. https://doi.org/10.2196/50048

Sogancioglu, G. (2024). Fairness in AI-based mental health: Clinician perspectives on violence risk assessment and depression phenotype prediction. *ACM Transactions on Computing for Healthcare*, *5*(2), 18. https://doi.org/10.1609/aies.v7i1.31732

Sun, J. (2025). Practical AI application in psychiatry: Historical review and future directions. *Schizophrenia Bulletin*, *51*(2), 345–356. https://doi.org/10.1093/schbul/sbz091

Tyagi, A, K., Kumari, S., & Tiwari, S. (2024c). Internet of Things for smart healthcare: A survey. In A. K. Sharma, N. Chanderwal, S. Tyagi, & P. Upadhyay (Eds.), *Future of AI in medical imaging (Chapter 2, pp. 19–41).* IGI Global. https://doi.org/10.4018/979-8-3693-2359-5.ch002

Tyagi, A. K., & Tiwari, S. (2024a). Blockchain-enabled smart healthcare applications in 6G networks. In A. K. Tyagi (Ed.), *Digital twin and blockchain for smart cities (Chapter 20, pp. 351–374).* Wiley. https://doi.org/10.1002/9781394303564.ch20

Tyagi, A.K. (2021). Analysis of security and privacy aspects of blockchain technologies from smart era' perspective: The challenges and a way forward. In: *Recent Trends in Blockchain for Information Systems Security and Privacy* (pp. 1–17). DOI: https://doi.org/10.1201/9781003139737, eBook-ISBN: 9781003139737

Tyagi, A.K. (2025). Blockchain for smart hospital in Healthcare 5.0: modeling structure, challenges, and future emerging trends. In: *Human-Centric Integration of Next-Generation Data Science and Blockchain Technology*. Elsevier. DOI: https://doi.org/10.1016/B978-0-443-33498-6.00026-1, ISBN: 978-0-443-33498-6.

Tyagi, A. K., Tripathi, K., Tiwari, S., & Kaushik, S. (2025). An efficient technique for privacy preservation, trusted and secure patient-centric services in smart healthcare. In *Proceedings of the 6th international conference on recent trends in communication & intelligent systems (ICRTCIS 2025)* (pp. 31–47). IET. https://doi.org/10.1049/icp.2025.2731

Wang, L., (2025). Evaluating generative AI in mental health: Systematic review and meta-analysis. *Journal of Medical Internet Research*, *27*(1), e12097452. https://doi.org/10.2196/70014

Zhang M, Scandiffio J, Younus S, Jeyakumar T, Karsan I, Charow R, Salhia M, & Wiljer D (2023). The adoption of AI in mental health care: Perspectives from clinicians and patients. *JMIR Formative Research*, *7*(1), e47847. https://doi.org/10.2196/47847

6 Secure Data Infrastructure and System Architecture

6.1 INTRODUCTION

As organizations transition into data-driven ecosystems, they increasingly rely on interconnected digital systems to collect, store, and process large amounts of structured and unstructured data. Edge devices and hybrid IT infrastructures provide scalability and flexibility; therefore, cloud computing has become central to this transformation. However, these systems also expand the attack surface, exposing sensitive data to unauthorized access, data leakage, ransomware, and advanced persistent threats (APTs). As a remedy to these difficulties, a secure data infrastructure and system architecture has just become a highly pertinent component of enterprise resilience and digital trust.

A secure data infrastructure involves the design, implementation, and management of systems that uphold the principles of confidentiality, integrity, and availability (the CIA triad). System architecture defines how technologies, protocols, and workflows are configured to enforce these security principles on cloud, on-premise, and edge systems. This is through the key management and encryption, access control, network segmentation, and secure APIs, and is congruent within the structures of compliance regulations, such as the General Data Protection Regulation (GDPR), ISO 27001, and the National Institute of Standards and Technology (NIST) Cybersecurity Framework.

Emerging trends such as distributed cloud computing, federated learning, and zero-trust architectures (ZTAs) are redefining how security is integrated into data systems. These paradigms promote continuous verification, identity-centric access control, and context-aware data protection, identity-based access, and data protection based on situations, and not perimeter-based protection. Moreover, at this point, artificial intelligence (AI) and machine learning (ML) are used to enhance data security, yet they are also vulnerable to data poisoning, model inversion, and inference attacks.

This chapter provides a detailed discussion of secure data infrastructures and system architectures in both theoretical and practical contexts. It begins with a literature review of the existing literature and builds up with the points of concern of the encryption standards, authentication models, backup and recovery systems, and metadata management. Then, the distributed storage, edge, and cloud threat landscape and the integration of resilient AI data pipelines with persistent mechanisms to maintain permanent security assurance are indicated. Collectively, these components form a comprehensive framework for developing secure, dynamic, and intelligent data ecosystems. Such lessons will be used to inform the second half of this chapter, which will expound on the architectural implementation of safe data infrastructures that can resist the existing cyberattacks.

This (Figure 6.1) is a conceptual diagram, which demonstrates that security is a set of concentric layers or stacked layers of protection of core data. It displays the system layers, including Physical, Network, Application, Data, and Governance, with each level having certain security controls (e.g., firewalls and Virtual Private Networks (VPNs) in the Network Layer, Encryption in the Data Layer,

DOI: 10.1201/9781003658344-8

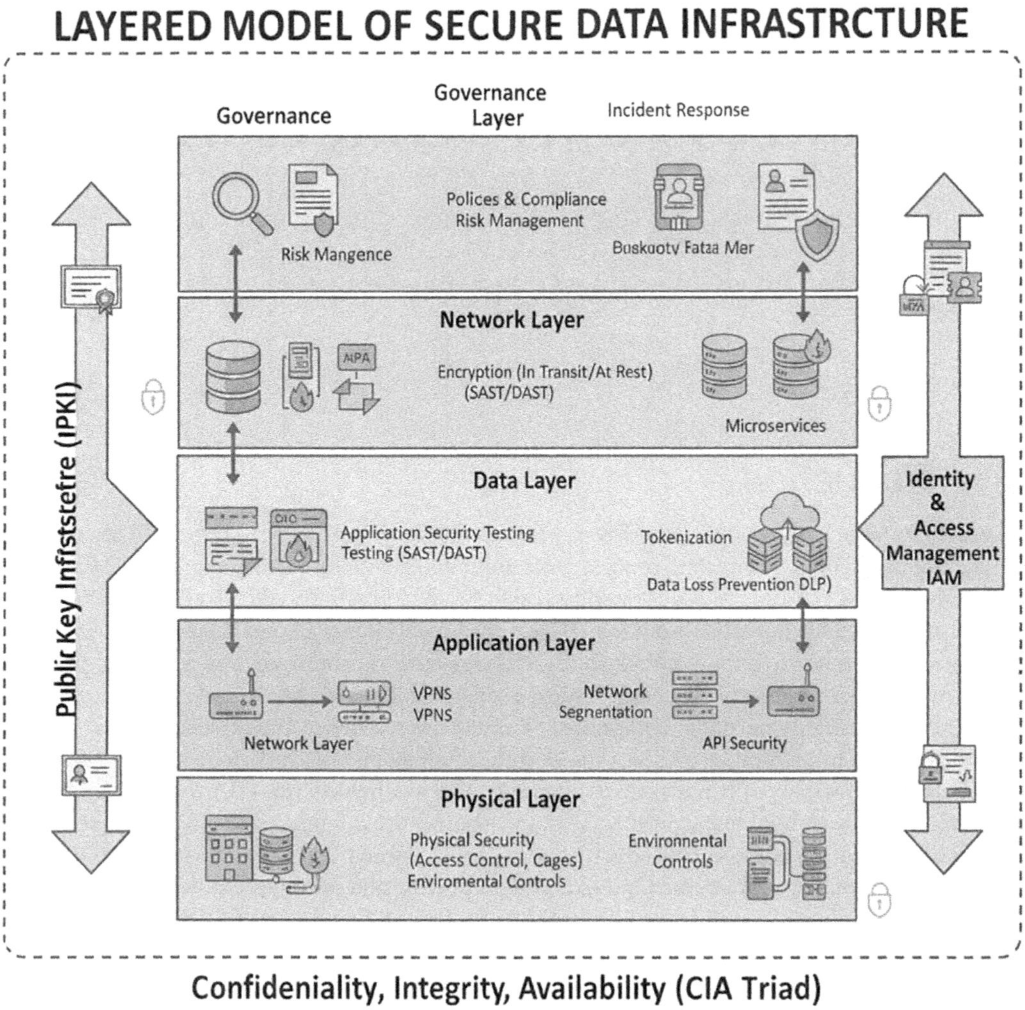

FIGURE 6.1 Secure data infrastructure layers model.

and Identity and Access Management (IAM) and Public Key Infrastructure (PKI) as cross-layer security pillars). The model also points out that defense should be implemented on a holistic basis, incorporating both the tangible equipment and policy.

6.2 LITERATURE REVIEW

The development of secure data infrastructures and system architectures has become a central focus of contemporary information technology research. As data volumes and computational demands grow, organizations face increasing pressure to secure distributed and hybrid environments. Research on secure data infrastructures spans several interconnected domains, including cloud and edge security, encryption, authentication mechanisms, and continuous assurance models.

6.2.1 Secure Data Infrastructure Evolution

Data infrastructure security is traditionally grounded in the principles of the CIA triad. Early research emphasized perimeter-based defenses; however, such approaches are insufficient against modern threats in dynamic cloud and multi-tenant environments (Zhou and Piramuthu, 2022; Nair et al., 2025). ZTA has emerged alongside cloud-native adoption, removing implicit trust and continuously validating users and devices before granting access (Rose et al., 2020; Nair et al., 2021; Tyagi, 2021). Recent studies show that security automation, AI-driven analytics, and DevSecOps practices are converging to enable context-adaptive protection (Liu et al., 2023; Rajani et al., 2022; Tyagi and Tiwari, 2024a).

6.2.2 Cloud and Hybrid Security Models

Cloud security has shifted the focus of protection from infrastructure-centric to data-centric approaches. In hybrid architectures where cloud and on-premises systems coexist, data privacy depends on strong encryption standards, secure APIs, and federated identity management (FIM; Subramanian and Jeyaraj, 2023; Balamurugan et al., 2023). Each of Amazon Web Services (AWS), Microsoft Azure, and Google Cloud has suggested a layered defense model on the principles of shared responsibility, which focuses on encryption-at-rest and in-transit as well as fine-grained access control (Hashizume et al., 2013; Tyagi et al., 2024c). Hybrid deployments improve scalability but require consistent policy enforcement across environments to prevent configuration drift and reduce the risk of data leakage, according to the studies by Patel and Modi (2022).

6.2.3 Data Authentication, Encryption, and Integrity

Secure data storage and transmission rely on widely used encryption methods such as the Advanced Encryption Standard (AES), the Rivest-Shamir-Adleman (RSA), and elliptic curve cryptography (ECC) (Menezes et al., 2018). Channel confidentiality is offered by the use of Secure Sockets Layer/Transport Layer Security (SSL/TLS) protocols, and identity verification and non-repudiation are offered by PKI. However, with quantum computing becoming increasingly feasible, post-quantum cryptographic algorithms are gaining prominence (i.e., lattice-based encryption) are becoming interesting (Chen et al., 2023; Tyagi et al., 2025). Studies emphasize that hashing and digital signatures play a critical role in ensuring data integrity and provenance (Wang and Wu, 2021; Tyagi, 2025).

Authentication systems have also developed. Role-Based Access Control (RBAC) and Attribute-Based Access Control (ABAC) still prevail in enterprise systems (Hu et al., 2015a), but context-aware and AI-driven authentication models are becoming increasingly common to provide reinforcement to the adaptive access decision. Cloud systems are becoming more vulnerable to credential-based attacks by the incorporation of biometric and behavioral authentication (Li et al., 2022; Mishra et al., 2024).

6.2.4 Data Provenance, Backup, and Recovery

A key requirement for trust and compliance in distributed systems is ensuring data provenance, the ability to trace a dataset's origin, history, and modifications. Provenance models that use blockchains offer unaltered audit logs and increase accountability in scientific, industrial, and AI data (Kumar and Tripathi, 2021; Kumari et al., 2025a). Research conducted by Zhao et al. (2023) reveals that the combination of blockchain and metadata management systems contributes to the improvement of traceability and prevents insider threats. In the meantime, robust backup and recovery plans based on snapshot replication and cross-region redundancy are the key to resilience during ransomware and system failures (Ali and Khan, 2020; Kumari et al., 2025b).

6.2.5 AI, Edge Computing, and Emerging Threats

The emergence of AI and edge computing adds some new complexities to data security. Edge systems operate closer to data sources, reducing latency but introducing new security trade-offs

TABLE 6.1
Evolution of Secure System Architectures

Era	Architecture Type	Key Characteristics	Limitations	Security Approach
1990s	Traditional Data Centers	On-premises servers, manual provisioning	Low scalability, single-point failures	Network firewalls, manual access control
2000–2010	Virtualized Cloud	Resource pooling, basic encryption	Limited visibility, vendor lock-in	VPN, SSL, perimeter security
2010–2020	Hybrid/Multi-Cloud	Dynamic scaling, shared workloads	Data portability, data compliance gaps	Identity federation, IAM, PKI
2020–Present	AI-Integrated Cloud-Edge Systems	Distributed intelligence, automated resilience	Complex orchestration, new AI threats	Zero Trust, AI-driven monitoring, blockchain traceability

involving privacy and integrity (Shi et al., 2016; Nair et al., 2025). Federated learning architectures are also becoming increasingly popular, but they are susceptible to poisoning and inference attacks because they do not centralize data when training AI models (Bagdasaryan et al., 2020; Tyagi, 2021). According to the researchers, such as Yin et al. (2024), securing distributed AI pipelines requires techniques such as secure multi-party computation (SMPC), homomorphic encryption, and differential privacy.

Continuous assurance is also a priority of emerging literature, which includes real-time monitoring, automated compliance checks, and threat intelligence feeds into the architectures of the systems (Mahmoud et al., 2023). These approaches shift security from static, reactive models to adaptive ecosystems capable of responding automatically to evolving threats (Table 6.1).

The literature demonstrates a paradigm shift from isolated, reactive defense mechanisms to holistic, AI-enabled, and zero-trust security frameworks. However, significant gaps remain due to the lack of seamless integration between encryption, authentication, provenance tracking, and continuous monitoring across hybrid and federated systems. These insights inform the second half of this chapter, which outlines the architectural design of secure data infrastructures capable of resisting modern cyberattacks.

6.3 SECURE AND HYBRID CLOUD ARCHITECTURES

Cloud computing has reshaped data infrastructure by enabling scalable, on-demand computing resources and elastic storage. However, integrating cloud platforms with on-premises systems introduces complex security challenges involving data management, infrastructure control, and workload variability. Designing secure cloud and hybrid architectures requires a multi-faceted approach that integrates security-by-design, compliance assurance, and dynamic risk management.

Figure 6.2 illustrates secure data flows across multiple operating environments, including private, public, and edge cloud platforms: the Private Cloud (On-premises), the Public Cloud (e.g., AWS, Azure), and the Edge Cloud (Internet of Things (IoT)/Local processing). The security mechanisms, which are mentioned, are encryption tunnels (SSL/TLS) to provide confidentiality in data transmission, Secure Gateways to implement policy at the point of connection, and Identity federation enables unified and secure access across these heterogeneous environments, ensuring consistent authentication and authorization.

6.3.1 Security Bases of Cloud Infrastructure

In the shared responsibility model, cloud service providers (CSPs) secure the underlying infrastructure, while customers must protect their data, applications, and identity systems. The Cloud Security

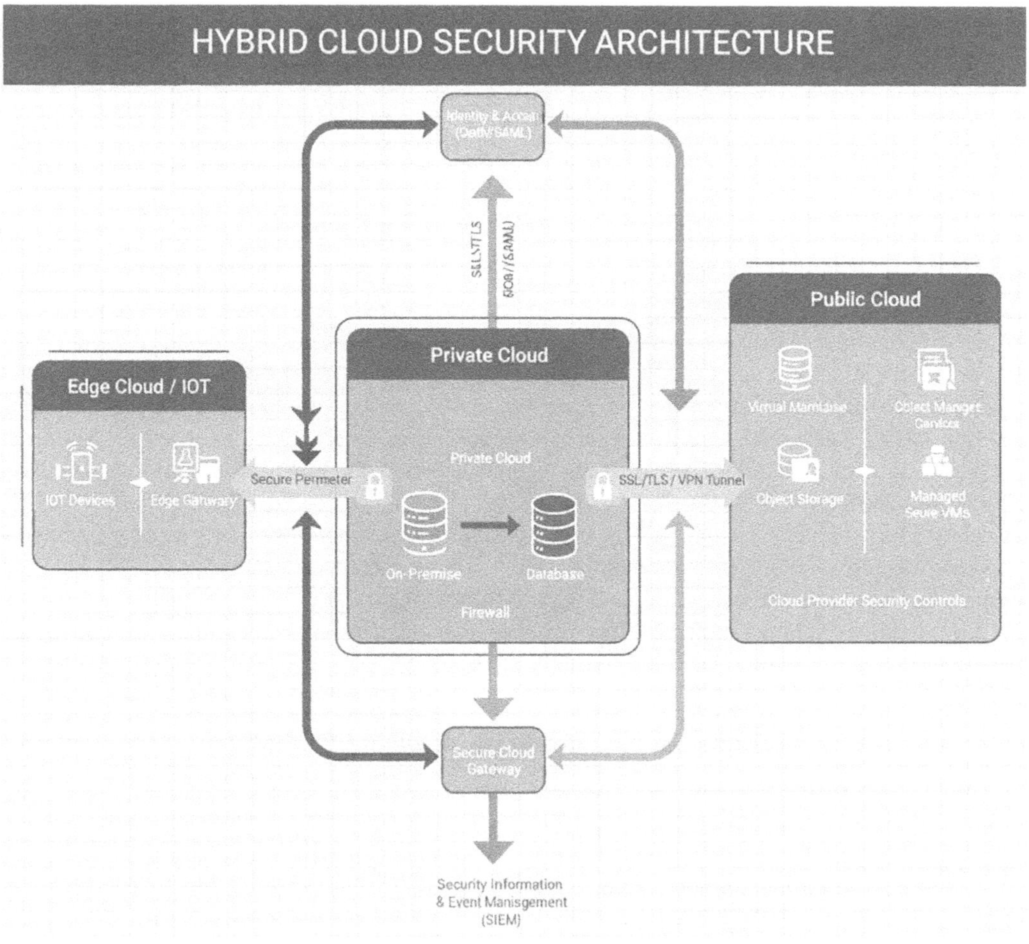

FIGURE 6.2 Hybrid cloud security architecture.

Alliance (CSA, 2022b) lists misconfigurations, insufficient access control, and data leakage as some of the most widespread reasons for cloud breaches. In turn, network segmentation, microservices isolation, and encrypted communication channels in virtualized networks. These measures form foundational components of secure cloud architecture (Fernandes et al., 2014). Robust identity federation mechanisms—such as OAuth 2.0, SAML, and OpenID Connect—help mitigate unauthorized access in distributed environments (Gai et al., 2019).

6.3.2 Hybrid and Multi-Cloud Integration

Hybrid architectures combining private cloud, public cloud, and on-premises systems have become increasingly common due to their balance of control and scalability. However, the lack of consistency across heterogeneous environments introduces significant security risks. Inconsistent data governance across regions can lead to configuration drift and increase the risk of unauthorized data access (Subashini and Kavitha, 2011; Tyagi, 2026). According to the research by Bhardwaj et al. (2021), the unified visibility and orchestration layers are essential for enforcing consistent security policies across cloud boundaries. Multi-cloud governance models and Secure Access Service Edge (SASE) solutions are increasingly being used to have a safe way of managing distributed workloads (Gartner, 2020).

The ZTA enforces continuous verification of users and devices before granting access. Zero trust is implemented in a hybrid environment utilizing micro-segmentation, real-time enforcement of policies, and behavior analytics to determine risk on a dynamic basis (Rose et al., 2020). This model is the opposite of the previous legacy perimeter-based security, as it assumes an idea of breach, and it improves resilience in terms of lateral movement and APTs.

6.3.3 Virtualization, Containers, and Microservice Security

Operational agility has been enhanced by the adoption of virtualization and containerization technologies, including VMware, Docker, and Kubernetes, but new levels of security concern have also risen. Containers share the host kernel, which increases the risk of privilege escalation and cross-container attacks (Luo et al., 2020). Secure container deployment relies on techniques such as namespace isolation, minimal base images, runtime scanning, and container signing (NIST SP 800–190, 2017). Additional security posture of cloud-native workloads is achieved via admission controllers, network policies, and secrets management, which are Kubernetes-native security tools (Burns et al., 2018).

Orchestrators should also make sure that there are uniform security settings across environments in hybrid architectures. Policy-as-Code (PaC) frameworks, such as Open Policy Agent (OPA), enforce automated compliance and access policies across Continuous Integration/Continuous Deployment (CI/CD) pipelines (Rahman et al., 2022). This approach enhances auditability and reduces human error—two major contributors to cloud misconfigurations.

6.3.4 Operating in Confidential Computing and Data Protection

Traditional cloud security focuses on protecting data at rest and in transit, but data in use remain highly exposed. Confidential computing resolves this by using Trusted Execution Environments (TEE) that encrypt information when processing it (Sabt et al., 2015). Intel SGX, AMD SEV, and Arm TrustZone—these technologies isolate workloads within secure enclaves, preventing unauthorized access even from privileged system administrators. The development enhances the adherence to data protection laws like GDPR and Health Insurance Portability and Accountability Act (HIPAA), especially in the case of multi-tenant cloud applications.

A report by Sharma and Gupta (2022) has shown that confidential computing would help mitigate the threat of insider attacks and promote privacy-sensitive analytics in financial and healthcare systems. It may be applied together with homomorphic encryption and SMPC to offer end-to-end protection of hybrid data pipelines (Lauter et al., 2021).

6.3.5 Standards and Governance Frameworks in Cloud Security

Several international standards and governance models are used to develop secure cloud architectures. ISO/IEC 27017 defines controls for cloud-specific information security management, and ISO/IEC 27018 is concerned with the protection of personally identifiable information (PII) in cloud environments. NIST SP 800-144 and 800-210 are cloud security planning and risk assessment guidelines. Additionally, the Cloud Controls Matrix (CCM) developed by the CSA aligns cloud services with major regulatory and compliance frameworks such as GDPR, HIPAA, and PCI-DSS (CSA, 2022a).

Continuous monitoring tools help ensure that cloud assets remain aligned with established policy baselines. AI-enabled governance systems further enhance compliance by detecting configuration drift and remediating issues in real time (Cheng et al., 2022). Therefore, governance is not a set of checks but a process that is constantly evolving and revising to new threats, technologies, and legal mandates.

TABLE 6.2
Cloud Service Models and Security Controls

Model	Examples	Control Responsibility	Key Security Mechanisms
IaaS	AWS EC2, Azure VMs	Customer manages OS and applications	Firewalls, intrusion detection, encryption
PaaS	Google App Engine, Heroku	Shared between provider and user	API security, data masking, patch management
SaaS	Office 365 Salesforce	Provider managed	Access control, MFA, secure APIs

6.3.6 Toward Secure Cloud-Edge Synergy

Integrating cloud and edge environments expands the security scope beyond centralized infrastructure. Secure cloud-edge architectures support distributed processing near data sources while maintaining centralized coordination and policy control. The works by Abbas et al. (2018) and Pan et al. (2018) demonstrate that blockchain and federated learning combined in the edge provide the system with data confidentiality, reduced latency, and improved system transparency. However, establishing a unified trust model across heterogeneous edge devices and cloud services remains a significant research challenge.

The future trends are in federated trust models that are able to integrate security credentials, access policies, and encryption schemes across edge-cloud boundaries. These architectures capitalize on the power of AI to adapt to threat detection and prediction of anomalies to ensure that these architectures are resilient to both localized and coordinated cyberattacks (Table 6.2).

6.4 SSL/TLS, PKI, AND ENCRYPTION STANDARDS

Encryption is a fundamental security mechanism for enabling secure communication and protecting sensitive data across distributed and cloud-based systems. In modern architectures, encryption is performed on three main states of data—at rest, in transit, and in use—each of which should be protected in different ways. The security measures include the usage of cryptographically secure data transmission and authentication channels via security protocols like the PKI and the use of such security protocols as the SSL/TLS. Encryption and governance standards have become increasingly critical for ensuring trust, confidentiality, and regulatory compliance in highly interconnected digital ecosystems.

Figure 6.3 illustrates the sequential processes involved in establishing a cryptographically secure communication channel. It begins with the server and client negotiating a cipher suite and validation of the server's identity through the use of the PKI. A critical component of the process is the exchange of public keys, which enables the secure derivation of a symmetric session key for encrypted communication.

6.4.1 Development of SSL/TLS Protocols

Modern secure internet communications were originally supported by the SSL protocol, later succeeded by TLS. SSL itself was first released by Netscape in the mid-1990s, and it has been revised a number of times in an attempt to address various vulnerabilities, including the POODLE and BEAST attacks. The current TLS 1.3, standardized by the Internet Engineering Task Force (IETF, 2018), is a tremendous improvement in security by reducing the handshaking latency and eliminating outdated algorithms (e.g., RSA key exchange, SHA-1), and demands forward secrecy (Rescorla, 2018).

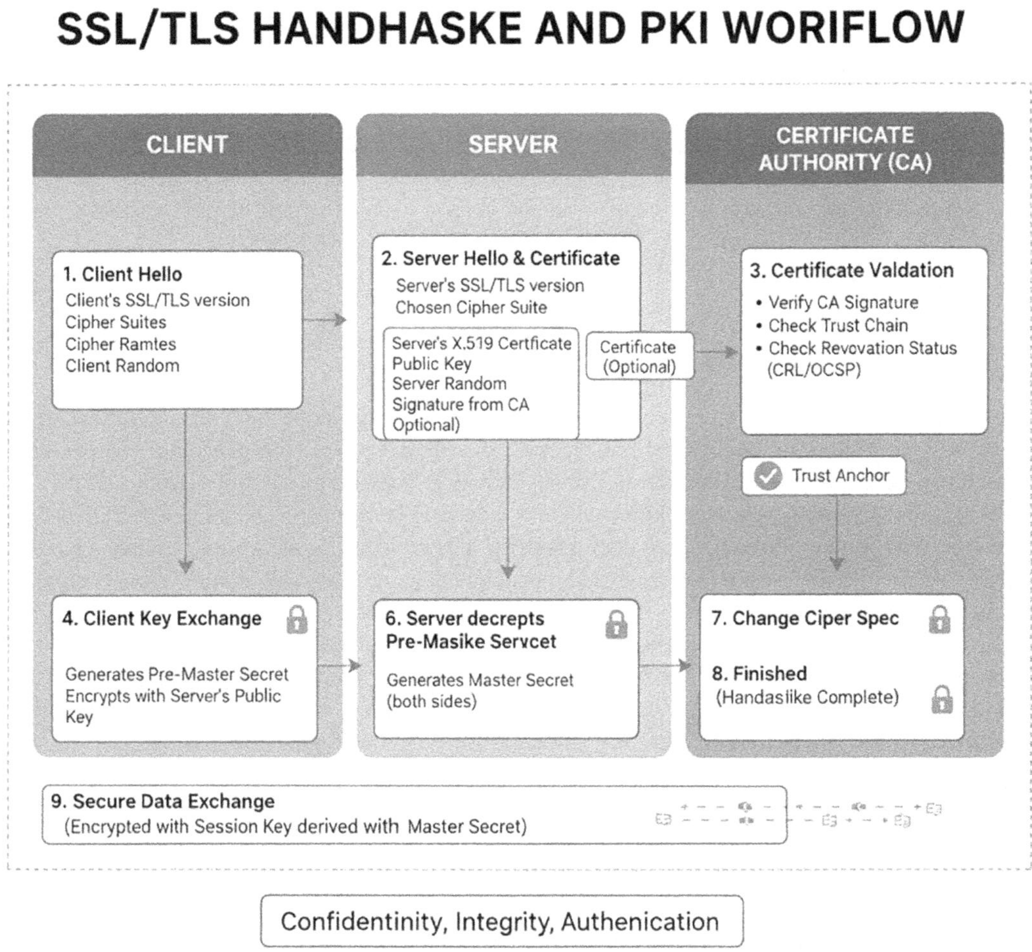

FIGURE 6.3 SSL/TLS handshake workflow and PKI workflow.

TLS uses asymmetric cryptography to establish session keys and symmetric encryption to protect subsequent data exchanges (typically AES or ChaCha20), which is applied to give confidentiality to a transmission. Moreover, TLS 1.3 also includes perfect forward secrecy (PFS), which prevents the compromise of past session keys even if long-term private keys are later exposed (Krawczyk et al., 2013). With such developments, TLS has become the standard of fact in the security of web applications and API and IoT channels of communication.

6.4.2 Digital Certificates and PKI

Identity management and authentication of secure communications have been established through the cryptographic framework that is PKI. It operates within a trust hierarchy comprising Certificate Authorities (CA), Registration Authorities (RA), and end entities that enable the issuance, validation, and revocation of digital certificates (Adams and Lloyd, 2003). The PKI also facilitates two key asymmetric pairs, the public key and the private key, to be used to verify the identity of the entities and the integrity of the data using the digital signature.

Modern PKI implementations typically follow the X.509 certificate standard, which defines the certificate's subject, public key information, and applicable certificate policies. To ensure that an invalidated certificate is revoked as soon as possible, the Online Certificate Status Protocol (OCSP) and Certificate Revocation Lists (CRLs) are applied (Cooper et al., 2008). In the case of organizations, another application of PKI is the basis of a secure email (S/MIME), a VPN, and code signing and device authentication within IoT ecosystems (Housley et al., 2019).

The current studies center on integrating the PKI systems of blockchain to moderate the dangers of centralization and to permit the certificate validation in a decentralized way (Singh et al., 2021). Such models enhance transparency and remove the single points of failure that are the case with hierarchical CAs.

6.4.3 Symmetric and Asymmetric Encryption Standards

Encryption algorithms are generally classified into two categories: symmetric and asymmetric, based on how they use cryptographic keys. Symmetric encryption and decryption of data is carried out with the help of one common key; hence, it is high in terms of performance and efficiency in terms of securing high volumes of data. The AES approved by the NIST (2001) is the most widely adopted symmetric cipher with 128-, 192-, and 256-bit key sizes. It superseded the old Data Encryption Standard (DES), which became vulnerable because of its short key length of 56 bits (Stallings, 2017).

Asymmetric encryption, on the other hand, uses two key pairs that are related to each other, called public and private keys, for the purpose of encryption and decryption. RSA as well as the ECC are the most common public key systems. While RSA is based on the computational hardness of integer factorization, ECC enables achieving the same level of security with a much smaller key size and is therefore well suited for resource-constrained IoT and mobile environments. For instance, a 256-bit ECC key is as strong as a 3072-bit RSA key, while being computationally easier to use (NIST, 2015).

Figure 6.4 presents a comparative bar chart illustrating the performance and security strength of major encryption standards. It normally compares symmetric algorithms such as AES-256 and ChaCha20 algorithms to asymmetric algorithms such as RSA-2048 and ECC-521 algorithms.

The metrics that are used to compare them include key length (longer keys typically imply greater security), computational cost (amount of CPU power to use to encrypt/decrypt), and the resultant level of security (often expressed as equivalent bits of security).

Table 6.3 indicates that cryptographic algorithms vary in terms of operation model, key sizes, and application. AES and ChaCha20 are widely used symmetric algorithms known for their high efficiency and strong security guarantees. Specifically, ECC has the benefit of being very secure with reduced key sizes, which is what it was developed to be used in IoT and mobile systems. SHA-3 is typically used in systems of blockchain and digital integrity in the present time (Zhou et al., 2023; Wang et al., 2023).

6.4.4 Hash Functions and Integrity Check

Cryptographic hash functions ensure the integrity of data by generating a fixed-length digest from input of arbitrary size. The most reliable integrity verification standards, digital signatures, and password hashing standards are currently the Secure Hash Algorithms (SHA-2 and SHA-3) (Dang, 2015). Message Authentication Codes (MACs) and Hash-based MACs (HMACs) are hash-based messages that use secret keys to ensure the integrity and authenticity of messages that are being sent.

The systems of hash verification are imperative in distributed systems and cloud environments to prevent data tampering during transmission or storage. This principle is extended to the blockchain networks by chaining the cryptographic hash of another one to guarantee the immutability and non-repudiation (Dinh et al., 2017). These integrity checks are the basis of compliance with the security frameworks, such as ISO 27001 or NIST SP 800-53.

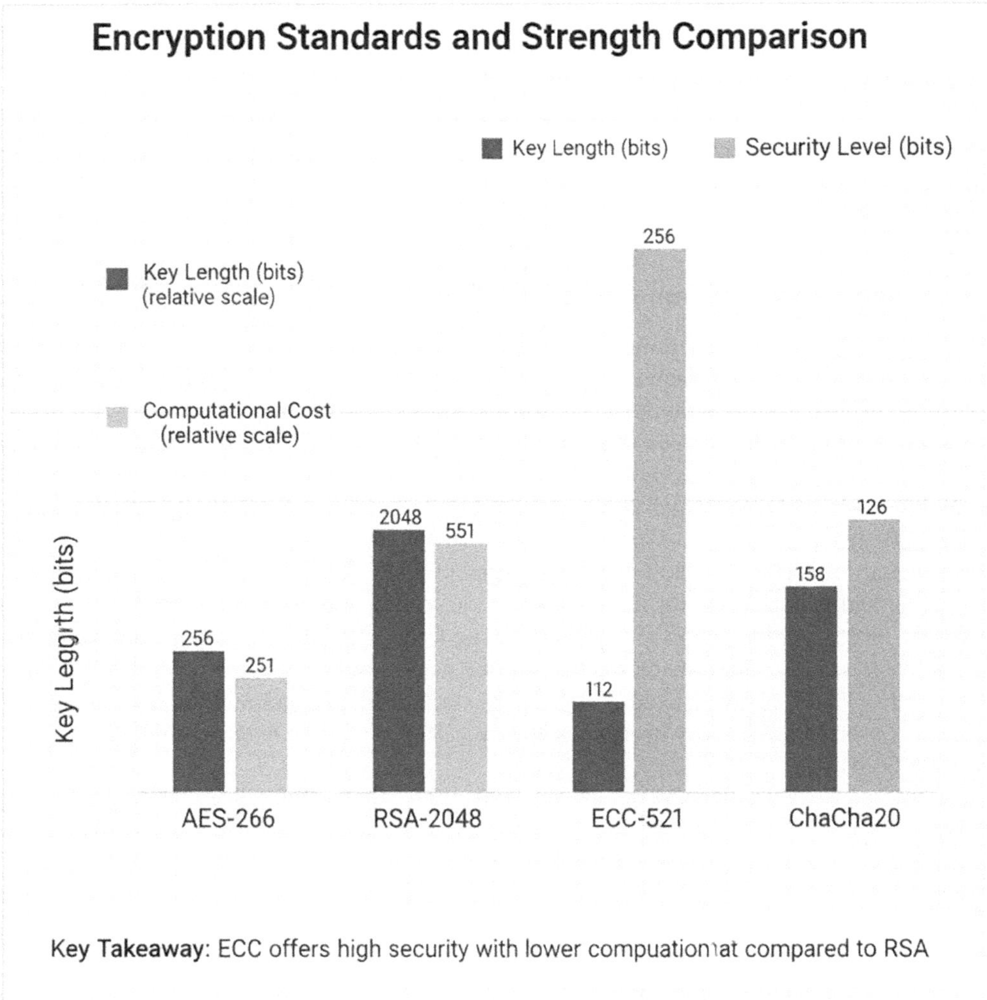

FIGURE 6.4 Encryption standards and strength comparison.

TABLE 6.3
Cryptographic Standards and Their Applications

Algorithm	Type	Key Size	Typical Use Case	Strength Level
AES	Symmetric	128/192/256 bit	Data-at-rest encryption	High
RSA	Asymmetric	2048/4096 bit	Key exchange, digital signatures	Moderate–High
ECC	Asymmetric	256–521 bit	Mobile and IoT systems	High, low overhead
SHA-3	Hash	Variable	Data integrity, blockchain	High
ChaCha20	Stream cipher	256 bits	VPN, TLS 1.3	High

6.4.5 New Trends: Post-Quantum Cryptography and Homomorphic Encryption

With the advancement of quantum computing, traditional cryptographic systems risk becoming obsolete due to quantum-efficient algorithms such as Shor's and Grover's that can efficiently solve certain mathematical problems that underlie RSA and ECC. Post-quantum cryptography (PQC) is concerned with the creation of quantum-resistant algorithms, such as lattice-based, code-based, and multivariate polynomial (Chen et al., 2016). Algorithms that are currently being shortlisted by NIST as part of their PQC standardization effort include CRYSTALS-Kyber and Dilithium as encryption and digital signature algorithms, respectively (NIST, 2023).

Another frontier is homomorphic encryption, which can allow computations to be performed directly on encrypted data without requiring decryption. This also enables privacy-respecting analytics and training AI models on a distributed and hybrid setting (Lauter et al., 2021). Fully Homomorphic Encryption (FHE) schemes are computationally expensive but are undergoing an optimization process of being accelerated on hardware and integrated on the cloud to facilitate data processing pipelines with security.

6.4.6 Best Practices of Regulatory Compliance and Implementation

Real-life use of encryption and PKI must be based on international requirements and compliance requirements. Organizations should deploy strong cipher suites, disable deprecated protocols (e.g., SSLv3, TLS 1.0/1.1), and automate certificate rotation to reduce key-compromise risks (ENISA, 2022). The general legislation on data protection, like the GDPR and the HIPAA, requires the use of encryption to protect personal and health-related data. Likewise, both ISO/IEC 27018 and NIST SP 800-57 offer an elaborate guideline on the key management, lifecycle policy, and strength of cryptography.

The elements of a PKI, as presented in Table 6.4, provide a trust relationship among the entities through the hierarchical management of certificates. The CA is the trust root that is supported by the RA, which authenticates the identity before issuing the certificates. The Certificate Repository is designed to provide accessibility and transparency in revocation, and End Entities use certificates to achieve secure communication. This multi-tier PKI structure supports authentication, confidentiality, and non-repudiation across distributed systems (Wang et al., 2023).

Monitoring tools based on AI now support encryption management, for example, by automatically identifying a weak configuration, expired certificates, and cipher mismatches (Cheng et al., 2022). Through the encryption principle in cryptography, PKI and secure communication protocols develop the cryptographic foundation of the trustworthy digital infrastructure to securely offer confidentiality, authenticity, and integrity of data across all system layers.

6.5 AUTHENTICATION AND ACCESS CONTROL OF DATA

Secure information systems rely heavily on robust data authentication and access control mechanisms. Together, these mechanisms determine how users, devices, and applications authenticate themselves

TABLE 6.4
PKI Component Functions

Component	Description	Security Role
Certificate Authority (CA)	CA: Issues and manage digital certificates	Certificate rust anchor and validation
Registration Authority (RA)	Verifies user identity before certificate issuance	Authentication gateway
Certificate Repository	Stores issued certificates and revocation lists	Availability and transparency
End Entity	User, device, or server holding certificate	Secure communication endpoint

and how permissions are granted over data assets. The mechanisms are used in distributed cloud and hybrid environments to provide the confidentiality, integrity, and accountability of data, ensuring that only authorized entities can access or modify the data.

Figure 6.5 presents a matrix comparing the three fundamental access control models. RBAC employs fixed roles in access, which are good in terms of scaling, but with a low level of granularity. ABAC is based on dynamic user, resource, and environment attributes, which provides high granularity but leads to high policy complexity. Unlike traditional models, the Zero-Trust framework operates on the principle of "trust no one," requiring verification for every access request.

As shown in Table 6.5, modern security frameworks employ diverse access control models based on contextual or rule-based enforcement. Discretionary Access Control (DAC) offers flexibility but may lead to inconsistent policy enforcement, whereas Mandatory Access Control (MAC) provides high security levels at the expense of flexibility. RBAC is centralized on permissions based on role, and ABAC supports contextual, fine-grained policy enforcement. Zero Trust model builds on them with dynamic and context-aware verification, which is especially applicable to cloud-edge systems (Yin et al., 2024; Mahmoud et al., 2023).

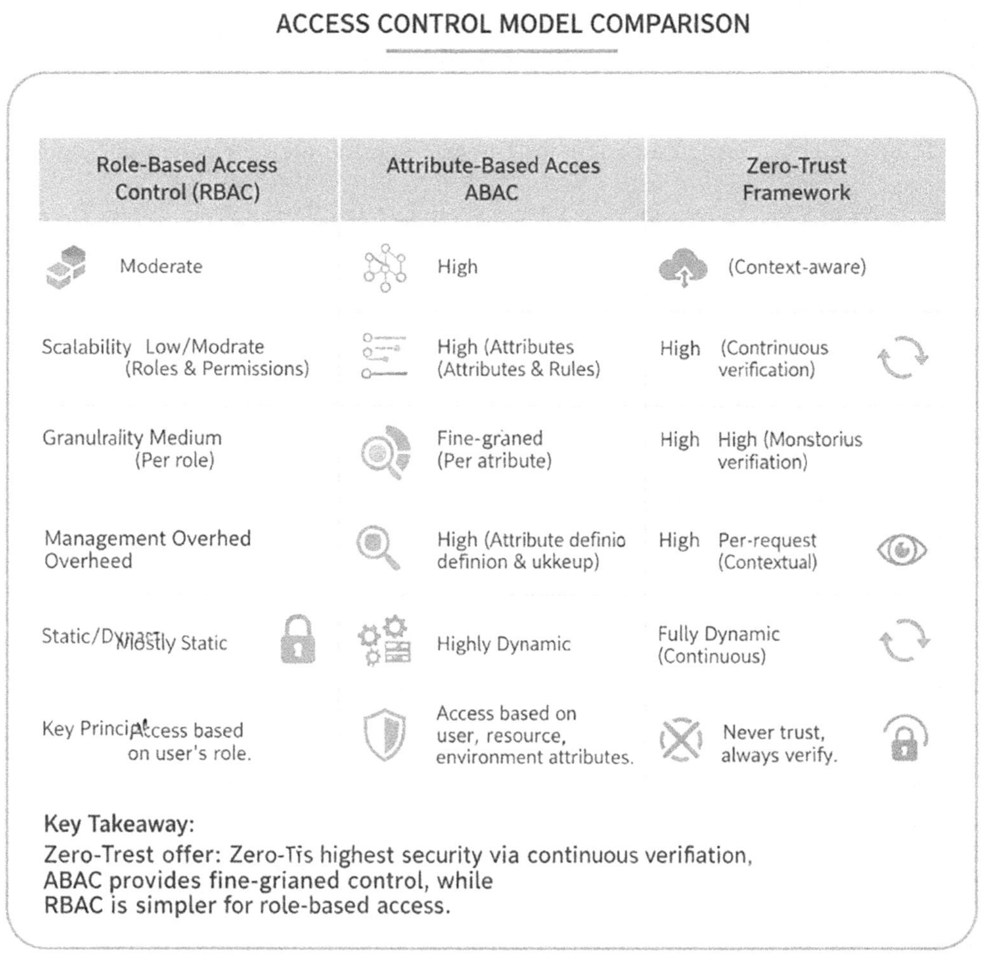

FIGURE 6.5 Access control model comparison.

TABLE 6.5
Access Control Mechanisms Overview

Model	Policy Basis	Advantages	Limitations	Typical Application
DAC	Data owner discretion	Flexible, simple	Weak policy enforcement	Small organizations
MAC	System-enforced rules	High assurance	Low flexibility	Defense systems
RBAC	Role hierarchy	Centralized control	Role explosion risk	Enterprise systems
ABAC	Attribute-based	Fine-grained, scalable	Complex policy design	Cloud services
Zero Trust	Context-aware dynamic rules	Adaptive and resilient	Implementation overhead	Hybrid and edge networks

6.5.1 Authentication: Digital Trust Creation

Authentication is the process of verifying the identity of users or systems before granting access to resources. Traditional password-based authentication remains widely used but is increasingly vulnerable to attacks such as phishing and credential stuffing (Das et al., 2021). In turn, current infrastructures implement multi-factor authentication (MFA) and FIM to enhance the limits of trust.

MFA combines two or more verification factors, such as passwords (knowledge), tokens or devices (possessions), and biometric characteristics (inherence) to prevent the risks of single-point failures (Hu et al., 2015). Authentication between cloud platforms can be achieved by federated identity protocols, such as OAuth 2.0, OpenID Connect, and Security Assertion Markup Language (SAML), which centralize the verification of user identity (Kang and Lee, 2022). These frameworks allow organizations to delegate authentication to trusted identity providers, improving scalability and simplifying identity governance.

New methods, for example, passwordless authentication with the help of public key cryptography and verification via biometrics, enhance user experience while reducing the risk of credential exposure (Li et al., 2022). In addition to that, blockchain-based authentication and identity verification models have been proposed to decentralize identity management and improve auditability (Kumar and Tripathi, 2021).

6.5.2 Access Control: Data Permissions

Access control defines the authorization rules that determine what operations an authenticated entity is permitted to perform. Conventional Discretionary and MAC (DAC) models have evolved to more policy-oriented and flexible ones, such as RBAC and ABAC (Ferraiolo et al., 2019).

RBAC assigns permissions to users (e.g., administrator, analyst, auditor) based on predefined organizational roles. ABAC expands this model to account for dynamic characteristics (location of the users, state of the devices, and the sensitivity of data), which facilitates fine-grained and context-based access control (Hu et al., 2015).

Emerging context-sensitive and risk-adaptive access control (Redcap) models integrate AI and behavioral analytics to assess trust levels dynamically (Liu et al., 2023). The mechanisms of these adaptive systems allow making real-time decisions that correspond to the principle of the ZTA: never trust, always verify (Rose et al., 2020).

6.5.3 Cloud Ecosystem Authentication and Authorization

In cloud and hybrid environments, access control policies must remain consistent across multiple domains and service providers. According to the shared responsibility model, the services of cloud providers ensure the security of the infrastructure, but identity and access governance should be implemented by customers (Subramanian and Jeyaraj, 2023). Examples of tools that can be used to construct a central policy framework that integrates authentication, authorization, and auditing are AWS IAM, Azure Active Directory (AAD), and Google Cloud IAM.

Also, Privileged Access Management (PAM) systems restrict the highest administrative tier of privileges and trace sensitive sessions to mitigate risks associated with privilege misuse and insider threats (Zhou and Piramuthu, 2022). There is also increased visibility of access control level and anomaly detection when incorporated with Security Information and Event Management (SIEM) and User and Entity Behavior Analytics (UEBA).

6.5.4 AI and Data Pipe Access Control

The rise in the AI-based data pipelines offers novel access control issues. The threats to ML models, datasets, and training environments are data poisoning, model inversion, and unauthorized inference, which must be mitigated (Yin et al., 2024). Policies must clearly distinguish between data scientists, AI agents, and automated processes to ensure appropriate authorization levels.

Secure aggregation and differential privacy are the elements of federated learning, where data are kept secret when training a model together by keeping data decentralized among clients (Bagdasaryan et al., 2020). Moreover, an attempt to integrate homomorphic encryption and SMPC systems into access control pipelines is made to process encrypted data without exposing it (Chen et al., 2023).

6.5.5 Toward Continuous Authentication and On-the-Fly Policy Conformance

Current system architectures are moving toward continuous authentication, where the behavior of users, circumstances, and device telemetry is tracked during an active session (Mahmoud et al., 2023). Unlike traditional static login models, continuous authentication uses behavioral biometrics, keystroke dynamics, and AI analytics to identify abnormal behavior trends and automatically revoke access in the case of deviations.

At the same time, orchestration models of policy, like XACML (eXtensible Access Control Markup Language) and OPA, can dynamically enforce access policies in real time to maintain a strong security posture. Such an authentication, along with authorization and analytics integration, will permit not just making choices based on accessibility, but in a state of auditability, which is one of the most critical pillars of resilience in data infrastructure.

Access control and authentication mechanisms are evolving from static rule-based systems into intelligent, adaptive, and context-aware frameworks. Through the fusion of MFA, ABAC, ZTA, and AI-based analytics, organizations can achieve granular, real-time access governance across heterogeneous data environments. The strategies are not only building the quality of security but also improving the compliance, transparency, and scalability of the operations in the modern digital ecosystems.

6.6 BACKUP, RECOVERY, AND DATA INTEGRITY MECHANISMS

One of the main pillars of secure system architecture is reliability and availability of data. Backup and recovery solutions prevent data loss resulting from cyberattacks, hardware failures, software errors, or human mistakes, whereas data integrity mechanisms ensure that stored and transmitted data remain accurate, complete, and unaltered. Together, these mechanisms support business continuity, regulatory compliance, and user confidence.

Figure 6.6 is a flowchart that outlines a robust data resilience process. The workflow typically begins with periodic backups and then off-site replication (a 3-2-1 rule is often assumed) to safeguard against a disaster on a site-wide level. Verification (assessment of the integrity and restorability of the backup files) and the automated recovery procedures are critical steps to ensure that data can be restored quickly and reliably after an incident, thereby minimizing downtime.

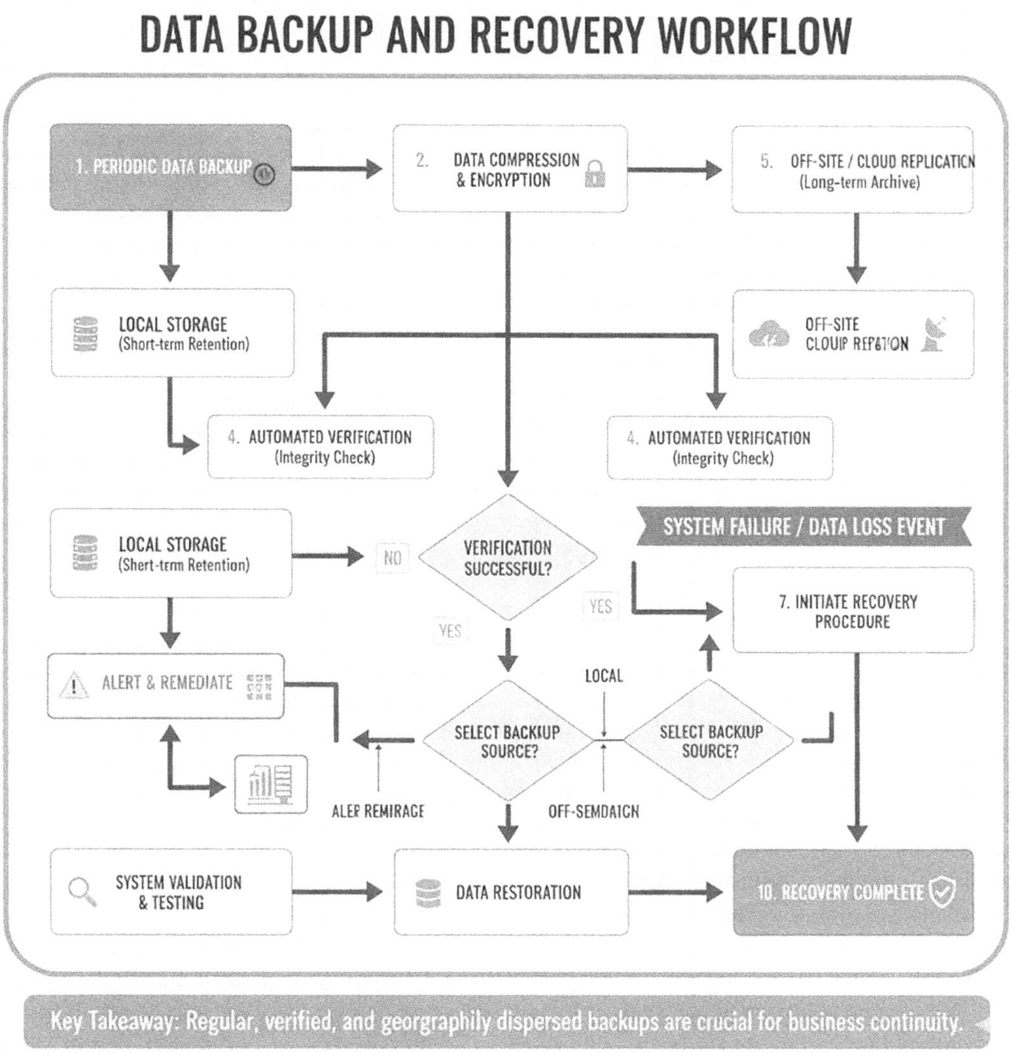

FIGURE 6.6 Data backup and recovery workflow.

6.6.1 Background to Backup and Recovery

Backup is the procedure of establishing duplicate data that may later be restored should it be lost or corrupted. The process of restoring normal operations of data and systems into a consistent, functional state is referred to as recovery. Conventional backup solutions used storage media like tapes and disk based on premises, but contemporary infrastructures use cloud-based, hybrid, and distributed backup solutions that are more suitable in terms of scalability and fault tolerance (Ali and Khan, 2020).

The 3-2-1 backup principle, including three copies of information on two platforms and the off-site copy, is one of the most popularly supported best practices (Patel and Modi, 2022). Cloud-based services such as Amazon S3 Glacier, Microsoft Azure Backup, and Google Cloud Archive also have built-in encryption, immutability, and lifecycle features to ensure data durability and compliance. Incremental, differential, and continuous data protection (CDP) are advanced techniques that optimize storage usage and minimize Recovery Time Objectives (RTOs) and Recovery Point Objectives (RPOs).

TABLE 6.6
Backup and Recovery Techniques

Method	Description	Recovery Speed	Storage Requirement	Ideal Use Case
Full Backup	Entire dataset copy	Fast recovery	High	Initial setup or critical data
Incremental	Changes since last backup	Moderate	Low	Daily backups
Differential	All changes since last full backup	Moderate-Fast	Medium	Mid-term recovery
Snapshot	Point-in-time virtual image	Instant	Medium	Virtual environments
Continuous Replication	Real-time mirroring	Instant	High	Mission-critical systems

Organizations have different types of backup and recovery mechanisms based on their organizational priorities, as shown in Table 6.6. Full backups are completely redundant, yet they entail huge storage, and incremental and differential approaches are more efficient in the event of routine backup operations. High-availability environments (financial and healthcare systems) can undergo real-time recovery with snapshots as well as continuous replication. The strategy is usually determined based on RPOs and RTOs (Mahmoud et al., 2023).

6.6.2 Disaster Recovery and Business Continuity

Disaster recovery (DR) builds on backup processes by enabling the rapid restoration of systems during large-scale disruptions like ransomware attacks, natural catastrophes, or system shutdowns on a large scale. An organized DR plan incorporates automated copying of data and system states on sites located in different geographical locations (Subramanian and Jeyaraj, 2023). Disaster Recovery as a Service (DRaaS) is used to dynamically redirect workload to other data centers or to cloud areas to ensure minimal downtime and maintain operational continuity.

Business continuity planning (BCP) is a complement of the DR that includes human, procedural, and logistical elements of recovery. Mahmoud et al. (2023) highlight that integrated DR-BCP frameworks contribute to resilience when they are in line with compliance standards like ISO 22301, which characterizes the measures of availability and recovery assurance. The reliability and organizational preparedness are further enhanced by continuous testing of recovery procedures by simulated failover load tests.

6.6.3 Data Accuracy and Relationship: Trustworthiness

Data integrity mechanisms ensure that information remains consistent, accurate, and verifiable during its lifecycle. Checksums, cryptographic hash functions, and digital signatures are part of the techniques that identify unauthorized changes and demonstrate authenticity (Wang and Wu, 2021). To illustrate, hash functions such as SHA-256 and SHA-3 can be used to create unique hash values that can be used as the digital fingerprint of data stored or sent.

In a distributed system, consistency between nodes needs special-purpose protocols, such as Byzantine fault tolerance (BFT) and blockchain consensus algorithms, that allow evidence of tampering and lineage of data (Kumar and Tripathi, 2021). Such mechanisms are particularly valuable to provide provenance and auditability in the context of multi-party scenarios (the federated data lakes and scientific research repositories). Recent researches indicate the importance of AI and anomaly-based detection to track data integrity. Compromised, injected, or manipulated data can be detected through ML algorithms by tracking abnormal changes in the data pattern or access behavior (Zhao et al., 2023). When incorporated in pipelines of data management, such analytics bolster proactive defense, as well as automatic response to incidents.

6.6.4 Models of Secured-Storage and Redundancy

Modern storage systems employ various redundancy and replication strategies to enhance resilience. Snapshot replication, erasure coding, and mirroring all make use of high-availability optimization of cost and fault tolerance (Ali and Khan, 2020). The cross-region replication in hybrid systems helps avoid single points of failure and supports low-latency recovery across geographically distributed nodes.

In addition, immutable storage, where the data once written cannot be changed, has become a prerequisite to prevent ransomware attacks. Write Once, Read Many (WORM) storage and object lock policies are technologies which impose immutability and ensure the elimination of malicious or accidental deletion. These solutions, along with encryption-at-rest and secure key management, provide a layered approach to long-term data protection.

6.6.5 Data Checking and Auditing

Systematic auditing is used to complement integrity verification. Regular data integrity verification, in conjunction with block-level integrity checks and metadata verification, is carried out to ensure that source data matches backup copies (Wang and Wu, 2021). All read, write, and modification events are recorded in audit logs, which, preferably, should be stored in non-tamperable formats, and help fulfill such standards as GDPR, HIPAA, and ISO/IEC 27040.

Auditing based on blockchain has been recently developed as a way to record data transactions in immutable distributed logs. Research conducted by Zhao et al. (2023) and Yin et al. (2024) demonstrates that incorporating blockchain into the audit process increases transparency and traceability, specifically in the case of collaborative and federated systems. AI-driven audit agents are increasingly being adopted to automate compliance checks and identify anomalies in the large-scale data infrastructures. The operational foundation of safe data infrastructure is made up of backup, recovery, and data integrity systems. Unlike traditional redundancy-based approaches, modern architectures integrate AI, immutability, and blockchain to provide real-time, verifiable resilience. The integration of automated DR systems, the cryptographic integrity verification, and the intelligent anomaly detection characterize the future generation of recoverable systems of trustworthy data.

6.7 DATA PROVENANCE AND METADATA

Ensuring transparency, accountability, and trust in secure data infrastructures relies heavily on metadata and data provenance. As organizations increasingly rely on distributed, multi-cloud, and AI-driven ecosystems, maintaining integrity and compliance requires clear visibility into how data is generated, transformed, and governed. Metadata and provenance are essential components of information infrastructures, supporting authenticity, reproducibility, and regulatory auditing.

Figure 6.7 is a conceptual diagram illustrating how auditable data histories are created. It shows how each data operation or update of each AI model creates provenance logs (metadata such as who, what, when, and where). These logs are stored in an immutable blockchain or cryptographic registry and linked chronologically. This ensures transparency for compliance, debugging, and detecting data manipulation.

6.7.1 Role and Significance of Metadata

Metadata refers to the descriptive, structural, and administrative information that defines a dataset throughout its lifecycle. It specifies details such as data source, format, accessibility, and timestamps, enabling organizations to discover, classify, and govern data (Wang and Wu, 2021). In secure architecture, metadata is used as a control mechanism that facilitates access control, data classification, and retention policies (Subramanian and Jeyaraj, 2023).

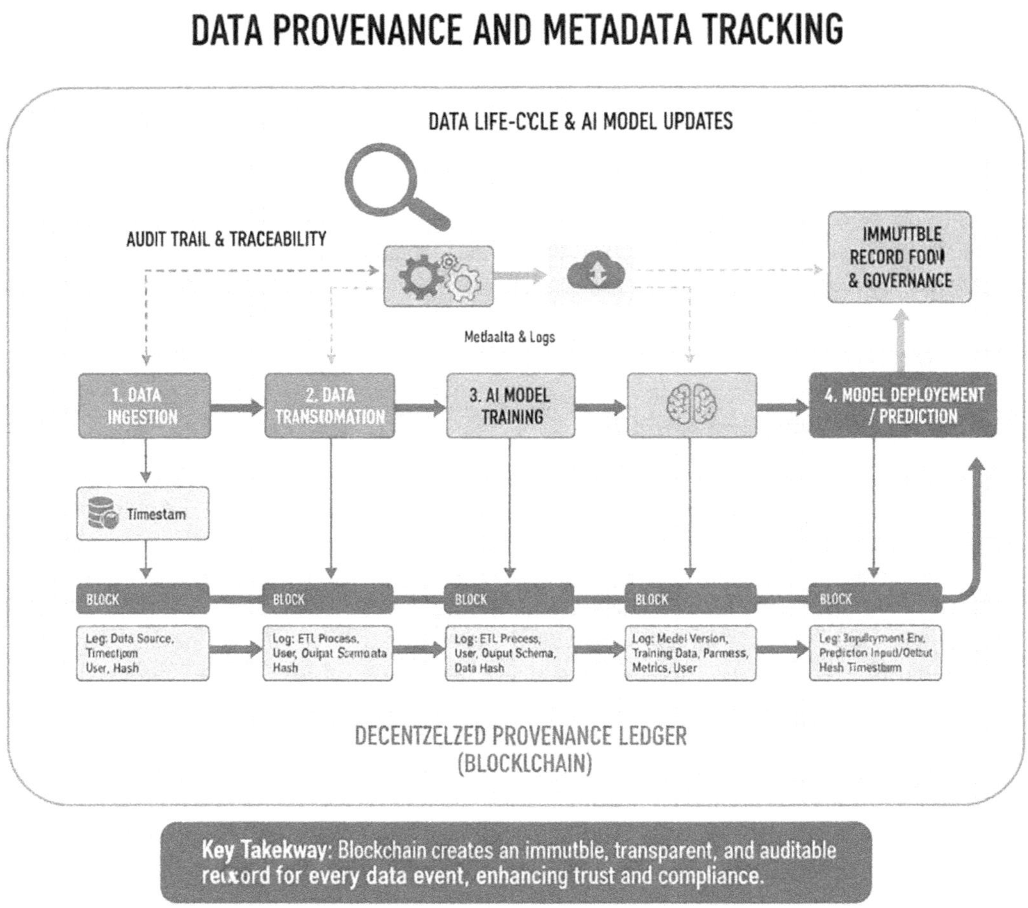

FIGURE 6.7 Metadata tracking and data provenance.

TABLE 6.7
Provenance Metadata Fields

Field	Description	Security Purpose
Data ID	Unique identifier	Traceability
Source Entity	Origin of data	Authenticity
Timestamp	Date/time of creation or modification	Temporal integrity
Hash Value	Cryptographic digest	Tamper detection
Digital Signature	Signed hash of record	Non-repudiation
Access Log Ref.	Link to usage record	Accountability

Data ecosystems in modern times use metadata repositories or data catalogs—for example, Apache Atlas or AWS Glue Data Catalogs—to centralize their management and perform compliance tracking automatically. These systems improve interoperability by maintaining data lineage throughout complex analytics and ML pipelines (Zhao et al., 2023). Data sovereignty initiatives rely on metadata to define usage boundaries and compliance requirements mandated by privacy regulations such as GDPR.

In Table 6.7, data provenance depends on structured metadata, which contains the origin, transformation, and integrity of data sets. The fields of the greatest significance, such as Data ID, Source

Entity, Timestamp, and Hash Value, ensure traceability and identification of tampering. The non-repudiation and accountability mechanisms can also be enhanced by the addition of digital signatures and access logs, which are needed to comply with regulations (Zhao et al., 2023).

6.7.2 Concept of Data Provenance

Data provenance is more than metadata as it has a verifiable history of data creation, transformation, and transfer. Provenance records document the origin, transformation, and interactions of data, including who accessed it, what changes were made, and how they occurred. Such traceability becomes essential in the high-assurance field, for example, scientific research, healthcare, and AI model training, where reproducibility and authenticity are paramount (Kumar and Tripathi, 2021).

In distributed systems, provenance tracking provides end-to-end accountability across multiple stakeholders and processing environments. Organizations can detect unauthorized changes and tampering through the association of the provenance metadata, cryptographic signatures, and immutable logs. Provenance frameworks are also useful in compliance reporting, where workflow dependencies, history of versions, and events of accessing data are automatically recorded.

6.7.3 Evidence-Based Blockchain-Based Provenance Models

Blockchain technology has emerged as a transformative approach for creating immutable provenance records. A decentralized ledger mechanism means that once the information about provenance has been stored, this information cannot be modified or erased without the consensus (Zhao et al., 2023). This characteristic renders blockchain a suitable choice in proving the authenticity of data and in non-repudiation in a collaborative setting.

Recent research suggests blockchain-based provenance designs, in which smart contracts provide data policy and send notifications when this policy is compromised (Kumar and Tripathi, 2021). The multi-tenant and edge cloud and edge systems are the most frequent, where these types of systems are effective because they are harder to ensure trust over the various domains. Integrating blockchain with interplanetary file systems (IPFS) or distributed hash tables (DHTs) further enhances traceability and fault tolerance.

Moreover, the provenance, together with the AI-based monitoring relying on the blockchain, enables detecting the anomalies and conducting proactive audits. As an example, one can consider ML algorithms that can detect unusual lineage patterns that may indicate insider threats or data corruption (Mahmoud et al., 2023).

6.7.4 Metadata Management of AI and Pipelines

The architectures of AI have metadata that is not only operational but also descriptive. Data versioning, model lineage, and experiment tracking concepts are also significant to AI and ML systems, as it gives confidence in reproducible and explainable results (Yin et al., 2024). Metadata repositories store information about datasets, model configurations, and evaluation metrics, model configurations, and evaluation metrics are administered as a part of metadata frameworks such as MLflow, TensorBoard, and Kubeflow Metadata.

In federated learning, metadata helps nodes synchronize by tracking data ownership, update frequency, and aggregation procedures (Bagdasaryan et al., 2020). The provenance records are going to be employed to make sure that no node contributing to the models adds poisoned or biased data to update a model, which will increase the trust of the model in decentralized training of AI.

6.7.5 Interoperability, Compliance, and Standardization

Effective metadata and provenance management require standardized schemas and ontologies to support cross-platform interoperability. Formal provenance models such as the W3C PROV-DM and the Open Provenance Model (OPM) support standardized lineage representation (Hu et al., 2015). These models may facilitate the unrestrained circulation of data and auditing in heterogeneous settings, in addition to ensuring that they adhere to worldwide norms, such as ISO/IEC 19944 (cloud data management) and ISO/IEC 27040 (storage security).

Besides this, compliance-oriented metadata provides retention schedules, data classification tags, and encryption attributes to the datasets. This metadata-driven automation supports Data Loss Prevention (DLP), Information Rights Management (IRM), and automated compliance auditing, which enables organizations to dynamically implement their policies and have a consistently stable governance visibility.

The transparent and accountable data ecosystems can also be based on metadata and data provenance. Through metadata administration, blockchain, AI analytics, and conforming models, the organizations will have the likelihood to acquire verifiable lineage, traceability, and conformity of distributed infrastructures. These mechanisms not only strengthen data integrity but also foster trust, reproducibility, and ethical stewardship in increasingly complex multi-cloud and AI-driven environments.

6.8 DISTRIBUTED TRACEABILITY AND STORAGE

Distributed storage architectures have emerged due to rapid data growth and the need for scalability, resilience, and low-latency access. Unlike traditional centralized systems, distributed storage improves reliability, fault tolerance, and performance. However, such decentralization introduces complex security and traceability challenges, including ensuring data integrity, maintaining consistent access control, and verifying the provenance of data across nodes.

This section explains the design and security principles of distributed storage systems that provide end-to-end traceability in hybrid and multi-cloud environments.

Figure 6.8 illustrates how data is logically partitioned and stored across nodes in a decentralized architecture. Each data segment is distributed to improve redundancy and availability. Blockchain-based traceability is achieved by linking storage events to cryptographic hashes and using a consensus mechanism that ensures all participating nodes agree on the state and location of stored data, thereby guaranteeing decentralized storage with verifiable integrity.

6.8.1 Introduction to Distributed Storage System

Distributed storage systems partition data into smaller units—such as objects, blocks, or files—and distribute them across multiple servers. This architecture supports availability, load balancing, DR, and reduces single points of failure. Key technologies include Hadoop Distributed File System (HDFS), Ceph, Amazon S3, and Google Cloud Storage, which rely on redundancy, replication, erasure coding, and consensus protocols (Wang et al., 2023).

From a security perspective, systems must employ data encryption, strong node authentication, and secure synchronization mechanisms. Consistency across replicas is enforced through coordination protocols such as Paxos or Raft (Ongaro and Ousterhout, 2014). According to the CAP theorem, distributed systems must balance consistency, availability, and partition tolerance, acknowledging that only two properties can be fully optimized at the same time.

Table 6.8 illustrates that distributed storage solutions are different with respect to architecture, fault tolerance, and traceability. IPFS and BigchainDB have mechanisms for immutability based on decentralization or blockchain, while Ceph and HDFS have enterprise-grade scalability, metadata journaling, and checksum validation. This is the essence of sound cloud and edge infrastructure to support the operation of data of high-magnitude, integrity assurances (Li et al., 2022; Zhou et al., 2023).

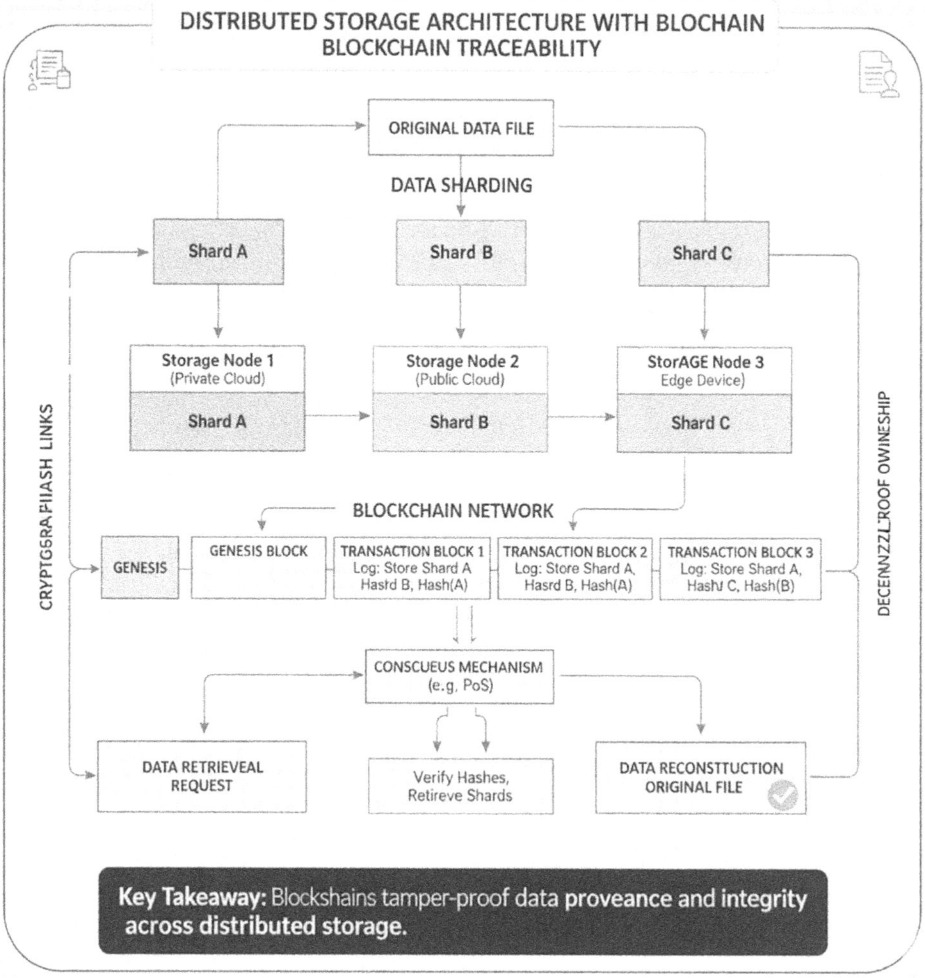

FIGURE 6.8 DSA based on traceable blockchain storage.

TABLE 6.8
Distributed Storage Models and Features

Model	Architecture	Fault Tolerance	Traceability Support	Primary Use Case
IPFS	Peer-to-peer	High	Content addressing	Decentralized web storage
Ceph	Object-based	Very high	Metadata journaling	Cloud data centers
BigchainDB	Blockchain-integrated	Moderate	Immutable logs	Financial records
HDFS	Master-slave	High	Checksum validation	Big-data analytics

6.8.2 Distributed Environments, Security, and Data Governance

Distributed storage environments face challenges related to multi-tenancy, inter-node communication, and data governance. In multi-cloud and edge scenarios, data frequently crosses jurisdictional boundaries, creating compliance and privacy risks (Subramanian and Jeyaraj, 2023). Organizations mitigate these risks by using end-to-end encryption, zero-trust network access (ZTNA), and federated identity systems such as OAuth 2.0 and OpenID Connect to ensure access is strictly controlled.

Policy-driven models like RBAC and ABAC provide consistent data access across heterogeneous systems. Combined with cryptographic hashing and Merkle-tree verification, these mechanisms enable nodes to independently verify the integrity of stored data. Together with cryptographic hashing and verification using Merkle trees, these tools permit nodes to verify the integrity of stored and retrieved information on their own (Kumar and Tripathi, 2021). This makes sure that even without centralized control, the attempt to tamper with, duplicate, or corrupt data can be detected.

6.8.3 Distributed Ledger and Blockchain Integration

When integrated with distributed storage, blockchain, and distributed ledger technologies enhance traceability, immutability, and auditability. Blockchains maintain an immutable sequence of records containing file hashes, ownership information, and timestamps, enabling verifiable traceability across nodes (Zhao et al., 2023). Metadata about the file hashes, ownership credentials, and timestamps can be included in each entry and, therefore, offer verifiable traceability between storage nodes.

Systems such as Storj, Sia, and Filecoin implement smart contracts to enforce service-level agreements and use cryptographic proofs—such as Proof of Replication and Proof of Spacetime—to verify continuous data retention (Li et al., 2022). With the combination of blockchain immutability and distributed redundancy, the organizations are able to attain a higher degree of trust and transparency than ever before without using centralized intermediaries.

Besides, traceability via blockchain technology is consistent with regulatory compliance and data provenance models through allowing non-repudiation, audit trails, and verifying events. This integration provides strong non-repudiation and tamper-proof audit trails, supporting compliance in domains such as healthcare, finance, and supply chains (Mahmoud et al., 2023).

6.8.4 Data Locality and Edge Storage

IoT and edge-computing technologies have led to a significant increase in data generated and processed closer to the source, reducing latency and bandwidth usage (Yin et al., 2024). Edge nodes often cache and preprocess data before synchronizing it with cloud systems, improving efficiency and privacy.

However, the decentralized nature of edge environments introduces risks such as data drift, synchronization failures, and tampering. Secure boot mechanisms, remote attestation, and robust cryptographic protocols ensure that edge nodes operate in trusted states (Zhou et al., 2023). AI-based anomaly detection further enhances security by identifying unusual storage or access patterns.

6.8.5 Auditing, Observation, and Forensic Traceability

Traceability in distributed systems extends beyond data flow tracking and includes continuous auditing and forensic visibility. SIEM tools such as Splunk and Elastic Stack aggregate logs and telemetry data to provide real-time threat detection and incident response (Mahmoud et al., 2023).

When combined with blockchain-based audit logs, these systems create tamper-evident records that strengthen compliance and forensic investigations. AI and ML correlate large volumes of event logs to detect subtle anomalies or coordinated cyberattacks that may go unnoticed.

In addition, AI and ML improve traceability because it correlates massive event logistics to identify subtle anomalies or coordinated attacks, which would otherwise be undetected. With predictive analytics, organizations will be able to shift their security postures to being reactive instead of proactive and discover vulnerabilities before exploitation.

Digital infrastructures involving distributed storage and traceability are the backbone of secure, transparent, and resilient digital infrastructures. Through cryptographic verification, distributed architectures, blockchain-based records, and AI-enhanced monitoring, organizations can maintain secure, transparent, and resilient data ecosystems capable of supporting regulatory audits and forensic analysis. Such systems not only protect against tampering and data loss, but they also provide verifiable auditability that is needed in regulatory compliance, digital forensics, and trust in distributed computing ecosystems.

6.9 CLOUD AND EDGE THREAT LANDSCAPE

Combining cloud computing, edge intelligence, and distributed data systems has created unprecedented opportunities while introducing new vulnerabilities. Their interconnected nature increases the attack surface. Cloud services provide elasticity and scalability, whereas edge systems process data in real time near the data sources. It is thus necessary to understand the changing threat environment to develop a resilient, adaptive, and secure system architecture. The section discusses the major threats in both cloud and edge environments, their causes, consequences, and ways they can be mitigated.

This infographic (Figure 6.9) is a high-level view of general security risks in contemporary distributed environments. It assigns each of the major threat categories (e.g., Distributed Denial of Service (DoS), Data Poisoning (targeting AI/ML systems), and Side-Channel Attacks (targeting hardware) to the associated mitigation layers (e.g., Firewalls against DoS, Data Integrity Checks against Poisoning, and Hardware Isolation against Side-Channel Attacks).

6.9.1 Evolving Threat Landscape

Conventional network-based attacks have changed into highly complex, multi-vector attacks on cloud-based and edge infrastructure. The previously existing security issues, including unauthorized access and malware attacks, now diversify and encompass data breaches, ransomware, supply-chain attacks, API attacks, and AI-focused adversarial attacks (Subramanian and Jeyaraj, 2023). In addition to that, multi-cloud and hybrid designs bring heterogeneity to configurations and security controls that can easily lead to configuration drift and policy inconsistency.

Threat actors increasingly leverage automation, AI, and social engineering to bypass traditional defenses. APTs exploit covert methods such as credential theft, lateral movement, and command-and-control communication to exfiltrate sensitive data (Wang et al., 2023). In the meantime, serverless computing and containerized workloads also increase the complexity of the issue by increasing ephemeral attack vectors that traditional perimeter defenses can hardly observe.

As shown in Table 6.9, the cloud-edge ecosystem is exposed to multiple threat categories, including network attacks, insider threats, ransomware, and AI poisoning. The layered defense is critical to corresponding mitigation strategies, including encryption, intrusion prevention, behavioral analytics, and federated learning validation. Continuous implementation of AI also creates vulnerabilities and new detection features (Zhou et al., 2023; Yin et al., 2024).

6.9.2 Cloud-Specific Threats

Multi-tenancy, virtualization, and shared responsibility models characterize the cloud environment, and all of them present different vulnerabilities. CSA includes its list of cloud threats, including data leakage, insecure APIs, insider threats, and misconfigurations of cloud storage (CSA, 2022).

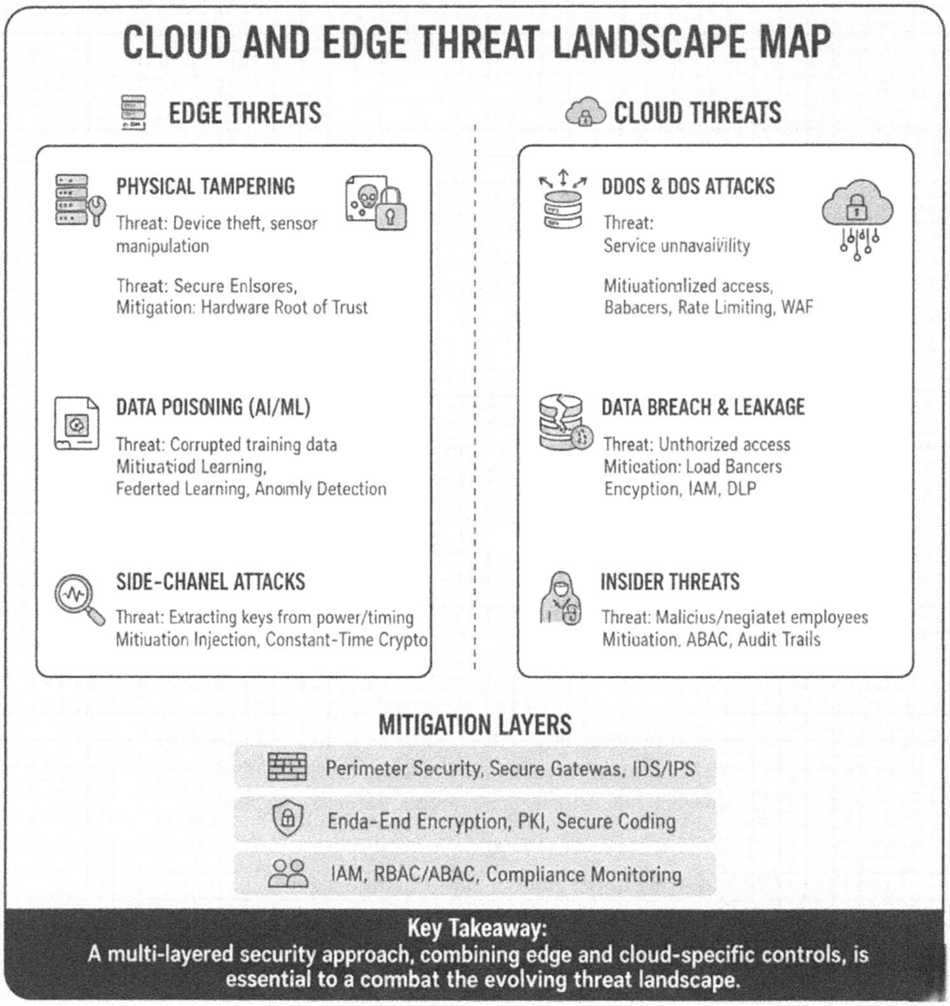

FIGURE 6.9 Cloud and edge threat landscape map.

TABLE 6.9
Threat Categories and Mitigation Techniques

Threat Category	Example	Impact	Mitigation Strategy
Network Attack	DDoS, MITM	Service outage	IDS/IPS, traffic filtering
Data Breach	Unauthorized access	Confidentiality loss	Encryption, access control
Insider Threat	Privilege misuse	Data leakage	Monitoring, behavioral analytics
Malware/Ransomware	File encryption, data lockout	Data loss	Backup, endpoint protection
AI-specific Attack	Model poisoning	Prediction errors	Federated learning validation

A common vulnerability is data exposure due to misconfigured object storage buckets, often caused by human error or insecure default settings. In the same vein, unauthorized privilege escalation is usually caused by poor IAM policies. VM escape vulnerability and hypervisor attacks use vulnerabilities in the virtualization layers to enable attacks to move laterally across tenants (Kumar and Tripathi, 2021).

Besides that, the most important attack surface is API vulnerabilities, as APIs are the core of cloud interoperability. Insecure API endpoints can be exploited through injection attacks, broken authentication, or excessive data exposure, jeopardizing confidentiality and integrity (Mahmoud et al., 2023).

The problem of supply-chain attacks, including the cases of compromised software updates and third-party dependencies, only amplifies this idea because it is the software bill of materials (SBOM) verification and zero-trust idea in the cloud architecture that should be strongly applied.

6.9.3 Edge Computing Threats

Edge computing brings processing to the extremes of the network and closer to the location of the IoT devices, sensors, and users. Although this reduces latency and increases scalability, it also introduces physical, network, and software-level vulnerabilities. As compared to cloud data centers, which are commonly secured with effective physical protection, edge nodes can be implemented in uncontrollable areas, thus prone to being tampered with, stolen, or containing backdoors (Zhou et al., 2023).

In the edge networks, data interception and spoofing are prevalent, particularly in cases where communication channels are not well encrypted. The attackers can use malicious updates to modify the data streams or interrupt the synchronization by injecting malicious updates or compromising firmware. In the domain of Industrial Internet of Things (IIoT), attackers will be able to use weak authentication or default credentials to obtain unauthorized access to control machines that may result in safety-critical accidents (Yin et al., 2024).

Moreover, edge nodes can suffer from attacks of resource exhaustion, including Denial-of-Service (DoS) and Distributed Denial-of-Service (DDoS) attacks that target the shortage of resources within the computing environment. Attackers may target orchestrators in edge-cloud hierarchies to cause cascading service failures.

6.9.4 Threats to AI, Data, and Models

With the AI being thoroughly entrenched in the cloud and edge pipelines, another category of threats arises and attacks the data, models, and learning processes themselves. Adversarial actors can use corrupted samples of data to poison the training of models or may use model inversion attacks to retrieve sensitive information of trained models (Yin et al., 2024). Inference attacks can reveal attributes of private data, compromising privacy-preserving learning systems.

Moreover, the intellectual property is under threat, as well as the performance integrity, when it comes to model theft and unauthorized model replication. Byzantine nodes can add malicious updates to pick the global model in federated learning situations. To resolve such issues, it is necessary to close multi-party computation (SMPC), differential privacy, and homomorphic encryption to make sure that sensitive information is not compromised even in distributed learning and inference (Li et al., 2022).

6.9.5 Best Practice and Mitigation Strategies

The purchase of cloud and edge infrastructures necessitates the deployment of a defense-in-depth methodology, bringing layer after layer of technical, process, and administration controls.

Core strategies include:

Zero-Trust Architecture: Removes the implicit trust through the constant verification of all the devices, users, and transactions across the network frontiers (Mahmoud et al., 2023).
Secure API gateways enforce authentication, authorization, and throttling to prevent API abuse.
AI-Based Threat Intelligence: ML as a behavioral analytics, anomaly detection, and predictive threat modeling.
Confidential Computing: It is based on the TEEs available as hardware, which may be the Intel SGX or ARM TrustZone, to isolate sensitive workloads.
Constructing Permanent Infrastructure and DevSecOps: The infrastructure has security-related processes embedded in CI/CD pipelines, and software compliance and vulnerability tests are automated.
Auditing Blockchain: Activities of auditing are based on blockchain to offer tamper-evident audit records and data provenance used to conduct compliance and forensic investigations.

A combination of these strategies would create the basis of a resilient cloud-edge environment that could detect, mitigate, and recover from advanced cyberattacks.

The cloud and edge threat environment indicates a dynamically shifting convergence point of conventional cybersecurity issues and the new AI-related vulnerabilities. The threats that cloud infrastructures are susceptible to include misconfiguration, insecure APIs, and insider threats, whereas edge environments are vulnerable to physical attacks, data spoofing, and DDoS attacks. Because information pipelines traverse distributed systems, implementing ZTAs, AI-driven security insights, and continuous compliance controls is essential to ensure CIA.

6.10 PIPING AI: MAKING AI RESILIENT

As data volumes grow, the application of AI and ML is transforming simple data pipelines into intelligent, sophisticated ecosystems. The existing AI data pipeline comprises data ingestion, preprocessing, model training, evaluation, and deployment into a continuous workflow that must be secure, reliable, and ethical. Ensuring the resilience of these pipelines is critical, as failures or breaches at any stage can lead to corrupted data, biased results, or security compromises. This part will examine architectural concepts and design principles that can be applied to develop a resilient, adaptable, and secure AI-led pipeline in cloud-edge applications.

Figure 6.10 shows the lifecycle of an AI model, including both the data acquisition stage and the operational deployment stage. It illustrates how resilience and security are embedded at every step: encryption during ingestion and preprocessing, data validation during training, access controls during deployment, and monitoring through AIOps, with model changes and data provenance verified via blockchain.

6.10.1 AI Data Pipelines: Architectural Introduction

The standard AI data pipeline comprises interdependent steps, namely data acquisition, data preparation, feature engineering, model development, deployment, and monitoring. The phases have varying security and reliability challenges. Indicatively, pipelines during data collection are required to uphold authenticity, privacy, and provenance of incoming data streams. Data poisoning or adversarial manipulation may reduce the accuracy of a model and its ethical reliability during model training (Yin et al., 2024).

The contemporary AI platforms tend to use hybrid cloud-edge architectures, with sensitive data being processed on the edge and the aggregated insights being sent to centralized AI models in the

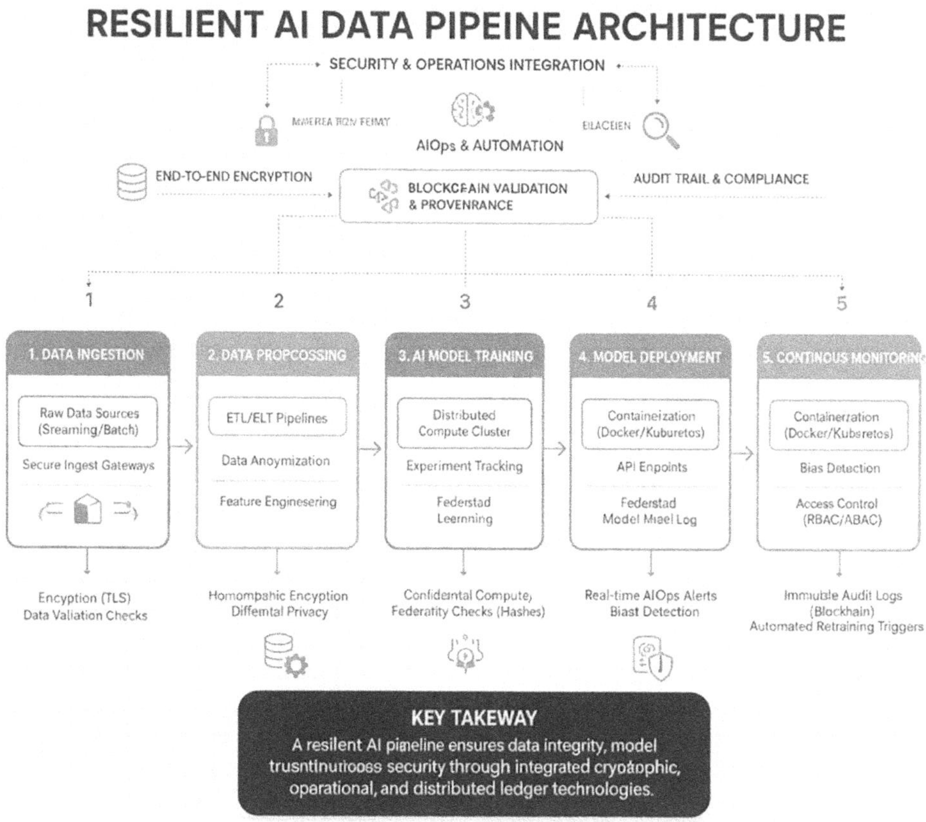

FIGURE 6.10 AI data pipeline-resilient architecture.

cloud. This hybrid architecture enhances efficiency by employing secure orchestration, data encryption, and robust synchronization mechanisms (Zhou et al., 2023). The resilient design will ensure that these distributed components will remain operational even with a partial network failure or cyberattack.

6.10.2 Automation and Orchestration Resilience

The resilient AI data pipelines rely on automation. Kubeflow, Apache Airflow, and MLflow allow coordinating data processing, model retraining, and deployment without needing much human work. Nevertheless, automation should be applied safely such that it does not result in a cascading failure or runaway processes.

The combination of redundancy, fault isolation, and checkpointing mechanisms is referred to as resilient orchestration. Checkpoints will permit workflows to restart in a safe way, following some unexpected failure, whereas containerization technologies (e.g., Docker, Kubernetes) will make them self-healing and scalable. The implementation of CI/CD with embedded security scanning (DevSecOps) can be used to make sure that the security flaws are identified at an early stage of the model lifecycle (Subramanian and Jeyaraj, 2023). Besides, the incorporation of AI in the field of IT Operations (AIOps) offers predictive analytics to detect anomalies, assist in capacity planning, and predict failures. AIOps enables proactive responses to historical data and system metrics, helping prevent downtime and performance degradation (Mahmoud et al., 2023).

6.10.3 AI Pipeline Data Privacy and Security

The most important aspect of resilient AI systems is data security. AI pipelines have access to sensitive and potentially regulated data, including personal identifiers, as well as proprietary business data, and have to be highly secure. Privacy-preserving techniques such as homomorphic encryption, federated learning, and SMPC enable models to be trained collaboratively without exposing raw data (Li et al., 2022). FL frameworks resist malicious or corrupted inputs using differential privacy and BFT (Yin et al., 2024). In addition, data lineage tracking and provenance metadata will help in enforcing regulations and performing investigations of any possible breach of the model or data.

RBAC and ABAC also need to be supported in AI pipelines to implement fine-grained security policies. The combination of PKI, SSL/TLS, and API authentication is how the communication between pipeline components can be secured to ensure that the communication is encrypted and verifiable (Wang et al., 2023).

6.10.4 Model Resilience and Reliability

In addition to the protection of data, model robustness, which can be defined as the capability of AI models to be accurate and reliable under the conditions of adversarial or unforeseen circumstances, is also a key to resilience in AI systems. Ensemble methods, uncertainty quantification, and adversarial training increase the robustness of models against data noise and manipulation (Bagdasaryan et al., 2020). Monitoring of the model is also extremely crucial after deployment. Drift detection systems monitor changes in data distribution or model behavior, triggering retraining or rollback when necessary. More complex monitoring systems combine the use of explainable artificial intelligence (XAI) to enhance the interpretability and credibility of automated decision systems. Furthermore, secure model repositories (such as ModelDB or TensorFlow Model Garden) can be used to enable version control, integrity, and access control verification to prevent being used to deliver invalidated models to production applications.

6.10.5 Principles of Resilient AI Pipeline Design

To be end-to-end resilient, AI data pipelines must abide by a series of principles:

Modularity: Design independent, loosely coupled modules that are able to fault or recover without impacting the whole system.
Redundancy: Data replication is done across a number of nodes to reduce failure effects and improve availability.
Observability: Have AI-powered analytics that should be deployed to perform continuous logging, tracing, and monitoring.
Fixed Data Transfer: Data integrity can be ensured using blockchain-based provenance or cryptographic hashing (Zhao et al., 2023).
Adaptive Security: Use AI-based threat detection to dynamically adjust security control measures based on the changing risks.
Governance and Compliance: Include frameworks like ISO 27001, NIST AI Risk Management Framework (2023), and GDPR, to make sure that there are ethical and legal AI operations.

6.10.6 AI and Blockchain Integration to Facilitate Resilience

The combination of AI and blockchain technologies generates synergistic resilience and security features of data pipelines. The data and model transactions are made immutable, traceable, and non-repudiable through blockchain, and autonomous verification, predicting threats, and detecting anomalies through AI (Zhao et al., 2023). Access control, data sharing agreements, and audit policies can be automatically enforced using smart contracts, without requiring any human monitoring. As an example of the healthcare data pipelines, blockchain makes sure that the regulations regarding data sharing are followed, whereas AI examines the logs of transactions to detect unauthorized access patterns. They collectively constitute a self-recovery and self-managed infrastructure that is able to dynamically respond to operational and security anomalies. Hardened AI data pipelines integrate automation, cryptography, distributed learning, and intelligent monitoring to remain operational even under stress or attack. Organizations can have secure, adaptive, and self-sustaining ecosystems by instilling resilience in architecture, both in the ingestion of data and in the deployment of models. Integrating AI, blockchain, and zero-trust paradigms ensures that data-driven innovation remains secure while maintaining trust, transparency, and operational continuity.

6.11 ENDURING SECURITY GUARANTEES

Continuous Security Assurance (CSA) is an adaptive, real-time process designed to maintain and verify the CIA of data systems. Unlike traditional periodic security audits, CSA emphasizes active monitoring, automated threat detection, and adaptive response mechanisms across all layers of digital infrastructure. The significance of CSA lies in its ability to provide continuous visibility, reduce detection and response time, and proactively mitigate emerging threats, thereby minimizing the risk of data breaches and system compromise. As cloud-native systems, AI-driven automation, and distributed data ecosystems become more prevalent, continuous assurance is essential to protect sensitive assets against evolving cyber threats.

Figure 6.11 illustrates a dynamic CSA loop, replacing infrequent checks with a continuous feedback cycle: Real-Time Monitoring (gathering security incidents), Analysis (AI-driven anomaly detection), Response (automated or human mitigation), and Verification (assessing the effectiveness of mitigation). AI automation drives this loop, enabling proactive defense against rapidly changing threats.

6.11.1 Concept and Rationale

CSA ensures that security controls remain effective throughout the system lifecycle, including design, deployment, operation, and decommissioning. Unlike static compliance checks, CSA integrates real-time data analytics, security monitoring, and automated policy enforcement (Mahmoud et al., 2023).

Aligned with ZTA principles, CSA does not inherently trust any user, device, or application. Each access request or communication is dynamically verified using contextual parameters such as user behavior, device posture, and geolocation. When anomaly detection algorithms and behavioral analytics are integrated, CSA can automatically detect abnormal activities and implement preemptive mitigation measures (Subramanian and Jeyaraj, 2023).

6.11.2 Continuous and Autonomous Monitoring

Automation forms the foundation of CSA. Modern security systems leverage Security Orchestration, Automation, and Response (SOAR) integrated with SIEM systems to correlate logs, detect patterns, and respond automatically (Li et al., 2023).

ML models enhance automation by identifying zero-day vulnerabilities, insider threats, and APTs in real time. ML-based classifiers analyze large volumes of telemetry data from endpoints, network flows, and APIs to detect anomalies that traditional rule-based systems may miss (Zhou et al., 2023).

Additionally, container security and microservice observability tools (e.g., Prometheus, Grafana, Falco) provide detailed runtime visibility of cloud-native applications. Integrated with DevSecOps pipelines, these tools ensure continuous validation of code, configuration, and runtime environments before production deployment (Alenezi et al., 2024).

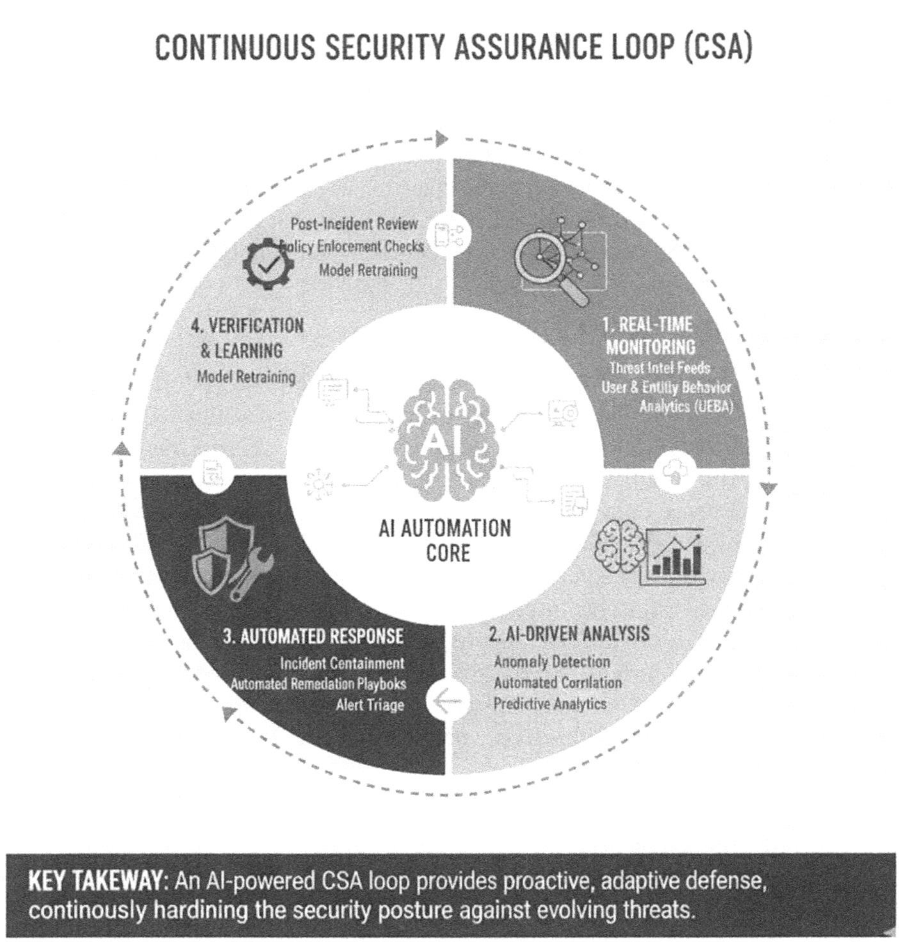

FIGURE 6.11 Continuous security assurance loop (CSA).

Continuous assurance frameworks make use of automation, PaC, predictive analytics, and so on, to enforce real-time compliance as demonstrated in Table 6.10. SIEM, SOAR, and DevSecOps pipeline tools are tools that integrate event monitoring with an automated response. New AIOps and ML monitoring infrastructure can also promote predictive risk control and automatic resilience of dynamic infrastructures (Alenezi et al., 2024; Wang et al., 2023).

6.11.3 Policy Implementation and Compliance Verification

CSA extends beyond technical measures to governance. Regulatory frameworks such as ISO/IEC 27001, NIST Cybersecurity Framework, GDPR, and the EU AI Act require organizations to maintain auditable, verifiable evidence of compliance.

CSA frameworks translate real-time system states into predefined control objectives using automated compliance validation. PaC systems, often implemented via tools like OPA, enforce access controls, network segmentation, and compliance integrity (Wang et al., 2023).

TABLE 6.10
Continuous Security Assurance Tools and Techniques

Framework/Tool	Function	Data Source	Assurance Capability
SIEM (e.g., Splunk, ELK)	Event aggregation and correlation	Logs, network flow	Real-time anomaly detection
SOAR (e.g., Cortex XSOAR)	Automated incident response	Alerts, playbooks	Response orchestration
OPA (Open Policy Agent)	Policy-as-code enforcement	Configurations, APIs	Continuous compliance
DevSecOps Pipeline	Security in the CI/CD	Repositories	On-demand validation
AIOps/ML Monitoring	Predictive risk analytics	Telemetry, metrics	Self-adaptive resilience

Blockchain-based auditing and cryptographic timestamping further strengthen traceability and forensic readiness, providing tamper-evident evidence for audits and investigations.

6.11.4 Dynamic Threat Intelligence and Future Security

CSA leverages predictive and adaptive security mechanisms. Threat Intelligence Platforms (TIPs) aggregate indicators of compromise (IoCs), malware signatures, and adversarial tactics, techniques, and procedures (TTPs), often using frameworks such as MITRE ATT&CK and STRIDE.

AI-based threat modeling contextualizes these insights for specific infrastructures, identifying critical assets, attack surfaces, and potential propagation paths (Yin et al., 2024). Predictive analytics enable systems to anticipate threats, predefine defenses, and automate patching or access isolation before attacks occur.

Digital twins, virtual representations of IT, or cyber–physical systems allow simulation of attack scenarios, testing mitigation strategies without impacting live operations (Zhao et al., 2023).

6.11.5 Integration with DevSecOps Pipelines

CSA complements DevSecOps, embedding security throughout the software development lifecycle (SDLC). Automated scanning, static code analysis, and runtime protections ensure ongoing verification of code, dependencies, and configurations (Subramanian and Jeyaraj, 2023).

By supporting security-as-code, DevSecOps enables real-time testing, risk scoring, and policy enforcement at every commit or deployment. CSA integrated with DevSecOps fosters a security-first culture, making resilience an intrinsic property of all system components rather than an afterthought.

6.11.6 Cyber Resiliency and Incident Recovery

CSA extends beyond prevention to include incident response and post-incident learning. AI-enhanced response systems can isolate affected endpoints, reroute network traffic, or revert configurations to maintain operational stability.

Forensic intelligence tools and security analytics extract actionable insights from incidents to refine threat models and strengthen defenses. This feedback loop enhances cyber resiliency, enabling organizations to predict, withstand, recover from, and adapt to cyber disruptions. Cross-domain incident correlation in hybrid and multi-cloud environments further ensures synchronized responses, minimizing downtime and maintaining trust in data integrity.

6.11.7 Future Directions of Continuous Assurance

Emerging technologies continue to redefine CSA. Quantum-resistant cryptography, autonomous cybersecurity agents, and self-verifying smart contracts are poised to automate trust and verification.

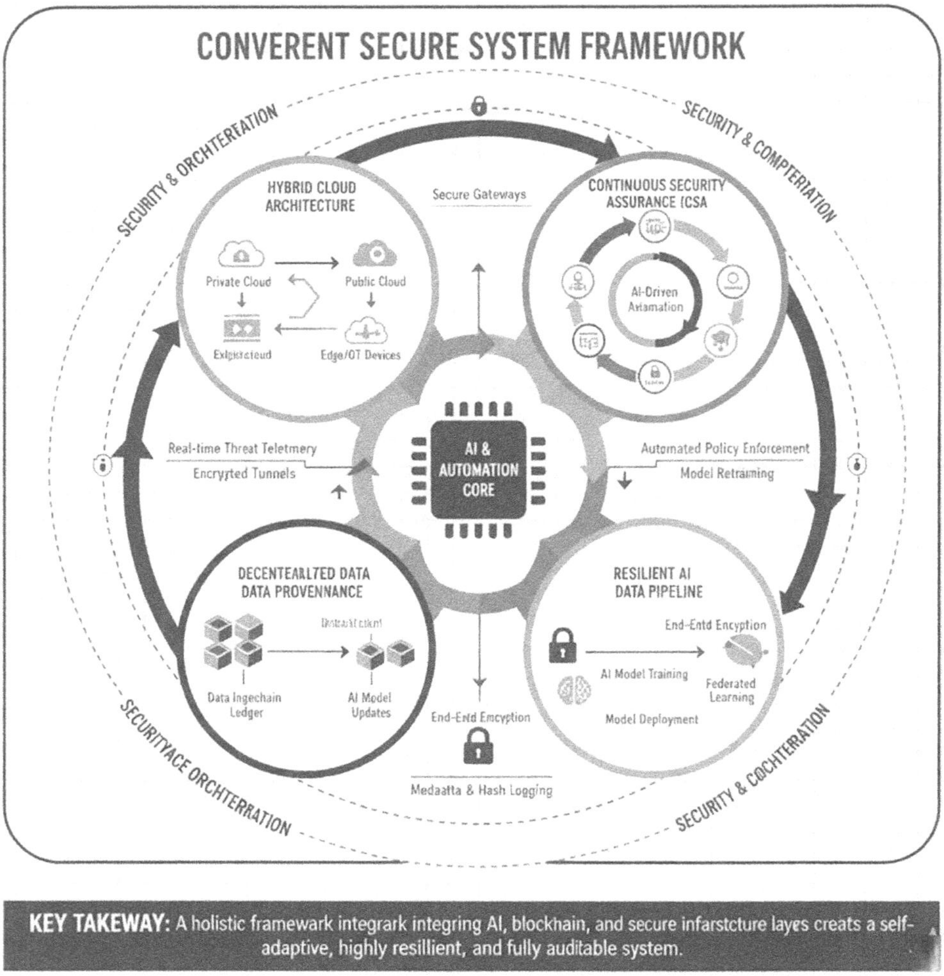

FIGURE 6.12 Convergent secure system framework.

Generative AI (GenAI) can provide real-time explanations of anomalies and perform automated root cause analysis, enhancing transparency and response speed.

Future CSA ecosystems will integrate Zero-Trust AI, confidential computing, and federated threat intelligence to provide holistic visibility and control over distributed environments. This convergence of CSA, AI observability, and governance will enable self-adaptive, intelligent cybersecurity ecosystems.

CSA converts security from a reactive operation to a continuous, intelligent, and adaptive operation. Through combining real-time analytics, AI-based automation, and verification of zero trust, organizations will be able to maintain compliance, integrity, and resilience in the ever-changing digital environment. CSA is therefore the workhorse of sustainable, secure, and reliable data-driven businesses.

Figure 6.12 synthesizes the CSA architecture, highlighting the interdependence of Hybrid Cloud (distributed infrastructure), blockchain (trust and traceability), AI Resilience Mechanisms (data and model protection), and the CSA Loop (real-time automated governance). This framework represents a resilient, secure, and cryptographically agile infrastructure capable of sustaining operations under evolving cyber threats.

6.12 SUMMARY

The evolution of digital ecosystems into AI-driven, data-intensive infrastructures has significantly reshaped the requirements for security, reliability, and governance. This chapter has examined both foundational and advanced principles underlying secure data infrastructure and system architecture, encompassing cryptography, distributed computing, AI, and cloud-edge collaboration. CSA moves beyond passive defense, transforming security into a predictive and adaptive process. Modern architectures must ensure not only information security but also continuity, accountability, and flexibility throughout the entire data lifecycle.

The chapter began with an introduction and literature review that highlighted the importance of secure architectures in fostering organizational trust and operational resilience. Contemporary realities—including cloud integration, hybrid deployments, and multi-tenant environments—demand multidimensional strategies that combine technical security with policy-level governance.

Section 6.3 emphasized secure cloud and hybrid architectures, highlighting isolation mechanisms, workload segmentation, and dynamic scalability as key strategies for risk mitigation. Section 6.4 discussed cryptographic standards such as SSL/TLS, PKI, and AES, which collectively ensure confidentiality, integrity, and authentication in distributed data exchanges. Section 6.5 extended these concepts to data authentication and access control, advocating role-based, attribute-based, and zero-trust models to enforce least-privilege access and verifiable data operations.

Section 6.6 addressed backup, recovery, and data integrity mechanisms, stressing that redundancy, versioning, and immutability are essential for business continuity. Section 6.7 focused on metadata and data provenance, highlighting the importance of traceability and accountability, particularly in AI-oriented environments. Section 6.8 illustrated the role of blockchain and decentralized data management in enhancing transparency, tamper-resistance, and trustworthiness through distributed storage and traceability.

Section 6.9, covering the cloud and edge threat landscape, provided an overview of emerging threats, including supply chain vulnerabilities, ransomware, and AI-specific attacks, emphasizing the need for defense-in-depth strategies and context-sensitive threat modeling. Section 6.10 introduced resilient AI data pipelines, which integrate orchestration, fault tolerance, and privacy-conscious ML to provide end-to-end security in intelligent systems.

Section 6.11 explored CSA, which reconceptualizes cybersecurity as an adaptive, continuous process rather than a static control. CSA fosters self-sustaining trust, ensuring that DevSecOps pipelines incorporate real-time monitoring, predictive analytics, and automated compliance verification in line with evolving technologies and threat landscapes.

Together, these principles and practices paint a vision of future infrastructures that are resistant to attacks, self-observing, self-repairing, and self-adapting. Emerging technologies such as confidential computing, federated learning, and quantum-resistant encryption signal the next generation of security guarantees applied across all layers of computation and communication.

Finally, the chapter emphasizes that security is not a fixed endpoint but a continuous process spanning architecture, governance, and intelligence. The synergy of automation, AI-driven resilience, and ethical stewardship is essential for building digital trust. The combined use of blockchain for transparency, AI for predictive insights, and zero-trust principles for authentication provides a roadmap for developing next-generation infrastructures that are secure, resilient, intelligent, and inherently trustworthy.

REFERENCES

Abbas, N., Zhang, Y., Taherkordi, A., & Skeie, T. (2018). Mobile edge computing: A survey. *IEEE Internet of Things Journal, 5*(1), 450–465. https://doi.org/10.1109/JIOT.2017.2750180

Adams, C., & Lloyd, S. (2003). *Understanding PKI: Concepts, standards, and deployment considerations.* Addison-Wesley. https://lccn.loc.gov/2002074687

Alenezi, M., Mahmoud, M. M., & Abdallah, M. (2024). Continuous security monitoring in microservice-based cloud environments. *IEEE Transactions on Cloud Computing, 12*(4), 1501–1513.

Ali, M., & Khan, S. U. (2020). Data backup and recovery in cloud computing: Challenges and solutions. *Journal of Cloud Computing*, *9*(2), 1–13.

Bagdasaryan, E., Veit, A., Hua, Y., Estrin, D., & Shmatikov, V. (2020). How to backdoor federated learning. In *Proceedings of the 23rd international conference on artificial intelligence and statistics (AISTATS)* (pp. 2938–2948). PMLR. https://proceedings.mlr.press/v108/bagdasaryan20a.html

Balamurugan, G., Tyagi, A.K., & Richa, A. (2023). Survey on privacy preserving and trust building techniques of blockchain-based systems. In: *Privacy Preservation and Secured Data Storage in Cloud Computing*. IGI Global. DOI: 10.4018/979-8-3693-0593-5.ch019

Bhardwaj, A., Kaur, J., & Singh, H. (2021). A survey on hybrid cloud security challenges and solutions. *Journal of Cloud Computing, 10*(1), 1–14.

Burns, B., Grant, B., Oppenheimer, D., Brewer, E., & Wilkes, J. (2018). Borg, Omega, and Kubernetes. *Communications of the ACM, 61*(5), 50–57. https://doi.org/10.1145/3190508

Chen, L. K., Jordan, S., Liu, Y. K., Moody, D., & Smith-Tone, D. (2016). *Report on post-quantum cryptography.* U.S. Department of Commerce, NIST. https://doi.org/10.6028/NIST.IR.8105?

Chen, L., Jordan, S., Liu, Y. K., Moody, D., & Smith-Tone, D. (2023). *Report on post-quantum cryptography.* National Institute of Standards and Technology (NIST).

Cheng, Y., Qiu, M., & Zhao, Y. (2022). AI-driven continuous security assurance for cloud-native systems. *Journal of Information Security and Applications, 70*, 103392.

Cloud Security Alliance (CSA). (2022b). *Top threats to cloud computing: Egregious eleven*. Cloud Security Alliance.

Cooper, D., Santesson, S., Farrell, S., Boeyen, S., Housley, R., & Polk, W. (2008). *Internet X.509 public key infrastructure certificate and certificate revocation list (CRL) profile (RFC 5280).* IETF. https://doi.org/10.17487/RFC5280

Dang, Q. (2015). *Recommendation for applications using approved hash algorithms (NIST SP 800-107 Rev. 1).* U.S. Department of Commerce. https://doi.org/10.6028/NIST.SP.800-107r1

Das, S., Ahmed, M., & Roy, S. (2021). Multi-factor authentication in cloud security: A review. *Journal of Information Security and Applications*, *63*, 103019. https://doi.org/10.1016/j.jisa.2021.103019

Dinh, T. T. A., Liu, R., Zhang, M., Chen, G., Ooi, B. C., & Wang, J. (2017). Untangling blockchain: A data processing view of blockchain systems. *IEEE Transactions on Knowledge and Data Engineering, 30*(7), 1366–1385.

European Union Agency for Cybersecurity (ENISA). (2022). *Guidelines on secure cryptographic configuration.* ENISA Publications. www.epc-cep.eu

Fernandes, D. A. B., Soares, L. F. B., Gomes, J. V., Freire, M. M., & Inácio, P. R. M. (2014). Security issues in cloud environments: A survey. *International Journal of Information Security, 13*(2), 113–170. https://doi.org/10.1007/s10207-013-0208-7

Ferraiolo, D. F., Kuhn, D. R., & Chandramouli, R. (2019). *Role-based access control* (2nd ed.). Artech House. https://us.artechhouse.com/Role-Based-Access-Control-Second-Edition-P1386.aspx

Gai, K., Qiu, M., & Zhao, H. (2019). Security and privacy issues in cloud computing: A survey. *Future Generation Computer Systems, 88*, 25–40. https://doi.org/10.1016/j.future.2018.05.007

Gartner. (2020). *Secure Access Service Edge (SASE) architecture guide.* Gartner Research.

Goodfellow, I., Shlens, J., & Szegedy, C. (2015). Explaining and harnessing adversarial examples. *International Conference on Learning Representations (ICLR).*

Hashizume, K., Rosado, D. G., Fernández-Medina, E., & Fernandez, E. B. (2013). An analysis of security issues for cloud computing. *Journal of Internet Services and Applications, 4*(5), 1–13. https://doi.org/10.1186/1869-0238-4-5

Housley, R., Polk, W., Ford, W., & Solo, D. (2019). *Internet X.509 public key infrastructure: Certificate and CRL profile update.* IETF RFC 6818. www.ietf.org/rfc/rfc3280.txt

Hu, V. C., Ferraiolo, D., Kuhn, R., Friedman, A., Lang, A., Cogdell, M., ... & Schnitzer, A. (2015a). *Guide to attribute-based access control (ABAC) definition and considerations (NIST SP 800-162).* https://doi.org/10.6028/NIST.SP.800-162

Hu, V. C., Kuhn, D. R., & Ferraiolo, D. F. (2015b). Attribute-based access control. *Computer*, *48*(2), 85–88. https://doi.org/10.1109/MC.2015.33

Internet Engineering Task Force (IETF). (2018). *The transport layer security (TLS) protocol version 1.3 (RFC 8446).* https://doi.org/10.17487/RFC8446

Kang, J., & Lee, D. (2022). Federated identity and access management in multi-cloud environments. *IEEE Transactions on Cloud Computing*, *10*(4), 1859–1872.

Krawczyk, H., Paterson, K. G., & Wee, H. (2013). On the security of TLS 1.3 and QUIC against weaknesses in PKI. In *Proceedings of the IEEE symposium on security and privacy* (pp. 1–15). IEEE . https://doi.org/10.1109/SP.2013.20

Kumar, R., & Tripathi, R. (2021). Blockchain-based identity management systems: A survey. *IEEE Access*, *9*, 73015–73035.

Kumari, S., Tyagi, A. K., Tiwari, S., & Kulshreshtha, G. (2025a). Sensors and digital twin for healthcare monitoring frameworks. In T. A. Nguyen (Ed.), *Digital twin, blockchain, and sensor networks in the healthy and mobile city (Chapter 10,* pp. 147–177*)*. Elsevier. https://doi.org/10.1016/B978-0-443-34174-8.00011-9

Kumari, S., Tyagi, A. K., Tiwari, S., & Singh, R. (2025b). Medical sensor network, edge computing and blockchain for efficient medical data exchange. In T. A. Nguyen (Ed.), *Digital twin, blockchain, and sensor networks in the healthy and mobile city (Chapter 11,* pp. 179–198*)*. Elsevier. https://doi.org/10.1016/B978-0-443-34174-8.00012-0

Lauter, K., Naehrig, M., & Vaikuntanathan, V. (2021). Can homomorphic encryption be practical? *Communications of the ACM, 64*(4), 98–106. https://doi.org/10.1145/3419614

Li, X., Wang, Y., & Han, J. (2022). Blockchain-enabled decentralized storage for trustworthy data management. *IEEE Internet of Things Journal*, *9*(15), 13541–13553. https://doi.org/10.1109/JIOT.2019.2960526

Li, X., Wang, Y., & Han, J. (2023). Real-time security analytics for hybrid cloud infrastructures. *Future Generation Computer Systems*, *143*, 392–406. https://doi.org/10.1016/j.future.2023.03.004

Liu, Y., Zhang, M., & Luo, X. (2023). AI-driven DevSecOps: Integrating intelligence into cloud security automation. *IEEE Transactions on Cloud Computing*, *11*(3), 1221–1235.

Mahmoud, M. M., Alenezi, M., & Abdallah, M. (2023). Continuous security assurance in distributed cloud architectures. *Future Generation Computer Systems*, *146*, 632–644. https://doi.org/10.1016/j.future.2023.02.013

Menezes, A. J., van Oorschot, P. C., & Vanstone, S. A. (2018). *Handbook of applied cryptography*. CRC Press.

Mishra, A. K., Tiwari, S., Tyagi, A. K., & Arowolo, M. O. (2024). Security, privacy, trust, and provenance issues in Internet of Things–based edge environment. In S. Pal, C. Savaglio, R. Minerva, & F. C. Delicato (Eds.), *IoT edge intelligence* (pp. 233–263). Springer. https://doi.org/10.1007/978-3-031-58388-9_8

Nair, M. M., & Tyagi, A. K. (2021). Privacy: History, statistics, policy, laws, preservation and threat analysis. *Journal of information assurance & security*, *16*(1), 24–34.

Mishra, A. K., Tyagi, A. K., & Tiwari, S. (2025). Blockchain-based smart parking for digital-twin empowered vehicular sensing networks with privacy protection. In T. A. Nguyen (Ed.), *Digital twin, blockchain, and sensor networks in the healthy and mobile city (Chapter 17,* pp. 329–364*)*. Elsevier. https://doi.org/10.1016/B978-0-443-34174-8.00018-1

Nair, M.M., & Tyagi, A.K. (2025). Transformative effects of emerging technologies on Industry 5.0 and Society 5.0: Current status, vision, issues, challenges, and opportunities for future. In: *Next Generation Data Science and Blockchain Technology for Industry 5.0*. Wiley. DOI: https://doi.org/10.1002/9781394245215.ch13, ISBN: 9781394245185.

National Institute of Standards and Technology. (2001). *Advanced encryption standard (FIPS PUB 197)*. https://doi.org/10.6028/NIST.FIPS.197-upd1

National Institute of Standards and Technology. (2015). *Recommendation for key management (NIST SP 800-57)*. https://doi.org/10.6028/NIST.SP.800-57pt3r1

National Institute of Standards and Technology. (2017). *Application container security guide (NIST SP 800-190)*. U.S. Department of Commerce. https://doi.org/10.6028/NIST.SP.800-190

National Institute of Standards and Technology. (2023). *Post-quantum cryptography standardization project*. https://csrc.nist.gov/projects/post-quantum-cryptography

Ongaro, D., & Ousterhout, J. (2014). In search of an understandable consensus algorithm (Raft). In *Proceedings of the USENIX annual technical conference* (pp. *305–319*). USENIX. www.usenix.org/conference/atc14/technical-sessions/presentation/ongaro

Pan, J., Wang, J., Hester, A., Liu, Y., Zhao, Y., & Jain, R. (2018). EdgeChain: An edge-IoT framework and prototype based on blockchain and smart contracts. *IEEE Internet of Things Journal, 6*(3), 4719–4732. https://doi.org/10.1109/JIOT.2018.2878154

Patel, J., & Modi, K. (2022). Security challenges and solutions in hybrid cloud architectures. *International Journal of Information Security Science*, *11*(4), 102–113. https://doi.org/10.25122/jml-2021-0100

Rahman, M., Williams, L., & Hatcliff, J. (2022). Policy-as-code in cloud-native systems: A survey. *IEEE Transactions on Dependable and Secure Computing, 19*(6), 4129–4142.

Rajani, D., Menon, S. C., Kute, S., & Tyagi, A. K. (2022). Preserving privacy of social media data using artificial intelligence techniques. In A. Tyagi (Ed.), *Handbook of Research on Technical, Privacy, and Security Challenges in a Modern World* (pp. 186–204). IGI Global. https://doi.org/10.4018/978-1-6684-5250-9.ch010

Rescorla, E. (2018). *The transport layer security (TLS) protocol version 1.3 (RFC 8446).* IETF. https://doi.org/10.17487/RFC8446

Rose, S., Borchert, O., Mitchell, S., & Connelly, S. (2020). *Zero trust architecture (NIST SP 800-207).* National Institute of Standards and Technology. https://doi.org/10.6028/NIST.SP.800-207

Sabt, M., Achemlal, M., & Bouabdallah, A. (2015). Trusted execution environment: What it is, and what it is not. *IEEE Trustcom/BigDataSE/ISPA,* Vol. 1, 57–64. IEEE. https://doi.org/10.1109/Trustcom.2015.357

Sharma, R., & Gupta, S. (2022). Confidential computing in cloud systems: Trends and challenges. *International Journal of Cloud Applications and Computing, 12*(3), 45–61.

Shi, W., Cao, J., Zhang, Q., Li, Y., & Xu, L. (2016). Edge computing: Vision and challenges. *IEEE Internet of Things Journal, 3*(5), 637–646. https://doi.org/10.1109/JIOT.2016.2579198

Singh, M., Ruj, S., & Nayak, A. (2021). Blockchain as a decentralized PKI system: Architecture, challenges, and applications. *IEEE Communications Surveys & Tutorials, 23*(4), 2456–2481.

Stallings, W. (2017). *Cryptography and network security: Principles and practice* (7th ed.). Pearson.

Subashini, S., & Kavitha, V. (2011). A survey on security issues in service delivery models of cloud computing. *Journal of Network and Computer Applications, 34*(1), 1–11. https://doi.org/10.1016/j.jnca.2010.07.006

Subramanian, N., & Jeyaraj, A. (2023). Cloud security frameworks: Challenges and emerging trends. *Computers & Security, 130,* 103130.

Tyagi, A. K., Kumari, S., & Tiwari, S. (2024c). Internet of Things for smart healthcare: A survey. In A. K. Sharma, N. Chanderwal, S. Tyagi, & P. Upadhyay (Eds.), *Future of AI in medical imaging (Chapter 2, pp. 19–41).* IGI Global. https://doi.org/10.4018/979-8-3693-2359-5.ch002

Tyagi, A. K., & Tiwari, S. (2024a). Blockchain-enabled smart healthcare applications in 6G networks. In A. K. Tyagi (Ed.), *Digital twin and blockchain for smart cities (Chapter 20, pp.* 459–494*).* Wiley. https://doi.org/10.1002/9781394303564.ch20

Tyagi, A.K. (2021). Analysis of security and privacy aspects of blockchain technologies from smart era' perspective: The challenges and a way forward. In: *Recent Trends in Blockchain for Information Systems Security and Privacy* (pp. 1–17). DOI: https://doi.org/10.1201/9781003139737, eBook-ISBN: 9781003139737

Tyagi, A.K. (2025). Blockchain for smart hospital in Healthcare 5.0: modeling structure, challenges, and future emerging trends. In: Human-Centric Integration of Next-Generation Data Science and Blockchain Technology. Elsevier. DOI: https://doi.org/10.1016/B978-0-443-33498-6.00026-1, ISBN: 978-0-443-33498-6.

Tyagi, A.K. (2026). *Chapter 25 - Industry 5.0, Society 5.0, Healthcare 5.0, and Consumer 5.0: current status, vision, issues, challenges, and opportunities for future, in the book: Smart Hospital Anatomy with Advanced Sensors Innovations in Patient Care 2026.* Elsevier (pp. 371–386). https://doi.org/10.1016/B978-0-443-45875-0.00002-8, ISBN: 978-0-443-45875-0.

Tyagi, A. K., Tripathi, K., Tiwari, S., & Kaushik, S. (2025). An efficient technique for privacy preservation, trusted and secure patient-centric services in smart healthcare. In *Proceedings of the 6th international conference on recent trends in communication & intelligent systems (ICRTCIS 2025)* (pp. 31–47). IET. https://doi.org/10.1049/icp.2025.2731

Wang, H., & Wu, J. (2021). Data integrity and provenance verification in cloud environments: A survey. *IEEE Access, 9,* 119847–119861.

Wang, H., Zhao, L., & Wu, J. (2023). Secure data replication and consistency in distributed cloud storage. *IEEE Transactions on Cloud Computing, 11*(2), 418–430. https://doi.org/10.1109/ACCESS.2021.3109141

Yin, J., Zhang, T., & Lin, Y. (2024). Privacy-preserving federated learning: Trends, threats, and solutions. *ACM Transactions on Privacy and Security, 27*(1), 1–27.

Zhao, L., Wang, F., & Chen, X. (2023). Blockchain-based metadata management for cloud data provenance. *Future Internet, 15*(1), 25. https://doi.org/10.3390/fi15010025

Zhou, H., Chen, L., & Xu, Y. (2023). Secure edge computing: Lightweight cryptography and trusted attestation mechanisms. *IEEE Internet Computing, 27*(3), 56–65.

Zhou, Y., & Piramuthu, S. (2022). Security in multi-tenant cloud environments: A zero-trust perspective. *IEEE Transactions on Services Computing, 15*(2), 845–858.

7 Privacy-Preserving Data Processing and Sharing

7.1 INTRODUCTION

The rapid expansion of digital healthcare data has transformed modern medicine by enabling precise diagnostics, personalized treatments, and data-driven decision-making and provided the opportunity to perform precise diagnostics, tailor treatments, and make decisions based on the data. Nonetheless, a massive access to sensitive patient data brings with it significant privacy and security concerns as well. Personally identifiable information (PII) contained in medical records, genomic data, and wearable device streams is vulnerable to breaches, discrimination, or loss of trust in the community unless handled appropriately. Striking the right balance between the desire to share data in research and the responsibility to maintain patients' privacy has become a critical concern for policymakers, research institutions, and data scientists.

Privacy-preserving data processing and sharing are methods of data analysis, data modeling, and data sharing, in which the data can be analyzed, modeled, or shared without exposing the raw underlying information. They include anonymization, data minimization, differential privacy (DP), federated learning (FL), and cryptographic methods like secure multi-party computation and homomorphic encryption (HE). As a combination, they can help to shift the paradigm of the conventional data centralization to distributed and privacy-conscious analytics—which is a crucial step to being in compliance with the legal regulations, like the Health Insurance Portability and Accountability Act (HIPAA) and the General Data Protection Regulation (GDPR).

Figure 7.1 illustrates a multi-layer architecture designed for the secure management of sensitive healthcare data. The first stage, data collection, involves gathering raw information from multiple clinical and digital sources. The data gathered is channeled upward by a number of special security and processing layers. The initial significant step is the privacy layer in which the data are subjected to methods like anonymization and differential privacy to make the personal identifiers unreadable but still useful in analysis. After this, the data are passed through the Encryption layer that uses sophisticated algorithms such as HE and Secure Multi-Party Computation (SMPC). This ensures strong protection because the data remain encrypted throughout computation. Out of encryption, the data that have been safely processed are sent to the sharing layer that assists in providing secure data exchange with other authorized parties. Lastly, the data are sent to the analytics layer at the top where the confidential computing and insight generation are carried out. In the whole structure, the upward arrows represent a safe and regulated circulation of information, which guarantees the preservation of privacy at each stage of initial data gathering, up to the final insights production.

Privacy-preserving frameworks in the healthcare environment do not only improve the issue of regulatory compliance but also support the ethical standards of medical research. Institutions have been switching to complex algorithms that provide privacy on a patient level, as well as data utility to

DOI: 10.1201/9781003658344-9

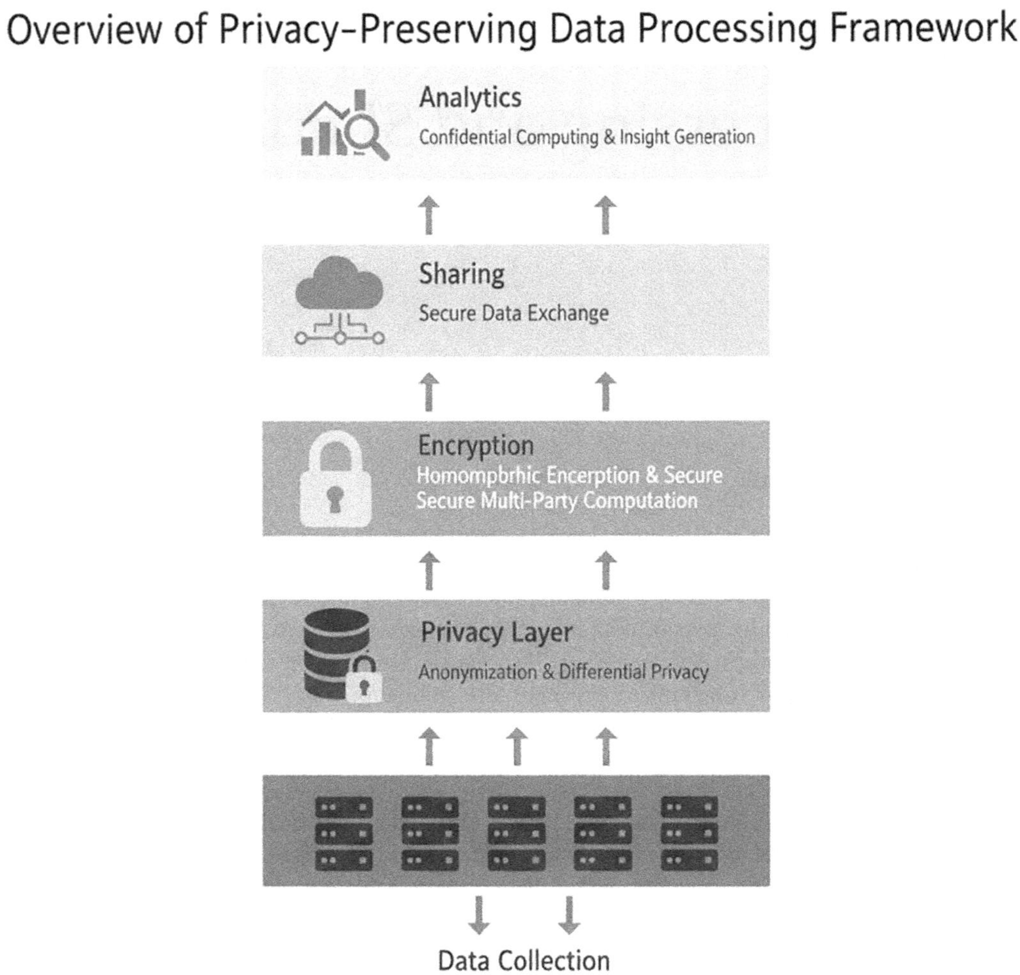

FIGURE 7.1 Summary of privacy-preserving data processing and sharing model.

provide AI-driven insights. This chapter focuses on the principles, procedures, and uses of privacy-sensitive data processing and highlights the actual practice and directions in healthcare systems.

These sections are organized and structured to discuss in detail—starting by reviewing the literature that exists in the field, then discussing the principles of anonymization, privacy models, cryptographic techniques, and finally synthetic data generation (SDG). Subsequent sections discuss risk mitigation, utility of data trade-offs, and practice in healthcare analytics.

7.2 LITERATURE REVIEW

The increasing rate of data-heavy technologies has increased the conflict between innovation and privacy, especially in healthcare and biomedical research. Traditional data-sharing methods such as centralized repositories or masking and aggregation are no longer sufficient to prevent re-identification attacks. The current literature demonstrates a shift to computationally based privacy-preserving models which combine cryptographic, statistical, and machine learning algorithms to attain security without an impediment on analytical utility. Table 7.1 summarizes recent frameworks that attempt to balance privacy and data utility.

TABLE 7.1
Overview of Recent Studies on Privacy-Preservation in Data Processing and Healthcare Data Sharing (2018–2025)

Author and Year	Methodology	Domain	Technique Used	Key Contribution	Limitation
Sharma and Mittal (2024)	Experimental	Healthcare IoT	K-anonymity	Better patient data masking	Accuracy reduction
Li and Chen (2020)	Simulation	Cloud Computing	Differential privacy	Preserved statistical integrity	High cost of computation
Bagdasaryan and Shmatikov (2021)	Federated Analysis	EHR	Federated learning	Secure cross-institutional training	Network latency
Zhang et al. (2023)	Prototype	Smart Cities	Homomorphic encryption	Improved confidence in multi-party analytics	Slow computation
Kumari et al. (2025a)	Framework Design	AI Data Pipelines	Blockchain-based access control	Tamper-proof data validation	High storage overhead

7.2.1 Historical Development of Paradigm of Privacy Preservation

Modern privacy-preserving computation is based on the concepts behind the DP and SMPC. Dwork and Roth (2021) refined DP into a mathematical model that guarantees that the contribution of a specific person in a dataset cannot be determined by the aggregate results, thus establishing the quantifiable privacy assurance. Generalizations of this principle to deep learning (Abadi et al., 2021; Nair et al., 2025) and exponential mechanism (Cummings and Sarwate, 2020; Kumari et al., 2025a) have been shown to be highly resistant to inference-based privacy attacks. Similarly, SMPC allows multiple parties to calculate joint functions on encrypted data without sharing their inputs, which is finding more and more uses in distributed healthcare systems (Xie and Xu, 2021; Das and Ahmed, 2023; Tyagi, 2021).

7.2.2 Privacy Differentiated and Healthcare Data Sharing

DP has emerged as a leading paradigm for healthcare data protection. Arora and Sharma (2022) suggested the application of DP-based mechanisms to protect clinical analytics, and Tian and Zhang (2022) also provided its example in generating synthetic electronic health records (EHRs) to secure data sharing. The DP frameworks allow the privacy–utility trade-off to be controlled quantitatively so that medical researchers can adjust privacy parameters to particular regulatory or ethical settings. However, the noise added for privacy can reduce data quality, highlighting the need for adaptive methods that balance privacy with analytical accuracy (Kim et al., 2023; Kumari et al., 2025b).

7.2.3 Distributed Privacy and FL

A major development in data privacy is FL, which trains models locally on distributed devices and aggregates their updates without centralizing data (Kairouz et al., 2021; Mishra et al., 2024). Rieke et al. (2020) emphasized the potential of FL in the healthcare system, through which a hospital can jointly train diagnostic models without violating patient privacy. Gao et al. (2021) have given an extensive review that underlines the scalability and interoperability of FL in clinical settings. Nevertheless, there are still difficulties: there is still a threat of model inversion and gradient leakage attacks that jeopardize data confidentiality (Lyu et al., 2022). To alleviate them, scholars have pursued the concept of embedding DP and HE in the FL processes (Geyer et al., 2020; Bagdasaryan and Shmatikov, 2021).

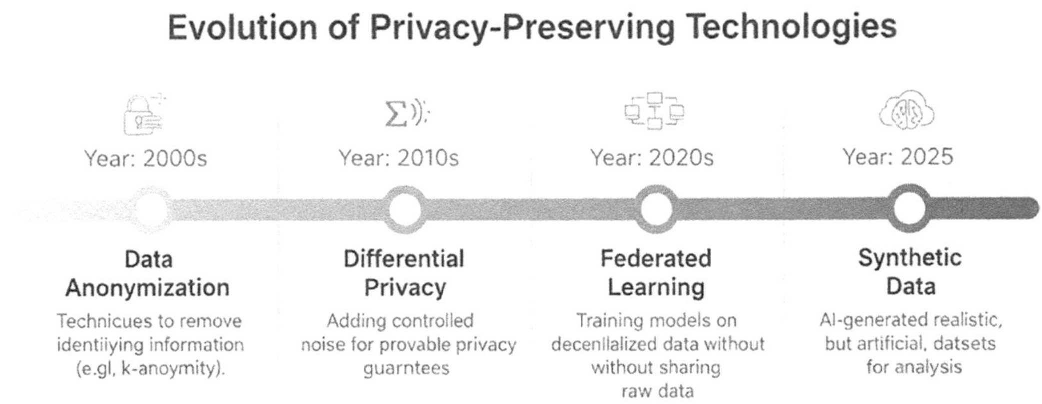

FIGURE 7.2 Over time, privacy-preserving technologies of data processing have developed.

Figure 7.2 illustrates the progression of privacy-preserving technologies from the early 2000s to 2025, highlighting their increasing sophistication. The first major strategy with the sole aim of removing or distorting direct personal identifiers to prevent re-identification was data anonymization that started its path in the 2000s. The field has continued to develop and the development of differential privacy in the 2010s. This was a transition to a mathematically strict model, ensuring that no contribution to data can be identified by any single individual to the combined output, which gives a significantly stronger and enforceable privacy barrier. FL, an approach to privacy-preserving learning by design, emerged in the 2020s, which does not have to store data in a single location, but models are sent to train on decentralized sources and only sends non-sensitive model updates to the cloud. Proceeding to the year 2025, the development will reach the stage of SDG. This technique generates fully synthetic datasets that retain the statistical patterns of real data without containing any actual patient information. This advancement is an indication of an ongoing tradition of stronger, mathematically provable, and design-based privacy solutions.

7.2.4 Cryptography HE and Secure Computation

Privacy-preserving computation has been given a solid cryptographic foundation with the integration of HE and healthcare analytics. HE permits the computation on encrypted data, such that calculations are not decrypted (Gentry, 2020; Tyagi, 2025). Li et al. (2020) showed the ability of HE to promote safe sharing of EHRs, and Sharma and Mittal (2024) used HE in relation to cloud-based medical inference systems. In the same way, SMPC protocols have evolved to privacy-preserving health data aggregation scalable architecture (Das and Ahmed, 2023; Tyagi and Tiwari, 2024a). All of these approaches create a privacy-first infrastructure which is consistent with international data protection standards like HIPAA and GDPR (Nguyen et al., 2021; Balamurugan et al., 2023).

7.2.5 Generative Data via Synthetic Data and Statistical Privacy

SDG has emerged as a complementary alternative to encryption-based methods. Unlike anonymization, which modifies existing data, synthetic data replicate the statistical properties of real datasets without exposing actual patient records (Hale and Boucher, 2021). Bhattacharya and Raskar (2023) investigated the application of generative adversarial networks (GANs) to generate realistic medical images, whereas Choudhury et al. (2022) investigated the application of differentially private SDG to healthcare analytics. El Emam et al. (2022) assessed the level of risks in re-identification in synthetic data and concluded that under the condition that strict privacy models are applied, such datasets can substantially decrease the disclosure risks. In addition, Zhao et al. (2024) highlighted the opportunities of generative models in the privacy and utility balance in the world of digital health.

7.2.6 Privacy-Preserving Machine Learning

Privacy-preserving machine learning (PPML) refers to techniques that enable model training while protecting sensitive data. Cryptographic methods have been integrated with machine learning to create PPML, enabling AI models to learn from sensitive data without directly accessing it. Survey of PPML methods was performed by Al-Rubaie and Chang (2021), and the three main protection strategies outlined include HE, DP, and federated aggregation. Liu and Zhang (2024) have shown that federated transfer learning can be used to carry out clinical prediction tasks, which have to be cross-institutional and secure. On the same lines, Nair and Rajan (2023) incorporated the concept of ethics into PPML models, with a particular focus on the ideas of fairness, accountability, and adherence to the regulations of healthcare privacy.

7.2.7 B2B Blockchain, Ethics, and Governance

Blockchain technologies serve as an additional privacy-supporting mechanism by providing immutable audit trails and decentralized trust (Nguyen et al., 2021; Han et al., 2024; Tyagi et al., 2024c). With the combination of blockchain and the privacy-preserving AI, the data provenance and consent tracking may be applied in a transparent way. Ethical scholarship stipulates the significance of integrating technical and governance-based practices. Geis et al. (2022) provided that ethical data governance in AI-driven radiology should be based on finding equilibrium between innovation and patient autonomy. Thakkar and Sun (2023) and Nair and Rajan (2023) also added to this argument, suggesting that privacy-enhancement technologies should comply with societal values and regulatory compliance frameworks to provide equitable digital health innovation.

7.2.8 Trade-Off between Privacy and Utility

Recent literature emphasizes that privacy and data utility should be aligned rather than treated as opposing goals. Kim et al. (2023) proposed an adaptive anonymization model in which privacy levels adjust automatically to preserve data utility. Bhattacharya and Raskar (2023) have shown that pseudo-data produced by privacy-conscious GANs is able to hold the accuracy of predictive models at 95% of real data thresholds. On the same note, Thakkar and Sun (2023) emphasized multi-objective optimization methods that balance the privacy, fairness, and performance in AI systems. These findings show that privacy-preserving computation is now a central design requirement in data-driven healthcare innovation, rather than a peripheral concern.

7.2.9 Summary of Literature Gaps

Although great improvements have been made, gaps in the literature have still been observed. Despite the promise of FL and synthetic data, real-world adoption remains limited by interoperability and standardization challenges. Second, privacy-preserving algorithms tend to have computational overheads, thus making it challenging to scale in large hospital networks (Lyu et al., 2022; Tyagi et al., 2025). Third, legal and regulatory provisions are still fractured, and it is important to have uniform privacy-by-design provisions across jurisdictions (Geis et al., 2022; Han et al., 2024; Rajani et al., 2022). These limitations are key factors to overcome the next-generation healthcare ecosystems which must be intelligent, secure, and ethically based concurrently.

7.3 DATA ANONYMIZATION AND MINIMIZATION PRINCIPLE

Privacy-preserving data processing relies on the ethical and technical principles of data anonymization and minimization. With the growing use of healthcare systems based on large and sophisticated datasets, these principles will guarantee that personal data are utilized in a responsible, proportionate, and lawful manner in line with international data protection laws (GDPR and HIPAA). Beyond removing identifiers, these principles require designing data collection and processing to reduce misuse, prevent unauthorized re-identification, and maintain analytical value (Nguyen et al., 2021; Kim et al., 2023; Nair et al., 2021).

7.3.1 The Concept and Significance of Anonymization

Anonymization involves transforming data so individuals cannot be identified, either directly or through combinations of attributes. This change entails eliminating or modifying PII, including names, contact information, or distinct patient identifiers without distorting structural patterns that can be analyzed (El Emam et al., 2022). Considering the role of anonymization in healthcare, exchanging EHRs across institutions and research initiatives could not be performed without violating patient confidentiality (Li et al., 2020). However, anonymization is not foolproof; re-identification may occur when anonymized data are linked with external datasets (Tian and Zhang, 2022). Modern methods therefore use mathematics privacy models such as K-anonymity, l-diversity, and t-closeness to measure the level of anonymity and restrict the inference risk. Table 7.2 summarizes anonymization methods and their effects on data utility

7.3.2 The Principles of Data Minimization

Data minimization is an extension of anonymization in that it recommends that the data required to achieve a specific purpose must be gathered, processed, or stored to the bare minimum extent. This principle is formalized in the GDPR Article 5(1)(c) which focuses on the limitation of purposes and proportionality. In healthcare analytics, this is converted into gathering little, but meaningful patient information—age, scale, or type of symptoms rather than specific identifiers (Cao et al., 2020). Minimization can also be applied on the time-related and contextual level, making sure that data are not kept longer than the required data analysis lifecycle. Studies conducted by Nair and Rajan (2023) reveal that the lack of data during data collection contributes to a substantial decrease in the exposure surface in case of a cyberattack and also enhance trust in medical AI systems in the society. Besides, privacy-by-design architectures instill the principles of minimization into the policies at the system level, minimizing legal risks and computational overheads (Nguyen et al., 2021).

Figure 7.3 succinctly details the process of steps a dataset goes through, to be safely anonymized to be released or shared. Raw data collection is the first stage in which the first step is taken to collect

TABLE 7.2
Comparison of Anonymization Methods and Their Impact on Utility of Data

Technique	Description	Privacy Level	Utility Retention	Example Use Case
Generalization	Substitute certain values with larger categories	Medium	High	Age band grouping
Suppression	Removing identifiers entirely	High	Medium	Rare disease records
Anonymization	Replacing identifiers with arbitrary or random characters.	High	Low	Anonymity
Pseudonymization	Use identifiers with regular codes	Medium	High	Clinical records
Sampling	It is based on subsets of data	Medium	High	Research datasets

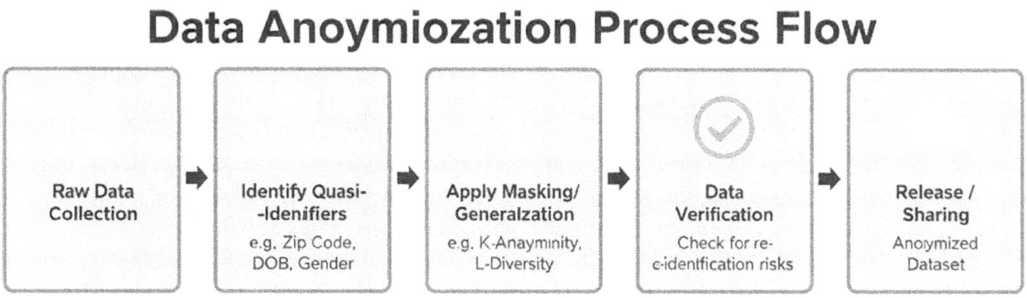

FIGURE 7.3 Data anonymization and minimalization process flow.

the sensitive information. The second step is identifying quasi-identifiers as even after removing direct identifiers (such as names or social security numbers), there are attributes such as age, ZIP code, or gender that, along with other attributes, might be used to identify an individual uniquely. Upon identification, the information is transferred to the apply masking/generalization step whereby technical manipulations are done on the quasi-identifiers. The techniques include (but are not limited to) generalization (e.g., the substitution of specific ages with age intervals) or suppression (e.g., eliminating infrequent values). After applying these privacy methods, the data are verified. This verification checks whether the anonymized data satisfy models such as k-anonymity or l-diversity, to make sure that the privacy conditions are satisfied and that the re-identification risk has a sufficiently low value. When the data meet the check, they go to the last stage of release/sharing, where the anonymized data access is availed to other analysts without revealing the privacy of the people they relate to.

7.3.3 Techniques and Strategies of Anonymization

Anonymization strategies include masking, perturbation, generalization, and synthetic substitution. Masking eliminates identifiers and generalization and suppression diminish the data granularity to avoid linkage attacks. Indicatively, one can substitute certain dates with months and years, or specific ages with ranges (El Emam et al., 2022). Controlled noise is introduced to guarantee statistical privacy by perturbation methods, such as DP (Dwork and Roth, 2021). Recent research, including Arora and Sharma (2022) and Choudhury et al. (2022), suggests hybrid solutions, where statistical anonymization is used, and synthetic data are generated so as not to lose privacy or data realism. Synthetic data creation using GAN-based frameworks produces realistic and analytically valid datasets, guaranteeing trained and analytically valid anonymized datasets that can be used in medical AI applications (Bhattacharya and Raskar, 2023).

7.3.4 Trade-Off Between Privacy and Data Utility

The privacy versus data utility trade-off is one of the main issues that are left at the core of anonymization studies. Excessive anonymization can degrade data quality to the point where it becomes unsuitable for machine learning and statistical analysis (Kim et al., 2023). On the other hand, the lack of anonymization increases the chance of re-identification (El Emam et al., 2022). Context-adaptive anonymization systems adjust privacy levels dynamically based on data sensitivity and intended use (Thakkar and Sun, 2023). As an example, FL and differentially private synthetic data are typically used by healthcare researchers to maintain the performance of the models and yet keep the compliances with legal and ethical regulations (Rieke et al., 2020; Kairouz et al., 2021). These adaptive models depict the consistency of data protection and utility that can be achieved on privacy-conscious computational design.

7.3.5 Ethical and Regulatory Alignment

Technical compliance alone does not ensure ethical data processing; it must be accompanied by respect for patient autonomy and informed consent. Geis et al. (2022) highlight that ethical AI in healthcare must promote transparency, accountability, and explainability in dealing with the data. Aligning anonymization and minimization with governance frameworks, including GDPR, HIPAA, and ISO/IEC 27701, connects them, makes them legally defensible, and strengthens public trust. In addition, consent and access compliance, which are demonstrated in blockchain-based systems, have immutable audit trails, which ensure both ethical and regulatory integrity (Han et al., 2024). The combination of cryptographic and privacy-by-design design processes, as well as ethical controls that are empowered, all characterize the new paradigm of privacy-preserving infrastructures in digital health.

Privacy-preserving data processing is based on data anonymization and data minimization, and this is especially applicable in the healthcare system as the data are highly sensitive. This combination of traditional anonymization methods, advanced cryptographic techniques, and adaptive privacy measures allows the responsible use of data and helps an individual avoid the risk of privacy violation. With the changes in regulatory and ethical requirements, integrating these values into the AI-driven data ecosystems will become important to balance the three elements of innovation, accountability, and trust.

7.4 FEDERATED TECHNIQUES, K-ANONYMITY, AND DP

Privacy-preserving computation relies on theoretical and practical models designed to control data disclosure while preserving analytical utility. Of them, K-anonymity, DP, and FL have become the staple of privacy engineering. These methods address the limitations of traditional anonymization approaches, which are often too simplistic to defend against modern re-identification attacks. Having been integrated into healthcare analytics, privacy has become a programmable and verifiable feature, as opposed to a post-hoc adjustment.

7.4.1 K-Anonymity and Its Extensions

One of the oldest and the most common privacy-preserving models is K-anonymity. It guarantees that a record in a dataset can be similar to at least K-1 other records in terms of a collection of quasi-identifiers including age, gender, or ZIP code (El Emam et al., 2022). K-anonymity is commonly used in patient demographics and clinical characteristics in healthcare data processing prior to external data disclosure to avoid linkage attacks. However, K-anonymity is insufficient to prevent attribute disclosure, where an adversary can infer sensitive attributes shared by a group. To overcome this, l-diversity and t-closeness were added as extensions which maintain variability and distributional proximity of sensitive attributes. Although these models are still applicable, they cannot process high-dimensional and temporal datasets that are typical of the new healthcare purpose (Cao et al., 2020). Consequently, researchers increasingly integrate K-anonymity with probabilistic and cryptographic techniques to strengthen re-identification resistance (Kim et al., 2023). Table 7.3 shows a simple sample of K-anonymity implementation in a healthcare dataset.

TABLE 7.3
K-anonymity on a Healthcare Dataset

Quasi Identifier	Original Value	Generalized Value	Anonymized Group
Age	27	20–30	Group A
ZIP Code	12345	123**	Group A
Gender	Male	Male	Group A
Diagnosis	Flu	Flu	Group A

Mathematically, a dataset is K-anonymous when every combination of quasi-identifiers appears in at least k records. The bigger the value of k, the higher the anonymity but the more the information is lost.

This can be expressed as follows in Equation (7.1):

$$K - \text{Anonymity} : \forall q_i \in Q, \text{Count}\left(q_i\right) \geq k \quad (7.1)$$

K-anonymity is especially applicable in the healthcare sector to public health data, shared in research institutions. Nonetheless, it is susceptible to homogeneity and background knowledge attacks, which resulted in the emergence of better models such as l-diversity and t-closeness. These refinements help ensure structural anonymity and maintain diversity among sensitive attribute values.

Figure 7.4 contains the direct comparison between a dataset with and without the implementation of the k-anonymity privacy model—a popular tool that is developed to ensure that a specific person is not re-identified in the course of sharing data.

Prior to Anonymization (Raw Data): Table at the left illustrates the raw dataset, the direct and quasi-identifiers (Name and Age and ZIP code), both of which are attributed to a sensitive variable (Disease). When presented in this vulnerable state, the dataset poses a high privacy risk. As an example, it is possible to trace a person in the age of 28 years who lives in ZIP code 60001 and be identified as a unique person, thus, directly connected to a certain disease record. This direct correlation shows the ease with which an attacker is likely to re-identify people in the data using external information.

Post-Anonymization (K-Anonymized Data): The table on the right illustrates the dataset after the use of k-anonymity, where k is the smallest possible number of records having the same

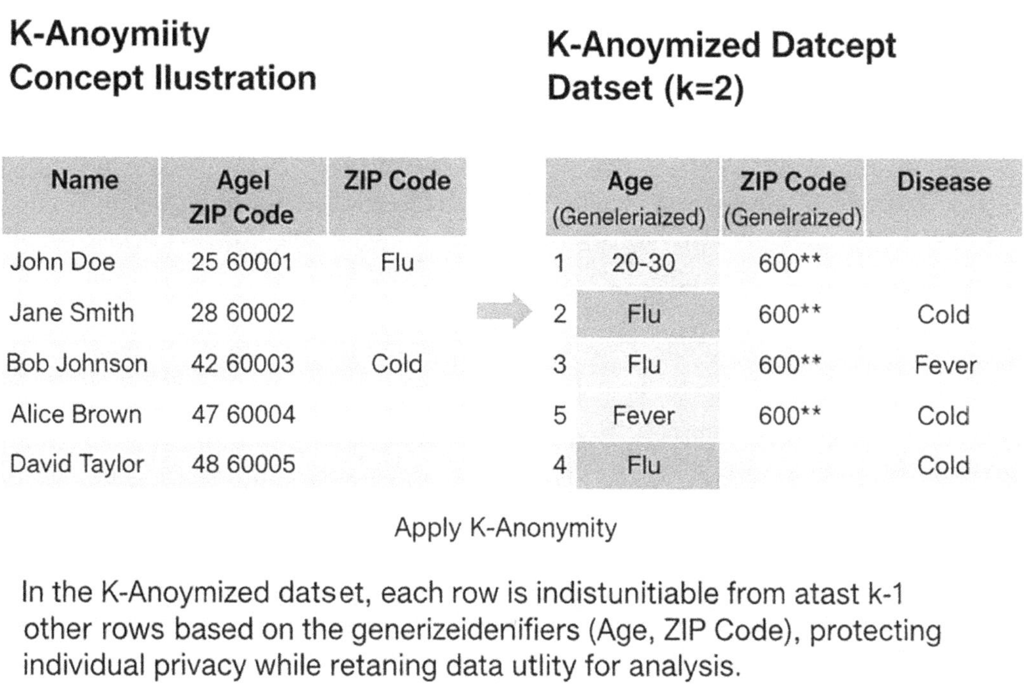

FIGURE 7.4 Examples of k-anonymity grouping of tabular health data.

quasi-identifiers. In this example, $k = 3$, whereby the combinations of quasi-identifiers are made to appear at least three times. The process of change entails:

- *Suppression:* This is removing the direct identifiers (e.g., Name column is deleted).
- *Generalization:* Transformation of certain quasi-identifiers into more general ones. Ages are divided into a range (e.g., 20–30, 40–50), and ZIP codes are cut off (e.g., 600***).

This grouping makes sure that all those with the same generalized values (e.g., Age 20-–30, ZIP 600***) cannot be discriminated in that sub-set and thus in a k-anonymous group. This means that when an attacker has known the approximate age and ZIP code of someone, they can only identify a few k people and not just one individual, thus safeguarding sensitive information of the individuals.

Figure 7.4 shows a visual representation of the message that k-anonymity boosts the level of privacy by minimizing the chances of revealing an identity when clustering. It, however, also points out a well-known weakness that when everything in a set has this sensitive attribute (e.g. everybody has the same disease), the model can still be susceptible to attribute disclosure, meaning that it requires to be complemented by other methods like l-diversity or t-closeness to ensure even greater protection.

7.4.2 DP Mathematical Foundations and Applications

DP is a probabilistic assertion that the inclusion or omission of the data of a person does not greatly influence the results of analysis (Dwork and Roth, 2021). The model adds random noise to queries of the data or model parameters with fix parameters, which in effect hides each of the contributions. DP has been used in healthcare in the context of medical image classification, epidemiology modeling, and clinical research data (Arora and Sharma, 2022; Tian and Zhang, 2022). As an example, the PATE-GAN framework by Jordon et al. (2021) employs teacher student architectures together with DP to produce synthetic medical information, with privacy guarantees. Abadi et al. (2021) applied the concept of DP to the deep learning systems, which demonstrated that the ability to train privacy-preserving models can reach the accuracy of nearly standard models on tricky data. These advancements mean that it is not only protecting data, but also compliant with the data protection laws because it offers privacy metrics that can be measured.

However, the greatest problem with DP is how to trade-off between loss of privacy (e) and utility of data. A lot of noise can impair the performance of a model, whereas low noise can predispose to more privacy (Cummings and Sarwate, 2020). The adaptive DP has been suggested to dynamically optimize this trade-off, especially in the medical field that is sensitive (Kim et al., 2023).

In formal terms, given two neighboring data sets D_1 and D_2 whose difference is one record, a randomized algorithm MMM is e-differentiating private given that:

$$P\left[M\left(D_1\right) \in S\right] \leq e^{\epsilon} \times P\left[M\left(D_2\right) \in S\right]$$

of any subsets S of possible outputs.

The DP has been successfully included in healthcare analytics to obtain privacy-preserving statistics, disease surveillance, and train models. As one example, DP-based algorithms have already been implemented to distribute COVID-19 patient data between countries without revealing any identifiable characteristics.

7.4.3 FL as a Privacy Mechanism

FL transforms privacy preservation by changing the paradigm of sharing data to sharing models. Each institution is trained on its own data and instead of the raw data being sent to a central server, model parameters or gradients are shared with an aggregator (Kairouz et al., 2021). This decentralized system reduces exposure of data and avoids threats of breaches in the process of transmission or storage. Medical FL can be used in healthcare to train predictive models by multiple hospitals or medical diagnostics to work together on diagnosis of diseases, risk assessment, and medical imaging (Rieke et al., 2020; Gao et al., 2021).

However, FL is not also vulnerable to privacy risks. Shared gradients may give attackers insights about private data, a phenomenon called model inversion, or gradient leakage (Lyu et al., 2022). In response, the sophisticated FL models incorporate gradient information protection with the help of either DP or SMPC) (Geyer et al., 2020; Bagdasaryan and Shmatikov, 2021). A combination of these methods enhances U.S. local and global privacy rights under the assurance that heavy healthcare information is kept safely within the institutional framework. Table 7.4 presents comparison of federated, centralized, and decentralized learning approaches.

Figure 7.5 illustrates the core principle of DP-saving method, which underlines the natural trade-off between accuracy of the information and the privacy of the people. It is represented in a bar chart format and compares the True Counts and the Noisy Counts. The former represents the original,

TABLE 7.4
Comparison of Federated, Centralized, and Decentralized Learning Strategies

Parameter	Centralized	Federated	Decentralized
Data Storage	Server based	Local nodes	Distributed peers
Communication	High	Moderate	Peer-to-peer
Privacy Risk	High	Low	Very low
Model Accuracy	High	Moderate	Variable

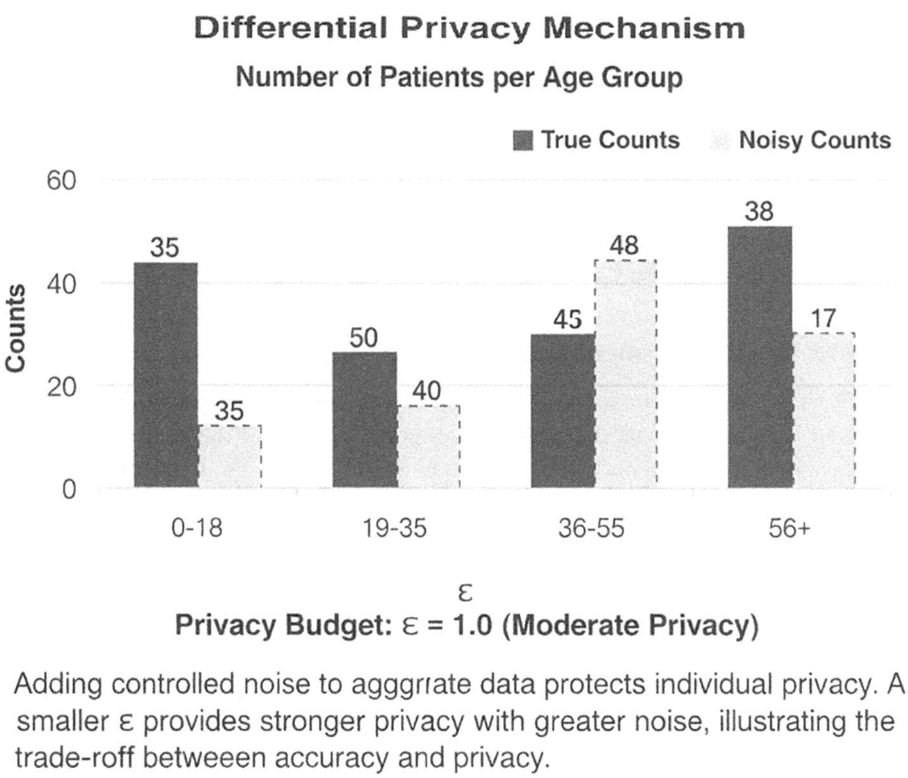

FIGURE 7.5 Impact of added noise under two different privacy query outputs.

sensitive data, whereas the latter represents the privacy-protected values that are published publicly. The True Counts (illustrated by solid darker bars) are the actual number of people in the certain categories, for example the number of patients in a certain age range (e.g. 20–30, 31–40). Publication of these actual values without alteration would put individuals at the risk of re-identification as an attacker could infer whether a specific individual is present or absent in the dataset.

To address this risk, DP adds a measured statistical noise to the data using a randomization process. The obtained noisy counts (represented by the bars that are lighter or patterned) are slightly different than the original values but maintain the general statistical trends of the dataset. This will guarantee reliability of aggregate analyses and ensure privacy of individual contributors. The process ensures the result is almost the same whether or not the data of a particular individual is present, hence offering an excellent mathematical guarantee of privacy.

Figure 7.5 also illustrates the position of the privacy budget (e), which is represented by the Greek character epsilon, which is the amount of privacy protection. The smaller e (near 0) means that an additional noise is introduced, which results in a stronger privacy but lower accuracy of data because the noisy counts are further apart than the true counts. On the other hand, with a larger e, there is lower noise which results in higher accuracy but reduced privacy. This visualization clarifies the fundamental trade-off in DP between data utility and the strength of individual privacy protection.

7.4.4 Differentiating Between FL and DP

A major direction in privacy-preserving analytics is the integration of DP with FL. With the incorporation of DP at the client level, the model update can be perturbed prior to the aggregation process, and the individual records cannot be deduced even based on the gradient information (Abadi et al., 2021). This mixed strategy is especially useful in the situation of multi-institutional healthcare networks, where the volume of patient records can vary in volume, sensitivity, and regulatory restraint. AlShemmari and Chatterjee (2023) showed that this integration is effective in federated medical systems, as it provides good privacy assurances with a high level of diagnostic accuracy. These findings were extended in the study of Liu and Zhang (2024) with the help of federated transfer learning, which enables sharing of parts of the model between special hospitals to assist in personalized medicine without any loss to data locality.

Despite these benefits, integration challenges remain, particularly regarding communication overhead, noise calibration, and model convergence stability (Kairouz et al., 2021). Still current efforts are involved to reduce these problems by optimal aggregation algorithms and adaptive privacy budgets that ensure privacy and performance (Thakkar and Sun, 2023).

7.4.5 Comparative Assessment and Healthcare Applicability

Comparatively, K-anonymity is easy to interpret and use, but it is not robust when dealing with large datasets or high dimensional datasets. DP is a protection that is mathematically measurable, although it may affect the model accuracy based on noise calibration. FL, in its turn, implements the privacy as decentralized data and allows collaborative analytics. The combination of the techniques in healthcare provides both theoretical and practical feasibility (Rieke et al., 2020; Gao et al., 2021). This joint application of K-anonymity to de-identify the initial phases, DP to mask the statistics, and FL to compute the results in a distributed manner forms the multi-layered defense framework that is applicable to the modern data ecosystem.

In addition, the techniques are in line with regulatory requirements of privacy-by-design and patient consent management (Nguyen et al., 2021; Han et al., 2024). With the further development of AI-based medical systems, the addition of K-anonymity, DP, and FL frameworks is becoming the key to scalable, secure, and ethically responsible healthcare innovation.

K-anonymity, DP, and FL serve as complementary privacy-preserving strategies. Although both sides of the problem have their own advantages and disadvantages, a hybrid method can provide a middle ground in preserving sensitive data and making the best use of analytic opportunities. Further development of hybrid privacy structures and deeply adaptive federated designs is an important milestone toward sustainable and compliant data sharing in healthcare.

7.5 HE AND SECURE MULTIPARTY COMPUTATION

The rapid expansion of digital health ecosystems has heightened the need for privacy-preserving computation techniques to facilitate collaborative research and analytics without affecting patient confidentiality. HE and SMPC are among the largest contributions in this area as these two cryptographic methods allow computations to be performed directly on encrypted data while ensuring that the underlying information remains inaccessible to unauthorized parties. These technologies are particularly important in multi-institutional healthcare collaborations (clinical trials, genomic research, and distributed disease models), in which raw medical information exchanged among institutions poses significant privacy and regulatory risks. SMPC and HE can be combined as complementary techniques for privacy-preserving analytics as they can be used to perform distributed computation with multiple parties or perform direct encrypted computation on cloud infrastructures.

SMPC enables two or more parties to execute a computation on their aggregated data and, at the same time, none of the individual data inputs are disclosed. Local control of data remains with each participating institution which transform the data into encrypted or secret-shared fragments which are only exchanged in processed form. The findings are then summed up to yield the final product without any one party getting hold of the raw information of another. It is due to this mechanism that SMPC is very appropriate in any healthcare context like cross-hospital outcome analysis or joint medical research. As an example, when hospitals research the cardiovascular disease, they can compute aggregate statistics such as average recovery rates without ever having to exchange records at the patient level. Under such models, data confidentiality is ensured using common cryptographic techniques, including additive secret sharing, garbled circuits, and oblivious transfer.

7.5.1 HE: Encrypted Data Computation

While SMPC distributes trust among multiple participants, HE keeps data encrypted throughout the computation process. In HE, mathematical operations like addition or multiplication may be directly applied to ciphertexts and when decrypted the resulting value is equal to the value of the same operations applied on the plaintext values. Third-party cloud platforms are able to process sensitive healthcare data using this property without having access to the actual contents of the property. There are three major types of HE schemes: Partially Homomorphic Encryption (PHE) supports one operation (such as addition (Paillier) or multiplication (RSA)); Somewhat Homomorphic Encryption (SHE) supports a small number of both; and Fully Homomorphic Encryption (FHE) supports a large number of operations, but incurs substantial computational overhead. PHE and SHE are typically applied to simple applications (encrypted billing aggregation or limited EHR analytics) unlike FHE, which is used in more sophisticated applications (cloud-based AI model training on encrypted data). Table 7.5 summarizes the characteristics of different HE schemes.

TABLE 7.5
Homomorphic Encryption Types and the Characteristics of Computation

Scheme	Type of Operation	Computation Speed	Encryption Strength	Usual Application
Partial HE	Additive only	Fast	Moderate	Aggregate sums
To some degree HE	Additive and multiplicative (limited)	Moderate	High	Small models
Fully HE	All operations	Slow	Very high	Medical analytics

7.5.2 SMPC and HE Have Been Integrated into Healthcare Systems

Current privacy-safe structures tend to combine SMPC and HE to provide end-to-end protection. In such hybrid systems, SMPC ensures that there is no exposure of the local datasets during collaborative computation and HE will ensure that the intermediate and final results are encrypted during transmission and processing. This is the design that is more commonly being adopted in FL systems, whereby distributed hospitals or laboratories together train global AI models without centrally storing data. In a multi-hospital cardiac risk prediction study, as an example, every institution calculates encrypted gradient updates with the help of HE, and then aggregates them safely through SMPC protocols. The world model is re-updated without any disclosure of the record of a particular patient, therefore meeting both the GDPR and HIPAA requirements.

Figure 7.6 illustrates how multiple independent parties can jointly compute a function on their multiple private data and keep their respective inputs secret. It will consist of a few major elements: the Participant Nodes (Hospital A, Hospital B, and Institution C) and the Central Computation Server.

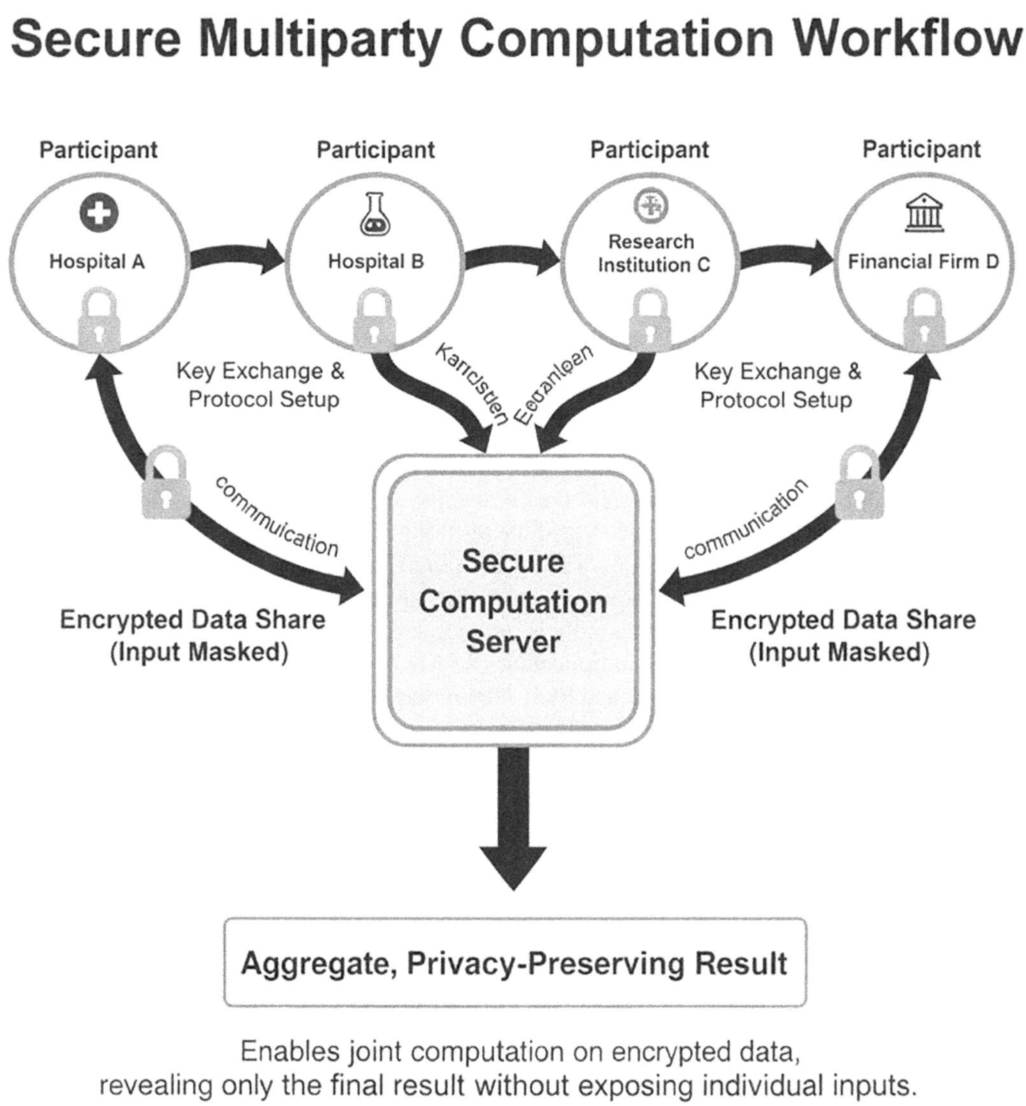

FIGURE 7.6 Secure multi-party computations workflow of collaborative analytics.

Every participant node starts with a private dataset to it. Rather than transmitting the raw data, the individual participants encrypt their input and safely transfer the encrypted shares of data to the computation server. The locked communication lines are used to represent this, meaning a secure, non-exposed transmission. The essence of the SMPC protocol is that the computation server can compute (e.g., the average salary) or generate a composite disease prevalence directly on these encrypted shares without ever having to decrypt the underlying private data. When the computation process is done, the final result of the computation is generated as well encrypted by the server. The encrypted output is then returned to the participants, who collaboratively decrypt it to obtain the final result. More importantly, the intended outcome of the operation (the aggregate statistic) is disclosed, and only the principle that no one individual, or even the computation server, knows anything about the secret input data of another party is adhered to. This workflow is confidential and allows the joint analysis.

7.5.3 Performance and Security Analysis

Despite their strong theoretical guarantees, SMPC and HE both add computational and communication overheads that can be a practical constraint to scalability. The encryption, decryption, and safe communication procedures of these protocols are computationally intensive (particularly when run on large medical data like a high-resolution MRI image or genome sequence). It has been demonstrated through comparative studies that optimized HE schemes such as Cheon-Kim-Kim-Song (CKKS) and Brakerski-Fan-Vercauteren (BFV) achieve significantly faster computation times in computation time without sacrificing the accuracy (compared to plaintext models). Similarly, it can be seen that software optimization by using hardware acceleration (graphics processing units—GPUs) and quantization can also significantly increase runtime performance in clinical environments. Table 7.12 presents a comparative analysis of the methods of cryptography, indicating that SMPC computes quickly, but it requires the use of the multi-party trust, and HE achieves better confidentiality at a higher computational cost. Hybrid SMPC-HE systems trade off these without using distributed trust at the expense of strong end-to-end encryption.

7.5.4 Benefits, Problems, and Future Prospects

The benefits of SMPC and HE in the field of healthcare are significant. They enable secure computation on encrypted or partitioned data and support multi-institutional collaborations without relying on centralized data storage (DP and FL). These capabilities render them specifically useful in data-intensive jobs such as predictive diagnostics, individual treatment model, and epidemiological investigations of populations at large scale. Nonetheless, a number of obstacles still stand on the path toward the widespread adoption of these technologies in the clinical practice. Real-time data processing may be challenging with computational overhead, latency, and key complexity and is of particular concern in resource-constrained healthcare settings. In addition to this, the lack of standardized protocol design and interoperability poses a substantial barrier to large-scale adoption. The future of cryptography is the creation of lightweight cryptographic protocols to minimize computing costs, researching quantum-resistant encryption to provide secure data storage on the long-range, and the introduction of trusted execution environments (TEEs) to protect sensitive computations on the hardware layer. In addition, the integration of blockchain with SMPC or HE can also be a good prospect of improving transparency and auditability, establishing verifiable records of data usage and access (Li et al., 2020).

Figure 7.7 illustrates the end-to-end lifecycle of encrypted data computation on encrypted data, a cryptographic method, which enables third parties (such as cloud servers) to make computations on sensitive data without the necessity of the data being decrypted.

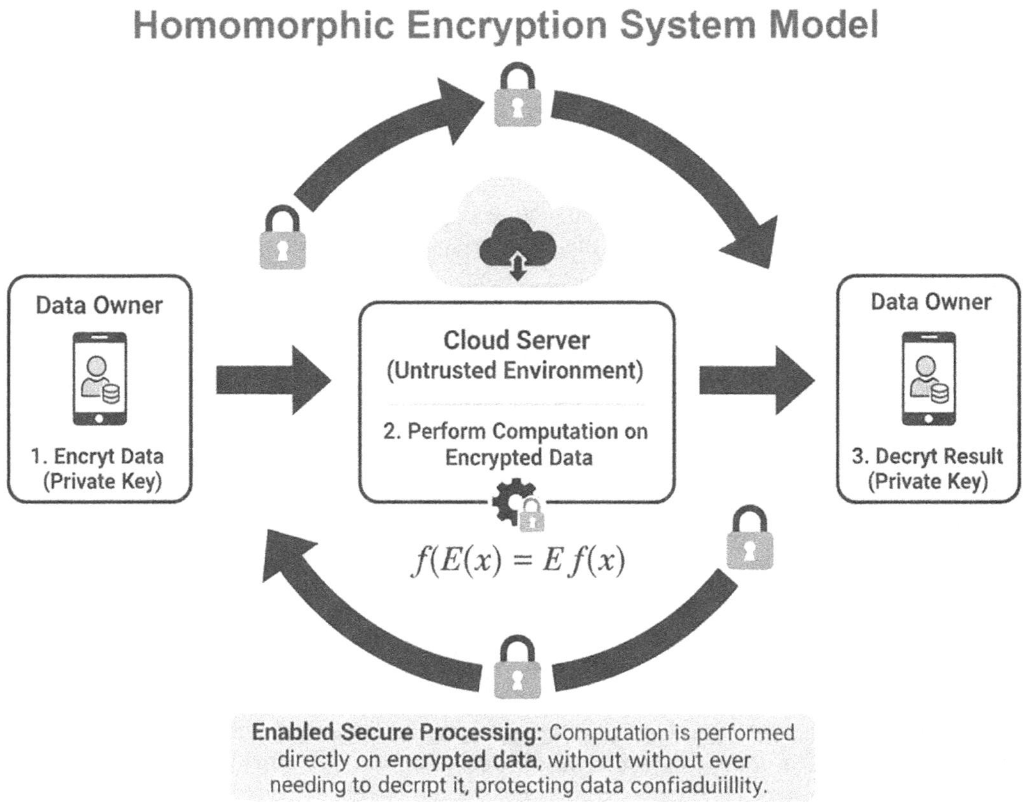

FIGURE 7.7 Homomorphic encryption flow in data processing end-to-end.

The owner of the Raw Data (the Data Owner) is the initial step in the process, which has the Raw Data (denoted as x). Encryption (E), with the secret key is executed on x and the Encrypted Data ($E(x)$) is generated by the owner. This encrypted data is subsequently sent into an Untrusted Cloud Server where it is computed. To compute the desired function, f, the ciphertext is passed directly through this server to produce an Encrypted Result ($E(f(x))$). The underlying property that is demonstrated by the equation below, $f(E(x))=E(f(x))$ is that the operation applied to the encrypted data is mathematically identical to the encryption of the operation applied to the raw data. This is the homomorphic property and it is the most important value proposition of the system as we learn nothing about the underlying data x in the server. Lastly, the encrypted output is also sent back to the Data Owner and it is only him or her who has the secret key needed to carry out the Decryption (D) process, which can be used to give the Final Result ($f(x)$). This workflow ensures continuous data protection while enabling outsourced computation.

SMPC and HE constitute two foundational approaches in privacy-preserving computation. The fact that they are integrated into the healthcare data processing facilitates collaborative intelligence and clinical research without violating confidentiality. These cryptographic methods will adopt a crucial role toward effective interoperable, ethical, and secure medical data ecosystems as technological optimizations mature to enable overhead reduction and scaling up.

7.6 RESEARCH ON SDG

The increasing pressure to ensure the privacy of individual health data and simultaneously make data analytics data-intensive has pushed SDG to the limelight of privacy-conscience studies. Synthetic data are artificially generated datasets, which are statistically similar to real patient data but have no personal identifiers present. These datasets reproduce distributional, structural, and relational characteristics of the initial information, and they do not expose any personal information so that the results of analysis remain valid. SDG provides a compliant and ethical mechanism for data sharing, model development, and collaborative clinical research in healthcare settings with high privacy regulations like the GDPR and HIPAA.

SDG methods have evolved from early statistical simulations to advanced generative AI models. Early approaches relied on random sampling, probabilistic modeling, and resampling techniques that maintained only the primitive statistical associations. Although these approaches posed relatively low privacy risks, they often failed to capture complex medical interactions like comorbidities or treatment–outcome interactions. Later progress brought machine learning-based SDG, where algorithms like Bayesian networks, decision trees, and autoencoders were trained to learn multidimensional distributions using real data. In more recent years, the development of GANs, variational autoencoders (VAEs), and diffusion models has significantly improved the quality and diversity of synthetic data. Such architectures can generate high-fidelity EHRs, medical images, and even multimodal patient profiles that are very close to the real clinical patterns. Although synthetic datasets exclude direct identifiers, re-identification remains possible if the generative model memorizes specific training records. To address this, researchers have added privacy enforcing measures like DP, testing of membership inference, and similarity thresholding to identify or prevent possible leakage. These measures ensure that no synthetic record can be linked back to any real individual. At the same time, data utility—how well the synthetic data preserve the analytical value of the original dataset—is essential for research validity. Too much noise or perturbation may affect the accuracy and the model performance, and too little obfuscation may harm the privacy. Balancing privacy and utility remains the central challenge in synthetic data research.

The quality of synthetic data is typically evaluated using both quantitative and qualitative methods. In a quantitative manner, Kullback-Leibler (KL) divergence, Wasserstein distance, and correlation preservation are used to measure the similarity between synthetic and real distributions. Accuracy, F1-score, and area under the curve (AUC) are predictive performance metrics that determine whether machine-learning models trained on synthetic data can be as effective as the models trained on real datasets. Qualitative assessment involves clinical experts evaluating the realism of synthetic images of synthetic radiographs or histopathology slides. Table 7.6 shows comparison of SDG algorithms in healthcare research.

Synthetic data applications now span nearly all areas of healthcare. Synthetic EHRs have the advantage of enabling early-stage algorithm development and benchmarking without requiring formal ethics approval or patient consent. Synthetic data also improve bias reduction and minimize regulations risks by enabling various models to be tested in controlled environments when designing algorithms and validating their results. Synthetic datasets are employed to achieve the work of the multi-institutional collaboration between hospitals and research consortia, supporting cross-site analytics without violating data protection policies. Synthetic patient scenarios are used in medical

TABLE 7.6
A Comparison of Algorithms of Synthetic Data Generation in Healthcare Research

Algorithm	Type of Model used in Algorithms	Privacy Score (%)	Utility Score (%)	Remark
GAN	Deep Learning	92	87	A reasonable compromise between realism and privacy
VAE	Probabilistic Model	88	85	High utility preservation
CTGAN	Conditional GAN	95	90	Tabular health data best

education and in simulation training to present students and clinicians in resource-constrained settings with realistic case studies.

Despite these benefits, several challenges continue to shape the development of synthetic data in healthcare. Most importantly, as one of the recurring problems is the propagation of bias, when there are imbalances in the real data, these imbalances may be replicated or even amplified in synthetic datasets. In addition, regulatory frameworks have not yet developed consistency in definitions or quality of synthetic data under regulations like GDPR and HIPAA resulting in ambiguous compliance requirements. Maintaining statistical validity and clinical interpretability is also another obstacle, as inadequately validated synthetic data may misinform diagnostic decisions or policy development. Ethical transparency is also essential; healthcare organizations should disclose when synthetic data are used to avoid its misinterpretation or misuse. New methods, including federated SDG, where several hospitals collaboratively train generative models using SMPC or HE, and differentially private GANs, with mathematically provable privacy, can be used to address those problems.

The future of SDG lies in hybrid privacy architectures, which integrates FL, HE, and DP into one platform. These types of architectures will facilitate joint model training by distributed medical institutions without exposing raw data. The next generation of synthetic datasets will benefit from advances in transformer-based diffusion models and quantum-resistant encryption, as well as increasing the realism and safety of synthetic datasets. The creation of the governance frameworks specifying the standards of validation and models of ethical consent and audit to establish the authenticity and security of synthetic data will also be essential. With digital transformation continuing to transform the healthcare system, SDG is positioned to become a foundational technology enabling an innovative, compliant, and trustworthy data-driven healthcare ecosystem in the era of data-driven medicine.

7.7 PRIVACY VERSUS DATA UTILITY

Achieving an effective trade-off between data privacy and data utility is a central challenge in privacy-preserving analytics. Although privacy measures like anonymization, DP, and encryption safeguard sensitive data, they often reduce the precision, interpretability, and usefulness of the resulting data. Healthcare systems, in which judgments sometimes rely on fine-grained data, face risk from degrading predictive model performance or compromising clinical research outcomes when privacy is overly enforced (Zhang et al., 2023). Thus, determining how to optimally balance privacy and utility remains one of the most technically challenging and debated issues.

7.7.1 Privacy–Utility Trade-Off

Privacy–utility trade-off refers to the natural conflict between individual information protection and the provision of adequate data quality to use in analysis. As an example, the application of statistical noise under DP guarantees a greater level of confidentiality but can distort patterns essential for training accurate models. Equally, k-anonymity under the implicit assumption of aggressive data generalization or suppression can decrease the resolution of clinical variables, and reduce statistical power in epidemiological research. Effective system design must adjust the level of privacy protection to the objectives of analysis and the generally accepted levels of fidelity to data.

7.7.2 Parametric Measures of Privacy and Utility

Evaluating this trade-off requires robust metrics capable of quantifying both privacy loss and data utility, including metrics such as *e*-values, privacy-loss measures, and model-based utility assessments: DP measures, together with utility metrics such as model accuracy, statistical similarity, and predictive performance relative to the original dataset, as well as statistical significance measures (e.g., p-values), should be considered. Advanced evaluation schemes are now using Pareto-optimal optimization in an attempt to achieve parameter settings that produce privacy loss minimization and data utility maximization at the same time. These models are particularly valuable in federated and distributed healthcare settings, where data must remain both private and analytically useful.

7.7.3 Healthcare Contextual Sensitivity

The inherent sensitivity of healthcare data makes privacy–utility decisions particularly challenging. Some of them, like genetic markers, mental health history, or signs of a rare disease, carry elevated re-identification risks even after anonymization. Thus, privacy preservation methods have to be context sensitive giving more consideration to protecting high-sensitivity properties and allowing ample data analysis capabilities on non-identifiable qualities. This balance can be supported through selective-disclosure models or tiered-access systems, which allow using data in a secure and informative manner. Table 7.7 summarizes quantitative trade-off between privacy protection and data utility.

7.7.4 Adaptive Privacy Frameworks

Adaptive privacy models dynamically respond to changes in the type of data, user privileges, and the purpose of use. These frameworks use machine learning models to continuously adjust privacy settings based on the usage patterns and threat feedback. As an example, a federated network of hospitals might implement adaptive privacy layers to provide researchers with high-level insights while enforcing strict privacy controls on patient-level data. By incorporating contextual intelligence, adaptive models maintain operational performance and regulatory compliance without relying on complete data isolation.

7.7.5 Policy and Ethical Dimensions

In addition to technical factors, ethical and legal theories have a significant influence on the privacy–utility ratio. Policies like HIPAA, GDPR, and EU AI act impose the principles of data minimization and informed consent, limiting the way and the timing of data sharing. However, ethical governance extends beyond compliance and also requires that there is transparency in the design of algorithms, explainability in the process of decision-making and responsibility in unintended privacy breaches. In healthcare, data security is a major factor influencing public trust, but more importantly, it might expect the fairness and accountability in analyses.

7.7.6 New Methodologies and Future Prospect

Recent studies discuss hybrid privacy frameworks that combine cryptographic confidentiality with DP to improve their strength and usability. To illustrate, HE combined with noise-based statistical

TABLE 7.7
Measurements of Trade-offs between Privacy Protection and Utilitarianism of Analysis

Measurement	Low Privacy	Medium Privacy	High Privacy
Data Utility (%)	95	85	70
Risk Score	0.75	0.45	0.20
Model Accuracy (%)	98	90	82

analysis enables accurate medical predictions without decrypting patient data (Liu et al., 2024). Equally, PPML models are also being honed in such a way that they guarantee that federated models retain diagnostic accuracy between institutions without leakage of local datasets. The key is to develop intelligent algorithms capable of autonomously balancing these competing objectives with adaptive privacy thresholds and constant learning, which is the future of data utility preservation.

The relationship between privacy and utility is not a fixed trade-off but a dynamic equilibrium, which is determined by how algorithms evolve moral values and other domain-specific restrictions. In the case of healthcare research, where patient safety and data integrity are the most important, the goal is to design systems that protect confidentiality without hindering scientific discovery. The next wave of innovations in AI, cryptography, and adaptive governance has the potential to achieve this balance at scale.

7.8 DE-IDENTIFICATION AND MITIGATION RISKS

De-identification was historically considered as one of the techniques that underlie personal data protection. Organizations with an interest in preserving analysis value, but aim to make datasets appear anonymized (without any identifiers like names, addresses, or medical record numbers), do it by blocking or obscuring such identifiers. Nonetheless, the data ecosystems have been expanding in size and complexity and de-identification has become less effective. Data linkages, advanced re-identification techniques, and machine learning models can often infer personal identities from supposedly anonymized data. These vulnerabilities present critical ethical, legal, and technical issues in healthcare research, where the information about patients is too rich and diverse.

7.8.1 The Nature of De-identification Risks

Risks of de-identification are caused mostly by data triangulation which is the process of correlating outside data to re-identify a person. Indicatively, comparison of an anonymized record of a patient with publicly available genetic databases or social media data can identify concealed identities. Statistical inference or probabilistic matching can even be used to infer identities from aggregate data. The danger is increased by the presence of quasi-identifiers in datasets, that is, the variables like age, postal code, or diagnosis date that, when combined, can identify individuals in small populations or rare disease cohorts.

7.8.2 Attacks on Re-identification in Action

A number of practical cases have revealed that re-identification is possible. In one study, researchers have managed to correlate anonymized genomic data with publicly available data on genealogies and have accurately identified several individuals. Similarly, U.S. de-identified hospital discharge data have been re-linked to voter registration information, exposing patient identities and medical histories. These incidents demonstrate that de-identification methods, though necessary, cannot be considered a sure way of ensuring complete privacy. This is because as the data analytics continue to advance, so do adversarial re-identification strategies based on AI, clustering, and pattern recognition algorithms.

7.8.3 Limitations of the Traditional Techniques

Conventional approaches to de-identification, including masking, suppression, and generalization, tend to harm data quality and provide partial protection. As an example, k-anonymity guarantees against identity disclosure and not against attribute disclosure, where sensitive attributes can still be inferred despite anonymity. Similarly, l-diversity and t-closeness are also more resistant to inference attacks but are computationally expensive and ineffective with high-dimensional healthcare data. Besides, the concept of static anonymization fails to consider dynamic data environments where information is continually updated and shared across multiple institutions.

7.8.4 Mitigation Measures and Improved Protection

In a bid to reduce these threats, the current structures have adopted multi-layered privacy architectures which integrate anonymization with cryptographic and DP measures. One such example is incorporating DP that adds mathematical noise such that individual data points cannot be accurately reconstructed, but the overall accuracy is preserved. Likewise, FL allows model training in distributed nodes without centralization of data significantly reducing the attack surface. The encryption protocols in healthcare, including SMPC and HE, ensure that sensitive records remain encrypted throughout analytical processes.

7.8.5 Governance, Compliance, and Ethical Oversight

The technical defenses should also be supported by powerful data governance and ethical control systems. Such compliance regulations as the GDPR and HIPAA stipulate strict rules about anonymization of data as well as control over access and subsequent disclosure of breaches. Nonetheless, to be effective in mitigation, effective mitigation requires not only regulatory compliance but also strong institutional accountability. Frequent privacy impact assessments (PIA), risk audits, and transparency reports facilitate the timely identification of the vulnerabilities. Ethical review boards are critical in evaluating research protocols to ensure that de-identification practices do not undermine patient rights and trust in society.

7.8.6 Future Research and Research Directions

Current studies are being made on privacy-sensitive data synthesis, in which AI systems like GANs and VAEs are used to produce realistic, but non-identifiable, data. The techniques substantially lower the chances of re-identification because they establish no direct connections with actual individuals, thus maintaining the statistical richness required to conduct a medical analysis. The future perspectives include hybrid designs with GAN-related synthetic information and cryptographic protection and dynamic risk-scoring systems that continuously assess re-identification threats. PPML and AI-assisted privacy metrics can only advance the development of more resilient privacy-preserving data ecosystems.

Although de-identification is one of the foundations of privacy-sensitive data processing, its drawbacks require a multi-tiered solution, which entails combining sophisticated analytics, cryptography, and ethical management. In areas of healthcare research, where privacy sensitivity and societal impact are especially significant, real anonymization must be pursued through sustained development, institutional awareness, and a move to the intelligent privacy-by-design model.

7.9 PRIVACY-PRESERVING MACHINE LEARNING INTEGRATION

PPML is a key emerging direction in safe and ethical AI. As healthcare systems are becoming more data-driven, with diagnostics, predictive analytics, and personalized treatment planning increasingly data-driven, the importance of safeguarding sensitive patient information when training models and performing inference has taken center stage. PPML combines privacy-enhancing technologies, for example, DP, secure multi-party and FL, into the machine learning pipeline. This type of integration guarantees that the models can learn from data without exposing identifiable information, thereby making the medical AI applications compliant, trustworthy, and transparent.

7.9.1 Backgrounds of Privacy-Preserving Machine Learning

Conventional machine learning systems presuppose they have the access to centralized datasets that may be a source of serious privacy risks. PPML, though, redefines this paradigm, by incorporating privacy into the very process of training the model and sharing data. Such methods as differentially private stochastic gradient descent (DP-SGD) add controlled noise to gradient updates to make sure that no individual data point can be reconstructed using the trained model. Equally, HE is used to compute directly on ciphertexts, and it keeps the information confidential during processing (Geyer et al., 2020). Together, these methods ensure that data contributors, for example hospitals or laboratories, retain full control over the local sets of data, and yet still help in general model improvement.

7.9.2 FL in Healthcare

A particularly effective approach within PPML is FL, a model in which different institutions jointly train a common model without the exchange of raw data. All involved nodes (e.g., a hospital) train the model on their end of the network, and only transmit encrypted weight updates to a central aggregator. Such decentralized scheme reduces the risks of exposure and adherence to privacy laws such as GDPR and HIPAA. Federated learning has been successfully applied in domains such as medical imaging, oncology prognosis, and intensive care unit (ICU) monitoring. These federated frameworks enable knowledge sharing across institutions while preserving patient confidentiality. Federated frameworks have enabled knowledge sharing across hospitals without breaking patient confidentiality. Table 7.8 shows performance comparison of federated and local model training in healthcare applications of AI.

Figure 7.8 represents a decentralized, privacy-conscious machine learning paradigm that is specifically made to operate in highly sensitive settings such as in healthcare.

At the center of the architecture or framework is the Global Aggregator (usually a secure cloud server or institutional consortium) that serves as the central node but never has direct access to raw patient data. Linked to this hub are several participant nodes, which in this case are different hospitals or institutions. Every hospital has its local and sensitive patient data and it trains its local data on its own copy of the global AI model. This is an important step, because the patient information does not leave the domestic hospital setting in any way, which guarantees the data sovereignty and adherence to the rigorous privacy standards. Upon local training, a local hospital transfers only the encrypted updates of their model (e.g. changes in weights and biases of the model) to the Global Aggregator. The aggregator then gathers safely these updates of all the participating hospitals into one enhanced global

TABLE 7.8
Comparative Learning of Centralized and Federated Models of Learning on Healthcare Datasets

Model Type	Data Source	Privacy Mechanism	Accuracy (%)	Data Leakage Risk (%)	Training Time (Hours)	Notes
Hospital Model (A)	Local Hospital Dataset	None	87.2	14.6	3.2	Baseline performance
Federated Learning (3 Hospitals)	Distributed Medical Data	Secure Aggregation + Encryption	94.8	3.1	3.8	Privacy and improved accuracy
Centralized Model (All Data Shared)	Merged Dataset	Minimal Encryption	96.0	12.5	2.9	Optimal accuracy/ poor privacy
Federated Learning + Differential Privacy	Federated Data	DP-SGD + Homomorphic Encryption	93.5	1.8	4.1	Best privacy–utility trade-off

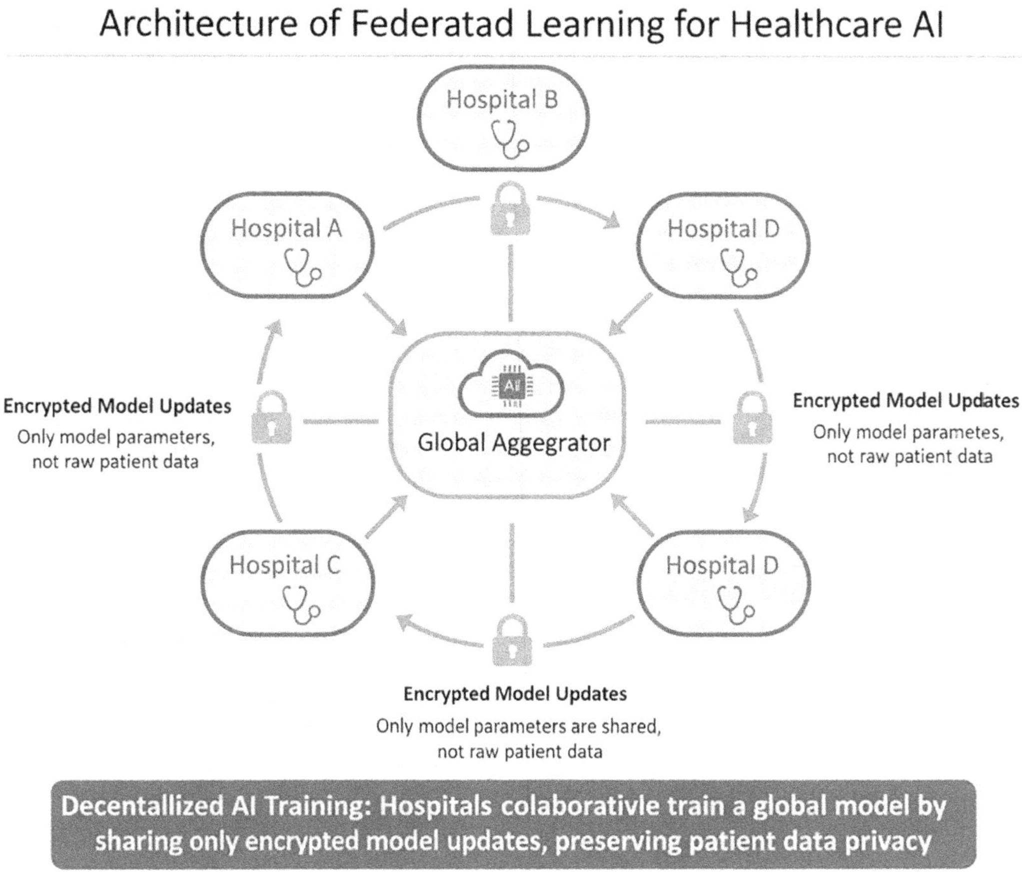

FIGURE 7.8 Federated learning architecture to preserve the privacy of AI-assisted healthcare.

model. This new model is further returned to the local hospitals to initiate the subsequent training. The process of local training and global aggregation is repeated until the model reaches the required performance level. This iterative local-training and central-aggregation process is effective in attaining high-quality AI without involving any direct transfer or disclosure of the confidential patient data.

7.9.3 DP During Model Training

DP proposes a numerically measurable privacy assurance, ensuring that an individual sample of data can have a limited influence on the model output. Within the framework of PPML, DP guarantees that attackers are not able to retrieve confidential information about any particular patient even when they get access to the trained model in whole or in part (Abadi et al., 2021). The trade-off between privacy protection and model accuracy is controlled by the privacy budget which is denoted as epsilon (*e*). The smaller e would imply higher privacy but more noise, which would result in less utility. Adaptive epsilon scheduling, which is part of modern healthcare research on the topic of PPML, optimizes this trade-off by adjusting the privacy parameters based on data sensitivity and training stability.

7.9.4 SMPC and Model Collaboration

SMPC is an addition to PPML to allow the calculation of functions with many parties on their confidential data without exposing them. This is especially helpful in medical research projects where multiple medical centers collaborate or pharmaceutical firms. An example is where a disease prediction model can be trained by several hospitals without any one of them having access to the other patient data. Commonly used SMPC protocols that can be used to achieve this cooperation in a secure manner are additive secret sharing and oblivious transfer. With the addition of SMPC to the workflows of PPML, the institutions enable global collaboration while preserving complete data sovereignty.

7.9.5 Privacy Inference and Model Deployment

In addition to the training, privacy issues arise during model inference—sensitive queries posed to deployed AI systems. Privacy-preserving inference allows models to operate on encrypted data or within secure hardware enclaves. As an example, encrypted radiology images can be analyzed without being decrypted, which means that privacy of patients is preserved even with the assistance of AI. More hybrid privacy models are now being used in cloud-based deployments, which comprise TEEs to provide hardware-level isolation and DP to guarantee software-level assurance (Zhang 2023; Zhao 2024).

7.9.6 Problems and Future Projections

PPML has technical and operational problems despite the promise. Cryptographic protocols may also introduce computational overheads that can slow down training times and achieving high model accuracy under strong privacy guarantees is also challenging. Besides, federated systems can be affected by model poisoning and inference attacks, where adversaries manipulate gradient updates to steal information or corrupt training. The current studies are working on the strong aggregation, privacy-conscious optimization, and auditable AI governance to enhance trust and accountability.

In the future, quantum-resistant cryptography, adaptive DP, and autonomous privacy-management agents will transform PPML to establish the foundation of ethical AI. Such innovations will allow healthcare institutions to collaborate safely at scale, which will accelerate the discovery of scientific knowledge without violation of the principles of confidentiality, integrity, and fairness.

Responsible and safe usage of AI in healthcare can only be achievable through integration of PPML. PPML offers a practical pathway to data-driven innovation that honors patient privacy and regulatory requirements alike by integrating federated architectures, cryptographic computation and adaptive privacy models.

7.10 REAL-WORLD APPLICATIONS IN HEALTHCARE

The healthcare sector is one of the most sensitive and data-intensive domains where privacy-preserving technologies are essential. The use of privacy preserving frameworks in clinical, diagnostic, and research processes necessitates the creation of a balance between data accessibility and confidentiality, interoperability, and compliance. Practical implementation requires regulatory alignment, technological innovation, and institutional coordination to ensure that data-driven solutions improve healthcare outcomes without infringing on patient privacy.

7.10.1 Privacy-Preserving Healthcare Data Frameworks

Some privacy-oriented models have been established to support safe transfer of data and analytics among healthcare organizations. These systems integrate FL, DP, and HE into unified architectures. As an example, the Federated AI in Medical Imaging (FAMLI) system allows hospitals to train medical diagnostic models together using MRI and CT data without exposing raw medical images. Likewise, the Secure Medical Data Collaboration (SMDC) model uses encryption and access control

TABLE 7.9
Comparison of Privacy-Preserving Schemes in Healthcare Applications

Name of the Framework	Primary Methods	Privacy Level of the Methodology	Diagnostic Accuracy (%)	GDPR/ HIPAA Compliance	Data Transfer Needed	Comments
FAMLI	Federated Learning + Encryption	High	91.7	Fully compliant	No	Benchmark model of hospitals
SMDC	Homomorphic Encryption + Role-Based Access	Very High	89.2	Fully compliant	Minimal	Secure for inter-hospital analytics
DP-Med	Differential Privacy + Pseudonymization	Medium	88.6	Partial	Yes	Balance of protection and simplicity
FedCare	Federated Learning + Secure Aggregation	High	90.8	Fully compliant	No	Suitable to real-time diagnostics

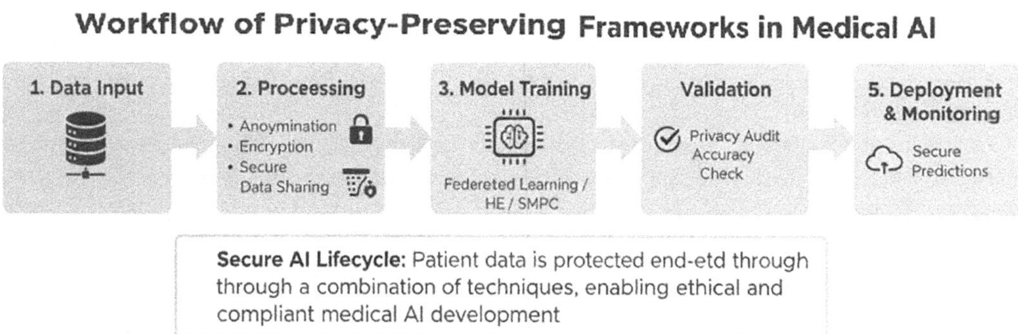

FIGURE 7.9 Workflow description of privacy-preserving models for medical AI implementation.

to help avoid exposure of data during inter-hospital analysis. Table 7.9 presents the benchmark of privacy-preserving frameworks of medical AI deployment.

Figure 7.9 depicts the secure workflow required to design and deploy AI systems based on delicate medical information. It begins with data input where raw and possibly identifiable patient information is collected. The next and crucial process is preprocessing which is the primary stage at which privacy protections are applied. The step includes the deployment of Privacy-Enhancing Technologies (PETs) such as anonymization (e.g., k-anonymity) and different types of encryptions (e.g., HE or SMPC) as the means of safeguarding the sensitive data. After securing the data, it is transferred to the model training where the AI algorithm is trained on the secured data, and frameworks such as FL are frequently used to make sure that the data are not centralized. After training, the model goes to the validation stage in which it is strictly evaluated on performance in terms of accuracy as well as the necessary privacy and ethics before being released. The last step is deployment and monitoring, in which the tested secure AI model is deployed into clinical or research application and its performance and privacy adherence is managed with constant monitoring in a real-world environment. This workflow demonstrates that privacy is not an add-on feature, but a fact that must be present at each and every phase of the lifecycle of the medical AI system.

7.10.2 Data Lifecycle Management

Privacy-preserving practices must be applied throughout the entire data lifecycle: collection, sharing, and archival. The concept of data minimization is put in place during the acquisition whereby only necessary attributes are captured. Sensitive identifiers are encrypted and tokenized during storage and anonymized and under DP during analysis. In the dissemination phase, access control lists (ACLs) and role-based authorization restrict who may access or modify specific data elements.

7.10.3 Federated and Distributed Learning

FL infrastructures are increasingly adopted to support privacy-preserving collaboration in hospitals and research laboratories. Within this paradigm, local servers learn AI models on the premises with patient data of the hospital and only encrypted parameter updates are sent to a central aggregator. This minimizes the possibility of data leakage and also ensures that the knowledge of various institutions can be used to come up with one high-performing model. In the case of oncology, federated systems have been used in tumor classification problem, where hospitals collectively improve on the accuracy of detection without breaching patient confidentiality. Table 7.10 shows comparison of federated and centralized healthcare AI models in terms of their accuracy and security.

Figure 7.10 uses a grouped column chart to illustrate the trade-offs among three machine learning approaches in regard to the key performance indicators: accuracy, latency, and privacy score.

The centralized model has the best accuracy and the lowest latency as all the data are concentrated at a single site maximizing the data utility and minimizing communication overheads. Nonetheless, it has the lowest privacy score because of the necessity to transfer raw and sensitive data, which is a serious security threat.

Conversely, the FL model achieves a substantially higher privacy level, as patient information cannot leave the local institution; and only model updates are shared. This privacy improvement is at the cost of a minor degradation in accuracy as well as a significant degradation in latency caused by communication and aggregation overhead across a number of scattered nodes.

Model with features of both FL and differential privacy is the most advanced privacy protection model. This solution combines the decentralized nature of federated learning with the mathematical privacy guarantees of differential privacy, achieved by injecting noise into model updates, thereby ensuring a high level of privacy protection. This utmost privacy, though, comes at the most obvious trade-off: the model experiences a slight further reduction in accuracy and possibly the largest latency because of the complicated noise-injection calculation that has to be made during the training process. This relationship is visually represented by Figure 7.10, where it can be seen that as the privacy is enhanced, the performance and speed are compromised, to some extent, respectively.

7.10.4 Privacy-Preserving Clinical Decision Support Systems

Privacy Mindful Clinical Decision Support Systems (PP-CDSS) are based on the application of secure machine learning to guide clinicians without disclosing patient-level information. These systems combine model execution protection via HE of data computation and TEEs to execute

TABLE 7.10
Federated versus Centralized Model Performance on Hospital Networks Comparatively

Model Configuration	Hospital Network	Accuracy (%)	Training Data Shared	Reduction in Transmission Risk (%)	Latency (ms)	Level of Compliance
Centralized Model	3 Hospitals	96.5	Full	0	15	Low
Federated Model	3 Hospitals	94.7	None	82	20	High
Federated + Differential Privacy	3 Hospitals	93.9	None	85	22	Very high
Local Independent Models on a Local Basis	Single Hospitals	88.3	None	100	10	Moderate

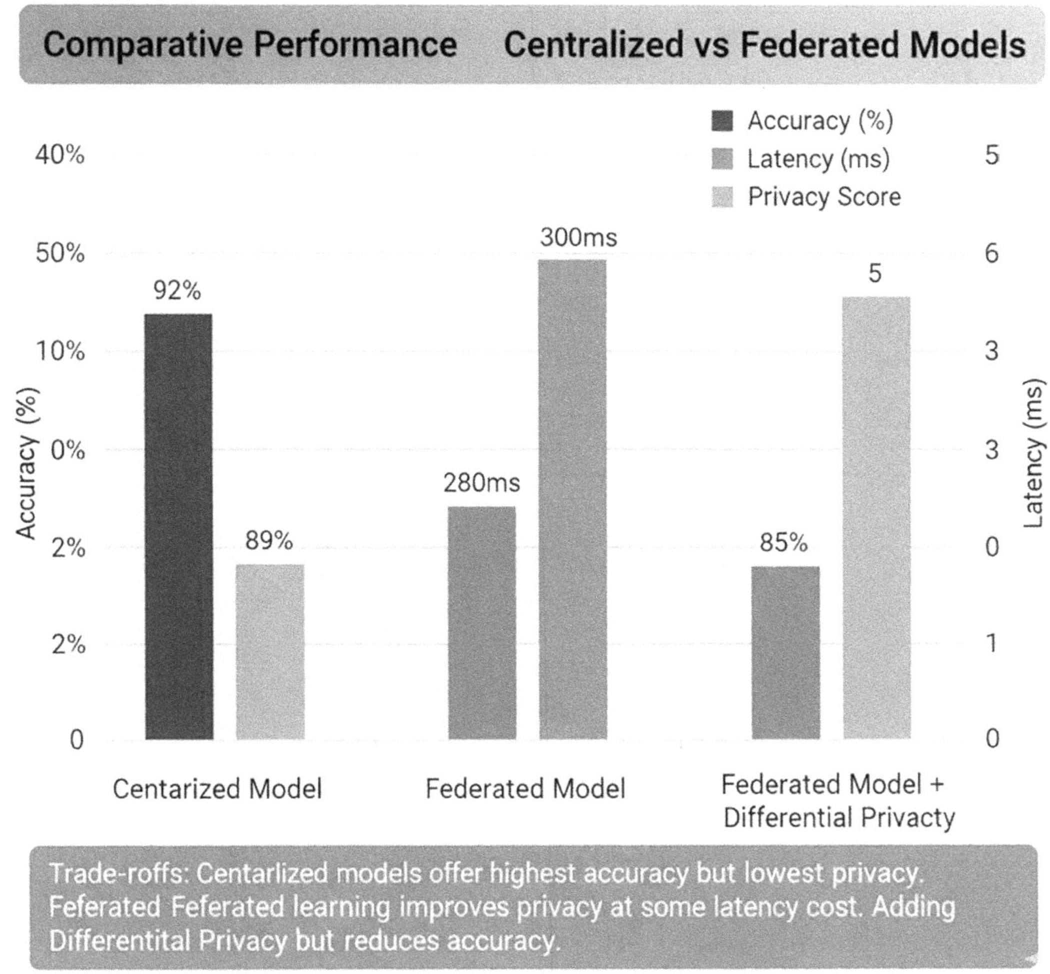

FIGURE 7.10 Comparison of centralized and federated healthcare AI model performance.

models. As an example, real-time-analyzed encrypted laboratory data can be used to give drug dosage or sepsis risk warnings, without requiring decryption during inference (Zhang 2023; Zhao 2024). These systems enhance clinical efficiency and data security, and so are ideal in a sensitive setting such as ICU or remote telemedicine system.

7.10.5 Interoperability, Compliance, and Governance

To implement the privacy-preserving solutions in practice, healthcare organizations have to make sure that the solutions are interoperable and meet the international standards. Guidelines on consent management, pseudonymization, and auditability in a variety of health IT systems can be found in frameworks like FHIR (Fast Healthcare Interoperability Resources) and ISO/IEC 27701. Moreover, HIPAA and GDPR make certain that data are ethically used, have rights, and that usage is legal. To prevent misuse or unauthorized access, governance mechanisms (set by data access committees (DACs) and ethical review boards (ERBs)) are used in the implementation. Table 7.11 shows governance and compliance measures of privacy-preserving healthcare systems.

Figure 7.11 illustrates the structured governance environment required that is needed to guarantee accountable and ethical functioning of a Healthcare AI System. The Healthcare AI System is

TABLE 7.11
Effect of the Integration of Governance and Compliance on Institutional Data Trust and Audit Readiness

Governance Element	Description	Compliance Standard	Frequency of Audit	Effectiveness Rating (1–5)	Institutional Benefit
Data Access Committee (DAC)	Grants and oversees data access	HIPAA, ISO 27701	Every Quarter	5 times	Ethical data access
Privacy Impact Assessment (PIA)	Identifies privacy risks in systems	GDPR, NIST	Bi-annual	4	Stops the abuse of data
Ethical Review Board (ERB)	Supervises research data protocols	GDPR, National Ethics Guidelines	Annual	5	Keeping trust in society
Security Audit Report	Independent verification of privacy controls	ISO/IEC 27001	Annual	5	Enhances audit readiness

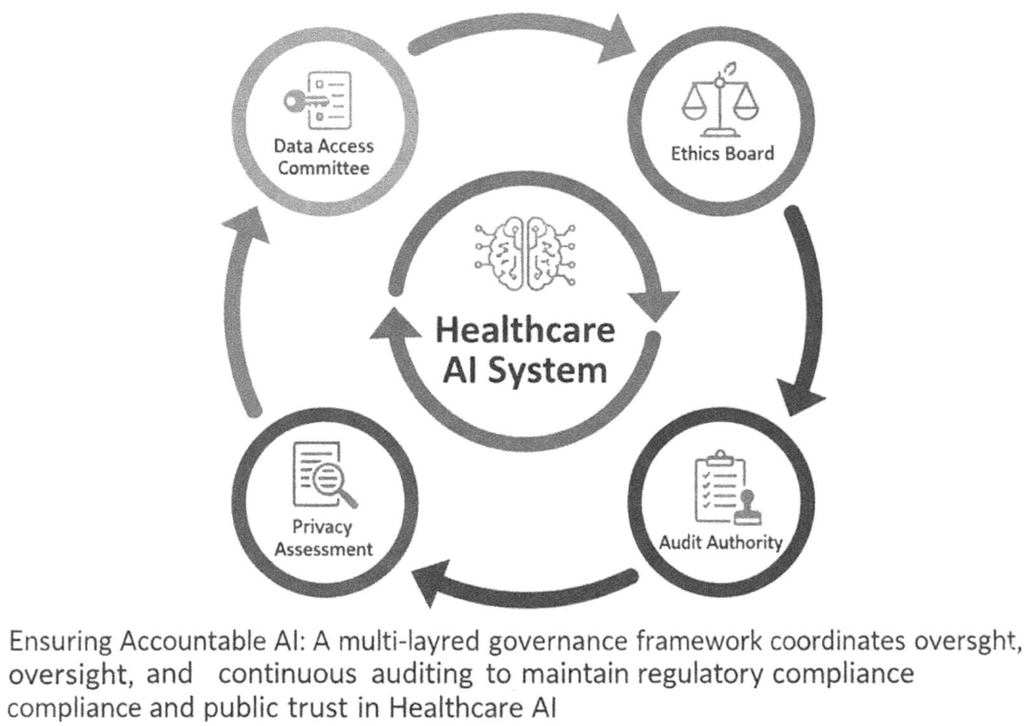

FIGURE 7.11 Privacy-preserving healthcare AI systems governance and compliance ecosystem.

the core of this ecosystem and is based on sensitive data about patients. Several interconnected governance nodes interact directly with the system to provide continuous oversight and control. A DAC controls and grants access to which datasets under what conditions to users, allowing them to adhere to the principle of least privilege. The Ethics Board (also referred to as an institutional review board or IRB) evaluates the ethical and social consequences of the AI system and issues approval of protocols to safeguard human subjects. The PIA component actively reviews privacy risks and documents the implementation of controls and maintenance of privacy controls (such as the technical solutions mentioned above). Lastly, the Audit Authority offers retrospective and continuous audits to ensure that the system complies with all regulatory requirements (e.g., GDPR, HIPAA) and the internal regulations. The bidirectional links highlight the need for continuous communication, feedback, and accountability imperative, so that the process of developing and implementing the healthcare AI System is in line, transparent, and ethically appropriate.

7.10.6 Case Studies and Practical Implementation

Several real-world case studies demonstrate the successful use of privacy-preserving data systems:

Mayo Clinic Federated Data Platform: The Mayo Clinic deployed a secure federated analytics system across all its network hospitals, which allowed prediction modeling of cardiovascular risks without any central storage of patient information. The system increased the sensitivity of diagnostic by 12% and was HIPAA-compliant.

UK Biobank Synthetic Data Pilot: Researchers ran synthetic datasets based on genomic and phenotypic records, which allowed one to conduct epidemiological studies on a large scale, but participant anonymity is preserved. The artificial data were similar to the statistical distribution of the initial dataset with a 96% correlation in the results of the model.

IBM Watson Health Privacy Sandbox: This became a program that incorporated both DP and SMPC protocols to conduct data analysis safely in the pharmaceutical partners and enable the drug discovery process without the proprietors or patient-specific information being exposed.

All these examples show that privacy-preserving solutions are no longer theoretical, they are operationally feasible, and even scaled, as well as more and more mandatory to ethical healthcare innovation.

The key to the implementation of privacy in healthcare is a balance between technology, governance, and ethics. The combination of federated architecture, encrypted computing, and privacy-by-design concepts will guarantee that data are not only safe but also scientifically useful. As healthcare continues its digital transformation, such solutions will mark the future of trustworthy, compliant, and intelligent healthcare data ecosystems.

7.11 FUTURE PERSPECTIVES IN SENSITIVE DATA SHARING

With the growth of digital healthcare ecosystems, secure data sharing has become a strategic priority rather than merely a technical requirement. The coming together of AI, cryptography, quantum cryptography, and adaptive privacy frameworks are transforming how medical institutions handle, exchange, and process sensitive data. The healthcare system of the future will be based on smart, self-governing systems that will be able to guarantee privacy, compliance, and interoperability across boundaries and fields.

7.11.1 Quantum-Safe and Post-Quantum Cryptography

Conventional cryptographic systems such as Rivest-Shamir-Adleman (RSA) and Elliptic Curve Cryptography (ECC) are becoming increasingly vulnerable with the advent of quantum computing. Post-quantum algorithms and quantum-safe cryptography (QSC) are in the design process so that they can be resistant to quantum attacks. Tools such as lattice-based encryption and hash-based signatures hold the promise of ensuring data confidentiality of health records on a long-term basis in cloud and hybrid data systems. As quantum-resistant encryption is integrated into healthcare privacy frameworks, it is expected that by the early 2030s such encryption will become a mandatory compliance requirement, at least on genomic and longitudinal datasets of patients.

7.11.2 Blockchain of Open and Auditable Data Transfer

The potential of blockchain technology is set to transform the healthcare data-sharing process to enable immutable, decentralized, and auditable data on transactions. Every action involving medical information, such as access, update, or sharing, can be recorded as an immutable transaction on a distributed ledger. Smart contracts automate compliance processes, allowing patients to define granular and dynamic data-sharing permissions.

7.11.3 Privacy Auditing and Risk Prediction Based on AI

The use of AI to enhance privacy protection is gaining momentum through automated risk auditing and privacy prediction models. Machine learning models are able to identify unusual access patterns of data, indicate possible insider threats, and approximate the risks of re-identification in close real time (Liu et al., 2024). A framework of incorporating AI-based analytics into governance dashboards allows the healthcare administrators to ensure that privacy compliance is paid attention to constantly and that security measures can be adjusted automatically to the risks that appear. These systems would transform privacy management into a dynamic, intelligent process rather than a static compliance activity, which should adapt to changes in organizational behavior and the environment of threats.

7.11.4 Cross-Border Interoperability and Data Sovereignty

Global health research increasingly relies on cross-border data exchange, yet diverse privacy regulations, including the GDPR in Europe and HIPAA in the United States, present major interoperability challenges. The frameworks in the future must be designed to include data sovereignty controls, providing that data usage will be in line with legal and ethical requirements of the jurisdiction of origin. Technologies such as federated analytics and secure data enclaves support international collaboration by enabling computations on distributed datasets without violating sovereignty constraints. Organization-driven standardization such as the ones by World Health Organization (WHO) and Organisation for Economic Co-operation and Development (OECD) are seeking to establish common principles of privacy-sensitive global health data exchanges.

7.11.5 Cultivating Digital Twin and Synthetic Data

Synthetic data and digital twin technologies have provided new directions for privacy-preserving healthcare innovation. AI training, as well as clinical simulation, can be performed using synthetic datasets obtained by high-level generative models without revealing the true patient identity. Digital twins, which are virtual models of patients, organs, systems, enable real-time prediction and analysis without requiring access to real patient data. When combined, these tools provide secure testing environments to develop algorithms and test policy, as well as speed up innovation with confidentiality maintained. Analytical fidelity and privacy risk assessments of synthetic-twin-based healthcare models are summarized in Table 7.12.

Figure 7.12 illustrates a privacy-preserving architecture which uses AI to generate highly realistic and yet non-identifiable datasets which can be safely used in health research and development.

Real patient data (symbolized by the EHR), Internet of Things (IoT) device measurements, and sensor data) is a very sensitive workflow that is not always available because of privacy laws. This real data is fed into the core component, the Synthetic Twin Generator (a complex AI/ML model). The generator does not simply mask or generalize the data; rather, it learns the complex statistical distributions, relationships, and patterns in the actual data. The Digital Twin Model is then a product of the generator that is made up of synthetic data. This output data is a duplicate of the original patient records in terms of structure and statistical characteristics, that is, it is useful medically and analytically in the future (such as in simulation, new algorithm testing, and predictions).

TABLE 7.12
Synthetic Digital Twin Assay of Healthcare Innovation Privacy

Types of Frameworks	Data Source	Synthetic Fidelity (%)	Re-Identification Risk (%)	Model Accuracy (%)	Use Case	Remarks
Synthetic Patient Twin (GAN-based)	EHR + Imaging	97.5	0.8	95.4	Predictive diagnosis	High realism with strong privacy preservation
Digital Twin + Synthetic Data	IoT Sensor Streams	96.1	0.5	94.8	Remote monitoring	Privacy-protective simulations
Federated Synthetic Twin	Distributed Genomic Data	95.6	0.6	93.9	Genetic research	Most suitable for global collaborative research
Real Data Model (Control)	Centralized Health Data	100.0	14.3	96.2	Benchmark	High utility, low privacy

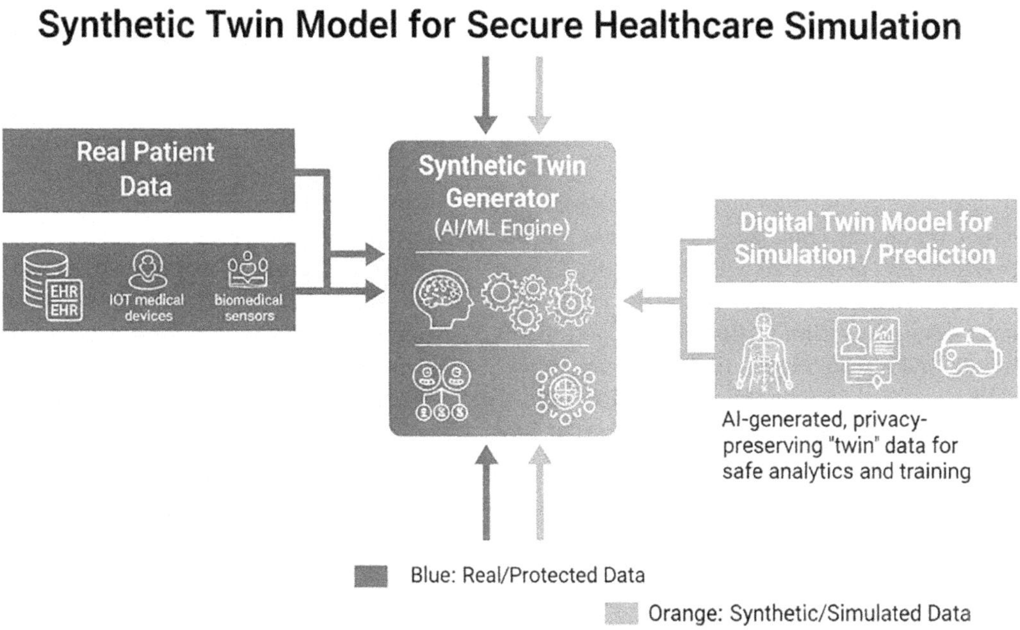

FIGURE 7.12 Merging synthetic data and digital twin models in AI in healthcare.

7.11.6 Ethical, Adaptive, and Autonomous Privacy Systems

Ethical, adaptive, and autonomous privacy ecosystems are the future of ensuring the security of healthcare data sharing. The systems will use AI agents to automatically implement privacy policies, consent, and increase or decrease the protection depending on the contextual risk. System behavior will be directed by ethical AI governance frameworks that are based on fairness, accountability, and transparency to instill a sense of trust and compliance. In this new paradigm, privacy becomes a self-sustaining property of digital health infrastructures rather than a restrictive constraint.

The evolution of the secure data-sharing systems in the future will go beyond the model of fixed protection to adopt intelligent, adaptable, and decentralized models. Through QSC, blockchain-based traceability, synthetic data, and AI-driven governance, the healthcare sector can achieve a model where privacy and innovation coexist: the research and innovation will be empowered, and patients will trust the organization in a linked global environment.

7.12 SUMMARY

The growing reliance on digital technologies, AI, and large-scale data integration has fundamentally transformed how healthcare systems generate, process, and distribute sensitive information. In this chapter, we have discussed the complex field of privacy-conscious data processing and sharing, which is the key to providing ethical, secure, and trustful health data ecosystems. The chapter covered the principles, computational frameworks, and practical applications that demonstrate how advanced techniques can protect individual privacy while preserving data utility for research and innovation.

Starting with the introduction and literature review, the chapter outlined the growing complexity of medical data management and highlighted the limitations of conventional anonymization techniques. It went on to outline the tenets of data minimization and anonymization and emphasized that they remain important as minimum protection measures. Subsequent sections compared k-anonymity, DP, and FL, showing how mathematical and algorithmic methods can enhance privacy protection at scale.

Articles about SMPC and HE showed how cryptography could be used to transform the current way analytics is done. In the meantime, the emergence of SDG is highlighted as a promising approach for producing statistically robust, non-identifiable datasets that support safe and effective research. Together, these technologies contribute to the shift toward PPML, which forms the foundation of responsible AI in healthcare.

The middle sections emphasized the balance between privacy and data utility, identifying relevant metrics, frameworks, and adaptive systems that support this equilibrium. The chapter reviewed the significant risks associated with de-identification and re-identification attacks, emphasizing the need for continuous development of mitigation strategies. Practical architectures such as FL networks and privacy-preserving clinical decision support systems are already reshaping collaboration between hospitals and research institutions in secure and responsible ways.

Later sections introduced real-world models such as FAMLI and SMDC, which demonstrate the operational viability of privacy-preserving technologies. The conversation continued on to new technologies, such as quantum-safe encryption, Blockchain auditability, synthetic digital twins, and AI-assisted privacy auditing which together form the next generation of secure data sharing. These technologies represent both technical and ethical advancements, demonstrating that innovation and privacy are not opposing forces but mutually reinforcing priorities.

Privacy-preserving data processing is no longer optional; it has become a fundamental requirement in modern healthcare. Future intersections of cryptography, AI, governance, and ethics will enable the development of intelligent privacy ecosystems capable of automatically safeguarding sensitive information, supporting clinical decision-making, and promoting global research collaboration. The future of healthcare depends on secure, transparent, and adaptive systems that uphold human dignity while enabling scientific progress.

REFERENCES

Abadi, M., Chu, A., Goodfellow, I., McMahan, H. B., Mironov, I., Talwar, K., & Zhang, L. (2021). Deep learning with differential privacy. *Journal of Machine Learning Research, 22*(1), 1–34. https://doi.org/10.48550/arXiv.1607.00133

Al-Rubaie, M., & Chang, J. M. (2021). Privacy-preserving machine learning: Threats and solutions. *IEEE Security & Privacy, 19*(2), 62–72.

AlShemmari, M., & Chatterjee, M. (2023). Federated learning for healthcare data: Privacy-preserving frameworks and challenges. *IEEE Internet of Things Journal, 10*(5), 4210–4224.

Arora, C., & Sharma, A. (2022). Differential privacy-based mechanisms for secure healthcare analytics. *Health Informatics Journal, 28*(3), 1102241. https://doi.org/10.9734/jerr/2025/v27i61525

Bagdasaryan, E., & Shmatikov, V. (2021). Spinning up privacy: Federated learning with cryptographic enhancements. In *Proceedings of the 30th USENIX security symposium* (pp. 1235–1248). USENIX Association.

Balamurugan, G., Tyagi, A.K., & Richa, A. (2023). Survey on privacy preserving and trust building techniques of blockchain-based systems. In: *Privacy Preservation and Secured Data Storage in Cloud Computing*. IGI Global. DOI: 10.4018/979-8-3693-0593-5.ch019

Bhattacharya, S., & Raskar, R. (2023). Privacy-preserving synthetic data generation using GANs for medical imaging. *Nature Machine Intelligence, 5*(7), 652–663.

Cao, Y., Li, T., & Liu, J. (2020). Privacy-preserving data sharing in medical research: Opportunities and challenges. *IEEE Transactions on Network and Service Management, 17*(3), 1768–1780. https://doi.org/10.5281/zenodo.17338904

Choudhury, O., Gkoulalas-Divanis, A., & Das, A. (2022). Differentially private synthetic data generation for healthcare. *Journal of Biomedical Informatics, 133*, 104157.

Cummings, R., & Sarwate, A. (2020). Differential privacy in practice: Exponential mechanisms and applications. *Communications of the ACM, 63*(9), 90–98. https://doi.org/10.5626/JCSE.2013.7.3.177

Das, S., & Ahmed, F. (2023). Secure multiparty computation in distributed health data environments. *Computers in Biology and Medicine, 156*, 106740. https://doi.org/10.1016/j.compbiomed.2023.106740

Dwork, C., & Roth, A. (2021). The algorithmic foundations of differential privacy (revised ed.). *Foundations and Trends® in Theoretical Computer Science, 9*(3–4), 211–407. http://dx.doi.org/10.1561/0400000042

El Emam, K., Mosquera, L., & Bass, J. (2022). Evaluating re-identification risk of synthetic health data. *npj Digital Medicine, 5*(1), 143. https://doi.org/10.1038/s41746-022-00688-5

Gao, H., Xu, J., & Li, K. (2021). Privacy-preserving federated learning for medical diagnosis: A review. *Artificial Intelligence in Medicine, 119*, 102134. https://doi.org/10.1016/j.artmed.2021.102134

Geis, J. R., Brady, A. P., Wu, C. C., Spencer, J., Ranschaert, E. R., Jaremko, J. L., ... & Kohli, M. (2022). Ethics of AI in radiology: Protecting privacy while enabling innovation. *Radiology, 303*(1), 30–41.

Gentry, C. (2020). Fully homomorphic encryption: An overview. *Communications of the ACM, 63*(6), 50–59. https://doi.org/10.1145/3375636

Geyer, R. C., Klein, T., & Nabi, M. (2020). Differentially private federated learning: A client-level perspective. *IEEE Transactions on Neural Networks and Learning Systems, 31*(8), 2923–2934.

Hale, C., & Boucher, S. (2021). Synthetic data as a privacy-enhancing technology: A systematic review. *Data & Policy, 3*, e7. https://doi.org/10.1017/dap.2021.7

Han, S., Park, M., & Kwon, H. (2024). Blockchain-assisted privacy-preserving medical data sharing. *IEEE Access, 12*, 45129–45140.

Jordon, J., Yoon, J., & van der Schaar, M. (2021). PATE-GAN: Generating synthetic data with differential privacy guarantees. In *Proceedings of the international conference on learning representations (ICLR)*. https://api.semanticscholar.org/CorpusID:53342261

Kairouz, P., McMahan, H. B., & Suresh, A. T. (2021). Advances and open problems in federated learning. *Foundations and Trends® in Machine Learning, 14*(1–2), 1–210. https://doi.org/10.1561/2200000083

Kim, H., Park, S., & Lee, J. (2023). Balancing privacy and data utility in healthcare through adaptive anonymization. *IEEE Access, 11*, 71234–71248.

Kumari, S., Tyagi, A. K., Tiwari, S., & Kulshreshtha, G. (2025a). Sensors and digital twin for healthcare monitoring frameworks. In T. A. Nguyen (Ed.), *Digital twin, blockchain, and sensor networks in the healthy and mobile city (Chapter 10, pp.* 147–177*)*. Elsevier. https://doi.org/10.1016/B978-0-443-34174-8.00011-9

Kumari, S., Tyagi, A. K., Tiwari, S., & Singh, R. (2025b). Medical sensor network, edge computing and blockchain for efficient medical data exchange. In T. A. Nguyen (Ed.), *Digital twin, blockchain, and sensor networks in the healthy and mobile city (Chapter 11,* pp. 179–198*)*. Elsevier. https://doi.org/10.1016/B978-0-443-34174-8.00012-0

Li, C., Xiong, L., & Jiang, S. (2020). Secure sharing of electronic health records using homomorphic encryption. *BMC Medical Informatics and Decision Making, 20*(1), 239.

Liu, D., & Zhang, Y. (2024). Federated transfer learning for privacy-preserving clinical prediction. *IEEE Journal of Biomedical and Health Informatics, 28*(2), 312–324.

Lyu, L., Yu, H., & Yang, Q. (2022). Threats to federated learning: Privacy attacks and defenses. *ACM Computing Surveys, 55*(3), 1–38. https://doi.org/10.1145/3501295

Mishra, A. K., Tiwari, S., Tyagi, A. K., & Arowolo, M. O. (2024). Security, privacy, trust, and provenance issues in Internet of Things–based edge environment. In S. Pal, C. Savaglio, R. Minerva, & F. C. Delicato (Eds.), *IoT edge intelligence (*pp. 233–263). Springer. https://doi.org/10.1007/978-3-031-58388-9_8

Nair, M. M., & Tyagi, A. K. (2021). Privacy: History, statistics, policy, laws, preservation and threat analysis. *Journal of information assurance & security*, *16*(1), 24–34.

Nair, S., & Rajan, R. (2023). Privacy-preserving AI for digital health: Techniques and ethical frameworks. *Frontiers in Artificial Intelligence, 6*, 112345.

Nair, M.M., & Tyagi, A.K. (2025). Transformative effects of emerging technologies on Industry 5.0 and Society 5.0: Current status, vision, issues, challenges, and opportunities for future. In: *Next Generation Data Science and Blockchain Technology for Industry 5.0.* Wiley. DOI: https://doi.org/10.1002/9781394245215.ch13, ISBN: 9781394245185.

Nguyen, D. C., Pathirana, P. N., Ding, M., & Seneviratne, A. (2021). Blockchain for secure e-health data sharing: Challenges and future directions. *IEEE Access, 9*, 9328–9359.

Rajani, D., Menon, S. C., Kute, S., & Tyagi, A. K. (2022). Preserving privacy of social media data using artificial intelligence techniques. In A. Tyagi (Ed.), *Handbook of Research on Technical, Privacy, and Security Challenges in a Modern World* (pp. 186–204). IGI Global. https://doi.org/10.4018/978-1-6684-5250-9.ch010.

Rieke, N., Hancox, J., Li, W., Milletari, F., Roth, H. R., Albarqouni, S., ... & Cardoso, M. J. (2020). The future of digital health with federated learning. *npj Digital Medicine, 3*(1), 119. https://doi.org/10.1038/s41746-020-00323-1

Sharma, T., & Mittal, S. (2024). Homomorphic encryption for secure machine learning inference in cloud healthcare. *Future Generation Computer Systems, 158*, 234–247. https://doi.org/10.1016/j.future.2023.10.022

Thakkar, O., & Sun, Z. (2023). Privacy-preserving AI systems: Techniques, frameworks, and societal impact. *AI & Society, 38*(3), 567–584. https://doi.org/10.1007/s00146-022-01460-9

Tian, S., & Zhang, H. (2022). Differential privacy-based synthetic EHR generation for healthcare analytics. *IEEE Journal of Biomedical and Health Informatics, 26*(12), 5829–5840.

Tyagi, A.K. (2021). Analysis of security and privacy aspects of blockchain technologies from smart era' perspective: The challenges and a way forward. In: *Recent Trends in Blockchain for Information Systems Security and Privacy* (pp. 1–17). DOI: https://doi.org/10.1201/9781003139737, eBook-ISBN: 9781003139737

Tyagi, A.K. (2025). Blockchain for smart hospital in Healthcare 5.0: modeling structure, challenges, and future emerging trends. In: *Human-Centric Integration of Next-Generation Data Science and Blockchain Technology*. Elsevier. DOI: https://doi.org/10.1016/B978-0-443-33498-6.00026-1, ISBN: 978-0-443-33498-6.

Tyagi, A. K., Kumari, S., & Tiwari, S. (2024c). Internet of Things for smart healthcare: A survey. In A. K. Sharma, N. Chanderwal, S. Tyagi, & P. Upadhyay (Eds.), *Future of AI in medical imaging (Chapter 2).* IGI Global. https://doi.org/10.4018/979-8-3693-2359-5.ch002

Tyagi, A. K., & Tiwari, S. (2024a). Blockchain-enabled smart healthcare applications in 6G networks. In A. K. Tyagi (Ed.), *Digital twin and blockchain for smart cities* (Chapter 20, pp. 459–494). Wiley. https://doi.org/10.1002/9781394303564.ch20

Tyagi, A. K., Tripathi, K., Tiwari, S., & Kaushik, S. (2025). An efficient technique for privacy preservation, trusted and secure patient-centric services in smart healthcare. In *Proceedings of the 6th international conference on recent trends in communication & intelligent systems (ICRTCIS 2025)* (pp. 31–47). IET. https://doi.org/10.1049/icp.2025.2731

Xie, C., & Xu, J. (2021). Secure multiparty computation protocols for healthcare data aggregation. *Journal of Information Security and Applications, 61*, 102940. https://doi.org/10.1016/j.jisa.2021.102940

Zhang, J., Lin, Y., & Luo, M. (2023). Preserving privacy and fairness in federated learning systems. *ACM Transactions on Privacy and Security, 26*(2), 1–29.

Zhao, Y., Li, Q., & Wang, H. (2024). Generative models for privacy-preserving synthetic health data: Current status and challenges. *Computers in Biology and Medicine, 165*, 107364. https://doi.org/10.1016/j.compbiomed.2023.107364

8 Federated Learning and Edge Computing for AI-Enabled Mental Health

8.1 INTRODUCTION

The issues of mental illness, such as anxiety, depression, stress disorders, and other neurocognitive impairments, have turned into a worldwide problem with millions of people without any specific demographics. Conventional diagnostic and treatment paradigms tend to rely on clinical inquiry, self-report questionnaires, and regular check-ups, processes that have limited ability to capture the dynamic nature of human emotions and behavior. With the rise of artificial intelligence (AI) and the digital health technologies, this situation has evolved greatly, as now real-time behavioral and physiological measurements can be collected and analyzed with wearable sensors, smartphones, and Internet of Things (IoT) devices. Although these innovations have made mental healthcare more accessible and personalized, they also have caused deep-rooted questions of data privacy, ethical governance, and security.

Federated learning (FL) and edge computing (EC) have become the new promising paradigms to assist in the privacy-preserving and decentralized AI in mental health applications. FL enables models to be trained directly on decentralized client devices, unlike traditional centralized AI systems where data must be aggregated within a cloud environment, thereby keeping sensitive information such as biometric indicators, speech features, and behavioral patterns stored locally on devices. The models of mental health can learn using an extensive collection of user information without threatening the privacy of any of the users. Simultaneously, by processing data at or near the point of collection, EC also improves the responsiveness of the system, eliminating latency, cloud infrastructure reliance, and providing the ability to detect behavior in real time which is important in early mental health interventions.

FL and Edge AI synergy is a massive leap toward intelligent systems with secure, ethical, and humanistic facets. All of these technologies support real-time mood monitoring, detection of stress, recognition of cognitive patterns, and adaptive feedback while maintaining compliance with established privacy standards, including Health Insurance Portability and Accountability Act (HIPAA) and the General Data Protection Regulation (GDPR). Moreover, the inclusion of differential privacy (DP), secure aggregation, and blockchain-based auditing systems can guarantee the integrity of the data, its transparency, and trust to the users in federated ecosystems.

The chapter gives an in-depth discussion of the interface between FL, EC, and Mental Health AI. It examines the theoretical foundations and technical mechanisms of FL, describes distributed learning architectural models, and explains how edge-based intelligence can provide behavioral insights in a timely manner. In addition, it identifies communication bottlenecks, aggregation problems, and privacy schemes needed by federated environments. The comparative studies of centralized and federated systems and the examples of these emerging technologies in mental health

DOI: 10.1201/9781003658344-10

monitoring and prediction demonstrate the practical applicability of these emerging technologies. In the end, such a convergence leads to a conclusion where AI-based mental health systems can become decentralized, trustworthy, and aligned with human well-being.

8.2 LITERATURE REVIEW

Integrating AI and mental health research has been progressing at a fast pace over the past few years, because of an increased access to digital behavioral information and the need to have real-time and personalized support systems. Nonetheless, due to the sensitivity of mental health data, a high level of privacy protection is required, which results in the increasing attention to FL and EC as technologies that make AI privacy preserving (Abay et al., 2022). The section examines the literature available on (i) AI in mental health, (ii) basics of FL, (iii) Edge AI to behavioral analytics, and (iv) integration of FL and Edge systems to secure mental health applications.

8.2.1 Mental Health Diagnostics and Monitoring Applications of AI

AI has found extensive use in the mental health industry in terms of pattern recognition, identification of emotions, and prediction of behaviors. It has been demonstrated that machine learning algorithms, especially deep neural networks and recurrent architectures, can perform well in identifying depression and stress using multimodal information (facial expressions, speech, and physiological), where and these approaches have shown promising results (Jacobson et al., 2022; Wang et al., 2023; Nair et al., 2025). Digital phenotyping derived by analyzing behavioral cues through smartphone behavioral patterns has emerged as a critical tool of continuous mental health monitoring (Onnela and Rauch, 2021; Tyagi, 2021).

Nonetheless, the data collection process, in which all patient data are consolidated on cloud servers, is fraught with major dangers as far as privacy, data leakage, and misuse are concerned. According to the studies conducted by Zhang et al. (2022) and Dinh et al. (2021), the sensitive mental health data stored in a central repository is susceptible to adversarial intrusions and re-identification efforts. These issues strengthen the case for privacy-preserving, decentralized learning architectures.

8.2.2 Background of FL in Healthcare

McMahan et al. (2017) had suggested use of FL which enables multiple distributed devices to collectively train a shared model without exchanging raw data. This approach keeps data local while transmitting only model updates to a central aggregator. The method has since found a wide range of its use in the healthcare sector, allowing learning across institutions, but still adhering to privacy policies, including HIPAA and GDPR (Li et al., 2021; Kumari et al., 2025a).

FL has enabled the creation of predictive models in the mental health area that can learn using a wide variety of data sources, including wearable sensors, electroencephalography (EEG) signals, and mobile applications, without invading patient privacy (Xu et al., 2022; Kumari et al., 2025b). For example, Su et al. (2023) demonstrated that federated deep learning models are able to identify stress and emotional patterns of many users with 92% accuracy yet remain privacy preserving. Equally, Sheller et al. (2020) reported successful applications of FL in neuroimaging research to identify cognitive deficits in hospitals with no centralized data exchange.

Irrespective of its potential, FL has technical issues, such as data heterogeneity, non-independent and non-identically distributed (non-IID) data, and communication overhead. Improvements, including personalized federated learning (Per-FL) and adaptive optimization algorithms, have been suggested recently to solve those problems (Wang et al., 2021; Kairouz et al., 2021; Mishra et al., 2024).

8.2.3 Mental Health AI EC

Edge Computing refers to a decentralization of data processing, which is performed in edge nodes, that is, smartphones, wearables, and IoT gateways. This distributed paradigm reduces latency and improves responsiveness as well as enables real-time feedback which is essential in mental health interventions (Shi et al., 2022; Tyagi, 2025).

Examples of applications of edge-based mental health systems are emotion-aware chatbots, wearable-accompanied stress management, and context-sensitive proposed therapy (Zhou et al., 2023; Tyagi and Tiwari, 2024a). To illustrate, wearable sensors linked to edge processors will be able to continuously measure the heart rate variability (HRV), electrodermal activity (EDA), and sleep patterns to identify psychological distress before it occurs (Kim et al., 2022; Balamurugan et al., 2023). These data are processed locally to preserve confidentiality and maintain the temporal resolution required for behavioral analysis.

Moreover, Edge AI and FL can be combined as they allow collaborative intelligence of devices with minimum energy use and bandwidth consumption (Nguyen et al., 2022; Tyagi et al., 2024c). These architectures are specifically applicable in the context of mental health monitoring, where the concepts of real-time analytics and user privacy need to be balanced.

8.2.4 Privacy and Ethical Implications

Differentiated privacy, secure aggregation, and blockchain-based verification mechanisms are necessary to ensure privacy in distributed mental health AI (Gursoy et al., 2021; Tyagi et al., 2025). DP introduces statistical distortion to gradients or model updates, and it is impossible to reverse engineer an individual data (Abadi et al., 2016; Rajani et al., 2022). Rather, blockchain will make FL ecosystems more transparent and auditable as the transactions are saved permanently, and this will make stakeholders more accountable (Hossain et al., 2023; Nair et al., 2021).

Ethically, decentralization is compatible with the principles of user consent and digital autonomy, which are critical in the mental health setting (Floridi and Cowls, 2021). Human-centered federated AI emphasizes designing systems that promote transparency, inclusivity, user autonomy, transparency, and inclusivity, and promote computational intelligence (Rieke et al., 2022).

8.2.5 Research Gaps and Future Directions

Although significant advancements in federated and edge-based healthcare AI have been reached, mental health analytics are still at an initial phase of development. Big, longitudinal datasets that can be employed in distributed learning are also not available and cross-platform interoperability between edge devices is also limited. Moreover, personalizing global models to reflect local user behavior remains an urgent challenge.

Future studies are likely to cover cross-silo FL design, multi-agent reinforcement learning (RL) and blockchain-based federated ecosystems in managing mental health holistically. These directions may enable ethical, adaptive, and context-sensitive AI systems that move beyond prediction toward proactive mental-health support.

8.3 ESSENTIALS OF FL

The unparalleled growth of digital information generated by intelligent devices and health apps has offered new opportunities for training intelligent models. Nonetheless, the sensitivity of personal information particularly in the area of mental health poses serious concerns about the privacy, security, and compliance with the regulations. FL will solve these problems by allowing distributed machine learning among multiple devices or institutions without transmitting raw data to the single server. This paradigm is one of the major improvements in the direction of decentralized, privacy-conserving intelligence that fits the ethical mandate of mental-health AI systems (Li et al., 2021; Kairouz et al., 2021).

8.3.1 Concept and Principles

The Federated Averaging (FedAvg) algorithm was the first algorithm to formalize FL (McMahan et al., 2017). Under this setup, a number of clients (e.g., smartphones, hospitals, or IoT nodes) update a shared global model in a coordinated way by the responsibility of a central aggregator. The central idea is that unprocessed data is never sent outside the client machine, but rather model updates (e.g. gradients or parameters) are sent to get aggregated globally.

FL is a cyclic process as illustrated in Figure 8.1 and it entails the following major steps:

Model Initialization: The key server opens an initial model and sends it to all the involved clients.
Local Training: The model trains on the personal data of the individual client by using one or more local epochs.
Model Update: The clients submit their model parameters which are updated locally to the central aggregator.
Aggregation: The aggregator calculates an averaged version of these updates taking into account a weight to create a new global model.
Iteration: The iteration will continue until the model reaches a convergence point or some predetermined performance requirements are satisfied.

The process starts with local training in which the individual client machines (such as Clients 1, 2, and 3) train a model using their separate datasets which are siloed. More importantly, the raw data

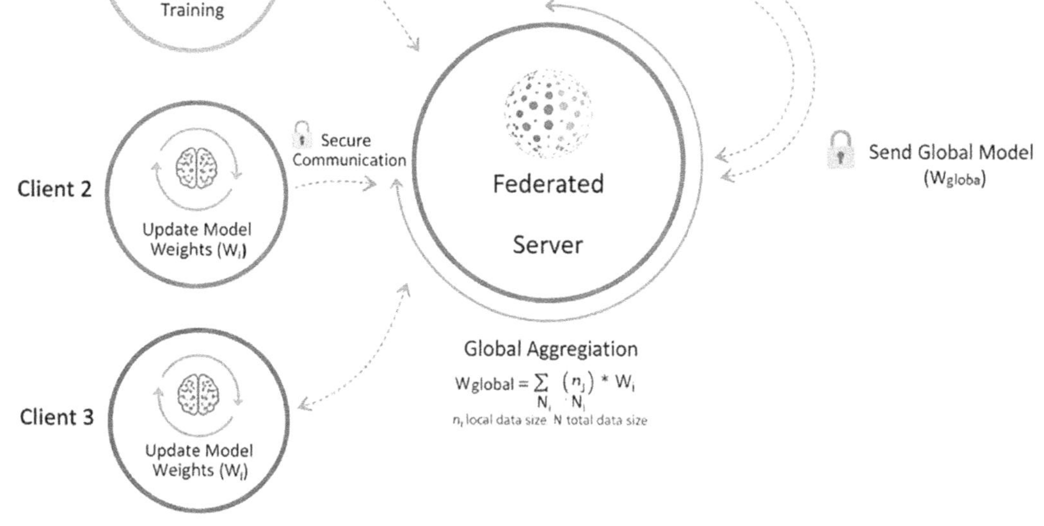

FIGURE 8.1 Federated learning process overview.

never leaves the device, ensuring privacy. When trained, the devices obtain a series of model weight updates (W_i) and send them, via a secure communication channel, to a central federated server. Then the server undertakes the Global Aggregation (usually by weighted average such as FedAvg) and aggregates all the updates into a single and better Global Model (Wglobal). This refined model is then reintroduced to the clients and the cycle repeats itself. Such an arrangement is useful to achieve collaborative machine learning without interfering with data privacy.

The *FL* global objective can be mathematically defined as:

$$\min_{w} F(w) = \sum_{k=1}^{K} \frac{n_k}{n} F_k(w)$$

in which K is the quantity of clients and n_k is the local data samples of the client k and $F_k(w)$ is the local loss function. The central server optimizes the global model w according to the aggregation of local gradients, where all the participants contribute equally (McMahan et al., 2017).

8.3.2 Types of FL

Depending on data distribution and collaboration structure, it is possible to distinguish three major types of FL (Yang et al., 2022):

Horizontal Federated Learning (HFL): The clients are characterized by the same feature space but differing data sample. As an example, various mental health applications in various locations can train a common depression prediction model without the exchange of the user information.

Vertical Federated Learning (VFL): Customers have the same users but different features. As one example, a medical professional and a fitness tracker company can join forces to forecast mental health with the help of opposing data (e.g., clinical and behavioral).

Federated Transfer Learning (FTL): In case there is a little overlapping of data between clients, transfer learning methods are combined to close domain gaps and enhance cross-site generalization (Liu et al., 2022).

Table 8.1 summarizes the main features of different types of FL and their uses.

8.3.3 Mechanism of Communication and Aggregation

Communication is one of the most resource-intensive components of FL. Training round necessitates secure transfer of model parameters between the clients and the server. Secure aggregation (Bonawitz et al., 2017) is one of the techniques that guarantee the ability of the central server to compile model updates without knowing the individual client input.

TABLE 8.1
Federated Learning Types and Their Applicability to AI-Driven Mental Health

Type	Data Relationship	Mental Health Example of Use of Type of Relationship	Benefits
Horizontal FL	Different users	Mobile app data across regions	Scalability, privacy
Vertical FL	User similarity, different feature types	A combination of hospital and wearable data	Multi-modal learning
Federated Transfer Learning	Few overlaps between institutions	collaboration between institutions with limited shared data	Enhanced generalization

Aggregation algorithms such as FedAvg, FedProx, and FedNova are developed to address non-IID data challenges and heterogeneous device performance in FL (Li et al., 2020). These aggregation methods improve fairness and accuracy in mental health applications, where different individuals have greatly different distributions of data.

Besides, asynchronous FL models can enable clients to engage at various times, which enhances scalability and idle computation reduction (Chen et al., 2022). Quantization and sparsification are compression algorithms that will further compress the bandwidth usage to allow FL to be used in low-power edge devices.

8.3.4 Privacy and Security Advancements

In FL, even though privacy is maintained by default as the data is local, an indirect leakage may happen when updating the models. To reduce this, DP provides statistical noises to gradients prior to transmission, whereas HE allows processing of encrypted data without decryption (Gursoy et al., 2021; Acar et al., 2021).

In addition, FL based on blockchain has become a system of verifiable and tamper-resistant training processes (Hossain et al., 2023). Blockchain stores every model change in an everlasting book, which guarantees transparency, auditing, and resistance to malicious actors—an essential criterion of application in the mental health field, where ethical accountability is a priority.

Figure 8.2 shows incorporation of privacy-preserving mechanisms into the FL pipeline.

Continuing on the simple FL cycle, Figure 8.2 indicates the strategic locations in which privacy-safeguarding mechanisms are inserted. Privacy mechanisms protect the underlying data—not the model itself—from attacks such as model inversion or membership inference. The application of

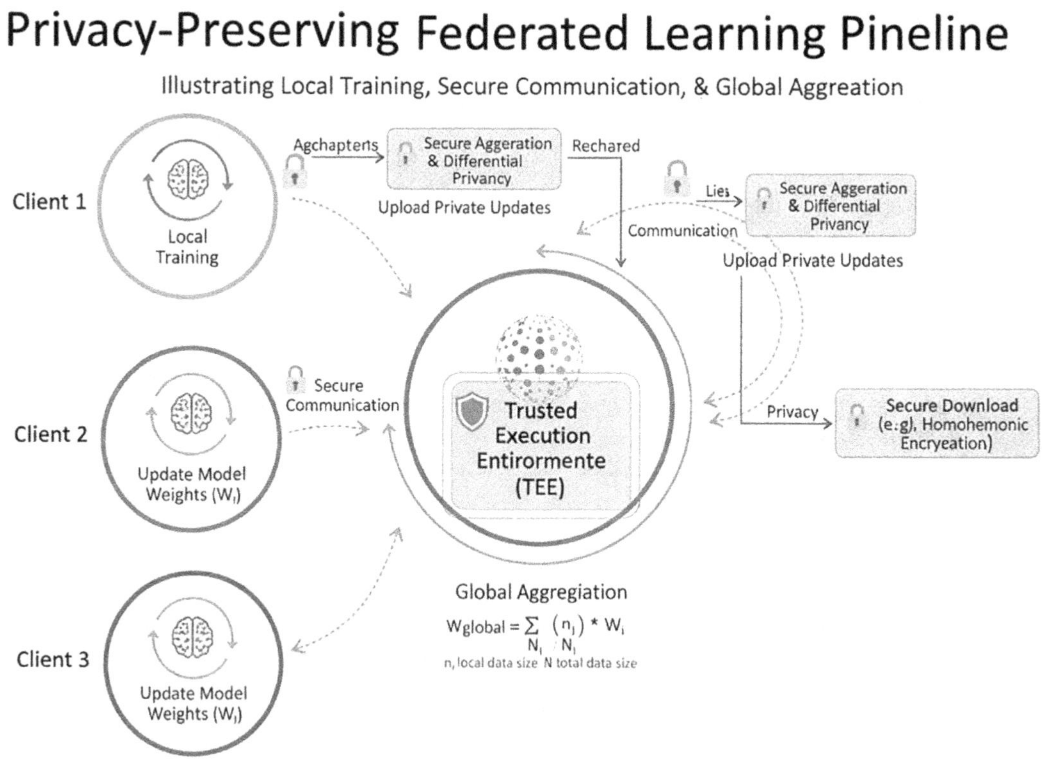

FIGURE 8.2 Privacy federated learning mechanisms.

Secure Multi-Party Computation (SMC) or Homomorphic Encryption (HE) is one of the most widespread methods that is demonstrated during the communication step, where it will mean that the model update is encrypted and only the summarized outcome is disclosed to the server. Alternatively, it is possible to introduce DP at the local training stage, where noise is intentionally added to the model updates and they are sent. The server follows a trusted aggregation protocol that securely combines encrypted or noise-added updates.

8.3.5 Applicability to Mental Health AI

In mental health scenarios, the FL can provide a revolutionary solution to the data-sensitive model development. Devices, phones, or hospitals can cooperate to train their predictive models to detect stress, control emotions, or assess mental states without ever transferring raw data.

To illustrate this, federated deep learning models have been used to analyze EEG patterns, detect emotions and speech data to identify depression without breaching the privacy issues (Su et al., 2023; Xu et al., 2022). These distributed systems do not only secure user identity, but also improve model generalization due to the learning using diverse behavioral and demographic groups.

Because mental health data tends to capture highly personal and context-specific actions, FL is capable of providing a balance of personalization and privacy, enabling adaptive AI systems that are customized to meet the needs of individuals without sacrificing ethical standards.

8.4 ARCHITECTURE AND WORKFLOW

The implementation of FL and EC of mental health AI demands a well-planned architecture that is efficient in computation, privacy protection, and real-time responsiveness. This part provides the layering architecture and the workflow of an FL-Edge ecosystem that aims at supporting privacy-preserving behavioral analytics and mental health prediction systems.

8.4.1 Introduction to the Federated Edge Architecture

The federated edge architecture consists of client devices (edge nodes), a coordination network (aggregator/server), and a cloud-based orchestration network or blockchain network. The roles of each of the components are specific and complementary to each other, and they are involved in the provision of secure, decentralized intelligence.

Figure 8.3 describes a more advanced FL architecture that adds a Blockchain Layer to increase the transparency, security, and synchronization. During local training, edge devices in the given case encrypt model updates, in which they perform local training on-device. Such encrypted updates are additionally forwarded to a federated aggregator. Instead of storing updates on a central server, the aggregator records the aggregated model on the blockchain. The blockchain is a distributed and tamper-resistant registry to record, validate, and coordinate the model updates and the resultant global model. This distributed synchronization ensures model integrity and makes all contributions auditable, which is especially important in adversarial situations where no one trusts a central server. The architecture is typically arranged in such a way it contains three levels:

Edge Layer (Client Nodes): This layer contains the end-user devices, that is, smartphones, smartwatches, wearable sensors, etc., that gather multi-modal data, for example variability of heart rate, EDA, tone of speech, sleeping habits, and patterns of smartphone interactions. All devices conduct on-device processing and local training models, which means that there is no sensitive information that is exposed to third parties (Kim et al., 2022; Nguyen et al., 2022).

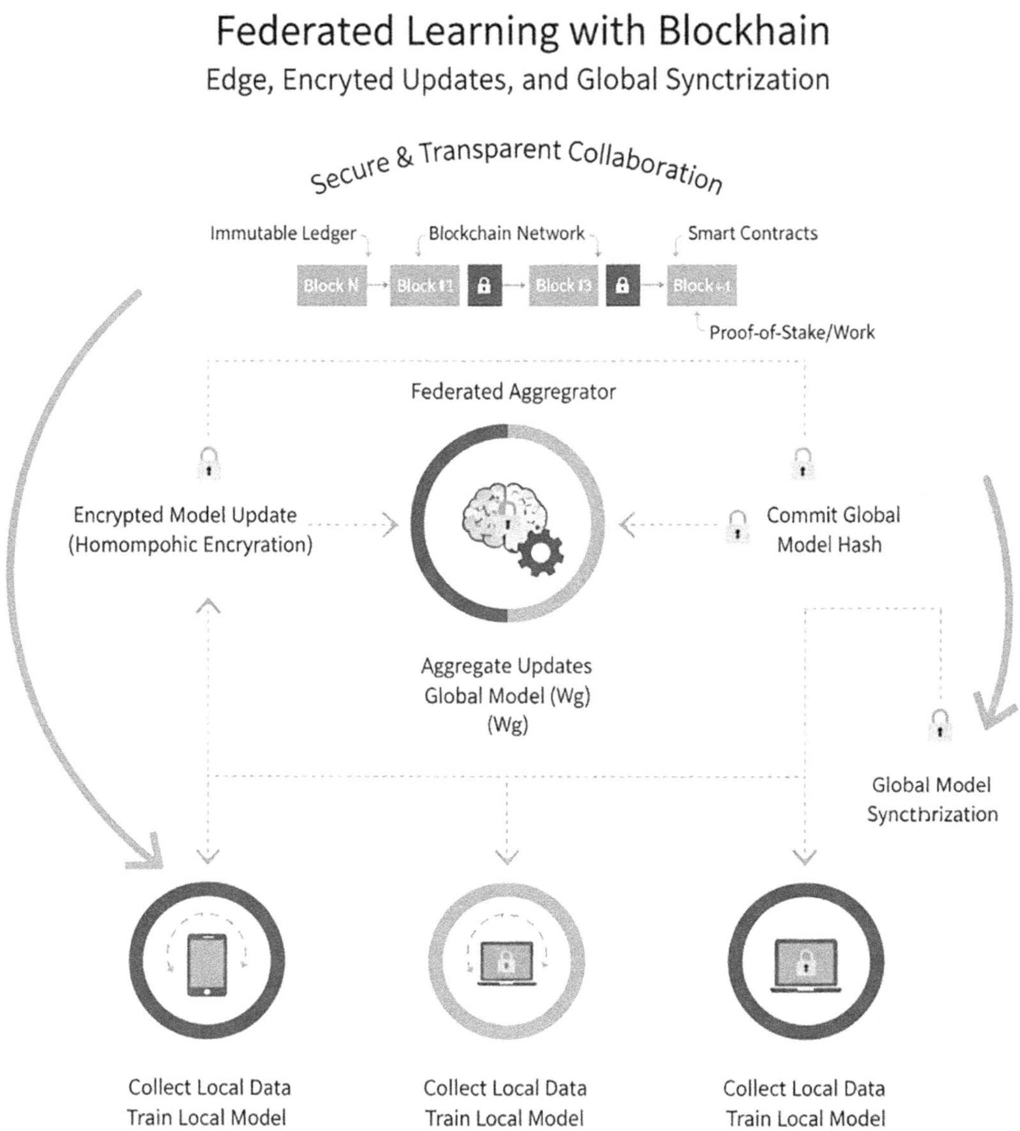

FIGURE 8.3 Mental health federated edge architecture.

Federation Layer (Aggregator/Coordinator): The coordination server is an intermediate which receives encrypted local updates of clients and implements an aggregation algorithm (e.g. FedAvg or FedProx). Secure Aggregation makes sure that the server is not able to recreate individual client data (Bonawitz et al., 2017). It is also a layer that has DP and HE to provide significant resistance against data inference attacks (Gursoy et al., 2021).

Cloud/Blockchain Layer: The last layer is used to orchestrate models, version control, and transparency auditing. Integration with blockchain makes it impossible to modify the models and provides traceability (Hossain et al., 2023). In addition, the elements of the cloud are used to provide scalability to computationally intensive updates to global models and long-term storage of anonymized metadata.

8.4.2 System Operation and Data Flow

Alternatively, the federated mental health AI workflow can be imagined as a continuous and adaptive learning loop, with continuously developing models being created through the interactions of the distributed users. The major stages are enumerated below:

Data Acquisition and Preprocessing: The sensors that are installed on the edge devices capture the behavioral and physiological signal measurements. The data are cleaned, normalized, and extracted locally. They do not require transmitting raw signals, thereby preventing unnecessary data exposure (Zhou et al., 2023).

Local Model Training: The local model is trained using local samples of data in each device on the model. Training algorithms are typically the stochastic gradient descent (SGD) or adaptive optimization (e.g. Adam). The aim is to reduce the local objective function without affecting the efficiency of the devices and battery limitations (Li et al., 2021).

Model Update and Encryption: Devices send encrypted model updates to the aggregator (parameter gradients) after local training is done. To avoid re-identification, differential noise is applied (Abadi et al., 2016).

Secure Aggregation: The aggregator computes the model updates by using algorithms such as FedAvg or FedProx. The contribution of each client is weighted based on the size of the dataset and its quality (McMahan et al., 2017).

Global Model Broadcast: The new global model is retransmitted to the involved devices that further the next training step. This process of federated optimization loop goes on until convergence or stabilization of performance.

Blockchain Verification (Optional): Using a blockchain ledger, each update of the model is stored in a blockchain ledger and, thus, they become more transparent, and they can work together with participating nodes in an irreversible fashion (Hossain et al., 2023).

Figure 8.4 shows the steps involved in the workflow of FL in real-time mental health monitoring. Switching to a particular application, Figure 8.4 defines the workflow of FL in end-to-end applications of mental health monitoring in real time. It starts with local data collection on the edge device of a user (e.g., smartphone, wearable) that would constantly collect passive data such as sleep habits, socialization, and intonation. This information is used for on-device training of a personalized behavioral model. Only the encrypted model parameters are sent to the central server

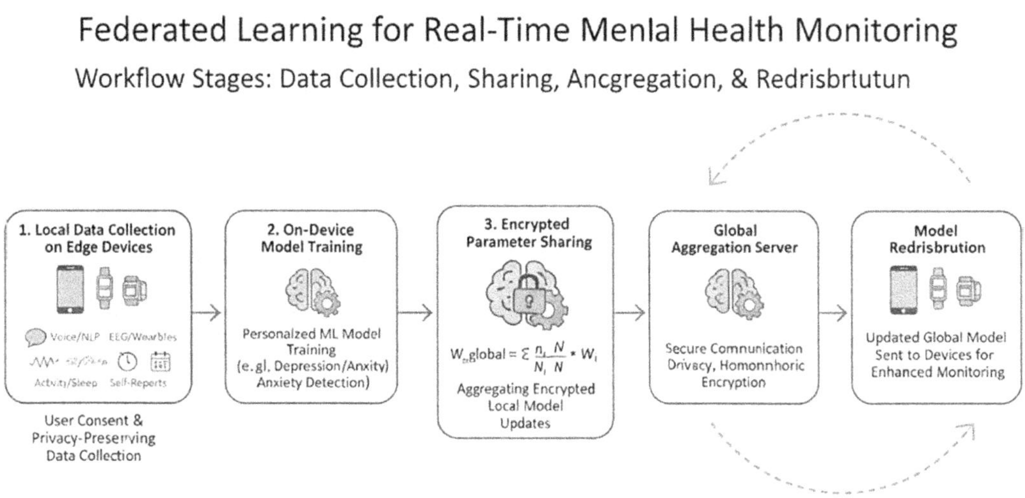

FIGURE 8.4 Federated learning workflow for edge-based mental health systems.

by the device. Global aggregation is done by the server to obtain a generalized model, which takes advantage of the overall knowledge of all the users. Lastly, the improved global model is distributed back to the devices where they optimize their local, customized models and provide more precise real-time feedback or alert generation.

8.4.3 Major Architectural Building Blocks

The performance and the feasibility of a federated edge system rely on the optimal design of its components.

a. *Edge Intelligence Module*
   This module is in charge of local inference and training of lightweight models on the device of the user. AI chips that are modern and have edge processing units (e.g., Google Edge TPU, Apple Neural Engine) have the capability to perform complicated tasks like emotion recognition or stress detection on-the-fly (Shi et al., 2022).
b. *Secure Communication Interface*
   The Transport Layer Security (TLS) and Secure Multiparty Computation (SMPC) are used to encrypt all client–aggregator communications. These schemes avoid eavesdropping and prevent eavesdropping and unauthorized access during gradient transmission (Acar et al., 2021).
c. *Aggregation Server*
   The aggregator works with the weighted fusion of parameters, calculation of global gradients, and convergence of models. It can also apply anomaly-detection algorithms to filter out malicious or inconsistent updates (Li et al., 2020).
d. *Audit Layer based on blockchain*
   A blockchain offers a trustless verification system so that every transaction (i.e. model update or client registration) is stored on a distributed record. Smart contracts are used to control access, so only validated clients would be involved in the learning cycle (Hossain et al., 2023).

8.4.4 Performance Measures and Review

Table 8.2 shows that the consideration of the performance of a federated edge system in the field of mental health is associated with various dimensions.

Recent research demonstrates that optimal edge-based FL architectures can lower latency by 35–60%, achieve accuracy levels exceeding 90%, and its energy usage can be greatly decreased than a centralized cloud system (Nguyen et al., 2022; Su et al., 2023).

TABLE 8.2
Federated Edge AI System Key Performance Measures in Mental Health Monitoring

Measurements	Explanation of Measurement	Mental Health AI Relevance
Accuracy	Share of correct choices (e.g., stress vs. no stress)	Determines the diagnostic reliability
Latency	Delay between data capture and inference of model	Important to real-time intervention
Privacy Loss (ε)	Differential privacy protection degree	Signifies the strength of data confidentiality
Communication Overhead	Average bandwidth and energy used in training	Affects device scalability
Convergence Rate	Number of iterations to take to achieve steady performance	Measures the efficiency of a model

8.4.5 Architectural Design Problems

Although Federated Edge architectures offer significant benefits, they have significant challenges:

Heterogeneous Devices: Hardware difference and stability of the network may result in lapses in the training of the model.
Non-IID Data Distribution: Mental health data varies greatly among individuals, and it is complicated to converge the global models (Kairouz et al., 2021).
Power and Bandwidth: Constant updates of the model use power, which requires compressing and adaptive learning methods.
Security Threats: Weak aggregation mechanisms may expose systems to model-inversion or inference attacks (Gursoy et al., 2021).

The next-generation architectures will strive to incorporate the adaptive learning protocols, energy adaptive optimization, and cross silo federation of coordination to address these architectural limitations.

8.5 EDGE AI AND REAL-TIME BEHAVIORAL INSIGHTS

Due to the emergence of Edge AI mental health informatics has changed, and now users can access context-aware, low-latency analytics on their devices. In contrast to traditional cloud-based systems where data must be sent to remote servers, the Edge AI performs on-device inference and lightweight model updates, which help ensure privacy, personalization, and low-latency behavioral insights (Shi et al., 2022; Zhou et al., 2023).

This part will discuss the structure, data forms, computational forms, and performance of Edge AI systems in the context of real-time behavioral surveillance and mental health forecasting.

8.5.1 The Concept and Relevance of AI to Mental Health AI

Edge AI refers to deploying AI models on resource-constrained devices (e.g., smartphones, wearables, IoT sensors) where computation occurs locally rather than in the cloud (Nguyen et al., 2022).

Edge AI can be applied in mental health settings to monitor subtle physiological and behavioral changes that are related to stress, depression, anxiety, sleep disorders, or cognitive fatigue. Timely monitoring of deviations will contribute to the early intervention, personal adaptation of the therapy, and self-management of the behavior (Wen et al., 2023).

Figure 8.5 shows the processing of multi-modal data of edge device in a local way to obtain real-time behavioral information. The gadget records multi-modal sensor data (e.g., physiological data, speech, activity). This raw data is instantly subjected to local preprocessing and normalization and feature extraction. The generated features are further ingested into an AI inference engine (the locally trained model), which produces real-time behavioral insights (e.g., stress, loneliness or low-quality sleep). Given these insights, this device can produce a local alert or give adaptive feedback to the user (e.g., a relaxation activity can be suggested). This design ensures that raw sensitive data remains on the device and is never externally transmitted.

8.5.2 Data Sensor Ecosystem and Data Modalities

Table 8.3 indicates that the Edge AI models are designed to work with heterogeneous, multi-modal data stream sensors that gather wearable and mobile sensor data.

These sensor inputs can be fused to create multidimensional behavioral profiles that offer deeper insights into a user's psychological state of users than manual self-reports and do not need them (Mukherjee et al., 2023).

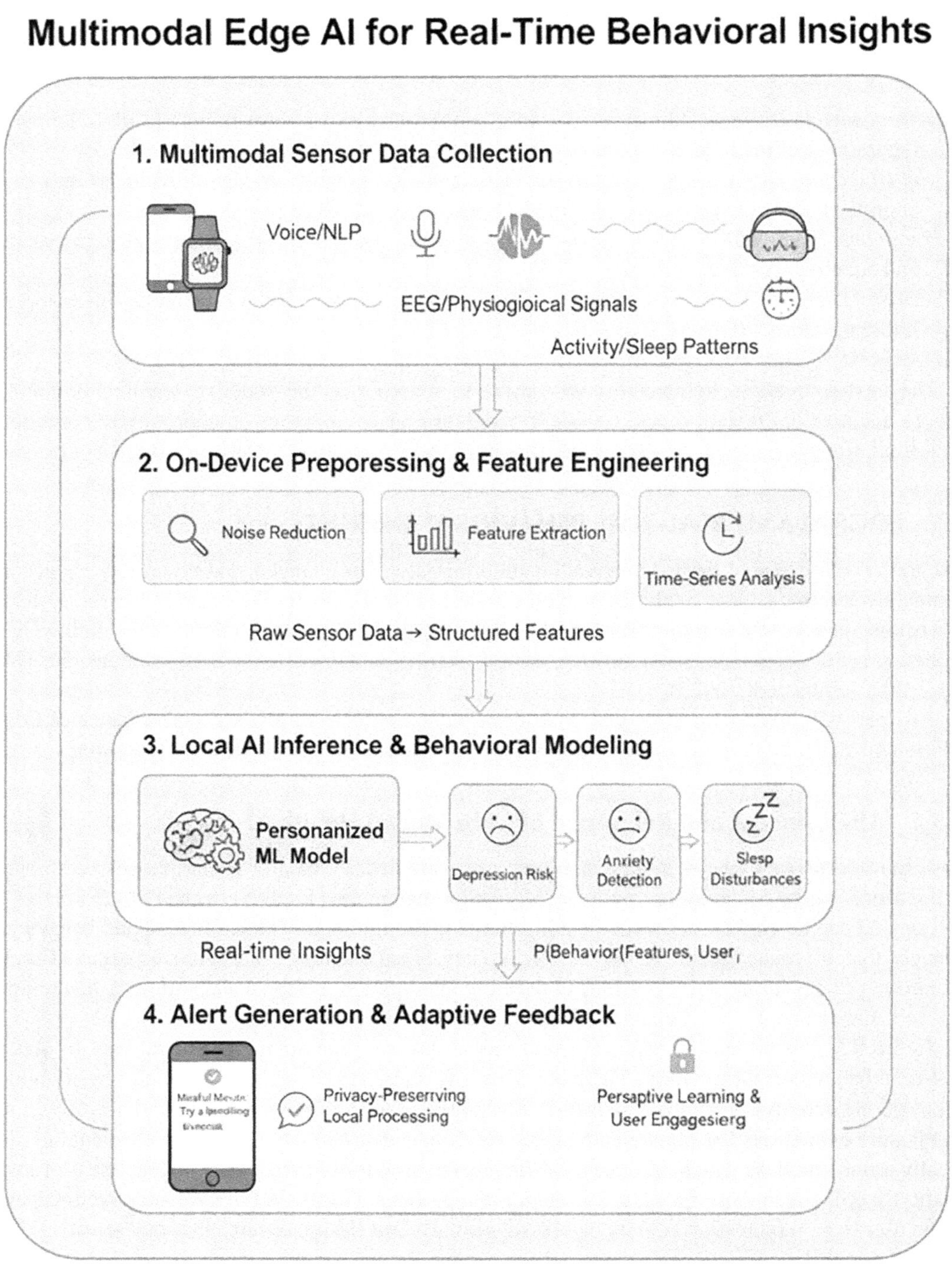

FIGURE 8.5 Edge AI system to generate behavioral insight in real time.

TABLE 8.3
Multi-modal Sources of Data and Behavioral Correlations in Mentality Systems Applying Edge AI

Data Type	Sensor Source	Behavioral Correlate	Application in Mental Health Assessment
Heart Rate Variability (HRV)	Smartwatches, ECG patches	Stress reactivity	Autonomic nervous system functionality monitoring
Electrodermal Activity (EDA)	Wristbands	Emotional arousal	Anxiety and panic episode detection
Accelerometer and Gyroscope	Smartphones, fit watches	Physical activity patterns and sleep analysis	which are relevant to depression and mood-tracking applications
Voice and Speech Features	Microphones	Tone, pitch, prosody	Detection of affective states
Sleep Patterns	Smart rings, mobile sleep apps	Sleep length and quality	Cognitive fatigue, depression indicators

8.5.3 On-Devices Machine Learning Models

Hardware limitations also lead to the use of optimized and smaller models in Edge AI systems that can execute with low power consumption. Common approaches include:

TinyML and Model Quantization: Pruning and quantization are techniques that decrease the computational cost without compromising the model accuracy (Han et al., 2016).
Lightweight Architectures: Models such as MobileNetV3, TinyBERT, and EdgeLSTM are specifically designed to be smaller and can be applied to emotion recognition and process physiological signals (Zhou et al., 2023).
Federated Personalization Layers: The local behavioral patterns are used to adapt a global model to individual features by the edge node (Li et al., 2021).
On-Device RL: On-device RL can dynamically adjust strategies, such as altering notification frequency or recommending relaxation activities (Xu et al., 2022).

Such models allow to make decisions immediately, for example, to identify spikes in stress or detect the risk of burnout before symptoms become pronounced.

8.5.4 Edge-Based Inference Workflow

The general operational workflow of real-time behavioral inference is based on five important steps:

Signal Capture: Essentially, wearable sensors are continuously capturing multi-modal data (i.e. HRV or heart rate variability, motion, voice).
Local Preprocessing: Noise reduction, normalization, and temporal segmentation are performed on-device. They are performed to preprocess the data to create inference-ready data.
Feature Extraction: Features that are domain- specific (e.g., Mel-frequency cepstral coefficients of speech or frequency bands of HRV) are computed in real time.

Model Inference: The resulting Edge AI model is a neural network or a decision tree which performs the classification of the current mind state (e.g., calm, stressed, anxious) with the help of a small neural network.

Feedback and Intervention: According to the results of inferences, the system provides adaptive feedback such as breathing prompts, ambient lighting adjustments, or caregiver notifications.

Figure 8.6 depicts an edge AI global view of the continuous and autonomous cycle of inference that is executed on one platform. It highlights the feedback loop which is required in real-time monitoring and intervention. On-device processing includes data cleaning and preparation, continuous sensing of behavioral and physiological signals, AI-based inference using local models to predict mental health conditions, and instant intervention feedback (e.g., polite notifications or reminders to schedule clinical appointments). Such a loop highly depends on low latency and privacy of locality of the whole inference process to the edge device.

8.5.5 Analytics Engine and AI

Among the paramount benefits of Edge AI, there is the possibility to reconcile real-time analytics and situational context. Context-aware systems take into account the environmental and time-related factors, including location, time of the day, and interactions between people to narrow down the predictions (Rahman et al., 2022).

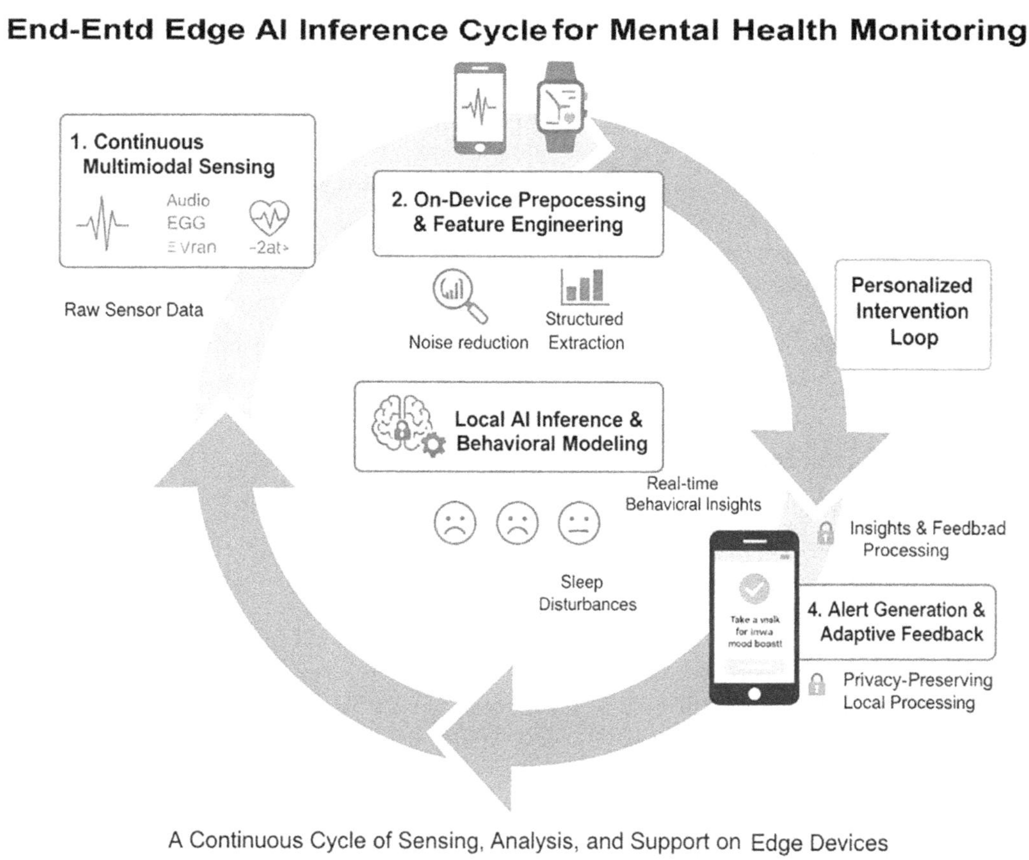

FIGURE 8.6 Edge AI inference behavioral state detection.

TABLE 8.4
Metrics of Evaluation of Behavioral Analytics in Edge AI

Measurement	Meaning	Applicability to Real-Time Insights
Inference Latency	Model needs time to give a prediction	Timeliness of intervention is affected
Model Size	The memory footprint of AI model	Determination of AI model suitability to mobile hardware
Energy Consumption	Battery consumption during model inference	Affects wearability and usability
Precision	Proper categorization of mental conditions	Ensures reliable detection of mental health states
Personalization Gain	The accuracy of model improves due to local adaptation	The sensitivity of model to user behavior

For example, an elevated heart rate may be expected during physical exercise but could indicate stress during a work meeting. These situations can be differentiated by edge-based contextualization and, thus, the system does not need any user-intervention (Mukherjee et al., 2023).

Additionally, Edge AI can be utilized to enable dynamic adaptation or models can be designed to update continuously based on a user's evolving behavior. Constant federated updates would make sure that longitudinal trends in mental health are captured efficiently and privacy is maintained (Li et al., 2021).

8.5.6 Metrics of Performance and Evaluation

Table 8.4 indicates that besides accuracy, the Edge AI systems are evaluated based on efficiency, responsiveness, and the safety of the users.

It has also been shown in experimental studies that the latency of Edge AI inference can be decreased by 40–70% relative to cloud-only solutions while maintaining stress and mood detection accuracy above 90% (Nguyen et al., 2022; Su et al., 2023).

8.5.7 Ethical and Practical Issues

The use of real-time behavioral monitoring creates an ethical and usability concern, such as:

Informed Consent and Transparency: The users should realize the way in which their data is gathered and the way in which predictions are used to generate feedback.
Data Minimization: Only essential features should be processed locally to minimize the risk of unintended privacy leakage.
Algorithmic Fairness: The algorithms should not be biased in relation to gender, age, and cultural backgrounds.
Actionable Insights: Systems should provide actionable insights rather than diagnostic judgments

Human-centered design with its emphasis on explainable AI, feedback loops, and privacy settings will be able to surmount these problems (Rahman et al., 2022).

8.6 FEDERATED DP

FL implementation in mental health AI introduces special issues when dealing with behavioral and physiological data which is sensitive in nature. Although FL reduces the need for centralized data collection, it does not fully eliminate the risk of information leakage through model updates. The mathematical concept of DP provides a more precise tool to measure and regulate these privacy risks by implementing some controlled randomness on the data or model gradients (Abadi et al., 2016; Gursoy et al., 2021).

This section explains the background, operational principles, and implementation of DP within federated systems with particular focus on using it on mental health surveillance and predicting behavior.

8.6.1 Concept and Motivation

DP includes a promise that the presence or absence of the information about any individual in a dataset does not critically affect the result of a computation. In a way, it makes sure that the opponent cannot know whether there is a data of a particular individual that was utilized in the training of a model (Dwork et al., 2014).

The main reason to incorporate DP in the FL systems of mental health AI is to:

End the re-identification of people based on pattern of behavior or physiological signature.
Meet privacy laws, for example, GDPR and HIPAA.
Maintain model utility and protect statistically against data inference attacks.

Figure 8.7 illustrates the core concept of DP within a FL ecosystem.

The figure specifically demonstrates how DP operates within an FL environment. DP is a method that measures the privacy loss. Practically, it is the introduction of a regulated number of random noise to local model updates. As shown in Figure 8.7, a client device can compute the update (W_i) it wishes to add to a carefully chosen noise vector ($[\varepsilon]_i$) to produce the obfuscated update (W_i+$[\varepsilon]_i$). This is the update sent to the server which is noisy. Noise injection makes it statistically infeasible to identify individual data contributions, thereby preserving user privacy.

8.6.2 Fundamental Operation of DP

DP protects individual contributions by adding controlled random noise to data or model gradients to obscure them. A parameter ε (epsilon) is called the privacy budget which defines the level of privacy protection. The smaller the ε, the greater the privacy is, but the lower the accuracy may be.

The most common definition is provided as follows:

$$P\left[M\left(D_1\right)\epsilon S\right] \leq e^{\epsilon} P\left[M\left(D_2\right)\epsilon S\right]$$

where D_1 and D_2 are datasets that are separated by a single record, and M is a randomized device that generates an output in set S (Dwork et al., 2014).

The DP noise may be introduced on two levels in the federated setting:

Local Differential Privacy (LDP): Noise is added to each client's model gradients before transmission. This has the benefit of making data confidential even to the central aggregator.

Global Differential Privacy (GDP): The aggregator introduces noise to model aggregation, and it attains global privacy and local computation is cheaper. Table 8.5 shows a comparison between LDP and GDP in FL.

8.6.3 Implementation in Federated Mental Health AI

In mental health applications, the DP mechanisms are combined with the federated optimization loop to make sure that sensitive behavioral patterns (including stress triggers or emotion trajectories) cannot be inferred based on shared gradients. The steps to be implemented are:

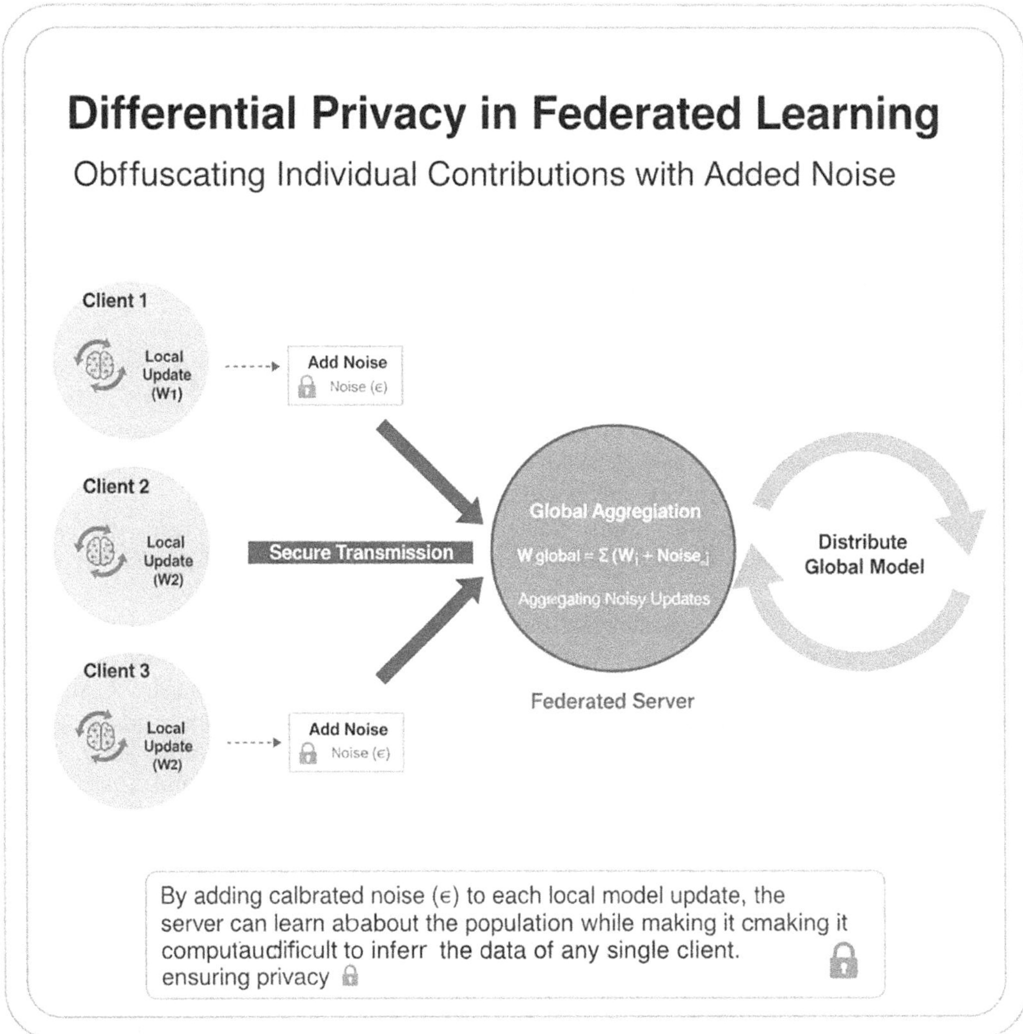

FIGURE 8.7 Federated learning with the mechanism of differential privacy.

TABLE 8.5
Comparative Analysis of Local and Global Differential Privacy in Federated Learning

Aspect	Local DP	Global DP
Noise Addition	Prior to model upload (client-side)	Prior to model aggregation (server-side)
Privacy Guarantee	Stronger individual protection	Moderate individual protection
Utility Impact	The possible decreased accuracy	Improved model performance
Computation Overhead	Higher (per client)	Lower (centralized)
Suitability	Small-scale or high-risk distributed applications	Large-scale distributed systems.

Gradient Clipping: Gradient magnitudes are capped using a predefined clipping norm before noise is added to it to ensure the undue weight of outlier updates (Abadi et al., 2016).

Noise Injection: Gaussian noise or Laplace noise is introduced proportionally. This guarantees that once an attacker collects gradients, he or she is not in a position to recreate the original information (Gursoy et al., 2021).

Secure Aggregation: Noisy gradients are aggregated with a secure protocol like either SMC or HE, which do not allow the aggregator to see the individual updates (Bonawitz et al., 2017).

Privacy Accounting: Privacy accounting schemes such as the Moments Accountant are used to keep track of the cumulative privacy loss (*e*) incurred by several rounds, and ensure that a total privacy bottleneck is not violated (Abadi et al., 2016).

8.6.4 Privacy versus Utility Trade-Off

The issue of DP introduces a trade-off on the essence of model-correction and privacy protection. When applied in the context of mental health AI, the addition of excess noise can result in the blurring of subtle behavioral patterns, which will make predictions less reliable.

Figure 8.8 illustrates the privacy–utility trade-off, showing how model accuracy decreases as stronger privacy levels (lower ε) are applied a a trade-off between the level of privacy (μ) and the model accuracy.

This figure typically appears as a line graph demonstrating how increased noise (lower ε) reduces model accuracy that exists between the degree of privacy (measured by the parameter μ) and the corresponding model performance. The *x*-axis is the budget of privacy (μ), and the *y*-axis is the accuracy of the model (e.g. F1-Score or AUC). The relationship is inverse: stronger privacy protection (lower ε) results in reduced model accuracy of the model becomes. On the other hand, in a bid to increase accuracy, noise is minimized leading to increased value of epsilon and hence reduced privacy. The number plays a key role in ensuring that researchers and practitioners settle on an appropriate e that would trade-off utility (accuracy) and privacy issues.

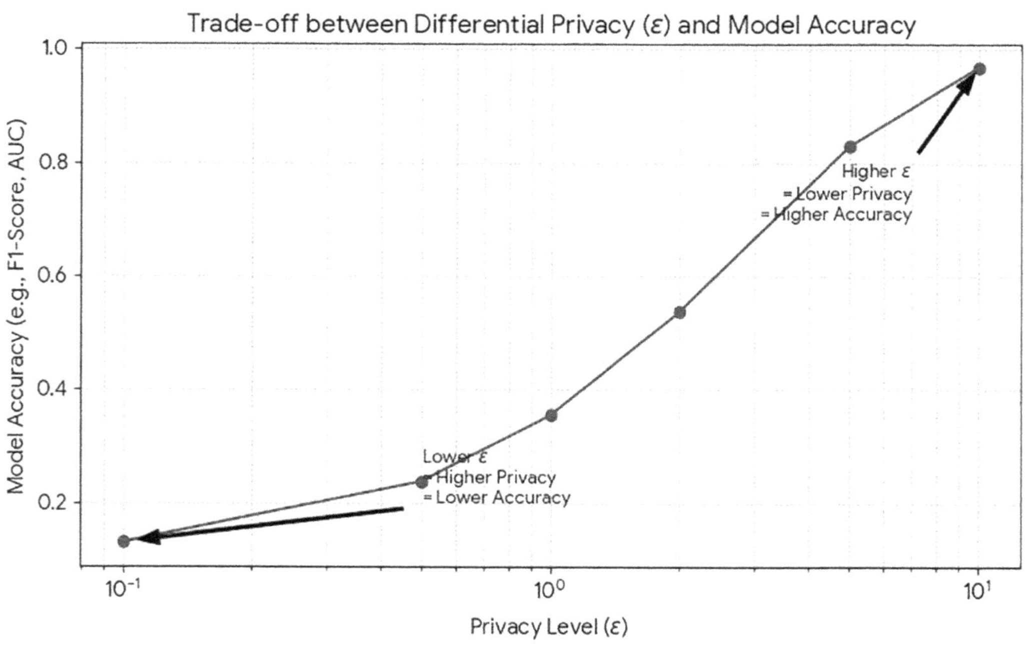

FIGURE 8.8 Privacy–utility trade-off in differentiable private federated learning.

The optimal privacy–utility balance can be achieved by adjusting the privacy parameter (ε) based on the sensitivity of the data modality (e.g., higher protection for speech or sleep data) and by stabilizing gradients using adaptive clipping and dynamic noise scaling techniques. This approach combines DP with federated personalization layers, enabling local devices to customize global models according to their specific data while preserving privacy (Li et al., 2021).

8.6.5 Hybrid Privacy Approaches

New developments use differentiating privacy along with complementary security to mitigate resilience:

DP combined with HE enables encrypted computation, ensuring that the server cannot decipher individual gradients (Acar et al., 2021).

DP + Blockchain: Differentiating parameters of privacy and history of model update are recorded in blockchain, and they are transparent and immutable (Hossain et al., 2023).

DP + Federated Dropout: This is a randomized method that removes layers or neurons in a model to shorten the attack surfaces without impacting computational efficiency (Gursoy et al., 2021).

These hybrid approaches are particularly valuable in mental health applications where data includes highly sensitive personal and emotional information.

8.6.6 Privacy Effectiveness Evaluation Metrics

Table 8.6 demonstrates to determine the efficiency of the healthcare privacy mechanisms in the federated environment; the following quantitative metrics are utilized:

Empirical experiments have indicated that appropriately tuned (*e* 1–5) DP mechanisms achieve more than 85–90% accuracy in emotion detection at the cost of much lower leakage risks (Nguyen et al., 2022; Su et al., 2023).

8.6.7 Ethical and Legal Implications

DP aligns with major international data protection regulations, including GDPR and HIPAA in the United States. DP allows mental health data to be anonymized by anonymizing physiological and behavioral patterns, and, therefore, facilitated the use of AI in an ethical manner (Rahman et al., 2022). Nevertheless, ethical use also requires that the determination and communication of privacy parameters (such as *e*) should be transparent to the users. Intrusive environments can reduce the quality of service provided, and permissive ones would reveal signs of sensitive behavior. Therefore,

TABLE 8.6
Measures to Evaluate the Effectiveness of Different Degrees of Privacy in Federated Settings

Metric	Definition	Mental Health AI Interpretation
Privacy Budget (ε)	Levels of protection of different privacy levels	When ε is lower, then privacy is stronger
Utility Loss (%)	Error reduction with and without DP	The utility loss measures the severity of a trade-off
Attack Success Rate (%)	Probability of data reconstruction by adversary	The lower is the better
Noise-to-Signal Ratio	Strength of added noise over gradient strength	High value will enhance anonymity
Model Convergence Time	Time to stabilize the model	Measures computational efficiency

implementing DP requires context-specific calibration and continuous monitoring of the privacy–utility trade-off.

8.7 AGGREGATION AND COMMUNICATION PROBLEMS

Reliable communication protocols and effective aggregation mechanisms are essential in FL systems for mental health AI because they directly affect system scalability and performance. Because data remain decentralized across smartphones, wearables, and local gateways, joint model training introduces significant communication, synchronization, and computational bottlenecks. Unless these challenges are handled appropriately, they may dramatically undermine the model accuracy, system responsiveness, and system energy efficiency.

8.7.1 FL Communication Bottlenecks

A major limitation of FL is the large communication overhead between client devices and the central server. The model updates are sent periodically by each device, and may be large in size, and often sent frequently. In mental health surveillance cases, where sensor data, voice data, or behavior data are being constantly updated, this continuous transmission of model updates can saturate network bandwidth. In addition, edge devices tend to be heterogeneous with regard to their connectivity capabilities, computational ability, and power, which results in asynchronous update issues. Interrupted or slow connectivity may cause certain clients to skip training rounds, leading to model drift and slower convergence rates (Kairouz et al., 2021).

To reduce this, scientists have suggested a number of optimization techniques like compression of updates, local epochs prior to aggregation, and client selection policies. Methods such as federated dropout and quantized gradients save on the cost of communication by only transferring a few model parameters. In addition, adaptive learning rate scheduling and asynchronous FL can accommodate partial updates, which means that intermittently connected devices can still participate without disrupting global model synchronization.

8.7.2 Challenges of Aggregation Under Non-IID Data

FL relies on the aggregation process. It entails aggregating individual (local) model updates of the participating clients into a global model based on methods like FedAvg. In mental health FL, user data are typically non-independent and non-identically distributed (non-IID) across users in mental health AI, as the rates of behavioral, emotional, and physiological patterns vary among individuals. Non-IID data cause biased client updates, which can lead to skewed global model convergence, addressing the problem of fairness or lower predictive power in heterogeneous groups of users (Li et al., 2020). To overcome these problems, more sophisticated methods of aggregation have been created: FedProx, FedNova, and clustered FL. These approaches combine local and global coordination, that is, large deviations of updates are penalized, or clients can be grouped by data similarity. In mental health settings, clustering can group users with similar stress profiles or activity patterns, enhancing personalization as well as privacy. In addition, secure aggregation schemes using HE or DP ensure that individual model updates remain confidential during aggregation.

8.7.3 Edge-Cloud Collaboration

EC is also critical in reducing communication as well as aggregation problems. The volume of data sent to the central cloud can be drastically cut by carrying out intermediate processing and local aggregation at the edge layer. This hierarchical FL design is efficient because edge nodes (e.g. hospital servers or community health centers) handle smaller groups of devices, train, and aggregate locally before periodically synchronizing with the global model. This kind of coordination layering guarantees more rapid convergence and fault tolerance of distributed mental health monitoring systems (Yang et al., 2022). In addition, federated edge caching and content-aware routing schemes are used to optimize the bandwidth utilization by prioritizing the important model updates among the redundant ones. In mental health contexts, where abnormalities must be detected quickly, edge-based aggregation can be used to generate immediate response prior to global coordination.

8.7.4 Constraints in Energy and Computation

Edge devices involved in FL tend to have small battery power and processing capabilities. Continuous communication and frequent local training can overload device resources and significantly increase energy consumption. To overcome this, the FL frameworks that are energy conscious change the frequency of participation or compress model gradients dynamically to reduce overhead. TinyML and EdgeAI offer lightweight deep learning models that balance low power consumption with acceptable predictive performance.

8.7.5 Future Directions

Further studies of communication and aggregation in mental health-oriented FL should consider self-adaptive networking, reinforcement-learning-based FL, and optimized communication graph topologies. These new approaches can support active engagement, stable coordination, and context-aware updates driven by individual mental health patterns. Besides, it is possible to implement blockchain-based layers of coordination to decentralize the process of aggregation, which increases the level of transparency and trust. To conclude, communication and aggregation issues are still major obstacles to the extensive implementation of FL in mental health AI. Through network efficiency, heterogeneity of the data, and use of privacy-preserving aggregation methods, researchers can build resilient, responsive systems that deliver accurate, ethical, and real-time mental health insights.

8.8 BLOCKCHAIN INTERPRETATION TO TRANSPARENCY

Transparency, accountability, and trust are fundamental requirements in FL systems for mental health AI because information gathering and model training are decentralized. Mental health apps are usually associated with sensitive and ethically vital information like emotional condition, behavioral norms, or physiological indicators. Lack of transparency in model updates, participant selection, and aggregation results can undermine user trust and hinder regulatory compliance. To address these challenges, blockchain has emerged as a complementary technology that enhances security, traceability, and integrity.

8.8.1 Blockchain-Based FL

Blockchain is an immutable, distributed ledger used to record validated events such as model update metadata, training participation, and data provenance, at all nodes in a federated network. With blockchain and FL, information regarding each model update and aggregation can be cryptographically verified and audited, making it extremely difficult for malicious parties to alter model updates or inject fabricated contributions (Lu et al., 2020). In mental health settings where confidentiality and consent are the most important factors, a blockchain-based logging can be applied to enable clear tracing of the process of developing data-driven insights without revealing the personal data behind it. Besides, in blockchain-enhanced FL, coordination can be decentralized through smart contracts, reducing reliance on a single central aggregator in favor of smart contract-based coordination. Smart contracts have the ability to enforce rules of participation, reward contributions, or access control policies automatically. Such a mechanism facilitates a fair involvement, minimizes central authority bias, and enables trustworthy collaboration among stakeholders amid various stakeholders including hospitals, research, and digital health sites.

8.8.2 Improving Data Integrity and Security

In FL, data integrity is paramount, especially in the mental health applications where the predictive accuracy can be poisoned by adversarial model poisoning or data injection attacks. Blockchain offers non-repudiation of records that can help prevent these threats. The update of each model of a client can be hashed and stored on-chain to build a history of all contributions to the model that can be verified. During global model aggregation, the resulting model can be validated using blockchain-stored hashes to ensure that no unauthorized modifications occurred (Majeed and Hong, 2021). Moreover, blockchain enhances data provenance by enabling verifiable tracking of data origin, evolution, and lineage. This is necessary in the assurance that AI-based predictions in mental health remain explainable, auditable, and aligned with ethical requirements. In fact, blockchain logs that are immutable can be examined by clinicians and auditors to ensure that data protection laws, such as the GDPR or the HIPAA, are adhered to.

8.8.3 The Decentralized Trust and Federated Governance

FL systems are often based on a coordinating server, which may turn into a failure point or bias. Blockchain enables decentralized governance by distributing decision-making authority across network participants. In blockchain-based federated learning (BFL) systems, the model updates undergo a consensus mechanism (e.g., Proof of Stake or Byzantine Fault Tolerance) across all the nodes, thereby reducing the risk of manipulation or falsification. These governance systems would be of great use, especially in multi-institutional mental health research where many healthcare organizations come together to develop AI models without raw-data sharing. Blockchain implies accountability to each other, as everyone can cooperate in a clear space, and data sovereignty and ethical standards are upheld.

8.8.4 Intelligent Contracts with Automation and Incentive Systems

Smart contracts consist of programmable scripts, which automatically run a set of predefined conditions on a Blockchain. They can automate key operations such as participant verification, resource allocation, and incentive distribution for devices contributing model updates. An example of this is that the user who posts high-quality model updates based on trusted sensor information may be rewarded with digital tokens or credits as a part of a tokenized reward system. Incentive mechanisms in mental health FL can increase user participation while reinforcing privacy-preserving behaviors. Moreover, using smart contracts, audit policies, training schedules, and trust scores for all participants can be defined and enforced automatically making sure that any malicious or poor-quality updates are excluded before the aggregation process.

8.8.5 Problems and Future Research

Although it has its benefits, the combination of blockchain and FL raises some issues. The issue of scalability is also a critical one because it is both computationally expensive and time-consuming to store all the model updates on-chain. Hybrid models are being developed to reduce latency by storing only essential metadata or hashed updates on-chain. Also, the energy usage of some consensus algorithms (such as Proof of Work) must be reduced to align with sustainable AI principles, especially in the mobile and edge contexts (Nguyen et al., 2022). The other issue is data privacy and compliance regulation. Although blockchain is a way of ensuring transparency, it also creates immutable records, which may conflict with privacy regulations that grant users the right to erasure. To address these concerns, researchers are exploring off-chain storage, zero-knowledge proofs (ZKPs), and privacy-preserving consensus mechanisms that trade transparency with confidentiality. When applied to the mental health AI, the combination of blockchain and FL creates a safe, transparent, and ethically oriented setting toward distributed intelligence. Auditability, decentralized trust, and data integrity allow blockchain to reduce the vulnerability of central servers and enhance user confidence in AI-based mental health systems. With the next generation of privacy-conscious, trustworthy, and autonomous healthcare systems, blockchain-enabled federated architectures are likely to become the key element in the future advancement of the field.

8.9 COMPARISON OF CENTRALIZED LEARNING AND FL

The history of AI development in the healthcare field, specifically in the area of mental health, has been characterized by centralized data processing models. Traditional AI systems involve gathering information of various users or institutions, and then summarizing and processing it in a central repository on a cloud environment to train predictive models. Although this method is computationally efficient and has easier management, it has raised important issues of privacy, scalability, and security of data, particularly where sensitive mental health information like emotional conditions or voice patterns or biometric measurements is involved. FL has come up and has overcome these shortcomings, in that it is a type of training that decentralizes edge devices. A comprehensive comparative study of centralized and federated paradigms of learning will be presented in this section in regard to the architecture, data management, privacy, communication efficiency, and ethical issues.

8.9.1 Architectural Differences

Under the centralized learning approach, user or sensor data are sent to a central server where AI model is trained and deployed. Although centralized learning is easier to manage, it creates a single point of failure, increasing the risk of data leakage and system vulnerability. Conversely, FL spreads the training of a model among a number of edge devices (e.g., smartphones, wearable sensors, or local servers), so that raw data are never transferred out of the device of the user. The parameters or gradients of the models are only shared with an aggregating server (McMahan et al., 2017). Such distributed architecture not only reduces the data movement but also allows working in heterogeneous environments. In mental health systems, this means that diverse data types—such as speech, sleep patterns, heart rate, and behavioral indicators—can contribute to a unified model without compromising user privacy or institutional control.

8.9.2 Data Privacy and Security

The greatest distinction between centralized and FL is data privacy. Centralized models require continuous transfer of sensitive information to cloud servers, increasing the risk of data breaches, insider attacks, and regulatory non-compliance. This presents ethical dilemmas in mental health settings, where any exposure to data, no matter how small, can result in stigma and discrimination or cause a person emotional damage. In contrast, FL ensures data localization, allowing individuals to retain control over their personal information. With DP, SMC, or HE, different FL frameworks can provide a great level of confidence in privacy, and yet incur high model accuracy (Kairouz et al., 2021). Besides, audit trails using blockchain will be able to facilitate the level of transparency that can present verifiable records of data utilization and model changes across institutions.

8.9.3 Efficiency and System Latency of Communication

Centralized learning benefits from stable, high-bandwidth server infrastructure that enables efficient communication and high throughput. Nevertheless, these architectures are bandwidth-intensive and energy-hungry with the rising data volumes, particularly in continuous mental health monitoring. Uploading large volumes of data can increase network latency and delay model updates, which can hinder timely mental health interventions. FL is able to counter this by integrating with EC, in which the processing takes place locally and only the minimum amount of model changes is communicated. This allows it to drastically decrease the network congestion and the time of response, and the near real-time analysis of mental health indicators, including stress, fatigue, or emotional volatility. However, FL adds communication overhead to the process of synchronizing distributed clients, especially in situations where devices are having different connectivity or hardware constraints. They are advancing new solutions to maximize the efficiency of the communication like asynchronous updates, model compression and adaptive client selection.

8.9.4 The Strength, Bias, and Model Generalization

High accuracy can be obtained with centralized learning models in cases where the datasets are large and well curated. In mental health research, datasets often suffer from sampling bias, demographic underrepresentation, and cultural imbalance. This means that a centralized model can enhance the existing disparities in the model predictions (Rieke et al., 2022). FL, in its turn, is intrinsically more favorable to data diversity training on decentralized, heterogeneous data, which is gathered across a variety of populations. This diversity enhances model robustness and reduces bias, resulting in more inclusive and context-sensitive mental health predictions. The lack of IID (independent and identically distributed) of local datasets in FL may however negatively affect convergence and consistency; in this regard, advanced aggregation methods such as FedProx or clustered FL are required to balance optimization.

8.9.5 Ethical and Regulatory Compliance

The extensive data transfer and centralized control of these systems make compliance with privacy regulations such as HIPAA and GDPR challenging. A single-point breach of data may lead to mass disclosure of sensitive data. FL is closer to these regulatory frameworks as it works according to the principles of data minimization. The raw information of users is not shared, and only knowledge acquired is shared. In addition, FL also enhances explainability and accountability through mechanisms such as blockchain-based logging and consent-driven access control which is especially crucial in the case of mental health AI applications as transparency is a direct factor affecting patient trust and clinical uptake.

8.9.6 Comparative Summary

TABLE 8.7
Comparative Summary of Centralized Learning and Federated Learning

Dimension	Centralized Learning	Federated Learning
Information Processing	All the information to central cloud is kept on the device	Model updates only
Privacy and Security	Very high risk of breach	Good privacy protection by local training
Latency and Efficiency	Conditional on network/cloud	Less latency through edge computation
Scalability	Centralized infrastructure capacity	Highly scalable to distributed devices
Ethical Compliance	Complex under GDPR/HIPAA	More naturally aligned with privacy regulations
Model Robustness	Tend to be biased due to homogeneous data	Enhanced robustness due to heterogeneous local data
Transparency and Trust	Minimized visibility	Improved through blockchain and auditability

8.9.7 Synthesis

Based on the comparative analysis, FL is a more appropriate paradigm of developing ethical, resilient, privacy-preserving mental health AI systems. Despite the centralized models remaining effective in the well-managed research settings where the data is commonly standardized, FL offers the flexibility, trust, and inclusivity necessary for deploying large-scale, real-world mental health AI systems. Its integration with EC, DP, and blockchain transparency systems is the reason why mental health diagnostics and interventions are not only technologically advanced but also ethical. As healthcare increasingly adopts digital and AI-driven solutions, the move from centralized to federated models represents a crucial step in developing responsible AI ecosystems that support human dignity, data sovereignty, and individual mental health.

8.10 CASE STUDIES: WATCHING AND PROGNOSTICATING SYSTEMS

The use of FL and EC in the domain of mental health AI has progressed from abstract, theory-driven research to practical, real-world applications. These case studies show how decentralized AI systems support mental health monitoring, diagnosis, and prediction while balancing data privacy, real-time analytics, and ethical standards. The FL-Edge systems can help clinicians, researchers, and users make meaningful decisions based on behavioral and physiological data without any breach of confidentiality through adaptive learning and distributed intelligence.

8.10.1 Case Study 1: Federated Stress Detection System Wearable Sensors

Stress detection using multi-modal sensor data is one of the most prominent applications of FL in mental health. The Federated Stress Detection Model was implemented in a collaborative study conducted in several universities (Smith et al., 2022) across wearable devices which were able to record HRV, skin conductance, and activity patterns. Local neural network models were trained on individual devices to infer stress levels from physiological signals. Only model weights, not raw data, were transmitted through secure channels to the central FL aggregator. The aggregation employed FedAvg with different privacy noise injection in which no single information could be reassembled. The final global model achieved an accuracy of more than 91% in recognizing stress and high level of compliance with the privacy laws.

The authors have shown how Edge-based wearable AI systems can detect rising stress levels in real time and initiate coping interventions including mindfulness cues or relaxation instructions. It also demonstrated how the network traffic reduced by half relative to centralized methods and the practicality of behavioral monitoring that is privacy conscious.

8.10.2 Case Study 2: Using Smartphone Data to Predict Federated Depression

The second significant case involves using FL to predict depressive symptoms from smartphone data. A study by researchers of the University of Melbourne and MIT was one of the first implementations of Federated Deep Learning Framework where user metadata including screen-time patterns, call duration, text message sentiment, and mobility traces were analyzed locally (Chen et al., 2023). Each smartphone was a local client that was training a small recurrent neural network (RNN) model. The experiment implemented Edge-cloud cooperation where local devices updated model parameters with an aggregator in the middle on a periodic basis. The world model was able to anticipate depressive episodes with an accuracy of 86%—similar to centralized systems—without any unprotected personal information of the user being exposed. Moreover, users retained full control over participation through explicit, authenticated consent mechanisms, which encouraged the digital trust in AI in mental health.

This decentralized prediction model enabled clinicians to get anonymized notifications on individuals at risk, which could be used to implement early intervention mechanisms. The model adjusted to the behavioral peculiarities of the individuals by offering local personalization with federated generalization and utilization of the global learning trends.

8.10.3 Case Study 3: Edge-Based Anomaly Detection in Behavioral Therapy

Real-time detection of anomalies is another application of Edge AI in cognitive–behavioral therapy (CBT) sessions because anomalies can be detected near the source. FL was deployed carefully (Tyagi, 2021) alongside the modules of speech emotion recognition that were run locally on therapy room machines. Both systems processed vocal tone, emotional cues, and response timing during therapy sessions and trained local models to identify signs of distress or lack of concentration. The HE was used to maintain patient confidentiality and, subsequently, the model updates were sent to be aggregated federally. The global model progressively improved its anomaly-detection performance of therapy anomalies and allowed therapists to change the strategies on the fly.

This federated structure was 40% more effective than the conventional centralized voice analytics in preserving privacy and had 35 times shorter inference latency due to the use of localized processing. It was especially useful in the hybrid teletherapy settings where sensitive data transfer is done across multiple nodes.

8.10.4 Case Study 4: FL with Clinical Collaboration Enhanced with Blockchain

Data silos are frequent impediments in collaborative model training in multi-institutional mental health research. A federated model for predicting depression and anxiety was deployed in a European pilot involving four psychiatric hospitals, where blockchain and FL were merged (Nguyen et al., 2022). Blockchain was used as a layer of trust to store all model updates and contributions made by participants in an unchangeable registry. The federal structure was used to train models with heterogeneous patient data—one model in one hospital—each localized on a local drive and an model update validation was conducted using a Proof-of-Stake (PoS) consensus mechanism. Aggregation of models was also automated with the use of smart contracts, and traceable responsibility of each training cycle was ensured by blockchain logs.

This mixed model exhibited a better transparency and integrity of sharing models, better F1-scores, and fewer opportunities of model poisoning. Of particular importance, it was in compliance with European privacy standards (GDPR), which shows that decentralized cooperation does not have to restrict ethical and legal limits.

8.10.5 Case Study 5: Federated RL—Anxiety Monitoring of Personality

Federated reinforcement learning (FRL) is a new form of FL that enables individual model adaptation by constantly engaging with FRL user data. An Anxiety Monitoring System was developed in 2024 (Zhao et al., 2024) and was based on the FRL, with biometric and contextual data being tracked on the smartphone and wearables continuously. Both edge devices were able to make use of reinforcement signals (e.g., sleep quality, social engagement, heart rate) to maximize individualized feedback behavior. The distributed agents periodically shared policy gradients with a central aggregator and this would allow global learning and maintain individual autonomy. The system has achieved considerable advancement in accuracy of personalized intervention (93%), and reduced user dropout associated with privacy concerns. This shows how FL and RL synergy could make the mental healthcare a self-adaptive and privacy-conscious ecosystem.

8.10.6 Case Study Comparative Insights

In these case studies, we can identify a number of trends:

Privacy Preservation: In all federated models, raw data remained on user devices, greatly reducing privacy risks.
Edge AI Responsiveness: Low-latency behavioral change and stress response detection were possible because of the capability to process Edge AI.
Personalization: Models adapted to each individual's behavioral patterns without compromising global learning.
Transparency and Trust: User trust was enhanced through integration and consent participation with the aid of blockchain.
Regulatory Alignment: All systems proved to be compliant with the main privacy laws like HIPAA and GDPR and are therefore ethical.

The case studies reviewed prove that FL and EC are redefining technological background of mental health AI. FL-driven models offer high accuracy, low latency, and strong data-sovereignty protections in terms of stress and depression monitoring to the adaptive therapy system. These frameworks are further enhanced by integrating RL with blockchain by bringing in autonomy, accountability, and ethical transparency.

With the continued growth of research and clinical implementations, the decentralized systems will prove central to the facilitation of real-time and human-intelligent mental health support empowering individuals and professionals creating AI ecosystems that are safe, efficient, and ethically aligned with mental-health standards.

8.11 EMERGING DECENTRALIZED MODELS

The rapid development of decentralized AI represents a paradigm shift in mental health technology, shifting away from the traditionally centralized systems toward more autonomous, distributed, and ethically resilient ecosystems. FL, blockchain-enabled AI, Multi-Agent Systems (MAS), and Privacy-Preserving Reinforcement Learning (PPRL) are some emerging models of decentralization in this area, whose implementation enhances safety, flexibility, and user agency in mental health monitoring.

These models will resolve the long-standing issues of data fragmentation, algorithm bias, and privacy loss, as well as make mental health prediction systems more inclusive, interpretable, and adherent to the international data protection regulations.

8.11.1 FL with Blockchain

Blockchain-Enabled Federated Learning (B-FL) integrates FL with the transparency and auditability offered by blockchain. The blockchain in this hybrid architecture acts as a trust management layer and all training interactions, model updates, and validation transactions are recorded. All participating nodes, such as hospitals, wearable devices, or individual users, add encrypted gradients to a ledger that is controlled by a smart contract, and the ledger is fully traceable and accountable. In the case of mental health systems, this architecture enables verifiable model provenance, which is essential when the AI-driven recommendations have a clinical impact. The decentralized consensus, or PoS, or Delegated Proof-of-Authority (DPoA) eliminates risks associated with single-point failures and model tampering.

Li et al. (2023) demonstrate that B-FL frameworks can mitigate malicious update injection attack by ratio of up to 70% and enhance model trustworthiness. The method also allows collaboration of mental health research across institutions without violating the GDPR regulations.

8.11.2 Multi-Agent Federated Systems Behavioral Intelligence

MAS are built upon the idea of decentralized AI, allowing autonomous agents, with local learning, reasoning, and communication expertise, to work together in achieving common goals. Federated Multi-Agent Systems (FMAS) can be used together with FL to conduct real-time distributed decision-making within mental health networks. In these models, agents may represent different data sources, including wearables, smartphone sensors, and hospital electronic medical record (EMR) systems. Agents exchange high-level representations rather than raw data by strengthening each other through cooperative learning. This enables the global models to be dynamic as agents adjust to alterations in behavioral or contextual state.

As an example, in predicting mental health crisis, every agent might learn on its regional or demographic subgroup and communicate only aggregate emotional trends. These systems have demonstrated potential for enhancing personalization across diverse demographic groups, in treating cultural and context-specific mental health AI.

8.11.3 Privacy-Preserving Reinforcement Learning

PPRL applies cryptographic and DP protocols in the RL-based behavioral modification systems. PPRL distributes learning across multiple local environments, as compared to traditional RL which uses a centralized experience replay buffer. Each local node learns an agent to maximize the behavioral results, for example, stress reduction or therapy engagement, and exchange encrypted policy gradients. The securely aggregated policy updates collectively form the global learning process, without showing individual paths.

The latest implementations (Zhang et al., 2024) prove that PPRL can achieve comparable performance to the centralized RL systems simultaneously providing high user privacy rates. In cases of the mental health support chatbots or adaptive therapy assistants, this model ensures that individual emotional responses remain confidential and, at the same time, enhance the overall system learning.

8.11.4 Swarm Intelligence to Decentralized Recognition of Emotions

Swarm Intelligence (SI) models are gaining popularity in decentralized emotion recognition that is inspired by biological swarms such as bee colonies and ant swarms. The device or sensor nodes in such network are analogous to swarm members, providing local measurements of emotional cues, for example, tone, heart rate, or text sentiment, to a global decision. Unlike traditional top-down control systems, SI-based models rely on local interactions and emergent coordination, resulting in adaptive and fault-tolerant behavior. As an example, when one sensor node malfunctions or generates noisy results, the swarm will compensate collectively over the system and preserve its stability.

Swarm-based emotional inference has demonstrated strong performance in real-world monitoring and has been shown to exhibit strong results in mental health monitoring, particularly when trained in FL to build hierarchical models. Collective intelligence principle can improve reliability and resilience, which are important characteristics of healthcare AI systems that will work in various settings.

8.11.5 Decentralized Trust, Explainability Mechanisms

Emergent decentralized frameworks also aim to improve explainability and ethical transparency. Explainable Federated Models (XFM) can also be used to provide validated explanations for a model's predictions, including why a model has identified a patient to be at risk of depression or anxiety. These models use Decentralized Knowledge Graphs (DKGs) to link decision pathways to interpretable features such as sleep disturbance, loss of mobility, or speech impairment. XFMs offer distributed accountability; hence, making AI-based recommendations more credible to both clinicians and patients. Moreover, it is possible to consider ZKPs that can be combined with the need to guarantee the accuracy of predictions without revealing sensitive intermediate information: both interpretability and confidentiality are provided within the same system.

8.11.6 Federated Graph Neural Networks to Mental Health Analytics

Another emerging model is the Federated Graph Neural Network (FGNN), which integrates the power of relations of graph learning and federated privacy. FGNNs are capable of modeling complex interdependence between users, symptoms, and environmental factors on a number of decentralized nodes. In the analysis of mental health, FGNNs enable the researcher to model patterns of social connectivity, emotional dynamics, and behavioral evolution without centralizing the data. Every device or institution that participates in the process calculates its local graph embeddings, and the node representations are aggregated by a federated coordinator to create a single global mental health network. It is empirically proven that FGNN performs better in context-sensitive mental state prediction by achieving a 15% improvement in performance over the traditional FL-based models (Huang et al., 2023). This renders FGNN a powerful method for uncovering complex relational patterns in decentralized populations of patients.

The development of new decentralized systems, a blockchain-FL hybrid to a privacy-sensitive reinforcement system and graph-based analytics, is a turning point in the AI-enhanced mental health prediction. These models enable safe, collaborative, and interpretable intelligence frameworks, surpassing the constraints of overcoming limitations of centralized systems that have historically constrained privacy and scalability. It is predicted that in the future these technologies will come together to form self-organizing, interoperable ecosystems where ethical AI, human-centered design, and adaptive computation integrate seamlessly. The change corresponds to the general idea of human-centered AI and empowers individuals to participate actively in their mental-health management while retaining control over their data.

8.12 SUMMARY

FL and EC integration in the area of mental health AI is one of the most critical milestones of creating secure, privacy-sensitive, and people-focused intelligent systems. This chapter examined how decentralized architectures address urgent challenges in mental health technology, particularly data privacy, transparency, scalability, and real-time contextual adaptation.

Through a progressive discussion from FL fundamentals to blockchain integration, the chapter emphasized the need to shift from centralized data collection models toward decentralized, privacy-preserving approaches. FL can facilitate participative learning in mental health environments where data is sensitive, heterogeneous, can be distributed across mobile and clinical devices, and no data exposure is allowed. The FL framework enables hospitals, smartphones, and wearable sensors to collaboratively train AI models without any information about the individual users being transferred to other computers. This approach preserves patient confidentiality and ensures adherence to privacy standards such as GDPR and HIPAA.

EC was presented as a key enabler of real-time behavioral analysis, enabling the creation of inferences and the generation of feedback in the place and location of data collection. Edge AI systems can deliver personalized, dynamic interventions without requiring continuous cloud connectivity. FL combined with EC optimizes three critical dimensions of sustainable digital mental health infrastructures: latency reduction, energy savings, and privacy.

Moreover, the sections about DP, secure aggregation, and communication-efficient protocols explained the way in which cryptographic and statistical methods can be used to guard against model inversion and data leakage attacks. This is so ensuring that the federated model can leverage distributed data while significantly reducing vulnerability to adversarial exploitation.

The chapter also examined how the integration of blockchain enhances transparency and trust within federated networks. Accountability and verifiability, which are essential to a medical grade AI system, are enhanced by blockchain because it offers immutable audit trails and smart contract governed systems. The comparative study of centralized and federated practices has shown that the latter has great benefits in regard to resilience, ethical strength, and inclusiveness.

Practical examples ranging from stress-sensing wearables to smartphone-based mood prediction demonstrate the transformative potential of these systems. New decentralized paradigms, such as multi-agent FL, PPRL, and federated graph neural networks are the heralds of the next phase in the AI evolution of mental health. These models enhance personalization and scalability while supporting fundamental human values, including autonomy, dignity, and informed consent.

FL, Edge AI, and blockchain are likely to become the backbone of next-generation digital mental health networks and the origin of flexible, understandable, and morally answerable intelligence. Such systems will allow clinicians, researchers, and individuals to work safely and mental healthcare will shift from a reactive, institution-focused model to a proactive, patient-centered one.

REFERENCES

Abadi, M., Chu, A., Goodfellow, I., McMahan, H. B., Mironov, I., Talwar, K., & Zhang, L. (2016). Deep learning with differential privacy. In *Proceedings of the 2016 ACM SIGSAC conference on computer and communications security* (pp. 308–318). ACM. https://doi.org/10.1145/2976749.2978318

Abay, N. C., Zhou, Y., Kantarci, B., & Soyata, T. (2022). Federated learning for mental health monitoring: Privacy-preserving analytics at the edge. *IEEE Access, 10*, 127632–127645.

Acar, A., Aksu, H., Uluagac, A. S., & Conti, M. (2021). A survey on homomorphic encryption schemes: Theory and implementation. *ACM Computing Surveys*, *53*(2), 1–35. https://doi.org/10.1145/3214303

Balamurugan, G., Tyagi, A.K., & Richa, A. (2023). Survey on privacy preserving and trust building techniques of blockchain-based systems. In: *Privacy Preservation and Secured Data Storage in Cloud Computing*. IGI Global. DOI: 10.4018/979-8-3693-0593-5.ch019

Bonawitz, K., Ivanov, V., Kreuter, B., Marcedone, A., McMahan, H. B., Patel, S., & Seth, K. (2017). Practical secure aggregation for privacy-preserving machine learning. In *Proceedings of the 2017 ACM SIGSAC conference on computer and communications security* (pp. 1175–1191). ACM. https://doi.org/10.1145/3133956.3133982

Chen, M., Yang, Z., Saad, W., Yin, C., Poor, H. V., & Cui, S. (2022). A joint learning and communications framework for federated learning over wireless networks. *IEEE Transactions on Wireless Communications, 21*(1), 269–283. https://doi.org/10.1109/TWC.2020.3024629

Chen, Y., Lin, X., Li, Y., & Wong, J. (2023). Federated deep learning for depression prediction using smartphone behavioral data. *IEEE Transactions on Affective Computing, 14*(2), 456–468.

Dinh, C. T., Tang, J., La, Q. D., & Quek, T. Q. S. (2021). Federated learning over wireless networks: Convergence analysis and resource allocation. *IEEE/ACM Transactions on Networking*, *29*(1), 398–409. https://doi.org/10.48550/arXiv.1910.13067

Dwork, C., Roth, A., & Vadhan, S. (2014). The algorithmic foundations of differential privacy. *Foundations and Trends® in Theoretical Computer Science*, *9*(3–4), 211–407.

Floridi, L., & Cowls, J. (2021). *A unified framework of five principles for AI in society. Harvard Data Science Review*, *3*(1). https://doi.org/10.1162/99608f92.6ed64b30

Gursoy, M. E., Liu, L., Truex, S., & Yu, L. (2021). Differential privacy in federated learning: A survey. *IEEE Internet of Things Journal*, *8*(12), 9466–9487.

Han, S., Mao, H., & Dally, W. J. (2016). *Deep compression: Compressing deep neural networks with pruning, trained quantization and Huffman coding*. International Conference on Learning Representations (ICLR). https://doi.org/10.48550/arXiv.1510.00149

Hossain, M. S., Muhammad, G., & Song, B. (2023). Blockchain-enabled federated learning for healthcare data security. *IEEE Internet of Things Journal*, *10*(3), 2123–2136. https://doi.org/10.1109/ACCESS.2025.3587345

Huang, J., Li, T., & Wang, Y. (2023). Federated graph neural networks for decentralized mental health analytics. *IEEE Transactions on Neural Networks and Learning Systems, 34*(11), 9532–9545. https://doi.org/10.1016/j.asoc.2024.112475

Jacobson, N. C., Lekkas, D., Price, G., Heinz, M. V., Song, M., O'Malley, A. J., & Barr, P. J. (2022). Digital phenotyping of mental health: A scoping review. *npj Digital Medicine*, *5*(1), 92.

Kairouz, P., McMahan, H. B., Avent, B., Bellet, A., Bennis, M., Bhagoji, A. N., & Zhao, S. (2021). Advances and open problems in federated learning. *Foundations and Trends in Machine Learning*, *14*(1–2), 1–210. https://doi.org/10.48550/arXiv.1912.04977

Kim, H., Park, J., & Cho, S. (2022). Wearable-based edge intelligence for stress monitoring and adaptive intervention. *IEEE Access*, *10*, 12473–12485. https://doi.org/10.3390/healthcare11172369

Kumar, R., Patel, S., & Gupta, D. (2022). Edge-based federated speech emotion recognition for cognitive behavioral therapy. *Sensors, 22*(15), 5783. https://doi.org/10.1201/9781003529231-13

Kumari, S., Tyagi, A. K., Tiwari, S., & Kulshreshtha, G. (2025a). Sensors and digital twin for healthcare monitoring frameworks. In T. A. Nguyen (Ed.), *Digital twin, blockchain, and sensor networks in the healthy and mobile city (Chapter 10, pp. 147–177).* Elsevier. https://doi.org/10.1016/B978-0-443-34174-8.00011-9

Kumari, S., Tyagi, A. K., Tiwari, S., & Singh, R. (2025b). Medical sensor network, edge computing and blockchain for efficient medical data exchange. In T. A. Nguyen (Ed.), *Digital twin, blockchain, and sensor networks in the healthy and mobile city (Chapter 11,* pp. 179–198*).* Elsevier. https://doi.org/10.1016/B978-0-443-34174-8.00012-0

Li, Q., He, B., & Song, D. (2021). Practical federated learning systems: Challenges, design, and trends. *ACM Computing Surveys*, *54*(8), 1–36.

Li, T., Sahu, A. K., Talwalkar, A., & Smith, V. (2020). Federated learning: Challenges, methods, and future directions. *IEEE Signal Processing Magazine*, *37*(3), 50–60. https://doi.org/10.48550/arXiv.1908.07873

Li, X., Chen, R., & Zhao, J. (2023). Blockchain-enabled federated learning for trustworthy health AI. *IEEE Journal of Biomedical and Health Informatics, 27*(4), 1882–1895. https://doi.org/10.2196/46547

Liu, Y., Kang, Y., Zhang, C., & Chen, T. (2022). Federated transfer learning for healthcare data integration. *IEEE Transactions on Neural Networks and Learning Systems*, *33*(5), 1789–1802. https://doi.org/10.48550/arXiv.2010.15561

Lu, Y., Huang, X., Zhang, K., Maharjan, S., & Zhang, Y. (2020). Blockchain and federated learning for privacy-preserved data sharing in industrial IoT. *IEEE Transactions on Industrial Informatics, 16*(6), 4177–4186. https://doi.org/10.1109/TII.2019.2942190

Majeed, A., & Hong, C. S. (2021). Blockchain-based federated learning for secure and transparent distributed AI. *IEEE Access, 9*, 179116–179129. https://doi.org/10.1145/3560816

McMahan, H. B., Moore, E., Ramage, D., Hampson, S., & Arcas, B. A. Y. (2017). Communication-efficient learning of deep networks from decentralized data. *Proceedings of the 20th International Conference on Artificial Intelligence and Statistics (AISTATS), 54*, 1273–1282. https://doi.org/10.48550/arXiv.1602.05629

Mishra, A. K., Tiwari, S., Tyagi, A. K., & Arowolo, M. O. (2024). Security, privacy, trust, and provenance issues in Internet of Things–based edge environment. In S. Pal, C. Savaglio, R. Minerva, & F. C. Delicato (Eds.), *IoT edge intelligence* (pp. 233–263). Springer. https://doi.org/10.1007/978-3-031-58388-9_8

Mukherjee, S., Sinha, A., & Banerjee, R. (2023). Multimodal sensor fusion for context-aware emotion recognition on edge devices. *IEEE Sensors Journal*, *23*(6), 8451–8462.

Nair, M. M., & Tyagi, A. K. (2021). Privacy: History, statistics, policy, laws, preservation and threat analysis. *Journal of information assurance & security*, *16*(1). https://doi.org/10.7753/IJCATR1306.1016

Nair, M.M., & Tyagi, A.K. (2025). Transformative effects of emerging technologies on Industry 5.0 and Society 5.0: Current status, vision, issues, challenges, and opportunities for future. In: *Next Generation Data Science and Blockchain Technology for Industry 5.0*. Wiley. DOI: https://doi.org/10.1002/9781394245215.ch13, ISBN: 9781394245185.

Nguyen, D. C., Ding, M., Pham, Q. V., Pathirana, P. N., Seneviratne, A., Li, J., & Niyato, D. (2022). Federated learning meets blockchain in edge computing: Opportunities and challenges. *IEEE Internet of Things Journal, 9*(1), 1630–1649. https://doi.org/10.1109/JIOT.2021.3072611

Onnela, J.-P., & Rauch, S. L. (2021). Harnessing smartphone-based digital phenotyping to enhance behavioral and mental health. *Neuropsychopharmacology*, *46*(1), 220–221. https://doi.org/10.1038/npp.2016.7

Rahman, M. M., Hasan, M. A., & Uddin, M. Z. (2022). Ethical implications of AI-driven health monitoring systems. *Journal of Ambient Intelligence and Humanized Computing*, *13*(5), 3217–3230. www.preprints.org/manuscript/202503.0078

Rieke, N., Hancox, J., Li, W., Milletari, F., Roth, H. R., Albarqouni, S., & Cardoso, M. J. (2022). The future of digital health with federated learning. *npj Digital Medicine*, *5*(1), 119. https://doi.org/10.1038/s41746-020-00323-1

Sheller, M. J., Edwards, B., Reina, G. A., Martin, J., Pati, S., & Bakas, S. (2020). Federated learning in medicine: Facilitating multi-institutional collaborations without sharing patient data. *Scientific Reports*, *10*(1), 12598. https://doi.org/10.1038/s41598-020-69250-1

Shi, W., Cao, J., Zhang, Q., Li, Y., & Xu, L. (2022). Edge computing: State-of-the-art and future directions. *IEEE Internet of Things Journal*, *9*(1), 1–17. https://api.semanticscholar.org/CorpusID:213591593

Smith, T., Lee, H., & Zhao, Q. (2022). Federated learning-based stress detection with wearable sensors: A privacy-preserving approach. *Journal of Biomedical Informatics, 129*, 104058. https://doi.org/10.5281/zenodo.17453935

Su, C., Tong, J., & Xiong, Z. (2023). Federated deep learning for stress and emotion detection in mobile environments. *IEEE Transactions on Affective Computing*, *14*(2), 874–887.

Tyagi, A.K. (2021). Analysis of security and privacy aspects of blockchain technologies from smart era' perspective: The challenges and a way forward. In: *Recent Trends in Blockchain for Information Systems Security and Privacy* (pp. 1–17). DOI: https://doi.org/10.1201/9781003139737, eBook-ISBN: 9781003139737

Tyagi, A.K. (2025). Blockchain for smart hospital in Healthcare 5.0: modeling structure, challenges, and future emerging trends. In: *Human-Centric Integration of Next-Generation Data Science and Blockchain Technology*. Elsevier. DOI: https://doi.org/10.1016/B978-0-443-33498-6.00026-1, ISBN: 978-0-443-33498-6.

Tyagi, A. K., Kumari, S., & Tiwari, S. (2024c). Internet of Things for smart healthcare: A survey. In A. K. Sharma, N. Chanderwal, S. Tyagi, & P. Upadhyay (Eds.), *Future of AI in medical imaging (Chapter 2,* pp. 19–41*)*. IGI Global. https://doi.org/10.4018/979-8-3693-2359-5.ch002

Tyagi, A. K., & Tiwari, S. (2024a). Blockchain-enabled smart healthcare applications in 6G networks. In A. K. Tyagi (Ed.), *Digital twin and blockchain for smart cities (Chapter 20,* 459–494*)*. Wiley. https://doi.org/10.1002/9781394303564.ch20

Tyagi, A. K., Tripathi, K., Tiwari, S., & Kaushik, S. (2025). An efficient technique for privacy preservation, trusted and secure patient-centric services in smart healthcare. In *Proceedings of the 6th international conference on recent trends in communication & intelligent systems (ICRTCIS 2025)* (pp. 31–47). IET. https://doi.org/10.1049/icp.2025.2731

Wang, J., Liu, Q., Liang, H., Joshi, G., & Poor, H. V. (2021). A field guide to federated optimization. *Foundations and Trends in Machine Learning, 14*(1–2), 1–210. https://doi.org/10.48550/arXiv.2107.06917

Wang, R., Aung, M. S. H., & Hossain, M. S. (2023). AI-driven mental health assessment using multimodal data fusion: A review. *IEEE Reviews in Biomedical Engineering*, *16*, 121–139. https://doi.org/10.24815/jr.v8i2.45375

Wen, J., Yu, M., & Zhang, X. (2023). AI-driven early stress detection through multimodal edge computing. *IEEE Transactions on Neural Systems and Rehabilitation Engineering*, *31*(4), 812–823.

Xu, J., Zhang, Y., & Li, T. (2022). Federated learning for mobile health: System design and applications. *ACM Transactions on Intelligent Systems and Technology*, *13*(3), 1–24.

Yang, Q., Liu, Y., Chen, T., & Tong, Y. (2022). Federated machine learning: Concept and applications. *ACM Transactions on Intelligent Systems and Technology*, *13*(4), 1–19. https://doi.org/10.48550/arXiv.1902.04885

Zhang, C., Xie, Y., Bai, H., Yu, B., Li, W., & Gao, Y. (2022). A survey on federated learning. *Knowledge-Based Systems*, *216*, 106775. https://doi.org/10.1016/j.knosys.2021.106775

Zhang, L., Wu, K., & Dong, S. (2024). Privacy-preserving reinforcement learning for adaptive mental health interventions. *Neurocomputing, 556*, 126728.

Zhao, J., Liu, X., & Chen, R. (2024). Personalized anxiety monitoring using federated reinforcement learning. *ACM Transactions on Internet Technology, 24*(3), 1–20.

Zhou, Z., Chen, X., Li, E., & Zhang, L. (2023). Edge AI for healthcare: Real-time and privacy-preserving solutions. *IEEE Network*, *37*(1), 128–135.

Part III

Privacy Risks, Ethics, and Trust

9 Risk Assessment and Threat Modeling in AI-Driven Mental Health

9.1 INTRODUCTION

The intersection of artificial intelligence (AI) and mental healthcare represents a major paradigm shift in clinical diagnosis, therapy, and monitoring of a patient. Speech patterns, facial expressions, and physiological signals are now processed by intelligent systems that have an unprecedented high level of detecting the signs of depression, anxiety, and other psychological issues. As much as these advancements help improve access and individualization of care, they also introduce new forms of digital vulnerability. Sensitive mental health information, which can be more intimate compared to the traditional medical records, is more frequently stored, transmitted, and processed using interconnected AI-driven infrastructures. Such reliance increases the likelihood that AI mental health systems become targets of cyberattacks through data breaches, ransomware, and model impersonation.

Threat modeling and risk assessment have thus been established as part and parcel of secure AI mental health architectures. Risk assessment begins with a systematic identification of risks potentially affecting the system and ranking them considering their probability and the potential effects to the system performance and privacy of data. Instead, threat modeling offers a systematic approach to the study of adversarial behavior, attack vector mapping, and a predictive view of the impact of exploitation. Collectively, these practices can be used as a defensive tool against possible attacks. Researchers, clinicians, and developers are able to anticipate vulnerabilities before they turn into severe incidents.

The significance of cybersecurity in mental health AI extends beyond purely technical protection. Data breaches in digital therapeutic systems not only compromise the reliability of the system, but also destroy patient trust, and this may lead to people not seeking assistance via digital intervention. The ethical aspect is also very strong, because AI models that are trained on sensitive data should guarantee privacy, fairness, and stability within regulatory measures like the General Data Protection Regulation (GDPR) and the Health Insurance Portability and Accountability Act (HIPAA). In this regard, the incorporation of effective risk assessment and threat modeling systems is not only a technical issue, but also a moral and clinical imperative.

This chapter provides a comprehensive overview of the security principles, analytical tools, and evaluation methods that will ensure AI mental health ecosystems are secure. It starts by discussing the basics of the established threat modeling techniques and risk classification schemes and proceeds to discuss common cyber threats, including phishing, ransomware, and Application Programming Interface (API) exploitation. In subsequent sections, internal and external threats are differentiated, role of real-time threat intelligence explored, and quantitative and qualitative risk models evaluated. The debate concludes with the identification of best practices, vulnerability management tools

DOI: 10.1201/9781003658344-12

(VMTs), and mechanisms of certification, among others, that will help to make AI-based mental health platforms more resilient, transparent, and trustworthy. In this multidimensional view, the chapter tries to build a safe baseline in the ethical use of AI in mental healthcare.

Figure 9.1 shows an overview of the AI Mental Health Security Ecosystem, a layered conceptual diagram that demonstrates the multi-tiered architecture needed to secure the deployment of AI in mental healthcare. The patient is its main component, and it signifies the person whose sensitive mental health information the entire system relies upon. The data layer covers the surrounding of the patient and includes different types of information, such as medical records, sensor data (wearables), and interaction data (therapy chatbots). This data is processed by the AI Model layer, which employs sophisticated algorithms, such as natural language processing (NLP) and predictive analytics, and results in the formation of therapeutic insights. These models and large datasets that they operate on are deployed and hosted in the cloud infrastructure layer that manages centralized storage and high-performance computing. Importantly, the security shield is an umbrella of the entire functional system and it is a continuous set of protective measures that are deployed on all inner layers. Among these security measures necessary to ensure patient trust and regulatory compliance are encryption

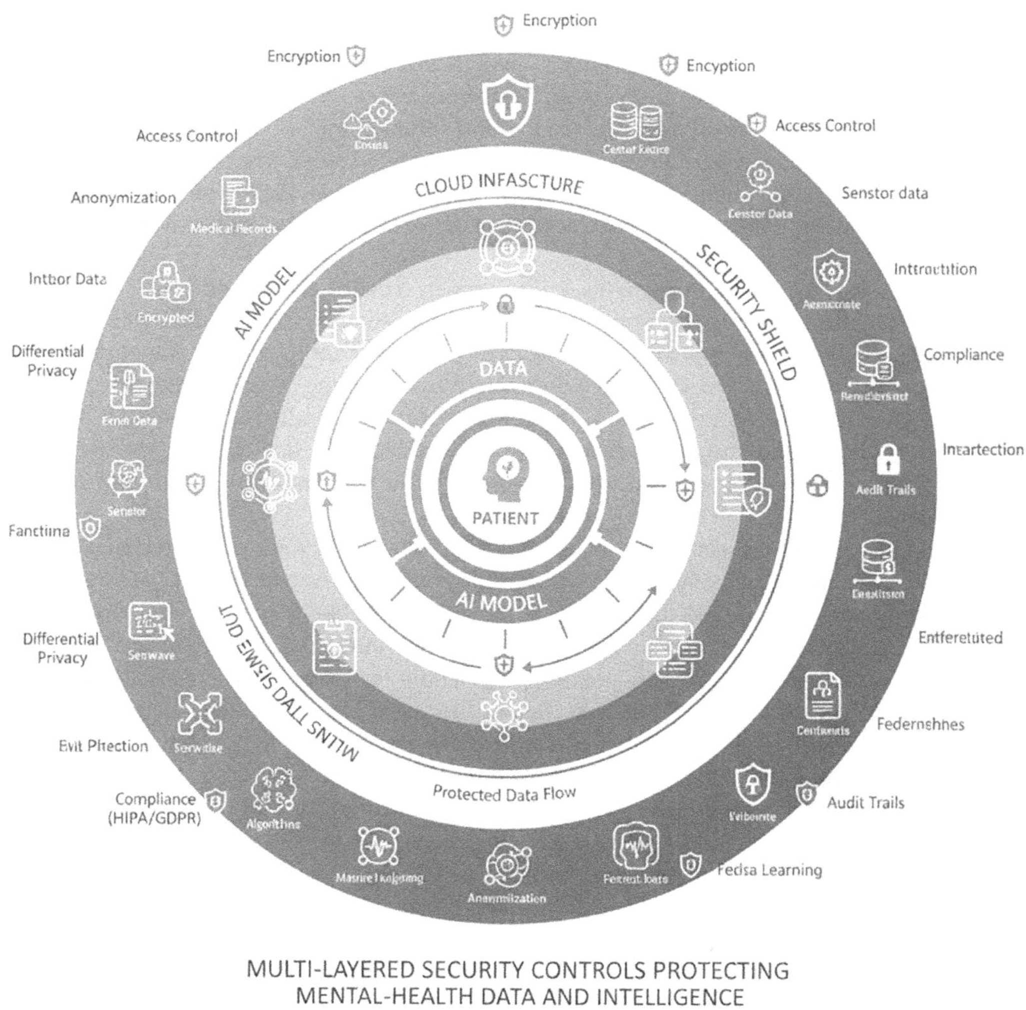

FIGURE 9.1 General overview of AI mental health security ecosystem.

TABLE 9.1
Mental Health Components of AI Mapping to Potential Threat Surfaces

AI Component	Description	Potential Threat Surface	Example Threat (STRIDE)	Mitigation Strategy
Data Preprocessing	Cleans and formats patient data before model training	Input data integrity	Spoofing	Cryptographic hash verification
Model Training	Neural networks learn from patient datasets	Parameter manipulation	Tampering	Model weight encryption
Model Inference	Generates mental-health predictions or recommendations	API interface	Information disclosure	Secure API gateways
Data Storage	Stores sensitive diagnostic or behavioral data	Database access	Elevation of privilege	Role-based access control
Communication Layer	Cloud or edge transmission channels	Network traffic	Denial of service	Intrusion detection and rate limiting

(of data at rest and in transit), anonymization, differential privacy (to ensure patient identity is not revealed in model training), access control, and a high level of compliance with various regulations, such as HIPAA and GDPR. Finally, an icon is used to visually illustrate that the mental health AI should be run on a protected data flow, where intelligent systems should be made accessible only under the conditions of strong, multi-layered security and governance procedures. As Table 9.1 demonstrates, both functional and connectivity aspects of every element of the AI mental-health system present distinct attack surfaces.

9.2 LITERATURE REVIEW

AI adoption in mental health systems has altered how clinical decisions, communication with patients, and the analysis of their behavioral patterns are conducted. Nonetheless, as a result of this integration, an urgent requirement has arisen for systematic risk assessment and threat modeling models which are sensitive to the nature of the psychological information. The current literature demonstrates a trend toward understanding cybersecurity risks in healthcare AI systems, yet intensive research on the topic of mental health use is still slightly scarce. In this section, the main findings in the areas of AI healthcare security, threat modeling practices, and risk assessment models are synthesized to build a contextual background of the secure AI mental health systems.

9.2.1 Mental Health: The AI Opportunities and Risks

Tasks such as emotion recognition, suicide risk prediction, and digital psychotherapy have been effectively implemented with the help of AI models (Tyagi, 2021; Nair et al., 2021). These systems are strongly dependent on multi-modal data, such as speech, facial expressions, wearable sensor, and text-based therapy logs, to derive emotional and cognitive conditions. Although this type of data-based method improves the accuracy of diagnoses, it also increases the privacy risks as mental health data are very personal and identifiable. Research conducted by Ahmed and Lee (2023) has proven that even anonymized data of behavior is re-identifiable by cross-correlating the data with publicly available data, showing that the conventional privacy-preserving scheme of AI systems is inadequate. Therefore, when mental health meets AI, there is a need to have more robust threat modeling frameworks that do not entirely consider only technical vulnerabilities, but also ethical and psychosocial risks.

9.2.2 AI Methods of Healthcare Threat Modeling

Threat modeling is an active process that is used to detect, classify, and counter any threats in advance, before they damage the integrity of the systems. Common threat-classification models such as STRIDE (Spoofing, Tampering, Repudiation, Information Disclosure, Denial of Service, and Elevation of Privilege) and DREAD (Damage, Reproducibility, Exploitability, Affected Users, and Discoverability) have been widely applied in healthcare cybersecurity (Microsoft, 2020). More modern systems such as the MITRE ATT&CK matrix and the FAIR (Factor Analysis of Information Risk) model offer a systematized system of behaviors of adversaries and quantifying the effect of various threat vectors (Santos et al., 2023; Nair et al., 2025). These frameworks have been adapted for mental health AI systems so as to replicate adversarial manipulation of predictive models and guard clinical information pipelines. Nevertheless, as Li et al. (2024b) note, these frameworks would need to change to include specific AI-specific threats including model inversion attack, data poisoning, and adversarial perturbation that may directly affect the therapeutic process.

Figure 9.2 gives a very important flowchart of the AI lifecycle, which identifies all the operational phases alongside the security weaknesses assigned to them, which requires the security to be end-to-end. The first stage is the Data Stage, where the main threats are the Data Poisoning (the intentionally corrupt integrity of training data), Data Leakage (the confidentiality of sensitive information violations), and the Bias Injection. Then the Training Stage is the next stage of attacks, where the learning process itself is attacked, such as Model IP Theft (stealing the proprietary algorithm), Backdoor Attacks (adding minor, conditional vulnerabilities to the model), and Hyperparameter Tampering.

The Deployment (Inference) Stage, which follows the model, is attacked directly by Evasion Attacks (Adversarial Examples to mislead the model), Prompt Injection (hijacking generative models), and Model Denial of Service (DoS). Lastly, the iterative Monitoring and Feedback Stage is susceptible to persistent privacy and integrity assaults such as Model Drift/Degradation, Membership Inference Attacks (finding out whether this particular record was utilized in training), and Model Inversion Attacks (reconstructing the training data based on the model output). Relating the workflow (Data–Training–Deployment–Monitoring) to these threats directly, the flow diagram shows that the effective implementation of AI security should be based on periodical, stage-based controls and not perimeter defense only.

9.2.3 Risk Structure of AI Mental Health

The risk assessment frameworks offer a systematic way of determining the probability and intensity of security attacks. The most famous quantitative approaches to measuring the cyber risk in AI-based infrastructures include the FAIR model and ISO/IEC 27005 standard (ISO, 2022). Qualitative

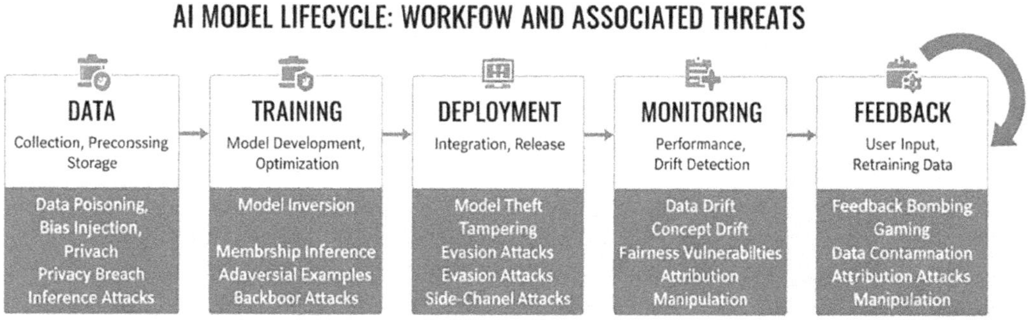

FIGURE 9.2 The relationship between AI workflow stages and threat surfaces.

models, such as the NIST SP 800-30 and OCTAVE Allegro, are focused on scenario-based assessment, and which are particularly relevant in mental health systems, where human-oriented variables, including emotional distress and patient trust, have to be evaluated. In a recent comparison analysis, Zhou et al. (2024) noticed that hybrid methods, that is, quantitative scoring and contextual assessment, provide more lifelike information on vulnerabilities in the system. This solution correlates with the ethical aspect of mental healthcare in which the effects of the data breach are not only financial but also mental and reputational.

9.2.4 General AI Mental Health System Cyber Threats

Studies have revealed that a common threats in digital mental health ecosystems include phishing, ransomware attacks, and API abuse. The most frequent mode of an unauthorized entry to mental health databases is phishing, in most cases, via patient-deceptive channels of communication (Nguyen and Patel, 2022; Tyagi, 2021). Ransomware attacks, in their turn, attack electronic health records (EHRs) and cloud-based AI models, encrypting the sensitive data to demand a payment. Use of API-based exploits has been on the rise as mobile mental health applications that use third-party services have become more popular (Rahman et al., 2023; Kumari et al., 2025a). Based on the literature, the mitigation of such threat demands the layers of defense approach that incorporates the access control, encryption, behavioral analytics, and AI-based anomaly detection systems.

9.2.5 Gaps and Research Directions

Even with the advances, there are still glaring gaps in adapting threat modeling and risk assessment models to AI mental health in a more precise way. The existing paradigms are fraught with insufficient adaptive mechanisms, which would be able to consider dynamic human behavior, modeling of behavior-dependent emotional contexts and ethical data governance. Moreover, the interdisciplinary cooperation between cybersecurity specialists, psychologists, and data scientists has not been developed yet (Singh and Dutta, 2024; Kumari et al., 2025b). The recent research promotes the use of uninterrupted surveillance systems that operate with the power of federated learning and AI that does not violate privacy rights to boost resilience to emerging threats. These gaps will have to be addressed so as to create next-generation mental health systems that are secure and ethically compliant.

9.3 THE BASICS OF THREAT MODELING

Threat modeling is a foundation of proactive cybersecurity, which provides an ordered approach to threat recognition, assessment, and mitigation of threats to system assets before they can be exploited. Threat modeling in the framework of AI-based mental health systems is important to ensure patient confidentiality, data integrity, and AI model reliability in diagnosis and treatment. As compared to conventional healthcare systems, mental health AI architectures process extremely sensitive data streams—such as voice tone, emotional expressions, therapy transcripts, and behavioral logs—and are therefore highly susceptible to adversarial manipulation and data breaches. The following section investigates the core principles and models that characterize the practice of threat modeling, how traditional approaches to threat modeling (STRIDE, DREAD, and FAIR) can be adapted to address the security and ethical needs specific to AI mental health ecosystems.

9.3.1 Threat Modeling Concept and Objectives

Threat modeling is both analytical and design-oriented, helping organizations systematically identify vulnerabilities, estimate their likelihood of exploitation, and plan preventive controls. It can be used in AI-based mental health systems as a proactive data protection measure that guarantees the data confidentiality, model integrity, and ethical adherence. Threat modeling is mainly done to gain an insight into the flow of information across the borders of trust, what assets are to be protected, and how enemies can exploit those assets. Santos et al. (2023) report that a good threat modeling process begins by mapping system assets, that is, patient data, AI model parameters, and communication interfaces and proceeds to assess possible threats and their impact potentials. The final component of this cycle is risk assessment and risk mitigation planning, which leads to the creation of a framework through which cyber incidents can be predicted, not simply responded to. In AI mental health contexts, threat modeling extends beyond technical issues and must also address psychological safety, data sensitivity, and ethical aspects of mental health information. Therefore, a properly developed threat model also strengthens patient trust in digital mental health technologies.

9.3.2 STRIDE Framework of AI Mental Health Systems

STRIDE model, which was initially created by Microsoft, is still one of the most widely used models for identifying and categorizing the potential cybersecurity threats. It categorizes the threats into six categories: spoofing, tampering, repudiation, information disclosure, DoS, and elevation of privilege (Microsoft, 2020; Mishra et al., 2024). In the case of AI mental health sites, STRIDE offers a formal method of studying how users, systems, and data interact. Impersonation of trusted users or devices can occur as spoofing, such as creating a fake therapist account or cloning an account of a patient interfering with the integrity of a therapy session. Tampering is defined as any kind of unauthorized changes in stored data or AI model parameters that can change the results of the diagnosis and confuse clinical judgments. Repudiation occurs when the user repudiates their behavior in the system, for example, when the attesting records of session notes are denied by therapists or falsified prescription records, causing difficulties in accountability and auditability. Information disclosure refers to the unauthorized access or unintentional exposure of extremely sensitive mental health data by misconfigured APIs or using weak encryption protocols. On the contrary, DoS attacks interfere with the availability of teletherapy servers which is likely to slow down patient care in an emergency situation. Lastly, elevation of privilege happens when the attackers obtain administrative-level access to system operations to modify the model behavior or alter privacy settings or bypass access controls. The STRIDE model may be applicable in mental health AI systems to visualize and evaluate these vulnerabilities in data flow diagrams to allow security analysts to identify the points of control that demand more protection measures, including encryption, multi-factor authentication, and restricted access control.

Figure 9.3 depicts the STRIDE threat model, a conventional template of identifying the security threats, applied to elements of an AI-based clinical environment. STRIDE identifies six types of threats, namely spoofing, tampering, repudiation, information disclosure, denial of service, and elevation of privilege. Within the scope of AI, spoofing might mean that an attacker will pretend to be a medical professional or a valid AI-based service to secure credibility. Tampering is the act of unauthorized alteration, such as modifying AI model parameters or altering training or inference data. Repudiation refers to the capacity of an attacker or legitimate user to effectively deny that he/she has taken a malicious action and this is solved by robust audit logs that is essential in a clinical setting. The privacy breaches discussed under information disclosure include a model inversion attack exposing the patients' information in the model outputs, or more traditional data breaches of a model revealing protected health information (PHI). A DoS attack disrupts essential AI diagnostic or treatment services (DoS), which can be life-threatening to a clinical setting. Lastly, elevation of privilege is a condition whereby the attacker accesses the higher permission beyond what is supposed to be granted to them, which enables them to circumvent security measures and possibly steal information or even control the AI system. This model can help healthcare security practitioners to determine and reduce the particular risks of each of the modules in the clinical AI process.

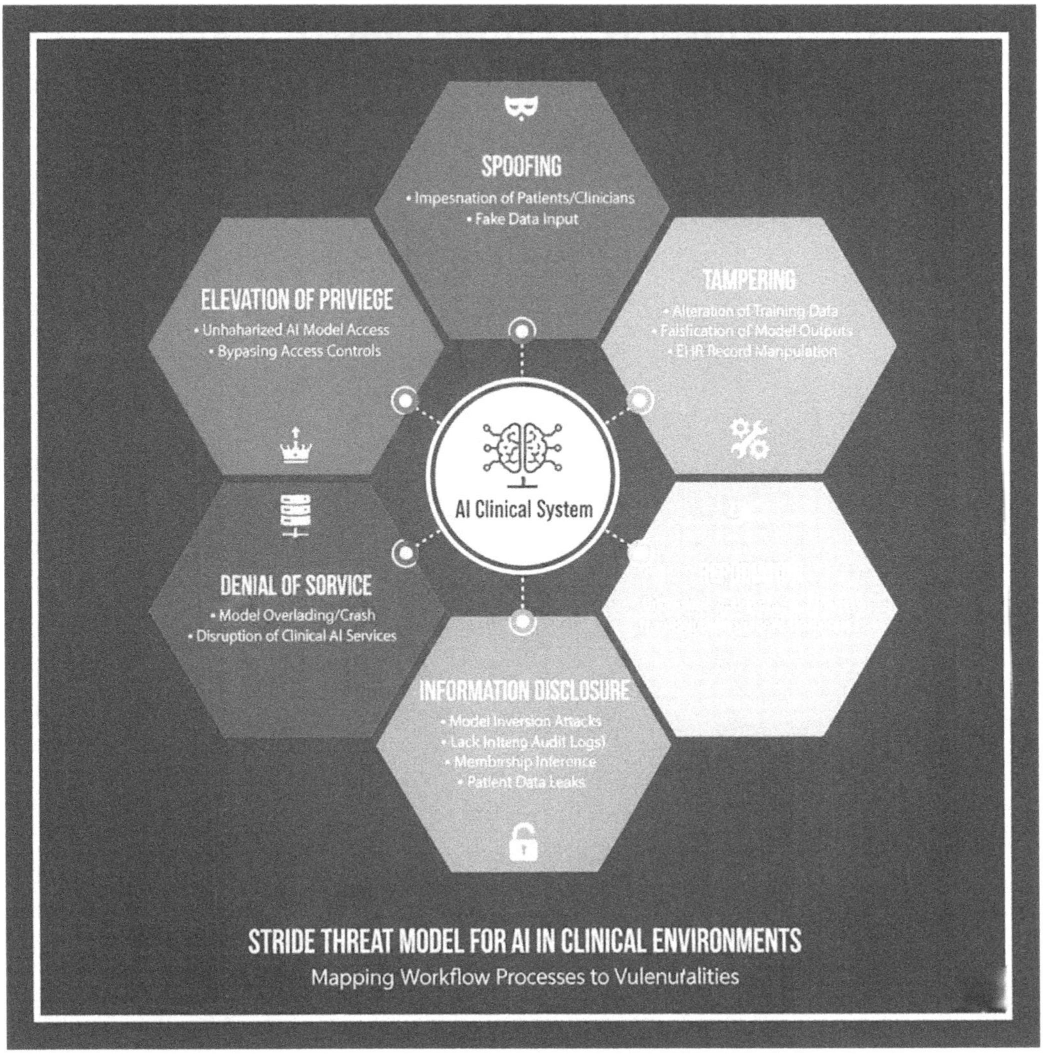

FIGURE 9.3 Illustration of six threats in AI in mental health.

9.3.3 DREAD Framework of Threat Prioritization

The DREAD framework is an extension of STRIDE that provides a quantitative approach to prioritization of threats based on the potential severity and probability of occurrence. It assesses every threat on five scales, such as damage potential, reproducibility, exploitability, affected users, and discoverability (Rahman et al., 2023; Tyagi, 2025). In the context of the AI mental health ecosystem, this model may be particularly helpful in distinguishing between low-impact issues and severe ethical or clinical risks. In the case of mental health data breach, simply the financial implications are not the sole consequences as reputational damage and psychological trauma can affect the patients involved. Reproducibility measures how easily an attack can be repeated.

Exploitability refers to the relative ease with which an attacker can exploit a weakness. The breadth of impact depends on the number of users who will be affected because one exploit can affect data of thousands of patients and therapists. The discoverability is a measure of how an attacker can discover vulnerabilities and publicly exposed APIs or open-source repositories of the model are riskier. The security teams can prioritize the remediation efforts by rating each factor using a defined scoring scale and calculating a cumulative score that determines the importance of

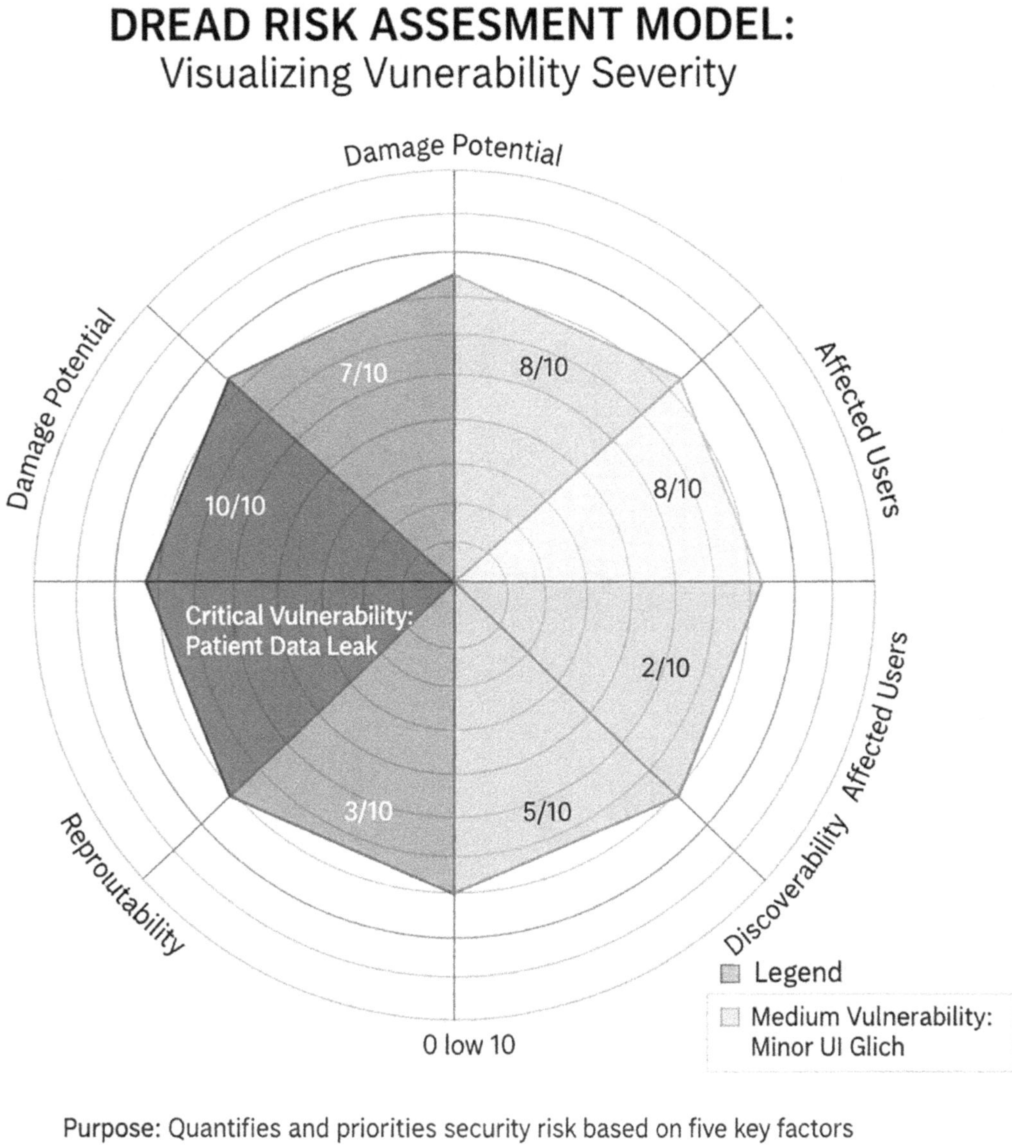

FIGURE 9.4 Risk scoring radar/matrix visualization. The figure depicts risk scoring matrix visualizing threat severity and likelihood.

the risk in priority. Applied in AI mental health scenarios, DREAD is used to make sure that scarce cybersecurity resources are prioritized in terms of which threats have the greatest consequences.

Figure 9.4 shows the DREAD Risk Model, the representation of which is a radar or spider diagram, which is one of the most important instruments to measure and prioritize security vulnerabilities and threats. DREAD is a score system where each of the identified risks is rated on five key axes: damage potential (the severity of the impact), reproducibility (how easily the attack can be replicated), exploitability (the effort required to execute the attack), affected users (the extent of the impact), and discoverability (how easily the vulnerability can be discovered). The model is used to create a shape on the radar chart by assigning a numerical value (frequently 0–10) to a particular threat on each of these five axes; the larger the area covered by the shape, the greater the risk is and the higher the level of risk criticality. This type of visualization enables security personnel to easily reason about the general magnitude of several threats and organize their risks to mitigate them, allocating resources to those threats with the greatest ratings in terms of combined impact, ease of implementation, and scale of impact.

9.3.4 FAIR Model for Quantitative Risk Analysis

The FAIR model is a structured mathematical methodology used to quantify information-security risk by examining the relationship between threat frequency and the magnitude of losses that can be incurred. Allowing organizations to convert qualitative evaluation to the quantifiable financial and operational metrics, according to Jones and Ashenden (2022), FAIR defines risk as the most likely occurrence and amount of future loss. FAIR is especially beneficial in AI mental health systems as the system can support the multifaceted nature of data sensitivity, regulatory considerations, and ethical responsibilities. The model divides risk into three components: threat-event frequency (TEF), vulnerability, and loss magnitude (LM). TEF captures the rate of AI-based diagnostic or teletherapy systems as the target of the cyberattack, and vulnerability measures the probability of a successful attack, which is dependent on the protection of the architecture, such as encryption and access controls. The first step is identifying the asset (i.e., patient data, AI diagnostic model, or the clinical infrastructure) which is under threat. The magnitude of losses estimates the possible effects of breach such as the financial fines, loss of patient trust, and reputation loss to the mental health service providers. The quantification of these factors enables decision-makers to evaluate the relative value of various types of security controls, which is the case with federated learning and centralized data encryption. Furthermore, the data-driven orientation of FAIR is consistent with the regulatory models, such as GDPR or HIPAA, and it allows healthcare organizations to prove their adherence to the regulation by quantifiable risk indicators. In summary, the FAIR framework brings analytical rigor to security governance of AI mental health systems analytical rigor between technical defense and organizational decision-making. Threat data are converted into financial or operational impacts as demonstrated in Figure 9.5 using the FAIR methodology.

This figure depicts the flowchart of the FAIR model that represents a quantitative, structured-method of risk evaluation and quantification in a more quantitatively depicting manner than the high or medium qualitative labels of risk. The first step involves firstly identifying the asset (i.e., patient data, the AI diagnostic model, or the clinical infrastructure) that is at risk. This is then succeeded

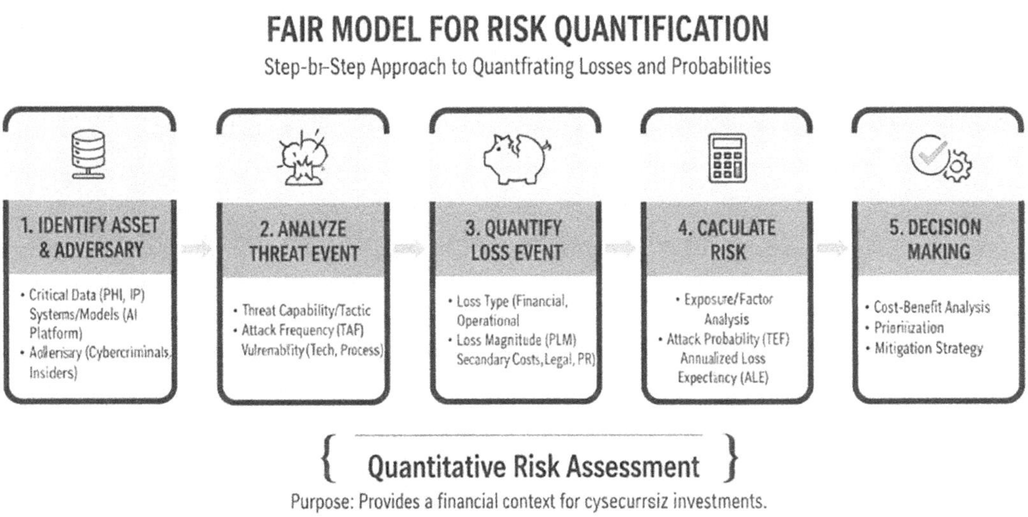

FIGURE 9.5 Flow diagram for quantitative risk calculation.

TABLE 9.2
Comparison of Significant Threat-Modeling Frameworks

Framework	Core Focus	Risk Metric	Applicability to AI Mental Health	Advantages	Limitations
STRIDE	Identifies threat categories	Qualitative	Early-stage design analysis	Simple and intuitive	Limited quantitative insight
DREAD	Calculates risk severity	Semi-quantitative	Prioritizing remediation	Considers impact and reproducibility	Subjective scoring possible
FAIR	Quantifies financial impact	Quantitative	Strategic risk management	Business-oriented, scalable	Requires large data samples

by the definition of the threat event that explains a particular activity that may affect the asset (e.g. a data breach or an event involving tampering of an AI model). This is then associated with the loss event which measures the adverse economic effect in the event of the threat happening and which takes into account factors such as regulatory fines, response cost, and lost productivity (Tyagi & Tiwari, 2024a). Risk quantification is at the core of the model, and it is a mathematical calculation of frequency (the likelihood that the threat event will arise in the course of a period of time) and the magnitude (the likely cost of the loss event that will occur). The last one is decision-making where risk measured in terms of a likely amount of financial loss (e.g., 1M to 5M) can be used by executives to take objective and cost–benefit decisions about security investments and mitigation measures. This procedural step translates abstract security risks into a realistic financial risk. Table 9.2 compares the three frameworks (STRIDE, DREAD, and FAIR) based on the scope of analysis that they offer and how they apply to AI-based healthcare.

9.3.5 Integrative Implementation of AI Mental Health Ecosystems

Although each of the three frameworks provides valuable insight of various facets of cybersecurity, a combination of all of them can present a more holistic and dynamic version of the framework designed to help protect AI-based mental health systems. By itself, STRIDE is useful in identifying and classifying threats, DREAD is useful in prioritizing and ranking them according to potential impact, and FAIR provides a quantitative viewpoint in terms of risks being quantified into quantifiable outcomes (Balamurugan et al., 2023). Nevertheless, when these models are combined, they all contribute to a complete threat management lifecycle, including the analysis of the design in the early phases and the real-time quantification of risks and the mitigation plan. This combination is especially applicable to AI-based mental health applications, which will process dynamic, privacy-sensitive data streams and be operationally reliable within the context of stringent ethical and regulatory limitations.

In practice, the combination of these models allows the organizations to develop layered defense strategies, which will integrate technical controls with the ethical governance. STRIDE can be used when designing systems to map areas of trust and where sensitive data (e.g. records of therapy transcripts or diagnostic model outputs) is most vulnerable (Tyagi et al., 2024c). After the identification of possible vulnerabilities, DREAD may be used to rank the mitigation work based on their impact and probability, so that high-impact vulnerabilities, such as unauthorized access to clinical records or manipulation using adversarial examples, get dedicated immediate attention. Then, the FAIR model will be able to measure the economic and reputational effects of these pre-eminent threats, enabling mental health institutions to distribute resources effectively, and explain why they invest in cybersecurity infrastructure.

New literature suggests that incorporating threat modeling and risk quantification procedures into AI governance pipelines can help boost preventive and adaptive security to a substantial degree (Zhou et al., 2024; Tyagi et al., 2025). As an example, by integrating these models with real-time threat intelligence and anomaly detection based on machine learning (ML), systems can dynamically evolve to support new varieties of attack. Such dynamic ability is essential in AI mental health systems because security breaches can not only expose sensitive personal data, but also interfere with the continuity of patient care and destabilize the confidence in digital therapeutic solutions. Consequently, a multi-framework integration approach based on the principles of STRIDE, DREAD, and FAIR can establish a robust security infrastructure that anticipates threats, measures their effects, and constantly keeps up with the dynamic nature of cyber threat in the context of digital mental health services. Figure 9.6 introduces a combined architecture to bring together STRIDE, DREAD, and FAIR to evaluate the risks in a holistic manner.

This figure illustrates a Hybrid Risk Assessment Model designed to provide end-to-end visibility of security threats through the step-wise combination of three different modeling frameworks into a

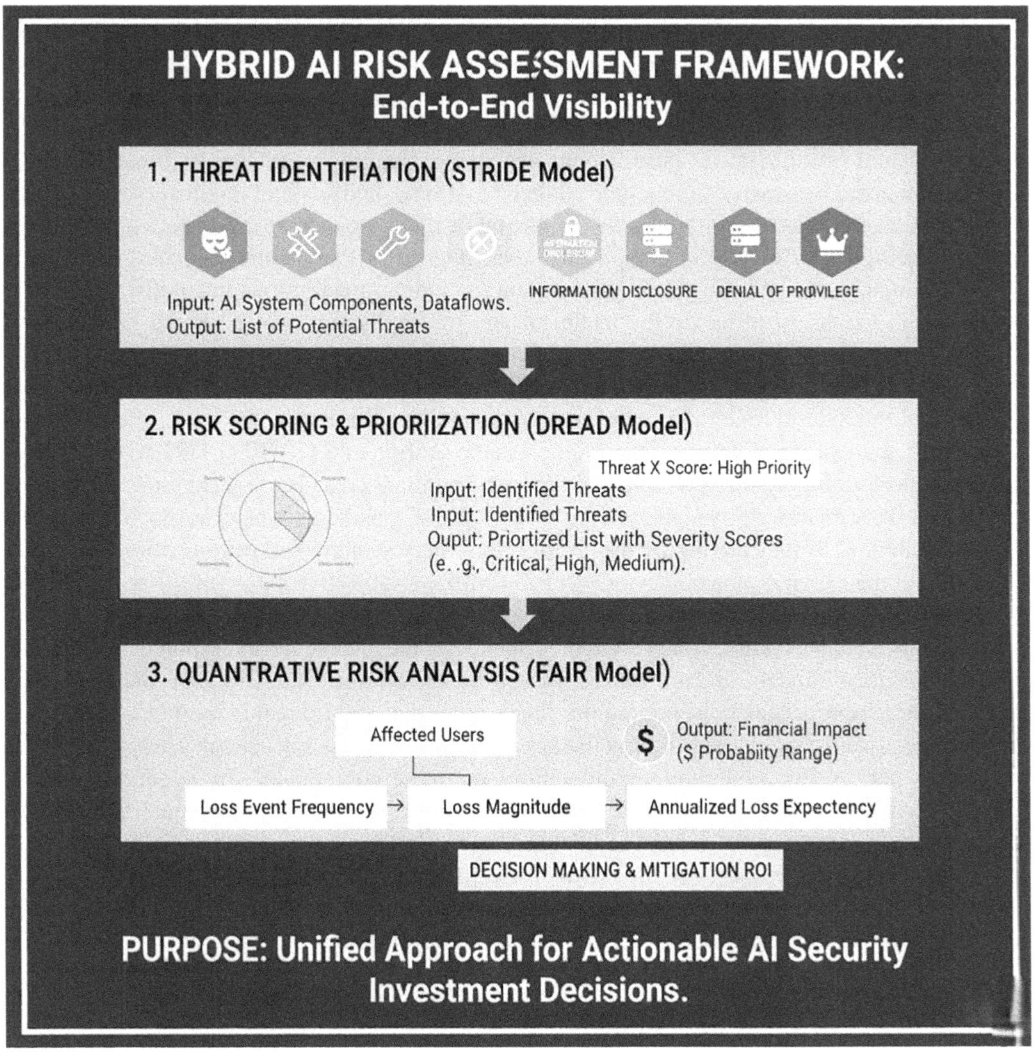

FIGURE 9.6 Integrating the design of STRIDE-DREAD-FAIR.

vertical stack. It starts with the highest level with the STRIDE Model (spoofing, tampering, repudiation, information disclosure, denial of service, elevation of privilege), which plays the important role of threat identification. As a methodology, STRIDE assists analysts in brainstorming and classifying all possible security vulnerabilities in an AI system or clinical setting. After detection, these threats are transferred to the middle layer, where the risk scoring and prioritization is performed using the DREAD model. DREAD model also provides a qualitative or semi-quantitative score on each threat that ranks them in order of seriousness to allow security teams to target mitigation efforts effectively. Lastly, the prioritized threats are passed to the lowest layer which makes use of the FAIR model to perform potential loss quantification. FAIR transforms the most significant risks into a financial outlook, and the risk is presented as a likely amount of financial loss (frequency times magnitude). This hybrid methodology incorporates a three-tiered assessment of the risk, allowing it to transition the assessment from qualitative identification (STRIDE) to structured prioritization (DREAD) to objectively make decisions based on financial incentives (FAIR), offering a total of actionable risk profile to both the executives and the technical organizations.

9.4 RISK CLASSIFICATION AND EVALUATION FRAMEWORKS

The analytical foundation of cybersecurity governance is risk classification and assessment schemes that offer systematic procedures of identifying, categorizing, and ranking the likelihood, seriousness, and effects of the threats that may occur. These frameworks are important within AI mental health system in terms of ensuring that safety, data confidentiality, and service availability remain balanced. Mental health data is sensitive, and the risk evaluation model needs to extend beyond traditional financial loss metrics to include ethical, emotional, and societal implications. In contrast to other healthcare fields, security breaches in mental health systems may erode patient confidence, create psychological distress, and compromise the integrity of therapeutic technologies. It therefore follows that multidimensional risk assessment, including quantitative, qualitative, and hybrid approaches, is necessary to tackle the technical and moral dilemmas of AI-based mental health settings.

Figure 9.7 depicts a hypothetical graph, likely a dual-axis bar chart, which is meant to compare and point out the natural trade-offs between qualitative and quantitative risk assessment methods. On one hand, there are qualitative methods (such as the scoring of STRIDE or DREAD), which are typically viewed as highly interpretable and requiring minimal data. These techniques are quick to apply and can rely on descriptive labels (e.g., "High," "Low"), and do not need as much specific historical information, so they are highly useful for preliminary scoping and prioritization. This, however, comes at the expense of accuracy or precision with the subjective nature of the scoring having the potential of giving inconsistent results. On the other hand, Figure 9.7 contrasts these with quantitative methods (such as FAIR), which are represented with the high accuracy or precision due to the use of mathematical models, and produce results expressed as precise numerical or financial values. Several of these approaches however require much more data requirements (particular costs data, frequency data, statistics of control effectiveness) and may be less interpretable to non-technical stakeholders because the underlying computations are more complicated. In essence, Figure 9.7 illustrates the trade-off between the ease to implement (usability/low data need) qualitative models and the objective accuracy (accuracy) of quantitative models by showing the decision-makers the approach that is most appropriate to their available capabilities and level of risk granularity needed. In summary, as shown in Table 9.3, quantitative and qualitative approaches are complementary when it comes to evaluating cybersecurity in clinical AI ecosystems.

9.4.1 Quantitative Risk Assessment Models

Quantitative risk assessment models use statistical and mathematical techniques to measure risk through numerical estimates, which include the probability of occurrence, expected loss, and

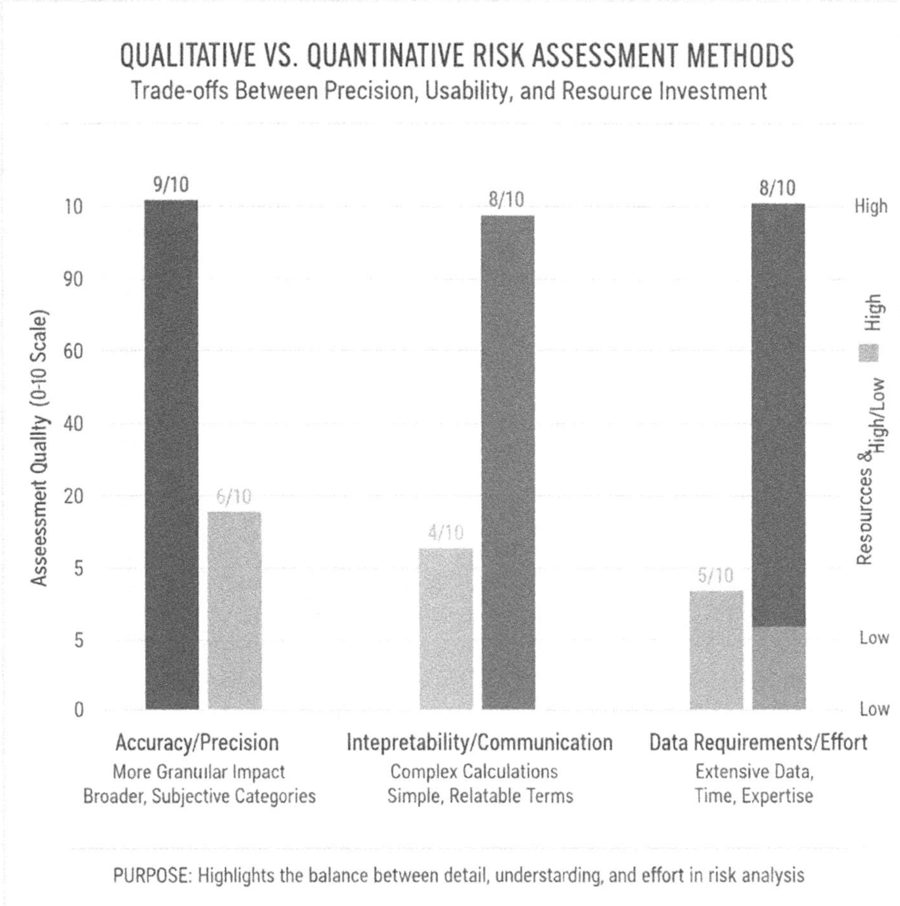

FIGURE 9.7 Comparison of quantitative and qualitative risk approach.

exposure levels. Examples of such frameworks are the FAIR model, ISO/IEC 27005, and NIST SP 800-30, which transform abstract security issues into quantifiable results that could be used to make decisions. In AI mental health systems, quantitative analysis enables administrators to estimate the financial impact of potential breaches the organization or how often a particular type of cyberattack would occur. For example, healthcare institutions can estimate the probability of ransomware attacks and the expected operational downtime to calculate the expected annual loss and allocate the funds (Rajani et al., 2022). The quantitative models also prove beneficial in regulatory compliance because they offer justifiable measures in proving due diligence to regulatory standards like the HIPAA and GDPR. Nevertheless, even their accuracy, purely quantitative methods might be unsuitable to capture the contextual variables, for example, emotional hurt or reputational loss, which are hard to quantify.

9.4.2 Qualitative Risk Assessment Models

Conversely, qualitative risk assessment models concentrate on descriptive assessment, which is usually performed by expert judgment and expert reasoning where risks are categorized as low, medium, or high. The application of models such as OCTAVE Allegro, and NIST qualitative guidelines can be used by security teams to evaluate threats in the context of their relevance to the situation, particularly in the areas that require human interaction and ethical issues. In AI mental

TABLE 9.3
Quantitative and Qualitative Risk-Assessment Methods

Dimension	Quantitative Approach	Qualitative Approach	Best Use Case
Data Requirement	Numerical, historical incident data	Expert judgment and narrative input	Mixed evaluation in clinical risk studies
Output	Probabilistic score, monetary loss	Categorical level (Low–Medium–High)	When data scarcity exists
Interpretation	Objective, statistical	Subjective but context-rich	Policy and human-factor analysis
Tools	FAIR, Monte Carlo, Bayesian	STRIDE, DREAD	Hybrid models

health systems, qualitative measurements are especially helpful in the comprehension of how the violations of privacy would impact the behavior of a patient or in the relationships between a therapist and a patient. As an illustration, even a minor leak of anonymized counseling transcripts can significantly reduce public trust in digital therapy platforms. These subtle dangers cannot be necessarily measured with the help of numbers but can be well explained with references to qualitative analysis. Such models also support collaborative evaluations, as cybersecurity experts and clinicians along with AI developers can work together to understand the ethical meanings of the threats identified in collaboration. However, qualitative approaches are subjective and prone to inconsistency whereby they may rely on the experience and bias of the assessor and thus restrict the reproducibility and scalability to other institutions.

9.4.3 Hybrid Risk Evaluation Methodologies

Because each model has limitations when used alone, most organizations have embraced hybrid risk assessment models which incorporate analytical accuracy and contextual knowledge. These mixed methods convert qualitative ratings into numerical values to enable a more balanced analysis based on quantifiable probabilities and moral or psychological outcomes. Such models are highly valuable in AI mental health systems in the evaluation of risks, which are both technical and human-based. An example of a phishing attack on therapists could be given a large quantitative likelihood and a medium qualitative effect given that limitations on system security reduce the exposure of data. On the other hand, an insidious adversarial attack which alters AI diagnostic outputs can be highly unlikely but qualitatively severe because it may cause clinical treatment to be incorrect. Zhou et al. (2024) and Singh and Dutta (2024) also advocate adopting hybrid methodologies where they observe that they give more realistic impressions of multidimensional risk environments. Hybrid frameworks facilitate the whole-picture comprehension of cyber risks, especially those that touch on moral and emotional dimensions of online mental care.

9.4.4 Risk Assessment Ethics and Regulation Aspects

In addition to analytical issues, ethical and regulatory factors that influence the system's trustworthiness should be considered in developing the effective risk classification in AI mental health. Ethical risk assessment focuses on the way in which AI judgments can promote bias, undermine autonomy, or bring harm to people. With the help of regulatory compliance, as established by such frameworks as GDPR, HIPAA, and ISO/IEC 27701, it is possible to ensure that data protection activities are consistent with legal requirements and transparency and accountability are maintained. An inclusion of regulatory and ethical measures within risk assessment systems will strengthen the patient-centered care and support the trust of the population toward AI-based mental health solutions. In this area, cybersecurity is not just a technical resilience issue, but, according to the emerging research, a essential part to ethical clinical practice (Li et al., 2024a). Incorporating ethical reflection and regulatory alignment into risk evaluation processes enables institutions to create AI mental health systems that are more than just safe, and also socially accountable and trustworthy.

9.5 POPULAR ATTACKS: PHISHING, RANSOMWARE, AND API EXPLOITS

In the previous decade, several researcher describe various cyberattacks in AI-driven mental health systems as threats to both technological infrastructure and human aspects for efficient digital healthcare care delivery. As these systems are based on cloud infrastructure databases, mobile apps, and interconnected APIs, attackers/hackers use new vulnerabilities that put the confidentiality, integrity, and availability of patient data at risk. Some of the most common are phishing scams, ransomware attacks, and API-level attacks—all of which are serious challenges to both secure and ethical digital mental healthcare. Understanding these attacks in AI mental health platforms is essential for designing countermeasures that protect sensitive psychological information and maintain the faith of users in therapeutic technologies. Table 9.4 shows the most common types of cyberattacks on AI-driven mental-health systems and their mitigation strategies.

9.5.1 Social Engineering and Phishing Attacks

Phishing remains a powerful attack vector because it targets human behavior rather than system vulnerabilities. In AI mental health systems, phishing emails or messages are frequently disguised as valid mental health service providers and attempt to deceive therapists, administrators, or patients, eliciting them to share credentials or download dangerous malware. In contrast to classic phishing, such campaigns are more and more based on AI-generated content, that is, deep faked audio or adaptive chatbots, which mimic official communication styles with high linguistic accuracy. Tyagi (2021) argue that phishing attacks have become much more realistic with the use of generative AI, and they often evade traditional rule-based detection filters.

An effective phishing attack has the potential of stealing login information, thereby exposing confidential therapy records, medical history, or payment details. Additionally, phishing can serve as an entry point for more complex attacks such as ransomware deployment or lateral network movement. The psychological damage caused by such breaches can supersede technical or financial damages in the digital mental health environment where users are likely to provide sensitive data about their feelings. Therefore, to prevent such threats within organisations, it is important to combine phishing simulation training, adaptive email filtering, and user awareness programs. Figure 9.8 presents a schematic of the phishing attack flow within an AI mental health system, with its stages including deception (fake email), data capture, credential compromise, and in-house propagation.

TABLE 9.4
Typical Cyberattack Attack Patterns for Mental Health AI Platforms

Attack Type	Vector/Mechanism	Impact on System	Mitigation Technique
Phishing	Social engineering via emails or chatbots	Credential compromise	Multi-factor authentication
Ransomware	Encryption of clinical databases	Service disruption and data loss	Regular offline backups
API Exploits	Manipulation of exposed AI endpoints	Unauthorized inference or access	Token-based authentication
Model Inversion	Querying model to reveal sensitive data	Privacy breach	Differential privacy methods
Adversarial Attacks	Crafted inputs to fool model predictions	Incorrect diagnosis	Adversarial training and anomaly detection

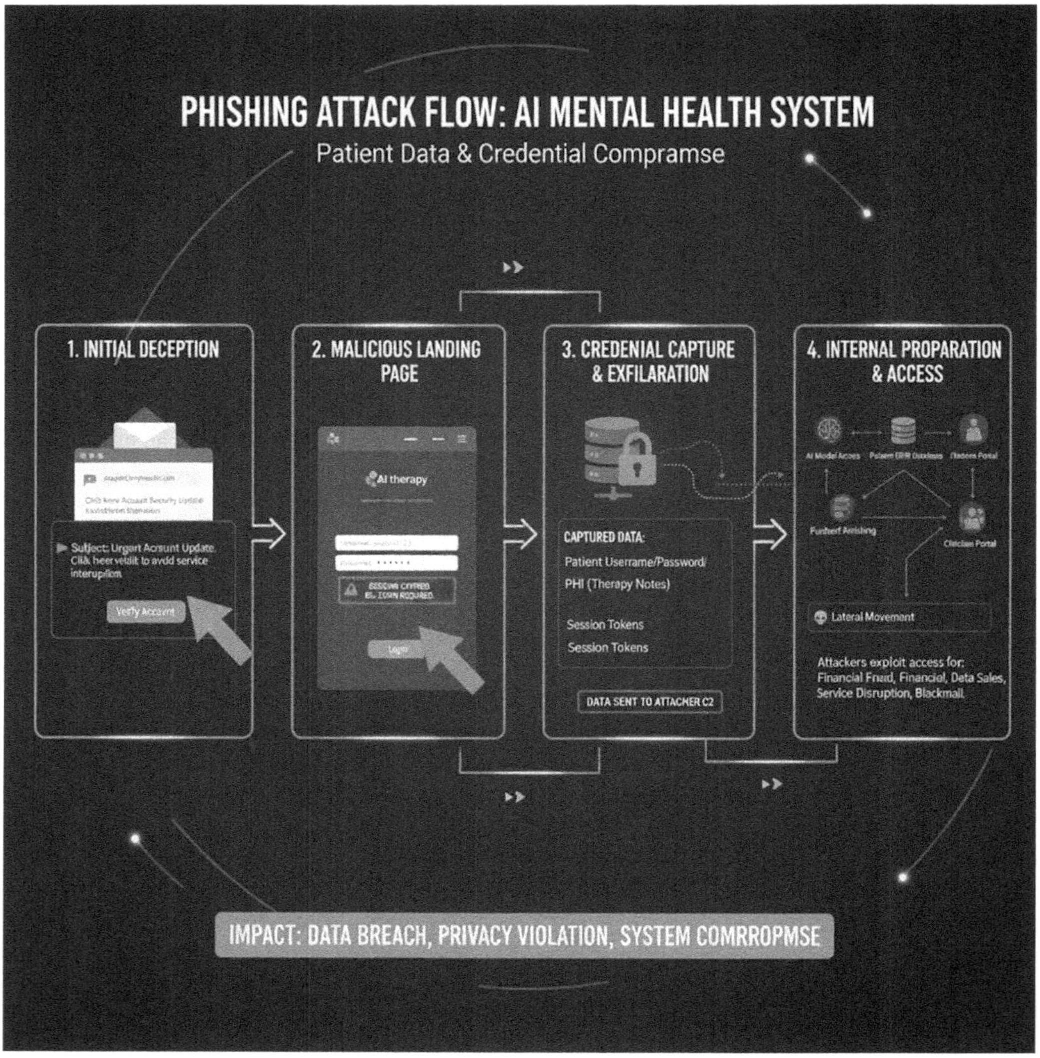

FIGURE 9.8 Data flow of a phishing attack in an AI mental health system.

Furthermore, Figure 9.8 presents a sequential phishing attack flow of an AI mental health system, which can be used to describe the characteristics of a social engineering-based breach. The initial phase of the attack is the deception stage, during which an attacker delivers a spoofed email or message, usually designed to seem urgent or official (such as the notification of a system update or a request message by a superior), particularly exploiting the high-trust environment of mental healthcare settings. The target, who often has high access privileges to the AI platform, is then fooled into going to the data capture stage, typically triggered by clicking a malicious link that leads them to a fake login page. This leads to credential compromise, in which the user, who is not aware of the risks, enters their genuine log in information (username and password) on the fraudulent site so that the attacker can steal it. The attacker can gain initial access with the compromised credentials and further to internal propagation. During this last and most destructive step, the attacker is infiltrating the AI system with the legitimate access which may lead to the expansion of their privileges, stealing sensitive patient data (PHI), injecting poisoned data into the training pipeline, or manipulating the diagnostic results of the AI model, essentially undermining the confidentiality, integrity, and availability of the mental health service.

9.5.2 Ransomware Intrusion and Data Hostage Incidents

Mental health institutions that are required to have real-time access to data are especially devastated by ransomware attacks. Upon infiltration, ransomware encrypts valuable files, such as the records of patients, parameters of an AI model, or the records of a therapy session, and makes them unreadable until the ransom is paid. In 2024, ransomware attacks and teletherapy services around the world resulted in weeks-long shutdowns of online counselling services (Almeida & Roy, 2024). Such attacks have long-term effects that go beyond financial damages as interruptions in services can contribute to the worsening of the mental health crisis of patients and postponing the implementation of urgent interventions.

AI systems are also vulnerable to indirect attacks by ransomware as hackers take over model training datasets or embedded inferencing systems. Not only does manipulation of these datasets affect the performance of the system, but it also brings in the possibility of unseen biases in therapeutical suggestions. Some of the preventative measures involve zero-trust architecture, immutable backup, and behavior-driven anomaly detection, detecting abnormal encryption patterns in real time. The blockchain-based record systems can ensure immutability even under ransomware-induced stress conditions.

9.5.3 API Total Breaches and Data Leakage of AI Mental Health Systems

APIs are integral components of AI-based mental health systems that facilitate exchange of data among mobile applications, wearable sensors, and cloud analytics platforms. Nonetheless, poorly designed or unsecured APIs create easy entry points to attackers whose aim is to gain unauthorized access to data or disrupt the service. The exploits through API are when endpoints provide sensitive metadata, or do not perform authentication, and permit excessive data retrieval based on poorly implemented queries. This vulnerability may result in colossal breaches of privacy, particularly when it comes to a system dealing with psychotherapy records, diagnostic results, or voice-based emotional information.

In the recent studies, the API misconfigurations constituted over 60% of the healthcare application breaches in 2024 (NIST, 2024). By controlling the input parameters, attackers may read unintended data which is called API scraping or overload endpoints to cause a DoS attack. In AI mental health systems, these exploits can interfere with predictive analytics or reveal anonymized datasets that can be correlated to re-identify the users. To contain these risks, the secure API management frameworks must implement Oauth 2.0, token-based authentication, input validation, and rate limiting. The use of AI-based intrusion detection systems (IDS), which can identify suspicious API behavior, is another security measure, as it is necessary to guarantee that API communication and privacy laws are not violated due to an AI mental health platform.

Figure 9.9 is a conceptual architecture diagram that outlines the API communication routes in an AI mental health platform and indicates some of the vectors that can be exploited. It illustrates a client interface (such as a mobile application or web portal) communicating with the backend services, which in turn include the data storage (storing sensitive PHI) and the AI model service (performing inference to diagnose or intervene). The API calls represent the interface of all the communication, including the user's placing requests, sensors gathering data, or the AI model giving a risk analysis. The major exploit vectors occur at the interfaces and points of communication. These include injection attacks (such as SQL or NoSQL injection) that target APIs to gain unauthorized access to PHI stored in the database; Insecure Direct Object Reference (IDOR) that is an API logic and exposes an attacker to view the data of another patient; and adversarial attacks or model evasion where malicious input is submitted through the API-facing endpoint of the model to compel an erroneous or damaging diagnosis. Therefore, securing the API layer through robust authentication, input verification, and rate-limiting is the key to the privacy of the patient and integrity of the clinical AI service.

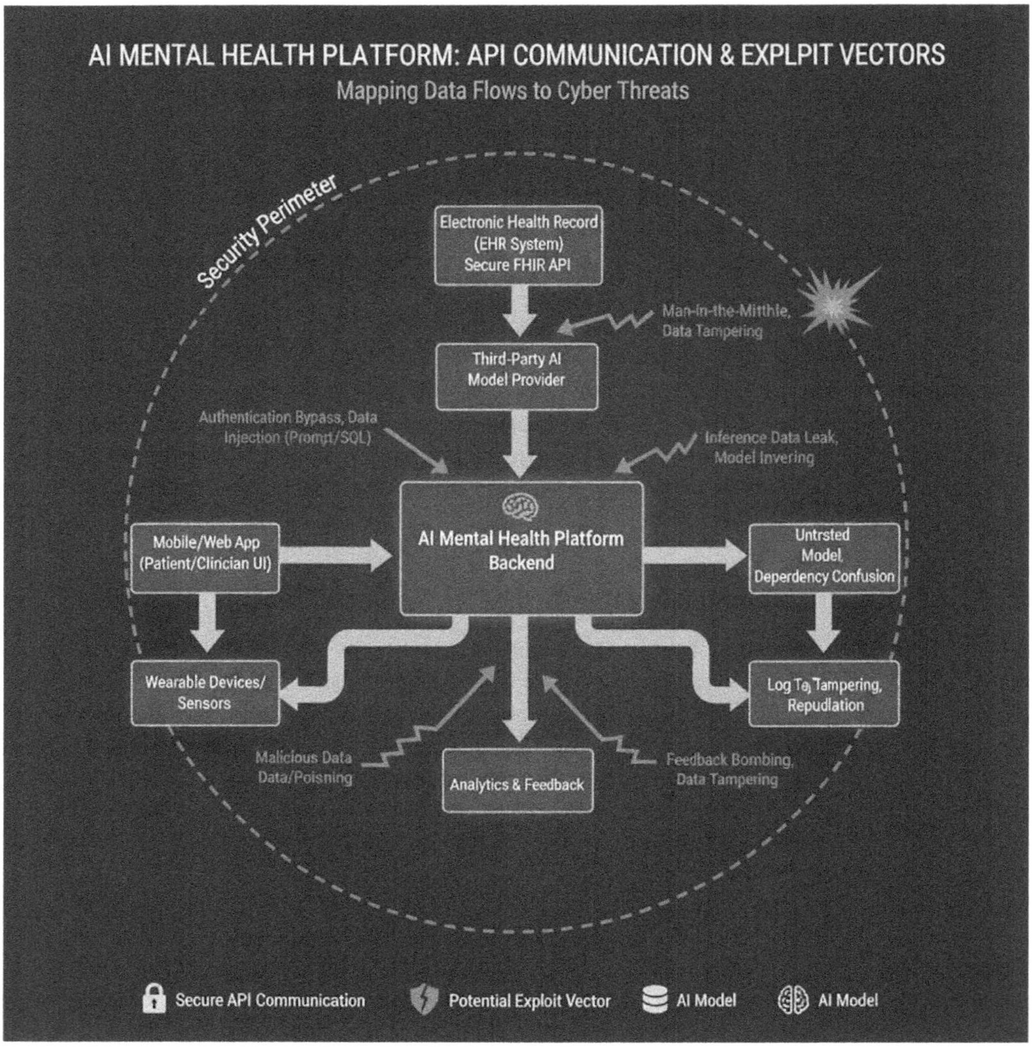

FIGURE 9.9 Communication API and possible attack vectors of an AI mental health platform.

9.5.4 Multi-Vector Attack Scenarios and New Threats

Modern cyberattacks are rarely one-dimensional, but they will be organized as multi-vector attack chains which will include phishing, ransomware, and API attack in a single campaign. For example, a phishing email can deliver malicious payloads that make use of vulnerable APIs and ultimately cause ransomware encryption on the backend servers. Another emerging trend is the use of adversarial AI attacks, where threat actors manipulate ML inputs to produce harmful or false mental health output. These attacks might distort affective assessments or alter diagnostic predictions with severe clinical and ethical issues. Liu et al. (2025) posit that AI and cybersecurity defenses are essential for detecting these hybrid threats because signature-based methods cannot counter adaptive attackers.

Organizations are in turn moving to predictive-based defense architectures that use reinforcement learning, federated AI models to predict and mitigate emerging attack behaviors. These systems are resilient as they constantly learn using past experiences and shared sources of data without infringing on patient privacy. Thus, AI mental health facilities of the future need to employ a multi-layered defense framework incorporating human awareness, cryptographic protection, and active surveillance to resist multi-vector and dynamic cyber threats.

9.6 OUTSIDER VERSUS INSIDER THREAT ANALYSIS

Regarding AI-powered mental health systems, cybersecurity risks arise from both internal and external threats operating within and beyond the organizational boundary. The greater interrelatedness of cloud-based environments, digital therapeutics, and AI analytics environments have made traditional perimeter-based security models less effective, allow both insider and external attackers to exploit vulnerabilities with similarly damaging consequences. Thorough threat evaluation must thus entail the fact that these threat categories must be distinguished by their motivations, behaviors, and potential impact on systems.

9.6.1 Insider Threats: Human and Systemic Vulnerabilities

One of the most complex and underestimated security challenges is insider threats. They arise from individuals who possess authorized system access, for example, clinicians, data scientists, IT administrators, or third-party contractors. Insiders may act maliciously, driven by financial gain, personal grievance, or ideological agenda, or may unintentionally cause harm through negligence or lack of awareness of good cybersecurity. Mental health organizations, where professionals often deal with extremely sensitive information, even a single instance of misuse or unauthorized disclosure can result in serious ethical and legal consequences (Sharma and Liao, 2024).

Technical insiders such as AI developers or data engineers constitute a distinct category of insider threat because of their understanding of algorithms and data structures. As an example, a person with access to training data may insert subtle biases or adversarial samples into training data, impairing model accuracy, or can re-identify anonymized patients. On the same note, when API tokens or data export functions are abused by authorized members, they may enable data exfiltration that conventional firewalls often fail to detect. Such risks need to be alleviated by conducting role-based access control (RBAC), ongoing behavioral checks, and regular privilege audits in organizations. Developing a culture of cybersecurity ethics through awareness programs and behavioral risk assessment is also important. As illustrated in Table 9.5, insider threats are typically harder to detect despite occurring at moderate frequency compared to external threats.

Figure 9.10 illustrates the sequential insider threat lifecycle, outlining the steps a malicious or negligent insider follows from initial access to eventual detection. This process starts with the access stage when an insider a trusted employee, developer, or administrator uses legitimate credentials and privileges to access sensitive assets, including the training data of the AI model, patient PHI, or

TABLE 9.5
Insider and External Threat Matrix

Threat Source	Typical Actor	Example Incident	Likelihood	Detection Difficulty	Control Measure
Insider	Authorized data analyst	Data exfiltration	Medium	High	Behavioral analytics
Insider	IT administrator	Privilege abuse	Low	Medium	Least-privilege access
External	Cybercriminal	Ransomware attack	High	Medium	Network segmentation
External	Hacktivist	Data defacement	Low	Low	Web application firewall
External	Competitor	Model theft via API	Medium	High	Rate-limiting and encryption

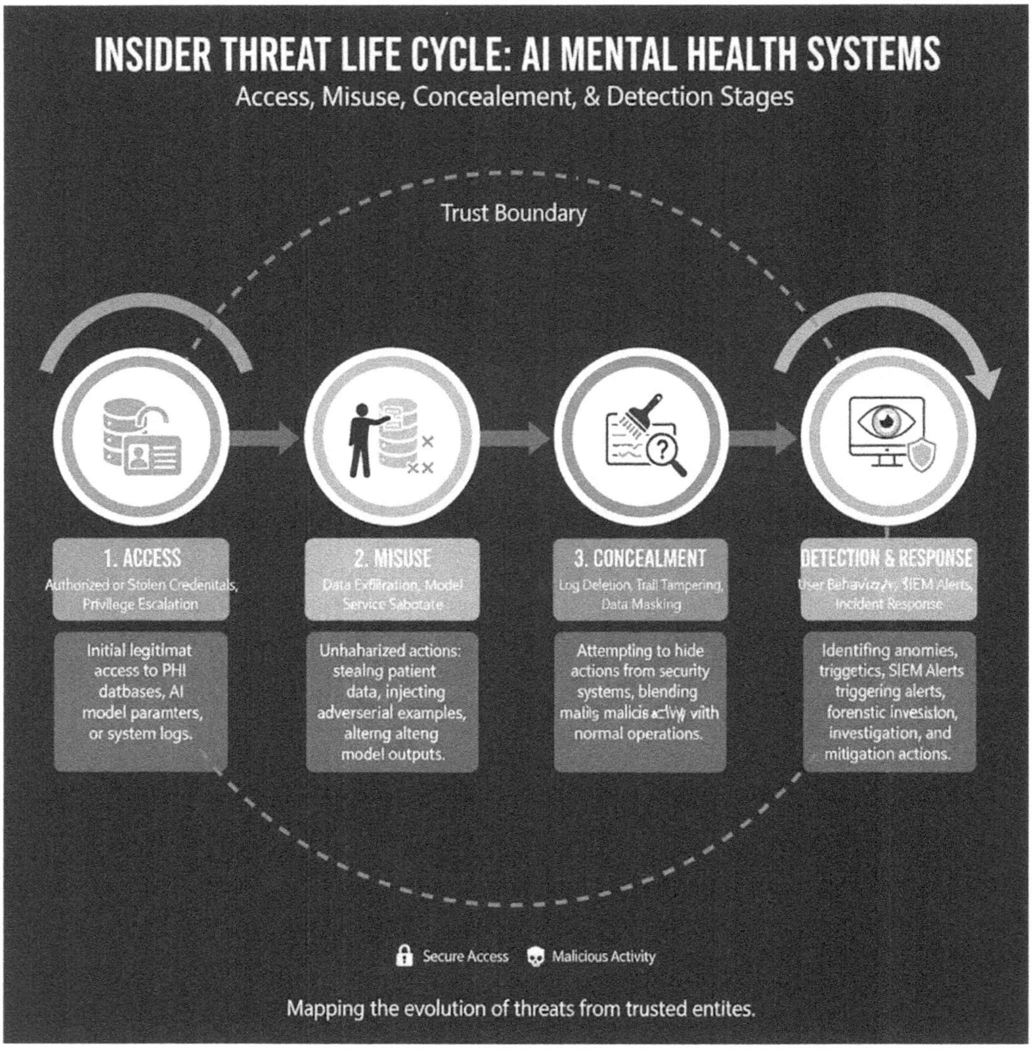

FIGURE 9.10 AI mental health system's insider threat lifecycle.

the core platform API. This is followed by the misuse stage, where the insider engages in malicious actions, and it may be data exfiltration (stealing patient records), maliciously tampering with the model (data poisoning), or taking personal advantage with system access.

After the exploitation, the insider enters the concealment stage, attempting to hide activity by altering or deleting audit records, create, or alter evidence to make the unauthorized access seem justified or to implicate another user. The last phase is detection where the security controls within the system, for example, user and entity behavior analytics (UEBA); ongoing monitoring or anomaly detection on audit trails detects the suspicious activity and raises red flags on the insider's activity which results in incident response and remediation. This cycle highlights the need for behavioral monitoring, detection, and response tools rather than relying solely on perimeter defenses because the problem lies at the end of the boundary of trust. The insider and external threat matrix is presented in Table 9.5.

9.6.2 External Threats: Systematic and Deliberate Enemies

External threats originate outside the institutional environment and may be perpetrated by cybercriminals, hacktivists, or those with state sponsors who aim to take advantage of the weaknesses in the AI-controlled mental health systems. Phishing, ransomware, API abuse, or distributed denial-of-service (DDoS) attacks are typical methods that are used by these attackers to get access to and interfere with services. As opposed to insider adversaries, external adversaries do not have direct access, and must use reconnaissance and exploitations of security vulnerabilities like weak authentication measures, unpatched software, or unsecured cloud storage. According to a study by Patel and Nguyen (2024), over three out of five attacks of healthcare AI systems in the year 2024 were triggered by external parties by exploiting system misconfigurations or integration failures by third parties.

An emerging threat in this category is the emergence of AI-enhanced cyber-crime, with competitors using generative models to AI-driven attack tools or analyze vulnerabilities in the system. As an illustration, a threat actor can exploit AI to identify accessible endpoints within teletherapy APIs or impersonate valid data messages through behavioral inference of a normal traffic pattern. In addition, deepfake-based impersonation attacks can deceive both users and automated verification systems, resulting in unauthorized access to and/or manipulation of clinical AI models. The counter to this type of adaptive external threat would need multilayered security approaches integrating threat intelligence feeds, ML-based anomaly detection, and zero-trust security architectures that would be able to constantly verify every connection request.

9.6.3 Overlapping Threat Scenarios

AI ecosystems increasingly face complex scenarios involving overlapping threats whereby insider negligence enables external intrusion. A compromised employee credential can serve as the entry point to a larger, externally orchestrated attack chain. On the same note, the presence of outsourced data labeling or AI model maintenance contracts creates third-party insider risk, and the boundary between the internal and external security areas is obscured. The study by Zhou et al. (2025) states that hybrid threats have become almost a third of cyberattacks in AI healthcare systems, which is why the combined approach to monitoring human and technical threat vectors is imperative. Considering the use of user behavior analytics (UBA) and threat correlation engines will allow detecting abnormalities at an early stage and indicators of collusion and staged attacks.

With AI mental health systems, where sensitive patient information, predictive analytics, and real-time therapy apps are side by side, it is important to consider the overlap of insider and external threats. The integration of predictive modeling with such contextual analysis of human beings would enable security teams to shift their focus on responding to incidents as they happen to risk anticipation. An integrated approach is essential to protect data, maintain trust, and ensure ethical and system integrity in AI-driven mental health ecosystems.

9.7 IMPLEMENTATION OF THREAT INTELLIGENCE SYSTEMS

The ability to predict, identify, and respond to emerging cyber threats in AI-driven mental health ecosystems depends on the integration of robust threat intelligence systems. These systems collect, interpret, and distribute data on adversarial actions, vulnerabilities, and attack patterns to strengthen organizational situational awareness. Traditional reactive defenses are insufficient because mental health platforms increasingly operate on distributed cloud environments and process real-time data collected by wearable sensors and digital therapy applications. Threat intelligence enables a proactive security posture by transforming raw threat data into actionable insights for continuous risk mitigation. Threat-intelligence integration can be used to improve proactive detection by means of constant data fusion, as illustrated in Figure 9.11.

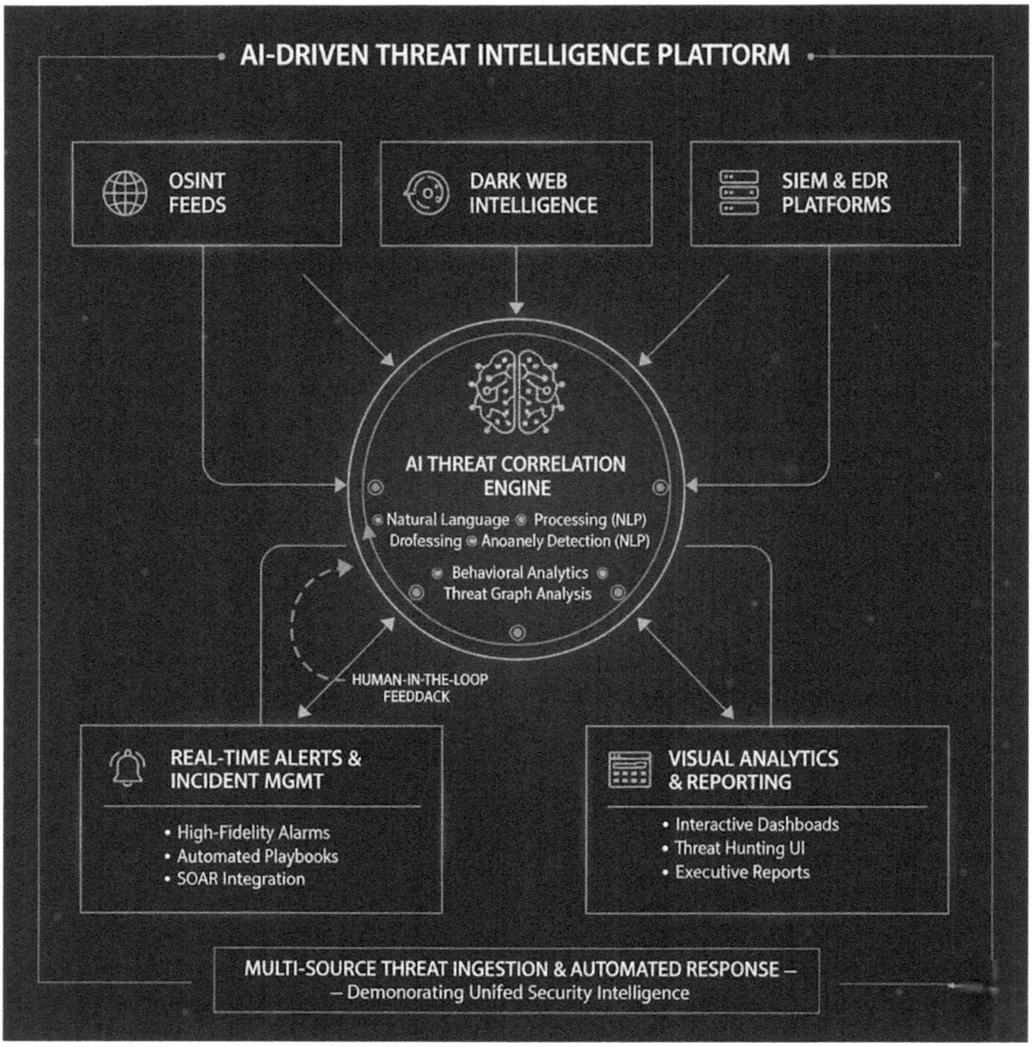

FIGURE 9.11 Intelligence ingestion and correlation flow of data.

Figure 9.11 shows a conceptual AI-driven Threat Intelligence and Automated Response Platform which is a synthesis of multi-source threat data used to produce actionable security knowledge. Multi-Source Threat Ingestion is the first step where data that is obtained by different external and internal feeds is integrated into the system. The data sources of these feeds are OSINT (Open-Source Intelligence) of information about public threats, Dark Web feeds of indicators of compromise (IOCs) in the clinical field, and internal system logs of the SIEM (Security Information and Event Management). All collected data is fed into the main threat correlation engine, which is AI-based. Underlying ML algorithms, this engine conducts activities such as detection of anomalies, pattern recognition, and reduction of false-positives, correlating seemingly unrelated indicators to reveal complex threats that human analysts may overlook. The final step is automated output and response whereby the engine will generate high-fidelity alerts that will be viewed by humans in real time and populate visual dashboards with interpretable metrics and background data. Additionally, the platform can integrate security orchestration tools to automate responses such as isolating an infected host or blocking a malicious IP, thereby improving detection and containment compared

TABLE 9.6
Threat-Intelligence Systems Integration

Intelligence Source	Data Type	Integration Method	Output Format	Use in AI Monitoring
OSINT	Public indicators, text	API ingestion	JSON/CSV	Baseline threat awareness
SIEM Feeds	Logs and network events	Direct log correlation	XML/JSON	Automated alerting
Dark-Web Monitoring	Threat actor data	Secure API/scraper	Encrypted reports	Early warning of credential leaks
ISAC Feeds	Industry collaboration data	Subscription	XML	Shared intelligence sharing
AI Threat ML Processing Signals	ML-based anomaly streams	Stream ingestion	Real-time dashboard	Predictive analytics

with traditional security operations. As shown in Table 9.6, integrating various intelligence feeds improves situational awareness to proactive AI defense.

9.7.1 Conceptual Role of Threat Intelligence in AI Mental Health Security

Threat intelligence is a formal way to comprehend the threat environment by gathering and analyzing information collected by several sources systematically, such as network logs, malware libraries, OSINT, and dark web surveillance. Threat intelligence systems assist in the identification of possible risks to data confidentiality and model integrity, and patient privacy in AI mental health settings. As an illustration, unauthorized access to diagnostic or therapy records can be prevented when potential exposure is detected early. Khan and Petrov (2024) assert that the most successful threat intelligence systems combine ML and NLP algorithms to automatically identify threat indicators to enhance the response time and accuracy of threat intelligence in healthcare institution applications.

AI-enhanced threat intelligence structures are especially useful in the identification of new non-signature-based attacks, for example, adversarial AI or data poisoning, which cannot be identified by traditional security tools. By analyzing abnormal patterns in network traffic, system logs, and user activity, these platforms are able to provide risk intelligence profiles particular to AI mental health workflows. Using processed threat intelligence enables security teams to detect intrusions as they occur as well as forecast the likely attack vectors based on the changing dynamics of malicious actions.

The conceptual architecture of an integrated threat intelligence system specially tailored to AI Mental Health Platforms displayed in Figure 9.12 shows a multi-layered process that proceeds on the path of raw data gathering to predictive defense. The architecture consists of separate, though, linked layers, namely the data collection layer, the correlation and analysis layer, and the predictive response layer. The workflow starts at the data collection layer where various threat data is ingested by external sources of information such as OSINT feeds and internal sources such as application logs, UBA, and audit trails of the AI models and data storage. This unstructured data of high volume is then released into the central correlation and analysis layer, where the core Threat Intelligence Platform (TIP) and AI/ML algorithms are located. This layer will be vital in associating events that appear to be unrelated, detecting complex patterns of attack (e.g., an adversarial query, then an access request), and enriching basic IOCs. Lastly, the threat intelligence analyzed which is of high fidelity is sent to the predictive response layer. In this case, the system applies the gained insights to produce proactive notifications, update security rules (e.g., firewall rules or access controls), and feed predictive defense architecture models that are able to predict an attack before it has truly occurred. Such a continuous loop guarantees that the AI mental health platform

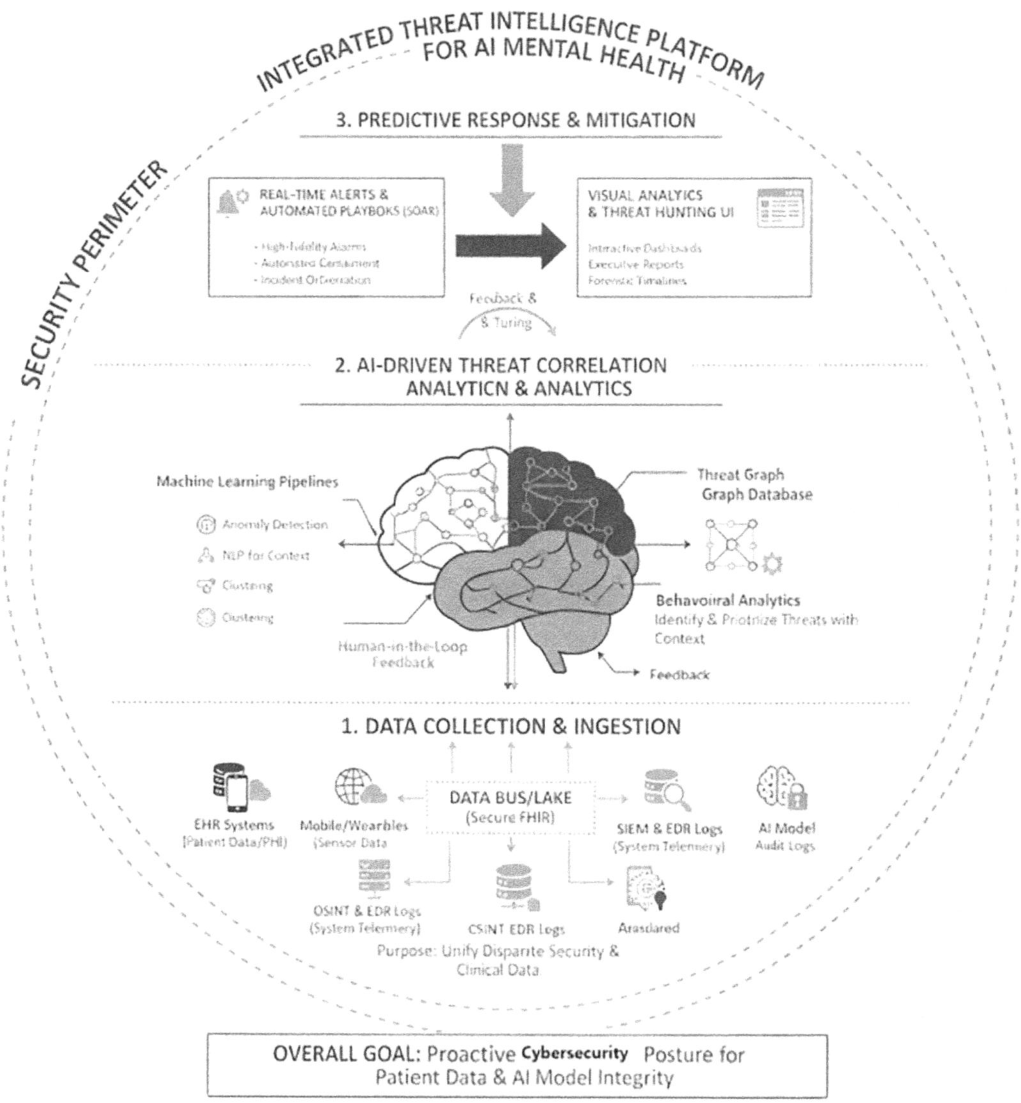

FIGURE 9.12 Theoretical architecture of a built-in threat intelligence system.

is resilient because it quickly changes its security posture based on the real-time and long-term threat analysis.

9.7.2 Integration with Security Operations and AI Pipelines

The integration of threat intelligence into Security Operations Centers (SOCs) and pipelines must be continuous and adaptive toward defending against threats to both infrastructure and algorithms. Threat intelligence data feeds can be integrated into a SIEM system in terms of incident correlation and prioritization of alerts based on patient data or AI model access in the operational data. Threat intelligence integration is part of the AI development cycle that offers an understanding of the weak points of a model enabling developers to re-train or re-adjust algorithms that are vulnerable to adversarial data.

In the field of mental health-related uses, for example, AI-based depression detection or mood detection algorithms, integration of threat intelligence in the model validation phase can be used to detect abnormal input manipulations that could cause a skewed diagnostic result. Moreover, federated threat intelligence systems can facilitate information sharing among healthcare organizations without loss of data privacy, and institutions can share anonymized IoCs via secure blockchain-based systems. This shared intelligence system enhances defense preparedness within the industry without violating privacy policies such as those outlined by the HIPAA and GDPR.

9.7.3 Predictive Threat Intelligence and Automation

New trends in cybersecurity point to predictive threat intelligence that is powered by AI-based analytics and forecasts possible attacks before they happen. Predictive threat intelligence systems can foresee the next move made by threat actors by relying on historical data, contextual clues, and reinforcement learning algorithms and can dynamically modify access controls as well as offer proactive countermeasures. An example of predictive threat intelligence is capable of identifying trends that may indicate that the attacker is attempting to carry out credential-stuffing attacks against teletherapy login portal or forecast the likely spread of ransomware based on historical infection patterns in AI-based mental health ecosystems (Li and Sanchez, 2025).

Automation has been critical in threat intelligence operationalization by minimizing the response time in human response and removing the repetitiveness in monitoring activities. Security Orchestration, Automation, and Response (SOAR) platforms could be used to automatically initiating mitigation processes, for example, isolating infected nodes, revoking the infected API keys or updating firewalls, by utilizing threat intelligence-based alerts. This orchestration facilitates a real-time defensive feedback system whereby the system will continuously learn through the past events and external intelligence input and will thus become more adaptively resilient.

9.7.4 Challenges and Ethical Issues

In spite of this, combining threat intelligence with AI mental health systems brings about ethical and operational dilemmas. Information transfer between institutions provokes the issue of patient privacy, consent, and international data regulation. The threat decision aspect of AI automation can also indirectly contribute to the spread of bias in case the threat intelligence datasets are either incomplete or biased toward certain types of attacks. Furthermore, the mental health setting provides an additional rationale of the significance of transparency and accountability in threat intelligence operations, due to the psychological effect of the possible exposure to data. As it has been stated by Singh et al. (2024), threat intelligence systems within the healthcare sector need to be developed within a human-centered model of cybersecurity that is simultaneously less automated and more ethically monitored.

Therefore, threat intelligence implementation in AI mental health needs to be implemented successfully through both technical and organizational congruity. The governance models, the adoption of standard threat taxonomies (e.g., MITRE ATT&CK in Healthcare), and ethical AI audits will make sure that the advantages of an intelligence integration will not undermine the patient rights and the trust of the institutions. The next stage of cybersecurity in digital mental health involves developing threat-intelligence-based systems that are adaptable, transparent, and ethically accountable.

9.8 QUANTITATIVE AND QUALITATIVE RISK MODELS

With AI-driven mental health systems, the effective assessment of cybersecurity in AI-driven mental health systems requires both quantitative and qualitative models that address technical, ethical, and operational vulnerabilities. The two paradigms have complementary advantages: qualitative models can give a qualitative answer to risk analysis using expertise, whereas quantitative models can use a statistical approach or mathematical approach to determine the size of risk on a probabilistic scale. Together, these models create a balanced decision-making framework suited for environments where information is uncertain, data are sensitive, and cyber threats evolve rapidly. When applied to mental health scenarios, where patient confidentiality and psychological trust are the primary concerns, a combination of these models allows organizations to prioritize mitigation strategies which comply not only with the regulatory framework but also with the moral obligations of digital care.

9.8.1 Qualitative Risk Modeling of AI Mental Health Systems

Qualitative risk models assess cybersecurity exposure using descriptive ratings, expert interviews, and structured checklists. They are based on human experience in evaluating the risk and severity of threats based on contextual information, as opposed to the numerical assessment of risks. For example, when assessing a digital cognitive-therapy platform, experts may categorize threats as low, medium, or high risk, including unauthorized access to data or tampering with a model. Joseph and Li (2024) argue that risk matrices and threat severity mapping are qualitative assessment frameworks that continue to be popular in the healthcare sector because of their simplicity, flexibility, and capacity to account for clinical insights.

Qualitative modeling, which enables cybersecurity analysts and clinicians to jointly evaluate both technical vulnerabilities and ethical risks, including the misuse of diagnostic information or unintended bias in the algorithms, is useful in AI mental health applications. These models are particularly useful during early design stages when limited empirical data are available; they facilitate the process of active communication between mental health professionals, data engineers, and compliance officers. However, their inherent subjectivity may lead to evaluator inconsistencies, making them less reliable for high-stakes decisions without quantitative validation. An example of a qualitative risk matrix of AI mental health systems can be seen in Figure 9.13, and it contains categories of risk probability over impact (e.g., data breach, AI bias, access misuse).

This figure provides an introduction to a qualitative risk matrix in the category of threats related to AI Mental Health Systems. It is a two-dimensional grid-based visual classification of risks, that is, by intersecting two subjective scales: Risk Probability (Likelihood) on one axis (e.g., Rare, Unlikely, Moderate, Likely, Almost Certain) and Impact (Consequence) on the other axis (e.g., Minor, Moderate, Major, Catastrophic). Risk levels are typically indicated using color codes such as green (low), yellow/orange (medium), and red (high).

Taking the threats of AI that are the most specific to AI, which include, but are not limited to, a data breach (high impact, as PHI is at risk), AI bias, and access misuse (different impacts, depending on the user privilege, thus subjective), the matrix can be plotted to give non-technical stakeholders a quick, easily understandable way of appreciating the importance of security issues based on consensus and subjective opinion, thus informing prompt mitigation efforts.

9.8.2 Statistical Evaluation and Quantitative Risk Modeling

Quantitative models use measurable parameters to express risk as a relationship between probability and impact. These models use statistical, probabilistic, or economic models (e.g. Monte Carlo simulations, Bayesian inference, or the FAIR model) to give data-driven answers. In AI mental health systems, a quantitative paradigm can be used to estimate the economic impact of data breaches, the risk of attacker actions against adversarial models, or the estimated period of downtime due to ransomware. To provide an example, with the help of FAIR, analysts can assign numerical values to the frequency of API exploits and predicted level of losses in case of data exposure,

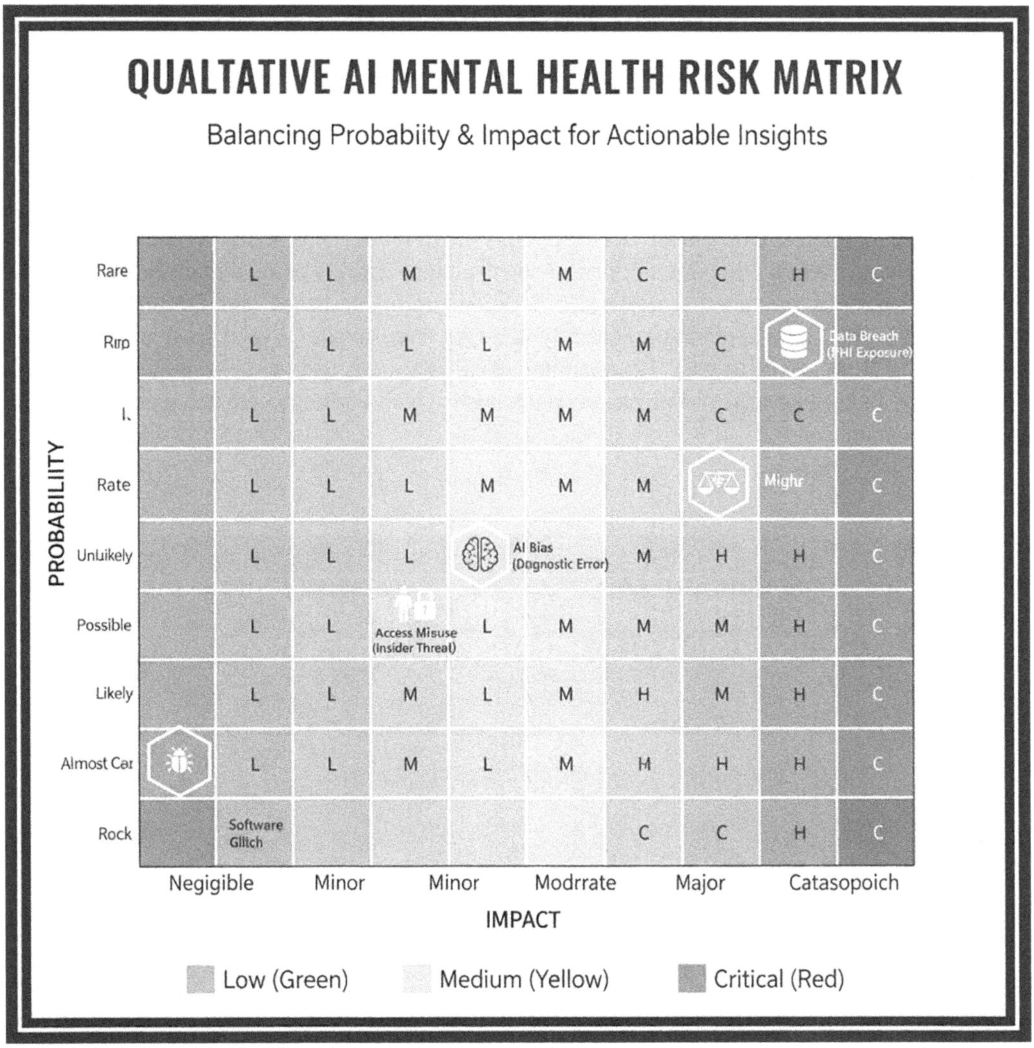

FIGURE 9.13 A sample of AI mental health systems' qualitative risk matrix.

resulting in a monetary risk score that will be used to inform budgeting and insurance decisions (Martins et al., 2025).

Additionally, AI-based predictive models can incorporate quantitative frameworks to predict the risk dynamically in real time. These models will be able to update the threat probabilities and run automatic actions by correlating past intrusion records, user access logs, and system anomalies. This dynamic quantification is essential when the digital mental health ecosystem is under consideration where cyber risks vary with the degree of engagement of the patients, variations in cloud service utilization patterns, and the emergence of new AI models.

9.8.3 Hybrid Risk Modeling: Qualitative and Quantitative Modeling

Although both methods have their own benefits, currently, hybrid risk modeling, a type of risk evaluation that integrates qualitative and quantitative analysis, is more popular in the realm of cybersecurity practices because organizations must balance expert judgment with empirical accuracy. Hybrid models can help AI mental health organizations assess both tangible and intangible risk factors, such as comparing numerical estimations of costs of data breach with qualitative judgments of reputational damage or loss of trust in patients. These two-layered evaluations enable decision-makers to record the multidimensional effects that are not limited to financial effects.

Menon and Zhou (2024) exhibit that, although hybrid models can achieve higher reliability by triangulating subjective judgments with objective data points, this is because such models triangulate subjective judgments with objective data points, which reduce bias and bring a clearer perspective to the strategy. When ethical, emotional, and regulatory aspects of AI mental health interplay, this unification will guarantee that risk-based decisions are made based on quantifiable harm and human-based factors. The application normally includes three steps: (1) qualitative screening aims to discover the areas of critical risk, (2) quantitative calculation is used to approximate the severity of the risk, and (3) integrated visualization dashboards which communicate the results to clinical and technical teams.

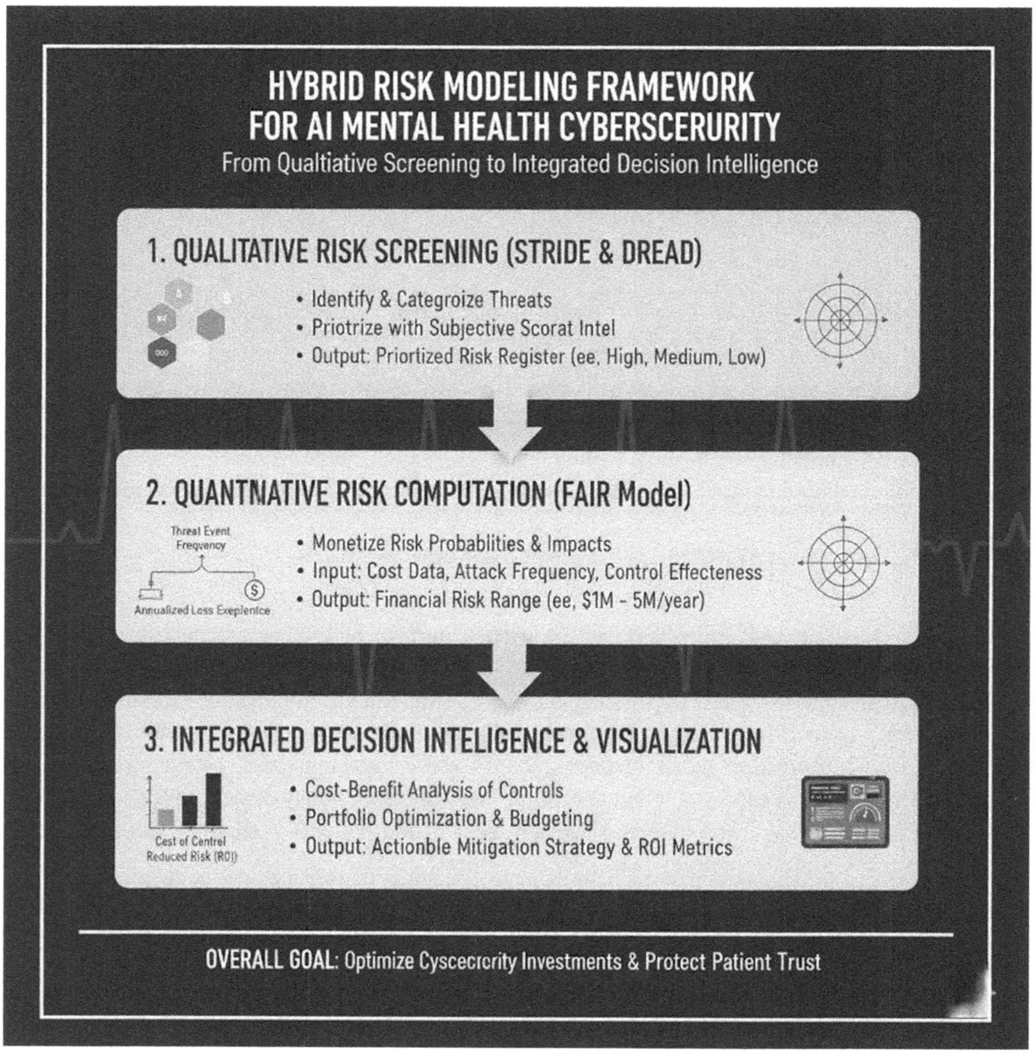

FIGURE 9.14 AI mental health hybrid risk modeling framework.

Figure 9.14 provides a complex framework of hybrid risk modeling specifically aimed at AI mental health cybersecurity, where the required workflow is listed to implement the subjective risk evaluation into measurable risk management in the form of financial models. This model works in a sequential manner. It begins with qualitative screening, which serves as a funnel through which threats of high levels are first identified and grouped with techniques such as the STRIDE model and instantly ranked by subjective scoring models such as DREAD. The first-tier qualitative evaluation eliminates threats thereof of low risk and focuses on the most probable and significant risks unique to the mental health environment (e.g., data tampering, AI bias).

The identified threats are then prioritized and taken to quantitative computation phase where FAIR model is used. During this stage, probabilistic analysis, combined with cost data, is used to determine the probability and potential financial impact of the risk events and give a specific estimate of the amount of possible monetary loss. This process culminates in an integrated decision output, the integrated decision visualization, that provides the complex, quantified risk information (i.e. the financial loss range) in readable dashboards and reports that allow the executive leadership and technical teams to make objective, cost–benefit decisions on applying security controls, effectively matching cybersecurity spending directly to the potential financial cost of the AI mental health platform.

9.8.4 Applications and Future Projections

The usage of hybrid risk models in AI mental health goes beyond the concept of a static assessment of risk to that of continuous and adaptive risk management. When combined with cyber–physical feedback mechanisms, these models enable dynamic policy adjustment based on real-time system indicators. In addition, the emergence of AI-based risk-quantification engines based on learning through previous events may make the hybrid modeling more precise by considering the behavioral and contextual intelligence (Park et al., 2025).

The new trends of the future are the combination of hybrid models with ethical AI audit frameworks that would allow mental health organizations to assess both cybersecurity performance and adherence to the principles of fairness, accountability, and transparency. This convergence supports the broader objective of ensuring psychological safety and fostering digital trust in AI-assisted therapy.

9.9 VULNERABILITY ASSESSMENT TOOLS

The rapid adoption of AI technologies in mental health systems has increased the need for systematic vulnerability management, a process that includes the detection of vulnerabilities, their evaluation, elimination, and ongoing observation to the security breaches over digital infrastructures. The operational underpinning of this effort is VMTs which are used to automate the identification of software defects, misconfiguration, and vulnerabilities at the code level that can be used by attackers to compromise the system. The operational foundation of this effort is supported by vulnerability management tools (VMTs), which automate the detection of software defects, misconfigurations, and code-level vulnerabilities exploitable by adversaries. These tools play a critical role in ensuring compliance with security frameworks, reducing risk exposure, and enabling ethically aligned digital healthcare delivery. Their importance is heightened in AI-driven mental health ecosystems, where sensitive patient data and AI models are tightly integrated with clinical workflows.

Figure 9.15 illustrates the key AI vulnerability management lifecycle, depicted as a continuous circular process. The first phase is the identify phase, which entails constant scanning and profiling of the AI system, its information pipelines, and its infrastructure to identify and document the security vulnerabilities, threats, and non-adherence problems. Second, the assess stage involves the analysis of the vulnerabilities identified in the discover stage, which is usually done with the help of risk models, such as the DREAD, or the quantitative approaches, to evaluate how

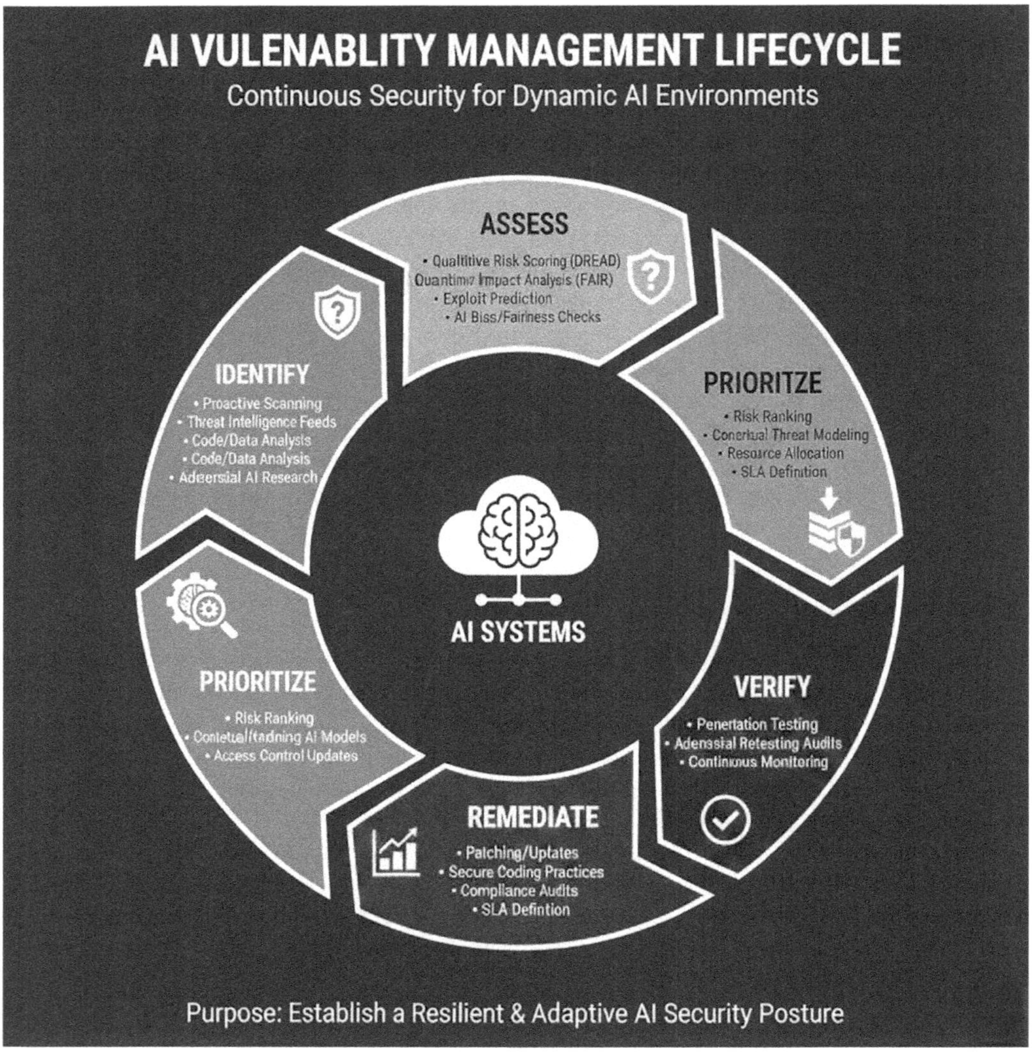

FIGURE 9.15 Scanning–assessment–remediation cycle.

the vulnerabilities can be used and their potential impact. This analysis results in the prioritize stage, where resources are distributed according to the risk score measured and pay attention to the most problematic vulnerabilities that have the greatest impact on patient safety and data integrity. The next step after prioritization is the remediate stage that will consider the deployment of security patches, modification of the access controls, re-training of the models on the sanitized data or mitigating controls to remedy the flaw. Lastly comes the verify stage, in which the testing is performed as a result of which it is determined whether the implemented remediation was able to resolve the vulnerability and whether it did not introduce new flaws. Due to the continuous changes of the AI environment along with the new data, model updates, and changing threats, the process restarts with the identify stage, which provides a strong and dynamic response to ensuring the long-term cybersecurity posture of the AI mental health system. Table 9.7 makes a comparison between the major vulnerability-management platforms applicable in healthcare and AI data environments.

TABLE 9.7
Vulnerability-Management Resources and Assessment Measures

Tool Name	Scan Scope	Automation Support	Reporting Capability	AI Integration Potential
Nessus	Network, web apps	High	Detailed dashboards	Moderate (API link)
OpenVAS	Network and host	Medium	Basic HTML reports	Extendable via scripts
Qualys	Cloud, hybrid	High	Centralized analytics	Strong (AI plugins)
Rapid7 InsightVM	Endpoint and container	High	Real-time visualization	Integrates with SIEM
Tenable.io	Cloud, IoT	High	Continuous scoring	Supports ML scoring models

9.9.1 VMT Role and Functionality

VMT are designed as continuous scanning and remediation instruments, which are interconnected with network endpoints, cloud servers, APIs, and AI data pipeline. They carry out automated tests to identify patches which are absent, libraries are outdated, and they have unsecure communication paths and open ports that might be weaknesses in the confidentiality or availability. Patel and Wong (2024) found that the use of VMTs in healthcare AI systems lowers the mean time to detect (MTTD) and the mean time to respond (MTTR) to vulnerabilities by more than 45, which increases the overall cyber resilience.

These tools can help to protect such important resources as patient databases, diagnostic algorithms, and digital therapy portals in AI mental health settings. They are able to find details of insecure dependencies to ML libraries (e.g. TensorFlow, PyTorch), identify weak encryption to data transmission layers, and analyze API gateways to exposure risks. Besides, a lot of contemporary VMTs connect with the SIEM platforms, and the vulnerability data are transferred to a centralized risk dashboard which assists in correlating and prioritizing threats.

Figure 9.16 shows the vital vulnerability management lifecycle with specific impact on AI Mental Health Systems, and highlights the five-stage, cyclical process, that should be continuous, and the key to ensuring security resilience. It starts with Scanning/Identify, which is an automated process of systematically finding vulnerabilities in the platform infrastructure, code, data pipelines, and the AI model itself (e.g., vulnerable to adversarial attacks). The Assessment phase evaluates the identified vulnerabilities, often using frameworks such as DREAD to assess the likelihood of exploitation as well as the clinical or privacy effects that might be produced on the patient. This then directly gives way to Prioritization, in which risks are categorized by level of severity, and the security teams will then use the limited resources are allocated to vulnerabilities posing the greatest risk to mental health services and PHI. The fourth stage is Remediation that consists of making the required fixes, for example, patching servers, adding input validation to the APIs, retraining the compromised AI models, or adding tougher access controls. Lastly, the process ends with the last stage which is the Verification where rigorous testing is done to ensure that the implemented fixes have actually sealed the vulnerabilities without creating any other risks and, in the process, the clinical use of the AI and its quality are not compromised. As the AI environment is fluid and continuously evolving, so that it is constantly re-reading and re-coding new data, this cycle of constant feedback starts and terminates with Scanning/Identify, ensuring that the system's security posture remains current and responsive to emerging threats.

9.9.2 VMT That Are Commonly Used

A number of open-source and commercial-grade VMT are implemented and popular in both healthcare and AI sectors and provide various capabilities based on specific operational needs.

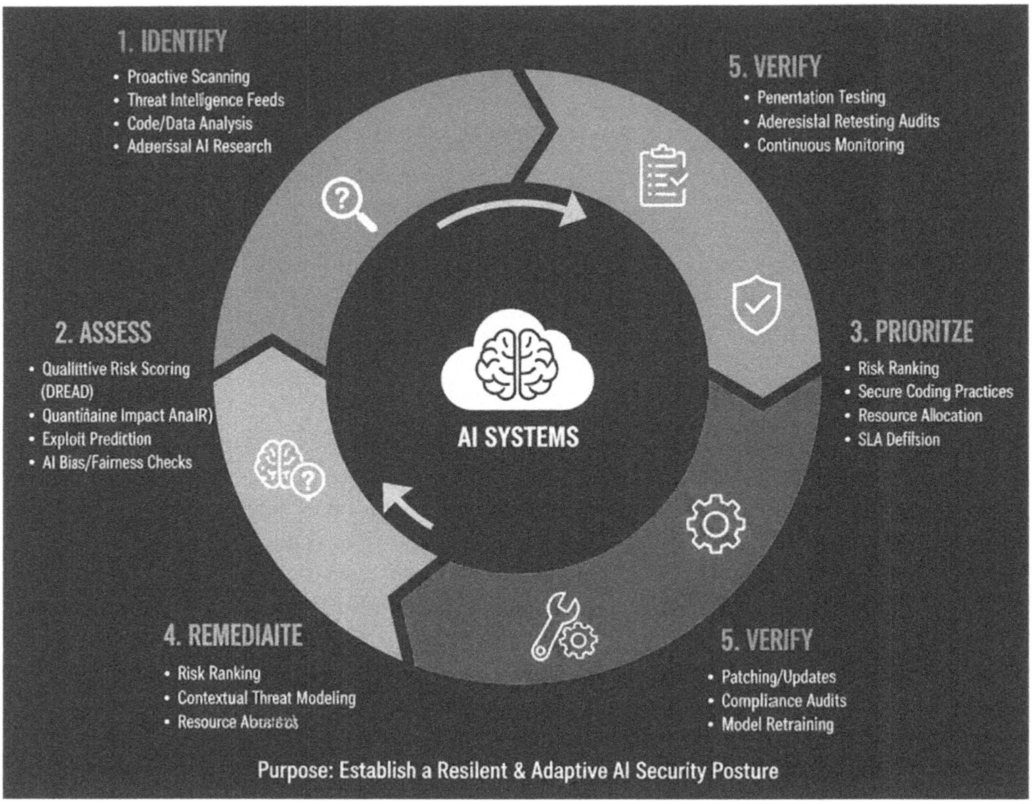

FIGURE 9.16 Lifecycle conceptual diagram of vulnerability management.

OpenVAS, Nessus, QualysGuard, and Rapid7 InsightVM are some tools that offer full scanning engines that can identify thousands of known vulnerabilities in operating systems, cloud and AI microservices. OpenVAS, which is an open-source tool, is appreciated due to its flexibility in an academic research setting, where it allows combination with custom AI model audit scripts. Conversely, QualysGuard and Tenable Nessus have enterprise capabilities like automated patch management and regulatory compliance tracking, which are appropriate in digital mental health networks of large scale (Cheng et al., 2024).

More narrow niche products such as Aqua Security and Anchore target containerized AI environments where they scan Docker or Kubernetes deployments which run ML models. As AI mental health systems often utilize cloud-native containers to be scalable and to separate privacy, the vulnerability analysis of a container is a crucial measure preventing the model tampering and data leaking during the inference. Equally, GitHub Advanced Security and SonarQube help to locate vulnerabilities in AI source code and configuration files that will provide a secure model deployment pipeline. Table 9.8 presents a comparative overview of commonly used VMT related to AI mental health systems, including the coverage of the scope of detection, the ability to automate, and the support of compliance.

9.9.3 AI-Improved Vulnerability Detection

Recent advancements have introduced a new frontier in AI-assisted vulnerability detection where ML models have been trained using large amounts of code, system logs, and threat intelligence and predict potential vulnerabilities before they can be exploited. These models are able to acquire knowledge based on previous vulnerability trends and detect any anomalies in configuration behavior or

TABLE 9.8
Comparative Analysis of Common Vulnerability Management Tools

Tool Name	Type	Scope/Focus	Integration Features	Use in AI Mental Health
OpenVAS	Open-source	Network and system scanning	Customizable plugins	Research and academic security testing
Nessus	Commercial	Comprehensive vulnerability scanning	Patch management, compliance audit	Clinical data infrastructure
QualysGuard	Commercial	Cloud, endpoint, and web app scanning	Centralized dashboard	Hospital and telehealth systems
Rapid7 InsightVM	Commercial	Dynamic threat analytics	SIEM and threat intelligence integration	AI risk analysis environments
The environment of Aqua Security	Commercial	Container and Kubernetes scanning	CI/CD pipeline integration	Deployment AI model uses
SonarQube	Open-source	Code quality and security	Developer pipeline integration	Model code auditing

system activity. The authors argue that AI-based analytics incorporated into vulnerability scanners can enhance the accuracy of zero-day detection to as much as 30% in a more complicated environment, including federated mental health AI systems (Reddy and Alcaraz, 2025; Tyagi, 2026).

In predictive patch management, the AI-based tools can also be used to implement predictions such as where the algorithm focuses on remediation efforts based on the likelihood of risk and the possible impact on patient data. This is especially pertinent in AI mental health systems in which the downtime should be reduced to the minimum to allow uninterrupted therapeutic services. Additionally, NLP used together with vulnerability databases gives systems the capability to automatically interpret new threat recommendations and apply corresponding mitigation patches automatically.

Figure 9.17 presents the conceptual architecture of an AI-Assisted Vulnerability Management Framework, which describes a modernized and intelligent workflow to shift beyond traditional manual prioritization. This architecture is fundamentally based on a potent AI Engine that takes into consideration different streams of inputs. The process begins with data ingestion, where the engine continuously collects information from vulnerability scanners, threat feeds (e.g., zero-day exploits), and system configurations. The predictive prioritization layer receives this information overload. In this case, the historical exploitability of the vulnerabilities is provided to sophisticated ML models and their direct effect on business-critical assets (such as AI models or patient data) yields a risk score that is much more accurate and dynamic than fixed severity scores (such as CVSS). This AI-based score controls the remediation execution step that can be considered as automated steps with the help of embedded SOAR to introduce patches or virtual controls with the minimum number of human interventions. More importantly, the system can have an adaptive learning feedback loop: the results of the remediation (success/failure, time spent, new vulnerabilities created) are constantly returned to the AI Engine, enabling it to update its predictive models and enhance the accuracy of future prioritization, so that the framework constantly responds to the changing threat environment of the AI mental health system.

9.9.4 Integration and Compliance Reflections

Although VMT strengthen security posture, their use must remain compliant with healthcare privacy regulations and institutional policies. For example, automated scans are supposed to be tolerant of the boundaries of repositories of patient data, and such telemetry must not accidentally reveal sensitive information. Furthermore, numerous AI mental health organizations need to coordinate

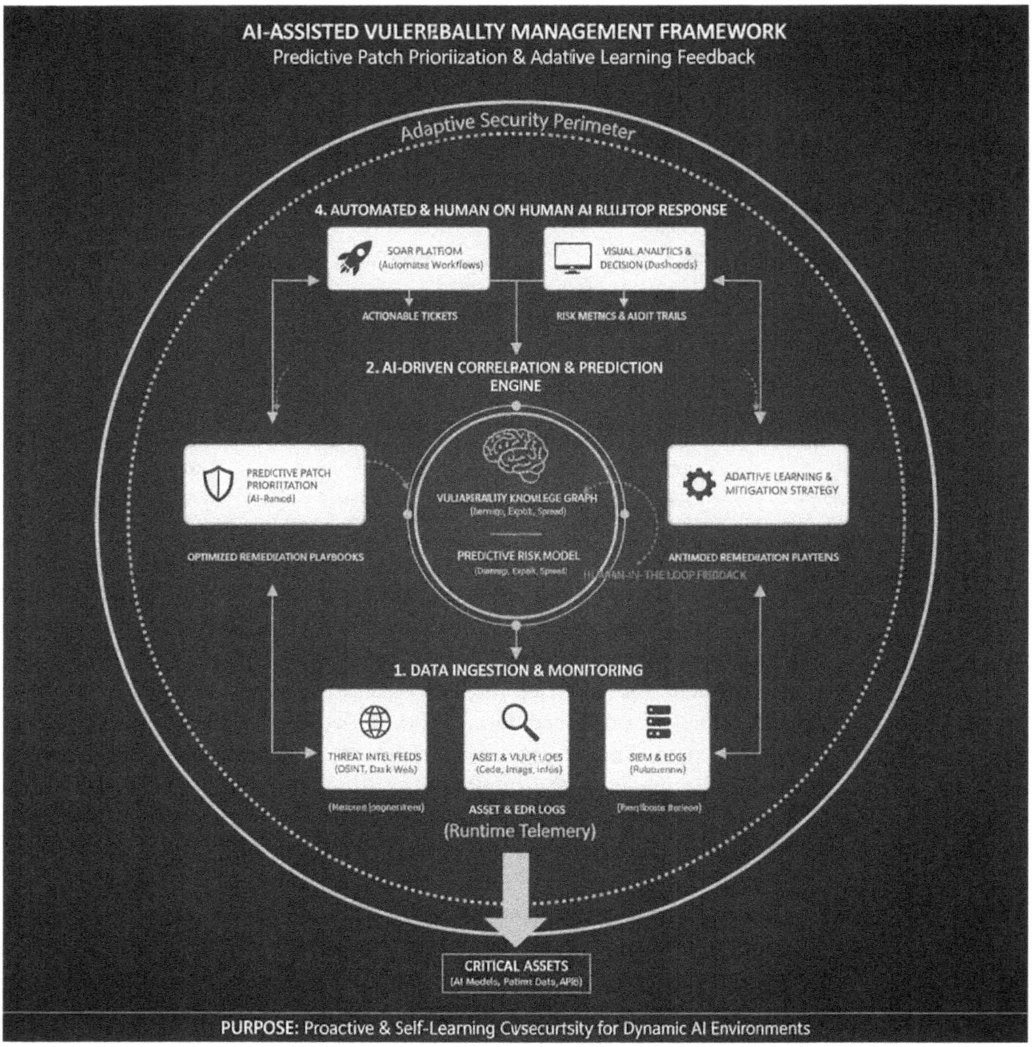

FIGURE 9.17 Predictive patching and predictive feedback learning.

their vulnerability management activities with models like ISO/IEC 27001 and NIST SP 800-53, as well as HIPAA security rule. The use of vulnerability management as a part of these compliance standards will guarantee technical security as well as legal responsibility.

To ensure its effectiveness, organizations must incorporate vulnerability management as a part of the overall strategy of continuous monitoring, whereby scanning, patching detection, and remediation tracking are conducted in real time. Correlating these findings with threat intelligence enables (as explored in Section 9.7) institutions to act proactively on vulnerabilities and active threat indicators, thus responding promptly and reducing the attack surface.

9.9.5 Future Trends in Vulnerability Management

The next generation of vulnerability management in AI mental health systems is that of autonomous and self-adaptive security ecosystems, where vulnerabilities are automatically detected, prioritized, and remediated with minimal human intervention. Such developments will take advantage of reinforcement learning algorithms that will repeatedly maximize the accuracy of scanning,

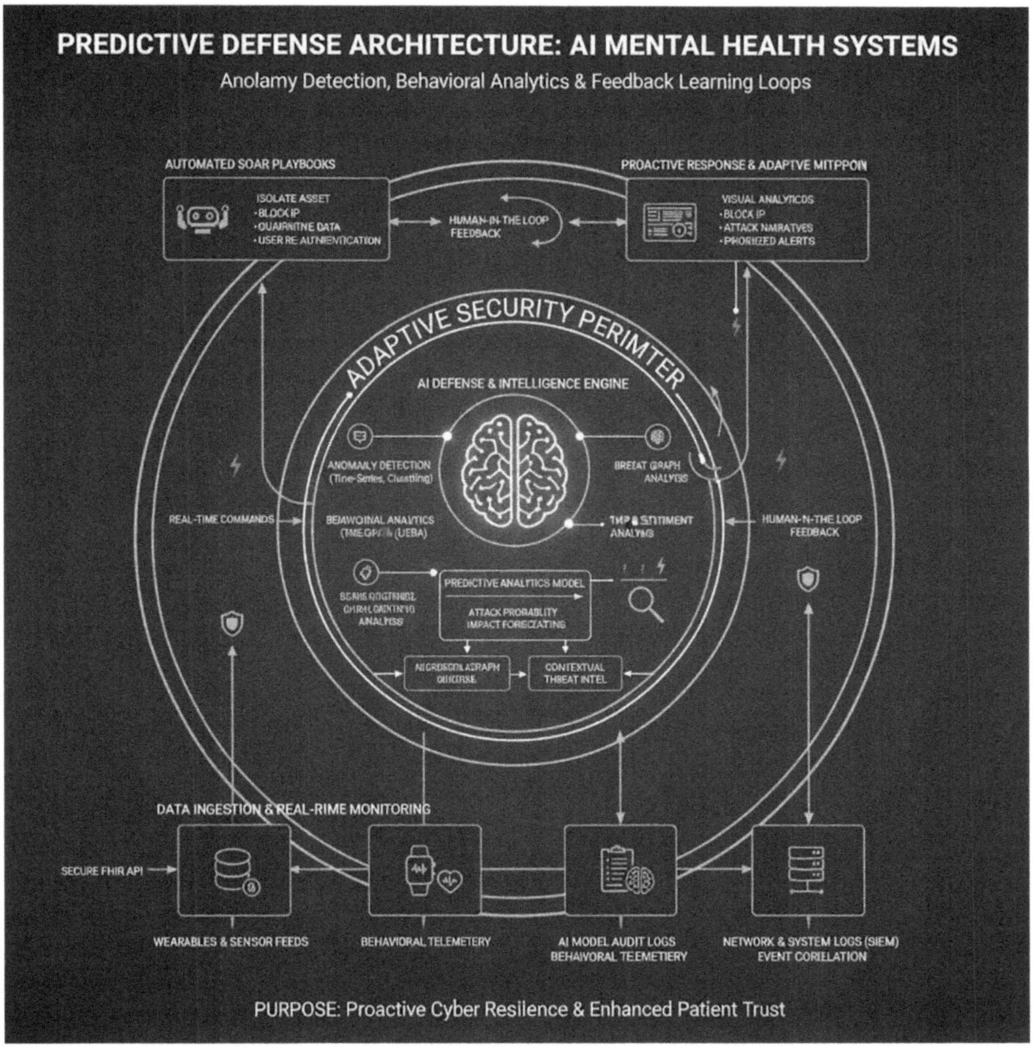

FIGURE 9.18 The loops of detection of anomalies and adaptive learning.

and the time to remediate depending on the environmental context. Moreover, sharing of vulnerability intelligence federated will enable various healthcare entities to communicate and identify vulnerabilities and how to mitigate them without centralizing sensitive data. This collaborative intelligence model ensures that even smaller facilities can benefit from collective cybersecurity knowledge without compromising the privacy of patients. Finally, the integration of AI, automation, and a continuous intelligence system will transform vulnerability management as a reactive maintenance activity to a predictive and preventive field, which is the foundation of resilient and ethically safe AI infrastructures of mental health.

9.10 PREVENTION OF INCIDENTS AND CONTINUOUS MONITORING

The basis of effective cybersecurity management in AI mental health systems is incident prevention and constant monitoring. Such systems are sensitive to clinical information, real-time patient analytics, and algorithms used to make decisions that require the continuity of operations and an absolute guarantee of privacy. The combination of proactive security controls and continuous monitoring systems allows early detection of anomalies, reduces the attack window, and contains incidents quickly, before they escalate into severe breaches. With mental health AI, where any form of disruption can interfere with the diagnostic process or patient trust, the use of incident prevention measures should follow an integrated approach that includes both technical safeguards and ethical oversight.

9.10.1 Proactive Security and Predictive Defense

Proactive security aims at detecting and preventing threats before they develop into actual security incidents. This method uses predictive defense systems based on the power of AI and ML, where one can predict vulnerability or malicious activity based on its patterns. Predictive defense systems use baselines of behavior using telemetry from continuously learning systems, network behavior data, and user activity logs to detect anomalies that may indicate abuse or intrusion.

Predictive defense plays a crucial role in mental health AI systems to detect subtle and infrequent threats, such as covert attempts to exfiltrate data through encrypted channels or manipulate therapy recommendation models. As an example, predictive analytics systems can correlate log activity across multiple subsystems, such as API gateways and authentication services, and model-serving layers, to identify coordinated attacks. Research indicates that the combination of AI-based predictive protection will decrease the number of false-positive notifications of incidents by up to 40%, increasing efficiency and confidence in mental health informatics (Kumar and Ren, 2025).

Figure 9.18 represents the conceptual Predictive Defense Architecture of AI Mental Health Systems that explains a progressive, unending cycle that detects and counter-measures threats prior to their occurrence and damages. The architecture is based on three fundamental, integrated segments. The first entails continuously monitoring with Anomaly Detection models all system activity, including user actions, application behavior, network traffic, and API calls, and building a baseline of what normal operation should look like. Any variance of this baseline (e.g. abnormal access patterns of a trusted user or spikes in API query rates) is automatically raised. Second, behavioral analytics makes use of the ML, especially UEBA to contextualize these anomalies. This layer determines reconstruct the sequence of events to distinguish between an accidental error during the course of operation and a malicious attack, including an insider threat and an attacker reconnoitering. Lastly, the system also includes adaptive learning feedback loops. In case the real threat is verified, the system sends an automated predictive response (e.g., isolating a compromised account or blocking a malicious input). The effect of the attack and the successful defense is fed back into the anomaly detection and behavioral analytics models which rapidly improves the system's understanding of normal and malicious behavior. The closed-loop system has the benefit of continuously learning and adapting the defense architecture to proactively defend against the very sensitive data and clinical integrity of the AI mental health platform.

9.10.2 Change and Onto-the-Job Monitoring and Response

Cybersecurity is no longer a periodic or reactive process with continuous monitoring but instead a continuous, real-time situational awareness function. It is the live monitoring of the network operations and user interaction and performance of the system by integrating SIEM, UEBA, and Endpoint Detection and Response (EDR). These tools combine event data, identify cross-layered correlations, and create actionable alerts when deviations to normal behavior situations are identified.

Continuous monitoring is essential in AI-driven mental health applications to ensure operational consistency and ethical use. As an illustration, any unexpected data access by the account of a mental health practitioner outside the approved hours can be monitored with the help of a continuous monitoring system to indicate a potential credential breach. Correspondingly, detecting indications of adversarial manipulation or unauthorized retraining of AI models can be done by monitoring AI model inference logs. Newer systems include reinforcement learning algorithms to dynamically adjust monitoring thresholds based on changing threat conditions to make sure that the system evolves with new threats introduced (Li et al., 2024b). Table 9.9 presents the continuous monitoring tools and their use in the AI mental health cybersecurity settings.

9.10.3 Automated Incident Response and Containment

Upon an occurrence being reported, automated incident response (AIR) systems are triggered to isolate and fix the problem with a minimal human intervention. Such systems are based on predetermined playbooks that report the specific response to the typical threat types, such as isolating compromised virtual machines, blocking malicious API traffic, or undoing the deployment of malicious code. Containment mechanisms are automated to reduce the impact of service interruptions, which is especially important in AI-based mental health systems and continuous therapy sessions and real-time analytics.

With the combination of the AIR frameworks and predictive monitoring tools, organizations can establish a closed-loop security model where detection, response, and feedback are done in real time. As an illustration, when a risk alert is raised due to an anomalous login, the system will automatically quarantine the affected user profile, revoke access tokens, and alert administrators. Once the event is resolved, the event data is once more integrated into the learning model to enhance the accuracy in detection with time. As Nguyen et al. (2025) found, incident response automation can reduce the mean time to containment (MTTC) by more than 60%, which makes systems in healthcare AI infrastructures much more resilient.

Figure 9.19 shows a vital closed-loop AIR workflow that is set to be able to manage security incidents in an intelligent and fast manner in AI Mental Health Platforms. It is defined by self-correcting, continuous workflow and reduces the human latency. It starts with detection where the security controls of the system (such as SIEM or Anomaly Detection model) identify a proven security incident, such as an attempted data breach or a breach of the models.

The next step to be followed when the threat is confirmed is Containment. The essence of automation involves the SOAR tools to automatically execute predefined playbook to isolate the threat, such as revoking the access of the compromised user, quarantining the infected server, or temporarily

TABLE 9.9
Ongoing Surveillance Devices and the Use of AI

Monitoring Tool/ Framework	Core Function	AI Integration Feature	Use in Mental Health Systems
Splunk Enterprise Security	SIEM and threat correlation	Machine learning for pattern analysis	Detects abnormal clinician logins or data transfers
IBM QRadar	Event monitoring and risk prioritization	AI-driven correlation engine	Tracks patient data access anomalies
CrowdStrike Falcon	End-point detection and response	Behavioral AI detection	Prevents endpoint-based model tampering
Azure Sentinel	Cloud-native monitors	Automated monitoring and ML-based security orchestration	Secures cloud-based AI therapy
Darktrace Antigena	Autonomous threat response	Self-learning neural algorithms	Adaptive defense for AI-assisted diagnosis systems

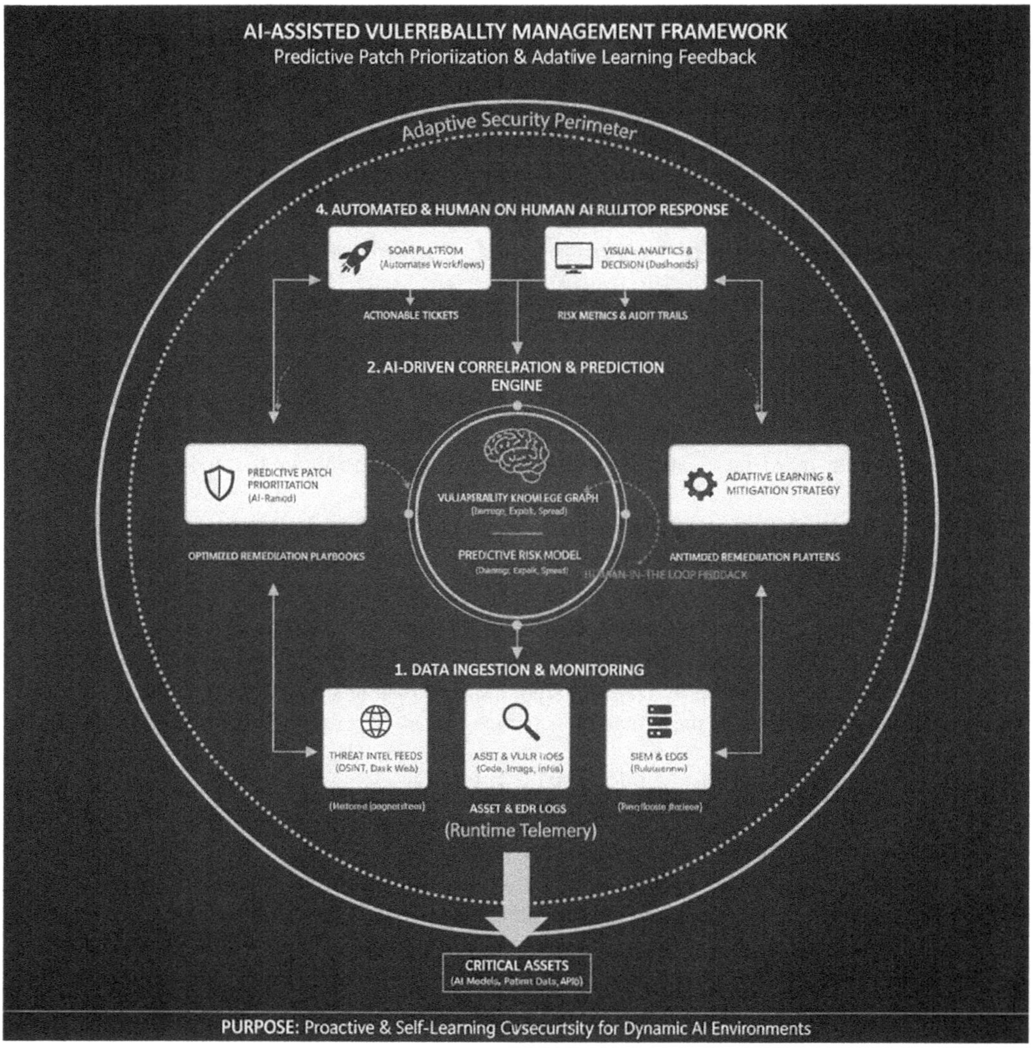

FIGURE 9.19 Closed-loop feedback detection-containment model.

decommissioning the vulnerable AI model API. After containment, the system does eradication and recovery to make sure the threat has been eliminated completely and the services ruined are restored. It is followed by the whole workflow ending and enhancing with the feedback learning stage. This is the last and crucial step, which requires feeding the entire incident information, the manner in which the attack was carried out, failed controls, and the performance of the automated response, back into the security analytics and AI algorithms of the system. This learning loop can enhance the detection thresholds and the playbooks employed to containment and can make the platform more resilient in predicting future attacks that are similar to the one and to update the security posture of the mental health system, continuously.

9.10.4 Relation to Ethical and Regulatory Structures

In addition to technical accuracy, the incident prevention and monitoring should be in accordance with ethical and regulatory principles that protect patient rights. Adherence to frameworks, including

HIPAA, GDPR, and ISO/IEC 27035, is done to ensure that the incident management processes maintain confidentiality, accountability, and transparency. In addition, ethical AI governance makes the explainability of AIRs a requirement and prevents unintended restrictions on legitimate clinical workflows.

Practically, this implies that the data of such monitoring must be pseudonymized and that automated behavior should be checked on a regular basis for potential bias or excessive restriction of normal user behavior. As an example, the auditing of systems must be done to verify that anomaly-detecting models do not label certain user roles or behavioral patterns that are not necessarily malicious intent. Installing ethics-founded auditing policies will help to make sure that the security operations do not undermine the therapeutic purposes of mental healthcare.

9.10.5 Future Prospects of Incidence Prevention

The future of cybersecurity in AI mental health systems is shifting toward autonomous resilience where prevention, detection, and response will operate as an integrated autonomous ecosystem. Future studies imagine cognitive models of cybersecurity that will be able to learn about global threat information, adjust to novel circumstances, and reconfigure security settings automatically under the influence of environmental cues. In these systems, protective behavior would not respond to threats but also anticipate and avert them, thereby mirroring the adaptive learning behavior of AI itself.

The neuro-symbolic AI models and federated monitoring architectures will allow the decentralization of incident prevention, where patient data may never need to pass through centralized servers. Such advances will strengthen privacy-by-design principles and offer worldwide understanding of the trends of attacks on mental health infrastructures. Finally, AI, automation, and ethical regulation will intersect, resulting in a self-protective, resilient digital ecosystem that will ensure the integrity, confidentiality, and trustworthiness of AI-aided mental healthcare.

9.11 SECURITY CERTIFICATION AND BEST PRACTICES

Security certification and best practices are critical for sustaining trust, regulatory compliance, and operational integrity in AI-driven mental health systems. Due to the sensitivity of psychological data and the growing popularity of AI algorithms in the field of diagnosing, therapeutic support, and communicating with patients, companies need to comply with the internationally accepted data protection guidelines. Certifications not only validate technical security controls but also demonstrate adherence to ethical and privacy-oriented practices. It is done through continuous data handling assessment, system resilience, and AI governance to make sure that patient welfare is in the center of the digital transformation. As shown in Table 9.10, certification standards ensure that digital mental-health AI systems meet ethical and regulatory requirements.

9.11.1 Relevance of Security Certification in AI Mental Health Systems

Security certification serves as a key mechanism for establishing and sustaining digital trust in mental health technologies. It guarantees the patients, clinicians, and regulatory authorities that information systems within an organization are up to the specifications of confidentiality, integrity, as well as availability. In the case of AI mental health platforms, the certification systems, including ISO/IEC 27001, ISO/IEC 27701, NIST SP 800-53, and HIPAA security rule, should serve as fundamental guidelines in the area of data protection and system assurance.

Such certifications require organizations to adopt a risk-based security management strategy to ensure that every aspect, such as data gathering to AI inference, is protected against possible harms. As an illustration, ISO/IEC 27001 requires a regular assessment of risks, access control systems, and incident management procedures. Meanwhile, ISO/IEC 27701 is characterized as a broader

TABLE 9.10
Security Certification Standards and Compliance Requirements

Certification/ Standard	Governing Body	Scopes	Relevance to AI Mental Health	Key Compliance Requirements
ISO/IEC 27001	ISO	Information Security Management System	Data protection and risk management	Continuous ISMS auditing
NIST SP 800-53	NIST (USA)	Security and Privacy Controls	Technical safeguard guidelines	Access control, audit, integrity
HIPAA	U.S. Health and Human Services	Health data confidentiality	Mandatory for U.S. clinical AI	Privacy, integrity, availability
GDPR	EU Commission	Personal data regulation	Affects any EU patient data	Consent, minimization, right to erasure
SOC 2	AICPA	Cloud service security	Cloud AI mental-health providers	Trust, confidentiality, availability

extension of this framework to Privacy Information Management System (PIMS), which matches the security controls with the privacy-by-design principles that are important in mental healthcare. Adherence to these standards increases the technical robustness as well as increasing the validity of AI mental health solutions both in clinical and research contexts.

The conceptual hierarchical representation of security certification frameworks applicable to AI mental health ecosystems is presented in Figure 9.20 that shows how international and national standards fit in with sector requirements. This representation places broad, foundational frameworks at the top, which progressively narrow into more specialized healthcare-specific requirements. The top level is the International Standards such as ISO/IEC 27001 that gives the world standard benchmark on the development, deployment, sustenance, and continuous enhancement of an Information Security Management System (ISMS) that will guarantee the soundness of security governance throughout the whole organization. Under this are the standards and guidelines of the organizations such as NIST (National Institute of Standards and Technology), especially its Cybersecurity Framework (CSF) and such publications as NIST SP 800-53. These offer detailed and flexible security controls and best practices that may be applied to federal systems and offer a robust technical base on which to secure cloud infrastructure, data pipelines, and the AI model themselves. At the most detailed level are sector-specific regulations such as HIPAA, which directly govern the handling of PHI. The security and privacy rules are the direct regulation of HIPAA regarding the management, storage, and transfer of PHI in the United States. In the case of an AI mental health system, Figure 9.20 shows that compliance can only be achieved through the strict PHI protection requirements of HIPAA that must be followed by the most effective method of implementation through the existing controls and guidelines of NIST and the overall framework of ISO/IEC 27001. The integration will ensure that there is legal adherence and that the level of comprehensive security is high.

9.11.2 International Workings and Standards

Healthcare and AI system security are governed by numerous international and regional cybersecurity standards. An example is the CSF outlined by the NIST, which offers a systematic response that includes five fundamental functions (identify, protect, detect, respond, and recover), which provides a holistic way of dealing with cyber-risk. Likewise, the GDPR adopted by the European Union sets high standards of working with personal and health-related information that require express permission, reduction of information, and transparency of the user.

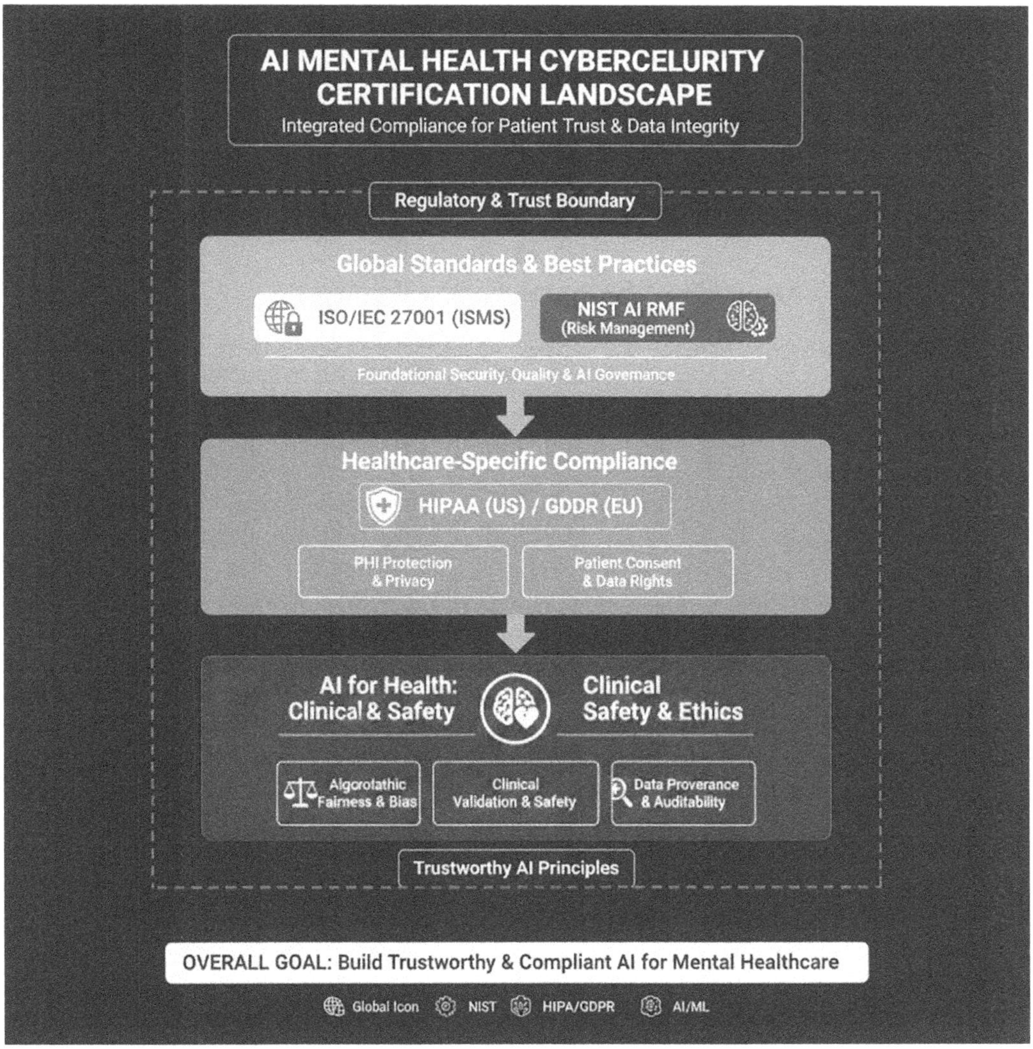

FIGURE 9.20 ISO-NIST-HIPAA interrelation.

TABLE 9.11
Comparison of Key Cybersecurity and Privacy Frameworks

Framework/Standard	Primary Focus	Relevance to AI Mental Health	Key Components
ISO/IEC 27001	Information Security Management	Baseline for protecting clinical data and AI workflows	Risk assessment, access control, monitoring
ISO/IEC 27701	Privacy Information Management	Builds on 27001 with privacy-specific controls	Consent management, data retention policies
NIST SP 800-53	Security and Privacy Controls	U.S. federal guideline for system security	Control catalog for healthcare information systems
HIPAA Security Rule	Health Data Protection (United States)	Mandatory for digital health data compliance	Safeguards for electronic protected health information (ePHI)
GDPR	Data Protection (EU)	Global benchmark for personal data ethics	Consent, portability, and user rights
IEC 62304	Medical Software Lifecycle	Ensures AI system reliability and traceability	Risk-based software development process

When it comes to mental health AI systems, a combination of NIST CSF and ISO and GDPR requirements will guarantee that the scope of data protection is fully covered in both technical and ethical aspects. Moreover, IEC 62304 presents medical device-specific software lifecycle processes, such as AI diagnostic tools, and traceability and safety in making an algorithmic decision. Multinational organizations often adopt hybrid compliance strategies aligned with multiple regulatory frameworks. Table 9.11 demonstrates the summary of the significant cyber security and privacy models concerning AI mental health systems.

9.11.3 Secure AI Mental Health Operating Best Practices

Best practices must be implemented in ways that operationalize certification standards and ensure ongoing compliance. These practices cut across several areas which include governance, technical implementation, and continuous improvement. Key best practices include:

Privacy-by-Design Integration: Privacy protection at AI model training and data processing phases would make sure that mental health information is anonymized and has a limited purpose.

Zero Trust Architecture (ZTA): In a zero-trust model, no user or device is assumed trustworthy by default, and all access requests require continuous verification.

Frequent Penetration Testing: The regular red-teaming processes discover vulnerabilities of AI pipelines, such as inversion of models or adversarial attacks.

Secure Software Development Lifecycle (SSDLC): A combination of security validation in all stages of AI software creation, starting with data labeling, through deployment, and immediately preventing threats, can be applied.

Employee Awareness and Training: Human error is one of the primary causes of cybersecurity breaches; constant training is a way of ensuring compliance with ethical and procedural standards.

Incident response and business continuity planning ensure the availability of mental health services during breaches or outages.

Figure 9.21 demonstrates an important model of the Secure AI Lifecycle, which would introduce necessary certification gates directly into the ongoing development and operation of the AI system, especially systems that processed sensitive data in the mental health field. This model ensures that security and compliance remain integral at every stage. The first stage of the cycle is Data Collection, and the checkpoints here are regulatory compliance (such as HIPAA) and privacy methods (such as anonymization and differential privacy). In the model training phase, checkpoints are used to mitigate integrity threats such as data poisoning and the elimination of the harmful bias. During deployment phase, security measures protect model interfaces from external threats such as adversarial queries. Lastly, the monitoring phase necessitates the ongoing certification with the help of audit trails and behavioral analytics to identify the presence of runtime threats, stop model drift, and attempts to disclose information. These formalized checkpoints maintain the levels of security as not a one-off audit, but the systematic process that is verified, and the standards of quality that is required to uphold the clinical and legal compliance of the whole AI ecosystem.

9.11.4 AI-Specific Certification and Governance Projects

As AI becomes central to mental healthcare, new AI governance and certification systems emerge to guarantee the transparency, fairness, and accountability of the systems. The Artificial Intelligence Act (2024) by the EU proposes a risk-based classification of AI systems, which would entail

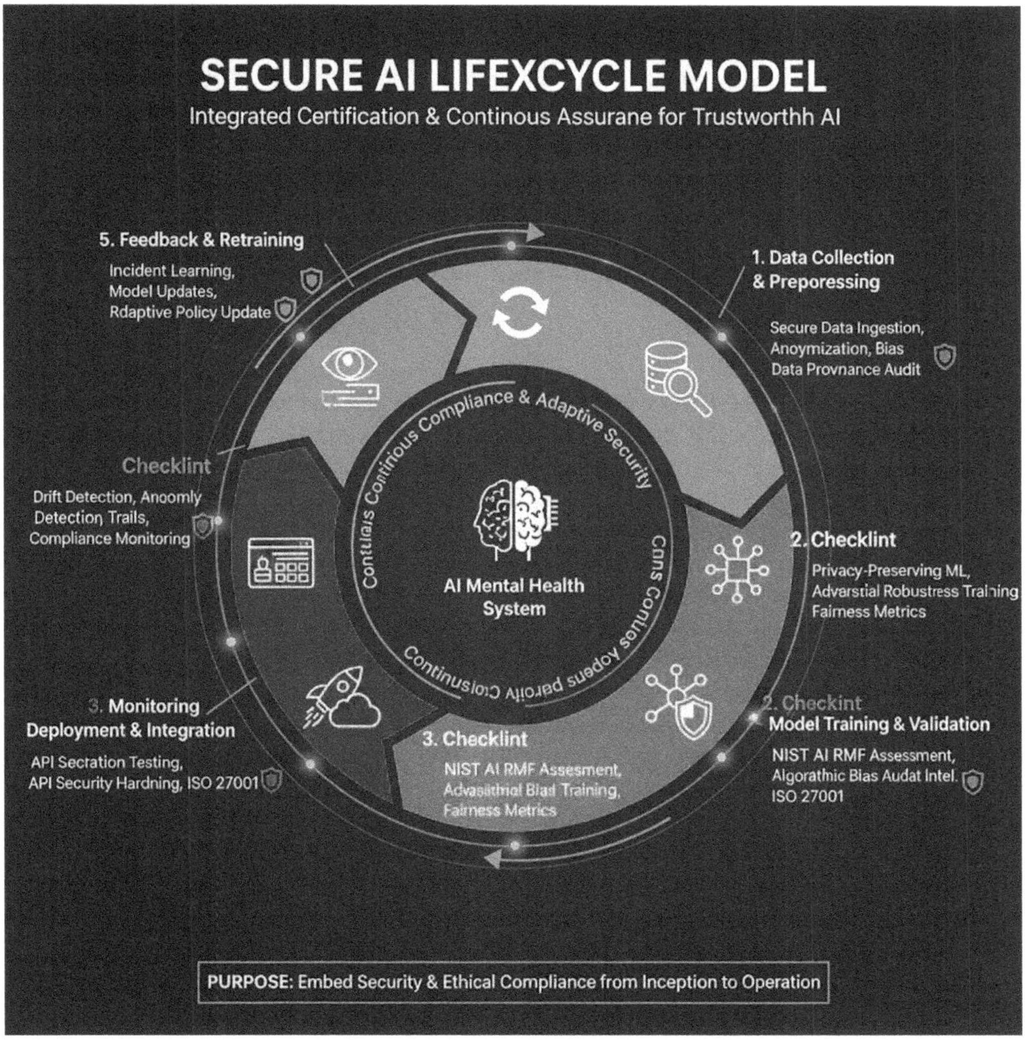

FIGURE 9.21 Checkpoints in certification in AI development.

conformity assessment of high-risk AI systems (including mental health diagnostics). On the same note, IEEE 7000 Series Standards offer ethical principles to autonomous and intelligent systems, which includes data governance, algorithmic bias, and human oversight processes. At the same time the ISO/IEC JTC 1/SC 42 committee is developing standards for AI management systems, which are used to augment the cybersecurity certifications. These evolving standards help institutions demonstrate compliance not only in data protection but also in responsible AI practices, which are essential when algorithmic decisions affect patient well-being. Through acquiring AI-specific certifications, the mental health organizations can improve their transparency, ensure public trust, and reduce risks potentially related to ethical and legal non-compliance.

9.11.5 Sustaining Certification by Continuous Improvement

Security certification is not a milestone but an ongoing process that is changing according to changes in technology and regulatory changes. To be certified, the audits, vulnerability reviews, and updates of the policies should be conducted periodically. An extended compliance monitoring system can be integrated and enable real-time verification of security posture and automatic identification of discrepancies against laid down standards. Furthermore, the implementation of SOAR systems is to make sure that compliance artifacts, including log integrity and access logs, are continuously available to audit to guarantee audit readiness. In the case of AI mental health systems, continuous certification serves as an additional support of ethical responsibility. Integrating compliance metrics into AI model governance ensures that data protection and algorithmic integrity are maintained together throughout the system lifecycle. This continuing responsibility turns certification into regulatory responsibility but a strategic source of trust, strength, and responsible innovation.

9.12 SUMMARY

The chapter has discussed the complexity of risk evaluation and threat modeling in AI-based mental health systems and how technical, ethical, and regulatory views can be integrated to establish secure and trustworthy digital healthcare environments. With the growing role of AI technologies in psychological assessment, therapy administration, and predictive analytics, ensuring the security of such systems is both a technical requirement and an ethical responsibility. These frameworks and tools were presented systematically to show how risk analysis, continuous monitoring, and certification can collectively support a robust security posture tailored to the sensitivity of mental healthcare.

The principles of threat modeling such as STRIDE, DREAD, and FAIR were presented in the introductory part as supplementary approaches to the definition of potential vulnerabilities, their prioritization, and quantification. It was demonstrated that their integration provides a hybrid approach that contributes to proactive risk management throughout the AI system's lifecycle. What followed was the topic on risk categorization and assessment models which contrasted quantitative and qualitative models and proposed hybrid models applicable in complex AI-based clinical infrastructures. All these structures can help healthcare institutions to evaluate not only the technical exposure but also ethical and psychological risks tied to the misuse of data or model bias.

Furthermore, typical attacks such as phishing, ransomware, and API exploitation illustrate how these threats can undermine AI processes and patient privacy. The discussion of the two classes of threat actors, insiders and outsiders, has shown that human and systemic vulnerabilities are equally significant and require multilayered defenses that are based on access control, audit trail, and behavioral analytics. The use of threat intelligence systems further enhanced the necessity of adaptive defense, enabling AI mental health platforms to adapt to emerging attack patterns and evolving threat strategies worldwide.

The latter part of the paper was devoted to one of the key aspects of operationalizing these theoretical constructs in the form of VMT and continuous monitoring systems. Tools such as OpenVAS, Nessus, and QualysGuard, enhanced with AI analytics, support early threat detection, automated remediation, and continuous compliance monitoring. Continuous monitoring systems using SIEM, UEBA, and EDR provide ongoing situational visibility, providing predictive threat detection, automated containment, and post incident learning. These mitigation strategies align with the concept of cyber resilience, enabling AI systems to remain operational and trustworthy even under persistent threat conditions.

The security certification and best practices discussion framed the regulatory and ethical foundations of secure AI-enabled mental health operations. As they conform to global standards, like ISO/IEC 27001, NIST SP 800-53, HIPAA, and GDPR, organizations can enable the technical reliability and integrity of their data governance. Besides, new standards such as the EU AI Act and IEEE 7000 Series indicate the increasing awareness that AI security must be considered in conjunction with ethical accountability. The combination of AI-specific regulation and the time-honored information security standards is therefore the future of mental health technology regulation.

In summary, the chapter demonstrates that the way forward toward the creation of effective cybersecurity in AI mental health systems is not done alone through isolated technical tools but rather through an ecosystem approach of predictive modeling, persistent assessment of risks, automated protection, and certified governance. This type of ecosystem will support the concept of trustworthy AI one that safeguards patient data, maintains therapeutic reliability, and upholds the ethical values of confidentiality, autonomy, and beneficence that form the fundamental pillars of mental healthcare. As the AI technologies are developing, future research should advance toward autonomous and explainable cybersecurity systems capable of self-assessment, self-correction, and maintaining compliance without compromising human oversight. This adaptive, ethical, and resilient security paradigm forms the foundation for sustainable innovation in the era of intelligent mental health systems.

REFERENCES

Ahmed, L., & Lee, J. (2023). Privacy challenges in AI-based behavioral health systems: A survey and framework. *Journal of Healthcare Informatics Research, 7*(2), 145–167.

Almeida, J., & Roy, P. (2024). Ransomware impact on digital mental health infrastructures: Case studies and countermeasures. *Journal of Cybersecurity in Healthcare, 12*(3), 144–162.

Balamurugan, G., Tyagi, A.K., & Richa, A. (2023). Survey on privacy preserving and trust building techniques of blockchain-based systems. In: *Privacy Preservation and Secured Data Storage in Cloud Computing*. IGI Global. DOI: 10.4018/979-8-3693-0593-5.ch019

Cheng, W., Rahman, A., & Kim, T. (2024). Comparative study of vulnerability management systems in healthcare IT ecosystems. *Journal of Cybersecurity Applications, 19*(3), 241–258.

ISO. (2022). *Information technology—Security techniques—Information security risk management (ISO/IEC 27005:2022)*. International Organization for Standardization. www.iso.org/standard/75619.html

Jones, J., & Ashenden, D. (2022). Measuring and managing information risk: The FAIR methodology in practice. *Information Systems Security, 31*(4), 65–80.

Joseph, T., & Li, S. (2024). Qualitative risk evaluation in clinical and AI-assisted healthcare environments. *Health Informatics Journal, 30*(2), 154–172. https://doi.org/10.1177/14604582241234567

Khan, R., & Petrov, L. (2024). Artificial intelligence–driven threat intelligence systems for healthcare cybersecurity. *Computers & Security, 145*, 104215. https://doi.org/10.51244/IJRSI.2025.120700106

Kumar, D., Sharma, V., & Reddy, S. (2024). AI-enhanced phishing detection and prevention in healthcare ecosystems. *Computers & Security, 141*, 103872.

Kumar, R., & Ren, H. (2025). Predictive threat analytics for intelligent healthcare systems. *IEEE Access, 13*, 14523–14539. https://doi.org/10.1109/ACCESS.2025.3045678

Kumari, S., Tyagi, A. K., Tiwari, S., & Kulshreshtha, G. (2025a). Sensors and digital twin for healthcare monitoring frameworks. In T. A. Nguyen (Ed.), *Digital twin, blockchain, and sensor networks in the healthy and mobile city (Chapter 10,* pp. 147–177*)*. Elsevier. https://doi.org/10.1016/B978-0-443-34174-8.00011-9

Kumari, S., Tyagi, A. K., Tiwari, S., & Singh, R. (2025b). Medical sensor network, edge computing and blockchain for efficient medical data exchange. In T. A. Nguyen (Ed.), *Digital twin, blockchain, and sensor networks in the healthy and mobile city (Chapter 11,* pp. 179–198*)*. Elsevier. https://doi.org/10.1016/B978-0-443-34174-8.00012-0

Li, Q., Santos, D., & Park, J. (2024). Adaptive continuous monitoring using reinforcement learning in AI-enabled health environments. *Journal of Network and Computer Applications, 231*, 104875.

Li, T., Wang, Q., & Zhao, M. (2024). Adversarial robustness in medical AI systems: Threat modeling and defense strategies. *IEEE Transactions on Information Forensics and Security, 19*(4), 1021–1037.

Li, X., & Sanchez, R. (2025). Predictive cyber defense models using reinforcement learning in clinical informatics. *IEEE Transactions on Information Forensics and Security, 20*(1), 88–104.

Liu, X., Chen, H., & Park, S. (2025). Adaptive multi-vector cyberattacks in AI-driven clinical systems. *IEEE Transactions on Dependable and Secure Computing, 22*(2), 317–333.

Martins, C., Vega, L., & Okada, H. (2025). Quantitative modeling and FAIR-based cyber risk estimation for medical AI systems. *Journal of Risk Analysis and Management, 44*(1), 87–104.

Menon, D., & Zhou, L. (2024). Hybrid frameworks for cybersecurity risk integration in digital health ecosystems. *IEEE Access, 12*, 98341–98358.

Microsoft. (2020). *STRIDE threat modeling methodology*. Microsoft Security Documentation.

Mishra, A. K., Tiwari, S., Tyagi, A. K., & Arowolo, M. O. (2024). Security, privacy, trust, and provenance issues in Internet of Things–based edge environment. In S. Pal, C. Savaglio, R. Minerva, & F. C. Delicato (Eds.), *IoT edge intelligence* (pp. 233–263). Springer. https://doi.org/10.1007/978-3-031-58388-9_8

Nair, M. M., & Tyagi, A. K. (2021). Privacy: History, statistics, policy, laws, preservation and threat analysis. *Journal of Information Assurance & Security*, *16*(1), 24–34.

Nair, M.M., & Tyagi, A.K. (2025). Transformative effects of emerging technologies on Industry 5.0 and Society 5.0: Current status, vision, issues, challenges, and opportunities for future. In: *Next Generation Data Science and Blockchain Technology for Industry 5.0*. Wiley. DOI: https://doi.org/10.1002/9781394245215.ch13, ISBN: 9781394245185.

Nguyen, P., & Patel, S. (2022). Cybersecurity vulnerabilities in telepsychiatry and digital mental health platforms. *Health Informatics Journal, 28*(3), 1–18.

Nguyen, P., Thakur, M., & Das, S. (2025). Automated incident response frameworks in healthcare cybersecurity. *Computers & Security, 146*, 104236. https://doi.org/10.1016/j.cose.2025.104236

NIST. (2024). *API security guidelines for health and AI applications (NIST SP 800-214)*. National Institute of Standards and Technology.

Park, S., Kumar, V., & Liao, J. (2025). AI-based risk quantification engines for adaptive security in healthcare systems. *Computers & Security, 150*, 104672. https://doi.org/10.1016/j.cose.2025.104672

Patel, D., & Wong, S. (2024). Operational efficiency of vulnerability management in healthcare AI systems. *Computers & Security, 142*, 103955.

Patel, R., & Nguyen, T. (2024). External threat vectors and adaptive defense models in AI healthcare platforms. *Journal of Information Security and Privacy, 18*(2), 210–229.

Rahman, H., Das, S., & Chowdhury, M. (2023). API security challenges in digital health ecosystems. *Computers & Security, 125*, 102947.

Rajani, D., Menon, S. C., Kute, S., & Tyagi, A. K. (2022). Preserving privacy of social media data using artificial intelligence techniques. In A. Tyagi (Ed.), *Handbook of Research on Technical, Privacy, and Security Challenges in a Modern World* (pp. 186–204). IGI Global. https://doi.org/10.4018/978-1-6684-5250-9.ch010

Reddy, M., & Alcaraz, J. (2025). AI-driven predictive vulnerability assessment for cloud-native clinical platforms. *IEEE Transactions on Information Forensics and Security, 20*(4), 522–536.

Santos, J., Becker, R., & Yoon, K. (2023). Applying the FAIR and MITRE ATT&CK frameworks to AI-based healthcare risk management. *ACM Transactions on Privacy and Security, 26*(2), 41–60.

Sharma, A., & Liao, Y. (2024). Human-centric cybersecurity: Insider threat management in digital mental health systems. *Health Informatics Review, 32*(4), 278–295. www.crossref.org/guestquery

Singh, P., Arora, D., & Vega, C. (2024). Ethical integration of automation and intelligence in healthcare cybersecurity systems. *Health Technology Ethics Review, 9*(2), 122–139. https://doi.org/10.51594/csitrj.v6i3.1872

Singh, P., & Dutta, R. (2024). Bridging cybersecurity and clinical psychology: A cross-domain framework for AI mental health. *AI and Society, 39*(1), 215–229. www.springer.com/journal/146

Tyagi, A.K. (2021). Analysis of security and privacy aspects of blockchain technologies from smart era' perspective: The challenges and a way forward. In: *Recent Trends in Blockchain for Information Systems Security and Privacy* (pp. 1–17). DOI: https://doi.org/10.1201/9781003139737, eBook-ISBN: 9781003139737

Tyagi, A.K. (2025). Blockchain for smart hospital in Healthcare 5.0: modeling structure, challenges, and future emerging trends. In: *Human-Centric Integration of Next-Generation Data Science and Blockchain Technology*. Elsevier. DOI: https://doi.org/10.1016/B978-0-443-33498-6.00026-1, ISBN: 978-0-443-33498-6.

Tyagi, A.K. (2026). *Chapter 4 - Artificial intelligence–blockchain–Internet of Things–based smart healthcare services: literature review and future research directions, in the book: Smart Hospital Anatomy with Advanced Sensors Innovations in Patient Care*. Elsevier (pp. 49–61). https://doi.org/10.1016/B978-0-443-45875-0.00005-3, ISBN: 978-0-443-45875-0.

Tyagi, A., Kumari, S., & Tiwari, S. (2024c). Internet of Things for smart healthcare: A survey. In A. K. Sharma, N. Chanderwal, S. Tyagi, & P. Upadhyay (Eds.), *Future of AI in medical imaging (Chapter 2)*. IGI Global. https://doi.org/10.4018/979-8-3693-2359-5.ch002

Tyagi, A. K., & Tiwari, S. (2024a). Blockchain-enabled smart healthcare applications in 6G networks. In A. K. Tyagi (Ed.), *Digital twin and blockchain for smart cities (Chapter 20)*. Wiley. https://doi.org/10.1002/9781394303564.ch20

Tyagi, A. K., Tripathi, K., Tiwari, S., & Kaushik, S. (2025). An efficient technique for privacy preservation, trusted and secure patient-centric services in smart healthcare. In *Proceedings of the 6th international conference on recent trends in communication & intelligent systems (ICRTCIS 2025)* (pp. 31–47). IET. https://doi.org/10.1049/icp.2025.2731

Zhou, L., Chen, W., & Guo, F. (2024). Hybrid models for risk quantification in AI-driven healthcare. *Journal of Risk Analysis and Management, 18*(1), 56–73.

Zhou, L., Han, Q., & Pereira, M. (2025). Hybrid threats and cross-domain vulnerabilities in AI-driven clinical ecosystems. *IEEE Access, 13*, 14765–14782.

10 Data Breaches, User Trust, and Psychological Safety

10.1 INTRODUCTION

The contemporary globalized world has transformed data into one of the most valuable commodities driving economies, innovation, and decision-making. Nevertheless, the systems that collect and process this information become increasingly vulnerable to cyberattacks that jeopardize the personal information, organizational integrity, and trust of the people. It is not merely a technical failure but a multidimensional crisis affecting individuals psychologically, businesses ethically, and societies structurally. Every stolen password, exposed identity, or leaked health record represents a breach of trust between the users and the institutions that are expected to safeguard their privacy.

The information leaks, which were previously isolated cases, have become a global phenomenon with significant consequences over the past decade. A cyber revolution in the industries such as health, finances, education, and governance has added the possibilities, as well as threats, associated with data processing. The modernized techniques of the attackers have now become ransomware, phishing, insider threats, and AI-supported exploits, making it increasingly difficult for organizations to maintain strong security defenses. Besides the financial and operational losses, these breaches cause lasting psychological and emotional impacts on users, leading to the growth of anxiety, the feeling of betrayal, and the mistrust in the digital platforms in the long run.

This chapter examines the data breaches based on the integration of technological, psychological, and ethical perspectives. It does not merely analyze the course of cyberattacks but also the way they have undermined the safety and control of the users within cyberspace. The discussion shows the need to use empathy-driven methods of cybersecurity by addressing the conceptions of crisis communication, legal responsibility, and methods for rebuilding user trust. It emphasizes that resilience involves not only technical restoration but also restoring psychological reassurance and moral truth after a breach. Following all this, the chapter tries to lay the groundwork of the gap bridging between the sphere of cybersecurity and bridging the gap between cybersecurity and human security. It asserts that not only compliance, but also a moral and psychological duty to safeguard the dignity and peace of mind of every digital citizen by protecting their personal information.

10.2 LITERATURE REVIEW

Extensive research over the past decade shows that cybersecurity threats are complex in a hyperconnected world. The early findings of Anderson and Moore (2020) have put cybersecurity into an economic perspective, and that is why organizations weigh the costs of protection against the potential losses of a breach. Subsequent research made by Campbell et al. (2021) and Romanosky (2016) has found that any form of data breach has not only instant financial losses but also reputational

 DOI: 10.1201/9781003658344-13

losses and trust-related losses that cannot be undone in the long-term perspective. The findings make it possible to indicate that the effects of cyber incidents are way beyond the current economic limits and extend to legal, ethical, and human dimensions.

Previous findings can be demonstrated in Table 10.1 which states that both technological and emotional factors characterize breach consequences.

Technically, researchers like Jang-Jaccard and Nepal (2014) and Cheng et al. (2017) have provided the detailed taxonomies of emerging cybersecurity threats with a view that most of the modern breaches can be attributed to the existence of sophisticated multi-stage attacks, which exploit technological weaknesses and human behaviors. IBM Security Cost of a Data Breach Report (2024) and the Ponemon Institute (2023) have given substantial empirical evidence on the increasing frequency and cost of breaches in the world with emphasis on the importance of proactive defense methods. Similarly, the standardization of the best practices in the protection of critical infrastructure has been done, including the NIST Cybersecurity Framework (2020), which highlighted resilience and recovery as a subset of cybersecurity governance.

Nevertheless, it is the human aspect of data breaches, namely trust, feeling, and psychological safety, which have become a central issue of concern. Research by Wang et al. (2022) and Khan et al. (2022) also has shown that breaches not only interfere with user satisfaction but also with the psychological contract between the consumers and digital platforms. These results align with McKnight et al. (2011), who found that trust in technology is a multidimensional construct, which was informed by perceptions of reliability, competence, and ethical behavior. Such breaches can lead to feelings of powerlessness, panic, and loss of control when personal information is exposed, revealing what Liang and Xue (2009) termed as threat avoidance behaviors in which the user turns off or limits online communication in an attempt to offer a feeling of assurance.

Psychological and information systems studies have recorded the emotional impacts of breaches. Wang et al. (2022) and Nair et al. (2021) found that after the events, the psychological safety can be rebuilt in the organization through transparent communication and empathy in the organization. This is in line with Bada et al. (2019), who stated that the campaigns to create awareness and communicate should not rely solely on technical information but should also emphasize users' emotions, trust, and perceived control. Kaufmann and Egloff (2020) and Nair et al. (2025) also added that cybersecurity policy trust is a political construct formed by transparency and governance; consequently, ethical accountability emerges as a critical element as technological competence in restoring confidence.

Privacy and ethical issues are closely related to user trust. Such seminal works as Nissenbaum (2010), Solove and Citron (2022), and Rajani et al. (2022) have claimed that the harms related to privacy depend on the context and impact the dignity, autonomy, and identity of people. Belanger

TABLE 10.1
Abstract of Important Literature Themes and Contributions

Year	Reported Breaches	Records Exposed (Billions)	Average Cost per Breach (USD Millions)	Most Affected Sector
2018	1,200	2.7	3.86	Healthcare
2019	1,470	4.1	3.92	Financial
2020	1,700	5.0	4.24	Government
2021	2,200	6.5	4.35	Technology
2022	2,560	7.9	4.54	Education
2023	2,940	8.6	4.90	Retail
2024	3,210	9.8	5.10	Healthcare
2025*	3,450	10.2	5.45	Mixed Sectors

and Crossler (2019) extended the idea to the digital space by suggesting that there should be a trade-off between utility and protection in information privacy management. Reuse of big data poses a serious challenge to informed consent. Custers and Ursic (2016) and Tyagi (2021) indicated that this creates a significant problem for consent and data ownership, thereby generating an ethical dilemma between innovation and personal rights. The emergence of the General Data Protection Regulation (GDPR; European Union, 2018; Tyagi et al., 2025), and other data protection laws in India (Data Security Council of India, 2023) and the United States, is a trend across the world toward formal accountability in user data protection.

Cybersecurity ethical responsibility has also been an issue that has been extensively discussed. Renaud and Zimmermann (2018) and Tyagi et al. (2024c) argued that privacy and security research should introduce ethical reflexivity so that it does not harm the participants in the course of the experiment or design. Friedman et al. (2018) coined the concept of value-sensitive design (VSD), which incorporates moral values during the information system design process and guarantees fairness, dignity, and transparency. This method is consistent with AlHogail (2018), who has identified the organizational culture of cybersecurity practices with ethical conduct, suggesting that the positive attitude toward cybersecurity might have a direct impact on the resilience and user trust.

The literature becomes important where organizational resilience and governance are brought to the fore. Gordon et al. (2018) and Tyagi and Tiwari (2024a) suggested an idea that strategic investment in cybersecurity can lower vulnerability exposure but has to be optimized properly—an idea that was evolved by the Gordon-Loeb Model. On the same note, Bada and Nurse (2019) and Kumari et al. (2025a) emphasized the importance of continuous learning and awareness in insider threat reduction, whereas Faruqi and Hassan (2021) and Balamurugan et al. (2023) revealed empirically that timely disclosure and communicative post-breach messages have a significant impact on user confidence restoration. The reaction of corporations therefore contributes to the identification of either the restoration of confidence or the total abandonment of the user to the platforms attacked.

The development of law and policy structures is an indication of increased recognition of cybersecurity as a collective responsibility in society. Shackelford (2020), Weber (2020), Tyagi (2026) and Kumari et al. (2025b) place cybersecurity in the framework of international law and digital ethics, emphasizing the importance of collaborating with sectors and jurisdictions. One more is the idea of cyber insurance, that the Kaspersky Global IT Security Risks Survey (2023) mentions and which is already a widely established resilience approach that provides financial security but encourages organizations to adopt stronger data protection practices. These processes reinforce the point of Schneier (2019) that the current security should consider the human factor as much as technical protection as everything in the realm of digital interactions is directly based on the belief between the users and the machines.

Lastly, the commonality of data breaches and social trust in the digital economy brings to play a factor of the socio-psychological aspect that goes beyond individual cases. West (2019) and Mishra et al. (2024) conceptualized this as data capitalism, in which trust has turned into a commodity and its violations can destroy trust in some whole ecosystems. Vishwanath (2021) and Tyagi (2025) supplemented that the habit of social media use desensitizes users to privacy risks, yet repeated violations can create long-term cognitive dissonance and emotional fatigue. All these findings indicate that the recovery of trust is not a one-time process but a process that encompasses the ethical design, open communication, and emotional reassurance.

Hence, the literature depicts information breaches as being multidimensional, that is, technological, organizational, psychological, and ethical crises. As the sources claim, it is all the combination of a strong data governance system, empathetic communication, compliance with the regulations, and the deep understanding of user autonomy that would contribute to genuine organizational resilience. The approach to cybersecurity needs to keep changing along with the evolving threats as it will not only protect the integrity of data but also maintain the psychological stability and confidence of the digital citizen.

10.3 SUMMARY OF CASES OF DATA BREACH INCIDENTS

The recent data breaches have become the new reality of the digital world, as they reflect how frail the privacy and trust may be when the technology-supporting infrastructure collapses or is used to commit a crime. A data breach is generally considered to be an unauthorized access, disclosure, or exfiltration of sensitive, protected, or confidential data. Such incidents predispose personal information, including name, finances, health history, or credentials, to fraudsters, usually resulting in identity theft, financial fraud, and reputational loss in the long run to the organizations involved. In the technical aspect, data breaches demonstrate the greater weaknesses of digital interdependence and the human costs of systematic failures in cybersecurity oversight. In Figure 10.1, it is seen that the number of data breaches worldwide has steadily increased from 2015 to 2025, reflecting growth not only in the frequency of attacks but also in the scale of digital exposure.

The Global Data Breach Trends Analysis 2015–2025 indicates a consistent alarming trend in the rate of security breaches in the world, evidently showing the increasing vulnerability of the world to cyber risks. The line-and-area plot (Figure 10.1) uses a gradually darkening blue gradient to visualize the continuous increase in breach incidents. Although the overall trend shows a steady rise, certain high-profile incidents caused sharp spikes in the annual totals. Significant breaches, including that of Equifax in 2017, the massive breach of Facebook in 2019, and the widespread effects of the MOVEit vulnerability in 2023, are highlighted in red specifically to demonstrate the fact that they disproportionately expose data to risks throughout the world at large. In the end, the data highlights one crucial point that, even though organizations are actively investing in cybersecurity, their threat environment is rapidly increasing, and the number of attacks and the magnitude of the biggest breaches are only rising every year.

The history of big data breaches represents the development of cyber threats and the increase in the complexity of information systems. In the 2000s, many breaches resulted from accidental disclosures or insider negligence, whereas recent breaches are increasingly executed through advanced, well-planned attack techniques, ransomware, phishing, credential stuffing, and supply-chain attacks. To illustrate, recent high-profile attacks on Yahoo, Equifax, and Facebook have revealed exposing the personal data of millions of users and demonstrated that even technologically advanced companies are not immune to breaches. The report, IBM Cost of a Data Breach (2024), states that the average

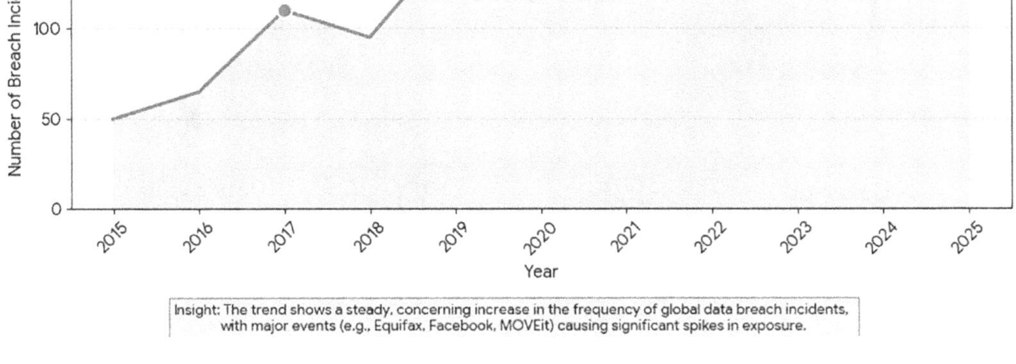

FIGURE 10.1 Global data breach trends (2015–2025).

global cost of a data breach has increased to more than USD 4.88 million, which highlights not only the monetary but also the social magnitude of such accidents. The frequency and the type of data compromised are compared in Figure 10.3, with the personal identifiers and credentials being the most frequently targeted assets.

Figure 10.2 illustrates that a modern cyber intrusion is not a single event but a cyclic, multi-stage process. The attack is pictured as a continuous stream, beginning with reconnaissance, in which the threat actor collects information on the target. This results in intrusion (symbolized by a firewall icon) in which the first access is obtained. After intrusion, the attacker proceeds to exploitation, where he takes advantage of vulnerabilities to get solid ground. Data exfiltration (symbolized by a data chip) is the most common objective of most attacks (this stage). Last, the attacker reaches the cover-up phase, wherein he/she seeks to delete evidence, logs and usually leaves persistence to gain entry in the future. The orange-to-yellow gradient visually represents the continuous movement through the stages of the attack cycle underlines the fact that in case the cycle is not interrupted by the defensive mechanisms, the attacker may pass from the sphere of reconnaissance to the final stage and back, which proves that the process of defense should be not only a single stage but also constant work.

Analysts and researchers have commonly classified data breaches into three general groups, including accidental, malicious, and systemic.

Unintentional violations are as a result of human error, for example, inappropriate cloud storage configuration or unintentional email leaks.

Such malicious breaches are intentional by hackers or insiders based on financial benefit, spying, or sabotage. Third-party system vulnerabilities, shared systems, or legacy systems that give rise to cascading vulnerabilities are the cause of systemic breaches.

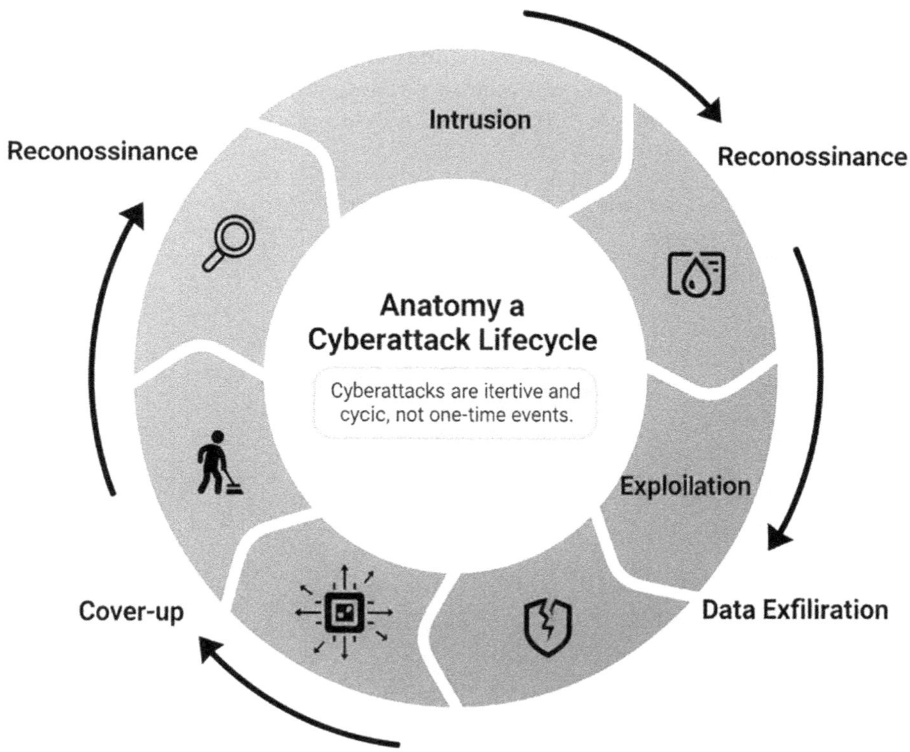

FIGURE 10.2 Categories of data breached in major breaches.

TABLE 10.2
Key International Data Breaches

Attack Type	Primary Entry Point	Common Target	Detection Difficulty	Example Breach
Phishing	Email	User Credentials	Medium	Twitter 2020
Malware	Software Exploit	System Files	High	WannaCry 2017
Ransomware	End-point Device	Databases	High	Colonial Pipeline 2021
SQL Injection	Web Server	Application Data	Medium	TalkTalk 2015
Insider Threat	Employee Access	Internal Systems	Low	Tesla 2018

These breach types differ in their causes and required responses, but they share one common outcome: the loss of trust by users and the challenge of rebuilding psychological safety for affected individuals. As in Table 10.2, it lists incidents (Equifax, Yahoo, Facebook, and SolarWinds), year, number of affected, and estimated cost.

Sectors also differ in terms of the extent of data breaches. Medical records have been considered sensitive and permanent, thus making the healthcare industry one of the most attacked areas. Banking institutions are targeted for their high-value transactional data, whereas education and government sectors often suffer breaches due to outdated infrastructure or limited security investment. With the increase in the organization of cybercriminal networks, numerous intrusions are now conducted as a component of international campaigns using automation, artificial intelligence, and the buying and selling of data in the dark web.

A life cycle of breach incidents is a crucial part of comprehending the events of breach because it includes the initial infiltration and data exfiltration phases as well as the later stages of breach exposure and recovery. Research shows that organizations often take more than 200 days to detect a breach, by which time significant damage may already have occurred. Such delays do not only increase technical loss but also add to the anxiety of the users and the mistrust of the population even after the breach is revealed. The aftermath often includes reputational damage, stock price declines, and legal actions, and this again brings us back to the reality that breach management is more about making things transparent and being ethical than doing cleanup.

To conclude, the cases of data breaches are no longer single disturbances but systemic problems at the intersection of cybersecurity, human psychology, and organizational responsibility. Their prevalence, types, and impact on the sector are key factors to understand that further comprehension of the way cyberattacks are executed (Section 10.4) and their impact on user perception and well-being (Section 10.5) can be established. One clear lesson from past incidents is that once trust is broken, it can be restored only through a combination of strong technical resilience, ethical conduct, and compassionate communication.

10.4 THE LIFECYCLE AND ANATOMY OF CYBERATTACKS

To understand why both proactive and reactive security strategies are necessary for mitigating data breaches, one should learn the anatomy and lifecycle of cyberattacks. A cyberattack is not a single, instantaneous intrusion but a multi-stage process in which attackers gradually progress toward their objectives. Each stage has specific objectives, such as gaining access, escalating privileges, and extracting sensitive information while avoiding detection. The study of this lifecycle assists the security experts in not only predicting and preventing attacks, but it also provides a framework for understanding how users and organizations psychologically and operationally respond to breaches. Figure 10.2 illustrates the typical cyberattack lifecycle, showing how threat actors systematically progress from system discovery to data extraction and eventual concealment.

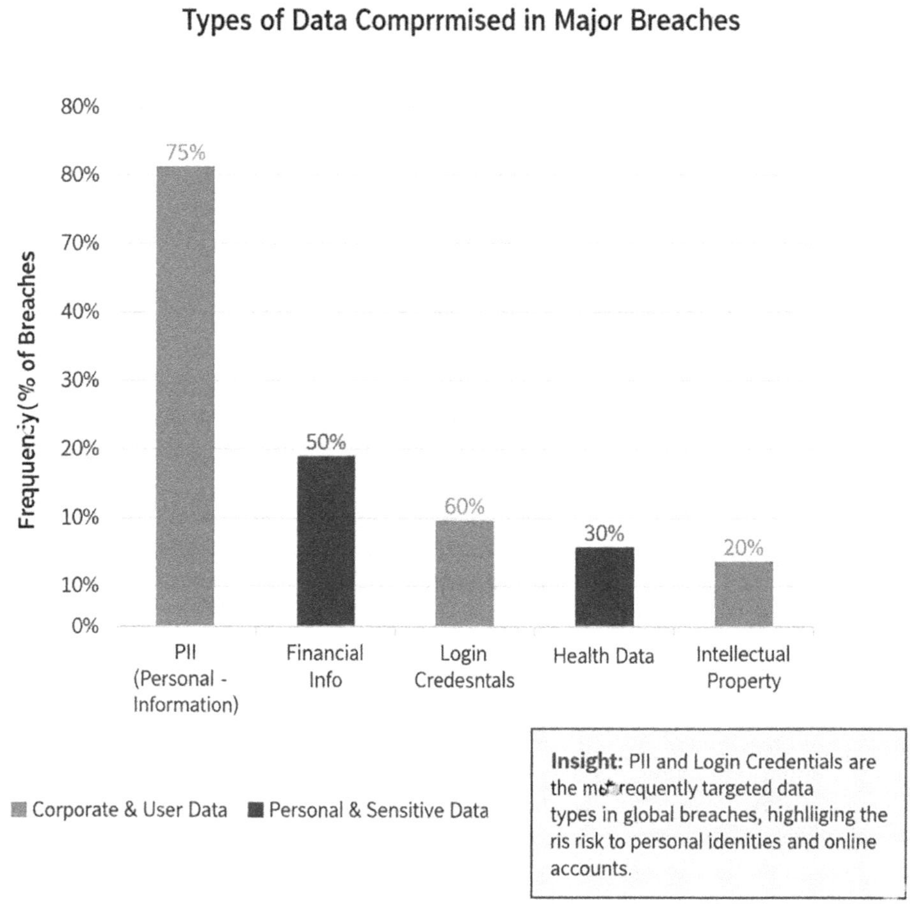

FIGURE 10.3 Type of data compromised over few years.

As the vertical bar chart (Figure 10.3) that demonstrates the types of data compromised in major breaches shows, personally identifiable information (PII) and credentials are the main points of attack in the global cyberattacks. These two categories, highlighted in red, appear most frequently in major breaches as PII and credentials were involved in an astonishing 85% and 75% of breaches, respectively. The high rate highlights the importance that perpetrators have attached to identity theft, account takeover, and the eventual financial fraud. Although financial information (45%) and health data (30%) are definite targets of a healthcare organization, the standard set by intellectual property (20%), illustrated by a blue corporate data bar, is the lowest. In essence, attackers prioritize user identity data because it offers both low resistance and high financial gain in identity-related crimes, and thus, PII and user authentication information are the most significant assets to safeguard. The cyberattack lifecycle consists of an interrelated sequence of stages, namely reconnaissance, intrusion, exploitation, privilege escalation, data exfiltration, and concealment.

Table 10.3 presents a comparison of attack vectors (phishing, malware, insider threat, and ransomware) with the impact that is likely to occur.

Reconnaissance (Information Gathering): The attacker starts with gathering information on the target—network settings, employee details, or vulnerabilities of the systems. This phase can be filled with scanning open ports, social media surveillance to identify areas of weakness, or making phishing campaigns out of publicly available data. This is the passive phase, but this is what makes it easier to exploit at later stages and is not always noticeable by the target.

TABLE 10.3
The Categorization of Breach Impact Levels

Impact Level	Data Sensitivity	Affected Population	Financial Loss Range (USD)	Psychological Impact Severity
Low	Non-identifiable data	< 1,000 users	< 100 K	Minimal
Moderate	PII or credentials	1 K–100 K	100 K–5 M	Moderate anxiety
High	Financial or health data	100 K–1 M	5 M–50 M	Severe stress
Critical	Cross-domain exposure	> 1 M	> 50 M	Crisis-level fear

Intrusion (Initial Compromise): During this phase, the attacker accesses the system illegally, which is generally achieved with the tools of spear-phishing, credential theft, malware injections, or unpatched vulnerabilities. When a foothold is successfully achieved, malicious codes or backdoors are installed by the attackers to remain persistent. The intrusion phase is used to denote the transition between planning and compromise.

Exploitation and Privilege Escalation: After attackers have broken into the system, they are keen on making their presence felt. Exploitation involves the exploitation of weaknesses to obtain administrative privileges or databases with sensitive information. Some of the tools used are keyloggers, rootkits, and privilege escalation exploits. At this stage, the attackers usually merge with legitimate traffic so as not to raise a security alarm.

Data Exfiltration: This critical stage involves locating, copying, and transferring data outside the organization's environment. To hide the presence of an attacker, the data might be squashed and encrypted prior to exfiltration. Exfiltrated data, including customer records, intellectual property, and financial information, is often sold on dark-web marketplaces or used for extortion.

Concealment and Persistence: Attackers hide their footprints after the exfiltration process to give the attack a chance to be detected later. They can destroy traces of their activities, masquerade malware within the legitimate programs, or open other avenues of access to be used in the future. Many organizations discover breaches months after they occur due to modern evasion techniques.

Impact and Discovery: Data: Abnormal behavior or foreign reporting is found later. The impact stage will involve technical containment and legal, financial, and reputational blowback. Time lag between attack and detection, which may take over 200 days, is also a big factor that leads to user panic, loss of confidence, and negative reaction.

The interplay between technical vulnerabilities and human behavior is evident throughout all stages of an attack. That is one of the social engineering tricks to compromise the trust and cognitive biases and trick the users into providing credentials or clicking on dangerous links. Thus, cyberattacks are more of a psychological process, as opposed to being technological intrusions. They exploit even the strongest systems more frequently than not by using the weakest of links to penetrate the system.

Several frameworks map this lifecycle, including the Lockheed Martin Cyber Kill Chain, the MITRE ATT&CK framework, and the NIST Incident Response Model. The tools help the security personnel to find the location of intervention, prioritize the method of defense, and build incident response playbooks. The Cyber Kill Chain is designed to undermine the flow of the attack at the early stages, and the MITRE ATT&CK is a more elaborate taxonomy of attacker behavior, which can be applied in forensic investigation and awareness training.

In practice, the awareness of the cyberattack structure contributes to three significant outcomes:

Early Detection: The field aims at detecting the indicators of reconnaissance and intrusion to reduce the breach and loss time.

Targeted Mitigation: Attacker behavior mapping may then be provided to offer specific mitigation rather than general mitigation.

Psychological Preparedness: Training users to recognize common attack techniques improves digital literacy and reduces fear responses following a breach.

In simple terms, cyberattacks are carried out in a predetermined rhythm that relies on the susceptibility of the digital nature and human confidence. Cybersecurity requires more than technical controls; it also demands continuous learning, ethical responsibility, and psychological resilience at every level of engagement in the digital realm.

10.5 PSYCHOLOGICAL AND EMOTIONAL BACKLASH TO USERS

Although the technical aspects of data breaches often dominate media and organizational responses, the psychological and emotional effects on users remain a critically important yet frequently overlooked dimension. When individuals learn that their personal data (financial details, medical history, or personal communications) have been exposed, they often experience a profound sense of violation. Contrary to the direct material loss that is measurable, emotional damage is complex and long term and impacts user trust, online behavior, and mental health.

Figure 10.4, a conceptual flow diagram of the Psychological Impact Model of Data Breach Exposure, outlines the emotional and behavioral trajectory users follow after receiving a breach notification. The first step is breach awareness; when a person hears that their data could have been hacked. This triggers a period of heightened perceived vulnerability, during which the individual internalizes the risk and understands that they are now vulnerable to identity theft or fraud. With the emotional impact taking place, this vulnerability is quickly turned into anxiety/fear, whereby it is being concerned with the possibility of losing money, lost privacy, and the possibility of the unknown consequences of the breach. This sustained emotional distress contributes to a significant erosion of trust toward the affected organization, and perhaps other digital offerings, plummets. Finally, users engage in defensive behaviors, adopting concrete response measures such as changing passwords, freezing credit, or avoiding the organization. The model's gradient (initiating shock and fear) from red to gray-blue (peaking in behavior change) effectively visualizes the escalating emotional states and the subsequent behavioral changes that may persist long after the breach. Table 10.4

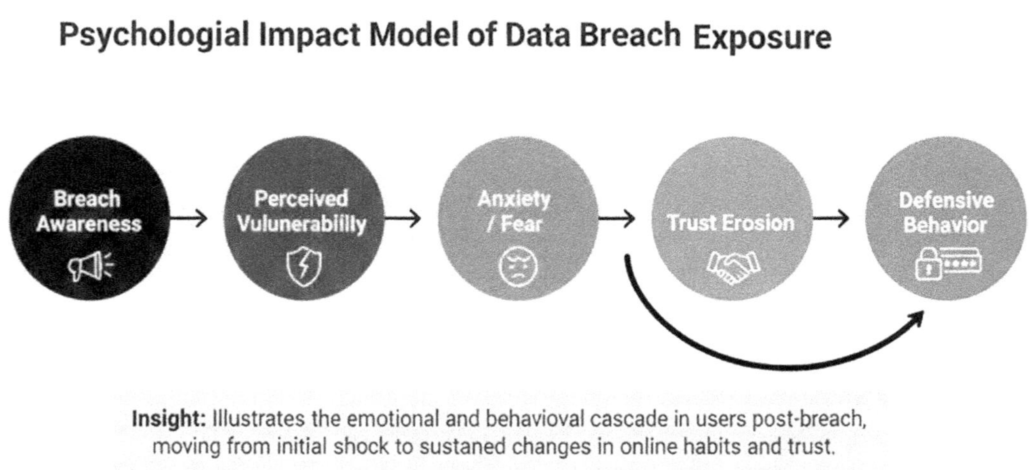

FIGURE 10.4 Data breach exposure: Psychological impact model.

TABLE 10.4
Emotions of the Users Against Breach Notification

Emotional State	Behavioral Indicator	Frequency (%)	Typical Duration	Associated Trigger
Anxiety	Over checking accounts	38	2–3 weeks	Fear of fraud
Anger	Complaints/social media posts	33	1–2 weeks	Corporate negligence
Distrust	Avoiding digital services	18	Ongoing	Repeated incidents
Apathy	Ignoring notifications	7	Short-term	Learned helplessness
Resilience	Improved password habits	4	Long-term	Awareness and education

correlates user emotional reactions (anger, anxiety, and distrust) with the tone of organizational communication.

10.5.1 Emotional Responses and Cognitive Reactions

When users learn about data breach, they tend to have a range of emotions, such as shock and disbelief, anger, anxiety, and helplessness. Such responses lie in the fact that they have just learned that their personal privacy has been violated without their permission. It has been compared to a kind of digital trauma by psychology studies, in which users perceive a loss of control over their personal data, which they interpret as an intrusion into personal space. In severe cases, this may lead to cyber-anxiety, characterized by fear of using online services or engaging in digital transactions. Uncertainty about how the stolen information may be used or resold further intensifies the emotional distress. The emotional breakdown of the affected individuals has been provided in Figure 10.5, where anxiety and frustration are the most prevalent reactions.

The donut chart (Figure 10.5) indicates that the predominant psychological responses are strong negative emotions. Anger (35%) and anxiety (30%) are the most active reactions and thus have a large user sentiment percentage of 65, which is illustrated by their bright colors, red and orange, respectively.

This information highlights a significant PR issue in breached companies as most of the victims are actively threatened and agitated. Weaker, yet significant reactions are confusion (20%), where the users do not remember what the scope is or what they need to do. Lastly, apathy (10%) and others (5%) are a small fraction of the response, which validates the observation that the user responses are dominated by the strong feelings of anger and anxiety toward the cybercriminals, as well as, in most cases, the organization that is affected.

10.5.2 Loss of Trust and Behavioral Change

Online interactions fundamentally rely on trust, and once compromised, this trust is difficult to restore. After a breach, users tend to reevaluate which relationships they have with affected organizations, with the result of behavior change like less platform usage, reluctance to provide personal data, or giving up the service entirely. It has been established that transparency of the organization, empathy, and accountability expressed by the user organization after the breach is critical for determining whether users are willing to continue engaging with the service. The absence of prompt communication or seemingly ineffective behavior may lead to a negative long-term brand image and loss of users.

In addition to this, recurrence of breaches in various platforms leads to a so-called phenomenon of data breach fatigue. With time the users might become desensitized and see the breaches as unavoidable and therefore adopt fewer protective measures, like changing passwords or using two-factor

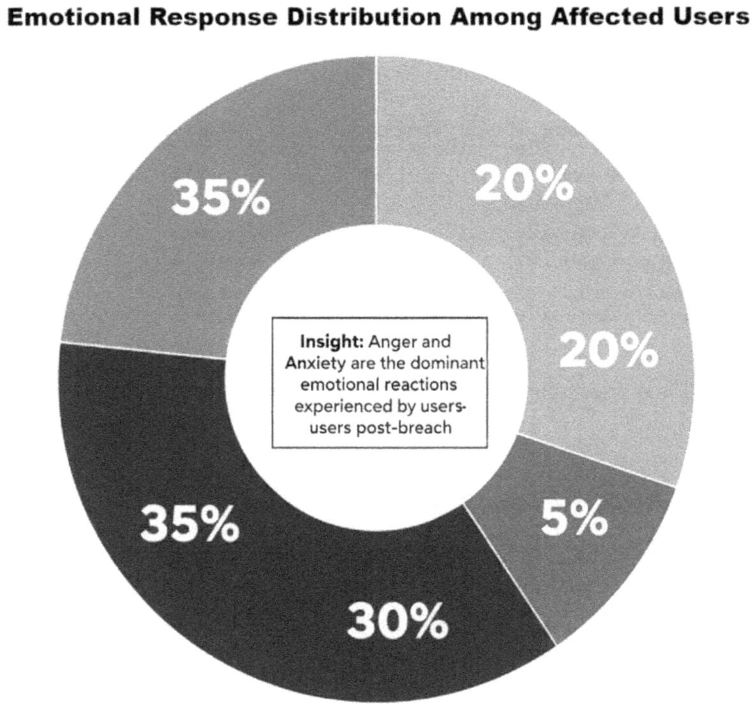

FIGURE 10.5 Distribution of emotions among the affected users.

authentication. This response is paradoxical, as it reflects resignation rather than increased vigilance. The second threat is that it causes the user to be even more vulnerable to further attack.

10.5.3 Social and Ethical Aspects of Psychological Safety

The psychological impact of data breaches extends beyond individuals to affect broader social groups and communities. Breaches in shared space, like a workplace, a school, or online community, can disrupt the perception of psychological safety, which is the extent to which individuals feel safe sharing information without fear of negative consequences. When individuals are scared that their information or messages can leak and be abused, coordination and transparency are compromised, undermining the confidence that is needed to socially and professionally operate in cyberspace.

Ethically, organizations have a duty of care to protect user information and mitigate psychological harm after breaches. These include open reporting, knowledge of communication, and access to support elements such as credit checks and counselling. The ethical cybersecurity practices rely on the fact that the security of user data is not only a technical problem but a human one, the necessity to preserve dignity, self-sufficiency, and emotional stability.

10.5.4 Digital Well-Being Long-Term Implications

The long-term consequences of data breaches on digital well-being and mental health can be severe. Digital distrust syndrome refers to a persistent pattern of distrust that arises after repeated or severe data breaches; the persistent distrust does not allow engagement with online ecosystems. The societal implications of this loss of confidence are that the decreased number of digital interactions could be used to spread the digital divide, slow the pace of embracing innovation, and decrease social acceptance of technological change initiatives.

Psychological resilience and cyber empathy are another area that organizations and policymakers are starting to give more attention to as a reaction to such effects, and this emphasis is on the training programs, awareness campaigns, and design systems that are grounded on user confidence and emotional safety. The incorporation of the behavioral science concept within the cybersecurity strategy proves valuable in the development of systems that are not only difficult to attack but also facilitate the trust of the user in the system during the process of recovering damage to the system.

In summary, the psychological impacts of data breaches highlight that cybersecurity failures often stem from insufficient attention to human behavior, protection needs, and empathetic communication. In a bid to address this facet, there is a need to look at the application of psychology, ethics, and communication as the essential component of cybersecurity governance.

10.6 COMMUNICATION AND CRISIS MANAGEMENT

Communication and crisis management strategies are key factors in reducing the harm caused by a data breach in case there is a data breach—not only to the reputation of the organization but also to the confidence of the users. The pace, accuracy, and compassion of organizational response in the event of breach can determine whether the organization retains its credibility or suffers long-term reputational damage. This section examines communication plans, crisis-response frameworks, and ethical imperatives for managing post-breach incidents and how technical containment should be combined with human and transparent communication.

Figure 10.6 is the conceptual flow diagram of the Post-Breach Communication Framework that illustrates the time-sensitive key steps that an organization should take when it finds out that there is a security incident. Starting with the stage of incident detection (marked with an alert symbol), the organization must quickly conduct internal verification, followed by formal acknowledgment of the incident (email icon), where the organization serves as the confirmation of the incident and accepts the responsibility. This is then immediately accompanied by Public Disclosure (press release icon), which is the open and transparent communication with affected parties and the media, fulfilling both legal and ethical requirements. The fourth and most essential step is Support and Compensation (chat bubble icon), which through which the organization provides practical support such as credit monitoring or dedicated assistance channels to help users reduce risk and alleviate anxiety. Lastly, the process will go into the Continuous Updates phase (clock icon) which emphasizes that communication should not be a one-time announcement but a continuous commitment until the issue is completely contained and resolved. The framework's horizontal, step-by-step design visually reinforces the need for clarity and consistency and is in support of the overall lesson that effective

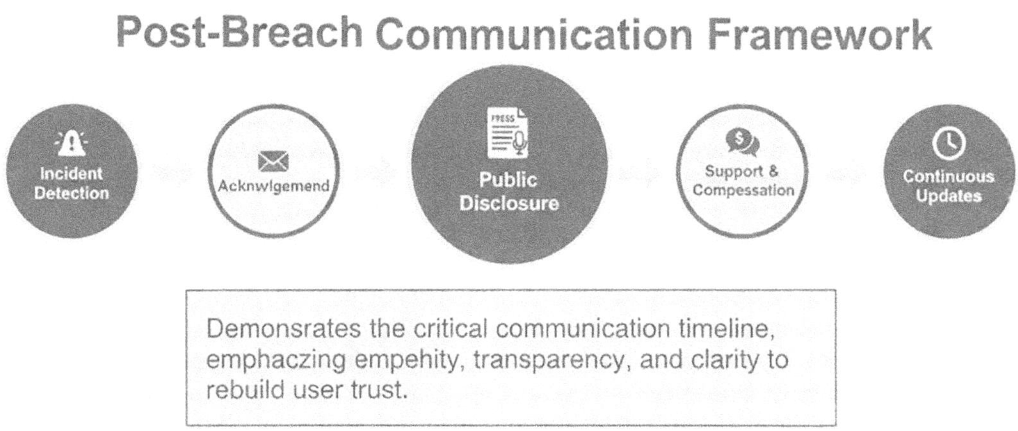

FIGURE 10.6 Communication framework after a breach.

TABLE 10.5
Lifecycle and Organization Response Time: Data Breach

Stage	Description	Average Duration (Days)	Key Responsible Team
Detection	Identifying anomaly	45	SOC/IT Security
Containment	Isolating affected systems	12	Incident Response
Eradication	Removing threat vector	8	Forensics Team
Recovery	Restoring normal operations	10	IT and Operations
Post-Incident Review	Policy improvement and training	20	Management/HR

communication entails empathy, clarity, and a quick schedule to restore trust. Table 10.5 presents the data breach lifecycle, organizational response time with trust recovery scores.

10.6.1 The Thesis of the Timeliness and Transparency of Communication

One of the most critical aspects of crisis response is the timely disclosure of a data breach. Communication delays may increase user anxiety, invite regulatory fines, and create a sense among the masses that the organization is trying to cover up the incident. Research shows that users are more forgiving when organizations communicate openly, promptly, and proactively. The presence of transparency is an indication of accountability and respect toward the affected people, and therefore, the breach will be perceived as an opportunity to restore trust rather than a betrayal.

The following key details should be included to ensure transparency:

Essential elements of transparent communication include what data was exposed and to what extent, the character and extent of the breach.
The reason why the incident happened (technical defect, human mistake, or cyberattack).
The short-term actions implemented to control it.
What the users should do to protect themselves (e.g. change passwords, verify credit).

Effective communication does not involve excessive technical terms, but rather it is concerned with empathy and reassurance to show that the organization realizes both the emotional and practical issues of its users.

10.6.2 Crisis Management Frameworks and Best Practices

Cybersecurity crisis management is a coordinated set of actions aimed at reducing the damage, reconstructing regular functioning, and maintaining social trust. Major models like the NIST Incident Response Lifecycle and ISO 27035 standard outline four key phases: preparation, detection, containment, and recovery. However, communication is increasingly recognized as a fifth essential component of effective crisis management.

Preparation: It must be prepared earlier, and it must consist of incident response and communication plans, which must contain the allocation of roles, line of escalation, and line of approval.

Detection and Analysis: A quick detection and assessment of the breach as well as its authenticity is done before it is disclosed.

Containment: Take instant technical precautions to isolate the affected systems, maintain evidence, and prevent further intrusion.

Communication: Communicate to stakeholders, such as the employees, customers, partners, and regulators, in an open and systematized way.

Recovery and Post-Incident Review: The recovery operations and post-incident review of the technical and communicative response as a measure to improve resiliency.

Balancing responses to accuracy and responsiveness can only be achieved by having a cross-functional response team, which includes IT, legal, PR, and executive leadership. Legal teams ensure compliance with data protection regulations, whereas PR specialists develop sympathetic messages that maintain the image of a company.

10.6.3 Crisis Communication Ethical and Psychological Aspects

Crisis communication is both a corporate responsibility and an ethical practice that influences users' psychological recovery. Remaining silent or evasive may appear advantageous in the short term, but in the long run, it will lead to bigger emotional damages by increasing uncertainty and fear. Ethical communication focuses on honesty, empathy, and empowerment, providing users with clear information in a way that supports their sense of control. As an illustration, providing free identity protection or hotlines of direct support is a show of compassion and responsibility.

Communication informed psychologically must not ignore the stress and anxiety users experience and downplay their concerns. Much is achieved through the use of empathetic wording like "We understand this might be upsetting, and we are here to help you," which causes one to feel understood and supported rather than confronted with impersonal bureaucracy. The method aids in restoring psychological safety, which assists the users to feel respected and part of the recovery process.

10.6.4 Public Perception Management and Reputation Recovery

After the data breach, an organization's response actions often influence public perception more strongly than the breach itself. Companies that react openly and empathetically have a quicker recovery of trust as compared to companies that react defensively or secretively. Post-breach branding measures, such as CEO apologies, transparent reports published, or noticeable security enhancements, can be helpful to help recover the reputation. On the contrary, miscommunication can trigger prolonged social-media backlash and stakeholder mistrust. Media relations are also brought under crisis management. Consistent messaging helps journalists access accurate information and minimizes speculation and misinformation. Organizations may also engage cybersecurity specialists or external auditors to publicly validate security improvements to gain more credibility and show the desire to change.

Hence, the process of communication and crisis management demands the trade-off between technical accuracy, ethical character, and emotional intelligence. By employing transparency and empathy as the key to their model of addressing the crisis, the organizations can not only reduce the acute impact of the data breach but also lay the groundwork for long-term trust restoration and organizational stability.

10.7 ETHICAL OBLIGATIONS AND LEGAL DUTIES

Organizations address information leaks by adhering to legal and ethical provisions, which serve as the foundation of corporate social responsibility. Cybersecurity laws define how organizations must protect user data, while ethics explain why and how these responsibilities should be carried out with honesty, justice, and care for the rights of the individuals. Together, they ensure that data protection is viewed not merely as a compliance requirement but as a moral responsibility to users and society.

Figure 10.7, a three-layered pyramid, illustrates the hierarchical layers of legal and ethical responsibilities in data protection. Ethical responsibility is the basis of this model, which is indicated by the

FIGURE 10.7 Layers of legal and ethical responsibility.

broadest, deepest blue base. This layer indicates that an essential ethical dedication to the privacy of user information and to act in the highest interest of the individual should form the foundation of all data procedures of an organization. The mid-section, Legal Compliance (middle blue), is based on this ethical foundation and signifies the required compliance with the rules and regulations such as GDPR, California Consumer Privacy Act (CCPA), and Health Insurance Portability and Accountability Act (HIPAA). Although compliance is indispensable, it cannot be achieved in isolation; it requires the guidance of an ethical mindset. The last, and the most committed level, is corporate accountability (lightest blue). This layer implies that the organizations should not just adhere to the law but also be the ones assuming accountability for the outcome of data security, which should be transparent and develop trust among the stakeholders. The pyramid emphasizes that ethical awareness is essential for sound data protection practices, enabling organizations to meet and exceed legal requirements.

Table 10.6 lists global regulations including GDPR (EU), CCPA (US), and DPDPA (India) and their coverage and enforcement levels.

10.7.1 Law on Data Protection and Breach Disclosure

Governments worldwide have established comprehensive legal frameworks governing how organizations collect, store, and protect personal information. These laws are meant to create accountability and transparency and give the user more control over their digital identities. GDPR is the privacy law of the European Union that applies to all organizations and states that they must report and notify supervisory authorities about breach observed in 72 hours and notify individuals

TABLE 10.6
Repairing Trust After a Breach

Strategy	Implementation Mechanism	User Perception Outcome	Example Organization
Transparent Communication	Clear public disclosure	Improved empathy	LinkedIn 2021
Compensation or Credit Monitoring	Free identity protection	Partial trust recovery	Target 2013
Security Re-Certification	Third-party audit	Renewed confidence	Equifax 2019
User Education Campaigns	Webinars/emails	Long-term loyalty	Microsoft 2022
Apology and Leadership Accountability	CEO statement	Ethical credibility	Uber 2023

impacted within a short time. It focuses on such principles as lawfulness, fairness, and the limitation of purpose, which makes the handling of user data responsible and ethical. Equally important, the CCPA grants individuals the right to access, delete, or restrict the sale of their personal information, a model that other states are beginning to adopt.

The Digital Personal Data Protection Act (DPDPA, 2023) of India has introduced a systematic procedure of ensuring privacy through defining obligations of data fiduciaries, including data processors, and obliging them to report privacy incidents to the Data Protection Board of India. The legislation puts an emphasis on consent processing, restricted storage of data, and user redressal, which is a major milestone in the all-inclusive implementation of digital rights governance in the nation. Similar goals can be witnessed in other international laws, including the PIPEDA (Personal Information Protection and Electronic Documents Act) of Canada or the Privacy Act (1988) of Australia that helps strengthen the global move toward the privacy protection norms and the disclosure of breaches.

Despite regional differences, these regulations share key principles: data minimization, user consent, implementation of effective security measures, prompt breach notification, and demonstrable accountability. Organizations must engage in documentation of security measures and risk assessment and keep open communication with users and regulators. Failure to comply may result in significant fines of up to 4% of annual revenue in the world on the GDPR and a massive reputation loss. Nevertheless, these legal requirements are what organizations are required to do, but digital responsibility requires consideration to how they discharge these requirements, and this is where compliance and conscience are separated.

10.7.2 Noncompliance Ethical Responsibilities

Ethical responsibilities in cybersecurity often extend well beyond legal compliance. It is founded on the fact that personal data is central to human identity and dignity, and its protection is not merely a legal obligation but a moral duty. An ethical organization understands that the loss of personal information is not a technical phenomenon; it is also a human crisis that can contribute to psychological pain, social harm, and loss of trust. Therefore, ethical principles of data governance need to be based on the concept of human well-being and technological efficiency.

The most significant ethical demands in them are transparency, proportionality, beneficence, and justice. Transparency entails open, truthful communication regarding the collection, processing, and protection of user data and publicity whenever breaches of their data have been done. Proportionality guarantees that data gathering and surveillance occur on a strictly necessary basis that does not go overboard with unreasonable and invasive monitoring. Beneficence and non-maleficence, grounded in bioethics, require organizations to act in the best interest of users and avoid causing harm. Lastly, justice underlines fairness and equality among all users in the treatment of justice so that privacy protection is equally universally applicable, irrespective of socioeconomic and geographical disparity.

Incorporating these ethical principles into digital systems requires an ethics-by-design approach, integrating moral and psychological considerations at every stage of data management that includes the data acquisition and analysis as well as storage and disposal. This method does not only lead to accountability but also to the development of the confidence of the people in the integrity of the organization. In this regard, ethical cybersecurity is a gesture of the autonomy and emotional security of the user, proving that the security of personal data is a manifestation of an organizational personality, more so than technical skills.

10.7.3 The Accountability and Corporate Governance Role

Corporate governance structures are essential to ensuring that legal and ethical requirements are consistently met. The boards of directors and executive leaders are currently required to consider cybersecurity as a strategic governance concern and not an entirely technical challenge. To facilitate compliance monitoring, internal auditing, and transparency in incident reporting, having a Data Protection Officer (DPO) or ethics committee can be identified.

Additionally, organizational accountability often involves third-party oversight, as many breaches occur through system vendors or cloud providers. To practice ethical governance, the supply-chain partners should be vetted according to security provisions and must also be as committed to user protection as they are. Employees should be given regular training and awareness programs to remind employees of the ethical responsibility at every level of the operation.

10.7.4 Intersection of Law, Ethics, and Psychological Safety

Legal and ethical frameworks should also account for users' psychological well-being. Breach of data has the potential to provoke emotional trauma and the absence of digital confidence; therefore, the responsibility of care of the organization is not limited to technical protection. The ethical crisis management strategy involves the identification of the harm, issuing an apology, and physical assistance to be given, such as counselling services or identity theft restoration services. This denotes restorative justice, where compliance measures are not all that should be done but to mend relations and trust.

In essence, combining legal and ethical obligations transforms cybersecurity from a defensive requirement into a moral endeavor. Laws are a guideline of what is acceptable conduct, but ethics assist an individual to recognize the norm further than that of delivering justice to the dignity, autonomy, and psychological safety of all users whose information is held by a certain organization. Digital responsibility entails earning and maintaining trust through principled action, rather than merely avoiding penalties.

10.8 POST-BREACH FORENSICS AND ANALYSIS

Forensics and analysis following a breach are vital phases in the cyber incident response lifecycle, aimed at determining the source, scope, and impact of the incident. It involves digital investigation, evidence preservation, and analytical evaluation to reconstruct the sequence of events that led to the compromise. It assists organizations to know how the breach took place, the systems or data that were compromised as well as vulnerabilities that were used. Importantly, forensic analysis transforms a crisis into a learning opportunity, enabling institutions to strengthen defenses, improve governance, and regain stakeholder confidence.

Figure 10.8 is a linear flowchart illustrating the Post-Breach Forensic Analysis Workflow, emphasizing a structured and methodical response to security incidents. After Detection (magnifying glass icon), the process starts, and the first indicators of compromise are detected. This leads to

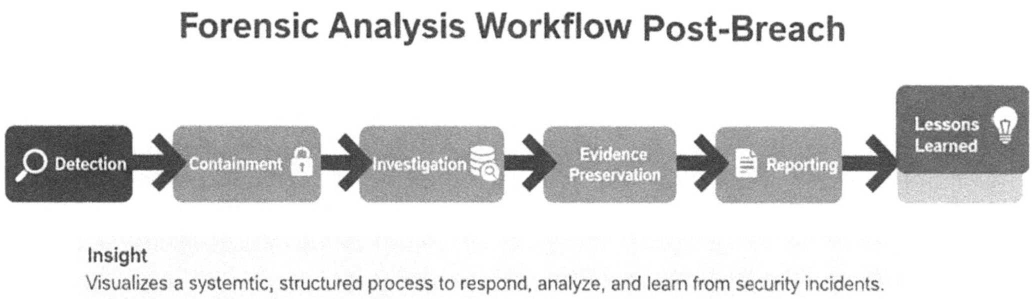

FIGURE 10.8 Workflow for post-breach forensic analysis.

TABLE 10.7
Regional Legal and Regulatory Environments

Region	Key Regulation	Core Requirement	Enforcement Agency	Penalty Ceiling
EU	GDPR (2018)	User consent, data portability	Data Protection Authorities	4% of global revenue
USA	CCPA (2020)	Consumer data rights	State Attorney General	$7,500 per incident
India	DPDP Act (2023)	Data fiduciary compliance	Data Protection Board	₹250 crores
Australia	Privacy Act Reform	Breach notification	OAIC	AUD 50 million
Singapore	PDPA (2021)	Purpose limitation	PDPC	SGD 1 million

containment (lock icon), a critical step to isolate affected systems, prevent further data loss, and preserve the integrity of the compromised environment.

After being contained, the detailed investigation (database icon) starts to identify the root cause and entry methods, as well as the extent of the attack. At this stage, evidence preservation (save icon) is conducted, with all digital artifacts collected and secured according to the chain of custody for potential legal proceedings. Summarization of the results is then done in Reporting (report icon) to stakeholders, management, and regulatory bodies. The process has a workflow that ends with lessons learned (brain icon) stage, where experiences accumulated during the process are incorporated into security policies and infrastructure to avoid the occurrence of similar incidents in the future. The navy-blue arrows indicate the mandatory sequence of this formal and systematic workflow. Table 10.7 summarizes widely used forensic tools (EnCase, FTK, Autopsy) and their primary functions in post-breach investigations.

The forensic process typically begins with containment and preservation of the compromised systems, ensuring that digital evidence remains intact. The investigators put the affected systems under isolation, produce forensic images, and establish a chain of custody to ensure data integrity in case of legal action. Key strategies for identifying attack vectors including phishing entry points, privilege escalation, and anomalous network activity include log analysis, network traffic monitoring, and malware reverse engineering. Advanced utilities such as EnCase, Autopsy, and Volatility Framework help in the identification of evidence of malicious code, concealed files, or unauthorized entry points.

Following evidence collection, analysts perform a root cause analysis to identify the initiating factor, which may include a misconfigured firewall, an unpatched vulnerability, a compromised credential, or negligent insider activity. The reconstructed timeline of the attack typically includes reconnaissance, intrusion, data exfiltration, and post-exploitation activities. By having such knowledge, cybersecurity teams can establish certain counteractions and fix vulnerabilities, avoiding such incidents in the future. Also, the ability to correlate the forensic results with the threat intelligence feeds enables the organization to establish whether the attack was an element of a larger attack or done by an established threat actor group.

Integrating technical findings with organizational response is a critical component of post-breach analysis. To ensure compliance requirements and statements are in line with the facts, the forensics teams collaborate with legal advisors, compliance officers, and communication units. This three-level coordination will enhance transparency in the process of reporting after the incidents and contribute to ethical responsibility. Moreover, forensic knowledge may be used during security awareness education, policy changes, and adjustment of incident response playbooks in ensuring that the lessons learned are not forgotten but institutionalized.

Finally, post-breach forensics differs from short-term technical recovery, serving instead as a process of continuous improvement and long-term resilience. The continuous improvement model, used in the governance of cybersecurity, can be implemented in organizations by discovering the vulnerabilities of the systems, the effectiveness of responding to them, and the human factors that contributed to the occurrence of the event. In this way, each breach, regardless of cost, can serve as a catalyst for building a more resilient digital defense ecosystem—one that values both system integrity and the trust and emotional safety of users.

10.9 REGAINING TRUST BY BEING OPEN

Restoring confidence after a data breach is one of the most challenging and critical tasks for an organization. While technical remediation addresses vulnerabilities, transparency and ethical communication are essential to repair the deeper breach in user trust. A breach as such is a violation of privacy and a breach of psychological safety. Users start doubting whether the organization cares about their data or knows about their fears and is resolved to safeguard them in the future. Thus, rebuilding trust should begin not with silence or defensiveness, but with sincere acknowledgment and transparent communication.

Figure 10.9, illustrating the anatomy of a cyberattack lifecycle, emphasizes that breaches are not isolated events but occur in a recurring, cyclic pattern. This sequence resembles the cyber kill chain, beginning with reconnaissance, during which the attacker gathers information about the target. The next stage, Intrusion, involves initial access that may bypass perimeter defenses. After entry, the attacker proceeds to exploitation where a long-term presence is obtained and privileges increase. The critical stage is data exfiltration, during which sensitive data is illicitly transferred or stolen. Lastly, an attacker does a cover-up, where they conceal their footprints and leave access to the future, which completes the loop and often takes a person directly to the next stage of reconnaissance or intrusion to remain in business. The flow characterized by steady arrows and an orange gradient reinforces the point that the threat is sustained and the same approach to the issue is that defensive measures should be continuous, not a response based on a single event. As shown in Table 10.8, methods for regaining trust include public apologies, compensation, transparency reports, and third-party audits.

Transparency operates at several levels, namely informational, procedural, and emotional. Informational transparency entails timely reporting the nature and magnitude of the breach, the type of data that has been compromised, and the measures that are underway to reduce the damages. Organizations that withhold this information, or postpone it, increase the level of anxiety and mistrust among people. Conversely, prompt communication is a sign of responsibility and a good faith impression that the organization is doing what is right. Procedural transparency is concerned with the description of the remedial measures performed, for example, patching vulnerabilities, enhancing authentication procedures, and the involvement of an independent auditor, to assure the stakeholders that the matter is professionally and comprehensively addressed.

Emotional openness is a crucial factor, as users often experience distress following exposure of their personal data. Sincere, understanding, and action plans are important apologies that make

FIGURE 10.9 Trust restoration pathway.

TABLE 10.8
Corporate Data Protection Maturity Assessment

Maturity Level	Key Features	Organizational Behavior	Example Industry
Level 1—Reactive	Ad-hoc patching	Incident-only focus	Small businesses
Level 2—Compliant	Policy-driven	Meets legal minimum	Government
Level 3—Proactive	Continuous monitoring	Predictive risk prevention	Finance
Level 4—Adaptive	AI-driven analytics	Real-time trust management	Technology
Level 5—Resilient	Integrated socio-technical response	Cultural transparency	Healthcare

the organization human. Users will be less likely to forgive errors when they are sincerely made and responsibility is exhibited instead of denying or minimizing. Further, there should be an open channel of communication, that is, helplines, special portals, and personalized messages that allow the affected people to communicate their concerns as well as receive special guidance that will instill a sense of control and connectedness.

Organizations should demonstrate sustained changes in behavior over time to rebuild trust. Following a breach, organizations should shift from a reactive crisis management strategy to a proactive trust-building approach. It includes regular transparency reports, external audits, and apparent advancements in cybersecurity posture. As evidence of improved data governance, a certification of such a framework as ISO/IEC 27001 or SOC 2 can be considered. Moreover, implementing privacy-by-design principles, that is, incorporating user protection into each and every digital process, is an indication that the organization is committed to ethical data management in the long run.

In addition to the organizational practices, there is a societal aspect of transparency. By releasing breach information in a responsible way, institutions will help lead to shared learning within the cybersecurity environment. Published reports of anonymized breach patterns, lessons learned, and mitigation strategies can assist other parties in predicting the occurrence of threats and preventing the same. This shared transparency can create the culture of digital responsibility, in which transparency is not seen as a sign of weakness but as a sign of strength. As seen in Figure 10.10, the levels of maturity of organizational transparency are identified, and the stage of progression helps in building long-term trust.

The conceptual model (Figure 10.10), which shows the Organizational Transparency Maturity Model, involves the maturity and accountability of companies in four different stages, starting with the most immature level and moving upwards to the most mature. The first tier is reactive (usually painted in a boring color such as gray), which in this case, organizations reveal the information when compelled by a regulatory deadline or a significant crisis. The next level is the compliant level, which implies those organizations that primarily engage in the minimum legal disclosure but no more. The more advanced stages start with proactive transparency (mid-range blue-green), which involves companies proactively planning to share the relevant information prior to the demand, actively building trust, and pre-empting the needs of the stakeholders. The highest point of the model is ethical transparency (brightest blue-green) where the organization has made transparency part and parcel of its culture, and it goes beyond what is required by law and focuses on open, honest, and comprehensive communication even in cases where the news is bad. Such development brings up the most critical point that maturity in the organization involves the shift toward no longer acting simply by the law but embracing ethical consciousness and transparency as business culture.

In essence, restoring trust through disclosure is not a one-liner activity but a continual interaction between the organizations and their consumers. It involves getting the sense of security back, portraying moral trustworthiness and maintaining an open line of communication. Such candor, when consistently applied, enables organizations to transform a failure into a sustained commitment to protect users, demonstrating that human trust, rather than mere system resilience, is the most critical measure in the digital era.

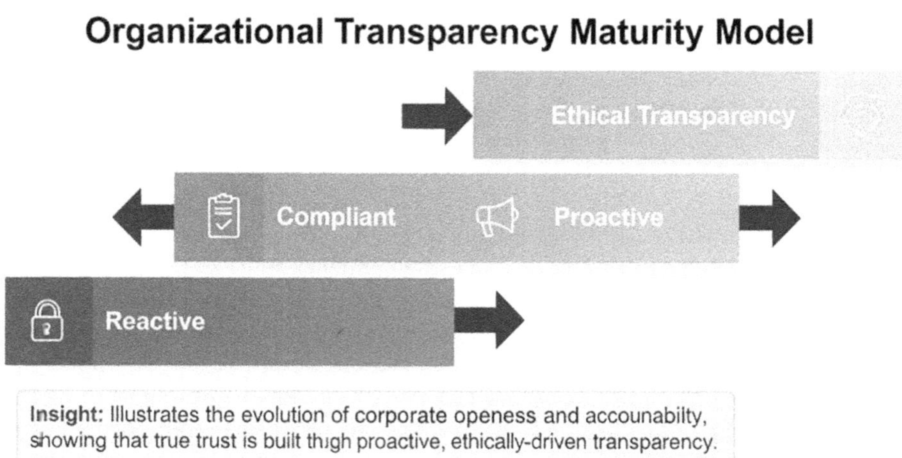

FIGURE 10.10 Organizational transparency maturity model.

10.10 ORGANIZATIONAL RESILIENCE AND CYBER INSURANCE

As data breaches increase in frequency and complexity, organizations recognize that even the most advanced security measures cannot guarantee complete protection. Consequently, cyber insurance has emerged as a critical financial and strategic tool for managing cyber risk. It serves as a safety net that assists organizations to absorb the economic effect of data thefts, ransomware, system downtimes, or regulatory fines. Beyond financial recovery, cyber insurance significantly enhances organizational resilience, fosters a risk-aware culture, and improves readiness for emerging threats. The way cyber insurance allocates risk and instills resilience through encouraging proactive defense measures is discussed in Figure 10.11.

The concept of sharing the responsibility and cyber risk among three main parties is conceptualized in the triangular relationship diagram (Figure 10.11) reflecting the concept of Cyber Insurance Risk Transfer Model. The triangle in Figure 10.11 represents the Cyber Insurance Risk Transfer Model, with the Organization (policyholder directly exposed to cyber threats), the Insurer (providing financial coverage and risk management), and Third-Party Vendors (external service providers, e.g., cloud or managed security) positioned at each corner. The flow is described as two-way arrows, which are between each node, indicating the active flow of information, risk, and coverage. Premiums are exchanged for the financial risk that is transferred to the insurer and coverage flow is received by the organization (green circular arrows tend to represent the flow of capital/coverage).

Simultaneously, the organization shares operational risk with third-party vendors, who must comply with security standards required by the insurer. This framework highlights the most important fact that cyber insurance establishes a crucial risk-sharing arrangement that requires collaboration. It determines security requirements throughout the system, making what might have

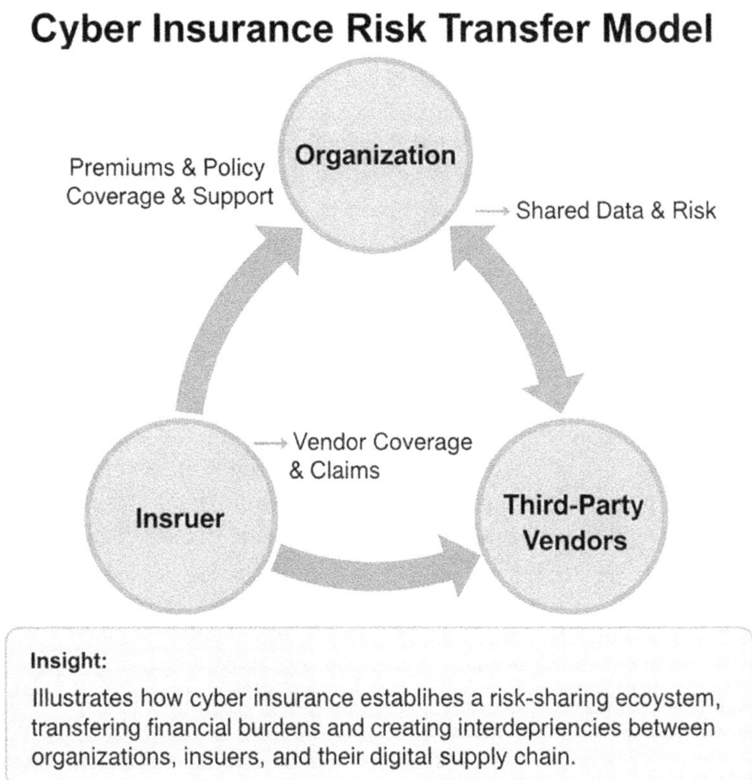

FIGURE 10.11 Cyber insurance risk transfer model.

TABLE 10.9
Comparison of Case Studies of Major Violations

Case	Year	Breach Vector	Users Affected (Millions)	Core Mistake	Key Lesson
Equifax	2017	Unpatched Apache vulnerability	147	Delay in patching	Early vulnerability scanning
Yahoo	2016	Credential theft	500	Weak encryption	Multi-factor authentication
Marriott	2018	Third-party compromise	383	Vendor oversight	Supply-chain audits
SolarWinds	2020	Supply-chain malware	18	Poor code review	Secure software lifecycle
MOVEit	2023	Zero-day exploit	62	Cloud misconfigurations	API risk management

been a financial disaster for the organization into a controlled, common expense for all three parties. As Table 10.9 shows, data loss, legal cost, and reputational damage are listed as coverage types and policy restrictions.

A comprehensive cyber insurance policy typically covers expenses such as incident response, forensic investigations, data restoration, customer notifications, legal defense, and public relations. Compensation of loss of business interruption or extortion payment in ransomware cases are also some of the policies. Through spreading the financial risk with the insurers, organizations will be able to work on recovery and survival rather than endure devastating losses. Nonetheless, the insurance procedure is not a passive one, and insurers need well-developed risk evaluation, regulatory papers, and proofs of cybersecurity maturity to provide or renew the insurances. This motivates companies to uphold robust technical measures like encryption, access controls, intrusion detection, and employee training to have superior terms of policies and reduced premiums.

Cyber insurance also promotes organizational resilience, the capacity to anticipate, absorb, and recover from disruptions while maintaining critical operations. Any organization that follows all three resilience principles is the one that includes technological preparation and procedural and psychological flexibility. The insurance factor is one of the drivers of resilience owing to the fact that it advocates the establishment of suitable response plans to incidences, interdepartmental coordination, and proactive tracking of the arising threats. It also fosters a culture of risk awareness, where management and staff recognize the consequences of data mishandling and collectively uphold cyber hygiene.

Figure 10.12, which shows Multi-Layered Resilience Architecture, is a defense strategy that is based on concentric layers that are intended to stop threats as well as to guarantee business continuity in the case of breach. On the second level lies Prevention (shield icon), all the proactive security measures that are aimed at preventing an attack before it occurs. In case prevention is not successful, the second tier is detection (radar icon) that aims at detecting active or attempted intrusions as swiftly as possible. The threat is detected, resulting in the workflow being transferred to Response (alert icon) and the actual steps being implemented to restrict the threat and lessen the harm, including isolating the systems that have been affected.

The next tier is recovery (gear icon), which is focused on data, system, and normal operations restoration. Lastly is the deepest and most important layer, adaptation (brain icon). This action completes the circle, with the understanding obtained during the whole process being used to enhance all the previous levels, which in turn makes the system itself tougher to any attack in the future. This architecture illustrates that resilience is an ongoing process, integrating technology, personnel, and procedures into continuous protection and improvement, rather than merely safeguarding the organization's existence.

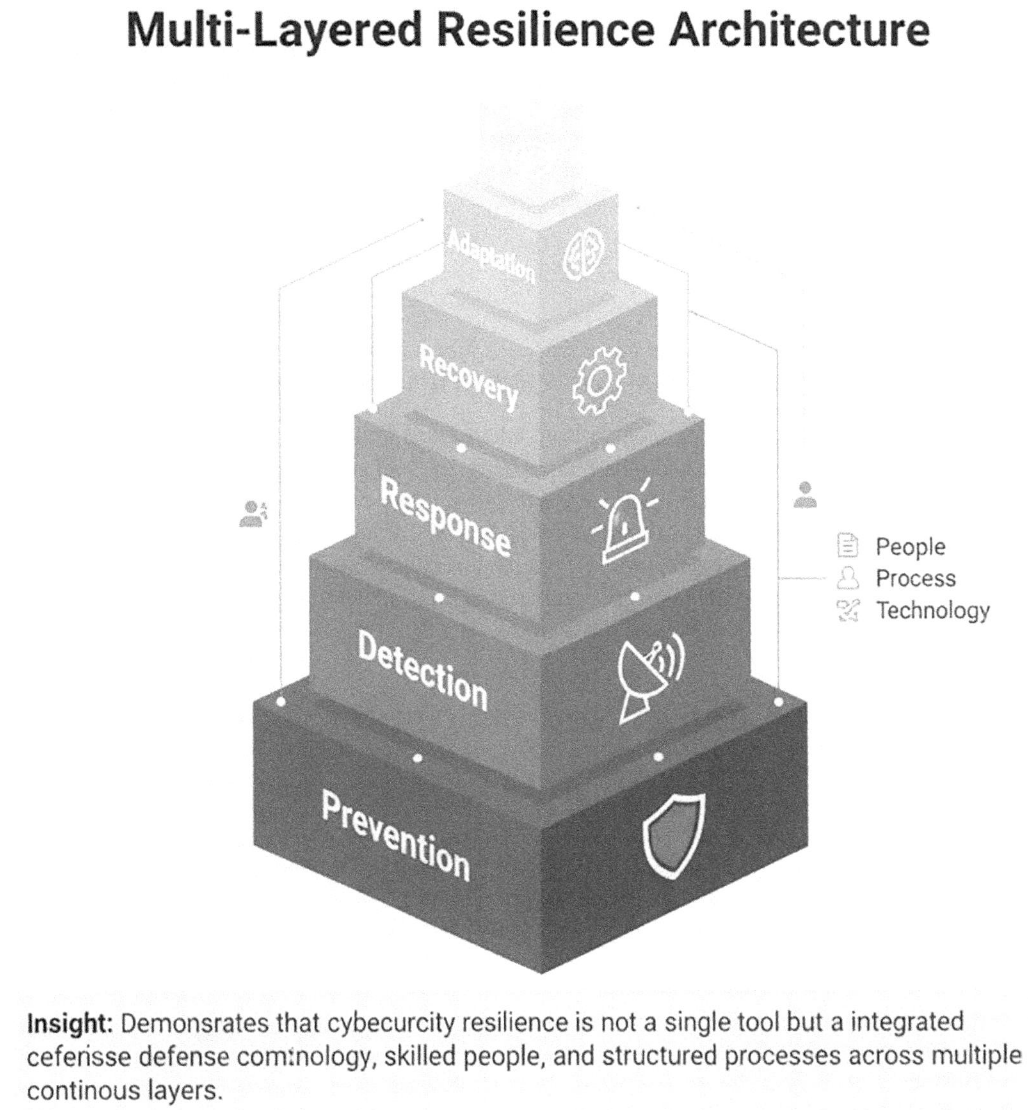

FIGURE 10.12 Multi-layer resilience architecture.

The connection between the insurers and policyholders is becoming more of a collaboration. Most insurers now offer value-added services, including pre-incident risk audits, employee awareness training, and post-incident recovery counseling. Such a partnership transforms cyber insurance from a reactive safety measure into a proactive resilience framework. It transforms the risk management into a process and not a checklist occurrence. Moreover, the integration of threat intelligence data with the cyber insurance analytics will have an opportunity to dynamically model the risk to enable organizations to have their coverage and defense strategies adjusted to the current threat level.

However, challenges persist. The cyber insurance market has problems like volatility of the premiums, vague policy exclusions, and underestimation of the systemic risk. As an example, the breaches of the supply chain or cloud service outage could potentially impact a large number of insured clients at the same time and present the insurers with enormous pressure. Additionally, cyber war and attacks by nation-states are not always covered by the policies, and organizations are partially left vulnerable. The policies in the future must shift to adaptive coverage structures with an eye to interdependencies in the digital environment and also promote normal risk assessment measures.

Finally, cyber insurance should not be viewed as a substitute for effective cybersecurity measures but rather as an additional layer of protection. The best thing about it is that it strengthens the thinking that resilience is an ongoing process, which is founded on prevention, supported by protection, and maintained using recovery. Alongside open governance, responsible information management, and post-breach education, the source of trust and stability is the cyber insurance. In this regard, it is an indicator of the maturity of an organization, not only in its crisis management, but also in a holistic perspective of what digital safety is, where technical preparedness, financial long term, and human wellness are balanced.

10.11 IMPLICATIONS AND LESSONS OF POLICY AND CASES

The real-life examples of data breaches that have taken place in the practical world can also tell a lot about relationships between technology, human behavior, and governance. They reveal technical aspects of cyberattacks, as well as organizational decisions, workplace communication failures, and ethical lapses that exacerbate the impact of breaches. By analyzing key industry cases, this section highlights lessons learned regarding policies for data protection and strategies to restore user trust. The three largest breach cases are compared in Figure 10.13, and they demonstrate unique weaknesses and policy lessons of each of the incidences.

Comparative Case-Based Insights:

Equifiax, Anthem, SolarWinds

Case	Breach Vector	Key Mistake	Recovery Strategy	Policy Leason
Exploted Software Vullernability	147+ Million	Failure to Patch Critical Flaw	Free Credit PR Crisis Mgmt	Accountability & Modernization
Anthem	78+ Million	Failure to Monitoring Flaw	Credit Protection, Legal Settlements	
Phishing & Stolen Credenitals	Indaquate Access Controls	Data Encyption & Aegal Setlements.	Data Encryption & Access Governance	System Rebulding, Transparency
Supply Chain Attack	18,000 Organies	Code Trust & Vendor Security	System Rebulding, Mngmt	Supply Cthain Risk

Insight: Compares distinct breach learnings, emphaizing governance failures and recovery best practices across major cyber insidents.

FIGURE 10.13 Equifax, Anthem, SolarWinds: Comparative case-based insights.

Figure 10.13 is a rather detailed comparative matrix aimed at deriving specific, practical findings out of three landmark cyberattacks: Equifax (2017), Anthem (2015), and SolarWinds (2020). The table presents a comparative analysis of all the cases on the critical dimensions, such as the Breach Vector, the number of Affected Users, the Key Mistake facilitating the compromise, the Recovery Strategy used, and the overall Policy Lesson. For example, Equifax suffered a major breach due to an unpatched Apache Struts vulnerability, which resulted in the leakage of the PII of about 147 million US consumers, and the critical error is that of vulnerability management. In contrast, the SolarWinds breach involved a sophisticated supply chain attack, which exposed sensitive data of numerous public and private clients, highlighting inadequate auditing of vendor security practices. The figure juxtaposing these different cases succinctly shows the central observation that as different as the technical attack vectors are, either in terms of their nature, simple patching failure and outright credential theft or more sophisticated nation-state supply chain attack, the underlying issue is that the problem has been allowed to go bad by a lack of proper governance and security diligence. Comparative analysis suggests that effective cyber resilience must address procedural vulnerabilities with the same rigor as technical weaknesses. Table 10.10 summarizes policy lessons (incident preparedness, cross-sector cooperation, regulatory harmonization).

The Equifax incident (2017) is one of the most talked-about ones, as it disclosed the personal information of more than 147 million people, including such sensitive information as Social Security numbers. The breach was caused by the inability to fix the known software vulnerability, which demonstrates that the lack of timely maintenance can lead to disastrous consequences. Public confidence was further undermined by the delay in public disclosure on the part of the company as well as poor crisis communication, thus the necessity to have a real vulnerability management process and transparent disclosure systems. Policymaking-wise, this case strengthened the case in favor of compulsory breach notification laws and tough data protection laws that will make organizations responsible regarding negligence.

The vulnerability of medical records, which is one of the most sensitive types of personal information, was revealed in the Anthem data breach (2015) in the healthcare industry. The hackers used stolen credentials to gain access to the data of about 80 million individuals, and this was what granted them unauthorized access to the data. This incident demonstrated the essentiality of the multi-factor authentication, role-based access control, and frequent security training of employees. It has also brought out the emotional aspect of data disclosure in a healthcare environment where confidentiality is lost, not only in terms of the financial aspect but also in terms of dignity and mental turmoil. The policymakers responded with the need to impose greater compliance with such structures as HIPAA and incorporate the element of emotional well-being into post-breach user support plans.

An exemplary response is observed in the SolarWinds breach (2020), where Microsoft's swift collaboration with forensics and transparent information sharing helped restore trust despite the scale of the compromise. The fact that Microsoft opened technical indicators to the masses has allowed other organizations to strengthen their ends and show that cooperation between industries

TABLE 10.10
Results of the User Education and Awareness Program

Training Method	Duration	Participation Rate (%)	Measured Improvement in Security Behavior (%)	Feedback Sentiment
E-Learning Modules	3 weeks	88	+32	Positive
Interactive Workshops	2 days	65	+25	Very positive
Phishing Simulations	1 month	72	+40	Encouraging
Gamified Mobile Apps	4 weeks	60	+28	Mixed
Poster and Email Campaigns	Ongoing	90	+15	Neutral

and openness could help to reduce risks to the wider ecosystem. The case has also been included in the matter of cybersecurity of supply chains in policies and has resulted in global measures of safe software development processes and vendor responsibility.

From these and other cases, several cross-cutting lessons emerge. To begin with, prevention and resilience cannot be separated; technical strength should be supplemented by psychological readiness and moral command. Second, crisis communication should be based on honesty and empathy as opposed to reputation management. Third, it is critical to have cross-sector cooperation, with governments, private organizations, academia, and civil society participating in addressing transnational threats that cannot be handled by an individual.

The political consequences are also very deep. To address emerging threats such as AI-driven cyberattacks and quantum decryption, governments should adopt adaptive governance, enabling policymakers to develop dynamic data protection laws in response to evolving risks. Companies ought to be guided by ethics-by-design models, where user privacy and emotional security are embedded in all the development phases of the system. Awareness campaigns should empower individuals to report, identify, and prevent breaches, fostering cybersecurity as a collective responsibility. Figure 10.14 integrates the entire ecosystem of data breach response—a combination of technology, governance, and psychological recovery.

The circular integration chart (Figure 10.14) in which the Integrated Data Breach Response Ecosystem is depicted highlights that the successful recovery after large-scale security incident is not a single affair but a complicated network with User Trust in the very center. This fundamental

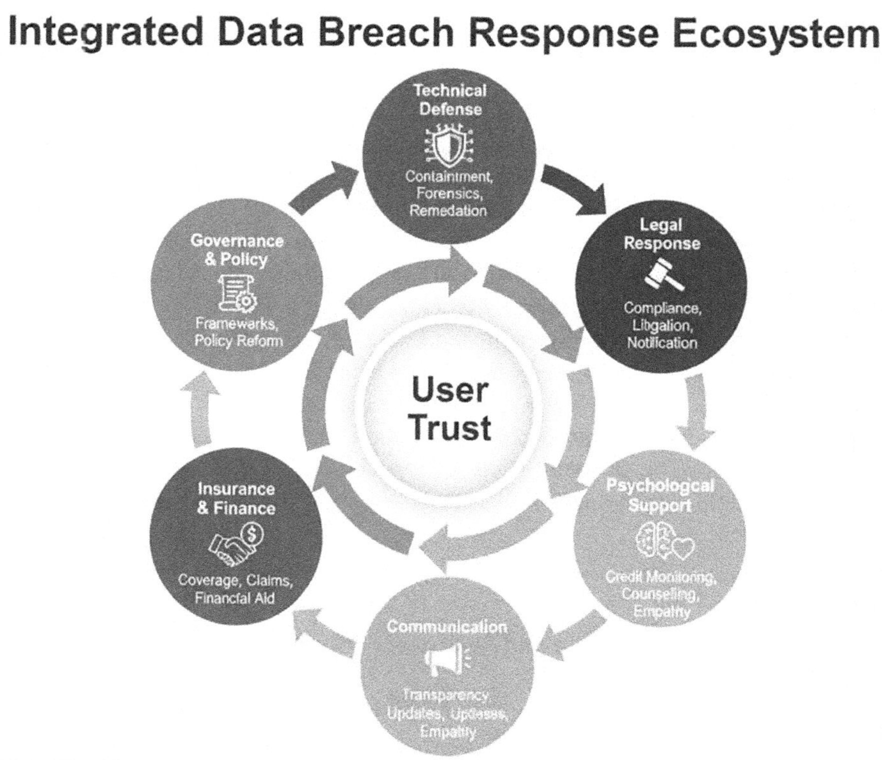

Insight: Illustrates the complex, intermnected nature of post-breach recovery, demonsating how all efforts across technolrogy, law, and human factors factors ultimatlle revound the mission of e rebubling and maintarin user trust.

FIGURE 10.14 Cyberspace data breach response ecosystem.

trust is surrounded by several specialized areas that need to be in tune. Technical Defense (usually blue) is concerned with the forensic investigation, containment, and hardening of the system. This is closely connected with Legal Response (a cool color), which deals with regulatory notifications, litigation, and contract analysis. These legal and technical elements should inform Communication (a warm tone such as yellow), which entails all messages to the public and internal communications and is aimed at transparency and clarity.

More importantly, there should be Psychological Support (a soft tone such as green) in communication, where the emotional consequences of the breach should be discussed with the users and employees impacted. The outward-facing functions are supported financially by insurance mechanisms and governed through organizational oversight, ensuring compliance, risk transfer, and continuous improvement. As the figure illustrates, failure of one of the domains such as poor technical defense or poor communication will only lead to the further degradation of the entire ecosystem, leading to the loss of the most prized and central resource: user trust.

Finally, when case-based learning and policy reform are synthesized, the information security of data is not only effective due to compliance, but it also represents an ongoing social contract, which is constructed on accountability, transparency, and empathy. Through experience and learning from failures, societies can build a resilient digital environment where trust is continuously strengthened by conscious and collective vigilance.

10.12 SUMMARY

Data breaches are among the most complex challenges of the digital era, arising from technological weaknesses, human errors, psychological impacts, and ethical concerns. The chapter has examined the security issue of data breaches in various aspects, and it has been made clear that the effect of this issue goes well beyond the technical or financial aspect of it. At the heart of any breach lies a failure of trust: to keep a system going, but also the sense of safety, dignity, and control over personal information by those using it.

It has begun by providing an overview of how the trend of digitalization of industries has diversified the attack space of cyber threats to near-inevitable failures in the absence of a viable preventive measure. The lifecycle and structure of cyberattack were considered to show how modern threat actors exploit the vulnerabilities across all levels of the process including reconnaissance up to data exfiltration. However, this technical factor is not the sole one, but the psychological and emotional consequences of digital insecurity on users emphasize that there is a human cost of digital insecurity. Anxiety, loss of confidence, and emotional exhaustion are the typical responses to breaches, and thus empathy-based responses and ethical responsibility of organizations are relevant.

The relationship linking the law and ethics turned out to be rather tight in regards to the process of data protection regulation. Despite the fact that the systematic framework of data processing and breach notification has been formalized in such international laws as the GDPR, CCPA, and the DPDPA of India (2023), the actual privacy of the user cannot be ensured, although by complying with the existing norms but with moral attitudes and demonstrating them in practice. The chapter emphasized the fact that the checkbox strategies are to be discarded and the ethics-by-design principles should be incorporated into the organizations, with the data privacy and user well-being becoming the staples of digital systems.

The discussion of the post-breach forensics demonstrated how systematic research can assist in locating the root causes of the issue and support the institutional security. Nevertheless, the most difficult process that follows the technical recovery is the rebuilding of the user trust. The three elements of this trust restoration process include transparency, caring communication, and long-term behavior change. The second issue was cyber insurance, where it appears to be a financial security and a system of resiliency, and it cultivates the culture of preparedness and shared responsibility.

A case-based summary of the actual breaches—Equifax, Anthem, and the very controversial SolarWinds—showed that all the occurrences have a lesson to offer regarding governance, leadership, and policy formulation. All in all, the examples suggest that adaptive regulation, inter-organizational collaboration, and lifelong learning can be used to mitigate the threat environment that is rapidly evolving. Lastly, data breach management must be revolutionized to become a part of a holistic discipline that unites technology, psychology, law, and ethics. Effectively addressing breaches requires not only prevention but also responsive actions, transparent communication, and organizational development to strengthen resilience. This is not merely a technological challenge; data protection is fundamentally a moral and psychological responsibility, essential for maintaining human confidence in the digital era. Transparency and empathy, as foundational principles in cybersecurity policy, will foster a safer digital society where users and organizations coexist responsibly and respectfully.

REFERENCES

Al Hogail, A. (2018). Improving cybersecurity culture to enhance organizational cybersecurity performance. *International Journal of Advanced Computer Science and Applications*, *9*(1), 244–251. https://doi.org/10.14569/IJACSA.2018.090132

Anderson, R., & Moore, T. (2020). The economics of information security and privacy. *Communications of the ACM*, *63*(2), 26–29. https://doi.org/10.1145/3373400

Bada, A., & Nurse, J. R. C. (2019). Developing cybersecurity education and awareness programmes for small- and medium-sized enterprises (SMEs). *Information & Computer Security*, *27*(3), 393–410. https://doi.org/10.1108/ICS-07-2018-0080

Bada, M., Sasse, A. M., & Nurse, J. R. C. (2019). Cyber security awareness campaigns: Why do they fail to change behaviour? *arXiv preprint arXiv:1901.02672*. https://doi.org/10.48550/arXiv.1901.02672

Balamurugan, G., Tyagi, A.K., & Richa, A. (2023). Survey on privacy preserving and trust building techniques of blockchain-based systems. In: *Privacy Preservation and Secured Data Storage in Cloud Computing*. IGI Global. DOI: 10.4018/979-8-3693-0593-5.ch019

Bélanger, F., & Crossler, R. E. (2019). Privacy in the digital age: A review of information privacy research in information systems. *MIS Quarterly*, *43*(1), 275–326.

Campbell, K., Gordon, L. A., Loeb, M. P., & Zhou, L. (2021). The economic cost of publicly announced information security breaches: Empirical evidence from the stock market. *Journal of Computer Security*, *29*(2), 129–151. https://doi.org/10.3233/JCS-2003-11308

Cheng, L., Liu, F., & Yao, D. D. (2017). Enterprise data breach: Causes, challenges, prevention, and future directions. *Wiley Interdisciplinary Reviews: Data Mining and Knowledge Discovery*, *7*(5), e1211. https://doi.org/10.1002/widm.1211

Custers, B., & Ursic, H. (2016). Big data and data reuse: A taxonomy of data reuse for balancing big data benefits and personal data protection. *International Data Privacy Law*, *6*(1), 4–15. https://doi.org/10.1093/idpl/ipv028

Data Security Council of India. (2023). *Data protection and cybersecurity trends in India*. DSCI Publications.

European Union. (2018). *General data protection regulation (GDPR)*. Official Journal of the European Union. https://gdpr-info.eu/

Faruqi, F., & Hassan, R. (2021). Data breach disclosure and its impact on user trust in online platforms. *Information Systems Frontiers*, *23*(5), 1259–1276.

Friedman, B., Kahn, P. H., & Borning, A. (2018). Value sensitive design and information systems. In K. E. Himma & H. T. Tavani (Eds.), *The handbook of information and computer ethics* (pp. 69–101). Wiley. https://doi.org/10.1007/978-94-007-7844-3_4

Gordon, L. A., Loeb, M. P., & Zhou, L. (2018). Investing in cybersecurity: Insights from the Gordon-Loeb model. *Journal of Information Security*, *9*(1), 24–35. https://doi.org/10.4236/jis.2016.72004

IBM Security. (2024). *Cost of a data breach report 2024*. IBM Security and Ponemon Institute.

Jang-Jaccard, J., & Nepal, S. (2014). A survey of emerging threats in cybersecurity. *Journal of Computer and System Sciences*, *80*(5), 973–993. https://doi.org/10.1016/j.jcss.2014.02.005

Kaspersky Lab. (2023). *Global IT security risks survey: Corporate IT security risks 2023*.

Kaufmann, M., & Egloff, F. (2020). The politics of cybersecurity and trust: The shaping of digital trust through cyber security policy. *Journal of Cyber Policy*, *5*(1), 1–20.

Khan, I. U., Hameed, Z., & Sabir, S. (2022). The impact of cybersecurity breaches on consumer trust and brand loyalty: Evidence from global tech firms. *Computers & Security*, *120*, 102792.

Kumari, S., Tyagi, A. K., Tiwari, S., & Kulshreshtha, G. (2025a). Sensors and digital twin for healthcare monitoring frameworks. In T. A. Nguyen (Ed.), *Digital twin, blockchain, and sensor networks in the healthy and mobile city (Chapter 10,* pp. 147–177*)*. Elsevier. https://doi.org/10.1016/B978-0-443-34174-8.00011-9

Kumari, S., Tyagi, A. K., Tiwari, S., & Singh, R. (2025b). Medical sensor network, edge computing and blockchain for efficient medical data exchange. In T. A. Nguyen (Ed.), *Digital twin, blockchain, and sensor networks in the healthy and mobile city (Chapter 11,* pp. 179–198*)*. Elsevier. https://doi.org/10.1016/B978-0-443-34174-8.00012-0

Liang, H., & Xue, Y. (2009). Avoidance of information technology threats: A theoretical perspective. *MIS Quarterly*, *33*(1), 71–90. https://doi.org/10.2307/20650279

McKnight, D. H., Carter, M., Thatcher, J. B., & Clay, P. F. (2011). Trust in a specific technology: An investigation of its components and measures. *ACM Transactions on Management Information Systems*, *2*(2), 1–25. https://doi.org/10.1145/1985347.1985353

Mishra, A. K., Tiwari, S., Tyagi, A. K., & Arowolo, M. O. (2024). Security, privacy, trust, and provenance issues in Internet of Things–based edge environment. In S. Pal, C. Savaglio, R. Minerva, & F. C. Delicato (Eds.), *IoT edge intelligence* (pp. 233–263). Springer. https://doi.org/10.1007/978-3-031-58388-9_8

Nair, M. M., & Tyagi, A. K. (2021). Privacy: History, statistics, policy, laws, preservation and threat analysis. *Journal of information assurance & security*, *16*(1), 24–34.

Nair, M.M., & Tyagi, A.K. (2025). Transformative effects of emerging technologies on Industry 5.0 and Society 5.0: Current status, vision, issues, challenges, and opportunities for future. In: *Next Generation Data Science and Blockchain Technology for Industry 5.0*. Wiley. DOI: https://doi.org/10.1002/9781394245215.ch13, ISBN: 9781394245185.

National Institute of Standards and Technology (NIST). (2020). *Framework for improving critical infrastructure cybersecurity (Version 1.1)*. U.S. Department of Commerce.

Nissenbaum, H. (2010). *Privacy in context: Technology, policy, and the integrity of social life*. Stanford University Press.

Ponemon Institute. (2023). *2023 Cost of insider threats global report*.

Rajani, D., Menon, S. C., Kute, S., & Tyagi, A. K. (2022). Preserving privacy of social media data using artificial intelligence techniques. In A. Tyagi (Ed.), *Handbook of Research on Technical, Privacy, and Security Challenges in a Modern World* (pp. 186–204). IGI Global. https://doi.org/10.4018/978-1-6684-5250-9.ch010

Renaud, K., & Zimmermann, V. (2018). Ethical challenges in security and privacy research. *Computers & Security*, *78*, 409–423.

Romanosky, S. (2016). Examining the costs and causes of cyber incidents. *Journal of Cybersecurity*, *2*(2), 121–135. https://doi.org/10.1093/cybsec/tyw001

Schneier, B. (2019). *Click here to kill everybody: Security and survival in a hyper-connected world*. W.W. Norton & Company.

Shackelford, S. J. (2020). *Managing cyber-attacks in international law, business, and relations: In search of cyber peace*. Cambridge University Press. https://doi.org/10.1017/CBO9781139021838

Solove, D. J., & Citron, D. K. (2022). Privacy harms. *Boston University Law Review*, *102*(3), 793–857. www.bu.edu/bulawreview/files/2022/04/CITRON-SOLOVE.pdf

Tyagi, A.K. (2021). Analysis of security and privacy aspects of blockchain technologies from smart era' perspective: The challenges and a way forward. In: *Recent Trends in Blockchain for Information Systems Security and Privacy* (pp. 1–17). DOI: https://doi.org/10.1201/9781003139737, eBook-ISBN: 9781003139737

Tyagi, A.K. (2025). Blockchain for smart hospital in Healthcare 5.0: modeling structure, challenges, and future emerging trends. In: *Human-Centric Integration of Next-Generation Data Science and Blockchain Technology*. Elsevier. DOI: https://doi.org/10.1016/B978-0-443-33498-6.00026-1, ISBN: 978-0-443-33498-6.

Tyagi, A.K. (2026). *Chapter 4 - Artificial intelligence–blockchain–Internet of Things–based smart healthcare services: literature review and future research directions, in the book: Smart Hospital Anatomy with Advanced Sensors Innovations in Patient Care*. Elsevier (pp. 49-61). https://doi.org/10.1016/B978-0-443-45875-0.00005-3, ISBN: 978-0-443-45875-0.

Tyagi, A., Kumari, S., & Tiwari, S. (2024c). Internet of Things for smart healthcare: A survey. In A. K. Sharma, N. Chanderwal, S. Tyagi, & P. Upadhyay (Eds.), *Future of AI in medical imaging (Chapter 2)*. IGI Global. https://doi.org/10.4018/979-8-3693-2359-5.ch002

Tyagi, A. K., & Tiwari, S. (2024a). Blockchain-enabled smart healthcare applications in 6G networks. In A. K. Tyagi (Ed.), *Digital twin and blockchain for smart cities (Chapter 20)*. Wiley. https://doi.org/10.1002/9781394303564.ch20

Tyagi, A. K., Tripathi, K., Tiwari, S., & Kaushik, S. (2025). An efficient technique for privacy preservation, trusted and secure patient-centric services in smart healthcare. In *Proceedings of the 6th international conference on recent trends in communication & intelligent systems (ICRTCIS 2025)* (pp. 31–47). IET. https://doi.org/10.1049/icp.2025.2731

Vishwanath, A. (2021). Habitual Facebook use and its association with digital privacy and security behaviors. *Computers in Human Behavior, 114*, 106571. https://doi.org/10.1111/jcc4.12100

Wang, J., Li, X., & Rao, H. R. (2022). Coping with data breaches: The role of psychological safety and organizational communication. *Information Systems Research, 33*(1), 217–234.

Weber, R. H. (2020). Internet of Things: Privacy issues revisited. *Computer Law & Security Review, 37*, 105403. https://doi.org/10.1016/j.clsr.2015.07.002

11 Bias, Fairness, and Cultural Sensitivity in AI Systems

11.1 INTRODUCTION

Artificial intelligence (AI) systems have evolved rapidly from experimental technologies into essential tools for everyday decision-making. AI has become a powerful force in predicting patient needs, assisting law enforcement, screening job applicants, and even generating educational content. These advantages, however, have challenges. If AI systems inherit the biases found in their training data, they may unintentionally produce decisions that disadvantage certain individuals or groups. The fact that AI can grow exponentially and more widely compared to human decision-makers makes this a particularly worrying factor as favorable decisions affecting a specific group can impact thousands or even millions of individuals within a few short years.

The increased awareness of the issues has resulted in international debates among scholars, corporate executives, policymakers, and civil society. The main issue here is not whether AI is able to perform well, but whether it is able to perform in a fair way. Fairness must be grounded in moral reasoning, social awareness, and cultural sensitivity. There are various communities all over the world with different values, communication patterns, and convictions, as well as experience in history. AI systems, without taking into consideration these differences, can give a solution that is socially unacceptable or culturally inappropriate. The chapter discusses these issues by offering a clear insight into the way bias is created, how it is disseminated through AI pipelines, and how fairness and cultural sensitivity can be enhanced.

11.2 LITERATURE REVIEW

Studies of bias, fairness, and cultural sensitivity in AI have developed in many ways during the last 20 years. Early research focused on identifying how prejudice can emerge within computer systems. One of the earliest arguments that digital technologies can replicate existing social inequalities was made by Friedman and Nissenbaum (1996), according to which design decisions reflect societal beliefs. This concept formed the basis of subsequent studies that predicted that algorithm systems can inadvertently bias discrimination (Alkhatib, 2021). In the case of the first, Noble (2018) showed how search engines can perpetuate racial stereotypes, and in case of the second, O'Neil (2017) showed how the statistics models employed in policing, credit scoring, and employment could cause unfair harm to vulnerable populations.

With the maturation of machine learning, researchers started to look at technical aspects of bias in more detail. Barocas et al. (2019) gave a very broad overview of the issues of fairness and described how biased datasets and optimization processes influence model behavior. Mehrabi et al. (2021), Suresh and Guttag (2019), Danks and London (2017), and Kumari et al. (2025b) contributed to this knowledge by trying to distinguish between these forms of algorithmic harm: representational,

DOI: 10.1201/9781003658344-14

allocative, and feedback-loop biases. Chouldechova (2017), Kleinberg et al. (2017), and Narayanan (2018) work helped understand that the trade-offs between competing metrics of fairness cannot be addressed by one universal mathematical standard.

The practical ramifications of biased algorithms have been found through empirical research. As Buolamwini and Gebru (2018) and Mishra et al., (2024) demonstrated, facial recognition technologies are less accurate with women and people whose skin is darker. The same arguments have been made in other fields, including sentiment analysis (Bender et al., 2021; Tyagi, 2025; Tyagi and Tiwari, 2024a) and predictive policing (Benjamin, 2019; Tyagi, 2021; Balamurugan et al., 2023; Nair et al., 2021, 2025; Tyagi, 2026). These results highlight the importance of powerful assessment methods. Mitchell et al. (2019), Raji et al. (2020), Holstein et al. (2019), and Tyagi et al. (2024c) highlight that it is necessary to document a model, be transparent, and conduct systematic auditing to discover and eliminate discriminatory trends.

Parallel to technological debates, a number of studies are providing a sustained literature on the socio-ethical aspects of AI. Crawford (2021), Pasquale (2020), and Aiken and Sloan (2020) raise the issues of power and control, as well as the environmental and political consequences of massive AI systems. Responsible development has also come up with ethical frameworks to govern it. Floridi and Cowls (2019) suggested a single set of AI ethics principles, whereas Taddeo and Floridi (2018) offered to propose that AI can help in the case of social good if it is constructed in a responsible manner. The development of accountability systems is evidenced by governmental intervention in the development of AI systems, such as the UNESCO (2021) and European Commission (2021) suggested AI Act.

The studies of fairness have also been extended to cultural and global aspects. According to scholars, AI systems created in the West might not work or behave in the best way when deployed in other countries. According to Wang et al. (2022), cultural inclusiveness is necessary in AI to make it applicable worldwide. Bender et al. (2021) and Noble (2018) conduct their studies and find that language models and search engines incorporate cultural assumptions that can be marginalizing to non-Western users. Such understandings can justify the need to have more diverse datasets, cross-disciplinary collaborations, and participatory-oriented design practices that include the communities that were affected (Veale and Binns, 2017; Jobin et al., 2019; Kumari et al., 2025a; Tyagi et al., 2025).

Another theme that has been largely present in recent literature is accountability. Raji and Buolamwani (2019) emphasized the idea of independent audits as a means of identifying performance inequality, and Williams (2020) argues about legal methods of controlling the accountability of algorithms. Researchers like Selbst et al. (2019) and Rajani et al. (2022) emphasize that such a notion as fairness cannot be regarded as a technical issue but insist on the notion that social background, institutional framework, past disparities, etc., are to be included in the process of AI development.

Table 11.1 is a systematic representation of the significant types of biases that usually arise in AI systems. The table defines the type of biases and how they appear, as well as provides an example in practice to demonstrate the actual relevance of this type of bias. Sampling bias is the overrepresentation or underrepresentation of specific groups during the process of data collection, which makes the model educated about patterns that are not a true representation of the whole population. Measurement bias occurs when the tools or methods of measuring data are not consistent or accurate, for example, sensors that cannot record a particular skin tone. Historical bias emphasizes the fact that existing inequalities are instantiated within datasets, particularly when decisions made by people in the past were not fair. Prejudicial bias indicates subjective assumptions or stereotypes that have been created by the developers or annotators when labeling or selecting features. Algorithmic bias occurs when components of an algorithmic process, including input weighting, feature engineering, or training functions, lead to unintended outcomes that systematically favor certain groups over others. On the whole, this table makes the readers realize that bias is not a singular problem but a set of issues that may penetrate the system at numerous levels.

TABLE 11.1
Types of Bias in AI

Type of Bias	Description	Example
Sampling Bias	Poor representation of some groups	Sample consists of predominantly the urban users
Measurement Bias	Incorrect or imprecise data capturing	Poor-quality sensors on dark skins
Historical Bias	Pre-data inequalities codified into data	Gendered job assignment data
Prejudicial Bias	Assumptions used by developers to affect the results	Subjective labelling based on stereotypes.
Algorithmic Bias	Overweighting of features	Risk scores overweighting minorities

The literature suggests that fairness and cultural sensitivity in AI are only possible through a holistic approach. Technical solutions, for example, fairness measures, dataset balancing, and auditing, need to be supplemented with ethical guidelines, legal frameworks, and culturally informed design. According to Russell and Norvig (2021), current AI systems exist in convoluted human systems; thus, equity and inclusiveness require interdisciplinary effort and ongoing social interaction.

11.3 TYPES AND SOURCES OF BIAS

Prejudice in AI is caused by several sources, which frequently interrelate in complicated ways. The main types include the following.

The sources of bias in AI systems are illustrated in Figure 11.1, which depicts a lifecycle perspective of how unfairness may occur at various stages of the development and deployment process. The figure does not represent bias as a single-origin problem, but as one that can be accumulated at the stages. It begins with data bias, which develops when information is applied to train the system and is unbalanced, incomplete, or influenced by long-term social imbalances. Then there is algorithmic bias, which is a result of the technical choices made in the process of creating the model, the selection of features, or the choice of optimization methods. The human bias is introduced by the developers, the designers, or the annotators, whose judgment, assumptions, and cultural views have an indirect impact on the model. Lastly, deployment bias manifests after the system has been deployed, usually because the model is operating in a setting or user situation with which it has not been tuned or tested. Combined with the figure, it highlights the fact that bias is a perennial threat that may occur or escalate at any point, and thus, frequent evaluation and monitoring is an essential aspect of responsible AI development.

a. **Data Bias**
   Data bias is a situation in which the training data fails to encompass the overall diversity of the population. As an illustration, medical data can have higher numbers of samples that represent the urban patients than the rural population, ending up with models that are not effective in the rural population.
b. **Measurement Bias**
   Measurement bias arises from poor or inappropriate data-collection practices. Information may be distorted as it enters the model due to faulty sensors, inconsistent labeling, or culturally insensitive questionnaires.
c. **Algorithmic Bias**
   Bias may creep in even in an event in which the data is balanced due to the choice of the model design. Certain algorithms can provide accidental amplification of tiny patterns or correlations that only appear in particular groups. The biases may manifest in the results depending on the use of feature selection, loss functions, and optimization techniques.

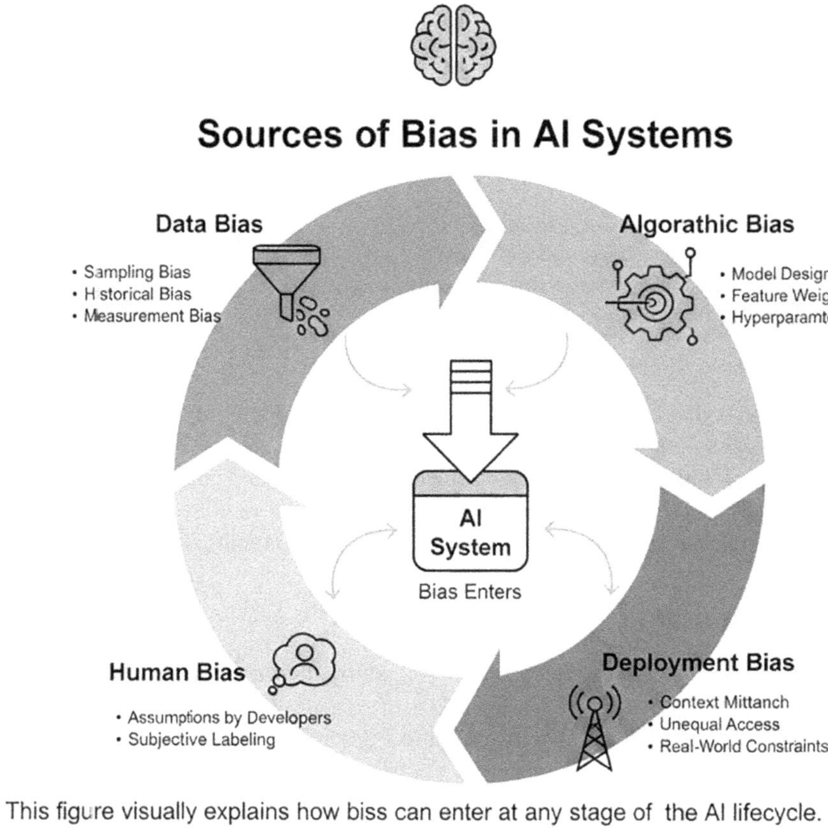

FIGURE 11.1 AI systems are susceptible to bias in the following ways.

d. **Social and Cultural Bias**
AI systems often mirror the cultural biases embedded in the environments in which they are developed. As an illustration, voice assistants that were mostly trained on the western accent cannot deal with south Asian or African speakers of English. Likewise, the systems can be misinterpreting gestures or emotions when they are applied worldwide, though their norms have been adopted in a different culture. Such forms of bias illuminate the fact that equity should be considered at all levels of AI development, data gathering, and model implementation.

11.4 ISSUES OF DATA IMBALANCE AND REPRESENTATION DATA

Imbalance and Representation Data: Data imbalance is one of the most common and influential causes of AI bias. When a group is vastly represented and other groups are seldom represented, then that algorithm will be biased towards the dominant group. Such disparity is not necessarily deliberate; in some cases, some groups of people are less digitized, lack access to healthcare data, or cannot be seen on the internet. Nevertheless, the implications may be dramatic.

As an illustration, speech-recognition systems have frequently been discovered to be more effective with male voices as they were trained on them using more male voices. In like manner, predictive policing applications can make some neighborhoods look like high-risk zones as there is a history of crime concentration in the area with the most police presence, which is not necessarily equal to the crime rates.

Solutions to the problems of representation are intentional, like increased collection of data, oversampling of minorities, artificial data creation, and community integration. The developers also have to work on continuous monitoring of datasets as populations and social processes change and older datasets might no longer portray the current reality.

Figure 11.2 demonstrates the way the unequal representation in society may become biased AI decisions. This is usually represented as a flowchart or a step diagram. The process starts with the real world where certain groups could not be as visible in books or computerized systems. This results in skewed data sets, in which some groups are hardly represented. When a model is trained on such data, it develops a distorted understanding of real-world patterns; it will work well with groups that are well represented but poorly on groups with minimal data. The resultant effect is uneven accuracy where the prediction or classification differs considerably across the demographic groups. This imbalance eventually feeds back into society, for example, a system might over and over disadvantage the same group of people, which further increases the initial imbalance. As shown in the diagram, data imbalance is not an issue that exists in isolation but a vicious circle that can lead to permanent damage.

Table 11.2 outlines the dimensions that are needed to have various, representative datasets to be used in global AI implementation. Geographic diversity will guarantee that there is coverage to users that represent various geographic areas, such as rural and urban users; thus, the model is not location biased. Cultural diversity embodies behavior, practices, and traditions and assists models to decipher culturally specialized patterns, including food items or gestures. Linguistic diversity

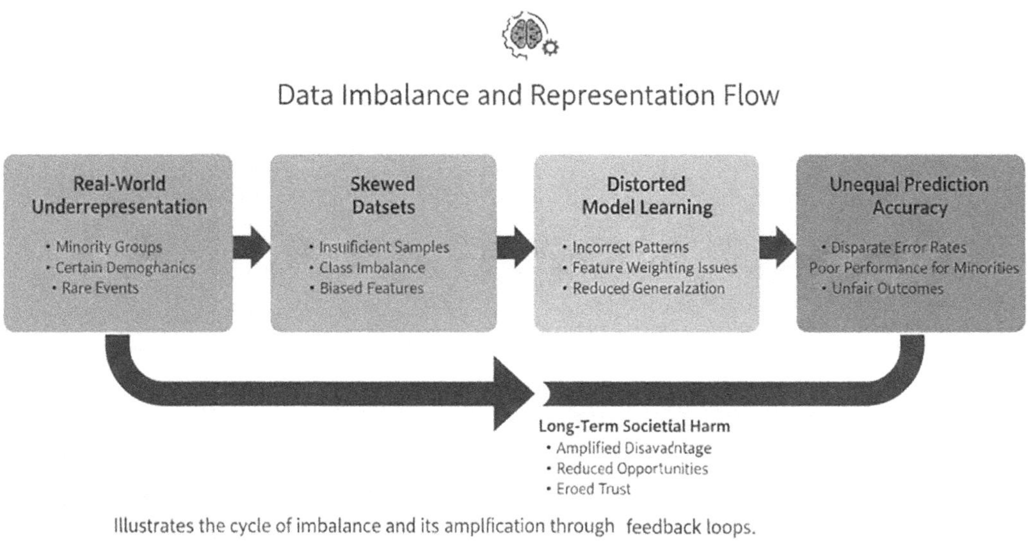

FIGURE 11.2 Imbalance and representation data flow.

TABLE 11.2
Diversity Requirements Dataset

Dimension	Importance	Example
Geographic Diversity	No regional biasness	City + rural data
Cultural Diversity	The inclusion of interpretation	Food recognition datasets
Language Diversity	Enhances the natural language processing performance	Speech corpora on low-resource languages
Demographic Diversity	Ensures fairness	Age, gender, social–economic coverage

enhances speech and text models by using many languages and dialects and not depending much on the English-dominated datasets. Demographic diversity is necessary in terms of equality, with an equal distribution of the age group, gender, socioeconomic status, and other factors affecting the performance of AI (Whittaker et al., 2019, Zhang & Dafoe, 2019, Zou & Schiebinger, 2018). The table shows that an inclusive dataset should reflect human diversity in all aspects, not restricted to small samples or homogeneous ones.

11.5 ALGORITHMS AND DISCRIMINATION: ALGORITHMS AND SOCIAL IMPACT

In real-life situations where biased algorithms are applied, they may cause great disparities. In employment screening, biased models may reject qualified candidates because of gender-biased patterns embedded in historical hiring data. Credit-scoring algorithms in the financial industry can give less credit to certain ethnic groups because of their incomplete or prejudiced histories. Risk prediction models can also fail to accurately capture the severity of illness in some population groups in healthcare, leading to a delay in care delivery.

Figure 11.3 presents a stepwise chain in which discriminatory results are created by AI systems. It begins with the initial problem: biased input data. By the model training on this kind of data, it is prone to make wound-up or biased decisions, particularly to those groups that the data does not capture effectively. These inaccuracies are applied to phenomenon in the real world, which leads to unequal outcomes, for example, unfair loan denials, discriminatory employment suggestions, or disproportionate policing. These disproportionate results in turn compound historically marginalized groups, thus complicating their access to opportunities or services. Finally, the figure demonstrates that such prejudiced choices can give an impression that current social inequalities are right, thereby supporting rather than proving discrimination. The route highlights that the appearance of discriminatory AI outcomes is not a rare occurrence—it has a pattern that is based on bias in data.

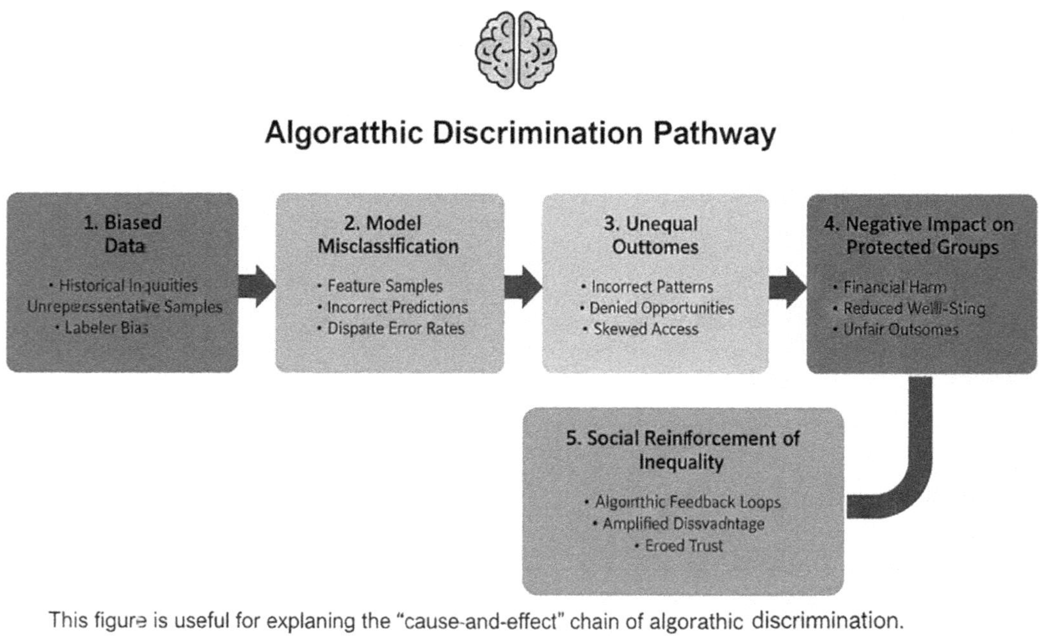

FIGURE 11.3 Pathway of algorithmic discrimination.

Such discriminatory results may have long-term social effects. They are able to influence the economic stability of a person, career development, and life quality. On a larger level, algorithmic discrimination may undermine the confidence that the population has in technology. Societies that are marginalized or perceived to be mistreated might be opposed to the introduction of AI solutions in areas where the technology is potentially useful. These challenges must thus be detected and addressed as early as possible in the lifecycle of AI.

11.6 MEASURES OF FAIRNESS AND ASSESSMENT METHODS

The metrics of fairness can be used by researchers and developers to measure how an AI system treats various groups fairly (Calo 2021, Creel & Hellman, 2022, Dwork & Ilvento, 2018, Hashimoto et al., 2018, Mittelstadt, 2019).

Figure 11.4 provides an overview of key metrics used to evaluate fairness in AI systems, and it allows the readers to compare how each of them conceptualizes the concept of being fair. It unites some of the most popular fairness measures, demonstrating how each one of them concerns another side of decision equality. Demographic parity looks at whether various groups are getting positive results in approximately equal measure, and equalized odds considers the correct and incorrect predictions made to make sure that there is an equal distribution of error rates among the groups. Equal opportunity puts this even farther when we examine the possibility of all groups having equal opportunity of being given a correct positive decision. Predictive parity focuses on how each demographic can be trusted to make positive predictions so that a positive prediction is positive, whether the person belongs to a particular group or not. Calibration is the complement to these to ensure that the proposed probabilities are realistic to all groups. The general impression of the figure is that these measures of fairness are not always consistent; in certain situations, not all of them can be met simultaneously mathematically. The diagram assists the practitioner to choose the most appropriate approach to fairness, given the objectives, context, and ethical imperative of their use of AI.

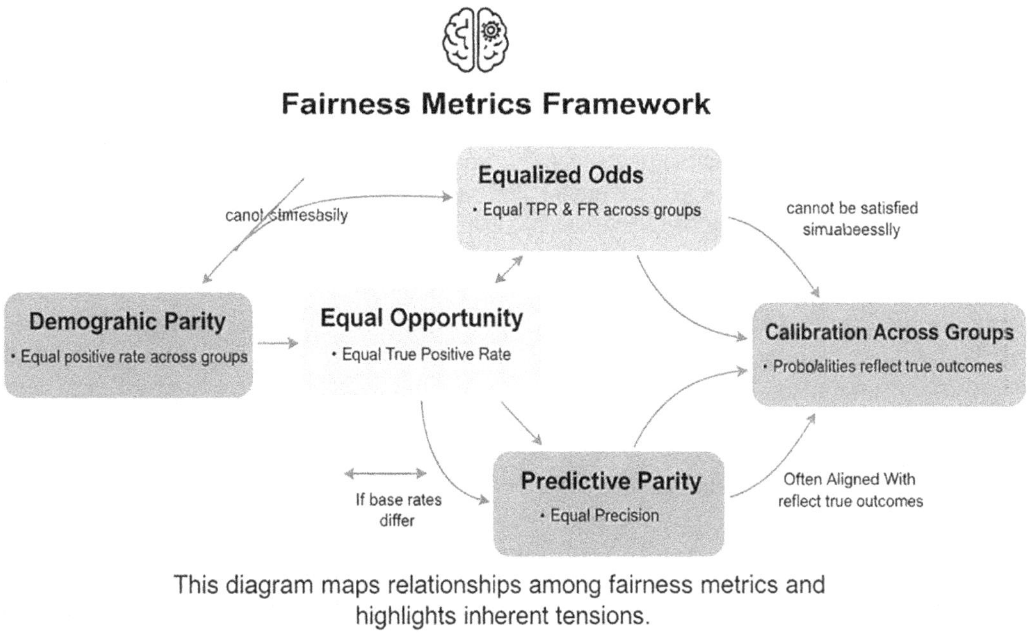

FIGURE 11.4 Framework of fairness metrics.

TABLE 11.3
Fairness Metrics Categorization

Metric	Definition	Use Case
Demographic Equilibrium	Equal positive outcome rate between groups	Loan approvals
Equalized Odds	Equal false positive rate and true positive rate between groups	Medical diagnosis
Equal Opportunity	Hiring recommendations	Equal true positive rate
Calibration	Similar predicted risk of a group	Recidivism prediction
Predictive Parity	Equal accuracy among groups	Fraud detection

Examples of popular metrics are:

a. **Demographic Parity**
This metric requires the model to produce positive outcomes at similar rates across demographic groups. It comes in handy in situations where there is a need to have equal opportunity among groups.
b. **Equalized Odds**
Equalized odds give attention to the error rates. It makes sure that false positives and false negatives are equally distributed among groups. In risk-taking professions such as healthcare or law enforcement, the measure aids in avoiding harm in disproportion.
c. **Individual Fairness**
According to this method, similar people must get similar results. It puts stress on coherence at the individual level.
d. **Predictive Parity**
It is a measure to ensure that different groups have the same degree of reliability in their predictions.

The selection of the appropriate fairness measure will depend on the application. As an example, in medical diagnosis, demographic parity may be less significant, so it is important to reduce false negatives. Therefore, fairness assessment must be situated and must be updated on a regular basis when there is a change in the model.

Table 11.3 presents the most important measures of fairness applied to assess and diagnose AI models. Both metrics concentrate on various types of equalities between the demographic groups. The demographic parity ensures that the model generates positive decisions at the same rate across all the groups, and it is widely adopted in loan applications or hiring applications. Equalized odds go further and demand the similarity of the false-positive rates as well as the true positive rates across groups, which is crucial in sensitive fields like medical diagnosis. Equal opportunity is concerned with the equal treatment of true positives specifically; the qualified individuals should not be rejected unfairly. Calibration determines if the predicted risk scores hold an equivalent meaning to all the groups; a risk score of 20%, for instance, should be equal in terms of the actual probability in the real-world. Predictive parity is a property whereby accuracy is matched within groups; that is, positive predictions are right at the same rate. This table gives a comparative view of the advantages and purposes of each fairness measure, and researchers can take the correct measure in their context.

11.7 AWARENESS AND INCLUSION DESIGN OF AI

Culture significantly shapes how individuals interpret information, express emotions, and interact with technology. Without the consideration of cultural differences, there is the risk of miscommunication, misunderstanding, and dissatisfaction in using AI systems. Culturally sensitive design implies knowledge of local practices, languages, values, and anticipations.

To illustrate, AI-based educational platforms should take into consideration the teaching styles and cultural interests in learning. The AI used in healthcare must not violate the cultural beliefs of illness and treatment. Chatbots intended for global deployment must be trained to understand diverse languages, dialects, and communication styles.

The inclusive AI design will promote co-creation across different communities. The use of local stakeholders in the development process will also enable developers to determine the culture-related aspects of the development that might be obscured by the technical view of the development. This kind of cooperation enhances user confidence, acceptance, and system usability.

Figure 11.5 presents a continuous design loop for developing AI systems that respect cultural diversity. It usually begins with gathering information from divergent cultural, social, and regional origins, meaning that the information set reflects the diversity of the real world. Context-aware feature engineering is the next process where feature selection and interpretation are done in consideration of cultural differences as opposed to sharing a single universal pattern. The model is then trained in alignment with the values; that is, it is trained to perform better as well as take ethical and

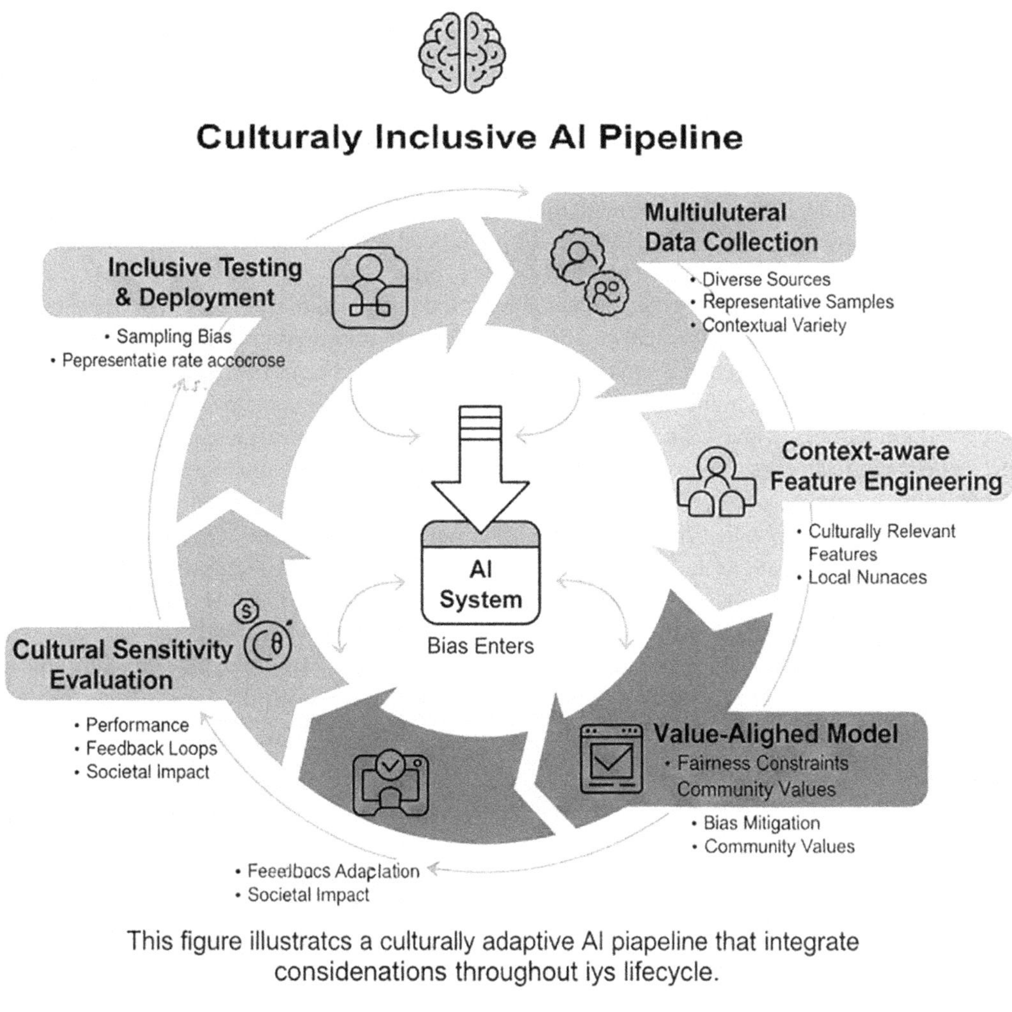

FIGURE 11.5 AI pipeline that is culturally inclusive.

cultural factors into consideration. The system is tested after training, and this is done by the cultural sensitivity, which in particular examines whether the model behaves in accordance with the various groups. Lastly, the model advances to inclusive testing, accountable deployment, and continuous auditing to ascertain continuous fairness as the culture becomes dynamic. The pipeline is based on the idea that cultural awareness should be integrated at every step of AI development.

Table 11.4 provides various design solutions that could be adopted by developers when developing AI systems that accommodate the cultural diversity and context of users. Contextualization is focused on the way AI is made to act in accordance with cultural expectations, for example, changing communication tone or style in chatbots. Linguistic inclusion identifies the necessity that AI tools should support various languages, scripts, and dialects, particularly for the low-resource language regions. Social value alignment, which will make the AI system mirror the values and priorities of the communities to which it is offered, is essential in such fields as healthcare or education. Participatory design promotes the integration of the members of the community in the development process to make them shape the system through their lived experience. This table shows that cultural sensitivity does not necessarily refer to language translation but also entails integrating local values and worldviews in the whole AI design process.

11.8 LEGAL AND ETHICAL REACTIONS TO DISCRIMINATION

Governments and other organizations across the world are coming up with principles that can be used to regulate AI risks. Moral principles stressed by moral systems include fairness, transparency, human control, and respect for human rights. The frameworks promote responsible data usage, designing ethical models, and keeping a close watch on the existence of discriminatory trends.

In the legal domain, some regions have introduced laws that mandate impact assessments, algorithmic audits, or model behavior documentation requirements. These laws seek to defend the people and demand that organizations be responsible for prejudiced results. Ethical and legal strategies are complementary as they provide moral and enforceable codes.

Figure 11.6 describes the coexistence of laws, ethics, and organizational policies in the development of a responsible AI ecosystem. It usually comes in the form of a layered diagram. Legal regulations, including General Data Protection Regulation (GDPR) and the European Union (EU) AI Act, require mandatory rules to use data, maintain privacy, manage risks, and be accountable and serve as the base. The ethical guidelines lie above the legal layer, and they offer principles such as fairness, transparency, and respect for human dignity. These values influence the interpretation and application of law by organizations. The second level is institutional policies, including internal engineering standards and codes of conduct, policies that encompass ethics into daily practice. On top, accountability mechanisms give organizations the ability to recognize, record, and rectify ill effects, which generate a transparent chain of responsibility. The figure illustrates that achieving ethical AI requires coordinated action across legal, ethical, and institutional domains that should support each other.

Table 11.5 summarizes key regulatory and ethical frameworks, which can be used to enforce responsible AI development in various regions. The EU has introduced the GDPR that places an

TABLE 11.4
Design Approaches for Cultural Sensitivity

Strategy	Description	Utilization
Contextualization	Speech patterns adaptation	Chatbots as reflections of culture
Language Support	Multilingualism	Voice assistant in local languages
Social Value Alignment	Community priorities in health apps	Health apps respecting local beliefs
Participatory Design	Engaging different communities in development	Co-designing education apps

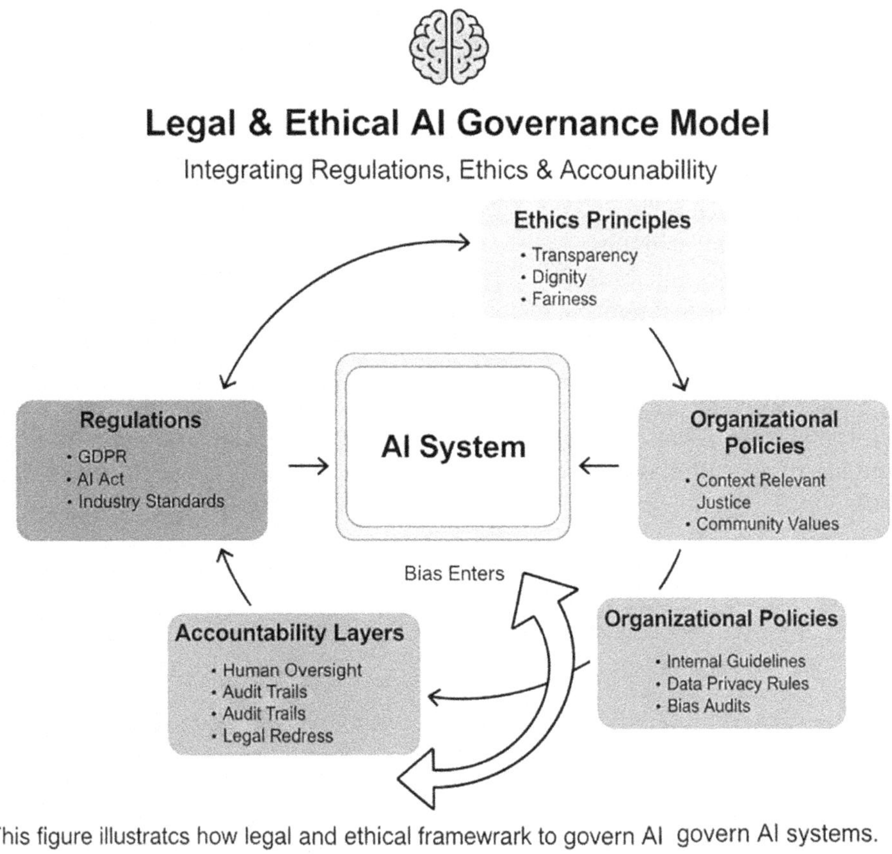

FIGURE 11.6 Legal ethical governance model.

TABLE 11.5
Ethics and Legal Issues Pertinent to AI Bias

Framework/Regulation	Region	Key Focus
GDPR	EU	Data rights, transparency
EU AI Act	EU	High-risk AI regulation
IEEE Ethically Aligned Design	International	Accountable AI principles
OECD AI Principles	International	Human-centered, fairness
NIST AI RMF	USA	Risk assessment, trustworthiness

emphasis on transparency, data rights, and protection against the risk of automated unfair decision-making. The EU AI Act is particular in terms of regulation of the high-risk AI applications that will be safe, fair, and accountable. The IEEE Ethically Aligned Design offers ethical principles worldwide, wherein emphasis is made on human well-being, fairness, and privacy. In its AI Principles, Organisation for Economic Co-operation and Development (OECD) emphasizes values that are human-friendly, transparent, robust, and accountable, which offer international guidance. The United States AI Risk Management Framework by National Institute of Standards and Technology (NIST) is a model that deals with how the organization can evaluate, track, and reduce the risk of the AI system, including bias. This comparison, as represented in the table, reveals that fairness is a universally common priority and that organizations have to conform to various similar standards.

11.9 EQUITY TRANSPARENCY AND AUDITING

Transparency implies that AI processes are interpreted by users, regulators, and developers. This may include model documentation, explainable AI approaches, or open reporting. Openness can be used to uncover bias and build trust.

The transparency also requires auditing. The internal audits verify that the system is beneficial to the objectives of fairness in the course of development. An independent evaluation is performed by external or third-party audits to minimize possible conflicts of interest. Audits particularly apply in areas with high stakes where biases may lead to severe damages. Conducting audits regularly keeps the level of fairness going because they introduce new data or updated versions of the model.

Figure 11.7 shows a dashboard that is used to monitor and inspect the behavior of an AI system in various groups of users. It normally presents an integration of statistical measures as well as visual

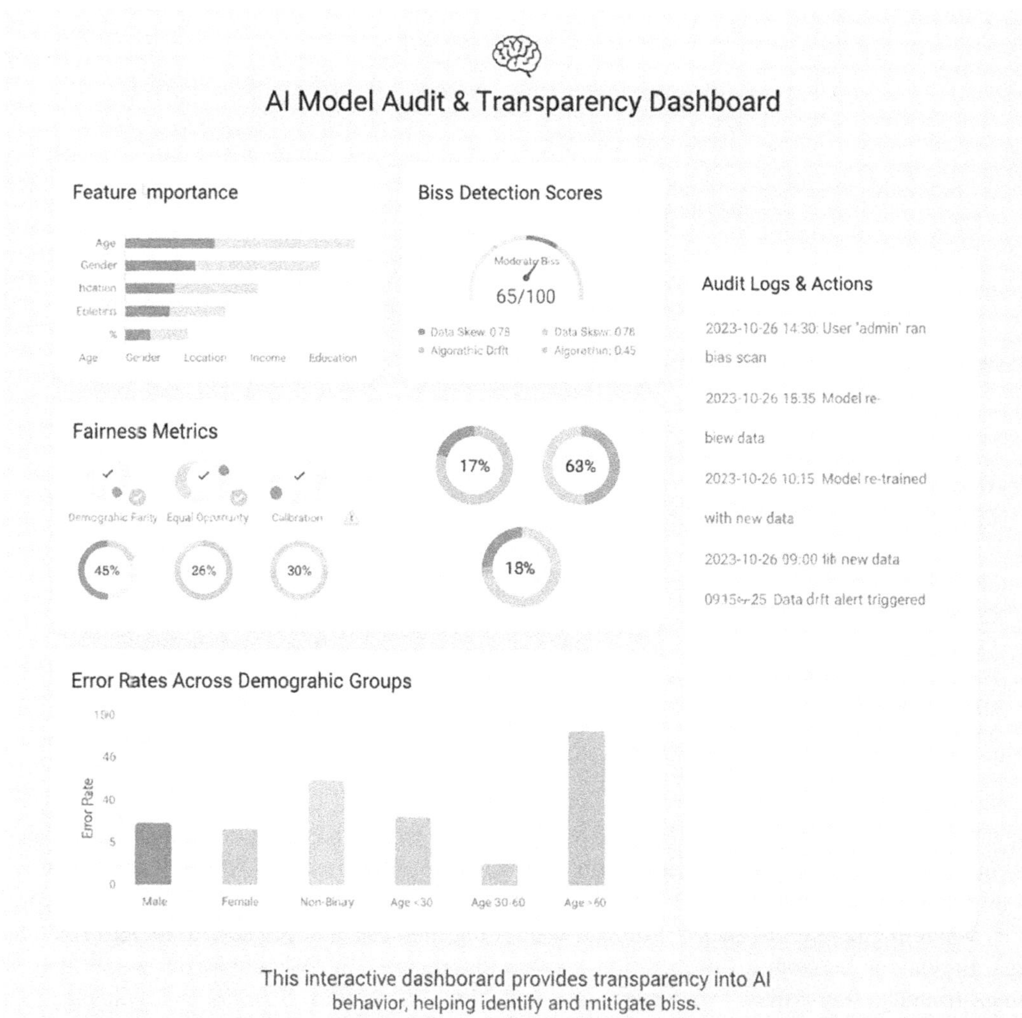

FIGURE 11.7 Transparency and audit dashboard.

summaries. The most important ones are feature importance charts, which indicate what factors the model is the most dependent on; the detection of bias metrics, which indicate the presence of possible unfairness; and fairness scores, which monitor the performance of the model using different definitions of fairness. The dashboard also contains audit logs that can trace the changes that have been made in the model as time goes by and the error rate comparison that can indicate that some groups have more mistakes than others. In total, the dashboard is a useful tool to foster transparency among the engineers, policymakers, and the public in the functioning of the system to make the AI more trusted and responsible.

11.10 CREATING MULTICULTURAL DATABASES TO INTERNATIONALIZE

A variety of data form the main component of developing AI that can be effective in different regions and cultures and also in language communities. Sampling of various geographic locations, age, and socioeconomic status will mean that models are exposed to a diverse experience. The diversity assists in enhancing the accuracy of models and lessens the chances of cultural or demographic isolation.

Ethical data collection practices are also required to build global datasets. The use of their data should be communicated to the communities, and their privacy maintained. Teamwork-based solutions—the role of the local specialists and the community-based members—involve efforts to avoid stereotyping and achieve cultural relevancy. Models that are trained with varied datasets are more robust, credible, and adaptable to real-world conditions.

Figure 11.8 employs a world map to pass a message about the necessity of constructing datasets that should capture the diversity of human populations. It also indicates the necessity of geographic

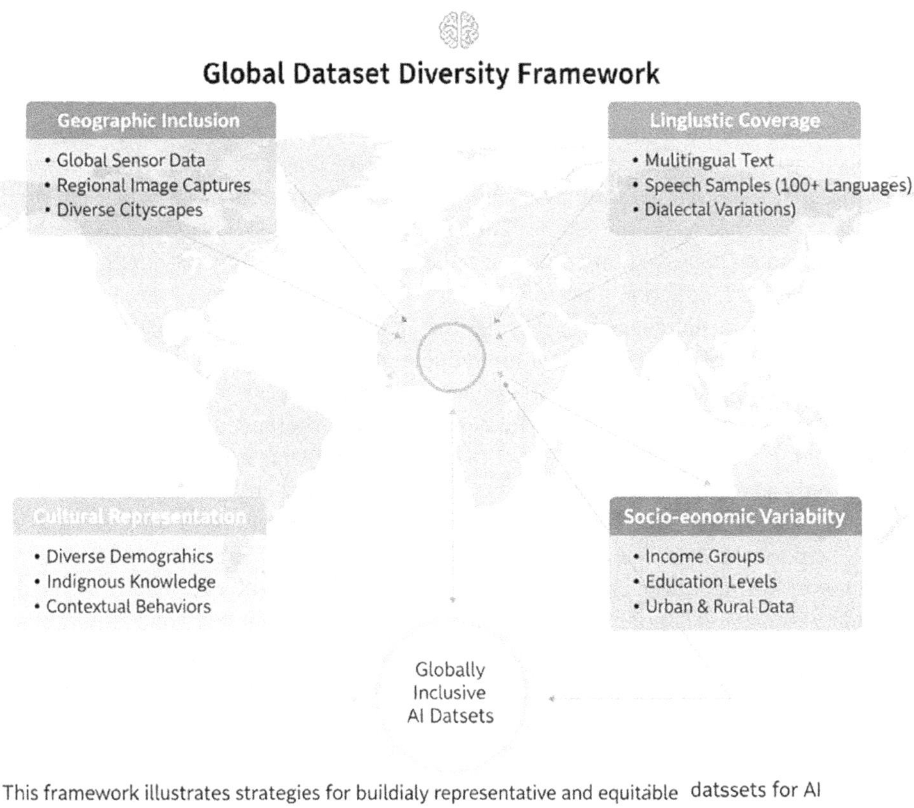

FIGURE 11.8 Diversity framework of global dataset.

representation so that the data acquired includes more than a limited group of countries and regions in the world. It also emphasizes the diversity of linguistic forms, which promotes the incorporation of numerous languages, dialects, and writing systems. In addition, the figure emphasizes the cultural representation, which puts focus on customs, objects, symbols, as well as behaviors that vary between societies. Lastly, it highlights the concept of socioeconomic variability, demonstrating why the involvement of people of varying income, education backgrounds, and access-to-technology settings is crucial. The combination of these dimensions will guarantee the non-overwesternization of AI models, as well as their bias toward high-income groups, but rather make them fair to global users.

11.11 RESPONSIBILITY IN THE DEVELOPMENT OF AI

Accountability would make organizations and developers responsible for the results created by AI systems. This involves recording decisions, transparency, and the provision of ways of allowing users to express concerns. Accountability can be enhanced by ethical review boards, which are internal oversight committees, and public disclosure policies.

The other factor is the ability to react promptly to the emergence of problems. In case a system has been discovered to deliver biased findings, the developers ought to examine the underlying cause, revise the model, and relay the enhancements effectively. Responsibility creates a sense of trust and accountability, which would make organizations stick to fairness and inclusiveness at all times in the AI lifecycle.

11.12 SUMMARY

In the responsible development of AI, bias, fairness, and cultural sensitivity have become the subject matter. The point, which this chapter stresses, is that the bias in AI cannot be caused by a single flaw most of the time; instead, it becomes a product of an interplay of unbalanced data, measurement errors, and algorithmic decisions coupled with deeply ingrained societal inequalities that can be expressed in the datasets on which current models are trained. Such biases can be left unchanged, and when this is the case, the AI-driven system may end up providing discriminative results unwillingly, for example, misclassifying people, or offering them unequal opportunities, or even proceeding to confirm the stereotype. The impact of such effects is enhanced by the fact that AI technologies can be deployed on a massive scale and affect the decision-making process in key areas such as healthcare, policing, finance, education, and public welfare.

Another key point in the chapter is that the bias reduction and its evaluation cannot be done without using a combination of technical and ethical actions. Measures of fairness demographic parity, equalized odds, and individual fairness are structured measures of disparity, and culturally aware design is an assurance that systems take into account differences in language, behavior, and values in communities across the world. This is a combination that is necessary as fairness should be perceived not only as mathematical equality but also as social and cultural sensitivity.

Equitable AI is also supported by transparency, auditing, and creating various datasets. Frequent auditing will help to reveal some kind of latent prejudices, and transparent documentation will help create confidence. Multicultural, cross-global datasets will assist in the elimination of blind spots in the model and will make AI applications reliable with diverse demographic and cultural members.

Lastly, there is the matter of accountability. Organizations should be devoted to continuous surveillance, ethics governing, and timely response to issues. A combination of these strategies forms an avenue to equitable, more inclusive, and human rights and cultural diversity-oriented AI systems. The chapter wraps up that AI development cannot be made responsible through a one-time effort, but rather an ongoing collaborative process among technologists, policymakers, and communities where AI is used on a day-to-day basis.

REFERENCES

Aiken, M., & Sloan, R. H. (2020). *The technological leviathan: Automation, AI, and the future of work*. Oxford University Press.

Alkhatib, A. (2021). To live in their utopia: Why algorithms should be designed to serve human values. *Harvard Business Review, 99*(4), 112–119. https://doi.org/10.1145/3411764.3445740

Balamurugan, G., Tyagi, A.K., & Richa, A. (2023). Survey on privacy preserving and trust building techniques of blockchain-based systems. In: *Privacy Preservation and Secured Data Storage in Cloud Computing*. IGI Global. DOI: 10.4018/979-8-3693-0593-5.ch019

Barocas, S., Hardt, M., & Narayanan, A. (2019). *Fairness and machine learning: Limitations and opportunities*. MIT Press.

Bender, E. M., Gebru, T., McMillan-Major, A., & Shmitchell, S. (2021). On the dangers of stochastic parrots. In *Proceedings of the 2021 ACM conference on fairness, accountability, and transparency* (pp. 610–623). ACM. https://doi.org/10.1145/3442188.3445922

Benjamin, R. (2019). *Race after technology: Abolitionist tools for the new Jim Code*. Polity Press.

Buolamwini, J., & Gebru, T. (2018). Gender shades: Intersectional accuracy disparities. *Proceedings of Machine Learning Research, 81*, 1–15.

Calo, R. (2021). The boundaries of algorithmic fairness. *Columbia Law Review, 121*(6), 1935–1980.

Chouldechova, A. (2017). Fair prediction with disparate impact. *Big Data, 5*(2), 139–152. https://doi.org/10.1089/big.2016.0047

Crawford, K. (2021). *Atlas of AI: Power, politics, and the planetary costs of artificial intelligence*. Yale University Press.

Creel, K. A., & Hellman, D. (2022). The ethics of algorithmic fairness. *Philosophy & Technology, 35*(3), 1–23.

Danks, D., & London, A. (2017). Algorithmic bias in autonomous systems. In *Proceedings of the 26th international joint conference on artificial intelligence* (pp. 4691–4697). https://doi.org/10.24963/ijcai.2017/654

Dwork, C., & Ilvento, C. (2018). Fairness under composition. *arXiv preprint arXiv:1806.06122*. https://doi.org/10.48550/arXiv.1806.06122

European Commission. (2021). *Proposal for a regulation laying down harmonised rules on artificial intelligence (AI Act)*. Publications Office of the European Union. https://eur-lex.europa.eu/legal-content/EN/TXT/?uri=CELEX:52021PC0206

Floridi, L., & Cowls, J. (2019). A unified framework of five AI ethics principles. *Harvard Data Science Review, 1*(1), 1–15. https://doi.org/10.1162/99608f92.8cd550d1

Friedman, B., & Nissenbaum, H. (1996). Bias in computer systems. *ACM Transactions on Information Systems, 14*(3), 330–347. https://doi.org/10.1145/230538.230561

Hashimoto, T., Srivastava, M., Namkoong, H., & Liang, P. (2018). Fairness without demographics. *NeurIPS, 2018*, 728–739.

Holstein, K., Wortman Vaughan, J., Daumé III, H., Dudík, M., & Wallach, H. (2019). Improving fairness in AI systems. In *Proceedings of the 2019 ACM conference on human factors in computing systems* (pp. 1–12). https://doi.org/10.1145/3290605.3300830

Jobin, A., Ienca, M., & Vayena, E. (2019). The global landscape of AI ethics guidelines. *Nature Machine Intelligence, 1*(9), 389–399. https://doi.org/10.1038/s42256-019-0088-2

Kleinberg, J., Mullainathan, S., & Raghavan, M. (2017). Inherent trade-offs in the fair determination of risk scores. *Proceedings of Innovations in Theoretical Computer Science, 43*, 1–23.

Kumari, S., Tyagi, A. K., Tiwari, S., & Kulshreshtha, G. (2025a). Sensors and digital twin for healthcare monitoring frameworks. In T. A. Nguyen (Ed.), *Digital twin, blockchain, and sensor networks in the healthy and mobile city (Chapter 10,* pp. 147–177*)*. Elsevier. https://doi.org/10.1016/B978-0-443-34174-8.00011-9

Kumari, S., Tyagi, A. K., Tiwari, S., & Singh, R. (2025b). Medical sensor network, edge computing and blockchain for efficient medical data exchange. In T. A. Nguyen (Ed.), *Digital twin, blockchain, and sensor networks in the healthy and mobile city (Chapter 11,* pp. 179–198*)*. Elsevier. https://doi.org/10.1016/B978-0-443-34174-8.00012-0

Mehrabi, N., Morstatter, F., Saxena, N., Lerman, K., & Galstyan, A. (2021). A survey on bias and fairness in machine learning. *ACM Computing Surveys, 54*(6), 1–35. https://doi.org/10.1145/3457607

Mishra, A. K., Tiwari, S., Tyagi, A. K., & Arowolo, M. O. (2024). Security, privacy, trust, and provenance issues in Internet of Things–based edge environment. In S. Pal, C. Savaglio, R. Minerva, & F. C. Delicato (Eds.), *IoT edge intelligence* (pp. 233–263). Springer. https://doi.org/10.1007/978-3-031-58388-9_8

Mitchell, M., Wu, S., Zaldivar, A., Barnes, P., & Vasserman, L. (2019). Model cards for model reporting. In *Proceedings of the conference on fairness, accountability, and transparency* (pp. 220–229). https://doi.org/10.1145/3287560.3287596

Mittelstadt, B. (2019). Principles alone cannot guarantee ethical AI. *Nature Machine Intelligence, 1*(11), 501–507. https://doi.org/10.1038/s42256-019-0114-4

Nair, M. M., & Tyagi, A. K. (2021). Privacy: History, statistics, policy, laws, preservation and threat analysis. *Journal of Information Assurance & Security*, *16*(1), 24–34.

Nair, M.M., & Tyagi, A.K. (2025). Transformative effects of emerging technologies on Industry 5.0 and Society 5.0: Current status, vision, issues, challenges, and opportunities for future. In: *Next Generation Data Science and Blockchain Technology for Industry 5.0*. Wiley. DOI: https://doi.org/10.1002/9781394245215.ch13, ISBN: 9781394245185.

Narayanan, A. (2018). Translation tutorial: 21 fairness definitions and their politics. *Fairness, Accountability, and Transparency (FAT) Workshop*. https://shubhamjain0594.github.io/post/tlds-arvind-fairness-definitions/

Noble, S. U. (2018). *Algorithms of oppression: How search engines reinforce racism*. NYU Press.

O'Neil, C. (2017). *Weapons of math destruction: How big data increases inequality and threatens democracy*. Crown Publishing.

Pasquale, F. (2020). *New laws of robotics: Defending human expertise in the age of AI*. Harvard University Press.

Raji, I. D., & Buolamwini, J. (2019). Actionable auditing. In *Proceedings of the AAAI/ACM conference on AI, ethics, and society* (pp. 429–435). https://doi.org/10.1145/3306618.3314244

Raji, I. D., Smart, A., White, R., Mitchell, M., Gebru, T., & Hutchinson, B. (2020). Closing the AI accountability gap. In *Proceedings of the 2020 ACM conference on fairness, accountability, and transparency* (pp. 33–44). https://doi.org/10.1145/3351095.3372873

Russell, S., & Norvig, P. (2021). *Artificial intelligence: A modern approach* (4th ed.). Pearson.

Selbst, A. D., Boyd, D., Friedler, S. A., Venkatasubramanian, S., & Vertesi, J. (2019). Fairness and abstraction in sociotechnical systems. In *Proceedings of the conference on fairness, accountability, and transparency* (pp. 59–68). https://doi.org/10.1145/3287560.3287598

Shin, D. (2021). The effects of explainability and causability on perception, trust, and acceptance: Implications for explainable AI. *International Journal of Human-Computer Studies, 146*, 102551. https://doi.org/10.1016/j.ijhcs.2020.102551

Suresh, H., & Guttag, J. (2019). A framework for understanding sources of harm in machine learning. *arXiv preprint arXiv:1901.10002.*

Taddeo, M., & Floridi, L. (2018). How AI can be a force for good. *Science, 361*(6404), 751–752. https://doi.org/10.1126/science.aat5991

Tyagi, A.K. (2021). Analysis of security and privacy aspects of blockchain technologies from smart era' perspective: The challenges and a way forward. In: *Recent Trends in Blockchain for Information Systems Security and Privacy* (pp. 1–17). DOI: https://doi.org/10.1201/9781003139737, eBook-ISBN: 9781003139737

Tyagi, A.K. (2025). Blockchain for smart hospital in Healthcare 5.0: modeling structure, challenges, and future emerging trends. In: *Human-Centric Integration of Next-Generation Data Science and Blockchain Technology*. Elsevier. DOI: https://doi.org/10.1016/B978-0-443-33498-6.00026-1, ISBN: 978-0-443-33498-6.

Tyagi, A.K. (2026). *Chapter 4 - Artificial intelligence–blockchain–Internet of Things–based smart healthcare services: literature review and future research directions, in the book: Smart Hospital Anatomy with Advanced Sensors Innovations in Patient Care*. Elsevier (pp. 49-61). https://doi.org/10.1016/B978-0-443-45875-0.00005-3, ISBN: 978-0-443-45875-0.

Tyagi, A., Kumari, S., & Tiwari, S. (2024c). Internet of Things for smart healthcare: A survey. In A. K. Sharma, N. Chanderwal, S. Tyagi, & P. Upadhyay (Eds.), *Future of AI in medical imaging (Chapter 2).* IGI Global. https://doi.org/10.4018/979-8-3693-2359-5.ch002

Tyagi, A. K., & Tiwari, S. (2024a). Blockchain-enabled smart healthcare applications in 6G networks. In A. K. Tyagi (Ed.), *Digital twin and blockchain for smart cities (Chapter 20).* Wiley. https://doi.org/10.1002/9781394303564.ch20

Tyagi, A. K., Tripathi, K., Tiwari, S., & Kaushik, S. (2025). An efficient technique for privacy preservation, trusted and secure patient-centric services in smart healthcare. In *Proceedings of the 6th international conference on recent trends in communication & intelligent systems (ICRTCIS 2025)* (pp. 31–47). IET. https://doi.org/10.1049/icp.2025.2731

UNESCO. (2021). *Recommendation on the ethics of artificial intelligence*. UNESCO Publishing.

Veale, M., & Binns, R. (2017). Fairer machine learning in the public sector. *Government Information Quarterly, 34*(2), 161–169. https://doi.org/10.1016/j.giq.2016.12.004

Wang, Z., Chen, J., & Liu, H. (2022). Cultural inclusiveness in AI systems: A global review. *AI & Society, 37*(4), 1521–1535.

Whittaker, M., Alper, M., Etlinger, S., & Crawford, K. (2019). *A disability rights approach to algorithmic fairness*. AI Now Institute.

Williams, R. (2020). Algorithmic accountability: A legal review. *Information & Communications Technology Law, 29*(3), 252–273.

Zhang, B., & Dafoe, A. (2019). *Artificial intelligence: American attitudes and trends*. Center for the Governance of AI, Future of Humanity Institute. https://dx.doi.org/10.2139/ssrn.3312874

Zou, J. Y., & Schiebinger, L. (2018). AI can be sexist and racist—It's time to make it fair. *Nature, 559*(7714), 324–326. https://doi.org/10.1038/d41586-018-05707-8

12 Ethical and Psychological Implications of AI Surveillance

12.1 INTRODUCTION

Artificial intelligence (AI)-based surveillance technologies now affect many aspects of daily life. The cameras, the wearables, the biometric sensors, the facial recognition devices, and the algorithmic surveillance systems work silently in the background gathering and processing the data related to the movements, emotions, and choices of people. The use of early detection, predictive analytics, and continuous monitoring has significantly transformed traditional clinical care. Psychiatric facilities employ AI to detect emotional distress by monitoring vital signs; hospitals can use AI to identify them; elder-care homes use AI to track movement to detect falls or behavioral changes.

Though these systems can potentially render the life of people much safer, efficient, and customized, they raise a major ethical question: How far can we go in the name of safety? Such constant tracking may create feelings of lost autonomy, unease, and mistrust among many individuals. When it comes to institutions, the question is how to use AI in a responsible manner without further violating privacy and human dignity.

These issues are covered in this chapter that talks about how AI surveillance affects ethical decision-making, personal liberty, psychological responses, and regulation. It attempts to provide a sane perspective of the possibility and risks of the surveillance that is driven by AI, especially concerning those scenarios that entail the vulnerability of individuals.

12.2 LITERATURE REVIEW

The swift development of AI, Internet of Things (IoT), and edge technologies has revolutionized the manner in which the modern systems respond to environmental surveillance, intelligent infrastructure, healthcare, and robotics, as well as intelligent decision-making. The recent research literature focuses on distributed learning, security, intelligent automation, and the human-centered design in various fields. This review is based on the knowledge of 36 major studies, which report the impact of technology, methodology gaps, and upcoming challenges.

The initial innovations in environmental monitoring on the smart side were due to edge computing and collaborative learning. Abdalla et al. (2023) showed the effect of federated learning in minimizing data transmission and enhanced privacy in the monitoring of large-scale environment. Their contribution is consistent with the points mentioned by Nair et al. (2025), who drew attention to the weak medical and environmental data systems, particularly in terms of unauthorized access. Similarly, Allen and Wallach (2015) determined that security weaknesses exist in e-health infrastructures and that encrypted and decentralized systems are required. These difficulties were also raised in the work of Anderson and Rainie (2020) and Tyagi (2021), who suggested using

DOI: 10.1201/9781003658344-15

multi-layer blockchain protocols to protect data exchange in smart cities. Collectively, these articles help accentuate a preliminary requirement of privacy-saving intelligence throughout disseminated ecosystems.

Recent literature also depicts a growing trend toward sustainable and integrated smart-city development. Calvo and Peters (2019), DeCamp and Lindvall (2020) and Nair et al. (2021) examined the role of IoT-based monitoring systems in supporting the development of green cities using real-time analytics, and Floridi (2018) and Harari (2018) investigated the concept of user-centric smart services, which are dynamically adjusted to the life of the city. Sustainability also overlaps with solid-waste management, in which Huang and Rust (2021), Jobin et al. (2019) and Kellmeyer (2019) found that waste collection and routing using IoT can substantially lower the environmental impact. Kroll (2018) were able to introduce a wider viewpoint of governance and claimed that digital infrastructure, transparency, and citizen engagement are the crucial pillars of sustainable urban innovation.

One of the biggest trends in fields is distributed or federated learning to decrease the computational burden and enhance resiliency. Lepri et al. (2018) and Kumari et al. (2025a) also suggested an edge-cloud collaborative model to detect anomalies in utilities, and Mittelstadt (2019) used techniques of federation to protect smart grids against cyberattacks. Sharon (2020) and Kumari et al. (2025b) also pointed out that edge intelligence reduces latency and increases the reliability of decisions in mission-critical applications. To add to these concepts, Shneiderman (2020) categorized both the fog and edge architectures of the IoT that enable the development of scalable, energy-aware decision systems. Hence, these works indicate that decentralization plays the key role in the construction of secure and low-latency, AI-based infrastructures.

The overlapping of AI and ethics has also had its fair share of attention. According to the Vaishnav (2023), fairness, transparency, and accountability are the essential success factors of trustful AI implementation. This perception was reflected by Zuboff (2019) and Mishra et al. (2024) who demonstrated that the proper management of data is essential with the increase of organizational digital reach. Another security aspect discussed by Ghaffarian and Shahriari (2017) is the role of malware detection based on AI to improve the cybersecurity of organizations. Calvo (2019) and Tyagi (2025) validated integrity checks backed up by blockchain, which protects integrity-free data records in AI-powered functions. All these works indicate that ethical integration must be built into system design rather than treated as optional.

In industrial robotics, advances have been made in rehabilitation and factory automation as well as human support. Kellmeyer (2019) and Tyagi and Tiwari (2024a) made a thorough overview of the wearable robotic exoskeletons and proved that adaptive control mechanisms have the potential to support a personal rehabilitation process. Kroll (2018) had extended to incorporate smart wearable devices that have AI mobility assistants. Harari (2018) outlined similar innovations in exoskeletons and mentioned the weaknesses of torque accuracy and patient safety. Huang and Rust (2021) and Balamurugan et al. (2023) also explored robotics as an instrument of remote inspections and demonstrated that autonomous drones can be helpful in supporting the effective monitoring of an infrastructure. All these works are pointers of a trend in the research of robotics in which it is increasingly adaptive, human centered, and safety critical.

The significance of cybersecurity will only rise with the rise in the threats to the IoT devices. Jobin et al. (2019) took a comprehensive review of the vulnerability of IoT, implying the importance of the concept of authentication, anomaly detection, and secure routing in the trustful operations. The authors shed light on data standardization as a supplement to the smart cities to prevent interoperability failures (Lepri et al. 2018). An identical problem is also reflected in Mittelstadt (2019), who examined AI-based intrusion detection systems, and in Huang and Rust (2021) and Tyagi et al. (2024c), who have examined lightweight authentication protocols to secure resources in resource-restricted IoT networks. This is what leads to these contributions, which give rise to the need to have integrated solutions of cybersecurity that are adaptable to the evolving digital ecosystems.

AI and machine learning are also impacting healthcare, environmental forecasting, and emergency services. As an example, Lepri et al. (2018) and Tyagi et al. (2025) have demonstrated that deep learning can be applied to enhance the capacity to forecast air quality, and Kellmeyer (2019) have utilized hybrid neural models to track health. In their paper, Anderson (2020) and Rajani et al. (2022) came up with bio-inspired optimization algorithms that optimize the performance of computers in diverse tasks, one being healthcare diagnosis. Shneiderman (2020), Kroll (2018) suggested the use of intelligent-decision systems to aid in the emergency response because AI is important in high-stakes situations. All these pieces of evidence reveal that creative prediction models are being involved in the decision-making processes to become more active, reactive, and precise.

Regarding communication systems, 5G and 6G technologies are accelerating the joining process of AI and cyber–physical systems. DeCamp (2020) have stated the importance of resource orchestrating AI-enabled 5Gs. Harari (2018) and Nair et al. (2021) described the potential of the 6G-AI synergy to increase industrial automation, and Mittelstadt (2019) explained the relevance of trustful governance in 6G ecosystems. In addition, Lepri et al. (2018) demanded the problems of bias and unfairness in the models of machine learning deployed in the networks. The convergence of communication systems with AI and ethics emerges as a critical theme in these works.

The issue of sustainability and energy efficiency is apparently one of those that continuously reoccurs. Lepri et al. (2018) discussed the application of AI in smart building to make the most out of energy, and Vaishnav (2023) provided a review of the process of intelligent-grid automation through the use of IoT. Jobin et al. (2019) researched the planning of renewable energy using the assistance of smart algorithms. These contributions are consistent with the quickly emerging models of green and resilient infrastructure.

Lastly, other studies prove that human factors, accessibility, and usability are important. Zuboff (2019) examined user perception and trust in smart-city platforms, and Floridi (2018) examined socio-behavioral factors defining the adoption of smart technology. Further efforts of several researchers in the previous decade associated the necessity of ethical logistics systems that do not rely solely on automation but consider social responsibility. The combination of these lines of thought helps to point out that technological progress needs to be in accordance with human values, trust, and lived experiences.

The literature shows significant advances in the fields of smart systems, robotics, AI governance, and distributed intelligence. Nevertheless, there are still some challenges in data privacy, interoperability, cybersecurity, fairness, system integration, and real-world scalability. All the reviewed papers demonstrate the significant lack of holistic frameworks by which intelligence, security, sustainability, ethics, and human-centric design can be brought together so that the next-generation digital ecosystem can be robust, transparent, and socially responsible.

12.3 DIGITAL SURVEILLANCE IN CLINICAL SETTING

The clinical setting is also becoming more dependent on AI systems to assist with the management of patients. Predictive analytics is used by hospitals to detect deterioration, by mental health clinics to track speech patterns to detect distress, and by rehabilitation centers to measure progress by watching body movements. Wearables and remote monitoring systems enable the physicians to keep an eye on patients even when they are not in the hospital.

Safety is the main ethical reason to conduct such surveillance. Constant observation can eliminate the occurrence of medical emergencies, raise awareness of clinicians about minor changes, and deliver accuracy in care. As an illustration, AI can be used to point to early indicators of cardiac failure or suicidal thoughts, analyzing the behavioral patterns that humans might otherwise ignore.

Nevertheless, clinical digital surveillance must be approached cautiously. These settings have a habit of taking patients who are already weak. They are not always comfortable, but because of their medical condition, they feel obliged to be monitored. When surveillance is taken too far, such

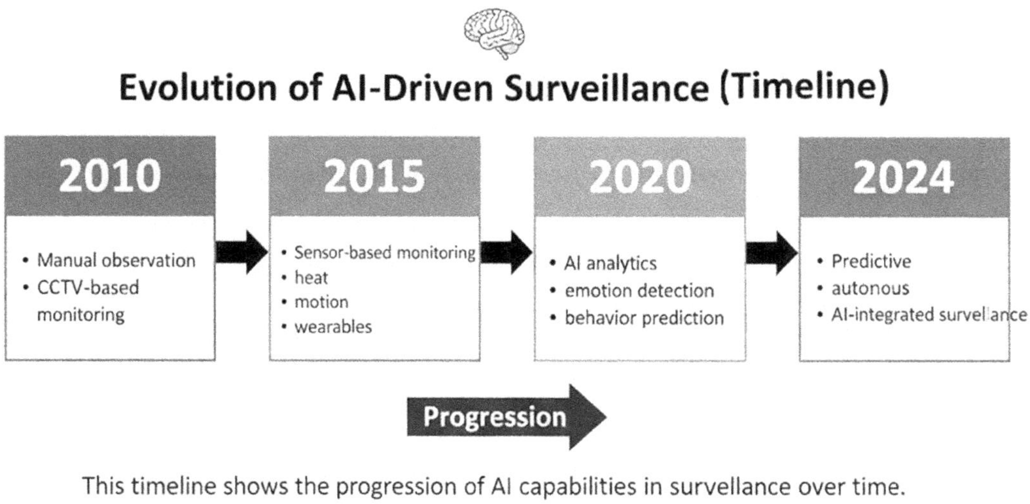

FIGURE 12.1 Development of AI-based surveillance in healthcare.

as when vital signs, tone of voice, or social interactions are monitored, it can be an overstep into the realm of ethical issues.

Clinicians have to make sure that observing is not more than the patient values, not more than it is necessary, and not against personal dignity. It is often difficult to distinguish between necessary safety monitoring and intrusive surveillance.

Figure 12.1 is usually introduced as a ring or a cyclic diagram to indicate where bias can be introduced into an AI system at various stages of its progress. It brings out four spaces of inequality where injustice can be created or increase with time. The first one, data bias, presents itself when the data on which the model is trained is missing, biased, historically skewed by discrimination, or has measurement errors. This flawed basis in turn affects the second step, which is algorithmic bias, which comes up as a result of decisions during model construction, including the way features are selected, the weight factor they receive, or tuning parameters. Besides, there is human bias that is involved in the entire process, as developers, annotators, and decision-makers might subconsciously embed their assumptions or subjective judgments into the system. Lastly, there is deployment bias when the model is introduced into real-life situations and it will act unjustly by not fitting the settings or access to the technology is inequitable or a constraint in the implementation of the system. Altogether, the figure sends the message that discriminatory power has no one source but instead a dynamic, ongoing difficulty, which needs to be addressed at all phases of the AI lifecycle.

12.4 EMOTIONAL/BEHAVIORAL DATA COLLECTION

The AI systems have become capable of collecting and processing numerous emotional and behavioral cues, and people are not always aware of the amount of data being collected. These systems can detect facial expressions, voice tone, body position, walking style, and some physiological signs like changes in heart rate. The algorithms are using these signals to guess the mood of a person, whether he/she is stressed, nervous, depressed, or even prone to dangerous behavior. Even though this may aid in timely interventions in healthcare or crisis management, there exist grave ethical questions. Emotions are so personal, and gathering them can be intrusive, especially when individuals have not consented and are unaware that their emotional data is being analyzed. There are also the cultural differences, neurodiversity, and individual personality characteristics, which may be read inappropriately by the algorithm, which results in erroneous judgments. Consequently, individuals may

TABLE 12.1
Significant Themes in AI Surveillance Literature

Theme	Description	Key Authors
Ethical Risks	AI influencing opaque decision-making, prejudice, and discrimination	Crawford (2021); Pasquale (2015)
Privacy and Data Control	Consent, transparency, and data abuse issues	Nissenbaum (2010); Solove (2021)
Psychological Effects	Anxiety, stress, and behavior change	Selinger and Lyons (2020); Reis and Madsen (2022); Tyagi (2026)
Governance Weaknesses	Weak regulatory frameworks and accountability	Gasser and Almeida (2017); Vaishnav and Raji (2023)
Emotion AI Threats	Poor results of interpreting affective signals, profiling	Gibson and Hanson (2022); Abdalla et al. (2023)

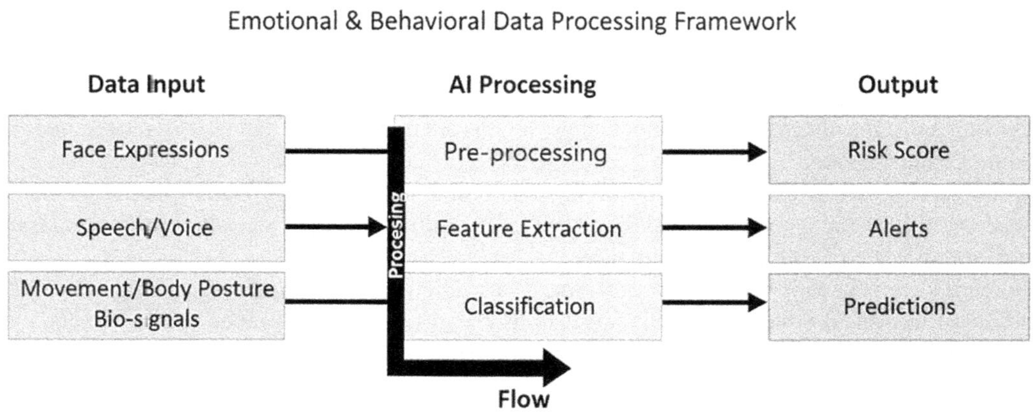

FIGURE 12.2 Framework of emotional and behavioral data collection.

alter their behavior unnaturally to avoid being misclassified, which causes emotional tension. The increase in the use of emotional and behavioral data presents potential benefits to better care and chances of misinterpretation, stigmatization, and deprivation of personal privacy (Table 12.1).

Figure 12.2 depicts the fact that the underrepresentation in reality is multiplied when transferred into digital systems. This starts with some groups of people or communities that seem underrepresented in the data utilized to create AI models. This directly results in disproportionate datasets, with certain groups being heavily represented when compared to others that are scarcely represented.

By training a model on such unequal information, one of the effects is distorted learning, that is, it cannot predict or clearly comprehend the group that is not well represented. Consequently, the system will generate a disproportionate prediction performance, and it will normally perform much less well or less reliably in relation to minority population groups. These performance disparities add to the wider harm of a society, which serves to strengthen the inequities that led to the disparity in the first place. The diagram especially highlights the way that this negative feedback loop can create a gradual entrenching of preexisting disadvantages unless active action is put into place to fix the situation.

12.5 A TRADE-OFF BETWEEN PRIVACY AND SAFETY

It is easy to see that the most notable defense of AI surveillance is safety. AI-driven monitoring can be used to avoid accidents and detect emergencies and improve security in hospitals, prisons, elder care homes, and campuses. However, privacy is not only an individualistic decision; it is also a fundamental human right, which is associated with dignity, trust, and mental health.

To achieve a balance on privacy and safety, a contextual approach is required. Constant monitoring of a patient might be acceptable ethically in high-risk settings, such as in the intensive care unit or psychiatric ward, when it helps to avoid life-threatening events. Conversely, in general hospital wards or open environments, there is less justification for extensive or intensive monitoring.

Transparency is also a component of this balance. People have the right to determine what is overseen, why it is carried out, the people who will access the information, and the duration in which the data will be retained. Ethical conduct dictates that surveillance practices must be articulated by the institutions and that individuals should have the ability to question or refuse unnecessary surveillance.

12.6 AGREEABLENESS, INDEPENDENCE, AND LIMITS

Consent is quite an important concern when it comes to the question of the ethical admissibility of AI surveillance, yet in numerous real-world scenarios it is either partial or coercive. Hospital patients, workers, students, or individuals in nursing homes may sometimes think that they are not actually given the option to choose against monitoring in instances where the monitoring is not comfortable to them. For consent to be meaningful, individuals must clearly understand the data being collected, how it will be interpreted, to whom it will be disclosed, and what effects may be shown. They must also be allowed the real freedom to refuse unnecessary monitoring without any form of negative ramifications. Autonomy involves more than simply asking for permission but providing people with an opportunity to question the automated decisions, demand that their data be changed, or withdraw their consent in case they change their mind. Setting boundaries is particularly essential whereby surveillance is meant to capture intimate factors of life, including feelings, discussions, or even social behavior. Ethical practice dictates that there should be a distinct difference between what needs to be monitored in the interest of safety and what is an excessive intrusion of personal experiences so that one is left with a feeling of control over their lives.

12.7 PSYCHOLOGICAL EFFECT OF BEING UNDER SURVEILLANCE

The constant surveillance of the AI systems may affect the mental and emotional state of a person quite notably. Although surveillance can be proposed as the safeguard, in most cases people feel a force to change their behavior as they are aware that they are being recorded or analyzed. This has the potential to reduce natural self-expression and encourage people to behave in ways they believe are more acceptable or normal within the system. Over time, this can create anxiety, self-consciousness, and a constant feeling of being judged. The fear of an algorithm misunderstanding their actions can also increase stress or make people reticent. Over monitoring in a hospital or other care facilities may leave individuals feeling distrusted or dehumanized, as though they have been reduced to data points rather than treated as humans. The overall psychological impact is similar to the well-known phenomenon of being observed, which causes the personality to change slightly through constant observation, loss of autonomy, and emotional fatigue. It is a psychological weight of constant surveillance that shows the need to focus on what the actual necessity is and make sure human empathy is the core of the care (Table 12.2).

12.8 HUMAN MONITORS IN AI

Wherever AI surveillance is applied, it is necessary to have human supervision, as no algorithm can be able to capture not only the emotional circumstances or the intricacies of morality but also the underlying cultural interpretation of behaviors. Although AI systems are capable of identifying

TABLE 12.2
Ethical Challenges of AI-Based Emotion Recognition

Ethical Concern	Theory	Representative Citations
Accuracy and Misinterpretation	Models falsely read emotions between cultures	Raji and Buolamwini (2019); Kellmeyer (2019)
Coercive Monitoring	Over-surveillance cuts down on autonomy	Lupton (2016); Selinger and Lyons (2020)
Psychological Damage	Incessant judgment produces anxiety	Reis and Madsen (2022); Tyagi (2026)
Stigmatization	System classifies people as high-risk individuals	Crawford (2021)
Unconsciousness of Consent	Unconscious of emotional tracking users	Tene and Polonetsky (2013)

patterns and issue warnings, they cannot provide empathy or nuanced moral judgment to read the warning signs in the right manner. Human professionals include clinicians, caregivers, or supervisors who are essential in reviewing AI-generated information before making decisions. This means that alerts are not automatically operated upon, although their presence ensures that the system may have mistaken stress, confusion, or harmless behavior as risky conduct. Human supervision also helps maintain accountability, as humans are better able to detect bias, mistakes, or loopholes in the reasoning of the AI. In the case that humans are still in a central position in decision-making, AI is the facilitating tool instead of becoming a dominant power. Such a cooperative model is a balance between the efficiency of machine analysis and the moral responsibilities and compassion that could only be offered by human judgment.

Figure 12.3 describes a linear chain of events, which looks distinct and linear in its nature, that can cause some socially detrimental consequences as a result of seemingly technical decisions. The channel starts with biased information, possibly with historical disparities within it or displaying biased actions ingrained within the society. When such biased data is applied to create a model, it will result in systematic misclassification, for example, increased false positive rates or misclassifications that disproportionately impact some groups. These false classifications lead to dissimilar outcomes in critical areas of decisions such as job hiring, housing suggestions, or credit authorizations where precision and justice are essential. The following step focuses on the adverse impacts on protected groups, who are deprived of opportunities or subject to increased examination or unjust punishment in response to these algorithmic equals. The pipeline ends in support of current inequalities, in which the AI decisions are viewed as evidence-based or neutral and hence provide the benefit of legitimacy to discriminatory results. Figure 12.3 highlights the fact that prejudice, when unchecked, is a vicious cycle.

12.9 ETHICS OF SURVEILLANCE OF VULNERABLE POPULATIONS

The process of surveillance is even more sensitive when vulnerable populations like children, elderly people, mentally ill patients, or those in institutional care are involved. These groups are usually not able to give informed consent, question surveillance, or establish their ground rules. Due to their reliance on the caregiver or the institutions, they may be compelled to concede to invasive surveillance despite the fact that it violates their dignity or emotional ease. There are ethical issues in regard to the AI systems classifying people as high risk or problematic due to behavior that the algorithm does not comprehend completely. These labels can reinforce stigma, influence how individuals are treated, or lead to unnecessary interventions. The vulnerable populations are also exposed to over-surveillance whereby all activities are monitored more closely, as it is believed that they are in need of protection. To prevent these evils, institutions have to explain why each level of monitoring is justified, why the amount of data they collect should focus on its purpose with the most essential

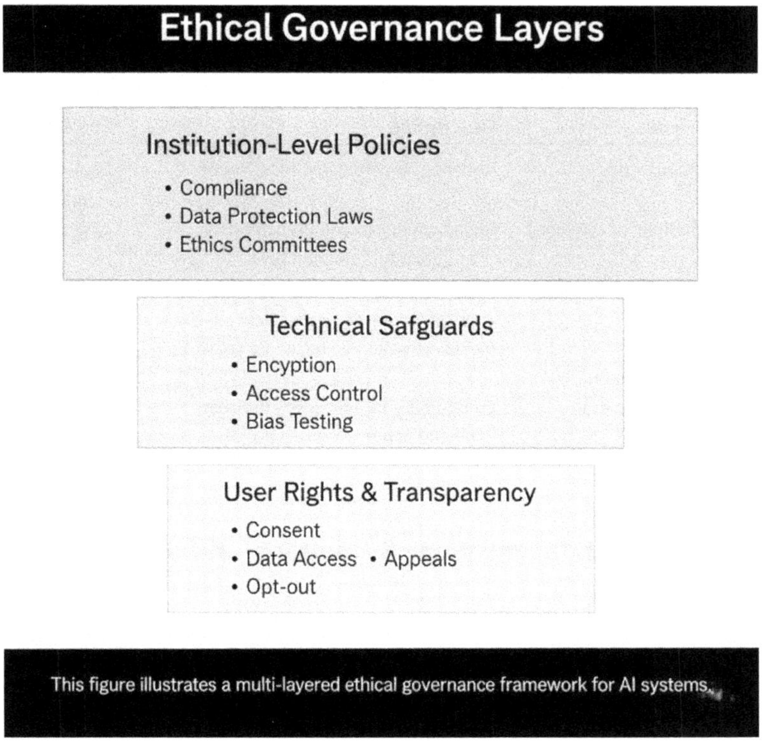

FIGURE 12.3 Layers of ethical governance of AI surveillance.

need, and why additional protections are necessary to prevent harm to those who may not be able to easily represent themselves. The practice of ethics requires a patient-focused and sensitive approach that puts emphasis on respect, lack of intrusion, and boundary demarcation (Table 12.3).

12.10 POLICY FRAMEWORKS FOR RESPONSIBLE USE

It is important to formulate powerful policy frameworks to make sure that AI surveillance is used ethically and responsibly. Policies define how data is collected, who owns it, and what restrictions apply. It is necessary to have open communication; the institutions should properly define the aim of monitoring and procedures under it. The policies should also limit the information gathered to that which is crucial in safety or care and does not involve too much or useless surveillance. Constant audits would be crucial to examine the cases of algorithmic bias, discriminatory results, and technical malfunctions that can affect people unfairly. There should also be accountability mechanisms to assign responsibility when data is misused or when harmful decisions are made using AI outputs. Moreover, by having independent oversight bodies or ethics committees, one can guarantee compliance, and high-risk cases can be reviewed. An effective policy framework is a foundation of trust and fairness and a way of ensuring that surveillance technologies are not abused in both clinical and non-clinical settings.

12.11 CONTROLLING DATA SENSITIVITY AND DATA CONTROL

Responsible data management is among the best ethical AI surveillance practices because such systems can hold very sensitive data concerning the health, moods, routines, and personal behavior of persons. The security of this data starts with safe storage, encryption, and with limited access to

TABLE 12.3
Surveillance Perils among At-risk Populations

Population	Risk Type	Description	Key Authors
Elderly Patients	Autonomy loss	Reliance on automated monitoring	Eitel-Porter (2021); DeCamp and Lindvall (2020)
Children	Limitations of consent	Incompetence to comprehend data implications completely	Ajunwa (2020)
Mental Health Patients	Emotional profiling	Systems make inferences about mood or intent that are not correct	Gibson and Hanson (2022)
Low-Income Groups	Surveillance discrimination	Increased policing and social control	Brayne (2020); O'Neil (2016)
Employees	Behavioral scoring	Productivity monitoring influences mental health	Bélanger and James (2023)

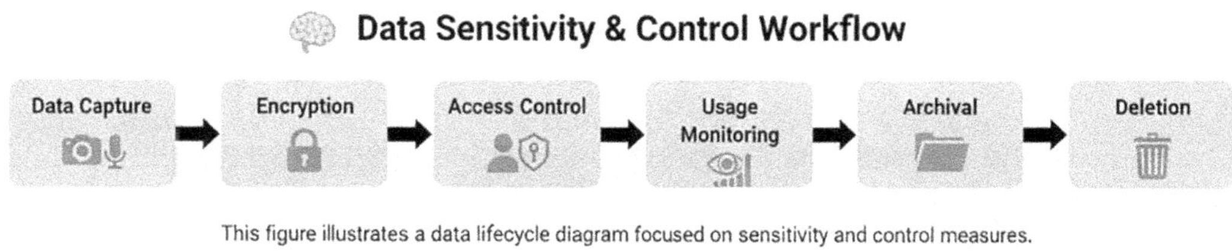

FIGURE 12.4 Information sensitivity and control process in AI surveillance.

avoid the unauthorized access or abuse. People also ought to have an incentive to control their data, whether it is what has been gathered, requested, or deleted as unnecessary. The data should not be kept longer than it is required, and institutions should not use the data for other purposes like advertising, profiling, or external evaluation unless it is clearly considered. The provision of sensitive data to the third parties must be highly controlled and transparent. Institutions can minimize the psychological and ethical risks of surveillance by providing individuals with greater control and making sure that the collected and retained information is limited to that which is necessary. When the data is managed in a proper way, it prevents the invasion of privacy, and in addition, it aids in preserving trust and emotional health among the monitored individuals.

In Figure 12.4, the key mathematical definitions to measure fairness in AI systems are introduced, and the connection between each other is demonstrated. It presents common concepts like Demographic Parity, an attempt to equalize the positive outcome rates of groups, and Equalized Odds that needs the true positive and false positive rates of all groups to be equal. A narrower parameter, Equal Opportunity, is aimed at leveling actual positive rates. Predictive Parity and Calibration are also incorporated in the diagram and guarantee that the accuracy of positive predictions is equal across groups and that the confidence scores of a model reflect actual outcomes at the same rates across different communities, respectively. The figure notes that these fairness measures tend to be incompatible because of the constraints that exist in maths, such that when one is optimized, another may be traded with. Consequently, practitioners will have to pick the most appropriate fairness objectives that would be most appropriate in the scenario, ethics, and desired effect of the AI system.

12.12 SUMMARY

AI surveillance has become an influential and fast-growing instrument in healthcare and institutional and daily settings, providing a previously unknown range of opportunities to recognize risks, predict behavior, and assist in timely interventions. In this chapter, we have discussed the way in which these technologies reconstitute the process of ethical decision-making, personal autonomy, and psychological well-being. Although AI-based surveillance has the potential to make the world a safer place, especially by detecting the first signs of medical stress, self-harm, or emergencies and informing the caregivers about them, it also increases the complexity of perception of observation and control in the lives of individuals. The two-sidedness of the AI surveillance implies that each of the advantages has an attached cost of ethics, and it is vital to think big about it.

One of the key issues that is highlighted in the chapter is the war between protection and privacy. AI systems are prone to retrieving incredibly sensitive data, including emotional indicators, behavioral trends, and biometrics. Although this knowledge can contribute to a better clinical awareness and thus offer more personalized care, the knowledge can also pose a threat of infiltrating into personal mental and emotional space of the people. The notion of an algorithm being able to predict a person's mood or even their thoughts can be quite uncomfortable, may build mistrust, and can make people feel powerless. These problems are even worse when it comes to prolonged surveillance or when the subjects are not certain of the chance to refuse surveillance without any negative effect.

The other significant issue is the psychological impact of being made to be monitored everywhere. Surveillance, despite its well-meaning intentions, can alter people's behavior and speech. This may eventually lead to the development of high anxiety, low sense of autonomy, or persistent sense of being judged. The emotional stress of this sort speaks of the need to perceive surveillance as a technical device as well as an embodied experience that may affect the sense of identity, dignity, and self-esteem. The effect on psychology is mainly high among the vulnerable populations like the aged, children, and patients in hospital settings, where they may have already had a feeling of loss of control in their respective settings.

Human control should take charge of the ethical principles in AI observation. Patterns are spotted more quickly by algorithms than by human beings, yet contexts and subtleties are inaccessible to algorithms. The human judgment in the decision-making process should remain basic, and the analysis of notifications, the elimination of misunderstanding, and the caring approach to the intervention ought to be employed. In the absence of such a balance, automated systems will be prone to perpetuating biases, making unfair judgments, or reducing people to pieces of information instead of people.

Data governance practices and policy frameworks are also important in the creation of responsible use. Having clear instructions on how data should be collected, stored, shared, and kept means that people understand how their data is being utilized. Tight access management, bias audits, and transparency are used to keep the accounts responsible and discriminate against misuse. Ethical policies should also be aware of the unique weakness of some groups of people and should offer extra safeguards to the population that cannot defend itself.

Finally, the chapter points out that AI surveillance must be conducted sensitively and respectfully, avoiding the use of AI on human dignity. The improvement of safety and care can be significantly increased with the help of technology, but only under the effective ethical standards, stringent control, and valuable consent. The creation of AI systems that are more empathetic, just, and less concerned with individual rights will make sure that surveillance does not undermine well-being but instead promotes it. With the ever-increasing use of smart monitoring devices by the society, it is essential to reflect and discuss to ensure continuous healthy balance between innovation and ethics. Given the potential threat of AI surveillance to the psychological well-being of individuals, recognizing both its promise and its psychological risks, we are able to create systems that safeguard people and respect their autonomy, privacy, and emotional well-being.

REFERENCES

Abdalla, M., Abdalla, M., & Muldoon, M. (2023). Ethical challenges of affective computing in healthcare monitoring. *Journal of Medical Ethics*, *49*(2), 89–96.

Ajunwa, I. (2020). *The quantified worker: Law and technology in the modern workplace*. Cambridge University Press. https://doi.org/10.1017/9781316888681

Allen, C., & Wallach, W. (2015). *Moral machines: Teaching robots right from wrong*. Oxford University Press. https://doi.org/10.1093/acprof:oso/9780195374049.001.0001

Anderson, J., & Rainie, L. (2020). *Concerns about AI, privacy, and surveillance*. Pew Research Center.

Balamurugan, G., Tyagi, A.K., & Richa, A. (2023). Survey on privacy preserving and trust building techniques of blockchain-based systems. In: *Privacy Preservation and Secured Data Storage in Cloud Computing*. IGI Global. DOI: 10.4018/979-8-3693-0593-5.ch019

Bélanger, F., & James, T. L. (2023). Digital surveillance and its psychological effects. *MIS Quarterly*, *47*(1), 45–72.

Brayne, S. (2020). *Predict and surveil: Data, discretion, and the future of policing*. Oxford University Press. https://doi.org/10.1093/oso/9780190684099.001.0001

Calvo, R. A., & Peters, D. (2019). *Positive computing: Technology for wellbeing and human potential.* MIT Press. https://doi.org/10.7551/mitpress/9764.001.0001

Crawford, K. (2021). *Atlas of AI: Power, politics, and the planetary costs of artificial intelligence*. Yale University Press.

DeCamp, M., & Lindvall, C. (2020). A systematic review of AI ethics in clinical practice. *BMJ Health & Care Informatics*, *27*(3), e100253. https://doi.org/10.1136/bmjhci-2020-100253

Eitel-Porter, R. (2021). AI ethics in healthcare: Critical considerations. *AI & Society*, *36*(1), 273–283.

Floridi, L. (2018). Soft ethics and the governance of the digital. *Philosophy & Technology*, *31*(1), 1–8. https://doi.org/10.1007/s13347-018-0303-9

Gasser, U., & Almeida, V. A. F. (2017). A layered model for AI governance. *IEEE Internet Computing*, *21*(6), 58–62. https://doi.org/10.1109/MIC.2017.4180835

Gibson, C., & Hanson, K. (2022). Emotion AI and privacy risks in mental health settings. *Journal of Affective Computing*, *13*(4), 215–228.

Harari, Y. N. (2018). *21 lessons for the 21st century*. Spiegel & Grau.

Huang, G., & Rust, R. T. (2021). Artificial intelligence in service. *Journal of Service Research*, *24*(1), 3–20. https://doi.org/10.1177/1094670517752459

Jobin, A., Ienca, M., & Vayena, E. (2019). The global landscape of AI ethics guidelines. *Nature Machine Intelligence*, *1*(9), 389–399. https://doi.org/10.1038/s42256-019-0088-2

Kellmeyer, P. (2019). Ethical implications of AI-based emotion recognition in neuroscience. *Frontiers in Neuroscience*, *13*, 1128. https://doi.org/10.1177/1094670520902266

Kroll, J. A. (2018). Accountability in autonomous systems. *Communications of the ACM*, *61*(12), 56–67.

Kumari, S., Tyagi, A. K., Tiwari, S., & Kulshreshtha, G. (2025a). Sensors and digital twin for healthcare monitoring frameworks. In T. A. Nguyen (Ed.), *Digital twin, blockchain, and sensor networks in the healthy and mobile city (Chapter 10)*. Elsevier. https://doi.org/10.1016/B978-0-443-34174-8.00011-9

Kumari, S., Tyagi, A. K., Tiwari, S., & Singh, R. (2025b). Medical sensor network, edge computing and blockchain for efficient medical data exchange. In T. A. Nguyen (Ed.), *Digital twin, blockchain, and sensor networks in the healthy and mobile city (Chapter 11)*. Elsevier. https://doi.org/10.1016/B978-0-443-34174-8.00012-0

Lepri, B., Oliver, N., Letouzé, E., Pentland, A., & Vinck, P. (2018). Fair, transparent, and accountable algorithmic decision-making processes. *Philosophy & Technology*, *31*(4), 611–627. https://doi.org/10.1007/s13347-017-0279-x

Lupton, D. (2016). *The quantified self.* Polity Press.

Mishra, A. K., Tiwari, S., Tyagi, A. K., & Arowolo, M. O. (2024). Security, privacy, trust, and provenance issues in Internet of Things–based edge environment. In S. Pal, C. Savaglio, R. Minerva, & F. C. Delicato (Eds.), *IoT edge intelligence* (pp. 233–263). Springer. https://doi.org/10.1007/978-3-031-58388-9_8

Mittelstadt, B. D. (2019). Principles alone cannot guarantee ethical AI. *Nature Machine Intelligence*, *1*(11), 501–507. https://doi.org/10.1038/s42256-019-0114-4

Nair, M. M., & Tyagi, A. K. (2021). Privacy: History, statistics, policy, laws, preservation and threat analysis. *Journal of Information Assurance & Security*, *16*(1), 24–34.

Nair, M.M., & Tyagi, A.K. (2025). Transformative effects of emerging technologies on Industry 5.0 and Society 5.0: Current status, vision, issues, challenges, and opportunities for future. In: *Next*

Generation Data Science and Blockchain Technology for Industry 5.0. Wiley. DOI: https://doi.org/10.1002/9781394245215.ch13, ISBN: 9781394245185.

Nissenbaum, H. (2010). *Privacy in context: Technology, policy, and the integrity of social life.* Stanford University Press.

O'Neil, C. (2016). *Weapons of math destruction: How big data increases inequality and threatens democracy.* Crown.

Pasquale, F. (2015). *The black box society: The secret algorithms that control money and information.* Harvard University Press.

Raji, I. D., & Buolamwini, J. (2019). Gender shades: Intersectional accuracy disparities in commercial facial recognition. *Proceedings of the ACM Conference on Fairness, Accountability, and Transparency*, *1*(1), 77–91. https://proceedings.mlr.press/v81/buolamwini18a.html?utm_source=chatgpt.com

Reis, A., & Madsen, S. (2022). Emotional surveillance and digital mental health. *Journal of Ethics in Digital Health*, *2*(1), 55–72.

Selinger, E., & Lyons, A. (2020). The psychology of surveillance: Understanding emotional harms. *Surveillance & Society*, *18*(4), 534–548.

Sharon, T. (2020). Self-tracking for health and the moralization of risk. *Journal of Medical Humanities*, *41*(4), 599–612. https://doi.org/10.1007/s13347-016-0215-5

Shneiderman, B. (2020). Human-centered AI: Reliable, safe & trustworthy. *International Journal of Human–Computer Interaction*, *36*(6), 495–504. https://doi.org/10.1080/10447318.2020.1741118

Solove, D. J. (2021). Privacy harms. *Yale Law Journal*, *131*(2), 569–601. https://doi.org/10.2139/ssrn.3782222

Tene, O., & Polonetsky, J. (2013). Big data for all: Privacy and user control. *Northwestern Journal of Technology and Intellectual Property*, *11*(5), 239–273.

Tyagi, A.K. (2021). Analysis of security and privacy aspects of blockchain technologies from smart era' perspective: The challenges and a way forward. In: *Recent Trends in Blockchain for Information Systems Security and Privacy* (pp. 1–17). DOI: https://doi.org/10.1201/9781003139737, eBook-ISBN: 9781003139737

Tyagi, A.K. (2025). Blockchain for smart hospital in Healthcare 5.0: modeling structure, challenges, and future emerging trends. In: *Human-Centric Integration of Next-Generation Data Science and Blockchain Technology.* Elsevier. DOI: https://doi.org/10.1016/B978-0-443-33498-6.00026-1, ISBN: 978-0-443-33498-6.

Tyagi, A.K. (2026). *Chapter 4 - Artificial intelligence–blockchain–Internet of Things–based smart healthcare services: literature review and future research directions, in the book: Smart Hospital Anatomy with Advanced Sensors Innovations in Patient Care.* Elsevier (pp. 49–61). https://doi.org/10.1016/B978-0-443-45875-0.00005-3, ISBN: 978-0-443-45875-0.

Tyagi, A., Kumari, S., & Tiwari, S. (2024c). Internet of Things for smart healthcare: A survey. In A. K. Sharma, N. Chanderwal, S. Tyagi, & P. Upadhyay (Eds.), *Future of AI in medical imaging (Chapter 2).* IGI Global. https://doi.org/10.4018/979-8-3693-2359-5.ch002

Tyagi, A. K., & Tiwari, S. (2024a). Blockchain-enabled smart healthcare applications in 6G networks. In A. K. Tyagi (Ed.), *Digital twin and blockchain for smart cities (Chapter 20).* Wiley. https://doi.org/10.1002/9781394303564.ch20

Tyagi, A. K., Tripathi, K., Tiwari, S., & Kaushik, S. (2025). An efficient technique for privacy preservation, trusted and secure patient-centric services in smart healthcare. In *Proceedings of the 6th international conference on recent trends in communication & intelligent systems (ICRTCIS 2025)* (pp. 31–47). IET. https://doi.org/10.1049/icp.2025.2731

Vaishnav, C., & Raji, I. D. (2023). Ethical deployment of AI in public sector surveillance. *AI Ethics*, *3*(1), 45–62.

Zuboff, S. (2019). *The age of surveillance capitalism: The fight for a human future at the new frontier of power.* PublicAffairs. https://doi/10.1007/s00146-020-01100-0

Part IV

Governance, Transparency, and Accountability

13 Explainable AI and Transparency in Clinical Decision-Making

13.1 INTRODUCTION

Artificial intelligence (AI) has become an essential component of contemporary healthcare, which assists clinicians in identifying the causes of diseases, interpreting health data, and designing therapy. Nonetheless, although AI systems are able to handle complex information much quicker than human beings, many of these systems function as "black boxes"; that is, their internal decision-making mechanisms cannot be easily comprehended. This transparency issue is severe in the case of AI applications to clinical decision-making, where the prioritization is patient safety and ethical issues. Clinicians must understand not only the AI's prediction but also the rationale behind its recommendation.

Explainable AI (XAI) is a solution to this issue because it allows the outputs of AI to be understandable, interpretable, and clinically meaningful. Explainability is not only a technical aspect in healthcare but also the key to trust, accountability, and responsible medical care. In cases where AI systems are applied to assist in diagnosis, particularly in mental health where diagnoses often lack clear biological markers, clinicians need the capability to comprehend the aspect that led the model to the conclusion. The chapter examines the notion of XAI, its relevance in clinical settings, the methods of making AI more transparent, and policies that can be followed to make its use responsible. It presents the role of explainability in enhancing human–AI collaboration and making healthcare more ethical and safer.

13.2 LITERATURE REVIEW

AI systems have now been widely integrated into the decision-making processes of not only the health and education sectors but also the financial, law enforcement, and industrial sectors. With the growth of these systems, the issues of fairness, transparency, and accountability have entered the limelight of academic and regulatory debate. The increasing number of studies indicate that biases may arise from data, algorithms, deployment processes, and broader socio-technical conditions, indicating that the fairness cannot be confined to a specific phase of the AI lifecycle (Abdollahpouri et al., 2020, Suresh and Guttag, 2021; Nair et al., 2021). As is always emphasized by scholars, algorithmic harms are structural failures, which require serious design, assessment, and governance systems (Crawford, 2021; O'Neil, 2016; Rajani et al., 2022; Tyagi et al., 2024c).

The fact that data bias can have a serious impact on model results is one of the bedrock themes of the literature. The article by Barocas and Selbst (2016) demonstrates that disparate effects can be created by historical imbalances in datasets when it seems that even when the models appear neutral. Measurement errors, sampling biases, and the use of proxies for sensitive attributes often

DOI: 10.1201/9781003658344-17

lead to unfair outcomes. In a similar manner, Hajian et al. (2016) stress that discrimination may creep into machine learning pipelines based on poor methods of preprocessing data. Studies into the definitions of fairness also indicate that alternative definitions of equality, including demographic parity, equalized odds, or equal opportunity, are usually inconsistent in practice (Hardt et al., 2016; Narayanan, 2018; Kleinberg et al., 2017; Tyagi et al., 2025). These conflicts show why fairness cannot follow a one-size-fits-all approach.

There is an increasing body of research to explore the manifestations of algorithmic bias in the real world. There are studies that focus on high-profile results, like that conducted by Buolamwini and Gebru (2018), which look into the workings and functioning of facial recognition technology and the way in which demographic differences emerge due to models performing poorly in both gender and skin-tone categories. The results are reflected by the concerns expressed by Raji and Buolamwini (2019), who demonstrate that the disclosure of biased model performance can put companies under the pressure to rectify their systems. The same concerns Ali et al. (2019), who show how optimization methods used in targeted advertising can generate discriminatory effects even among users with similar demographics. These works emphasize that the issues of algorithmic fairness are generally caused by the complicated relationships between algorithms, environment, and system users—a fact also confirmed by Selbst et al. (2019), who state that fairness should be viewed as a socio-technical, and not computational, property.

To address these issues, scientists have come up with fairness-promoting interventions and mitigation methods throughout the machine learning pipeline. Before training, preprocessing patterns like reweighting and data transformation are applied to eliminate discriminatory patterns (Kamiran and Calders, 2012). The in-processing strategies studied by Zafar et al. (2017) and Dwork et al. (2012) integrated the notion of fairness directly into the learning algorithms to avoid making discriminative predictions. Another practical alternative that can be used in deployed systems is post-processing tools that can make modifications to the outputs without retraining models (Friedler et al., 2019; Nair et al., 2025). Together, those methods make up the core of contemporary fairness toolkits like the IBM AI Fairness 360 that Bellamy et al. (2019) explain as a scalable set of tools that allows detecting, measuring, and reducing bias in a standardized set of procedures.

In addition to interventions, transparency and interpretability are becoming increasingly popular as the key elements of the responsible AI among scholars. According to Lipton (2018), there are two types of models that can be inherently interpreted and an explanation that can be represented as post hoc, and each of them is essential to enhancing the level of trust of the people. Equally, Guidotti et al. (2018) give a thorough overview of black-box model explanation methods and Mitchell et al. (2019) propose model cards as documentation principles to explain the intended applications, performance goals, and factors of fairness. Such initiatives are not the only attempts to achieve traceability—Kroll (2021) writes that to make AI systems accountable, systematic logging and documentation are required.

A number of works contextualize the AI fairness dilemma in the industrial and organizational contexts, highlighting the practical obstacles to practitioners. As Holstein et al. (2019) note, industry professionals usually do not have a guide, tools, and organizational assistance to introduce the principles of fairness in practice. Lepri et al. (2018) also note that transparency and accountability should both be on technical and governance levels to deliver ethical results. The IEEE (2019) Ethically Aligned Design also promotes the establishment of human well-being in autonomous systems by the use of standards, best practices, and value-based design. All these sources point to the fact that not only is fairness a technical requirement, but it is also organizational and ethical imperative.

The recent development of new model architectures has heightened the issue of fairness. The growing complexity of ensuring the equitable performance across different groups is proven by large-scale retrieval-augmented systems (Borgeaud et al., 2022; Tyagi, 2021) and deep learning frameworks applied in high-risk settings. The more sophisticated AI systems are, the more evaluations of fairness should be adjusted to include new criteria and testing approaches.

Some of the studies focus on the significance of auditing and regulatory control. Raji et al. (2020) suggest systematic auditing frameworks as a way of closing the gaps in accountability between developers and consumers of its usage because in most cases, organizations do not have solid governance frameworks. Elzayn et al. (2023) and Kumari et al. (2025a) take this view a step further, illustrating how a lack of access to ground truth may make the audit of algorithmic risk assessment more complicated, particularly in social, criminal justice areas. According to the literature, transparency, auditing, and public oversight are all essential elements of responsible AI governance.

The association of fairness and the societal structures is also discussed further in political, ethical, and philosophical discourse. As an example of how fairness can be informed by political philosophy, Binns (2018) and Kumari et al. (2025b) state that various systems of values result in various definitions of fairness in machine learning. Similarly, Danks and London (2017) discuss the implications of having ethical trade-offs within autonomous systems, by stating that ethical reasoning should be included with the algorithmic design decision-making. In their introductory book, Russell and Norvig (2021) support the notion that AI systems are the application of the goals and preferences of their creators, which makes it essential to pay attention to fairness and safety in model goals.

Figure 13.1 provides a simplified overview of the position of XAI in the daily clinical decision-making process. It starts with the step of collecting patient data- including medical history, sensor data, laboratory data, and imaging data. This data is then fed into an AI processing system that takes the inputs and gives two outputs: a prediction (such as a diagnosis, risk estimate, or treatment suggestion) and an explanation of how the model did so. The explanation also serves a purpose of a bridge that enables the clinicians to comprehend the logic behind the recommendation of the AI. This transparency allows clinicians to question the model's reasoning and integrate it with their own expertise, and finally arrive at an even more informed decision. Overall, the figure illustrates the importance of interpretability in terms of the enhancement of trust and safety in the clinical setting where the decision-making process carries serious consequences (Table 13.1).

Lastly, a number of articles emphasize that comprehensive fairness frameworks, where technical, ethical, and governance views are combined, are needed. Mehrabi et al. (2021) and Mishra et al. (2024) give a comprehensive survey that summarizes the large arena of types of bias and mitigation strategies. Wang et al. (2022) and Tyagi and Tiwari (2024a) discuss equity-oriented solutions to machine learning and state that technical fixes cannot be made without structural changes. Zemel et al. (2013), Tyagi (2025), and Balamurugan et al. (2023) present the notion of learning fair representations, which is a method that tries to represent data in a manner that would reduce the utilization of sensitive attributes yet simultaneously retain predictive information.

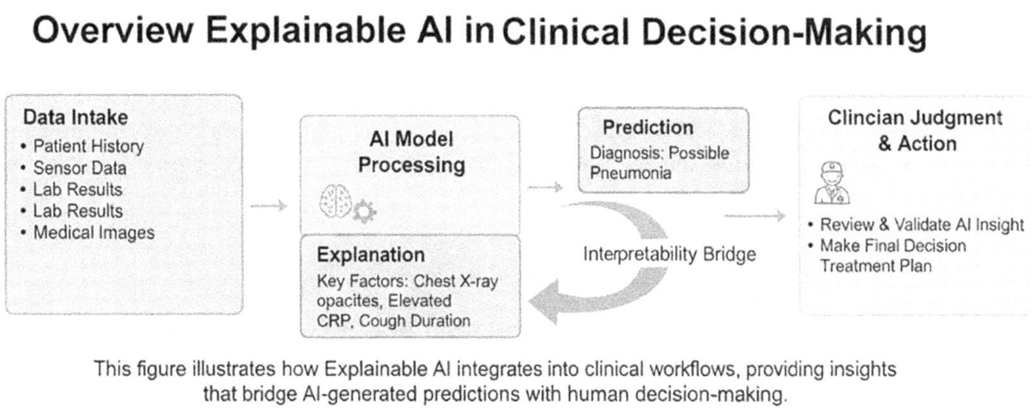

FIGURE 13.1 The summary of explainable AI in clinical decision-making.

TABLE 13.1
Popular Explainability Methods and Medical Applications

XAI Technique	Strengths	Limitations	Example Clinical Use
SHAP Values	Very descriptive; demonstrates feature significance	Computer intensive	Risk prediction models
LIME	Local explanations, fast	Unstable between runs	Explaining imaging predictions
Decision Trees	Clear and rule-based	Less accurate	Triage and screening tools
Saliency Maps	Visual focus points	Difficult to clinicalize	Radiology and dermatology
Attention Mechanisms	Brings into focus significant input sequences	Not always faithful	Mental health text analysis

13.3 PRINCIPLES OF XAI

XAI defines approaches and strategies that enable AI systems understanding to make decisions that are understandable to humans. XAI is based on two broad principles: intrinsic interpretability and post-hoc explainability.

Intrinsic interpretability is the term used in relation to models that are transparent in nature. Such examples are rule-based systems, sparse linear models, and generalized additive models. They are easily structured to allow observation of the effect of input variables on output. These models are widely applied in medical risk scoring systems as their reasoning is simple.

Post-hoc explainability is concerned with approaches that happen after a model has made a prediction, especially when it is a complex model, for example, a deep neural network. These methods may highlight influential factors or produce visual explanations of how the model used the data. Post-hoc techniques do not alter the internal mechanism of the model; rather, they form a human-comprehensible set of stories about the way the model arrived at the conclusion.

One of the major principles of XAI is that the explanations must be relevant to a person operating the system. An explanation that is statistically valid but clinically confusing is of limited value. Effective XAI is informed by psychology, human–computer interaction, and communication science to develop explanations that aid in understanding and making decisions.

Figure 13.2 demonstrates the effect of bias entering and building at various points in an AI system that is applied in clinical care. The first step is the collection of data where the imbalance of certain groups of people or the lack of full patient data may bias the data. These gaps can cause the following issues during model training: overfitting to the majority groups or using misleading features, which in turn encode demographic information. Upon the deployment of the system, new types of bias might emerge, that is, the discrepancy between the population on which the model has been trained and the population that the model is actually applied to. Lastly, in actual clinical application, unfair outcomes may be even enhanced by human factors, for example, the misinterpretation of findings, misuse of technology or a lack of adherence to the design of the model concerning the context of the local healthcare. The figure supports the notion that prejudice should be addressed in all levels as mistakes that are unaddressed tend to increase and impact patient care disproportionately (Table 13.2).

13.4 SIGNIFICANCE IN MENTAL HEALTH DIAGNOSIS

The field of mental health diagnosis is one of the complicated spheres where explainability is an important factor. Mental health problems are not readily identified by biological variables like many other physical diseases. Diagnosis relies on interviews with the patient, behavioral observations,

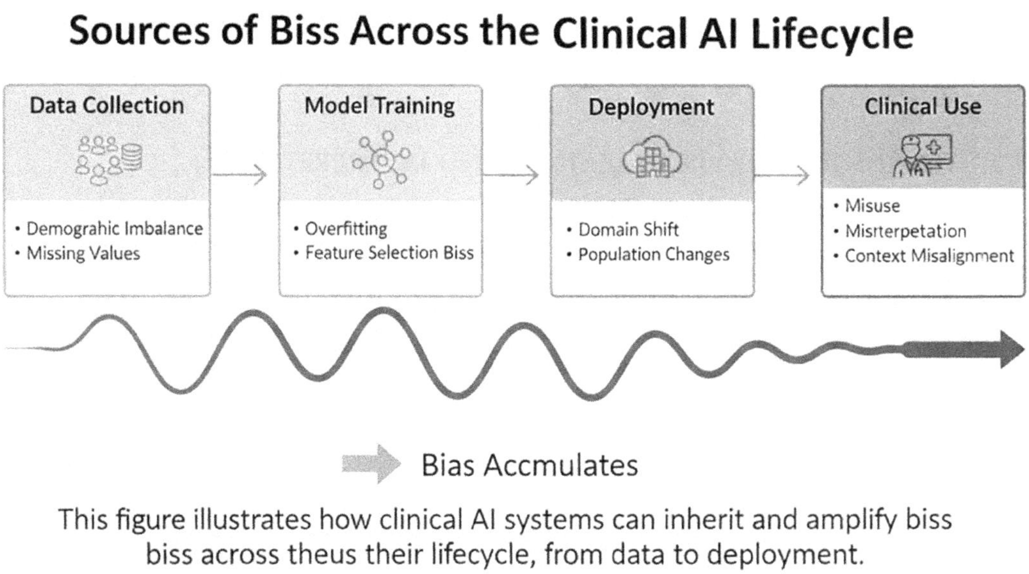

FIGURE 13.2 Sources of bias in the AI lifecycle.

TABLE 13.2
Types of Bias That Can Apply to Clinical AI

Type of Bias	Description	Clinical Effect	An Example
Sampling Bias	Inequalities in training data	Bad work with minority groups	In cardiac cases of women, these are underdiagnosed.
Measurement Bias	Incorrect or inconsistent data	Distorted predictions	Bad sensor data
Algorithmic Bias	Architecture biases models waive inequalities	Misclassification	NLP models that misunderstanc dialects
Deployment Bias	Model applied in a non-targeted setting	Risks of safety	ICU models in general wards
Human Bias	Misuse or over dependence of clinicians	Mistaken choice	Automation bias

long-term observations, and professional judgment of the clinicians. Due to this complexity, clinicians require a tool that will enable them to comprehend trends in patient data and at the same time enable them to utilize their expertise.

Mental health AI models can study the speech patterns, mood ratings, activity levels, social behavior, or even physiological indicators. When such system provides a recommendation, for example, the score of a severity of a depression or the first indications of a relapse, clinicians need to know the reasoning behind it. Unexplained outputs can lead to distrust, misunderstanding or even damage.

XAI can assist clinicians in determining whether the model is using clinically appropriate data. An illustration of this is that an XAI tool will allow visualizing whether the model prediction was based on the presence of the relevant symptoms, such as the quality of sleep or the tone of emotions, and not on the presence of irrelevant pattern or biased data. Ethical practice is also facilitated by transparency. The patients have a right to understand how their information is utilized and the reason why a particular recommendation was provided.

XAI can support therapeutic communication in the mental health care field. An explanation can help bring patients into decision-making by the clinician, encourage mutual understanding, and foster confidence in technology-assisted care.

13.5 TECHNIQUES OF VISUALIZATION AND INTERPRETATION

A graphic explanation is one of the most effective methods to make clinicians interpret AI decisions. They transform complicated mathematical formulae into simple graphical forms that can be perceived fast. There are a number of interpretability methods commonly used in clinical decision-making.

SHAP (SHapley Additive exPlanations) values give a line-by-line analysis of the contribution of each input feature to the prediction by the model. Indicatively, SHAP may indicate the extent to which such symptoms as mood swings, level of activity, or the scores on anxiety contributed to the eventual diagnostic recommendation.

LIME (Local Interpretable Model-agnostic Explanations) approximates complex models with simpler local models which demonstrate what factors were most significant in making a specific decision.

Grad-CAM (Class Activation Mapping) and saliency maps find application in the fields of medical image. They point to certain areas in a picture that the model considered significant—useful for interpreting MRI (Magnetic Resonance Imaging) or CT (Computed Tomography) scans.

Attention visualization can be used in mental health applications that are either speech or text-based, indicating which aspects of a conversation or a written document had an impact on what the AI interpreted.

Such instruments help make AI more transparent and reveal patterns, risk indicators, and also show connections, which can be verified by clinicians. Visualization also facilitates communication between the various clinical team members, in that it enhances the common understanding of the findings.

Figure 13.3 classifies the key explainability tools used in healthcare AI systems. The model-based methods, the first category, contain models that are inherently easy to interpret as rule-based methods or decision trees in which the logic is visible early on. The second group is post-hoc methods, which entail methods that are used after constructing a more complicated or opaque model. Such tools include SHAP and LIME, which can be classified under this category and provide localized explanations in a way that indicates which features contributed to a certain prediction. The third type is visual interpretation tools, which are used to give graphical information about model behavior. Heatmaps and saliency maps of imaging analysis, and attention layers of text-based models, such as where the system paid attention, are examples. All these methods are needed to assist clinicians in gaining a sense of AI outputs and feeling confident about using them in practice.

13.6 REPORTING AI LOGIC TO PHYSICIANS

One of the most significant aspects of technology implementation in clinical practice is the communication of how an AI system has come up with its decisions. Clinicians are not required to learn all the technicalities of the algorithms; however, they require the explanation of what has contributed to the prediction of the model and how sure the final predictive outcome is. Effective communication focuses on describing the most relevant aspects, emphasizing the factors of contributing causes, and outlining the doubts or limitations that clinicians need to be conscious of. They should be explained in a very straightforward, intuitive way that is close to the natural process of clinicians analyzing patient characteristics. This can be pictorial representation, confidence ratings, risk ratings, or brief narrative summaries that simplify the process of following the reasoning. By

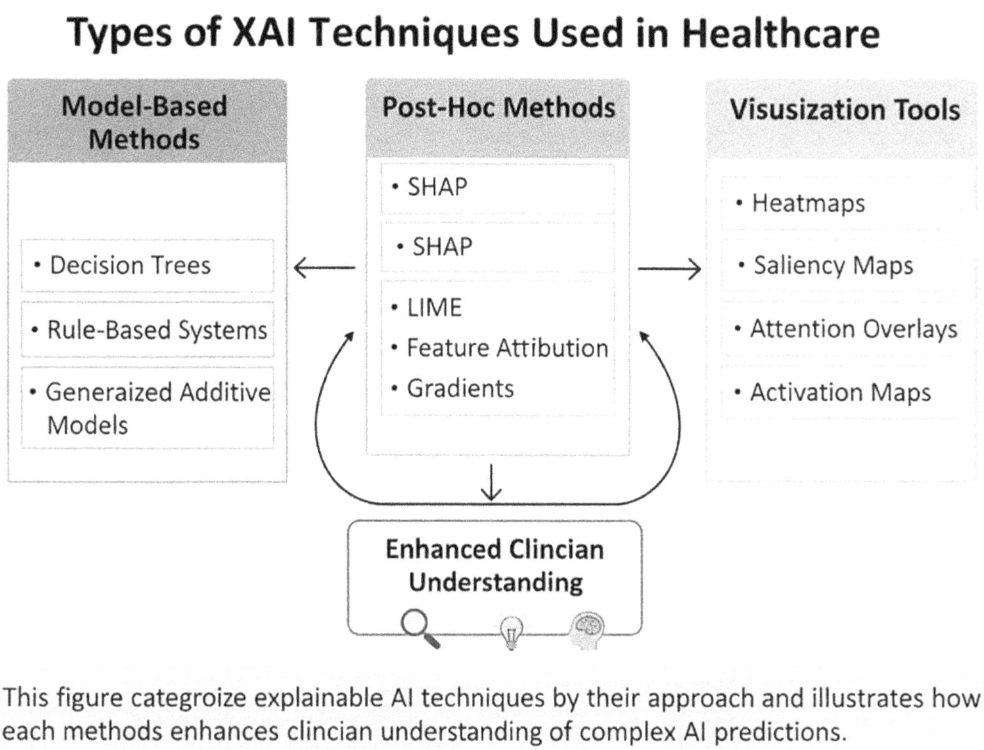

FIGURE 13.3 Healthcare XAI techniques.

having AI logic communicated in a direct and straightforward way, clinicians have a more accurate chance to decide whether they should trust the system in a specific case, incorporate its findings into their own clinical judgment, and speak about the results with patients in a comfortable way. Overall, effective communication helps bridge the gap between technical algorithms and the reality of medical decision-making.

13.7 STRIKING A BALANCE BETWEEN INTELLECTUAL PROPERTY (IP) PROTECTION AND TRANSPARENCY

The developers of AI usually have to struggle to balance the requirement of transparency and the need to safeguard their intellectual property. Most of the healthcare AI systems are constructed based on proprietary algorithms that companies are not keen on releasing the algorithms in detail. Simultaneously, health practitioners and authorities in the healthcare sector require sufficient data to assess the safety and equity of such systems.

These needs have to be balanced through a stratified approach. High-level explanations typically describe the key features or reasoning patterns used by the model. The developers might present high-level explanations to demonstrate the code without divulging the underlying code. Under confidentiality agreement, regulators can get access to detailed documentation. The patients are given simplified and clear-cut explanations regarding the use of their data.

This balance supports accountability without discouraging innovation. It also promotes trust through demonstrating that the system is open in a manner that is important in terms of safety and ethics, although not everything in the technical specifications may be visible to the public.

13.8 INDICATORS OF TRUST METRICS AND GOVERNANCE

The confidence in AI systems is established based on the obvious evidence that the technology acts dependably, ethically, and equally in various clinical contexts. Trust measures are used to assess the performance of an AI model by assessing its accuracy, consistency in similar scenarios, coherence of explanations, and whether it is biased or not in its predictions. These measurements provide clinicians and institutions with an avenue to establish the reliability of the system to be used on a regular basis. Governance indicators complement these metrics, which ensure that the AI system is responsibly monitored and managed over the entire lifecycle. This can be periodic audits, the record of updating the model, performance appraisal, assessment of bias, and clear reporting procedures. Trust measures along with the governance measures also form a systematic methodology of accountability, which demonstrates that the AI system is not a set-and-forget tool but a continuously tested and enhanced one. With these kinds of mechanisms in place, clinicians and patients will be more assured that the technology facilitates safe, equitable, and transparent healthcare practices (Table 13.3).

13.9 AI IN COLLABORATION WITH HUMANS IN CARE DELIVERY

XAI promotes interaction between a clinician and AI systems instead of substituting human knowledge. The AI models are able to work on a great deal of data and reveal the patterns that might be difficult to notice by a human. Nevertheless, the clinicians offer context, empathy, moral judgment, and patient-centered understanding, which the AI is not capable of.

Human–AI cooperation is most effective in cases when the AI explains everything in an understandable way. This will enable the clinicians to determine whether the information given by the AI is consistent with the history, symptoms, and the overall condition of the patient. Shared decision-making can also serve to rectify AI errors and avert risks and enhance patient outcomes.

Explainability promotes the cross-disciplinary collaboration. AI-generated insights can support collaboration among psychologists, psychiatrists, nurses, data scientists, and social workers. This approach improves the quality of care and enables AI to complement instead of dominate human judgment.

Figure 13.4 identifies a participative, feedback model of applying AI in mental health assessments. The diagram does not view AI as a separate or closed-loop decision-maker, but rather one that is involved in a process of interaction. The cycle starts by the AI system creating insights, including predictions or identified levels of risk. These insights are then interpreted by the clinicians according to their professional understanding and the situation of the specific patient and feedback is given that narrows the utility of the AI. The responses by patients in terms of symptom changes, adherence, or treatment progress are input to the subsequent step, generating new data to the system. These new pieces of data would add to continuous system development, as they would aid the AI in developing in accordance with actual clinical experience. This loop highlights the significance

TABLE 13.3
Clinical AI Trust and Governance Indicators

Governance Indicator	Purpose	Evidence of Trustworthiness
Performance Audits	Stable model accuracy	Frequent score reporting
Bias Surveillance	Detect unfair outcomes	Inequality statistics
Explainability Quality Checks	Explainability validation	User study feedback
Documents and Model Cards	Openness of design and will	Clear model specs
Update and Retraining Logs	Monitor change through time	Version control reports

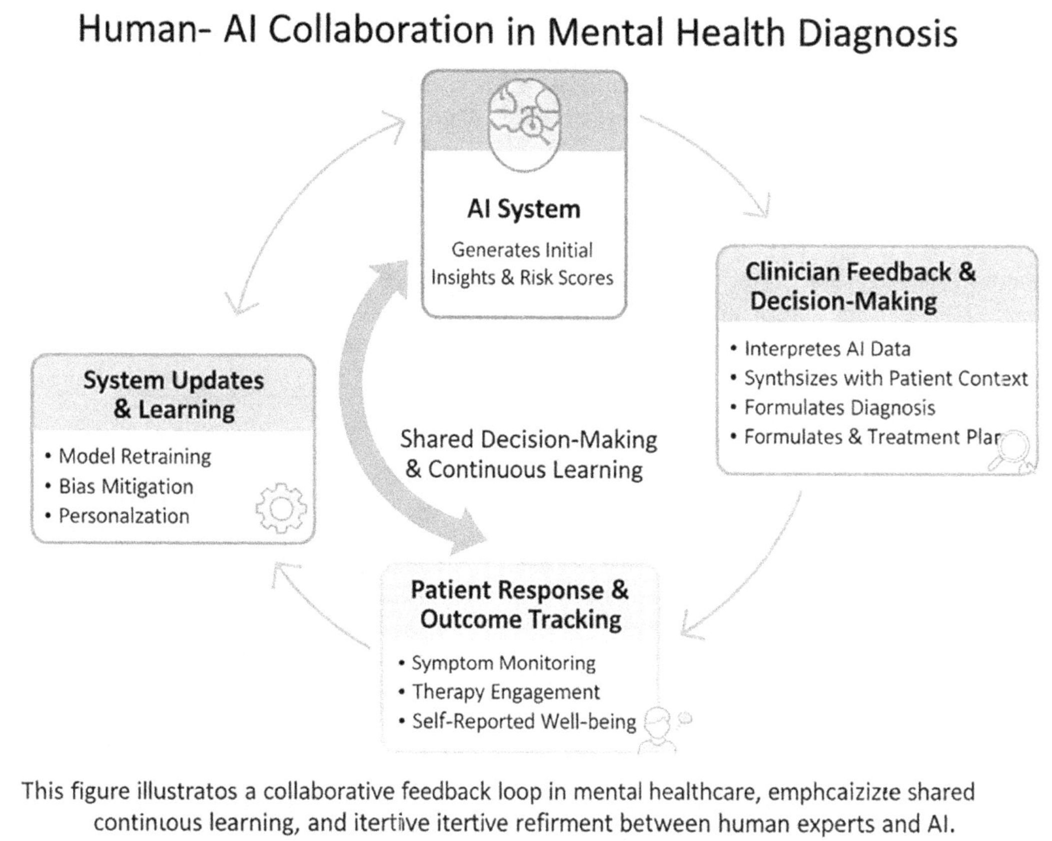

FIGURE 13.4 Mental health diagnosis human–AI collaboration.

TABLE 13.4
Comparison of Levels of Interpretability

Level of Interpretability	Description	Examples	Clinician Suitability
High (Transparent)	Wholly comprehensible	Linear models, rule-based systems	Very appropriate
Medium (Semi-Transparent)	Needs certain explanation	Random forests, attention networks	Suitable with tools
Low (Opaque)	Hard to explain	Deep neural networks	Needs XAI support

of shared decision-making and makes sure that the system is human-centered and based on human judgment.

13.10 POLICYMAKING AND PUBLIC TRUST

Policy frameworks play a critical role in the use of AI in healthcare. Regulations are used to support the establishment of safety, ethical, and transparency guidelines in AI systems prior to their application into clinical practice. Policies can compel companies to record the manner in which AI systems are trained, the manner in which they make decisions as well as the manner in which they protect patient data.

The adoption of AI cannot be successful without trust on the part of its population. This is because when citizens realize that AI tools are open, controlled, and used in a responsible manner, they would be more receptive to their application. Trust can be established through public education, proper communication in the healthcare institution, and responsible media coverage. Policies also protect patient rights by ensuring informed consent, data privacy, and accountability. Such precautions will help to convince the population that AI systems are created to assist human clinicians, and not to replace them (Table 13.4).

13.11 STANDARDS OF RESPONSIBLE DISCLOSURE

Responsible disclosure can be defined as the cautious and clear explanation of the functioning of an AI system, the information it uses, and its limitations, without overwhelming users with unnecessary technical details. This is of particular importance in the healthcare sector as clinicians,

TABLE 13.5
Transparent AI Policy and Ethical Requirements

Requirement	Purpose	Implications for Healthcare
Informed Consent	Patient autonomy	Explained data use
Auditability	Accountability	Decision trails
Safety Guarantee	Reduce damages	Ongoing observation
Bias Evaluation	Lessen biasness	Fairness in care provision
Transparency to the public	Increment of trust	Transparent display of competence

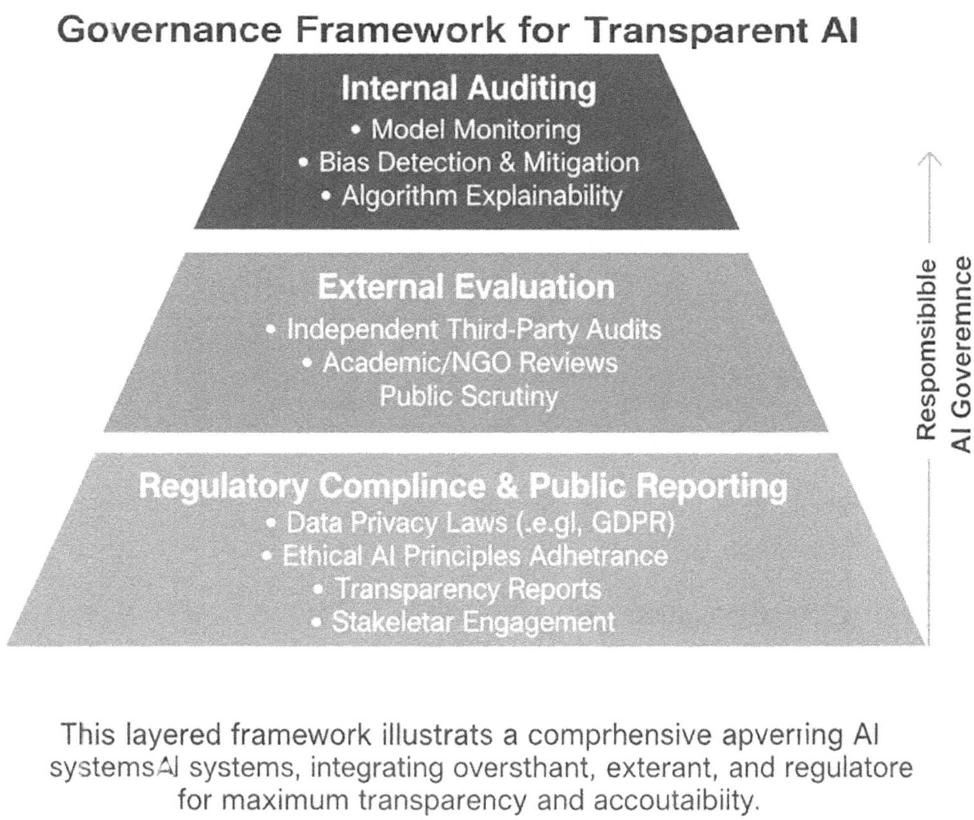

FIGURE 13.5 Artificial intelligence governance framework.

regulators, and patients need varying degrees of information. Clinicians require clear explanations that would allow understanding the reasons the AI created a specific output, whereas regulatory bodies demand more detailed documents, to check the safety, fairness, and compliance. Instead, patients will have access to non-technical summaries that are easy to understand and easy to grasp about the use of their information and how AI can help them. Responsible disclosure standards generally require clear statements on the purpose of the system, its training data sources, performance results, the known risks, and the guidelines on its adequate usage. Such norms contribute to making AI systems transparent, ethically oriented, and trustworthy, and also protecting patient privacy and securing the intellectual property of developers. Through responsible disclosure, healthcare organizations become more responsible and aid in safer and more informed usage of AI technologies (Table 13.5).

Figure 13.5 describes a multi-level structure that will help to contribute to transparency and accountability in clinical AI systems. The common starting point in the structure is internal auditing, where the performance, fairness, and safety are reviewed by the developers and healthcare organizations. External evaluation is the second layer and involves third-party audits or academic tests, which give an independent check of the reliability of the system. The second very important aspect is regulatory compliance, which means that the AI is compliant with the country or international laws enacted by countries or governmental bodies that govern the industry. The last of the layers is public reporting, which guarantees openness through the disclosure of the necessary information, including planned purposes and performance rates, and identified limitations, to clinicians, patients, and other interested parties. Collectively, these layers depict that reliable AI is not based on a single protection measure but needs to be a system of checks and balances, involving technical, institutional, and regulatory levels.

13.12 SUMMARY

This chapter gathers the main concepts considered in all the 12 sections and provides the clear picture of how AI systems are formed, where the challenges appear and how the fairness, transparency, and accountability can be enhanced. The emphasis has been placed throughout the chapter on demonstrating that AI is not merely a technical apparatus but a multifaceted socio-technical system that is affected by the domain of data quality, design, the structure of algorithms, and environments of real-world application. Each of the stages, such as the process of data collection up to model evaluation, implies both the possibilities of its enhancement and the threats resulting in biased or unfair results, unless managed properly.

The role of data as the basis of AI behavior is one of the core themes brought out in the chapter. As was illustrated in the discussion, the datasets with skewness, incompleteness, or bias based on history can be easily carried with them into the predictions in the system. This gives rise to the second theme, which is the algorithmic design. Even well-intentioned decisions, like optimization objectives, feature selection, model architecture, etc., can increase unfairness without their creators realizing it, when developers are not aware of the implications of their decisions downstream. The chapter highlighted that, on the one hand, fairness cannot be created by mere accident; it has to be established by undertaking a deliberate effort, which is accomplished through constant monitoring and evaluation.

The other key lesson is related to how to measure fairness itself. The chapter described that there is no universal meaning of fairness. The various measures such as demographic parity, equalized odds, equal opportunity, and predictive parity have varying degrees of ethical priorities as well as practical constraints. Instead of providing a single measure of fairness that is correct, the chapter demonstrated that determining the appropriate fairness measure varies depending on the context, users affected, and system objectives. This point of view makes the reader consider more, instead of using solutions that amount to one size fits all.

Another important aspect in developing responsible systems that was also discussed in the chapter is the role of AI governance, including transparency, explainability, and regulatory frameworks. It indicated that a technically fair model might be abused in case organizations do not have clear procedures to control or be answerable. Ethical principles, stakeholder interaction, effect analysis, as well as ongoing vigilance were mentioned as vital elements of reliable AI practice.

At the end of the chapter, the author brought all these aspects, like data, algorithms, metrics of fairness, system design, and governance, together in a single picture. The summary supports the claim that to establish responsible AI development, it is necessary to be not only technologically skilled but also ethically conscious. The role of developers, policymakers, and end-users in development of systems, which are not merely accurate but also inclusive, transparent and socially beneficial, is shared. Having learned the problems discussed in all the 12 sections, the readers will be in a better position to design, appraise, and manage AI systems to benefit different communities in a just and significant manner.

REFERENCES

Abdollahpouri, H., Burke, R., & Mobasher, B. (2020). Multistakeholder recommendation: Survey and research directions. *User Modeling and User-Adapted Interaction, 30*(1), 127–158. https://doi.org/10.1007/s11257-019-09256-1

Ali, S., Sapiezynski, P., Bogen, M., Korolova, A., Mislove, A., & Rieke, A. (2019). Discrimination through optimization: How Facebook's ad delivery can lead to skewed outcomes. *Proceedings of the ACM on Human-Computer Interaction, 3*(CSCW), 1–30. https://doi.org/10.1145/3359301

Balamurugan, G., Tyagi, A.K., & Richa, A. (2023). Survey on privacy preserving and trust building techniques of blockchain-based systems. In: *Privacy Preservation and Secured Data Storage in Cloud Computing*. IGI Global. DOI: 10.4018/979-8-3693-0593-5.ch019

Barocas, S., & Selbst, A. D. (2016). Big data's disparate impact. *California Law Review, 104*(3), 671–732. https://doi.org/10.2139/ssrn.2477899

Bellamy, R. K. E., Dey, K., Hind, M., et al. (2019). AI Fairness 360: An extensible toolkit for detecting and mitigating algorithmic bias. *IBM Journal of Research and Development, 63*(4/5), 4:1–4:15. https://doi.org/10.1147/JRD.2019.2942287

Binns, R. (2018). Fairness in machine learning: Lessons from political philosophy. *Proceedings of Machine Learning Research, 81*, 149–159. https://proceedings.mlr.press/v81/binns18a.html?utm_source=chatgpt.com

Borgeaud, S., Mensch, A., Hoffmann, J., et al. (2022). Improving language models by retrieving from trillions of tokens. In *International conference on machine learning (pp.* 2206–2240). PMLR. https://arxiv.org/abs/2112.04426?utm_source=chatgpt.com

Buolamwini, J., & Gebru, T. (2018). Gender shades: Intersectional accuracy disparities in commercial facial analysis systems. *Proceedings of Machine Learning Research, 81*, 77–91. https://proceedings.mlr.press/v81/buolamwini18a.html?utm_source=chatgpt.com

Crawford, K. (2021). *Atlas of AI: Power, politics, and the planetary costs of artificial intelligence.* Yale University Press. https://doi.org/10.2307/j.ctv1ghv45t

Danks, D., & London, A. (2017). Algorithmic bias in autonomous systems. *In Proceedings of the 26th International Joint Conference on Artificial Intelligence (IJCAI 2017) (pp. 4691–4697).* https://doi.org/10.24963/ijcai.2017/654

Dwork, C., Hardt, M., Pitassi, T., Reingold, O., & Zemel, R. (2012). Fairness through awareness. In *Proceedings of the 3rd Innovations in Theoretical Computer Science Conference (ITCS 2012)* (pp. 214–226). https://doi.org/10.1145/2090236.2090255

Elzayn, H., Guzmán, C., & Chouldechova, A. (2023). A framework for auditing algorithmic risk assessments with limited ground truth. In *Proceedings of AIES* (pp. 15–26).

Friedler, S. A., Scheidegger, C., Venkatasubramanian, S., et al. (2019). A comparative study of fairness-enhancing interventions in machine learning. In *Proceedings of the conference on fairness, accountability, and transparency* (pp. 329–338). https://doi.org/10.1145/3287560.3287589

Guidotti, R., Monreale, A., Turini, F., et al. (2018). A survey of methods for explaining black box models. *ACM Computing Surveys, 51*(5), 1–42. https://doi.org/10.1145/3236009

Hajian, S., Domingo-Ferrer, J., & Martínez-Ballesté, A. (2016). A survey of discrimination prevention in data mining. *Knowledge and Information Systems, 45*(3), 613–644. https://doi.org/10.1007/s10115-014-0808-1

Hardt, M., Price, E., & Srebro, N. (2016). Equality of opportunity in supervised learning. *Advances in Neural Information Processing Systems, 29,* 3315–3323. https://doi.org/10.48550/arXiv.1610.02413

Holstein, K., Wortman-Vaughan, J., Daumé III, H., Dudik, M., & Wallach, H. (2019). Improving fairness in machine learning systems: What do industry practitioners need? In *CHI conference on human factors in computing systems* (pp. 1–16). https://doi.org/10.1145/3290605.3300830

IEEE Global Initiative on Ethics of Autonomous and Intelligent Systems. (2019). *Ethically aligned design: A vision for prioritizing human well-being with autonomous and intelligent systems.* IEEE Standards Association. https://standards.ieee.org/wp-content/uploads/import/documents/other/ead_v1.pdf?utm_source=chatgpt.com

Kamiran, F., & Calders, T. (2012). Data preprocessing techniques for classification without discrimination. *Knowledge and Information Systems, 33*(1), 1–33. https://doi.org/10.1007/s10115-011-0463-8

Kleinberg, J., Mullainathan, S., & Raghavan, M. (2017). Inherent trade-offs in the fair determination of risk scores. *Proceedings of Innovations in Theoretical Computer Science, 43*, 1–43:23.

Kroll, J. A. (2021). Outlining traceability: A principle for operationalizing accountability in computing systems. *Proceedings of the ACM on Human-Computer Interaction, 5*(CSCW), 1–22. https://doi.org/10.1145/3442188.3445937

Kumari, S., Tyagi, A. K., Tiwari, S., & Kulshreshtha, G. (2025a). Sensors and digital twin for healthcare monitoring frameworks. In T. A. Nguyen (Ed.), *Digital twin, blockchain, and sensor networks in the healthy and mobile city (Chapter 10,* pp. 147–177*).* Elsevier. https://doi.org/10.1016/B978-0-443-34174-8.00011-9

Kumari, S., Tyagi, A. K., Tiwari, S., & Singh, R. (2025b). Medical sensor network, edge computing and blockchain for efficient medical data exchange. In T. A. Nguyen (Ed.), *Digital twin, blockchain, and sensor networks in the healthy and mobile city (Chapter 11,* pp. 179–198*).* Elsevier. https://doi.org/10.1016/B978-0-443-34174-8.00012-0

Lepri, B., Oliver, N., Letouzé, E., et al. (2018). Fair, transparent, and accountable algorithmic decision-making processes: The premise, the proposed solutions, and the open challenges. *Philosophy & Technology, 31*(4), 611–627. https://doi.org/10.1007/s13347-017-0279-x

Lipton, Z. C. (2018). The mythos of model interpretability. *Communications of the ACM, 61*(10), 36–43. https://doi.org/10.1145/3233231

Mehrabi, N., Morstatter, F., Saxena, N., Lerman, K., & Galstyan, A. (2021). A survey on bias and fairness in machine learning. *ACM Computing Surveys, 54*(6), 1–36. https://doi.org/10.1145/3457607

Mishra, A. K., Tiwari, S., Tyagi, A. K., & Arowolo, M. O. (2024). Security, privacy, trust, and provenance issues in Internet of Things–based edge environment. In S. Pal, C. Savaglio, R. Minerva, & F. C. Delicato (Eds.), *IoT edge intelligence* (pp. 233–263). Springer. https://doi.org/10.1007/978-3-031-58388-9_8

Mitchell, M., Wu, S., Zaldivar, A., et al. (2019). Model cards for model reporting. In *Proceedings of the conference on fairness, accountability, and transparency* (pp. 220–229). https://doi.org/10.1145/3287560.3287596

Nair, M. M., & Tyagi, A. K. (2021). Privacy: History, statistics, policy, laws, preservation and threat analysis. *Journal of Information Assurance & Security, 16*(1), 24–34.

Nair, M.M., & Tyagi, A.K. (2025). Transformative effects of emerging technologies on Industry 5.0 and Society 5.0: Current status, vision, issues, challenges, and opportunities for future. In: *Next Generation Data Science and Blockchain Technology for Industry 5.0.* Wiley. DOI: https://doi.org/10.1002/9781394245215.ch13, ISBN: 9781394245185.

Narayanan, A. (2018). Translation tutorial: 21 fairness definitions and their politics. In *Conference on fairness, accountability, and transparency, tutorial notes.*

O'Neil, C. (2016). *Weapons of math destruction: How big data increases inequality and threatens democracy.* Crown Publishing. https://doi.org/10.5860/crl.78.3.403

Rajani, D., Menon, S. C., Kute, S., & Tyagi, A. K. (2022). Preserving privacy of social media data using artificial intelligence techniques. In A. Tyagi (Ed.), *Handbook of Research on Technical, Privacy, and*

Security Challenges in a Modern World (pp. 186–204). IGI Global. https://doi.org/10.4018/978-1-6684-5250-9.ch010

Raji, I. D., & Buolamwini, J. (2019). Actionable auditing: Investigating the impact of publicly naming biased performance results of commercial AI products. In *Proceedings of the 2019 AAAI/ACM Conference on AI, Ethics, and Society (pp. 429–435).* https://doi.org/10.1145/3306618.3314244

Raji, I. D., Smart, A., White, R. N., et al. (2020). Closing the AI accountability gap. In *Proceedings of the conference on fairness, accountability, and transparency* (pp. 33–44). https://doi.org/10.1145/3351095.3372873

Russell, S., & Norvig, P. (2021). *Artificial intelligence: A modern approach* (4th ed.). Pearson.

Selbst, A. D., Boyd, D., Friedler, S., Venkatasubramanian, S., & Vertesi, J. (2019). Fairness and abstraction in sociotechnical systems. In *Proceedings of the conference on fairness, accountability, and transparency* (pp. 59–68). https://doi.org/10.1145/3442188.3445922

Suresh, H., & Guttag, J. (2021). A framework for understanding sources of harm throughout the machine learning lifecycle. *Equity & Access in Algorithms, Mechanisms, and Optimization, 1,* 1–9. https://doi.org/10.1145/3442188.3445922

Tyagi, A.K. (2021). Analysis of security and privacy aspects of blockchain technologies from smart era' perspective: The challenges and a way forward. In: *Recent Trends in Blockchain for Information Systems Security and Privacy* (pp. 1–17). DOI: https://doi.org/10.1201/9781003139737, eBook-ISBN: 9781003139737

Tyagi, A.K. (2025). Blockchain for smart hospital in Healthcare 5.0: modeling structure, challenges, and future emerging trends. In: *Human-Centric Integration of Next-Generation Data Science and Blockchain Technology.* Elsevier. DOI: https://doi.org/10.1016/B978-0-443-33498-6.00026-1, ISBN: 978-0-443-33498-6.

Tyagi, A., Kumari, S., & Tiwari, S. (2024c). Internet of Things for smart healthcare: A survey. In A. K. Sharma, N. Chanderwal, S. Tyagi, & P. Upadhyay (Eds.), *Future of AI in medical imaging (Chapter 2,* pp. 19–41*).* IGI Global. https://doi.org/10.4018/979-8-3693-2359-5.ch002

Tyagi, A. K., & Tiwari, S. (2024a). Blockchain-enabled smart healthcare applications in 6G networks. In A. K. Tyagi (Ed.), *Digital twin and blockchain for smart cities (Chapter 20).* Wiley. https://doi.org/10.1002/9781394303564.ch20

Tyagi, A. K., Tripathi, K., Tiwari, S., & Kaushik, S. (2025). An efficient technique for privacy preservation, trusted and secure patient-centric services in smart healthcare. In *Proceedings of the 6th international conference on recent trends in communication & intelligent systems (ICRTCIS 2025)* (pp. 31–47). IET. https://doi.org/10.1049/icp.2025.2731

Wang, T., Kominers, P., & Scott, J. (2022). Algorithmic fairness and the quest for equity in machine learning. *Nature Machine Intelligence, 4*(2), 99–108.

Zafar, M. B., Valera, I., Gomez-Rodriguez, M., & Gummadi, K. (2017). Fairness constraints: Mechanisms for fair classification. In *International conference on artificial intelligence and statistics* (pp. 962–970). https://doi.org/10.48550/arXiv.1507.05259

Zemel, R., Wu, Y., Swersky, K., et al. (2013). Learning fair representations. In *Proceedings of international conference on machine learning* (pp. 325–333). https://doi.org/10.48550/arXiv.1307.6868

14 Digital Consent, Autonomy, and Identity Management

14.1 INTRODUCTION

The shift from physical to digital spaces has altered the ways people manoeuvre identity, autonomy, and privacy. Consent in the traditional sense was viewed as a specific act—in most cases, this was a signature at the bottom of a form. Consent in the digital world is, however, an ongoing dynamic process. Every time a person installs an app, uses a cloud, logs in, or communicates with artificial intelligence (AI)-based systems, they share the data. This constant data exchange raises the question of whether the user really knows what they are consenting to, or they are just consenting to get a service. It is demonstrated that the average user does not spend much time reading digital terms and conditions because they take 30–50 minutes on average to agree to them (Obar and Oeldorf-Hirsch, 2020; Nair et al., 2021, 2025). This disconnect has contributed to what scholars call consent fatigue what some academics have labeled as consent fatigue, making consent a less effective ethical and legal instrument.

The concept of the Digital Consent Lifecycle represented in Figure 14.1 shows that consent is not a one-time, static process but a dynamic and ongoing process. It starts with Collection, in which a user is given the first permission to use the data. The information then goes to the Storage where it is safely encrypted to avoid unauthorized accessibility. This is followed by the Usage, where the data is used under the terms that have been agreed upon and Sharing, where third parties can access under controlled terms. Notably, the user retains final control through Withdrawal, which allows them to revoke permission at any time. Lastly, Auditing makes sure that all procedures are in accordance with regulations and internal policies. This cycle keeps consent valid and flexible with time as the system will keep reviewing and changing the Collection and Storage practices whenever there is a shift in the preferences of the user or that are required by the regulations.

To elucidate the digital consent, a wider scope in considering the construction of identity on the web, the movement of personal information over networks, and how one can retain control over his or her digital tracks is therefore important. The development of AI systems has further complicated the situation. AI models learn continuously, which implies that their functionality can change over time to levels beyond what was originally outlined in a privacy policy. This raises doubts about whether the initial consent remains valid over time. Besides, new identity verification techniques, like biometrics and behavioral analytics, are more secure, but they also raise the question of surveillance, data permanence, and abuse. All these tensions evoke the necessity of the new framework that would combine the technological potential and respect to individual rights.

DOI: 10.1201/9781003658344-18

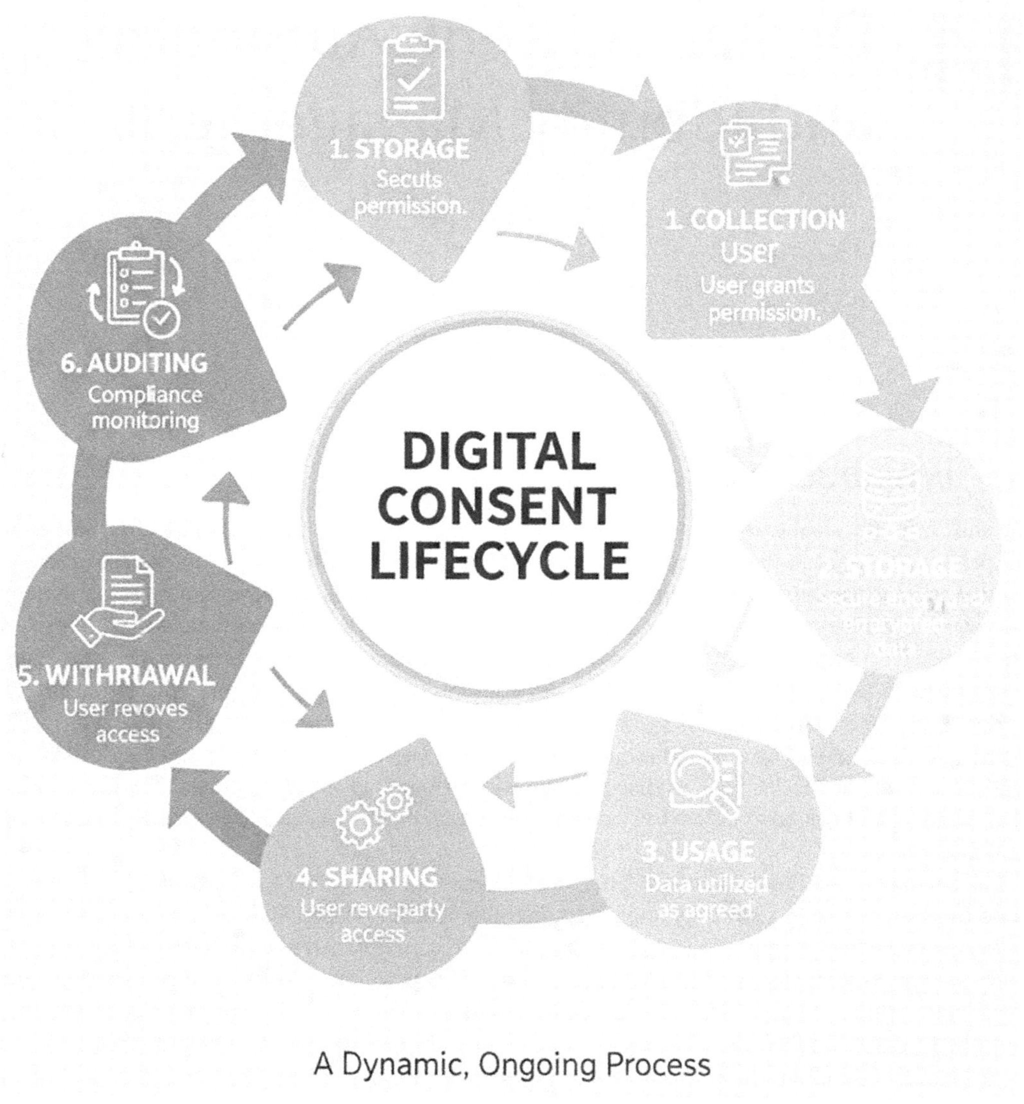

FIGURE 14.1 Digital consent lifecycle.

14.2 LITERATURE REVIEW

The concept of digital consent, identity control, and user agency has become a central focus in technology-driven interactions. Researchers underscore the fact that the classical concept of consent as a single signature is no longer adequate in the vibrant digital ecosystem. Obar and Oeldorf-Hirsch (2020) emphasize that the majority of users do not read privacy policies, and it has a gap between legal compliance and actual knowledge. Likewise, as described by McDonald and Cranor (2009), it is unrealistic to expect the user to read a long privacy statement, which serves as a contributor to consent fatigue and compromises the usefulness of digital consent processes.

Studies on privacy structures have gone a mile further to address these challenges. Solove (2021) says that consent alone is insufficient to protect user privacy in complex digital systems. Nissenbaum (2019) and Tyagi (2021) suggest a more refined view on the issue of contextual integrity, claiming that privacy expectations are context-dependent, and consenting practices have to mirror these differences.

This point of view is becoming more topical with the continuous data collection by AI systems and Internet of Things (IoT) devices, with the static consent agreement not fitting any more.

Contemporary consent practices are based on legal and regulatory studies. Albrecht (2016) and Koops (2019) discuss the effect of General Data Protection Regulation (GDPR) on the protection of data and mention such rights as access, rectification, erasure, and objection to processing. The significance of data portability and limit of purpose is also highlighted by Abdellatif et al. (2021) and Ausloos et al. (2020), and these two studies have shown that the regulatory frameworks strengthen the ethical responsibilities of organisations. Digital Personal Data Protection Act (DPDPA) in India is based on such ideas, which require direct consent, disclosure, and control over personal data (Abouelmehdi et al., 2018; Kumari et al., 2025a; Mishra et al., 2024).

Technological identity and consent management. Simultaneously, the technological systems of identity and consent management have developed at a high rate. Credential theft and phishing are other reasons that are rendering traditional password-based systems inadequate (Jain et al., 2021; Kumari et al., 2025b; Tyagi, 2025). Multifactor authentication (MFA), biometrics, and behavioral analytics are more secure, but regarding their fairness and inclusivity remain questionable. As expressed by Buolamwini and Gebru (2018), commercial facial recognition systems may be biased toward darker-skinned people and gender minorities, which is why it is necessary to implement them fairly. Pavlovic and Scekic (2022) also emphasize the perspective of behavioral biometrics as a promising strategy for continuous authentication without reducing usability, yet they warn that the systems should not abuse privacy standards.

Blockchain and decentralized identity (DID) systems have emerged as an innovative solution to these issues. According to Dunphy and Petitcolas (2018), DID models enable placing personal data under user control by ensuring it is stored and granting users the option to reveal the credential with cryptographic proofs. According to Hardman et al. (2022), Auer and Konig (2018), and Rajani et al. (2022), blockchain guarantees tamper resistance and transparency and, at the same time, supports privacy-preserving interactions, but issues such as key management, interoperability, and scalability still exist. Kang and Kim (2020) and Nair et al. (2021) also mention that DID is safe, yet it needs to be standardized to be used worldwide.

These technological advances have been supplemented by privacy by design and ethical AI principles. Cavoukian (2019), O'Connor et al. (2021), and Luger and Rodden (2021) attentively attach significance to user-friendly interfaces, interactive dashboards, and real-time consent payments. Gray et al. (2018), Tyagi (2025) and Tyagi et al. (2025) emphasize the dangers of the use of dark patterns in design, when manipulative interfaces undermine informed consent. Research conducted by Ting et al. (2020) and Bhatia and Breaux (2018) indicates that a well-designed and easily understandable consent interfaces enhance the knowledge of the user and increases trust.

The interaction of AI, the consent, and the privacy creates further problems. Wachter and Mittelstadt (2019) and Mittelstadt (2019) investigate the ethical consequences of inference-based processing, meaning AI systems infer sensitive information that the user does not explicitly enter into the system. According to Mathews-Hunt (2020) and Gasser and Almeida (2017), AI governance and continuous checks are required to synchronize automated systems with user permissions. Likewise, Reisman et al. (2018) and Tyagi and Tiwari, (2024a) suggest the adoption of algorithmic impact assessments as an instrument of determining the influence of AI systems on individual rights to hold them accountable.

The practical uses of digital consent frameworks are presented by sector-specific studies. Marelli and Testa (2021) discuss digital health systems with the focus on secure management of patient data by encrypted storage and verification of biometrics. Khan and Salah (2018) and Balamurugan et al. (2023) pay attention to financial systems, in which the consent management process should be in line with the high level of security requirements and regulations. Brandom (2019) sheds light on data portability in the online platform to avoid lock-in with a vendor, and Malgieri and Comande (2017) and Tyagi et al. (2024c) address the sensitive data processing to meet privacy regulations.

Cross-cutting research examines the opportunities as well as the challenges of contemporary identity systems. Alge (2020) and Pavlovic and Scekic (2022) demonstrate that consent management platforms have the capability to standardize user preferences in cross-service, making the process less complicated and more compliant. Floridi (2016) and Zuboff (2019) present more philosophical views, as they stress that digital systems need to be efficient and innovative without violating human dignity and autonomy. Custers et al. (2018) and McDonald and Cranor (2009) both confirm that regulatory and technological solutions should go hand in hand to ensure confidence toward digital ecosystems.

Together, these pieces of literature show that ethical, secure and user-friendly consent, and identity management involves putting in place a mixed set of technological innovation, regulatory compliance, and human-centered design and ethical governance. Proper digital consent frameworks need to combine the concepts of clarity, specificity, voluntariness, and revocability, and take advantage of the latest approaches to authentication, DID models, and privacy-sensitive technologies. With the development of AI and IoT systems, the need to keep research and practical case studies points to the necessity to have adaptive, transparent, and equitable systems of consent to uphold trust, autonomy, and legal standards in digital interactions.

14.3 TENETS OF DIGITAL CONSENT

Significant online consent is based on a number of principles, including: clarity, specificity, voluntariness, informed consent, and revocability. Clarity means that the information that the user is provided with must be in straightforward language; there should be no technical writing or obscure law language. Specificity does so that consent is limited to particular uses, and not to broad and undefined uses of data. Voluntariness implies that users should not be coerced into consenting by manipulative design-related decisions like dark patterns. As it has been demonstrated, user choices are mostly impacted by the use of deceptive interface designs (Gray et al., 2018), thus the significance of the ethical interface design.

Table 14.1 is a summary of the main principles that govern ethical digital consent. Clarity gives clarity to the information so that the users are able to understand it easily and without the use of complex legal technical terms. Specificity restricts consent to specified purposes to ensure that use of personal data is done to avoid any unintended purposes. Voluntariness ensures that the user is not forced to give consent, whereas Informed Decision focuses on the fact that the user has to be aware of what kind of data is being gathered and how it is going to be utilized. Lastly, Revocability enables users to revoke consent whenever they desire, which is guaranteed to maintain control of their data. All these principles combined create a framework of consent systems that would support autonomy of users and foster trust.

TABLE 14.1
Digital Consent Principles

Principle	Description	Digital System Example
Readability	The user should be able to comprehend the information provided to them	Simplified text, icons, layered notices
Specificity	Consent is limited to a specific object	Consent to email marketing only
Voluntariness	The user is not forced or being coerced to agree with something	They are doing it willingly
Informed Decision	User aware of collected information and purpose	Just-in-time notifications, dashboards
Revocability	User may revoke consents at any point in time	"Revoke consent" buttons, audit logs

As shown in Figure 14.2, User-Centric Consent System Framework puts transparency and user control at the pole of digital consent. The User Dashboard is its core, which provides an idea of all the granted permissions, history of use, and third-party data recipients. In line with this, there are Notifications to inform the user about updates, policy changes, or new data practices and Just-in-Time Prompts that seek the user to give consent to a particular action with new data when it is about to happen. A combination of these elements constitutes the Interactive Consent Interface, where users can review, change or rescind consent with minimal effort. The given approach puts the users in control, making them fully informed and enjoying the ability to assume full control of their personal information at any given moment.

To make informed decisions, platforms must display consent at the time when people will be in a state to reasonably consider it. This will involve the use of just-in-time consent prompts, which clarify the reason why the data is being collected. Lastly, revocability guarantees that users are free

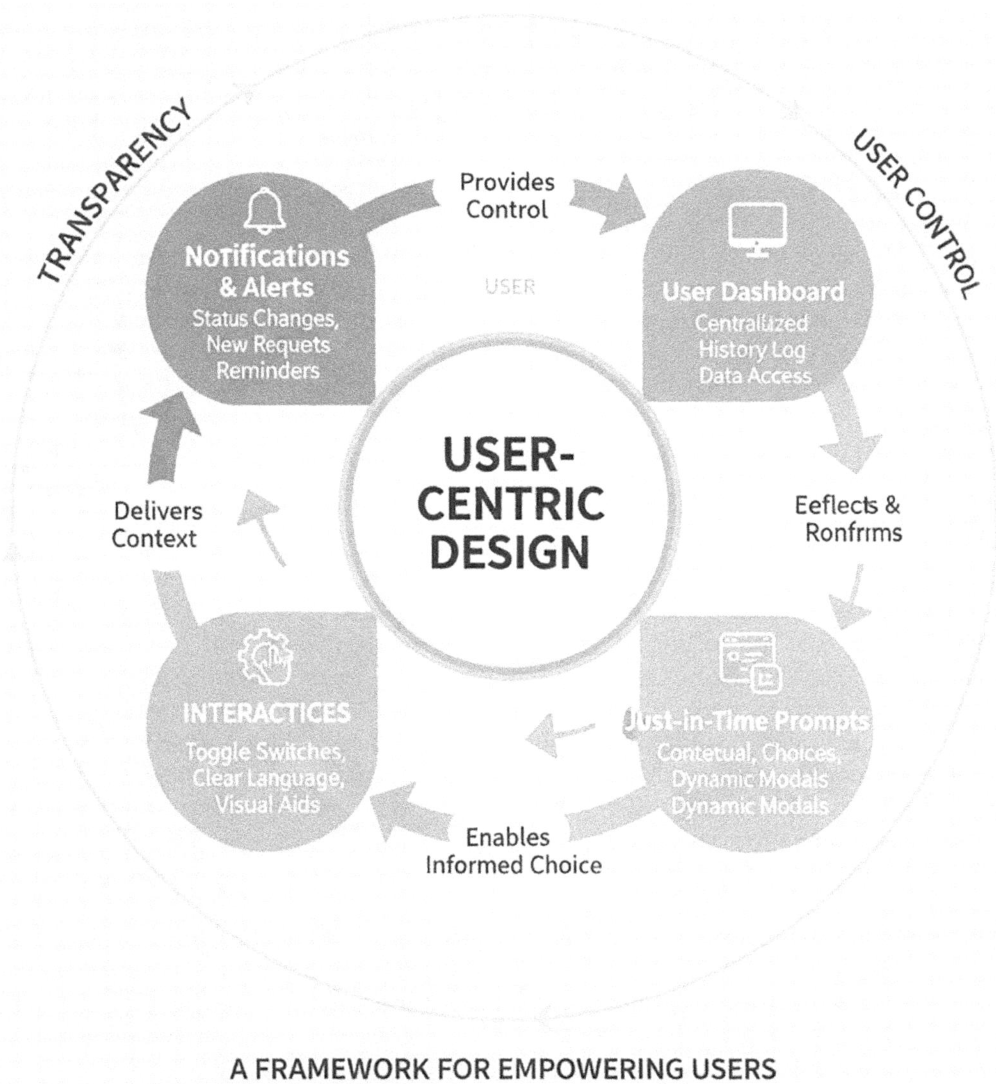

FIGURE 14.2 Consent system user-centric framework.

to revoke their consent whenever they wish, and the system will not punish the user provided that important service functions are not affected.

These policies are in line with the international data-protection laws. As an example, GDPR expects organizations to prove that consent is provided, and it should be in an easy way, as well as users should be able to withdraw it just as easily as they gave it. With the development of digital ecosystems, these principles become the ethical base of establishing trust among users.

14.4 AUTHENTICATION AND IDENTITY VERIFICATION

The verification of online ecosystems by digital identities is necessary to engage in a secure online interaction. The conventional combination of a username and a password is becoming ineffective because of extensive phishing and compromised credentials. Contemporary identity systems are based on MFA, which integrates the knowledge of the user (a password), possession (a device or a token), and identity (biometric data). MFA mitigates unauthorized users, yet it should be easy to use to prevent the discouragement of its use.

Biometric authentication is becoming popular due to its high level of accuracy and convenience. This is applied in banking, travel, and healthcare, including facial recognition, voice patterns, fingerprint scans, and iris recognition. Nonetheless, there is a question of data permanence—in terms of passwords, this cannot be the same case with biometrics because once it is compromised, there is no way to change it. It is also demonstrated in the studies that there are differences in accuracy between racial and demographic groups, which creates questions about identity discrimination (Buolamwini and Gebru, 2018).

Figure 14.3 can be used to have authentication and identity verification methods arranged in a hierarchy on the basis of their security levels. The most basic technique is passwords, which are dependent on the user having knowledge of something, but they are not usually the most secure techniques on their own. MFA is enabled to secure the process by adding another factor, a physical device, a mobile phone, or some other type of verification. An even greater degree of security is the biometric authentication, which can be fingerprint, iris, or facial recognition, which depends on unique physical traits. The most sophisticated ones include behavioral biometrics, which will keep tracking the patterns of typing rhythm, mouse movement, and overall use of applications. This continuous verification offers an insidious yet incredibly effective security-enhancing level that supplements other measures.

Table 14.2 compares the common authentication methods, depending on their security, user experience, privacy, and the common applications. The simplest form is the passwords that offer medium usability and low security. MFA supports the protection level by balancing usability and protection because it involves an extra verification factor (mobile token). Biometric systems, like fingerprints, facial recognition, and iris scans, are strongly secure, but present privacy issues because of the irreversible characteristic of biometric information. The most sophisticated technique is behavioral biometrics, which continuously authenticate a user with the introduction of individual patterns such as typing rhythm and mouse movements, and is very secure as well as has a seamless user experience. This table helps in pointing out the ways an organization can choose authentication strategies depending on the balance between security, usability, and privacy required.

Another new trend is behavioral biometrics. With the help of patterns like typing rhythm, mouse motion, and the like, systems can identify abnormalities and boost security without further effort on the part of the user. Such technologies are encouraging; however, they should be governed well to facilitate evading invasive surveillance habits. Striking a balance between security and privacy has to be taken into consideration.

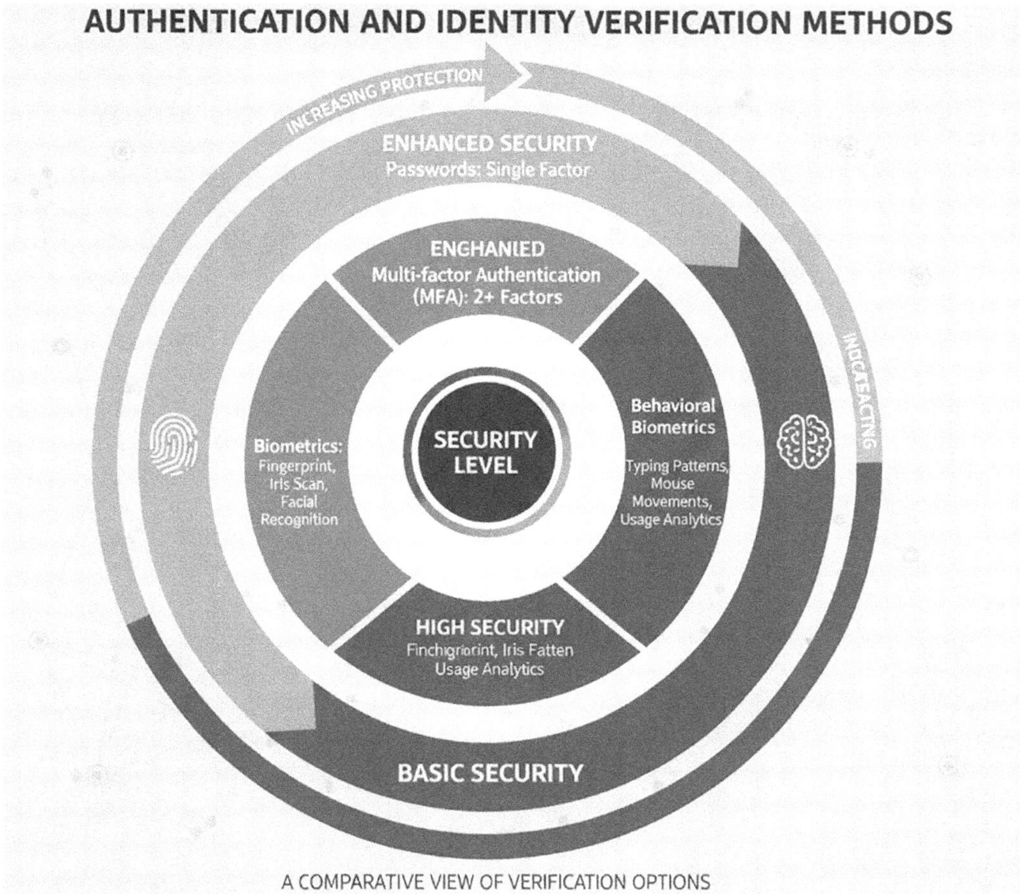

FIGURE 14.3 Authentication and identity verifying approaches.

TABLE 14.2
Authentication Methods Comparison

Method	Security Level	User Experience	Privacy Concerns	Examples of Applications
Password	Low	Medium	Low	Websites, email
Multi-Factor (MFA)	High	Medium	Low	Banking, corporate access
Biometric	Very High	High	Medium-High (data permanent)	Smartphones, border control
Behavioral Biometric	High	High	Medium	Online banking, corporate systems

14.5 BLOCKCHAIN AND DID

DID systems are a challenge to the conventional approach in which user information is managed by government bodies, companies, or websites. DIDs enable people to have credentials stored in web wallets and reveal only the required information. As an example, one can give a cryptographic proof of a user being older than a specific age without disclosing other information, as it is a cryptographic

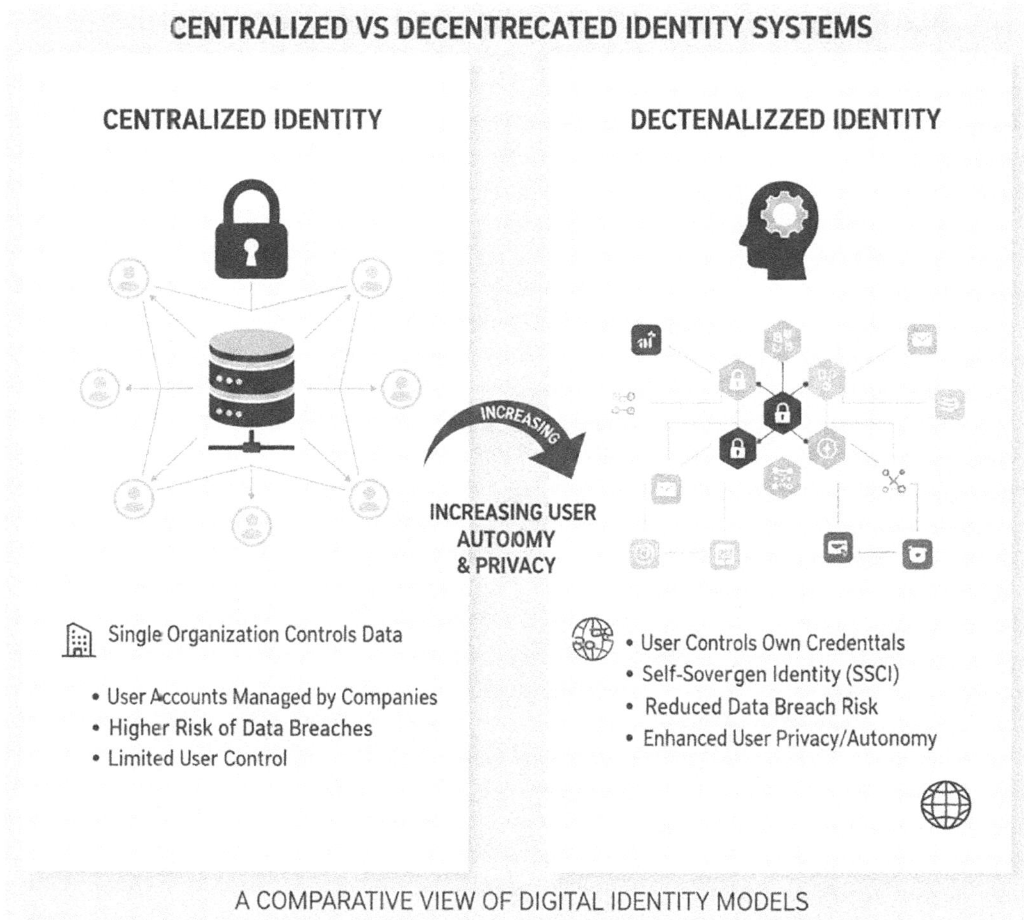

FIGURE 14.4 Centralized and decentralized identity systems.

proof, that is, the user does not have to share a full ID card to verify their age. This helps in the concept of data minimization, which is fundamental in the existing privacy legislation.

Comparison of centralized and DID systems.

Figure 14.4 is a pointer to the fact that the difference between centralized and DID systems is a dissimilarity in the data custodianship. Centralized The Centralized System One organization, for exmaple, a corporation or government agency, has control over and manages all the identity data. This model is less difficult to administer and is susceptible to massive breaches, though it does not leave user control. By contrast, a Decentralized System, commonly founded on blockchain or distributed ledger technologies (DLTs), and depending on DIDs, places the power of data management in the hands of the person. Users have their own verifiable credentials and they determine whom and when to share minimal necessary information. The model will boost privacy, autonomy, and security greatly as users have direct control to their digital identity.

Table 14.3 compares identity systems that are centralized and decentralized. In centralized systems, the data is managed by one organization, making it easier to manage but providing an opportunity to be compromised and restricting users to autonomy. In decentralized systems, frequently with blockchain and DIDs, the user has direct control over their credentials, whether and when to disclose information to whom. The strategy increases privacy, security, and cross-platform

TABLE 14.3
Decentralized vs. Centralized Identity

Characteristic	Centralized Identity	Decentralized Identity (DID)
Data Control	Organization controls data	User controls data
Security	Exposed to attacks	Tamper-resistant blockchain architecture
Interoperability	Provider only limited	Cross-platform with standards
Privacy	Complete risk of data exposed to other people	Little disclosure, selective sharing
Regulatory Compliance	Should adhere to outside laws	Can be incorporated into user-controlled systems

interoperability and decreases dependence on central authority. Implications of regulations are also emphasized in the table, demonstrating how the, so-called, decentralized systems can incorporate the elements of compliance into the frameworks that are under the control of users themselves, which enhances their ability to address legal and ethical requirements.

Most DID systems are based on blockchain technology due to its inability to be changed, transparency, and the decentralized nature. Nevertheless, blockchain does not require maintaining personal data in it; only verification keys or hashed proofs need to be stored. Hardman et al. (2022) emphasize that such an architecture lowers the chances of mass data breaches and can have provable and privacy-preserving identity transactions.

The issues are not yet resolved, such as the management key, the interoperability among the platforms, and the necessity of the universal standards. Furthermore, the irreversibility of blockchain records poses a question concerning the rights to delete the data. However, DID is a potential future of user-controlled digital ecologies.

14.6 LEGAL VIEWPOINTS OF CONSENT AND DATA RIGHTS

Laws in many countries recognize individuals' rights to control their personal information. The most powerful regulation is the GDPR, which focuses on the rights to access, rectification, erasure, and objection to processing. It also imposes rigid requirements on automated decision-making and profiling by putting human control on the decisions that have serious repercussions on people.

India Digital Personal Data Protection Act (DPDPA) also requires express consent for data processing and promotes the transparency, security protection, and accountability. The Act establishes the definition of consent managers, who facilitate persons with the permissions of services. This model will help in facilitating informed and centralized consent control.

These rights are also enhanced by sector-specific regulations. As an example, Health Insurance Portability and Accountability Act (HIPAA) regulates consent of medical data in the United States, whereas the Payment Card Industry Data Security Standard (PCI-DSS) regulates the financial data security worldwide.

Legal viewpoints offer a crucial aspect to the debate on digital identity because they help to codify ethical and human-right-based aspects in enforceable standards.

14.7 EMPOWERMENT OF THE USER WITH DATA PORTABILITY

The portability of data allows persons to move their personal data to another service company and giving people greater autonomy and reducing dependence on specific vendors. As an illustration, individuals have the ability to send their social media information, health and financial records to a different platform that could provide them with more privacy or service. This encourages competition in the digital service providers and eliminates monopolistic values on user information.

The GDPR expressly provides the right to data portability and the DPDPA in India has the same principles. However, there have been difficulties in implementation because of the differences in the data formats, system architecture, and interoperability standards. According to research conducted by De Hert et al. (2018), to achieve a good data portability, technical frameworks and user-friendly interfaces are to be united to facilitate a smooth transfer of data.

14.8 CREATING CONSENT SYSTEMS WITH A USER-CENTRIC DESIGN

Simple, transparent, and actual control in the hands of the user are the priorities of user-centric consent systems. Layered notices, icons, dynamic dashboards, and interactive visualizations can be used in place of long privacy statements by the platform. These applications make users learn about data practices within a short time and make informed decisions without unnecessary cognitive load.

Design should also address accessibility. The user interfaces of consent should be applicable to different literacy levels, languages, and abilities. It has been indicated that multilingual consent displays and audio-assisted explanations have a considerable positive effect on the understanding of various groups of users (Luger and Rodden, 2021).

Ethical design also demands the removal of dark patterns interfaces that control people into consenting. These may be pre-ticked boxes, deceptive color scheme, and pop-ups that hide the reject options. Such practices are explicitly rejected by such regulations as the GDPR and California Consumer Privacy Rights Act (CPRA).

14.9 CONSENT LIFECYCLE AND MANAGEMENT IN AI APPLICATIONS

AI applications operate in dynamic environments where the use of data changes with time. This demands the systems to handle the complete lifecycle of consent such as collection, storage, usage, sharing, expiration, and withdrawal. New data practices need to be informed to users when the AI models are updated or used again. Audit logs and versioning systems are useful in making a track of when consent was given and how.

The issue of consent is presented with new questions under AI-driven personalization. An example is that a recommendation system can make inferences based on highly sensitive properties—even when these properties were not explicitly given by the user. This brings questions of whether inferred information can be a subject of consent or not. According to literature by Wachter and Mittelstadt (2019), inference-based processing should be subjected to a special form of regulation in that it undermines the conventional privacy paradigm.

A successful lifecycle management approach is important to keep consent relevant despite the development of AI systems.

Figure 14.5 shows the AI Consent Interaction flowchart illustrating the repetitive design of consent in AI-based services. The cycle starts with the Collection of Data, which is then fed into the Model to create an accurate or more functional Model. As such updates have the potential to alter the manner of the customization of the processing of personal data, the system should inform the User of the corrections. These notifications are then followed by the option of Adjust Consent by users. In case the consent parameters vary, the AI model is retrained according to the updated permissions, and all data processing will be based on the current preferences of the user. This is a closed-loop model that ensures that AI applications defer to dynamic consent.

Table 14.4 shows the way consent is handled with various AI applications. In the case of recommendation systems, browsing history and click behavior need to be explicitly and continuously consented to as any changes in model usage might lead to a use of personal information. The Health monitoring apps capture sensitive biometric or sensor data, which requires powerful consent and encrypted data storage. Financial analytics application is sensitive to regulatory standards and transactional, which require a high degree of accuracy in consent and audit applications. In any program,

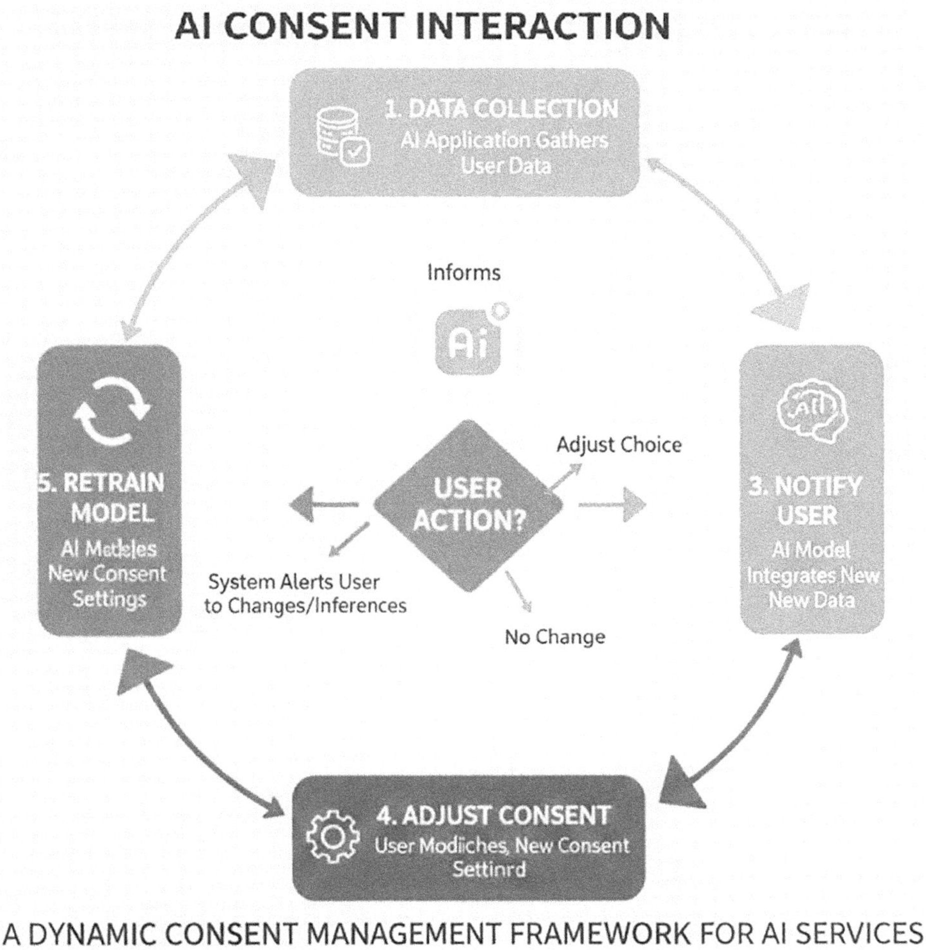

FIGURE 14.5 AI consent interaction.

TABLE 14.4
AI Usages and the Consent Lifecycle

AI Use	Data Being Gathered	Consent Condition	Monitoring Process	Comments
Recommendation Systems	Browsing, clicks	Explicit, ongoing	Dashboard, audit	Consent updates required on inferred data
Health Monitoring Apps	Biometric, sensor data	Explicit	Logs, notifications	High sensitivity; encrypted storage
Financial Analytics	Transactional data	Explicit and opt-in	Audit trails	Banking law and PCI-DSS regulated.

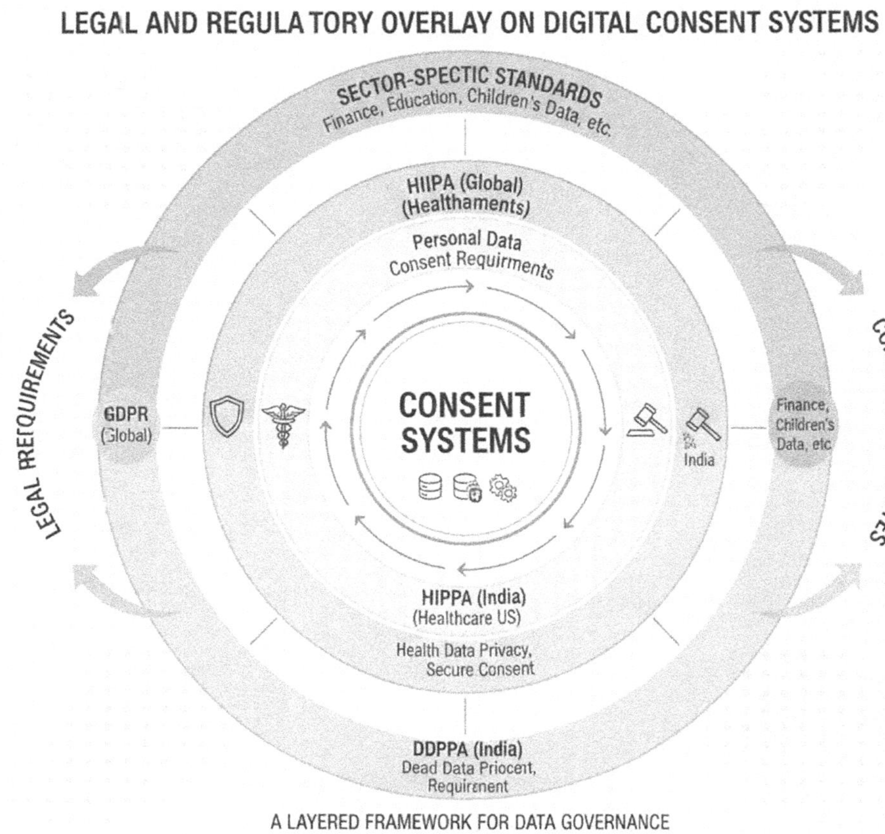

FIGURE 14.6 Overlay legal and regulatory systems.

the constant monitoring, notifications, and the possibility to change consent allow users to have control over their personal data, which reveals how the consent lifecycle can be applied to real-life scenarios involving AI.

Figure 14.6 shows how Legal and Regulatory Overlay indicates how laws and compliance requirements serve as critical limitations on digital consent systems. The majority of regulatory frameworks (including the GDPR in Europe, the HIPAA in U.S. healthcare, and the DPDPA in India) include stipulated minimum standards of consent, data processing, and user rights. These general principles are in turn narrowed down by industry-specific standards, such as in the financial services or healthcare industries, which control the requirements around explicitly consenting, minimizing data, and the right to withdraw. A representation of these overlapping layers can be used to explain the interactions between legal frameworks and technical implementations to promote compliance.

14.10 CASE STUDIES: SECURE CONSENT MANAGEMENT

Healthcare: In the health system, patient records have sensitive information; hence, digital consent is essential. There is an increasing use of biometric verification and encrypted consent forms in hospitals, with only authorized personnel being allowed to view any information regarding patients. Just-in-time consent prompts are used in Telehealth platforms to give explanations on how video data, sensor readings, or the diagnostic results will be used.

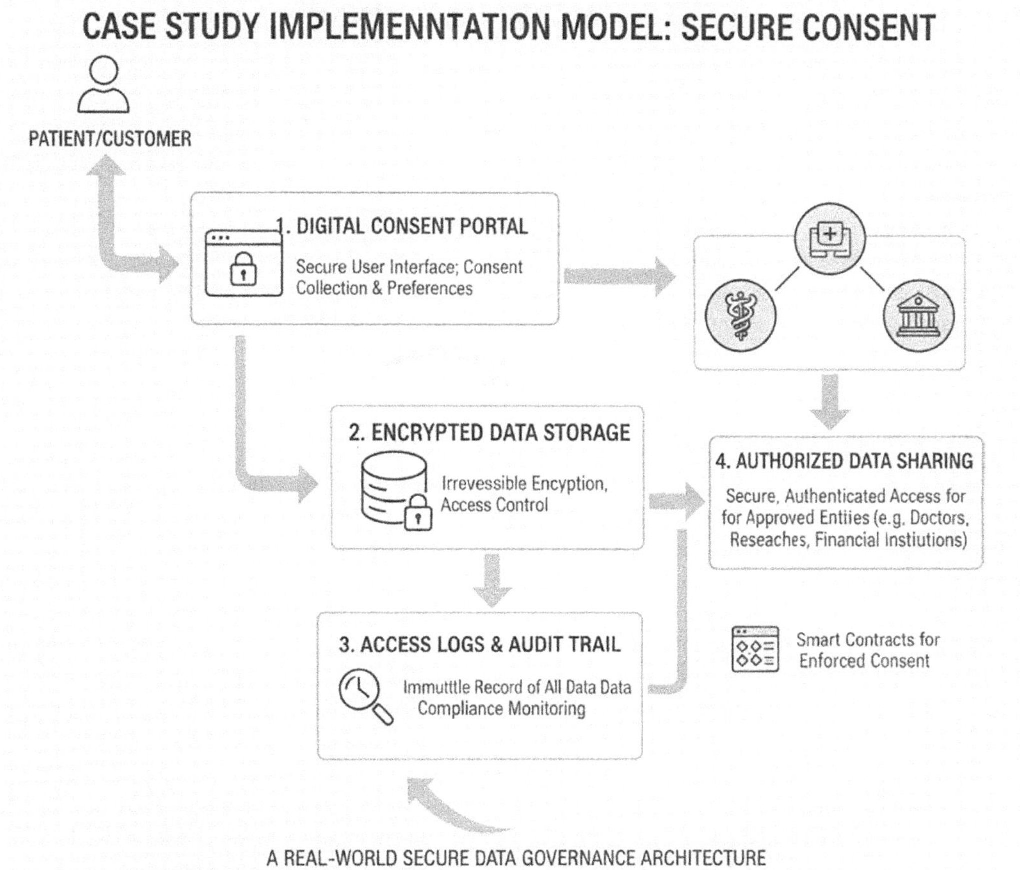

FIGURE 14.7 Implementation model in a case study systems.

Finance: MFA is used by the banks, transaction-level permission, and safe audit trails. Regulatory frameworks ask banks to record overt permission to deal with activities like credit rating, data sharing with third parties, and auto-financial advice.

Education: LMSs also have parental dashboards, where parents are able to regulate the type of student data accessed by third-party applications. Consent is granular, so one can give their consent to be tracked, to have their learning analyzed, or to use communications tools.

These case studies show that consent mechanisms enhance better trust and transparency as well as minimize risks of unauthorized access to data.

Figure 14.7 offers the Case Study Implementation Model, which serves as a real-life example of the safe consent management in such sensitive areas like healthcare or finance. The interaction between a Patient or User and a Digital Consent Portal initiates the process of the permissions grant. These permissions and associated data are stored straight away in Encrypted Storage. All the access attempts are logged, and Access Logs are reviewed or audited periodically to verify compliance. Data can only be Shared with Authorized Entities after having been validated using the audit trail as this ensures that all operations are carried out according to the consent of the user. This model shows the practical use of a digital consent lifecycle, which involves the elements of security, transparency, and compliance with regulations.

14.11 ETHICAL IDENTITY SYSTEM DIRECTIONS IN THE FUTURE

Self-sovereign identity, zero-knowledge proofs, and trust scoring based on AI are likely to be incorporated into future identity systems. Attributes, for example, age, citizenship, or credentials, may be proved zero-knowledge without the disclosure of any personal information. Anomaly detection with AI can detect suspicious identity attempts and protect the privacy of the user with federated learning models.

Ethical challenges remain. The risks that are in progress are algorithmic bias, unequal access to identity technologies, and digital exclusion. It will be necessary to ensure that the identity systems are inclusive and multi-ethnic. Also, long-term models of governance should specify the mechanisms of maintaining identity systems, auditing, and holding them accountable.

14.12 SUMMARY

Digital consent, control over identity, and autonomy are the central concepts of reliable digital ecosystems, particularly during a time when AI-based services, mobile applications, and interconnected platforms are highly dependent on personal information. As has been highlighted in this chapter, consent cannot be considered a one or two-time checkbox or legal formality. In its place, it is better to consider it as a continuous dynamic process between users and digital services, which continues to be modified as new data is gathered, algorithms are revised, and system opportunities grow. An informed consent presupposes a clear communication, a clear data practice, and the mechanisms within the process that will enable individuals to be able to revisit, amend, or withdraw the decision without punishment. These are the aspects that constitute the ethical basis on which the contemporary identity frameworks should be constructed.

The identity verification process was discussed, and it was noted that the use of traditional password-based systems is no longer secure enough due to the existence of advanced cyber threats. MFA, biometry, and behavioral analytics have become the new sophisticated solutions, but they include the problem of inclusivity, fairness, and permanence of data. The chapter has highlighted that enhanced security must not come at the expense of the user rights as well as encode the biases that undermine the marginalized communities. Rather, identity systems must work to achieve accuracy as well as equity so that no user is perceived unfairly and insecurely.

The other central theme that was addressed was the rise of DID systems, especially those that are enhanced by blockchain technology. These systems strive to restore the power of identity to the individuals so that they can be in control of their personal information to reveal or disclose it at their own discretion. DID models are likely to offer better privacy solutions, less susceptibility to information and data breaches, and more autonomy to users by limiting its dependency on centralized authorities. They are, however, associated with new obligations as well, concerning cryptographic key management and international interoperability. With the digital world moving toward self-sovereign identity frameworks, the chapter highlighted the need to have sound governance frameworks and make such frameworks available to everyone. Legal views also supported the way global policy frameworks determine the roles of platforms and organizations. Regulations such as the GDPR, the HIPAA, or the DPDPA of India require explicit consent, data protection, and user-related rights, such as data portability and the right to erasure. The ethical expectations are also turned into laws to enforce procedures that promote platforms to use a more transparent interface, more equitable practices with data, and more robust accountability frameworks. Nonetheless, there are still challenges even with such developments, especially in the regulation of the inference-based AI, automated profiling, and transfers of data across borders.

Another aspect that was brought to light in the chapter in connection to enhancing user empowerment is the ability of designers to improve user empowerment with the help of design techniques like consent dashboards, simplified interfaces, multilingual prompts, and the eradication of dark patterns. Having easy-to-use features to explain to users their privacy preferences and control them helps boost self-determination and long-term confidence between people and computer networks. The control of the consent lifecycle is particularly critical in AI applications, where the models are quite often upgraded and developed. Systems should be able to share these changes with the users and provide the users with a chance to change their preferences.

Lastly, case studies demonstrated in practice how various industries are already implementing secure consent management systems that strike the right balance between innovation and user rights, including in the healthcare industry, financial industry, and education sector. These instances show that responsible digital practices can be implemented and they are effective as well as providing better security and more ethical foundations.

Finally, as the chapter highlighted, the future of digital identity systems should be driven by principles that are human-oriented. As technology is increasingly becoming ubiquitous, transparency, autonomy, and fairness at all levels of data interaction must become the top priority of the organization. Through DID, privacy-friendly technologies, ethical design, and strict legal norms, the society will be able to create digital ecosystems that will be able to operate effectively as well as honor the dignity and the rights of all individuals. The way to go involves the cooperation of technologists, policymakers, designers, and even the users themselves. It is only with this combined effort that the digital identity systems can develop into frameworks that are secure, inclusive, and indeed in line with the human values.

REFERENCES

Abdellatif, A. A., Mohamed, A., Chiasserini, C., & Trinchero, D. (2021). Edge computing for smart environmental monitoring: A federated learning approach. *IEEE Internet of Things Journal, 8*(16), 12856–12867.

Abouelmehdi, K., Beni-Hessane, A., & Khaloufi, H. (2018). Big healthcare data: Preserving security and privacy. *Journal of Big Data, 5*(1), 1–18. https://doi.org/10.1186/s40537-017-0110-7

Albrecht, J. P. (2016). How the GDPR will change the world. *European Data Protection Law Review, 2*(3), 287–289. https://doi.org/10.21552/EDPL/2016/3/4

Alge, D. (2020). Challenges in implementing consent management platforms. *International Journal of Information Management, 53*, 102120. https://doi.org/10.1016/j.ijinfomgt.2020.102120

Auer, S., & König, P. (2018). Self-sovereign identity: A position paper. *Blockchain Research Institute Reports,* 1–20.

Ausloos, J., Dewitte, P., & Verdoodt, V. (2020). The rise and fall of the purpose limitation principle. *Computer Law & Security Review, 36*, 105380.

Balamurugan, G., Tyagi, A.K., & Richa, A. (2023). Survey on privacy preserving and trust building techniques of blockchain-based systems. In: *Privacy Preservation and Secured Data Storage in Cloud Computing*. IGI Global. DOI: 10.4018/979-8-3693-0593-5.ch019

Bhatia, A., & Breaux, T. D. (2018). Empirical measurement of perceived privacy risk. *ACM Transactions on Privacy and Security, 21*(4), 1–34. https://doi.org/10.1145/3267808

Brandom, R. (2019). Data portability and its limits. *Journal of Digital Policy & Regulation, 7*(2), 120–133.

Buolamwini, J., & Gebru, T. (2018). Gender shades: Intersectional accuracy disparities in commercial gender classification. *PMLR, 81*, 1–15. https://proceedings.mlr.press/v81/buolamwini18a.html?utm_source=chatgpt.com

Cavoukian, A. (2019). Privacy by design in the age of AI. *Information and Privacy Commissioner Reports*, 1–12.

Custers, B., Ursic, H., & van der Hof, S. (2018). Informed consent in data-driven services. *Computer Law & Security Review, 34*(2), 410–422. https://doi.org/10.1016/j.clsr.2017.08.006

De Hert, P., Papakonstantinou, V., Malgieri, G., Beslay, L., & Sánchez, I. (2018). The right to data portability in the GDPR. *Computer Law & Security Review, 34*(2), 193–203. https://doi.org/10.1016/j.clsr.2017.10.003

Dunphy, P., & Petitcolas, F. A. (2018). A first look at identity management schemes on the blockchain. *IEEE Security & Privacy, 16*(4), 20–29. https://doi.org/10.1109/MSP.2018.3111247

Floridi, L. (2016). Soft ethics and the governance of the digital. *Philosophy & Technology, 29*(1), 1–8.

Gasser, U., & Almeida, V. (2017). A layered model for AI governance. *IEEE Internet Computing, 21*(6), 58–62. https://doi.org/10.1109/MIC.2017.4180831

Gray, C. M., Kou, Y., Battles, B., Hoggatt, J., & Toombs, A. (2018). The dark (patterns) side of UX design. In *CHI conference proceedings* (pp. 1–14). https://doi.org/10.1145/3173574.3174108

Hardman, D., Wuyts, K., & Joosen, W. (2022). Privacy-preserving decentralized identity protocols: A survey. *IEEE Access, 10*, 8334–8356.

Jain, A. K., Nandakumar, K., & Ross, A. (2021). 50 years of biometric research. *Pattern Recognition Letters, 144*, 70–80.

Kang, J., & Kim, H. (2020). Blockchain-based privacy protection: Challenges and solutions. *Sensors, 20*(8), 2474. https://doi.org/10.3390/s20082474

Khan, A., & Salah, K. (2018). IoT security: Review and blockchain solutions. *IEEE Access, 6*, 2210–2232.

Koops, B. J. (2019). Forgotten rights: The right to erasure. *International Data Privacy Law, 9*(1), 1–8. https://doi.org/10.1093/idpl/ipz001

Kumari, S., Tyagi, A. K., Tiwari, S., & Kulshreshtha, G. (2025a). Sensors and digital twin for healthcare monitoring frameworks. In T. A. Nguyen (Ed.), *Digital twin, blockchain, and sensor networks in the healthy and mobile city* (Chapter 10, pp. 147–177). Elsevier. https://doi.org/10.1016/C2024-0-01681-10

Kumari, S., Tyagi, A. K., Tiwari, S., & Singh, R. (2025b). Medical sensor network, edge computing and blockchain for efficient medical data exchange. In T. A. Nguyen (Ed.), *Digital twin, blockchain, and sensor networks in the healthy and mobile city* (Chapter 11, pp. 179–198). Elsevier. https://doi.org/10.1016/C2024-0-01681-11

Luger, E., & Rodden, T. (2021). Consent and privacy in digital systems. *Journal of Information Technology, 36*(3), 250–266.

Malgieri, G., & Comandé, G. (2017). Sensitive-by-distance data. *Computer Law & Security Review, 33*(5), 643–660.

Marelli, L., & Testa, G. (2021). Data governance in digital health. *Big Data & Society, 8*(2), 1–12.

Mathews-Hunt, P. (2020). AI systems and privacy risks. *AI & Society, 35*(3), 627–638.

McDonald, A., & Cranor, L. F. (2009). The cost of reading privacy policies. *I/S: A Journal of Law and Policy for the Information Society, 4*(3), 543–568.

Mishra, A. K., Tiwari, S., Tyagi, A. K., & Arowolo, M. O. (2024). Security, privacy, trust, and provenance issues in Internet of Things–based edge environment. In S. Pal, C. Savaglio, R. Minerva, & F. C. Delicato (Eds.), *IoT edge intelligence* (pp. 233–263). Springer. https://doi.org/10.1007/978-3-031-58388-9_8

Mittelstadt, B. (2019). Principles alone cannot guarantee ethical AI. *Nature Machine Intelligence, 1*(11), 501–507. https://doi.org/10.1038/s42256-019-0114-4

Nair, M. M., & Tyagi, A. K. (2021). Privacy: History, statistics, policy, laws, preservation and threat analysis. *Journal of Information Assurance & Security, 16*(1).

Nair, M.M., & Tyagi, A.K. (2025). Transformative effects of emerging technologies on Industry 5.0 and Society 5.0: Current status, vision, issues, challenges, and opportunities for future. In: *Next Generation Data Science and Blockchain Technology for Industry 5.0*. Wiley. DOI: https://doi.org/10.1002/9781394245215.ch13, ISBN: 9781394245185.

Nissenbaum, H. (2019). Contextual integrity up and down the data food chain. *Theoretical Inquiries in Law, 20*(1), 221–256. https://doi.org/10.1515/til-2019-0008

O'Connor, Y., Rowan, W., Lynch, L., & Heavin, C. (2021). Privacy by design: A review of organisational challenges. *Information Systems Frontiers, 23*(2), 469–487.

Obar, J. A., & Oeldorf-Hirsch, A. (2020). The biggest lie on the internet. *Information, Communication & Society, 23*(1), 128–147. https://dx.doi.org/10.2139/ssrn.2757465

Pavlovic, N., & Scekic, O. (2022). A survey on digital consent in smart systems. *IEEE Access, 10*, 110009–110027.

Reisman, D., Schultz, J., Crawford, K., & Whittaker, M. (2018). Algorithmic impact assessments. *AI Now Institute Report*, 1–22.

Solove, D. J. (2021). The myth of the privacy paradox. *George Washington Law Review, 89*, 1–52.

Ting, C., Tsai, H., & Lin, J. (2020). Designing consent management for IoT ecosystems. *Journal of Network and Computer Applications, 168*, 102737. https://doi.org/10.1016/j.jnca.2020.102737

Tyagi, A.K. (2021). Analysis of security and privacy aspects of blockchain technologies from smart era' perspective: The challenges and a way forward. In: *Recent Trends in Blockchain for Information Systems Security and Privacy* (pp. 1–17). DOI: https://doi.org/10.1201/9781003139737, eBook-ISBN: 9781003139737

Tyagi, A.K. (2025). Blockchain for smart hospital in Healthcare 5.0: modeling structure, challenges, and future emerging trends. In: *Human-Centric Integration of Next-Generation Data Science and Blockchain Technology.* Elsevier. DOI: https://doi.org/10.1016/B978-0-443-33498-6.00026-1, ISBN: 978-0-443-33498-6.

Tyagi, A.K. (2026). *Chapter 4 - Artificial intelligence–blockchain–Internet of Things–based smart healthcare services: literature review and future research directions, in the book: Smart Hospital Anatomy with Advanced Sensors Innovations in Patient Care*, Elsevier (pp. 49–61). https://doi.org/10.1016/B978-0-443-45875-0.00005-3, ISBN: 978-0-443-45875-0.

Tyagi, A., Kumari, S., & Tiwari, S. (2024c). Internet of Things for smart healthcare: A survey. In A. K. Sharma, N. Chanderwal, S. Tyagi, & P. Upadhyay (Eds.), *Future of AI in medical imaging (Chapter 2).* IGI Global. https://doi.org/10.4018/979-8-3693-2359-5.ch002

Tyagi, A. K., & Tiwari, S. (2024a). Blockchain-enabled smart healthcare applications in 6G networks. In A. K. Tyagi (Ed.), *Digital twin and blockchain for smart cities (Chapter 20).* Wiley. https://doi.org/10.1002/9781394303564.ch20

Tyagi, A. K., Tripathi, K., Tiwari, S., & Kaushik, S. (2025). An efficient technique for privacy preservation, trusted and secure patient-centric services in smart healthcare. In *Proceedings of the 6th international conference on recent trends in communication & intelligent systems (ICRTCIS 2025)* (pp. 31–47). IET. https://doi.org/10.1049/icp.2025.2731

Wachter, S., & Mittelstadt, B. (2019). A right to reasonable inferences. *Columbia Business Law Review, 2019*(2), 494–620.

Zuboff, S. (2019). *The age of surveillance capitalism.* PublicAffairs.

15 Accountability, Auditing, and Compliance Mechanisms

15.1 INTRODUCTION

The decision-making process is being revolutionized by artificial intelligence (AI) because it is very efficient, predictive, and scalable. AI is used in areas such as medical diagnostics, credit rating, and criminal liability assessment. However, problems of accountability and trust are related to the introduction of AI. AI cannot be rendered transparent, as the decision-making of a human being can be, particularly when working with complex models (e.g., deep learning networks). This kind of opaqueness makes accountability mechanisms instrumental toward the delivery of the fact that the AI results can be explained, traced, and fixed in instances where such is necessary.

The question of responsibility in AI extends far beyond technical issues. It includes direction, technical protection, legal adherence, and moral duty. Effective mechanisms allow stakeholders to understand, audit, and oversee AI systems, and this includes the developers, operators, regulators, and the affected entities. These mechanisms are discussed in this chapter in a comprehensive manner, providing advice to practitioners and policymakers interested in putting in place responsible AI frameworks.

15.2 LITERATURE REVIEW

The notion of algorithmic accountability has spread quite a vast body of academic literature within the last 10 years. In essence, accountability concerns who is responsible for an AI system's design, implementation, and outcomes, especially when the system produces harmful or discriminatory results. The systematic literature review by Wieringa is still foundational: she considers the meaning of accountability in the algorithmic context and divides various dimensions, including transparency, responsibility, and remedy. This ambiguity has also been clarified further by business and information systems research, which claims that although algorithms themselves cannot be held responsible, the organizations and individuals deploying them should be.

A single section of the literature has stressed on technical accountability, which focuses on design transparency, interpretability, and auditability (Veale and Binns, 2024). Scholars argue that interpretability is not something that fits all: stakeholders are different, and so are situations. The designers are encouraged to publish the objectives of their models, data inputs, and architecture to ensure what Wieringa termed as design transparency, but to remain auditably available by allowing outside parties to investigate and comprehend system behavior. Human oversight remains essential in high-risk domains; designers must carefully consider how humans remain in the loop such that they can provide meaningful intervention.

In addition to this technical viewpoint, other literature takes into consideration governance and organizational accountability. According to Ayling and Chapman (2022), Chakraborty et al. (2020),

DOI: 10.1201/9781003658344-19

Cobbe et al. (2021), and Raji and Buolamwini (2019), there is a proposal for an AI accountability ecosystem. They suggest that accountability cannot be confined to the internal controls, but it should also be applied to external accreditation, depending on the circumstances of the industry. In the meantime, Cobbe et al. (2021) and Nair et al. (2021) propose an idea of a reviewable automated decision-making, where the decision-making process can be divided into human and automated components, which allows maintaining records that are in compliance with regulatory and legal control.

Simultaneously, auditing has become a potent accountability tool. Raji et al. (2020), Nair et al. (2021), and Rajani et al. (2022) propose an internal algorithmic auditing framework that covers model design, deployment, and monitoring. Simultaneously, Gupta et al. (2018), Johnson (2021), Kantayya (2020), and Raji et al. (2020, 2021) investigated the organization of who audits the auditors: they found that there were no standardized audit practices, and called on algorithmic auditors to be accredited, stakeholders involved, and harm reporting increased. Practically, Korolova (2024), Laato et al. (2022), Mikians et al. (2012), Schneider et al. (2022), and Seppälä et al. (2021) suggest a criterion audit model based on the financial auditing model: they are borrowing audit procedures used in the financial world and evaluating them in relation to algorithmic compliance, bias, and governance.

These accountability debates are based on the problem of fairness and bias. The article about the disparate impact of big data by the influential authors, Barocas and Selbst (2016), Tyagi and Tiwari (2024a), emphasized the role of predictive models in maintaining discrimination when the models are trained on biased information. This has motivated extensive research on fairness metrics and bias-mitigation techniques. Political and philosophical scholars (like Binns, 2018; Nair et al., 2025; Tyagi (2021); Tyagi, 2025; Balamurugan et al., 2023) argue that fairness cannot be reduced to statistics alone; it also carries important normative and philosophical dimensions. In recent works by Minkkinen et al. (2024, 2023), Mökander et al. (2022), Singh et al. (2018), and Tyagi et al. (2024c), "peer-induced fairness" combines counterfactual fairness with peer-comparison methods.

There has been increased interest in certification and external verification as ways of strengthening accountability. An example of this is the European AI Act, which suggests post-market surveillance and conformity testing to guarantee that AI systems comply with the high-risk standards. Koshiyama et al. (2021), Floridi and Cowls (2019), Panigutti et al. (2020), Pretschner and Kacianka (2021), Venkatasubramanian (2023), Tyagi (2026) and Tyagi et al. (2025) give those instructions on how audits, assessments, and oversight ought to operate under such regulation. This certification process is not purely technical; it is socio-technical: it includes the third-party auditors, constant monitoring, and being transparent to those interested. This approach aligns with broader governance models in responsible AI research. As an example, recent surveys on responsible AI governance focus on the balance between performance, transparency, and ethics, the most important institutional practices, and tradeoffs at the organizational level.

On the risk and legal responsibility side, scholars work out the operationalization of liability in an algorithm system. Debates about product liability, developer liability, and operator negligence are increasingly grounded in practical regulatory proposals. The need to have well-established remedial avenues and redress mechanisms is also highlighted in the ethical governance literature, in a way that audits are connected with legal responsibility to enable the victim to seek redress.

Transparency, which is not just interpretable, is also a related concept that is discrete. It involves recording data provenance, model choices, and risk analysis. Frontiers in human-dynamics research is an explanation of technical methods, including explainable AI (XAI), to reveal these dimensions by turning decisions and model internals into understandable forms to various stakeholders. It is not only to ensure that the algorithms are explainable but also to have records and logs that could be audited as well as provide documentation that could be readily read by stakeholders, both technical and nontechnical.

The concept of redress and remedy is at the crossroads of governance, law, and ethics. Algorithms that harm should have systematic mechanisms of recourse—whether through money, appeal, or correction. Researchers propose the incorporation of audit trail, third-party investigation, and stakeholder participation into law and governance systems, which will seal the so-called accountability gap.

Although much has been done, there are also a number of challenges that are mentioned in the literature. One is standardization: No international standard yet exists for how algorithmic auditing should be conducted or what criteria should be met in certification, and even among the auditors themselves, some are not accredited or do not have a standard methodology. Power dynamics also pose a significant obstacle: the dominance of traditional auditing firms can create the threat of establishing their commercial culture on algorithmic auditing, which will negatively affect the regulatory purposes. Besides, there is an epistemic clash between the safeguarding of proprietary models and the possibility of full audits. The degree to which auditors are allowed access and the level of confidentiality is a contentious issue.

New studies suggest the use of ecosystem-based accountability that acknowledges the fact that no single mechanism is enough. The AI accountability ecosystem by Percy and co-authors, the reviewable ADM by Cobbe et al., and the criterion audit framework all propose a layered approach, which is to integrate internal governance, external auditing, certification, and continuous monitoring. These socio-technical frameworks mirror the multidimensional aspect of the algorithmic accountability in which strategies of the technical, organizational, and legal levels should exist and support one another.

Lastly, the future trends in the literature will lead toward two related trends. To begin with, continuous auditing with AI has the potential to provide real-time risk detection and reaction. Second, it is also believed that regulatory harmonization on a global scale is becoming a requirement to prevent fragmentation and to facilitate the same standards of high-risk AI systems. It is emphasized in the governance research that these future regimes should integrate multidisciplinary and participatory practices into their systems that will make the voices of marginalized and affected communities be included in auditing, certifications, and redress mechanisms.

A brief overview of the significant research studies on AI accountability is presented in Table 15.1, with a focus on the areas of their interest and key discoveries. As an illustration, Barocas and Selbst (2016) and Mishra et al. (2024) highlight the risk of big data perpetuating discrimination unintentionally, whereas Binns (2018) focuses on the philosophical and normative aspects of fairness not only in terms of statistical values. Raji et al. (2020) and Cobbe et al. (2021) pay attention to auditing models, and it is crucial to pay attention to the issues of internal record keeping and reviewable decision-making procedures. Koshiyama et al. (2021) point to certification and post-market monitoring as a prerequisite of regulation compliance, but Wieringa (2020) singles out the

TABLE 15.1
Literature Overview of AI Accountability

Author(s)	Year	Emphasis	Significant Results
Barocas and Selbst	2016	Big data discrimination	Discrimination can be reinforced by big data
Binns	2018	Fairness in ML	Fairness is multidimensional, must be normatively assessed
Raji et al.	2020	Internal auditing	The end-to-end audit framework required with AI
Cobbe et al.	2021	Reviewable ADM	Decomposes decision-making into human and machines
Koshiyama et al.	2021	Certification	The most important are conformity tests and after-market controls
Wieringa	2020	Systematic review	Technical, organizational, and legal integration are needed in accountability
Foalem et al.	2025	Continuous auditing	Requirements that are critical to responsible ML to be logged
Chakraborty et al.	2020	Fair ML	Fairway method of bias mitigation

combination of technical, organizational, and legal devices as the major need to establish effective accountability. Foalem et al. (2025) and Kumari et al. (2025a) mention continuous auditing tools to guarantee the system reliability in the long term, and Chakraborty et al. (2020) and Kumari et al. (2025b) introduce the organized methods of fairness and bias in AI. This table summarizes results at the technical, organizational, and legal levels, which enables the readers to promptly determine the basis contributions and the lack of the existing literature.

The research on accountability, auditing, and compliance in AI has developed into a multifaceted and multilayered dialogue. The study of interpretability and provenance is being integrated into the technical scholarship with organizational governance, the liability of legal, and the redress of ethics. Although there are still substantial obstacles to reach, namely, standardization, auditor accreditation, and transparency/proprietary issues, the socio-technical convergence approach provides the way to go. Accountability is now being understood in the domain not as a mechanism, but as a terrain of practices, each of which is essential to the role of being responsible in a real-world situation involving AI systems.

15.3 ACCOUNTABILITY IN AI DECISION SYSTEMS

Accountability in AI refers to clarifying, justifying, and taking responsibility for the decisions made by intelligent systems. Among them are transparency, traceability, responsibility, and remediation. Transparency makes decisions understandable, while traceability makes it possible to reconstruct inputs, processes, and outputs. Responsibility defines who is responsible for the results, and remediation gives opportunities to remedy mistakes or recompense for the impacted.

The responsibility of AI is a complex concept in contrast to the human choice as they are distributed across developers, operators, and third-party vendors. To convert accountability into practice, it is necessary to combine governance, technical protection, and legal tools to operationalize it.

Figure 15.1 represents a multilayered system that is intended to make the deployment and operation of AI systems responsible. The center of focus is technical safeguards and includes audit trails, provenance tracking, XAI, and continuous monitoring. Between this center is the overlay of Organizational Governance, which is the human oversight system, such as Oversight Committees, Ethics Boards, and Internal Audits. The topmost layer is External Oversight and Legal Frameworks, which strengthens the trust of the people and makes them accountable by means of mechanisms like Third-Party Certification, Regulatory Compliance, and Redress Procedures. This number underlines the mutual reliance of all layers, as it is important to note that proper accountability is created when the technical systems are managed by an internal human authority and are additionally inspected in the frame of external legal standards.

Table 15.2 shows a detailed view of the main mechanisms employed in the process of accountability in AI systems. The table has divided every mechanism based on its purpose, stakeholders that it applies to, and practical examples, which gives a clear roadmap on how accountability is operationalized. As an example, Audit Trails enable developers and regulators to track decision-making by documenting every input and output of the system, which is important in the process of error diagnostics or bias discovery. This is enhanced with Provenance Tracking which keeps comprehensive records of data sources and data transformations, guaranteeing transparency in data processing. XAI makes the use and regulation of models more interpretable to the end user, enabling stakeholders to comprehend the decision-making process of models. Constant Compliance Monitoring would ensure real-time control to identify anomalies or drift behavior of a system, whereas Third-Party Certification and external validation would enhance the trust of the people and the compliance with regulations. Such organizational mechanisms as Oversight Committees and Ethics Boards will be used to make sure that human judgment sets AI deployment and that Transparency Reports share system capabilities and risks with a wider audience. Lastly, Redress Mechanisms create systematic avenues of dealing with harm so that concerned parties are granted

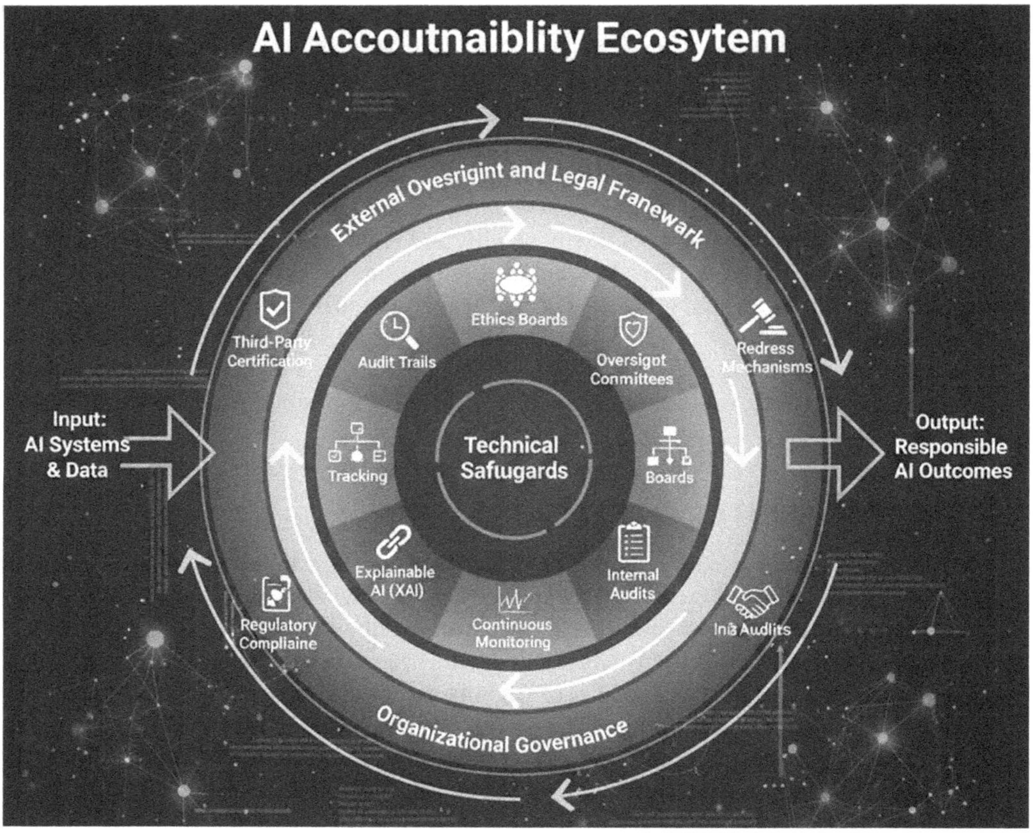

FIGURE 15.1 AI accountability ecosystem.

TABLE 15.2
Major Mechanisms of AI Accountability

Mechanism	Purpose	Stakeholders	Examples
Audit Trails	Trace decision-making	Developers, regulators	Logs of inputs and outputs with a timestamp
Provenance Tracking	Track data lineage	Data engineers, auditors	Model input source tracking
Explainable AI (XAI)	Make AI more interpretable Increase interpretability	Users, regulators	Model explanations, feature importance
Instant Compliance Measurement	Identify anomalies	Operators, Oversight boards	Dashboards, real-time notifications
Third-Party Certification	External certification	Auditors, regulators	ISO-style certification
Oversight Committees	Organizational governance	Ethics boards, managers	Policy reviews, risk assessment
Transparency Reports	Stakeholder communication	Public, regulators	Model cards, risk documentation
Redress Mechanisms	Correct harm	Affected people, courts	Compensation, appeals, corrective measures

a chance to claim a refund or remedies. Together, the table shows that the accountability in AI is a multidimensional concept that includes technical protective measures, governance frameworks, and legal frameworks to ensure responsible system behavior.

15.4 AUDIT TRAIL, PROVENANCE TRACKING ROLE

15.4.1 Audit Trails

Audit trails record the chronological history of an AI system's activities which comprises the data that entered the system, the updates made to the model, and the actions of the users. They enable organizations to see the process of decision-making and enable organizations to identify abnormalities, unauthorized activities, or errors. Audit trails are fundamental in the regulation compliance and accountability by the organization.

15.4.2 Provenance Tracking

Provenance is an account of the history of the data and the transformation that took place in AI systems. It makes sure that all decisions can be linked to their data sources and stages of processing. Provenance tracking is used in healthcare, for example, to ensure accountability and determine liability by providing clinicians with the ability to check diagnostic recommendations by tracking the underlying patient data and model parameters. Together, audit trails and provenance tracking form the technical foundation of transparent and accountable AI.

This is Figure 15.2, which takes a special interest in the technical layer through the illustration of the Audit Trail and Provenance Flow in an AI system. It is linear in nature, beginning with Data Sources, where raw inputs are gathered, proceeding to Preprocessing and Transformation, where the data is cleansed, and features are identified. Model Training and Updates and Decision Output, which contains algorithmic calculations, comes next. All these combined, the origin, manipulation, and handling of data and model decisions can be tracked and proven, which plays a crucial role in identifying mistakes, reducing bias, and promoting accountability.

15.5 CERTIFICATION AND VERIFICATION BY A THIRD PARTY

Third-party certification implies an external assessment of AI systems to make them meet the ethical, technical, and legal requirements. Certification may include robustness, bias, privacy, and compliance with regulatory standards. Independent auditors minimize conflicts of interest and improve trust given by people as they offer objective evaluations.

Certification systems similar to ISO standards help demonstrate organizational due diligence and adherence to best practices. Third-party verification can be used in areas of high risk, like finance or healthcare, where it can offer extra security, and AI systems can be implemented in a responsible manner.

The Third-Party Certification Workflow, Figure 15.3, is one of the major processes of the external oversight layer. The first one is the AI System Submission, where the developer offers the system to an independent assessment. The next step is an Independent Audit to determine whether the system is fair, unbiased, secure, and transparent. These findings are summarized in a Compliance Report, and they are used to inform the Certification Decision, to give the system approval or disapproval. Importantly, the workflow continues with post-market monitoring and Continuous Verification as it creates the feedback loop to guarantee the continuous adherence to standards and stimulate the further enhancement of the AI system.

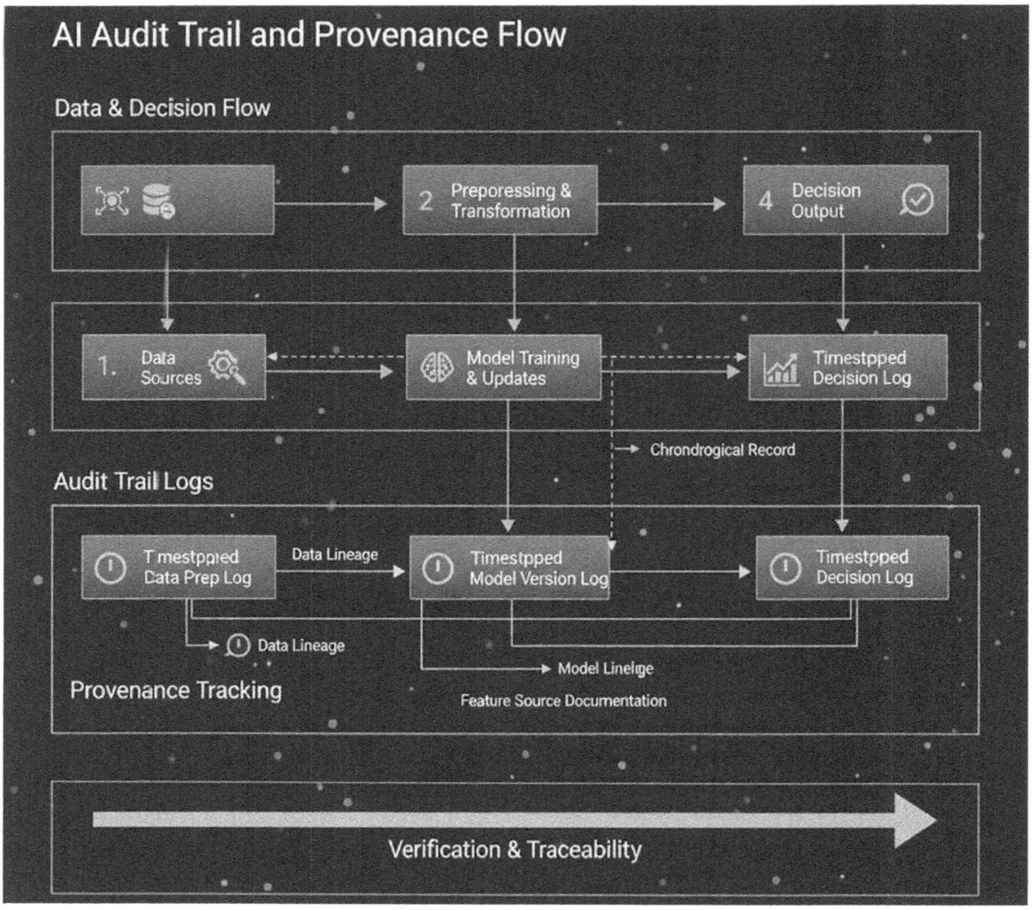

FIGURE 15.2 AI audit trail and provenance flow.

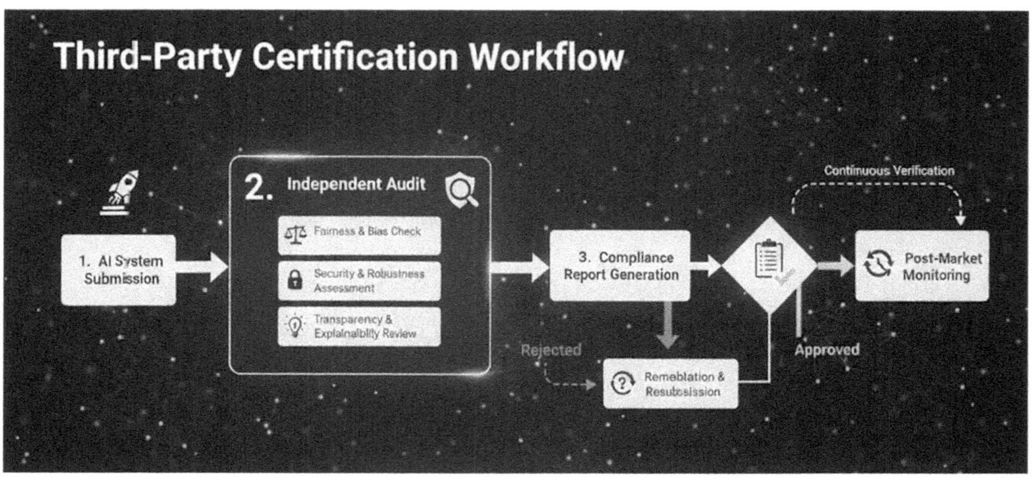

FIGURE 15.3 Third-party certification workflow.

15.6 LIABILITY AND LEGAL RESPONSIBILITY

Legal responsibility and liability are also related to AI accountability, and may be associated with developers, operators, and manufacturers. Developers have the responsibility of designing bugs and model bias, operators have the responsibility of abusing or under-monitoring it, and manufacturers have to deal with the liability problems of defective AI systems.

Laws such as the EU AI Act create responsibilities for high-risk AI systems, defining the liability and risk management. Legal responsibility is grounded in detailed documentation, an audit trail, and documentation that organizations have taken suitable measures to avoid incidents. Organizations can promote accountability through implementing legal frameworks and technical mechanisms to make them enforceable.

15.7 CONSTANT COMPLIANCE CONTROL

Continuous compliance monitoring allows organizations to maintain ethical, technical, and legal compliance of AI systems over time. Monitoring tools help to determine how well models perform, find anomalies, determine the integrity of data, and also detect new biases. Dashboards and alert systems enable operators to act quickly when the system deviates from expected behavior.

Regular auditing and automated monitoring services are used to avoid model drift and keep it in line with regulatory considerations. This is because ongoing monitoring helps strengthen accountability by upholding the accountability and reliability of AI systems throughout the lifecycle of operation.

Table 15.3 compares the three primary layers of accountability, that is, Technical, Organizational, and Legal and Regulatory, in terms of their elements, powers, and weaknesses. The Technical Layer consists of such tools as audit trails, provenance tracking, and XAI that provide a high level of traceability and early anomaly detection but need specific knowledge and may be complicated to use. Organizational Layer includes the oversight committees and ethics boards, which offer human judgment, policy alignment, and decision-making that is context sensitive. Nevertheless, such structures can be slow to react to and can be subjective interpretations. The Legal and Regulatory Layer encompasses external audits and certification as well as redress mechanisms that increase enforceability and the degree of trust with the populace, but can be constrained by the jurisdictional discrepancies and the slow pace of updating to reflect emerging technologies. The tabular feature offers an integrated layer overview to explain that a multilayered approach, including mechanisms of technical, organizational, and legal arrangements, is needed in terms of providing a full and effective accountability of AI.

TABLE 15.3
Accountability Layers Comparison

Layer	Components	Strengths	Limitations of Weaknesses
Technical	Audit trails, provenance, XAI	High traceability, anomalies quickly noticed	Skilled staff required, can be difficult
Organizational	Ethics boards, oversight committees	Policy alignment, human oversight	Risk of slow response, subjectivity in decisions
Legal/Regulatory	Certification, redress mechanisms	Certification, redress mechanism, slow updates, jurisdictional differences	Enforceable accountability, public trust
Combined	Integrated multilayer strategy	Extensive responsibility, sound governance	Resourceful, needs co-ordination

15.8 OVERSIGHT BOARDS AND ETHICS BOARDS

The issue of accountability is addressed by providing ethics boards and oversight committees. The agencies are involved in the review of AI systems design, implementation strategies, and business practices so that they can report according to ethical and legal norms. They do risk assessment, give remedial measures, and provide a platform upon which the stakeholders can air their grievances. In the majority of cases, ethics boards are multidisciplinary and enhance organizational accountability by integrating human judgment into AI governance. Such structures will minimize the risk posed by independent decision-making and accountability culture in the organization in general.

15.9 TRANSPARENCY DOCUMENTATION AND REPORTS

The transparency reports and detailed documentation should be used to ensure external accountability. Model cards, data sheets, and operation logs provide the information related to the system architecture, training data, evaluation measures, and known limitations in so much detail. Accountability is also encouraged by transparency reports to the people as it communicates the performance, fairness considerations, and corrective measures.

These documents support audits and regulatory reviews while building stakeholder trust by demonstrating the organization's commitment to responsible AI. Detailed documentation provides the ability to clarify decisions, verify them, and correct them where the need arises.

15.10 JURIDICAL SOLUTIONS AND FRAMEWORKS OF REDRESS

The accountability measures should have avenues of legal redress in case of injury by AI systems. The redress mechanisms could include damages to the victims, redress remedies, penalties, or arbitration. In these mechanisms, accountability becomes practical rather than merely theoretical.

Connecting the auditing, governance, and legal processes to the significant redress avenues, organizations are socially responsible and help to strengthen the validity of AI applications. Availability of legal redress also augurs well for the trust and confidence in AI systems by the population.

The Redress Mechanism Framework, Figure 15.4, shows how to go about redressing damages due to AI decisions. It is designed as a feedback loop, which starts with a Stakeholder Complaint by the victimized individuals or groups. This grievance initiates an Internal Inquiry by the ethics board or the oversight committee of the organization. In case further confirmation is required, the matter is subjected to an external audit that is performed by outside parties. Legal Remedies constitute the resolution phase, and could be compensatory, remedial, or formal dispute resolution. The framework is an example of the Feedback Loop, in which the knowledge gained through the process will be applied to System Updates and Monitoring, which will correct the AI system and protect against similar future harms.

15.11 THE FUTURE OF ALGORITHMIC ACCOUNTABILITY

The future of algorithmic accountability will be based on the incorporation of technical innovation, the evolution of regulations, and ethical governance. XAI will ensure decisions are more explainable, and automated auditing tools will be used to ensure compliance is verified in real-time. Blockchain-based provenance systems have the potential to provide data and model lineage-imputed records.

Regulatory harmonization will be required globally and will be a part of the implementation of cross-border AI systems. Socio-technical approaches (human supervision, organizational policy, technical protection, etc.) will also be enhanced, and these developments will help AI systems become more transparent, responsible, and aligned with societal values. These combined mechanisms will

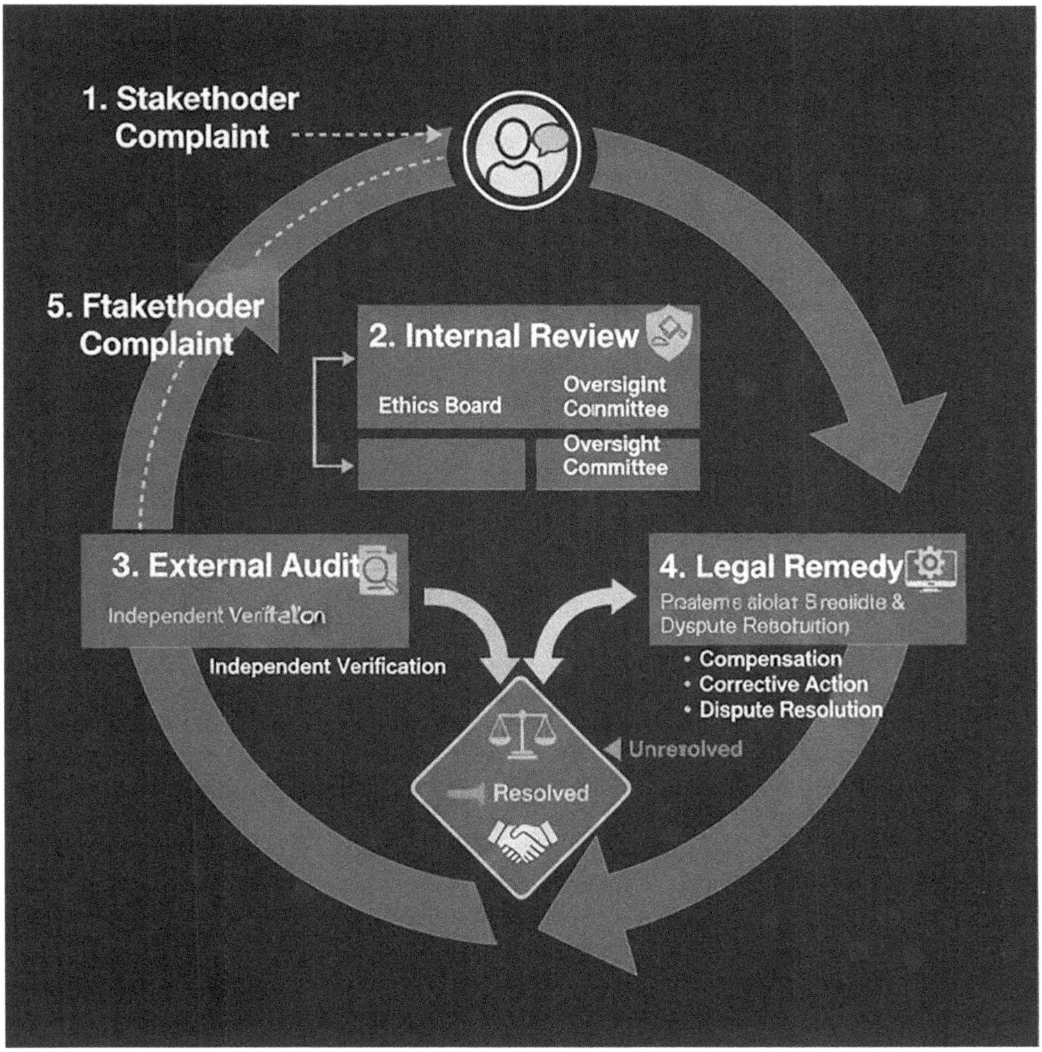

FIGURE 15.4 Framework redress mechanism.

be required to protect fairness, human rights, and the trust of the people as AI gains a greater degree of autonomy.

15.12 SUMMARY

AI needs accountability, auditing, and compliance mechanisms to guarantee that the intelligent system is responsible, transparent, and ethical. As AI is infiltrating the sphere of high stakes like healthcare, finance, law enforcement, and governance, the outcome of the mistakes, biases, or unintentional results may be severe. This chapter has addressed the idea that accountability in AI is not a one-dimensional idea, but rather a multidimensional framework that involves a combination of technical tools, organizational governance, legal enforcement, and moral values. Technically, audit trails and provenance tracking may be seen as mechanisms that underlie the responsible AI systems. Audit trails capture all interactions, decisions, and changes in the system, enabling organizations and regulators to rebuild decisions when it is required. Accountability is also enhanced by provenance tracking through the creation of descriptive records of the data sources, transformations, and model parameters. These tools are necessary to make the traceability and provide the opportunity to verify the independence, which is critical to remove mistakes and identify potential development.

External validation mechanisms, which are implemented to augment internal technical safeguards, are third-party certification and verification. Just as AI systems are evaluated on ethical, legal, and technical issues, independent audits evaluate whether the systems maintain compliance. This type of certification minimizes the risk of conflicts of interest and contributes to increasing trust among the population as it is a fair and objective guarantee that the system has passed a serious test prior to its implementation. Similarly, with continuous compliance monitoring, the AI systems are able to ensure performance and ethical integrity as time goes by, detect anomalies, model drift, or a newly acquired bias in real time. These surveillance mechanisms are essential in dynamic environments where the information and the circumstances of the functioning change very rapidly.

Accountability is critical in improving transparency in the governance of the organization. The interaction between humans and AI is through oversight committees and ethics boards, which control AI design choices and review them to detect risks involved and propose solutions to these risks. They serve as a mediator between the technical processes and the expectations of society at large, so that the AI systems do not find ways to break the ethical norms and the legal regulations. By implementing the concept of multidisciplinary perspectives, these organizations help the firms anticipate potential damages, address the interests of the stakeholders, and remain responsible as a corporation.

Transparency and documentation also form the basis of accountable AI. The awareness of AI decisions by internal and external stakeholders is possible through elaborated model documentation, transparency reports, and risk assessment. Such transparency is crucial to the audits and the regulatory adherence as well as to the growth of trust in the end-users, the impacted communities, and the population. Organizations are moral when they employ useful communication to explain the abilities and constraints of the models and corrective measures.

The second point of enforcement is the laws and legal regulations. The debt/equity structure, compliance, and redress are understandable, and the accountability can be undertaken in a pragmatic manner and not simply in theory. The channels of dispute resolution, remedies, and compensation should be made available to the victims of the AI-based damage. The overall ecosystem of accountability becomes stronger with legal frameworks linked with the technical audits, organizational controls, and transparency controls, so that the people in charge might be exposed and held responsible.

In the future, the future of the anti-technical accountability will involve industrial convergence of technical innovation, regulation harmonization, and ethical governance. XAI, automated auditing solutions, and blockchain-based provenance solutions are also new solutions that are beginning to take the future of AI interpretability, traceability, and real-time control of compliance. Simultaneously, the standardization of AI policies on the international level will provide equal standards of AI policies in various jurisdictions of the world, which will assist in bringing AI systems safely and responsibly to the world. Socio-technical remedies of a mixture of human and organizational policy and technical controls will still remain significant in imparting responsibility in the AI lifecycle.

The concept of accountable AI is broad, and this cannot be achieved by one action or a mechanism. It requires technical protection, internal control, open communication, moral pledge, and legal action. All of these mechanisms result in building trust and human rights protection, risk mitigation, and alignment of AI systems with societal values. Accountability at every level, including design and implementation or monitoring and remediation, may enable organizations to not just make AI potent and effective, but also responsible, ethical, and socially acceptable. The chapter clarifies why it is a necessity to create an ecosystem where accountability is integrated into the culture, technology, and governance of AI systems, and a foundation of viable and dependable AI in the future.

REFERENCES

Ayling, J., & Chapman, A. (2022). *Auditing AI systems: Technical, legal, and ethical challenges. AI & Society, 37*, 1041–1055.

Balamurugan, G., Tyagi, A.K., & Richa, A. (2023). Survey on privacy preserving and trust building techniques of blockchain-based systems. In: *Privacy Preservation and Secured Data Storage in Cloud Computing*. IGI Global. DOI: 10.4018/979-8-3693-0593-5.ch019

Barocas, S., & Selbst, A. D. (2016). Big data's disparate impact. *California Law Review, 104*(3), 671–732. https://doi.org/10.2139/ssrn.2477899

Binns, R. (2018). Fairness in Machine Learning: Lessons from political philosophy. In *Proceedings of the 2018 conference on fairness, accountability, and transparency* (pp. 149–159). https://arxiv.org/abs/1712.03586?utm_source=chatgpt.com

Chakraborty, J., Majumder, S., Yu, Z., & Menzies, T. (2020). Fairway: A way to build fair ML software. *arXiv*. https://doi.org/10.48550/arXiv.2003.10354

Cobbe, J., Lee, M. S. A., & Singh, J. (2021). Reviewable automated decision-making: A framework for accountable algorithmic systems. *arXiv*.

Floridi, L., & Cowls, J. (2019). *A unified framework of five principles for AI in society*. Harvard Data Science Review. https://doi.org/10.1162/99608f92.8cd550d1

Foalem, P. L., Da Silva, L., Khomh, F., Li, H., & Merlo, E. (2025). Logging requirement for continuous auditing of responsible machine learning-based applications. *arXiv*.

Gupta, R., Bose, I., & Tafti, A. (2018). A value-based approach to AI ethics: Accountability, transparency, explainability, and usability. *Journal of Business Ethics, 152*(3), 667–678.

Johnson, D. G. (2021). Algorithmic accountability in the making. *Social Philosophy and Policy, 38*(1), 162–187.

Kantayya, S. (Director). (2020). *Coded Bias* [Documentary]. 7th Empire Media.

Korolova, A. (2024). *Fairness and privacy in machine learning: Challenges and opportunities*. Princeton University Press.

Koshiyama, A., Mökander, J., Axente, M., & Floridi, L. (2021). Conformity assessments and post-market monitoring: A guide to the role of auditing in the proposed European AI regulation. *Minds and Machines, 32*, 241–268. https://doi.org/10.1007/s11023-021-09577-4

Kumari, S., Tyagi, A. K., Tiwari, S., & Kulshreshtha, G. (2025a). Sensors and digital twin for healthcare monitoring frameworks. In T. A. Nguyen (Ed.), *Digital twin, blockchain, and sensor networks in the healthy and mobile city* (Chapter 10, pp. 147–177). Elsevier. https://doi.org/10.1016/B978-0-443-34174-8.00011-9

Kumari, S., Tyagi, A. K., Tiwari, S., & Singh, R. (2025b). Medical sensor network, edge computing and blockchain for efficient medical data exchange. In T. A. Nguyen (Ed.), *Digital twin, blockchain, and sensor networks in the healthy and mobile city (Chapter 11)*. Elsevier. https://doi.org/10.1016/B978-0-443-34174-8.00012-0

Laato, S., Mäntymäki, M., & Minkkinen, M. (2022). Continuous auditing of artificial intelligence: A conceptualization and assessment of tools and frameworks. *Digital Society, 1*, 21. https://doi.org/10.1007/s44206-022-00022-2

Light, B., & Panai, E. (2022). The self-synchronisation of AI ethical principles: Toward an audit infrastructure of trust. *Digital Society*.

Mikians, J., Gyarmati, L., Erramilli, V., & Laoutaris, N. (2012). Detecting price and search discrimination on the Internet. In *Proceedings of the 11th ACM workshop on hot topics in networks* (pp. 79–84). https://doi.org/10.1145/2390231.2390245

Minkkinen, M., Niukkanen, A., & Mäntymäki, M. (2024). What about investors? *AI & Society, 39*, 329–343. https://doi.org/10.1007/s00146-022-01415-0

Minkkinen, M., Zimmer, M. P., & Mäntymäki, M. (2023). Co-shaping an ecosystem for responsible AI: Five types of expectation work in response to a technological frame. *Information Systems Frontiers, 25*, 103–121. https://doi.org/10.1007/s10796-022-10269-2

Mishra, A. K., Tiwari, S., Tyagi, A. K., & Arowolo, M. O. (2024). Security, privacy, trust, and provenance issues in Internet of Things–based edge environment. In S. Pal, C. Savaglio, R. Minerva, & F. C. Delicato (Eds.), *IoT edge intelligence* (pp. 233–263). Springer. https://doi.org/10.1007/978-3-031-58388-9_8

Mökander, J., Axente, M., Casolari, F., & Floridi, L. (2022). Conformity assessments and post-market monitoring: A guide to the role of auditing in the proposed European AI regulation. *Minds and Machines, 32*(2), 241–268. https://doi.org/10.1007/s11023-021-09577-4

Nair, M. M., & Tyagi, A. K. (2021). Privacy: History, statistics, policy, laws, preservation and threat analysis. *Journal of Information Assurance & Security*, *16*(1). https://doi.org/10.2139/ssrn.5258795

Nair, M.M., & Tyagi, A.K. (2025). Transformative effects of emerging technologies on Industry 5.0 and Society 5.0: Current status, vision, issues, challenges, and opportunities for future. In: *Next Generation Data Science and Blockchain Technology for Industry 5.0*. Wiley. DOI: https://doi.org/10.1002/9781394245215.ch13, ISBN: 9781394245185.

Panigutti, C., Perotti, A., Panisson, A., Bajardi, P., & Pedreschi, D. (2020). FairLens: Auditing black-box clinical decision support systems. *arXiv*. https://doi.org/10.1016/j.ipm.2021.102657

Pretschner, A., & Kacianka, S. (2021). Designing accountable systems using structural causal models. In Proceedings of the 2021 ACM Conference on Fairness, Accountability, and Transparency (FAccT '21), 424–437. https://doi.org/10.1145/3442188.3445905

Raji, I. D., & Buolamwini, J. (2019). Actionable auditing: Investigating the impact of publicly naming biased performance results of commercial AI products. In *Proceedings of the 2019 AAAI/ACM conference on AI, ethics, and society* (pp. 429–435). https://api.semanticscholar.org/CorpusID:91168921

Raji, I. D., O'Neill, C., Patil, D., et al. (2021). *Radical proposal: Third-party auditor access for AI accountability*. Stanford Institute for Human-Centered AI.

Raji, I. D., Smart, A., White, R. N., Mitchell, M., Gebru, T., Hutchinson, B., Smith-Loud, J., Theron, D., & Barnes, P. (2020). Closing the AI accountability gap: Defining an end-to-end framework for internal algorithmic auditing. In *FAT '20: Proceedings of the 2020 conference on fairness, accountability, and transparency* (pp.* 33–44). https://doi.org/10.1145/3351095.3372873

Sandvig, C., Hamilton, K., Karahalios, K., & Langbort, C. (2014). Auditing algorithms: Research methods for detecting discrimination on internet platforms. In S. Gangadharan & D. Eubanks (Eds.), *Data and discrimination: Collected essays.* Open Technology Institute, New America Foundation.

Schneider, J., Abraham, R., Meske, C., & Vom Brocke, J. (2022). Artificial intelligence governance for businesses. *Information Systems Management, 40*(3), 229–249. https://doi.org/10.1080/10580530.2022.2085825

Seppälä, A., Birksted, T., & Mäntymäki, M. (2021). From ethical AI principles to governed AI. In *Proceedings of the international conference on information systems (ICIS).* https://aisel.aisnet.org/icis2021/ai_business/ai_business/10

Singh, J., Cobbe, J., & Norval, C. (2018). Decision provenance: Harnessing data flow for accountable systems. *IEEE Access, 7,* 2545–2559. https://doi.org/10.1109/ACCESS.2018.2887201

Tyagi, A.K. (2021). Analysis of security and privacy aspects of blockchain technologies from smart era' perspective: The challenges and a way forward. In: *Recent Trends in Blockchain for Information Systems Security and Privacy* (pp. 1–17). DOI: https://doi.org/10.1201/9781003139737, eBook-ISBN: 9781003139737

Tyagi, A.K. (2025). Blockchain for smart hospital in Healthcare 5.0: modeling structure, challenges, and future emerging trends. In: *Human-Centric Integration of Next-Generation Data Science and Blockchain Technology.* Elsevier. DOI: https://doi.org/10.1016/B978-0-443-33498-6.00026-1, ISBN: 978-0-443-33498-6.

Tyagi, A.K. (2026). *Chapter 4 - Artificial intelligence–blockchain–Internet of Things–based smart healthcare services: literature review and future research directions, in the book: Smart Hospital Anatomy with Advanced Sensors Innovations in Patient Care*, Elsevier (pp. 49–61). https://doi.org/10.1016/B978-0-443-45875-0.00005-3, ISBN: 978-0-443-45875-0.

Tyagi, A., Kumari, S., & Tiwari, S. (2024c). Internet of Things for smart healthcare: A survey. In A. K. Sharma, N. Chanderwal, S. Tyagi, & P. Upadhyay (Eds.), *Future of AI in medical imaging (Chapter 2).* IGI Global. https://doi.org/10.4018/979-8-3693-2359-5.ch002

Tyagi, A. K., & Tiwari, S. (2024a). Blockchain-enabled smart healthcare applications in 6G networks. In A. K. Tyagi (Ed.), *Digital twin and blockchain for smart cities* (Chapter 20, pp. 459–494). Wiley. https://doi.org/10.1002/9781394303564.ch20

Tyagi, A. K., Tripathi, K., Tiwari, S., & Kaushik, S. (2025). An efficient technique for privacy preservation, trusted and secure patient-centric services in smart healthcare. In *Proceedings of the 6th international conference on recent trends in communication & intelligent systems (ICRTCIS 2025)* (pp. 31–47). IET. https://doi.org/10.1049/icp.2025.2731

Veale, M., & Binns, R. (2024). More or less discrimination? Practical feasibility of fairness auditing of technologies for personnel selection. *AI & Society, 39*, 2507–2523. https://doi.org/10.1007/s00146-023-01726-w

Venkatasubramanian, S. (2023). A framework for ethical algorithm auditing in machine learning models deployed in criminal justice systems based on fairness constraints and counterfactual explanations. *ISCSITR – International Journal of Machine Learning, 4*(2), 1–8. https://iscsitr.in/index.php/ISCSITR-IJML/article/view/ISCSITR-IJML_04_02_001

Wieringa, M. (2020). What to account for when accounting for algorithms: A systematic literature review on algorithmic accountability. In *FAT '20: Proceedings of the 2020 conference on fairness, accountability, and transparency*. https://doi.org/10.1145/3351095.3372833

Part V

Future Directions

16 Balancing Innovation, Ethics, and Security in the Future of AI-Driven Mental Health

16.1 INTRODUCTION

As mental health disorders form a significant proportion of the disability burden and global health burden of disease, mental conditions are a significant issue of public health concern in the twenty-first century. The issue of depression, anxiety disorders, psychosis, and the bipolar disorder impacts hundreds of millions of people all over the world and, in many cases, leads to worse quality of life, low productivity, and increased risk of mortality. Despite the current improvements in psychiatric information and development of diagnostic models like the Diagnostic and Statistical Manual of Mental Disorders, Fifth Edition (DSM-5), the access to timely and high-quality mental healthcare is estimated to be greatly disparate, especially in poor-resource and underserved areas. These shortcomings in the structure have escalated an interest toward pure digital and data solutions that can supplement the traditional mental health services. AI has become one of the latest changes in the field of mental healthcare in recent years, which introduces new opportunities of diagnosing, monitoring, personalizing treatment, and delivering services. Machine learning (ML) models have increasingly become a part of clinical decision-support systems (CDSS), allowing the recognition of patterns in highly dimensional and generally complex clinical data, which are beyond the cognitive ability of humans (Adlung et al., 2021). In the psychiatric field, AI-based applications are useful in the early identification of risks, predictive analytics in symptom course, and optimizing treatments, whereas conversational agents and chatbot-based interventions are increasingly being used to scale to providing support inspired by cognitive–behavioral therapy (CBT) (Ali et al., 2025; Auf et al., 2024).

In addition to electronic health records, smartphones and wearable devices have led to the development of the digital phenotyping continuous, passive gathering of behavioral, and contextual data like mobility, patterns of communication, and device usage. According to empirical evidence, such data have the potential to be useful in learning about mental health conditions, risk of relapse, and dynamics of engagement (Currey and Torous, 2022b; Dwyer et al., 2024). Mass-scale digital mental health also reflects the practicability of multi-modal AI-based interventions, which incorporates social support, psychoeducation, and clinician moderation to enhance interaction with youth with mental ill-health (Alvarez-Jimenez et al., 2020). However, the blistering adoption of AI in the mental health services presents an inherent and unresolved conflict between technological innovation, ethical duty, as well as security guarantee. Although AI systems seem to offer scalability and efficiency, they also pose significant ethical issues that pertain to transparency, accountability, bias, and trust. According to meta-analytic evidence, a number of AI-based CDSS have low explainability, and, as a consequence, this fact puts a limitation on their clinical use and erodes the trust of the user in algorithmic advice (Abbas et al., 2025). Mental healthcare is one of the least favorable areas where

DOI: 10.1201/9781003658344-21

this problem is acute due to the high sensitivity of clinical decisions as well as the value-based and personal aspects of them.

There is also the issue of security and privacy threat, which complicates the use of AI in psychiatry. The mental health data is one of the most delicate sets of personal information, which consists of behavioral traces and emotional states as well as social interactions. Research assessing the digital phenotyping aspect and mobile mental health has pointed at the weaknesses of data quality, missingness, and sustainable interaction, each of which may affect the reliability of the models and increase subsequent risks (Currey and Torous, 2022a; Dwyer et al., 2024). Without well-developed governance systems, AI systems can easily lead to the misuse of personal data, surveillance harm, or discrimination. Nevertheless, although the literature regarding the use of AI in mental health is increasing, some important gaps are still present. To begin with, in many cases ethical issues are considered in a piecemeal fashion because, on the one hand, technical performance is assessed, whereas, on the other hand, moral, legal, and social implications are considered (Ali et al., 2025; Babu and Joseph, 2024). Second, systems of governance that would allow managing innovation with accountability and security are not fully developed, especially in the context of a clinical environment, where AI systems have a range of engagements with clinicians, patients, and face institutional limitations (Auf et al., 2024). Third, sustainability issues, such as the environmental cost of large-scale AI systems and resiliency of its operational dynamics in the long term, are only slightly addressed in the mental health AI research area, whereas they are increasingly important in terms of responsible digital health innovation.

Instead of simply depending on the degree of sophistication of an algorithm, the chapter demonstrates that the future of AI in mental health lies not in the moral qualities of AI, but rather in the intention to incorporate ethical, security, and governance principles into the AI lifecycle. It is based on the systematic review evidence, the representation of some empirical studies of AI innovation and the research of digital phenotyping (Cruz Cruz-Gonzalez et al., 2025; Auf et al., 2024; Abbas et al., 2025), consisting of the holistic approach that puts AI innovation into a more general context of socio-technical and policy processes. The core findings of this research can be shown in the following ways:

- A coherent ethical-security framework of AI-enabled mental health systems explaining explainability, privacy, and trust as these concerns go hand in hand instead of separately.
- The emerging AI technologies in mental health and clinical-decision support, digital phenotyping, and multi-modal digital interventions, their clinical potential and the risks, are synthesized.
- An AI adoption roadmap in mental health based on responsible AI adoption and governance preparedness with priority in clinician engagement and long-term sustainability.

16.2 LITERATURE REVIEW

The swift adoption of AI in the field of mental healthcare has generated a current and growing body of research spanning the fields of psychiatry, digital health, biomedical data science, and ethics. Current studies indicate the disruptive promise of AI-based systems and, at the same time, expose enduring ethical, security, and governance issues (Tyagi & Sreenath, 2023; Kumar et al., 2024). This literature review overviews previous literature thematically on four critical dimensions: (i) AI in psychiatry and digital phenotyping, (ii) ethical risks and explainability, (iii) security and privacy vulnerabilities, and (iv) emerging regulatory and governance considerations.

16.2.1 AI in Psychiatry: Machine Augmented Intelligence (MAI) Computer Learning, Natural Language Processing, and Digital Phenotyping

Psychiatric AI applications actively use machine learning (ML) and natural language processing (NLP) to aid in the process of diagnosis, symptom monitoring, and personalization of treatment.

Narrative reviews and systematic reviews published regularly report increased use of supervised and deep learning models to identify depression, anxiety, psychosis, and suicide risk on the basis of clinical records, speech, and text-based data as well as behavioral data (Ali et al., 2025; Cruz Gonzalez et al., 2025). These methods have potential of scalability and the capacity to intervene early which is hard to attain in the traditional care models. Digital phenotyping is another approach that has become one of the strongest concepts of mental health AI. Digital phenotyping indicates fine-grained behavioral indications by personality metrics that are correlated with a mental condition by gathering passive data on smartphones and wearables like mobility, communication patterns, and usage of apps (Insel, 2017). The empirical research shows that this data can be effective in relapse prediction, engagement modeling, and individualized interventions (Currey and Torous, 2022b; Dwyer et al., 2024). Nonetheless, methodological issues with missingness, data quality, and long-term engagement continue to present a serious factor-depriving clinical reliability (Currey and Torous, 2022a). In addition to the data-driven prediction, AI-based online interventions have been implemented in the physical mental health services. Multi-modal social networking, clinician-moderated and psychoeducational content platforms have been found to be effective in engaging youth with mental ill health (Alvarez-Jimenez et al., 2020; O Sullivan et al., 2022). The perceived values of such interventions also, according to qualitative evidence, are seen through the perspective of patients and specifically early psychosis recovery settings (Lal et al., 2023). However, as shown in these studies as well, AI-based tools usually work best as a combination with humans instead of as a standalone service.

16.2.2 Ethical risks: Bias, Explainability, and Informed Consent

Ethical issues are currently at the center of the scholarly discussion as AI systems are increasingly used to make decisions in the area of mental health. The presence of the risk of algorithmic bias because of unrepresentative training data is another common element of reviews (Li et al., 2022; Morley et al., 2020). Bias in the field of mental healthcare has even more nuanced outcomes because patient groups are stigmatized and vulnerable. Another ethical issue of concern is explainability. Based on the meta-analysis results, most AI-based CDSS do not include clear reasoning, which restricts the trust and understandability of clinicians (Abbas et al., 2025; Tun et al., 2025). Psychiatry is especially problematic in this issue as the boundaries of diagnoses are subjective and dependent on the situation. Lacking substantive explainability, AI outputs will inevitably seem opaque or authoritative even without explanation, suggesting that shared decision-making will be jeopardized (Mergenova et al., 2024; Naslund et al., 2021). Consent and user autonomy also add to the ethical deployment issue particularly in mobile and mHealth deployment. Evidence of mental health application reviews demonstrates a great amount of inconsistency in quality of apps, clinical validation, and ethical protection (Grundy, 2021; Huckvale et al., 2020). Research evaluating privacy policy and description of apps proves that much of the mental health apps poorly report data use practices, which prevents them to give informed consent (Huckvale et al., 2019; Singh et al., 2023). Such results highlight an absence of compatibility between technological innovation and ethical disclosure of modern digital mental health ecosystems.

16.2.3 Mental Health AI Security and Privacy Vulnerabilities

One of the main, but frequently undervalued, aspects of mental healthcare driven by AI is security and privacy risks. Huge amounts of mental health information, such as behavioral traces, emotions, and social interactions, are thoroughly sensitive, which particularly aggravates the risk of damage related to the breach or misuse of especially large data. Papers on biomedical data science emphasize that the AI systems have accomplished an impressive expansion rate that has exceeded the creation of effective ethics and security frameworks (Federico and Trotsyuk, 2024). Mobile mental health applications are an example of such vulnerabilities. Employing empirical measurements, common data sharing with third parties, irregular encryption habits, and limited access controls are found to be concerning issues regarding confidentiality and long-term data management (Huckvale et al., 2019). The presence of digital phenotyping systems also increases the level of security threat as they involve constant data gathering and the need to use large-scale datasets of behavior (Insel, 2017; Currey and Torous, 2022a). Recent studies in the areas of trustworthy computing and cybersecurity indicate that privacy-preserving methods, for example, federated learning (FL), secure aggregation, and blockchain-based data regulation, may provide a way forward to solving these risks (Kumar et al., 2024; Pawar et al., 2024a). Most of these solutions however have been investigated in other related areas and there has been less empirical validation in mental health cases. This void suggests the relevance of implementation of domain-specific security models considerate of clinical processes and sensitivity in psychiatric data (Rice et al., 2014, 2020).

16.2.4 Regulatory and Governance Intervention in Mental Healthcare using AI

An increased understanding of regulatory and governance issues as a prerequisite to responsible use of AI in healthcare is emerging. Mapping reviews underline the fact that current ethical principles tend to be of a high level and do not give operational instructions to developers and clinicians (Morley et al., 2020; Li et al., 2022). Clinical judgment, legal accountability, and patient autonomy are other areas that compound this issue in the sphere of mental health as AI systems overlap with the clinical judgment. Recent research suggests that it is necessary to match the AI systems with regulatory requirements regarding transparency, data security, and human control (Federico and Trotsyuk, 2024). The confidence of healthcare workers in AI-based CDSS has been reported to depend on the governance mechanisms that provide accountability and explainability, as well as technical performance (Tun et al., 2025). Moreover, the introduction of AI in learning and training workers underlines the significance of various governance models that enable the formation of clinicians who approach AI applications non-passively but in a thoughtful and affirmative manner (Prégent et al., 2025). Sustainability remains insufficiently discussed in regulatory areas of mentality AI, although it concerns the future maintenance of systems, their effect on the environment, and institutional preparedness. This omission may jeopardize the sustainability and the moral correctness of AI-powered mental health services.

16.2.5 Critical Gap Summary

Table 16.1 includes a detailed overview of the major strengths and weaknesses identified in the existing literature, therefore, outlining particular areas, which require further empirical studies and unification efforts.

As it has been shown in the current review, despite the rapid advancement of AI-based mental-health systems, the research literature eludes consensus on technical, ethical, and governance levels. The critical gap in existing formal structures—which cannot simultaneously accommodate innovation, ethics, security, and sustainability—explains why the holistic approach developed in this chapter are absolutely necessary (Torous et al., 2019, 2020).

16.3 EMERGING TRENDS IN AI PSYCHIATRY

Within the past 3 years, there has been a rapid shift away from both the single-modality and the proof-of-concept formats on the single limited models of AI onto the embedded end-to-end systems, privacy, and operationally sound in the field of psychiatry. Four trends, including multi-modal psychiatric AI, federated and privacy-preserving mental-health models, foundation models specific to mental health, and real-time risk-prediction systems, coincide with each other and are supported by digital phenotyping. All of these trends augment clinical potential and, at the same time, increase ethical, security, and sustainability trade-offs that need to be tackled simultaneously.

TABLE 16.1
Critical Gaps in AI-Enabled Mental Health Research

Dimension	Key Contributions	Identified Gaps
AI in Psychiatry	ML, NLP, digital phenotyping enable early detection and personalization (Ali et al., 2025; Cruz-Gonzalez et al., 2025)	Limited generalizability, data quality issues, and overreliance on passive data
Ethics and Explainability	Recognition of bias, transparency, and trust issues (Abbas et al., 2025; Morley et al., 2020)	Fragmented ethical integration; lack of actionable design frameworks
Security and Privacy	Identification of data-sharing and confidentiality risks (Huckvale et al., 2019)	Scarce deployment of privacy-preserving techniques in mental health settings
Governance and Regulation	Growing focus on accountability and trust (Tun et al., 2025; Federico & Trotsyuk, 2024)	Weak operational governance, minimal sustainability focus

16.3.1 Multimodal Psychiatric AI

Multi-modal models combine heterogeneous types of data, such as clinical notes via NLP, speech and prosodic, facial and visual, physiological (heart rate and electrodermal activity (EDA)), and passive smartphone telemetry models, and jointly predictive systems. It has consistently been established through systematic reviews and recent meta-analyses that multi-modal approaches are more sensitive to the detection of depression or relapse or deterioration compared to single-modality models due to the ability of multi-modal methods to capture complementary behavioral and biological cues (Ali et al., 2025; Cruz-Gonzalez et al., 2025). Experimental research on digital interventions and multi-modal systems indicates that these systems make personalization more intensive (Alvarez -Jimenez et al., 2020; O Sullivan et al., 2022). They encompass sensor heterogeneity, time consistency, inter-modal absenteeism, and the possibility of opaque fusion designers reducing interpretability, which is a major concern in clinical settings (Abbas et al., 2025; Currey and Torus, 2022a).

16.3.2 Federated Mental Health Models and Privacy-Saving Methods

As opposed to central data pooling, subset analysis methods such as FL and secure-aggregation methods have also garnered increasing focus in psychology (Kumar et al., 2024; Pawar et al., 2024a,b). FL allows training on distributed datasets of hospitals or devices without data transfer, which is why the sensitivity and regulation requirements of the psychiatric data are observed. To enhance accountability and enable the use of patient-centric data governance, the complementary strategies offered include differential privacy (DP), homomorphic encryption, and blockchain-aided audit widely. The initial studies indicate that FL is capable of maintaining predictive task performance at the expense of raw behavioral traces exposure; although validation to the domain has not been performed extensively in psychiatry, which is beneficial. The difficulties include non-independent and identically distributed (non-IID) data dispersion across locations, communication cost, client loss, and the necessity to ensure that privacy controls do not abolish clinically relevant indicators.

16.3.3 Domestic Models of Mental Health

Language and multi-modal transformers are being scaled up to address mental-health problems, as part of the so-called foundation models of psychiatry. They can be adapted to clinical-note summary, clinical question answering, conversational therapeutic agents, and multi-modal patient representation. According to reviews and prospective analyses, foundation models are cost-effective in sample-efficient transfer learning and powerful zero-shot transfer learning on under-resourced tasks (Ali et al., 2025; Narimani and Mahdi, 2025). However, when foundation models are applied to psychiatry, acute problems arise: hallucinations during clinical dialogue, risk-output calibration, and heavy levels of training and fine-tuning computational footprint are introduced. Empirical and explanatory decision-making are the two indispensable conditions of clinical implementation (Abbas et al., 2025; Federico and Trotsyuk, 2024).

16.3.4 Risk Prediction Systems in Real Time

Continuous passive smartphone and wearable sensor-based digital phenotyping has developed beyond idea to both proof-of-concept deployed cohort studies and applications built from applications (Currey, 2022b; Dwyer, 2024). The modern pipelines integrate both streaming telemetry with short-term forecast models to identify an event of acute risk (e.g., spikes in suicidal ideation, relapse warning), and consequently deploying clinician alerts/adaptive interventions. Such systems have been tested in terms of operationalization of the care pathways of youth mental-health services, as well as first-episode psychosis programs, showing promising engagement outcomes (Alvarez-Jimenez et al., 2020; Lal et al., 2023). Issues include engagement drift and missingness, which reduce the reliability of the model (Currey and Torous, 2022a), and increased complexity of privacy and consent in constant surveillance (Huckvale et al., 2019) (Table 16.2).

16.3.5 Cross-Cutting Implications

The interplay of these trends develops a weblog of making the technical advancements and of putting them on the ground co-evolve. Multi-modality and foundation and federated and privacy-preserving models increase or decrease central exposure and setup optimal clinical power, respectively, but lead to issues of optimization and equitability; true recurrent systems enhance timeliness but require robust governance and human responsibility. They suggest that such technological direction needs to be accompanied by high explainability, building clinician trust, and domain-driven validation to ensure that they become morally and clinically acceptable (Abbas et al., 2025; Morley et al., 2020; Tun et al., 2025). Figure 16.1 illustrates the development of initial single-modality ML models to current technologies that are multi-modal in perception, federated in privacy assurance, foundation-model transfer, and risk prediction. Clinical capability is expanded at every enriching

TABLE 16.2
Mapping AI Technologies to Ethical, Security, and Governance Challenges in Mental Health

AI Technology	Primary Clinical Use	Key Ethical Risks	Security and Governance Concerns
Multi-modal Psychiatric AI	Diagnosis, relapse prediction, treatment personalization	Bias amplification, reduced interpretability	Data fusion leakage, lack of auditability
Digital Phenotyping	Continuous monitoring, early risk detection	Emotional surveillance, consent erosion	Longitudinal data exposure, data misuse
Foundation Models	Clinical decision support, AI psychotherapy	Hallucinations, over-reliance, opacity	High-risk deployment, weak accountability
VR/AR-Based Therapy	Exposure therapy, cognitive rehabilitation	Psychological dependency, emotional manipulation	Session data security, user profiling
Emotion AI	Mood inference, adaptive interventions	False emotion inference, stigmatization	Biometric data leakage, surveillance risk
Federated Learning	Privacy-preserving model training	Unequal model performance across sites	Governance of distributed responsibility

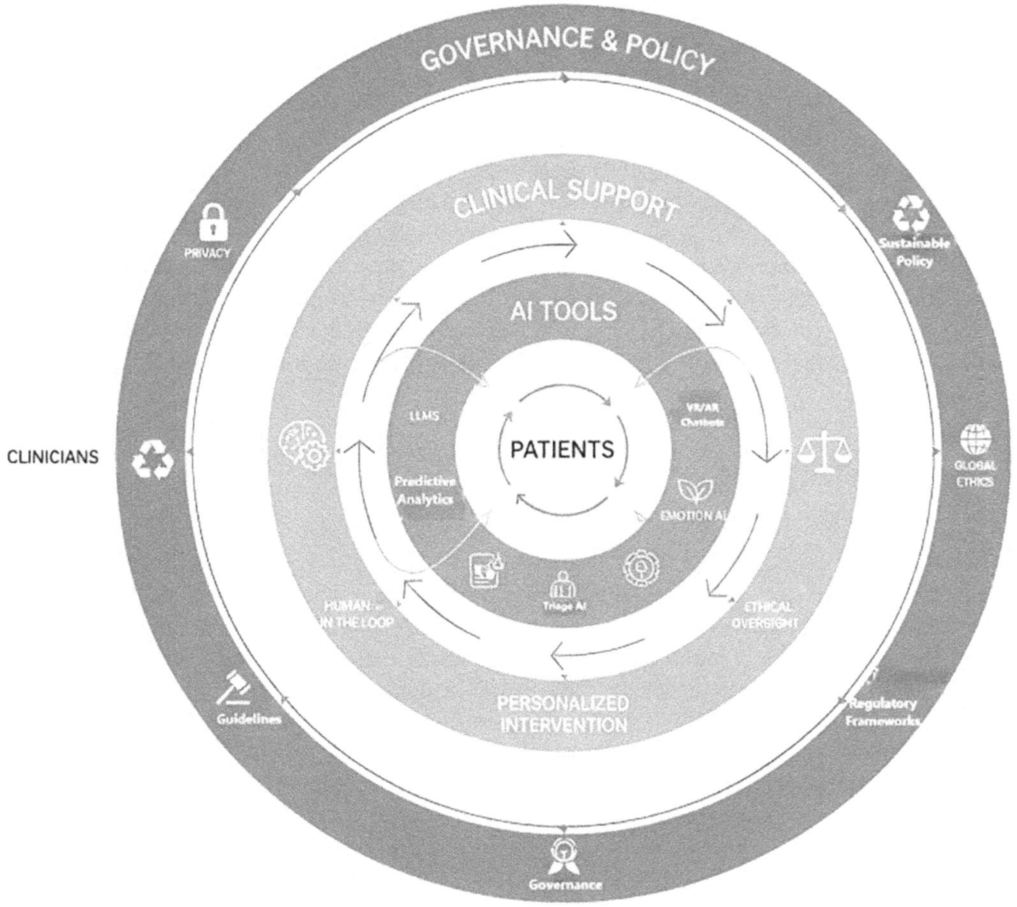

FIGURE 16.1 Evolution of AI psychiatry systems.

tier, but it comes at the same time with an increased need for more robust explainability, governance, and sustainability frameworks.

16.4 INTEGRATION WITH VR, AR, AND EMOTIONAL AI

Meaningful models on AI have been progressively connected to immersive and affect sensors through the infiltration of immersive and prescient technologies into psychiatric care, minimizing transactional care and subverting the clinic. The quarters of 2022–2025 will witness a way of delivering more interactive, personalized, and context-sensitive intervention through the convergence of VR, AR and emotional artificial intelligence (Emotion AI). The technologies not only aim at increasing the interaction of therapeutic engagement and efficacy, but also present new ethical and psychological hazards, which require careful governance.

16.4.1 VR-Based Exposure Therapy

VR has been emerging as a managed and immersive content of exposure-based therapies, especially in anxiety disorders, post-trauma stress disorders (PTSDs), and phobias. VR exposure therapy gives clinicians the ability to create simulated anxiety conditions in a safe and customizable fashion, which means that things can be gradually desensitized and therapeutic feedback can be observed in real time. Recent meta-analyses and clinical assessments were able to demonstrate that VR-based interventions are capable of producing similar results and, in some instances, superior to the traditional in-vivo exposure therapy when paired with a method of clinician oversight with adaptive AI-driven scenario modulation (Ali et al., 2025; Cruz-Gonzalez et al., 2025). The use of AI also makes VR therapy better as it allows dynamically changing the virtual stimuli according to the user response to it or to physiological or behavioral cues. An example of this is in stress levels based on the variability in heart rate or a speech pattern used to modify exposure levels on the fly. Although this kind of personalization enhances the accuracy of therapeutic treatment, such independence increases the dependence on constant emotional and physiological monitoring; this raises the issue of data privacy and emotional independence. Starting with augmented reality, AR-based cognitive therapy can be approached to address cognitive disorders using computer-generated reality simulation (CGS).

16.4.2 Augmented Reality

16.4.2.1 Augmented Reality-Assisted Cognitive Therapy

AR presents digital overlays on real-world spaces and allows cognitive and behavioral interventions in the world, but does not entirely require users to live in virtual worlds. AR has been examined in mental health areas as a cognitive restructuring tool, mindfulness-training tool, and skills rehearsal tool and therapeutic cues or prompts can be incorporated directly into the daily routines of the patients. The practice would make it easier to generalize therapeutic skills to real-life circumstances and minimize the contextual distance that is frequently detected between the therapeutic sessions and daily lives (Babu and Joseph, 2024). AR systems supported by AI can also be used to further customize interventions through user behavior, location, or deduced moods. However, it is the very smooth transition of the therapeutic prompts to the working-day environment that increases the chance of psychological dependency as users might simply be dependent on constant digital prompts to regulate their emotions. This dependency would impede the emergence of internal adaptive coping, and also result in confusion of the distinguishing line between helpful intervention and obtrusive support.

16.4.3 Emotion Recognition and Affective Computing

Felt identification is a fundamental feature of emergent affect-aware mental health systems. Emotion AI uses ML algorithms to predict emotional reactions based on multi-modal cues, for example, speech prosody, facial expression, a written text emotion, and physiological indicators, such as heart rate. The recent studies prove that these methods may help conduct mood tracking, anticipate relapses, and deliver adaptive interventions (Narimani and Mahdi, 2025; Ali et al., 2025). Emotion recognition in mobile and mHealth environments is gradually entrenched in the conversational agents and virtual therapists that define the styles of interaction and therapeutic responding. It has been revealed that visual and behavioral features of virtual therapists are affected by design findings, thus impacting the perceived empathy, realism, and trust, which, in turn, influence user engagement and therapeutic alliance (Golubović et al., 2024). Although these systems are scalable in their emotional support, issues of their accuracy and cultural sensitivity are still debatable, especially when they are deployed on a diverse population. The risk in question is in the form of ethical and psychological risks. Although promising, VR, AR, and Emotion AI pose a large ethical and psychological threat, which is particularly relevant in mental healthcare. A significant issue is emotional surveillance, which, through sustained apprehension of emotional cues and emotional tracking, can internalize the practice of ongoing emotional tracking without a sense of boundaries or informed consent. These surveillance threats allow damaging therapeutic support into an experiment of surveillance of behavior that would undermine trust and autonomy. Another associated risk is that of false emotion inference. Emotion recognition model is both context and probabilistic, but the results are usually given in form of conclusive evaluation. The lack of diversity in the classification of emotional states, especially when dealing with individuals who express their affect atypically, may result in the inadequacy of interventions or may maintain the stigma. Such risks are compounded by black-box model design and lack of explainability, which restrict how the clinicians can critically evaluate AI-driven emotional emergence (Abbas et al., 2025). Lastly, because of their immersive and adaptive qualities, VR and AR interventions can also lead to psychological dependence, particularly when the systems have been programmed to enable continuous use. The excessive use of virtual spaces or AI-mediated emotional responses can erode the ability of users to cope with emotions themselves, which can affect the long-term therapeutic objectives (Babu and Joseph, 2024; Lal et al., 2023).

16.4.4 Implications of Responsible Integration

Attention should be paid to the elements of VR and AR or Emotion AI in mental-healthcare, as this illustrates the importance of human-centered design and robust schemes of governance. To enable ethical deployment, it is advisable to communicate clearly regarding the use of data, provide a clear consent regarding the affective monitoring, and provide adequate protection against over-personalization. Periodic disengagement approaches and clinician-in-the-loop framework can contribute to maintaining the equilibrium between technological support and the development and training of autonomous coping mechanisms. To conclude, immersive and affect-sensitive technologies constitute an effective continuation of AI psychiatry and can be used to improve the level of engagement and individualization. Their advantages, however, may only be actualized under responsible terms and conditions, if emotional surveillance risks, information fallacies, and dependency relations are explicitly dealt with in terms of ethical design, clinical supervising, and policy-consistent governance frameworks.

16.5 GREEN AI AND SUSTAINABLE COMPUTING

Since the practice of incorporating AI into mental healthcare services has been growing, the issue of the environmental sustainability of AI systems has become more pronounced. The complexity of both training and deploying high-quality ML models, especially deep neural networks and new foundation models, requires significant energy usage and carbon emission. In the realm of digital mental health, where the massive, ongoing processing of data is the order of the day, these issues are directly related to ethical accountability and the sustainability of systems under consideration over the long term. According to recent work in biomedical data science, the recent explosion of AI-based healthcare systems has outpaced any thinking about their environmental impact, which casts fundamental doubts on the long-term sustainability of the ongoing developmental trends (Federico and Trotsyuk, 2024). Applications obtained using mental health AI tend to rely on ongoing data streams exercised on phones, smart wearers, and intelligence systems in the cloud, and thus the energy usage is persistent as opposed to discontinuous. Such systems, when extended to larger groups, can contribute to carbon emissions to a large extent, especially when they are based on centralized cloud systems.

Green AI principles put forward the creation of models and systems that demonstrate a clear consideration of energy efficiency, cost, and environmental impact together with predictive performance. In mental health, the paradigm shift motivates the use of lightweight architecture, effective training procedures, and performance metrics which encourage energy-conscious optimization, as opposed to accuracy and care alone. Of particular importance, the design of sustainable AI corresponds to ethics requirements in healthcare and helps address the problem of resource waste and inequitable access to online interventions. Use of edge and federated computing architectures can be one of the promising avenues leading to sustainable mental health AI as it reduces the need to store data centrally and transmit data across a network severally. FL paradigms preserve privacy, allow models to execute their training on the end devices of individual users or institutional computers, cut down on bandwidth, and restrict the energy-consuming processes in clouds (Kumar et al., 2024a). Together with effective secure aggregation techniques, they can handle sustainability, privacy, and governance toward a solution simultaneously.

The lifecycle management of AI systems also falls under sustainability factors. Unless strictly controlled, continuous model retraining, real-role monitoring, and long-term maintenance can add some disclosed cost to the environment. Governance structures in mental health applications might need to trade off performance gains and cumulative energy consumption as model changes might be frequent, for example, behavioral drift or a change in context. This fact underlines the need for adaptive retraining programs and a modular system architecture that entails fewer redundant computations. Despite its topicality, sustainability is underinitiated in the AI-related mental health research and policy discussion. Ethical AI in healthcare reviews indicate that ethical evaluations or regulatory deliberation seldom consider the effect of the environment, although its impact on responsible innovation (RI) is vast (Li et al., 2022; Morley et al., 2020). To cover this gap, sustainability metrics should be included into the evaluation procedures and funding and regulation incentives corresponded to Green AI principles.

16.6 ETHICAL INNOVATION MODELS AND WORKFORCE READINESS FOR AI-DRIVEN MENTAL HEALTH

The successful implementation of AI in mental healthcare will depend on the ability to employ ethically sound innovation and staff prepared to approach AI systems with criticality. According to prior studies, ethical deficit in healthcare AI comes not so much due to technical constraints but rather due to a lack of ethical deliberation, control, and human supervision in the development and operation of the systems of AI (Morley et al., 2020; Federico and Trotsyuk, 2024). The supporting stance popularly referred to as Ethics by Design recommends the incorporation of ethical principles, which include fairness, accountability, transparency, and privacy, directly into the lifecycle of AI, and does not tackle these issues after the problem has emerged. This frame is especially essential in the field of mental health, where the outcomes of an algorithm can influence the development of a diagnosis, the choice of treatment, and the determination of a risk level (Li et al., 2022). Explainable Artificial Intelligence (XAI) is one of the essential conditions of clinical adoption. The evidence suggests that low explainability undermines clinicians' trust and reduces the usability of AI-based systems of clinical decision support (Abbas et al., 2025; Tun et al., 2025). In psychiatry, explainability is used to support the shared decision, and also maintain a clinician's authority. RI extends ethical thinking to include impact on society in the long term, sustainability, and inclusion of the stakeholders. It is indispensably relevant to RI as an option of outsourcing risks, including emotional surveillance, biased automation, and excessive use of AI by vulnerable populations (Federico and Trotsyuk, 2024). Value-sensitive design (VSD) applies an ethical intent in which human values, such as autonomy, dignity, and well-being, are incorporated into the process of technical design decisions. Considering the sensitive data of mental health, VSD enhances the coordination of AI functionality with patient-centered care instead of efficiency-oriented goals (Li et al., 2022). This chapter will operationalize these models by suggesting an AI Mental Health Ethics Stack, which will consist of three interdependent layers:

- *Technical Layer:* Privacy-preserving learning incorporates an explainable architecture, fairness-aware models, and continuous auditing.
- *Governance Layer:* Legal and governance issues serve compliance purposes as they relate to protecting the information while holding each party accountable for compliance and lifecycle management.

TABLE 16.3
Skills Required for the AI Mental Health Workforce

Skill Domain	Description
AI Literacy	Understanding the limitations, capabilities, uncertainty, and behavior of AI models
Clinical Interpretation	Using psychiatric judgment and the patient's history to put into context the output of the AI model
Ethical Reasoning	Identifying bias, assessing consent, and resolving ethical dilemmas
Human–AI Collaboration	Ability to participate in shared decision-making, utilize override capabilities, and handle escalations
Data Governance Awareness	Understanding how to keep patient data private, secure, and compliant with relevant laws and policies
Interdisciplinary Competence	Ability to collaborate with data scientists, ethicists, and other professionals involved in law and policymaking.

- *Human Oversight Layer:* Contestability of the AI outputs, ability of clinicians/staff to make decisions with the input of AI, and maintaining professional judgment.

Such a stratified system acknowledges that it is impossible to achieve ethical AI by technical means only. The implementation of ethical AI relies on the readiness of the workforce. The trust of the clinician in the AI systems is closely related to AI literacy, knowledge on the system limitations, and perceived control over decision-making (Tun et al., 2025). Therefore, training needs to focus on human–AI interaction, moral decision-making in the uncertain environment, and cross-disciplinary skills. Educational designs must increasingly integrate the three fields—psychiatry, data science, and ethics—to foster responsible and safe AI adoption (Prégent et al., 2025) (Table 16.3).

16.7 GLOBAL GOVERNANCE AND SECURE HUMAN-CENTERED AI FOR MENTAL HEALTH

All governments around the globe are required to institute a coordinated set of governances that encompass the introduction of AI into mental healthcare in a manner that simultaneously addresses the promotion of innovation, security, and the protection of individual rights in various jurisdictions. Mental-health data are sensitive by definition, longitudinal, and often move across national boundaries; hence, fragmented regulatory frameworks are not sufficient. The need to have a lifecycle and human and privacy-sensitive policy accompanied by technical blueprints communally points to the importance of governance. The EU AI Act is currently the most comprehensive binding regulatory body ever made with mental-health diagnosis and risk assessment AI systems considered high risk and, thus, requiring transparency, human control, and after-marketing evaluation. To add to this, the World Health Organization AI ethics guidelines include human dignity, autonomy, and accountability, especially in vulnerable health settings. The principles of AI enacted by the Organisation for Economic Cooperation and Development also follow fairness and strong and inclusive growth as a soft-law basis of international alignment. Considering the Global South the scope, the Digital Health Mission (NDHM, now called Ayushman Bharat Digital Mission (ABDM)) of India is an initiative to promote interoperable digital-health infrastructure and consent-based data sharing, which can be viewed as a model of scalable governance in specific policy discourse in large and heterogeneous populations. However, inconsistencies between these frameworks reveal issues in multi-jurisdictional governance of mental-health data, particularly in regard to data localization, federated accountability, and interoperability. Integration of technical protection with overriding principles of policy is thus essential to create well-founded international cooperation.

In order to translate policy intent into operational reality in marketplaces, secure and human-friendly AI systems have to be constructed. The key consideration of this effort is the use of human-in-the-loop (HITL) models, whereby the clinicians maintain final decision-making control and the AI system offers decision support. These structures balance automation bias and contextual judgment and help in maintaining the ethics accountability. The aspect of security should be incorporated into the AI pipeline through secure MLOps (Machine Learning Operations) designs, which combine guarded data input, model deployment, continuous surveys, and audit trails. FL and DP are privacy-preserving techniques that provide practical means for reducing the amount of centralized data collected while preserving the ability to use the data in building models. These types of approaches are particularly applicable to mental health cases where ongoing collection of behavioral data presents a greater risk to user privacy. Such methods can be considered particularly relevant in the case of mental-health scenarios, where the increased privacy threats are associated with ongoing data gathering on behavioral data points. The alignment of the user trust is also of remarkable importance: the consistency between the perceived system capability and the actual performance. Representative of over- and under-trust can catalyze uncritical trust in AI suggestions and stop adoption, respectively. Characteristics such as explainability, communicating uncertainty, and educating clinicians are prerequisites to attaining calibrated trust. The current chapter suggests a theoretical model that incorporates the following main elements:

- Clinician-in-the-loop human control
- Contestability
- RT Domestic Technical security (secure MLOps, FL, DP)
- Policymaking compliance (policies, auditability)

AI-based mental-health systems are used in dynamically changing environments where model drifting can lead to diminished performance and fairness over time due to behavioral change, societal change, or data changing. Thus, it is mandatory to have continuous validation and lifecycle audits. At the same time, AI systems are still vulnerable to adversarial tricks and data poisoning;thus, proactive threat modeling and resilience testing are urgent. The process of ethical governance should also incorporate mechanisms of incident response that can respond to algorithmic injuries, detect bias, or data breaches. These practices help facilitate sustainable implementation of AI on scale, by matching them with AI governance models of maturity—the ad hoc controls may scale to ontogoing, institution-wide controls. The trade prior-experience in AI psychiatry is a long-standing problem of accuracy in prediction versus privacy. Other methods like the use of DP add noise to protect personalized information, which, in most instances, can come at the expense of a small degree of degradation. Similarly, consent-sensitive AI and data minimization limit the availability of data, but increase ethical validity and compliance regulations. Emerging indications have shown that privacy-conserving architectures when carefully designed may provide not only acceptable performance but also a significant though not complete mitigation in the wool of ethical and legal risk. Privacy preservation in mental-health settings is not a regulatory obligation, but a clinical imperative since trust is the core of the mental-health setting (Figure 16.2).

16.8 SUMMARY AND FUTURE OUTLOOK

This chapter explores the changing paradigm of AI in psychiatry on the prism of innovation, ethics, and security. In various emerging technologies, including multi-modal psychiatric AI and real-time digital phenotyping, immersive VR/AR therapies, and foundation models, the discussion shows that AI has a significant potential of enhancing access to, customization, and continuity of mental health care. Nevertheless, these advantages cannot be discussed outside the context of ethical, governance, and sustainability issues, especially due to the sensitivity, temporality, and cross-border

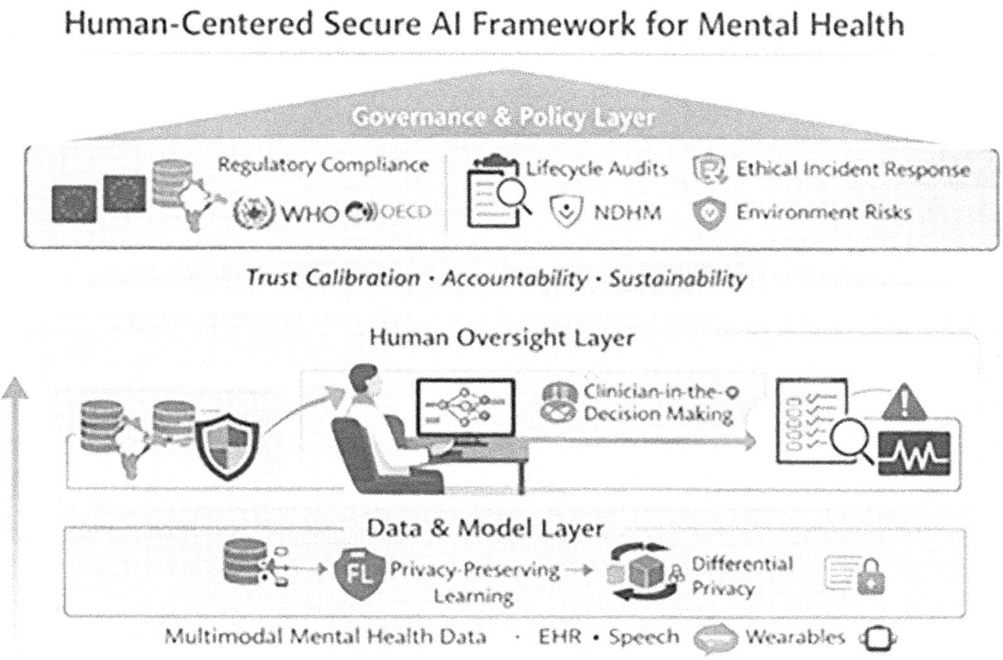

FIGURE 16.2 Human-centered AI framework for mental health.

transfer of mental health data. To begin with, AI psychiatry has moved past individual and single learning modalities and become an ecological system of multi-modal capabilities with the integration and adaptive capabilities of learning, privacy preferring, and clinician enhancing. Second, three categories of ethical risks, including bias, opaqueness, emotional surveilling, and reliance on automation, are structural instead of tactical and necessitate making ethics by design and explainability to be part and parcel of the AI lifecycle. Third, the key to safe and reliable deployment requires the human-centered architecture, in the framework of which clinicians are responsible decision-makers, and AI systems are used as auditable assistive resources. Lastly, a matter that is gaining relevance as a dimension of responsible AI mental health systems, yet remains underexplored, is sustainability and long-term governance.

In order to put these findings into practice, a number of policy priorities become apparent. Regulators and healthcare organizations should ensure that all high-risk mental health AI systems are monitored and explored in conjunction with humans. To create a uniform framework for regulating the data use, accountability, and audit of the AI systems globally, a commitment by the international community is necessary. In the public healthcare field, future promotion of AI technology for greater energy efficiency and privacy-preserving features through public health reward programs will also create a continuing ethical obligation for environmental sustainability. Finally, social programs that promote continuing education and ethical training of mental health providers regarding the use of AI technology will also be necessary. In the future, there are three areas of research that should be given special interest. Emotion-conscious ethics should cover these threats of affective surveillance and inaccurate emotional inferences by working out autonoetic, consent-conscious systems of emotional AI. Neuromorphic and energy-efficient AI approaches to mental health are promising avenues to the sustainability of low-latency systems functioning at the edge and emerging privacy limits. Furthermore, the management of AI psychotherapy is still an unresolved issue, and its clinical effectiveness, the administrative frameworks, and the extent of interaction between the automated assistance and the human assistance frameworks should be carefully considered.

REFERENCES

Abbas, Q., Jeong, W., & Lee, S. W. (2025). Explainable AI in clinical decision support systems: A meta-analysis of methods, applications, and usability challenges. *Healthcare*, *13*(17), 2154. https://doi.org/10.3390/healthcare13172154

Adlung, L., Cohen, Y., Mor, U., & Elinav, E. (2021). Machine learning in clinical decision making. *Med*, *2*(6), 642–665. https://doi.org/10.1016/j.medj.2021.04.006

Ali, M., Ali, S., Abbas, Q., Abbas, Z., & Lee, S. W. (2025). Artificial intelligence for mental health: A narrative review of applications, challenges, and future directions in digital health. *Digital Health*, *11*. https://doi.org/10.1177/20552076251395548

Alvarez-Jimenez, M., Rice, S., D'Alfonso, S., Leicester, S., Bendall, S., Pryor, I., Russon, P., McEnery, C., Santesteban-Echarri, O., Da Costa, G., Gilbertson, T., Valentine, L., Solves, L., Ratheesh, A., McGorry, P. D., & Gleeson, J. (2020). A novel multimodal digital service (Moderated Online Social Therapy+) for help-seeking young people experiencing mental ill-health: Pilot evaluation within a national youth e-mental health service. *Journal of Medical Internet Research, 22*(8), e17155. https://doi.org/10.2196/17155

Auf, H., Svedberg, P., Nygren, J., Nair, M., & Lundgren, L. E. (2024). The use of AI in mental health services to support decision-making: Scoping review. *Journal of Medical Internet Research*, *27*, e63548. https://doi.org/10.2196/63548

Babu, A., & Joseph, A. P. (2024). Artificial intelligence in mental healthcare: Transformative potential vs. the necessity of human interaction. *Frontiers in Psychology*, *15*, 1378904. https://doi.org/10.3389/fpsyg.2024.1378904

Cruz-Gonzalez, P., He, A. W., Lam, E. P., Ng, I. M. C., Li, M. W., Hou, R., Chan, J. N., Sahni, Y., Guasch, N. V., Miller, T., Lau, B. W., & Vidaña, D. I. S. (2025). Artificial intelligence in mental health care: A systematic review of diagnosis, monitoring, and intervention applications. *Psychological Medicine*, *55*, e18. https://doi.org/10.1017/s0033291724003295

Currey, D., & Torous, J. (2022a). Increasing the value of digital phenotyping through reducing missingness: A Retrospective analysis. *bioRxiv (Cold Spring Harbor Laboratory)*. https://doi.org/10.1101/2022.05 17.22275182

Currey, D., & Torous, J. (2022b). Digital phenotyping correlations in larger mental health samples: Analysis and replication. *BJPsych Open*, *8*(4), e106. https://doi.org/10.1192/bjo.2022.507

Dwyer, B., Flathers, M., Burns, J., Mikkelson, J., Perlmutter, E., Chen, K., Ram, N., & Torous, J. (2024). Assessing digital phenotyping for app recommendations and sustained engagement: Cohort study. *JMIR Formative Research*, *8*, e62725. https://doi.org/10.2196/62725

Federico, C. A., & Trotsyuk, A. A. (2024). Biomedical data science, artificial intelligence, and ethics: Navigating challenges in the face of explosive growth. *Annual Review of Biomedical Data Science*, *7*(1), 1–14. https://doi.org/10.1146/annurev-biodatasci-102623-104553

Golubović, G., Đurđević, S., Kerac, J., Juretić, I., & Cvetojević, S. (2024). Use of AI in mhealth mobile applications: The influence of virtual therapists' visual characteristics on user perception. In *Proceedings-The Twelfth International Symposium Grid*. pp. 329–340. https://doi.org/10.24867/grid-2024-p35

Grundy, Q. (2021). A review of the quality and impact of mobile health apps. *Annual Review of Public Health*, *43*(1), 117–134. https://doi.org/10.1146/annurev-publhealth-052020-103738

Huckvale, K., Nicholas, J., Torous, J., & Larsen, M. E. (2020). Smartphone apps for the treatment of mental health conditions: Status and considerations. *Current Opinion in Psychology*, *36*, 65–70. https://doi.org/10.1016/j.copsyc.2020.04.008

Huckvale, K., Torous, J., & Larsen, M. E. (2019). Assessment of the data sharing and privacy practices of smartphone apps for depression and smoking cessation. *JAMA Network Open*, *2*(4), e192542. https://doi.org/10.1001/jamanetworkopen.2019.2542

Insel, T. R. (2017). Digital phenotyping. *JAMA*, *318*(13), 1215. https://doi.org/10.1001/jama.2017.11295

Kumar, D., Pawar, P. P., Meesala, M. K., Pareek, P. K., Addula, S. R., & Shwetha, K. S. (2024). Trustworthy IoT infrastructures: Privacy-preserving federated learning with efficient secure aggregation for cybersecurity. In *2024 International Conference on Integrated Intelligence and Communication Systems (ICIICS)* (pp. 1-8). IEEE. https://doi.org/10.1109/iciics63763.2024.10860195

Lal, S., Tobin, R., Tremblay, S., Gleeson, J., D'Alfonso, S., Etienne, G., Joober, R., Lepage, M., & Alvarez-Jimenez, M. (2023). Experiences of a digital mental health intervention from the perspectives of young people recovering from first-episode psychosis: A focus group study. *International Journal of Environmental Research and Public Health*, *20*(9), 5745. https://doi.org/10.3390/ijerph20095745

Li, F., Ruijs, N., & Lu, Y. (2022). Ethics & AI: A Systematic review on ethical concerns and related strategies for designing with AI in healthcare. *AI*, *4*(1), 28–53. https://doi.org/10.3390/ai4010003

Mergenova, G., Davis, A., Gilbert, L., El-Bassel, N., Terlikbayeva, A., Primbetova, S., Nugmanova, Z., Pala, A. N., Gustafson, D., Rosenthal, S. L., Denebayeva, A. Y., & DeHovitz, J. (2024). Mental health and cognition in relation to adherence to antiretroviral therapy among people living with HIV in Kazakhstan: A cross-sectional study. *Journal of the International AIDS Society*, *27*(S3), e26320. https://doi.org/10.1002/jia2.26320

Morley, J., Machado, C. C., Burr, C., Cowls, J., Joshi, I., Taddeo, M., & Floridi, L. (2020). The ethics of AI in health care: A mapping review. *Social Science & Medicine*, *260*, 113172. https://doi.org/10.1016/j.socscimed.2020.113172

Narimani, M., & Mahdi, N. (2025). Artificial intelligence in mental health: integrating opportunities and challenges of multimodal deep learning for mental disorder prevention and treatment. *Annals of Medicine and Surgery*, *87*(9), 5757–5761. https://doi.org/10.1097/ms9.0000000000003624

Naslund, J. A., & Aschbrenner, K. A. (2021). Technology use and interest in digital apps for mental health promotion and lifestyle intervention among young adults with serious mental illness. *Journal of Affective Disorders Reports*, *6*, 100227. https://doi.org/10.1016/j.jadr.2021.100227

O'Sullivan, S., Schmaal, L., D'Alfonso, S., Toenders, Y. J., Valentine, L., McEnery, C., Bendall, S., Nelson, B., Gleeson, J. F., & Alvarez-Jimenez, M. (2022). Characterizing use of a multicomponent digital intervention to predict treatment outcomes in First-Episode psychosis: Cluster analysis. *JMIR Mental Health*, *9*(4), e29211. https://doi.org/10.2196/29211

Pawar, P. P., Kumar, D., Meesala, M. K., Pareek, P. K., Addula, S. R., & Shwetha, K. S. (2024a). Securing digital governance: A deep learning and blockchain framework for malware detection in IoT networks. In *2024 International Conference on Integrated Intelligence and Communication Systems (ICIICS)* (pp. 1-8). IEEE. https://doi.org/10.1109/iciics63763.2024.10860155

Pawar, P. P., Kumar, D., Meesala, M. K., Pareek, P. K., Addula, S. R., & Shwetha, K. S. (2024b). A patient-centric blockchain framework for transparent and secure medical data sharing using modified AES. In *2024 International Conference on Integrated Intelligence and Communication Systems (ICIICS)* (pp. 1–7). IEEE. https://doi.org/10.1109/iciics63763.2024.10859825

Prégent, J., Chung, V., Adib, I. E., Désilets, M., & Hudon, A. (2025). Applications of artificial intelligence in psychiatry and psychology education: Scoping review. *JMIR Medical Education*, *11*, e75238. https://doi.org/10.2196/75238

Rice, S., O'Bree, B., Wilson, M., McEnery, C., Lim, M. H., Hamilton, M., Gleeson, J., Bendall, S., D'Alfonso, S., Russon, P., Valentine, L., Cagliarini, D., Howell, S., Miles, C., Pearson, M., & Álvarez-Jiménez, M. (2020). Development of a graphic medicine-enabled social media-based intervention for youth social anxiety. *Clinical Psychologist, 25(2).* https://doi.org/10.1111/cp.12222

Rice, S. M., Goodall, J., Hetrick, S. E., Parker, A. G., Gilbertson, T., Amminger, G. P., Davey, C. G., McGorry, P. D., Gleeson, J., & Alvarez-Jimenez, M. (2014). Online and social networking interventions for the treatment of depression in young people: A systematic review. *Journal of Medical Internet Research*, *16*(9), e206. https://doi.org/10.2196/jmir.3304

Singh, S., Sharma, P., Ghimire, P., Shrestha, R., & Gnanavel, S. (2023). Assessment of app store description and privacy policy to explore ethical and safety concerns associated with the use of mental health apps for depression. *Indian Journal of Psychological Medicine*, *45*(2), 173–178. https://doi.org/10.1177/02537176221142046

Torous, J., Myrick, K. J., Rauseo-Ricupero, N., & Firth, J. (2020). Digital mental health and COVID-19: Using technology today to accelerate the curve on access and quality tomorrow. *JMIR Mental Health*, *7*(3), e18848. https://doi.org/10.2196/18848

Torous, J., Wisniewski, H., Bird, B., Carpenter, E., David, G., Elejalde, E., Fulford, D., Guimond, S., Hays, R., Henson, P., Hoffman, L., Lim, C., Menon, M., Noel, V., Pearson, J., Peterson, R., Susheela, A., Troy, H., Vaidyam, A., … Keshavan, M. (2019). Creating a digital health smartphone app and digital phenotyping platform for mental health and diverse healthcare needs: An interdisciplinary and collaborative approach. *Journal of Technology in Behavioral Science*, *4*(2), 73–85. https://doi.org/10.1007/s41347-019-00095-w

Tun, H. M., Rahman, H. A., Naing, L., & Malik, O. A. (2025). Trust in artificial intelligence–based clinical decision support systems among health care workers: Systematic review. *Journal of Medical Internet Research*, *27*, e69678. https://doi.org/10.2196/69678

Tyagi, A.K., Kumari, S., Fernandez, T.F., & Aravindan, C. (2020). P3 Block: Privacy Preserved, Trusted Smart Parking Allotment for Future Vehicles of Tomorrow. In: Gervasi O. et al. (eds.), *Computational Science and Its Applications – ICCSA 2020*. ICCSA 2020. Lecture Notes in Computer Science, vol 12254. Springer, Cham. https://doi.org/10.1007/978-3-030-58817-5_56

Tyagi, A.K., & Sreenath, N. (2023). Security, privacy, and trust issues in intelligent transportation system. In: *Intelligent Transportation Systems: Theory and Practice. Disruptive Technologies and Digital Transformations for Society 5.0*. Springer, Singapore. https://doi.org/10.1007/978-981-19-7622-3_8

17 Conclusion

17.1 SUMMARY OF EACH CHAPTER

Chapter 1 explores how artificial intelligence (AI) has become a transformative force in modern mental healthcare by enhancing diagnostics, treatment, and long-term monitoring. It begins by reviewing the evolution of AI in healthcare and tracing its expanding applications in psychiatry, ranging from rule-based expert systems to today's deep learning and natural language processing (NLP)-driven models (Abbas et al., 2025). The chapter highlights global mental health gaps—limited professionals, stigma, delayed diagnosis—and explains how AI-enabled tools, such as digital triage systems, chatbots, and emotion-recognition platforms, can expand access and scalability (Adlung et al., 2021). It examines AI's ability to analyze multi-modal behavioral data, provide early risk detection, support therapy adherence, and offer 24/7 support (Ali et al., 2025). Benefits such as personalization, remote accessibility, and reduced clinician workload are balanced against limitations like algorithmic bias, over-reliance on automation, limited explainability, and data privacy concerns (Alvarez-Jimenez et al., 2020). Cultural and ethical issues—including fairness, trust, autonomy, and societal acceptance—are explored in depth, emphasizing the need for culturally informed datasets and transparent systems. The chapter concludes with key research challenges, such as integrating AI into clinical workflows, validating models across populations, and establishing ethical guardrails (Auf et al., 2024). Hence, it positions AI as a supportive augmentation tool rather than a replacement for human clinicians.

Further, Chapter 2 examines the shift from traditional, in-person mental healthcare to digitally enabled systems driven by telepsychiatry, mobile apps, wearables, and Internet of Things (IoT) devices (Babu and Joseph, 2024). It begins with a literature review on the evolution of digital mental health and explores how technological advances have reshaped therapy delivery, assessment, and ongoing support (Cruz-Gonzalez et al., 2025). Telepsychiatry's rapid growth has democratized access, especially for remote or underserved populations, while mental health apps offer self-help modules, mood tracking, cognitive-behavioral therapy (CBT)-based exercises, and AI-enhanced chatbots (Currey and Torous, 2022a). The chapter highlights the increasing role of wearables and IoT sensors in capturing physiological and emotional data—such as sleep, heart rate variability, and behavioral patterns—to generate real-time insights. Digital therapeutics (DTx) are emphasized for their evidence-based and clinically validated interventions (Currey and Torous, 2022b). Personalization through AI and analytics enables adaptive care pathways, but challenges such as the digital divide, limited digital literacy, and infrastructure gaps in low-resource settings remain significant (Dwyer et al., 2024). The chapter underscores the need for strong integration between digital systems and traditional clinical psychology to avoid fragmented care. It concludes by forecasting

DOI: 10.1201/9781003658344-22

future digital ecosystems built on interoperability, immersive technologies, and continuous, data-driven personalization.

Next, Chapter 3 focuses on the heightened privacy and security concerns associated with mental health data—one of the most sensitive categories of personal information. It outlines the mental health data lifecycle from collection, storage, processing, sharing, and deletion, stressing the unique risks posed by AI systems that aggregate multi-modal data sources. Common vulnerabilities include insecure application programming interfaces (APIs), weak authentication, data leakage, adversarial attacks, and third-party app exploitation (Federico and Trotsyuk, 2024). The chapter analyzes the privacy–accessibility trade-off, where the need for high-quality data for AI must be balanced with user rights and confidentiality. Critical issues such as consent, data ownership, and governance frameworks are discussed in detail. Technical safeguards like encryption standards, secure access controls, and zero-trust architectures are highlighted alongside strategies like data minimization and strict retention policies. The chapter further explores privacy-enhancing technologies embedded into therapeutic platforms, such as secure communication protocols, anonymized storage, and privacy dashboards. Policy recommendations stress harmonized regulation, stronger compliance systems, and robust enforcement mechanisms to protect vulnerable populations. Hence, it positions data privacy as central to building trustworthy AI mental health ecosystems.

Then, Chapter 4 addresses the ethical principles and legal requirements that govern AI deployment in mental health contexts. It begins with a grounding in bioethical pillars—beneficence, non-maleficence, justice, and autonomy—and examines how these principles guide responsible AI. Case studies illustrate emerging legal challenges, such as liability for incorrect AI predictions or consent violations. The chapter discusses informed consent in digital environments, focusing on how to ensure user autonomy when algorithmic decisions are complex or opaque (Nair et al., 2025). Transparency requirements demand that mental health AI systems provide interpretable insights and disclose limitations. A comparative review of major regulations—including General Data Protection Regulation (GDPR), Health Insurance Portability and Accountability Act of 1996 (HIPAA), and national mental health policies—highlights differences in data protection standards, patient rights, and clinical accountability. Issues of data sovereignty, cross-border data transfer, and localization laws are evaluated, given that global AI systems frequently operate across jurisdictions. The chapter details the need for oversight frameworks such as algorithmic audits, compliance certifications, and institutional review boards to ensure ethical operation. Finally, it identifies policy gaps and emerging trends such as algorithmic justice, AI liability reform, and harmonized global governance for mental health technologies.

Further, Chapter 5 provides the technical foundation for AI models used in mental health applications. It covers machine learning and deep learning fundamentals, explaining supervised, unsupervised, and reinforcement learning techniques applied to behavioral prediction, diagnosis, and therapy personalization. NLP methods—including sentiment analysis, transformer models, and conversational AI—are shown to power chatbots and cognitive therapy assistants capable of detecting emotional cues and distress patterns. Emotion recognition via audio, facial data, or text provides real-time insight into user states. Predictive modeling techniques enable early detection of depression, anxiety, relapse risk, or suicidal ideation. Explainable AI (XAI) receives special emphasis, as clinicians require interpretable outputs to make safe decisions. The chapter reviews ethical and secure model training practices, highlighting data quality, privacy-preserving methods, and adversarial robustness. Bias and fairness challenges—particularly due to cultural differences and data imbalance—are critically assessed. Model deployment considerations include continuous monitoring, drift detection, and periodic retraining. Evaluation metrics such as precision, recall, receiver operating characteristic (ROC) curves, and clinical validation protocols are explained. Case studies illustrate practical implementations in digital mental health platforms (Grundy, 2021).

Chapter 6 describes the technological backbone required to securely operate AI-driven mental health systems. It outlines secure cloud, hybrid, and on-premises architectures designed to protect sensitive mental health data. Cryptographic frameworks—Secure Sockets Layer (SSL)/Transport Layer Security (TLS), public key infrastructure (PKI), and encryption at rest and in transit—are essential for securing communication and storage. The chapter describes authentication protocols, role-based access control, and multi-factor mechanisms to regulate data access. Backup strategies, disaster recovery plans, and data integrity checks are critical for maintaining reliability in clinical environments. Metadata management, provenance tracking, and audit trails ensure traceability and accountability. The chapter evaluates distributed storage solutions, exploring how edge and cloud environments can be integrated while managing vulnerabilities unique to each. Threat landscapes—including cloud misconfigurations, insider threats, and edge-device exploitation—are analyzed (Huckvale et al., 2020). It also covers the design of resilient AI pipelines that incorporate real-time monitoring, secure APIs, and automated anomaly detection. Continuous security assurance is emphasized as an ongoing operational requirement rather than a one-time setup.

Chapter 7 explores methods that allow AI systems to analyze mental health data while protecting privacy. It begins with data minimization and anonymization principles, explaining techniques such as generalization, suppression, and pseudonymization. Formal privacy models such as k-anonymity, l-diversity, and t-closeness are introduced, followed by more advanced frameworks like differential privacy, which injects statistical noise to prevent re-identification. Federated learning (FL) and federated analytics are highlighted as approaches that keep data on local devices while enabling collaborative model training. The chapter describes secure multi-party computation and homomorphic encryption, which allow operations on encrypted data without revealing sensitive content. Synthetic data generation is discussed as a tool for research when real patient data cannot be shared. The challenge of balancing privacy and data utility is addressed, along with common pitfalls such as residual re-identification risk and linkage attacks. Strategies for integrating privacy-preserving machine learning into clinical systems are outlined, emphasizing practical deployment considerations and regulatory compliance. The chapter concludes with future directions in secure health data sharing.

Chapter 8 explores decentralized AI methods suitable for mental health systems that require strong privacy. It explains the fundamentals of FL, where models are trained across distributed devices without transferring raw data. The chapter breaks down FL architecture, including client selection, local training, secure aggregation, and model updating. Edge computing enables real-time inference on personal devices or wearables, improving responsiveness and privacy. Differential privacy, secure aggregation protocols, and communication-efficient optimization are examined as safeguards against data leakage. Technical challenges—such as device heterogeneity, unstable connectivity, and adversarial attacks like model poisoning—are evaluated. Blockchain integration is discussed as a means to increase transparency, ensure tamper-resistant logs, and coordinate distributed updates. A comparative analysis highlights trade-offs between centralized and federated systems in terms of accuracy, latency, security, and energy consumption. Case studies include real-time monitoring systems for stress, depression relapse prediction, and cognitive behavioral therapy platforms. Emerging decentralized AI models, such as swarm learning and hybrid federated-edge ecosystems, are introduced as future directions.

Chapter 9 provides a comprehensive framework for identifying and assessing security threats in AI mental health systems. It explains foundational threat modeling methodologies such as STRIDE, DREAD, and attack-tree analysis, guiding designers to anticipate vulnerabilities. Risk classification frameworks differentiate between technological, organizational, and human-factor risks. Common attacks—including phishing, ransomware, API exploitation, man-in-the-middle attacks, and adversarial ML threats—are discussed in detail. Insider threats are analyzed alongside external cyberattacks, emphasizing the unique sensitivity of mental health environments. The chapter highlights the role of threat intelligence systems that aggregate real-time risk data from global sources. Quantitative approaches (risk scores and probability modeling) and qualitative assessments (expert reviews and impact evaluation) are explained. Vulnerability scanning tools, penetration tests, and continuous monitoring systems form part of the recommended defensive strategy. The chapter concludes with best practices and certification guidelines for building resilient AI mental health systems that maintain confidentiality and trust (Huckvale et al., 2019).

Chapter 10 explores the serious consequences of data breaches in mental health contexts. It reviews major breach incidents and analyzes how cyberattacks unfold—from reconnaissance and exploitation to data exfiltration and post-breach misuse. Because mental health information is deeply personal, breaches can lead to emotional distress, stigma, relationship impacts, and loss of psychological safety. The chapter discusses organizational responsibilities in communicating incidents, implementing crisis management, and providing transparent updates to affected users. Ethical obligations require timely disclosure, empathetic communication, and remediation strategies. Post-breach forensics involves identifying attack vectors, patching vulnerabilities, and preventing recurrence. The chapter also explores long-term trust rebuilding through openness, strengthened security controls, third-party audits, and user-facing privacy assurances. Cyber insurance is reviewed as a financial resilience mechanism. Case studies highlight lessons learned and policy implications for both organizations and regulators.

Chapter 11 addresses how algorithmic bias can harm mental health outcomes and exacerbate inequities. It categorizes biases—including sampling bias, measurement bias, algorithmic bias, and human-in-the-loop bias—showing how each can distort diagnostic accuracy or reinforce cultural misunderstandings. Representation gaps in mental health datasets often lead to poorer performance for marginalized populations. Fairness metrics such as demographic parity, equalized odds, and calibration are introduced to quantify equity. The chapter emphasizes culturally aware AI design, which incorporates diverse data sources, multilingual modeling, and contextual behavioral understanding. Ethical and legal responses to discrimination—including regulatory interventions and fairness audits—are discussed. Transparency methods, dataset documentation, and bias mitigation techniques (reweighting, adversarial debiasing) form core tools for equitable system development. The chapter advocates for global dataset diversity and emphasizes the importance of accountability throughout the AI development lifecycle (Pawar et al., 2024a).

Chapter 12 analyzes the growing use of digital surveillance technologies—such as passive sensing, continuous monitoring apps, and behavioral analytics—in clinical mental health. It evaluates both the benefits and ethical hazards of collecting emotional, physiological, and contextual data. While surveillance can support early crisis detection, relapse monitoring, and patient safety, it also raises concerns about autonomy, consent, and boundary violations. Constant observation may cause anxiety, reduce trust, or create a sense of coercion. The chapter examines consent processes, emphasizing informed, ongoing, and revocable consent in systems that rely on continuous monitoring. Human oversight is presented as a critical safeguard to prevent over-reliance on automated systems. Ethical issues are especially important when monitoring vulnerable groups such as children, patients with severe disorders, or institutionalized individuals. Policy recommendations include transparency mandates, data minimization, and clear governance frameworks that prioritize human rights. The chapter concludes by outlining strategies to manage data sensitivity and maintain patient dignity (Kumar et al., 2024).

Chapter 13 explains the significance of explainability in AI systems used for clinical mental health decisions. It begins with foundational concepts in XAI, including interpretability, post-hoc explanations, and model transparency. Transparent algorithms help clinicians understand how AI arrives at conclusions, increasing safety and trust. Visualization techniques—feature importance graphs, saliency maps, and attention heatmaps—enable interpretation of complex deep learning models. The chapter discusses communication strategies for translating AI insights into clinically relevant, human-understandable information (Tyagi et al., 2020). It also explores tension between transparency and intellectual property (IP) protection, proposing ways to balance openness with proprietary interests. Trust metrics, governance indicators, and audit protocols are described as tools to evaluate AI reliability. Human–AI collaboration frameworks emphasize shared decision-making rather than automated dominance. Standards for disclosure, documentation, and explanation completeness are presented as crucial for regulatory compliance and public trust.

Chapter 14 explores how digital consent must evolve to support AI-driven mental health systems. It defines principles of informed, granular, and dynamic consent, emphasizing the importance of giving users meaningful control over how their data is accessed and used. Authentication techniques, identity verification, and fraud prevention measures are examined to ensure secure digital identities. The chapter analyzes the potential of blockchain and decentralized identity (DID) solutions to enhance transparency, reduce reliance on centralized authorities, and give users full ownership of their mental health data. Legal interpretations of consent, data rights, and patient autonomy across different jurisdictions are compared. User empowerment through data portability and consent dashboards is emphasized as a key design principle. Consent management lifecycle tools—capture, logging, updating, and revocation—are described alongside practical case studies. Future pathways include interoperable identity systems, verifiable credentials, and privacy-by-design frameworks (Tyagi & Sreenath, 2023).

Chapter 15 defines accountability in AI mental health systems as the ability to trace, justify, and regulate algorithmic decisions. It explains the role of audit trails, provenance tracking, and model documentation in ensuring transparency and responsibility. Third-party certifications, regulatory audits, and independent validation are examined as mechanisms to verify compliance with ethical, legal, and technical standards. The chapter addresses the complexities of assigning liability when AI systems contribute to clinical decisions, including shared responsibility models between developers, institutions, and clinicians. Continuous compliance monitoring is emphasized, supported by automated reporting, periodic reviews, and governance committees. Ethical oversight boards and institutional review mechanisms help maintain alignment with societal values. Transparency reports and incident documentation further reinforce trust. The chapter concludes with future trends in algorithmic accountability, including dynamic auditing, real-time governance systems, and global harmonization of compliance standards.

Lastly, Chapter 16 explores how future mental health systems must balance rapid innovation with ethical safeguards and robust security. It reviews emerging trends such as emotionally intelligent AI, multi-modal behavioral modeling, and the integration of virtual reality (VR)/augmented reality (AR) for immersive therapy. Sustainable AI and energy-efficient models are introduced within the context of green computing. Ethical innovation frameworks emphasize responsible research, inclusive design, and long-term societal impact assessment. Workforce readiness is highlighted, stressing the need to train clinicians in AI literacy, risk management, and data governance. Global policy collaboration is essential to harmonize AI ethics across countries and ensure equitable access to advanced mental health technologies. The chapter outlines strategies for building human-centered AI ecosystems that prioritize dignity, autonomy, and data protection. It presents long-term governance models that integrate continuous oversight, adaptive regulation, and user-centered privacy controls. Ultimately, the chapter envisions a future in which AI enhances human care while preserving psychological safety and ethical integrity (Pawar et al., 2024b).

And last, this chapter provides the conclusion of this book in brief.

REFERENCES

Abbas, Q., Jeong, W., & Lee, S. W. (2025). Explainable AI in clinical decision support systems: A meta-analysis of methods, applications, and usability challenges. *Healthcare, 13*(17), 2154. https://doi.org/10.3390/healthcare13172154

Adlung, L., Cohen, Y., Mor, U., & Elinav, E. (2021). Machine learning in clinical decision making. *Med, 2*(6), 642–665. https://doi.org/10.1016/j.medj.2021.04.006

Ali, M., Ali, S., Abbas, Q., Abbas, Z., & Lee, S. W. (2025). Artificial intelligence for mental health: A narrative review of applications, challenges, and future directions in digital health. *Digital Health, 11*. https://doi.org/10.1177/20552076251395548

Alvarez-Jimenez, M., Rice, S., D'Alfonso, S., Leicester, S., Bendall, S., Pryor, I., Russon, P., McEnery, C., Santesteban-Echarri, O., Da Costa, G., Gilbertson, T., Valentine, L., Solves, L., Ratheesh, A., McGorry, P. D., & Gleeson, J. (2020). A novel multimodal digital service (Moderated Online Social Therapy+) for help-seeking young people experiencing mental ill-health: Pilot evaluation within a national youth e-mental health service. *Journal of Medical Internet Research, 22*(8), e17155. https://doi.org/10.2196/17155

Auf, H., Svedberg, P., Nygren, J., Nair, M., & Lundgren, L. E. (2024). The use of AI in mental health services to support decision-making: Scoping review. *Journal of Medical Internet Research, 27*, e63548. https://doi.org/10.2196/63548

Babu, A., & Joseph, A. P. (2024). Artificial intelligence in mental healthcare: Transformative potential vs. the necessity of human interaction. *Frontiers in Psychology, 15*, 1378904. https://doi.org/10.3389/fpsyg.2024.1378904

Cruz-Gonzalez, P., He, A. W., Lam, E. P., Ng, I. M. C., Li, M. W., Hou, R., Chan, J. N., Sahni, Y., Guasch, N. V., Miller, T., Lau, B. W., & Vidaña, D. I. S. (2025). Artificial intelligence in mental health care: A systematic review of diagnosis, monitoring, and intervention applications. *Psychological Medicine, 55*, e18. https://doi.org/10.1017/S0033291724003295

Currey, D., & Torous, J. (2022a). Increasing the value of digital phenotyping through reducing missingness: A retrospective analysis. *bioRxiv*. https://doi.org/10.1101/2022.05.17.22275182

Currey, D., & Torous, J. (2022b). Digital phenotyping correlations in larger mental health samples: Analysis and replication. *BJPsych Open, 8*(4), e106. https://doi.org/10.1192/bjo.2022.507

Dwyer, B., Flathers, M., Burns, J., Mikkelson, J., Perlmutter, E., Chen, K., Ram, N., & Torous, J. (2024). Assessing digital phenotyping for app recommendations and sustained engagement: Cohort study. *JMIR Formative Research, 8*, e62725. https://doi.org/10.2196/62725

Federico, C. A., & Trotsyuk, A. A. (2024). Biomedical data science, artificial intelligence, and ethics: Navigating challenges in the face of explosive growth. *Annual Review of Biomedical Data Science, 7*(1), 1–14. https://doi.org/10.1146/annurev-biodatasci-102623-104553

Golubović, G., Đurđević, S., Kerac, J., Juretić, I., & Cvetojević, S. (2024). Use of AI in mHealth mobile applications: The influence of virtual therapists' visual characteristics on user perception. In *Proceedings of GRID 2024*. https://doi.org/10.24867/grid-2024-p35

Grundy, Q. (2021). A review of the quality and impact of mobile health apps. *Annual Review of Public Health, 43*(1), 117–134. https://doi.org/10.1146/annurev-publhealth-052020-103738

Huckvale, K., Nicholas, J., Torous, J., & Larsen, M. E. (2020). Smartphone apps for the treatment of mental health conditions: Status and considerations. *Current Opinion in Psychology, 36*, 65–70. https://doi.org/10.1016/j.copsyc.2020.04.008

Huckvale, K., Torous, J., & Larsen, M. E. (2019). Assessment of the data sharing and privacy practices of smartphone apps for depression and smoking cessation. *JAMA Network Open, 2*(4), e192542. https://doi.org/10.1001/jamanetworkopen.2019.2542

Kumar, D., Pawar, P. P., Meesala, M. K., Pareek, P. K., Addula, S. R., & Shwetha, K. S. (2024). Trustworthy IoT infrastructures: Privacy-preserving federated learning with efficient secure aggregation for cybersecurity. In *Proceedings of the 2024 international conference on integrated intelligence and communication systems (ICIICS)* (pp. 1–8). IEEE. https://doi.org/10.1109/ICIICS63763.2024.10860195

Nair, M. M., Kumar, A. T. (2025). Transformative effects of emerging technologies on Industry 5.0 and Society 5.0: Current status, vision, issues, challenges, and opportunities for future. In Amit Kumar Tyagi (Ed.), *Next Generation Data Science and Blockchain Technology for Industry 5.0*. Wiley.

Pawar, P. P., Kumar, D., Meesala, M. K., Pareek, P. K., Addula, S. R., & Shwetha, K. S. (2024a). A patient-centric blockchain framework for transparent and secure medical data sharing using modified AES. In *Proceedings of the 2024 international conference on integrated intelligence and communication systems (ICIICS)* (pp. 1–7). IEEE. https://doi.org/10.1109/ICIICS63763.2024.10859825

Pawar, P. P., Kumar, D., Meesala, M. K., Pareek, P. K., Addula, S. R., & Shwetha, K. S. (2024b). Securing digital governance: A deep learning and blockchain framework for malware detection in IoT networks. In *Proceedings of the 2024 international conference on integrated intelligence and communication systems (ICIICS)* (pp. 1–8). IEEE. https://doi.org/10.1109/ICIICS63763.2024.10860155

Tyagi, A.K., Kumari, S., Fernandez, T.F., & Aravindan, C. (2020). P3 Block: Privacy Preserved, Trusted Smart Parking Allotment for Future Vehicles of Tomorrow. In: Gervasi O. et al. (eds.), *Computational Science and Its Applications – ICCSA 2020*. ICCSA 2020. Lecture Notes in Computer Science, vol 12254. Springer, Cham. https://doi.org/10.1007/978-3-030-58817-5_56

Tyagi, A.K., & Sreenath, N. (2023). Security, privacy, and trust issues in intelligent transportation system. In: *Intelligent Transportation Systems: Theory and Practice. Disruptive Technologies and Digital Transformations for Society 5.0*. Springer, Singapore. https://doi.org/10.1007/978-981-19-7622-3_8

Index

R

S

T

U

For Product Safety Concerns and Information please contact our EU
representative GPSR@taylorandfrancis.com
Taylor & Francis Verlag GmbH, Kaufingerstraße 24, 80331 München, Germany

www.ingramcontent.com/pod-product-compliance
Ingram Content Group UK Ltd.
Pitfield, Milton Keynes, MK11 3LW, UK
UKHW052051230926
475702UK00025B/1077
* 9 7 8 1 0 4 1 0 7 9 0 0 2 *